MW01626836

Richard Diebenkorn

The Berkeley Years

1953–1966

TIMOTHY ANGLIN BURGARD
STEVEN A. NASH
EMMA ACKER

Richard Diebenkorn

The Berkeley Years 1953–1966

Fine Arts Museums of San Francisco
Published in association with Yale University Press

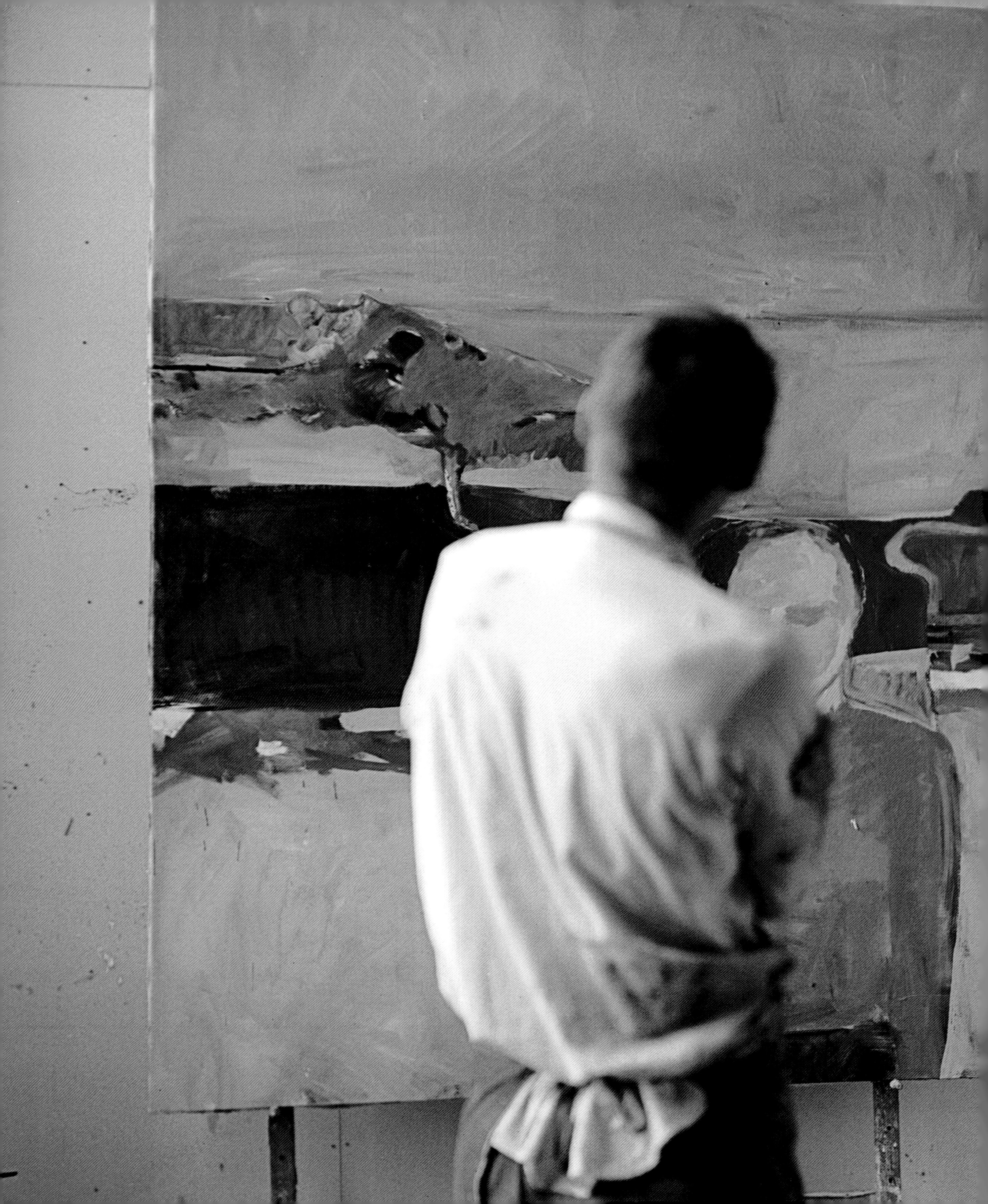

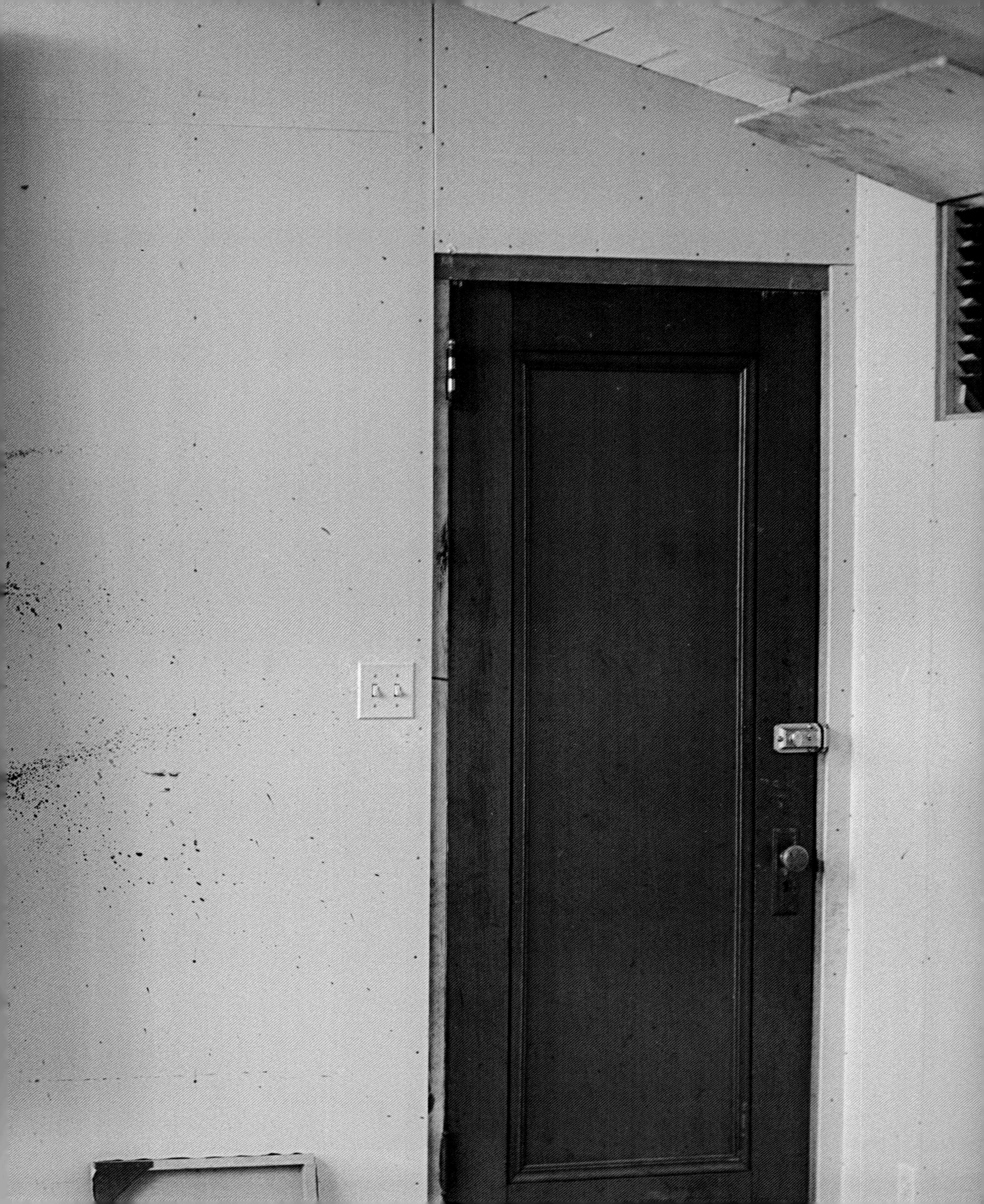

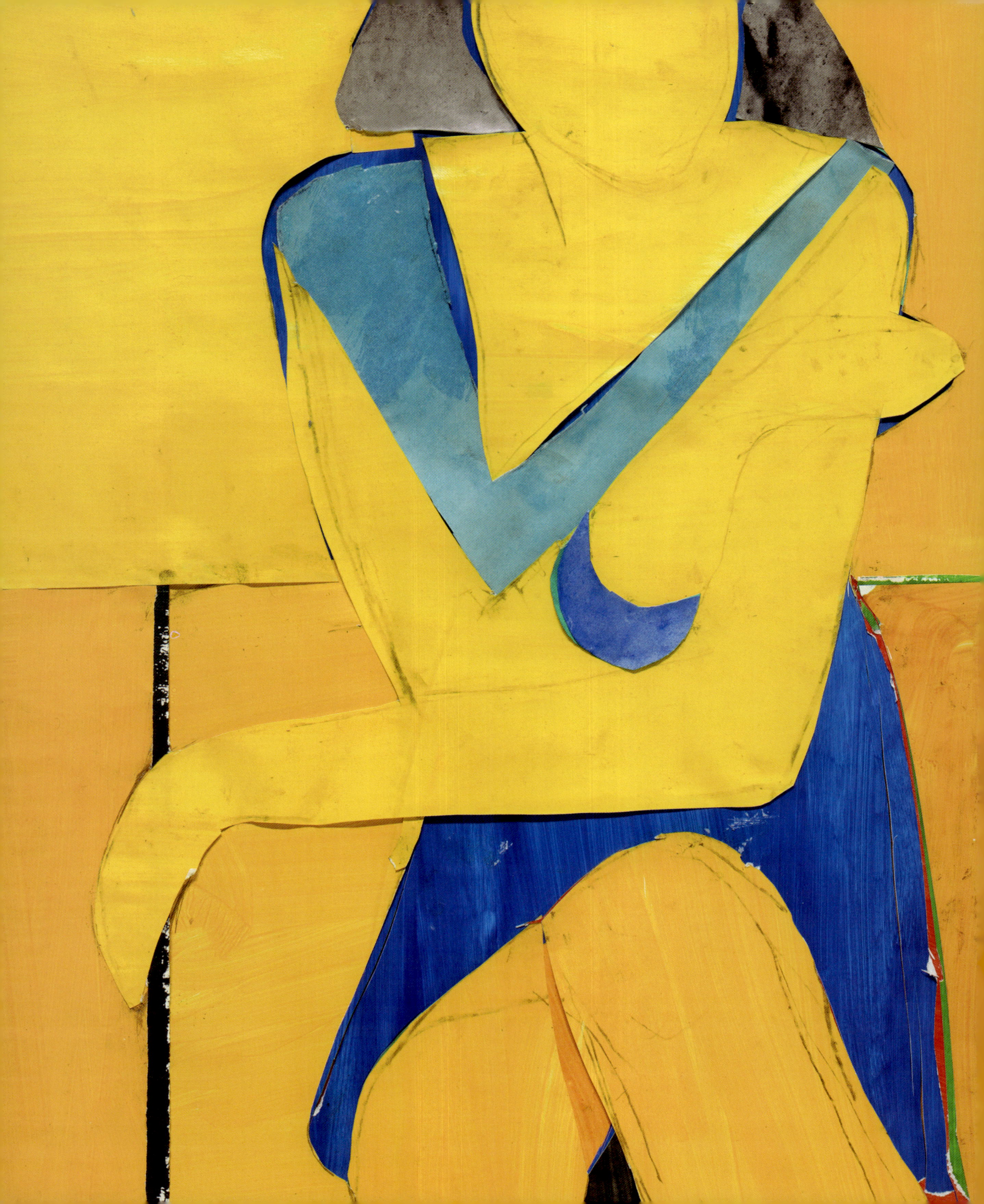

Contents

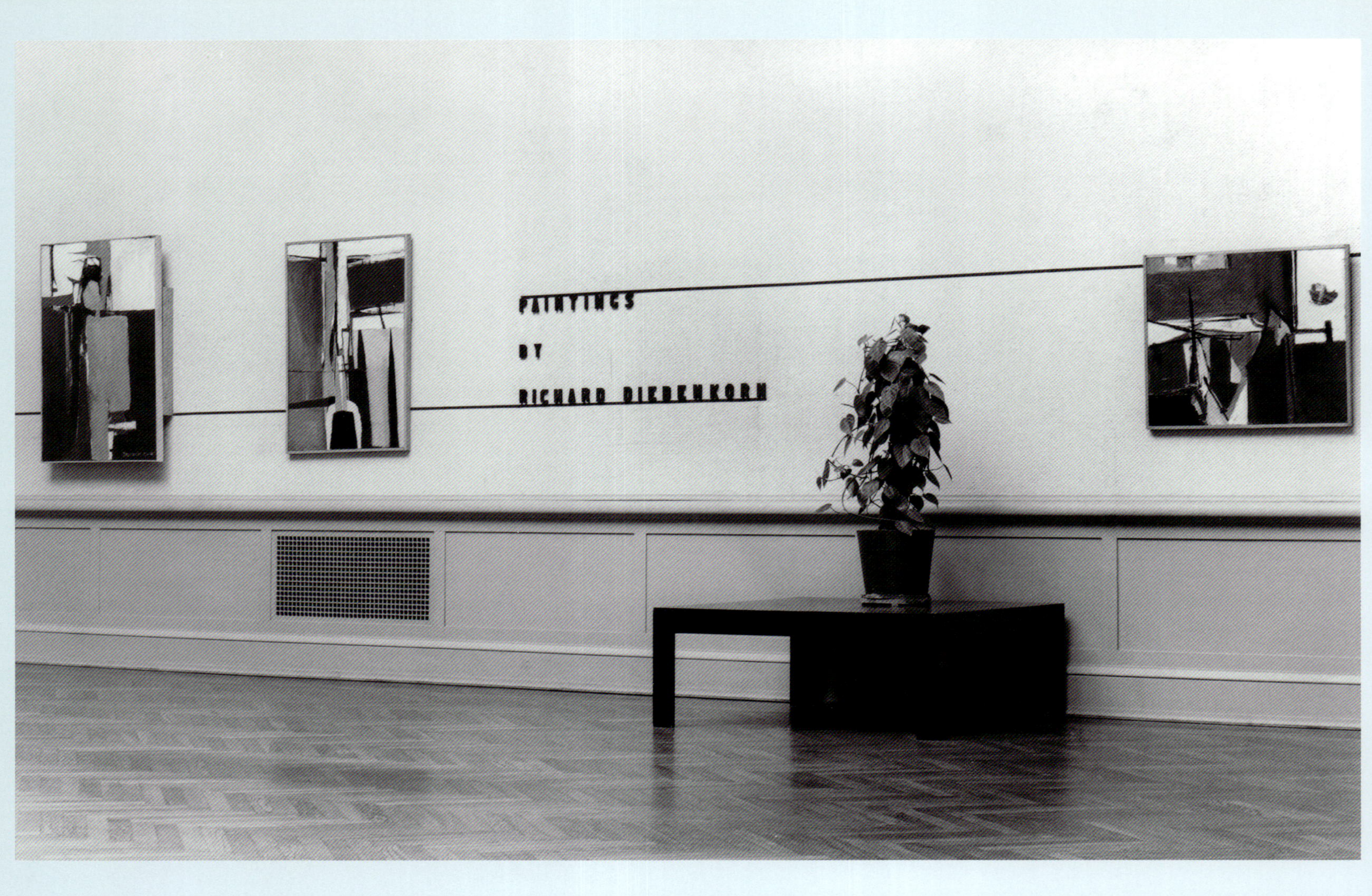

Installation view of the exhibition *Paintings by Richard Diebenkorn*, California Palace of the Legion of Honor, San Francisco, June 4–July 1, 1948

Foreword

DIANE B. WILSEY
President, Board of Trustees
Fine Arts Museums of San Francisco

In the summer of 1948, the California Palace of the Legion of Honor (now a part of the Fine Arts Museums of San Francisco) took the unprecedented but prescient step to give an exceptionally talented twenty-six-year-old artist his first solo museum exhibition. Sixty-five years later, Richard Diebenkorn is internationally acknowledged as one of the most influential American artists of the post–World War II era.

The artist's extraordinarily prolific Berkeley years, which spanned from 1953 to 1966 and generated both abstract and representational works, are the subject of this groundbreaking exhibition and catalogue, curated by Timothy Anglin Burgard, our Ednah Root Curator in Charge of American Art, and Steven A. Nash, Director of the Palm Springs Art Museum. During this monumental period, Diebenkorn was a pioneer of both Abstract Expressionism and the Bay Area Figurative movement, forging a modernist aesthetic uniquely his own. Exhibition viewers will be astonished by the breadth and depth of his work, which is not only intellectually rigorous, but also beautiful.

The Museums are proud to share a productive partnership with the artist's family and with the Richard Diebenkorn Foundation, the organization overseeing the artist's comprehensive catalogue raisonné project. We are grateful to them for sharing their expertise and extensive research archives, for providing logistical support for this catalogue, and for lending so generously to the exhibition.

The Fine Arts Museums' relationship with Richard Diebenkorn encompassed his entire career and included numerous exhibitions and publications featuring his work. The Museums currently house six major paintings by the artist, including the abstract *Berkeley #3* (1953) and the representational *Seawall* (1957), which are showcased in this exhibition, as well as many drawings and the largest archive of the artist's working proofs and published prints.

It is particularly appropriate to celebrate this stunning exhibition of Richard Diebenkorn's Berkeley-period works at the Fine Arts Museums of San Francisco, which have consistently supported and preserved the Bay Area's rich cultural heritage, while highlighting its national and international significance. It is my pleasure to share his legacy with our audiences.

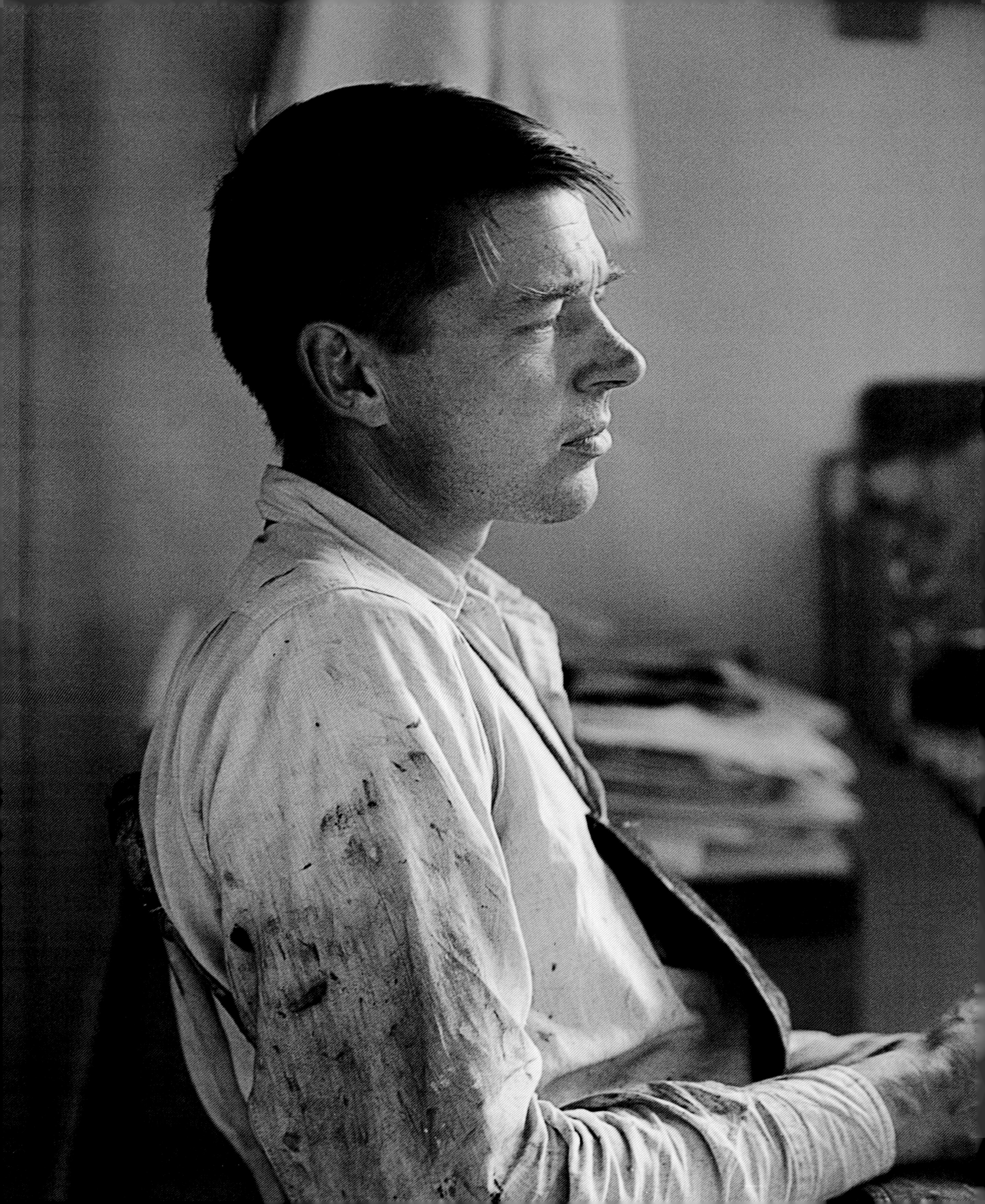

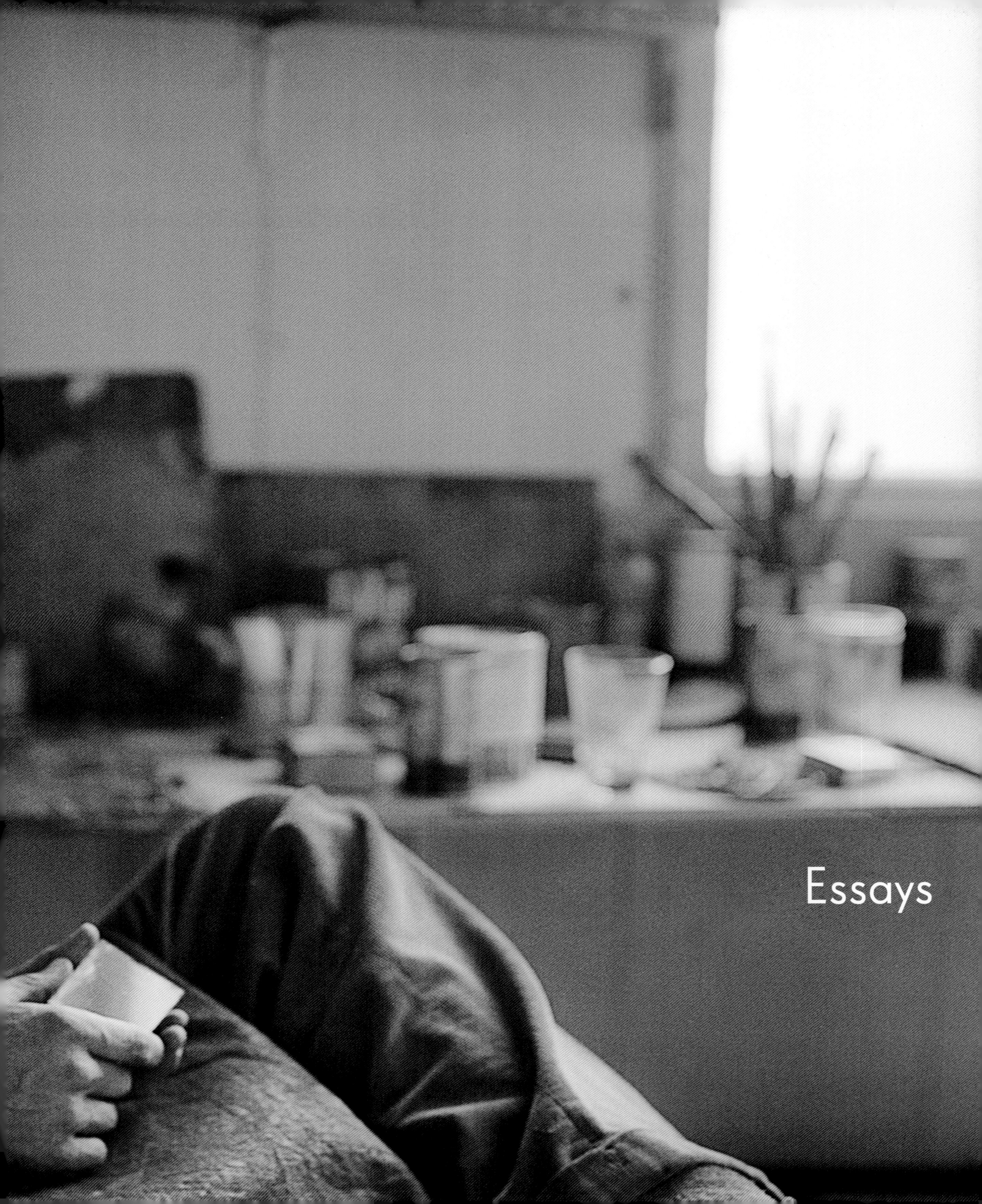

Essays

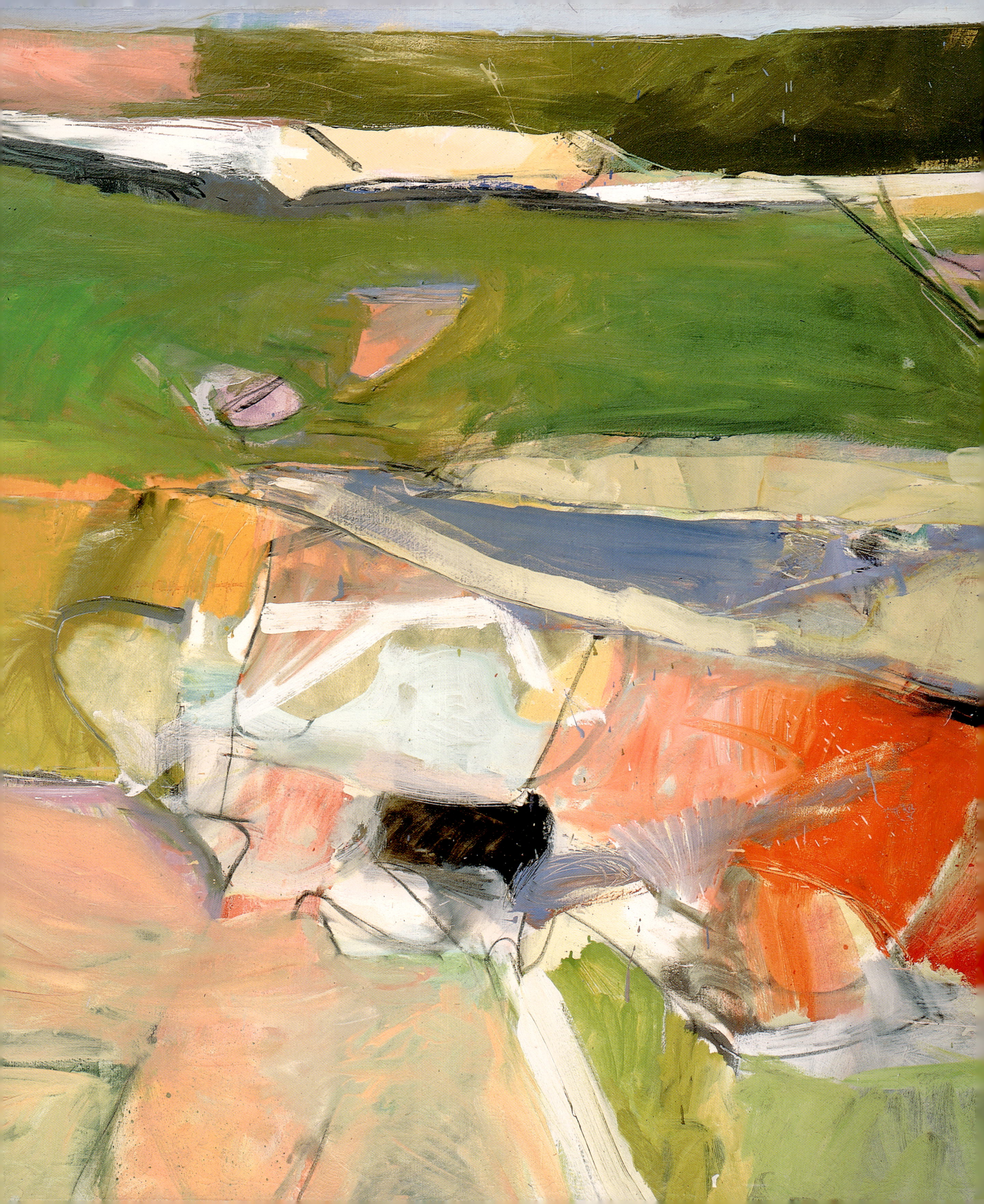

The Nature of Abstraction

Richard Diebenkorn's Berkeley Period

TIMOTHY ANGLIN BURGARD

Richard Diebenkorn (1922–1993) was one of the most significant and influential American artists working in the decades following World War II. Defying easy categorization, his varied career encompassed an early Abstract Expressionist phase (ca. 1946–1956), followed by a dramatic shift into representation (ca. 1955–1967), and then a return to abstraction (ca. 1967–1993) that centered on the celebrated Ocean Park series. Rejecting arbitrary allegiances to schools or movements, resistant to critical praise or censure, and dismissive of commercial concerns, Diebenkorn explored and extended the modernist tradition, making major contributions to the history of both abstraction and figuration.

To fully comprehend Diebenkorn's legacy, it is essential to examine the extraordinarily productive thirteen years he spent in Berkeley, California, beginning with his return to the San Francisco Bay Area in September 1953 and concluding with his departure in September 1966 for Los Angeles. During the Berkeley period Diebenkorn fully developed his working methods, favored themes, and artistic identity; earned critical recognition with his first New York gallery exhibitions of abstract (1956) and representational (1958) works; and gained wider acclaim through the *Art News* article "Diebenkorn Paints a Picture" (1957).[1]

Diebenkorn's work also entered public discourse during these years, alternately embraced or rejected by proponents of the New York and San Francisco Schools of Abstract Expressionism and by the opposing art-world factions advocating for either abstract or representational styles. Three decades later San Francisco Bay Area sculptor and painter Manuel Neri could still recall the impact of Diebenkorn's abstract Berkeley paintings: "God damn it, it was pretty strong stuff. It was just a type of painting we hadn't seen on the West Coast before. Diebenkorn had a wildness—not the controlled wildness of Hassel Smith, but an out-of-control feeling. Those were urgent times, wild times. He brought us a new language to talk in."[2]

The roots of Diebenkorn's Berkeley period can be traced to his family's move back to San Francisco in 1924. The artist grew up in the city's Ingleside Terraces neighborhood, attended Stanford University in Stanford and the University of California in Berkeley as an undergraduate, was both a student and an instructor at the California School of Fine Arts (CSFA, now the San Francisco Art Institute [SFAI]), and lived in Sausalito and Berkeley, two cities situated on San Francisco Bay. The man and his work were deeply influenced by both the nature and the culture of the San Francisco Bay Area. However, working within the confines of his various Berkeley studios (he was rarely a plein-air painter), he created work that was also defined by his responses to art of both the past and the present. As Diebenkorn observed, "I'm really a traditional painter, not avant-garde at all. I wanted to follow a tradition and extend it."[3]

Diebenkorn's abstract Berkeley-period works must be viewed as part of a creative continuum that encompassed his earlier studies as a graduate student and instructor at CSFA (1946–1949), as well as works made while he was living in Sausalito (1947–1949); completing a master's degree at the University of New Mexico in Albuquerque (1950–1952); and teaching at the University of Illinois at Urbana (1952–1953). During this formative eight-year period, Diebenkorn studied and assimilated precedents by some of the great modernist masters, including Paul Cézanne, Henri Matisse, Pablo Picasso, Clyfford Still, Mark Rothko, and Willem de Kooning. Almost immediately, Diebenkorn found common cause with the Abstract Expressionists (see fig. 1), gradually developing his own distinctive pictorial language of abstraction. In his successful application for the 1954 Abraham Rosenberg Fellowship that enabled him to work in his studio full time, Diebenkorn wrote that his art had reached a pivotal turning point:

> The emphasis in my development over the past year has changed from one of concern with the general form and style of my work, as part of an art movement [Abstract Expressionism], to a specific and personal application within a familiar frame directed toward developing those things, which, as an individual, I have to say.[4]

The first few years of Diebenkorn's Berkeley period (1953–1956), the primary focus of this essay, represent the artistic culmination of his first abstract period. In an extraordinary burst of creativity (he averaged around one painting every two weeks) the artist created his remarkable series of abstract Berkeley works. Of the fifty-eight extant paintings, fifty-six have "Berkeley" numbers (e.g., *Berkeley #1*) ranging between 1 and 67, and two (i.e., *Berkeley* and *Untitled*) have non-numbered titles.[5] The omission of individual descriptive names reflected an aversion—shared by many Abstract Expressionists—to overt narrative content in works that were supposed to be viewed primarily in formal terms.[6] The numbered titles signal his perception of these works as part of a series, although he did not envision its ultimate extent at its inception.

A profound dialogue between representation and abstraction defined Diebenkorn's Berkeley period. In 1955, at the height of his national success as an abstract artist, he shocked the art world with his dramatic shift to representation.[7] However, the Berkeley years should not be seen as comprising two discrete chapters—abstract and representational—but rather as encompassing an oscillation between these seemingly opposite poles.[8] Acknowledging these complexities, Diebenkorn observed, "One of the most interesting polarities in art is between representation, at one end of the stick, and abstraction, at the other end, and I've found myself all over that stick."[9] Further blurring the boundaries, nearly all of his representational works are "abstract" in the sense that they were created largely from his imagination, not from observed reality.[10]

Diebenkorn's intense physical engagement with his Abstract Expressionist works drew strength and power from the sublimation of their figurative elements, while his deep psychological involvement with his figurative works was alternately amplified or tempered by their abstract elements. The inherent tension between a dominant mode and a secondary mode that

FIG 1
San Francisco Bay Area artists represented in the exhibition *Younger American Painters*, Solomon R. Guggenheim Museum, New York, 1954, in *Glamour* magazine, June 1954

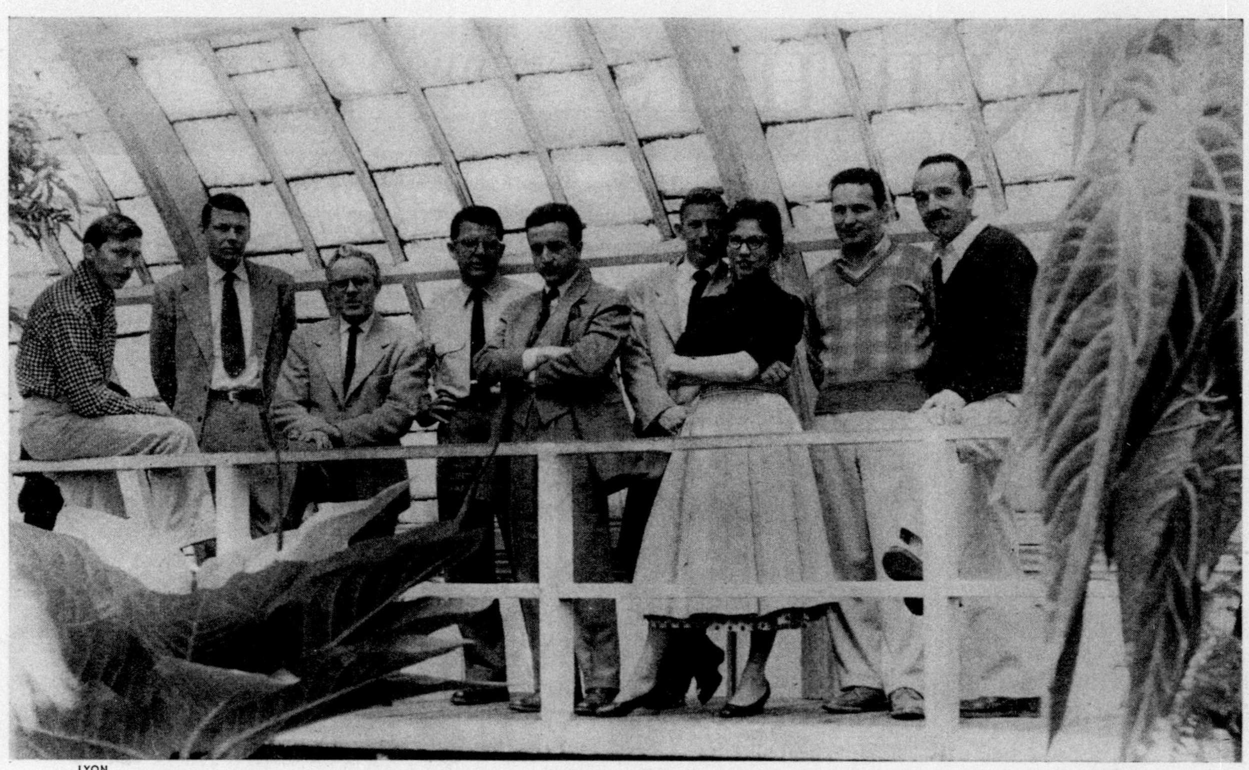

LYON

JAMES SWEENEY'S ART BETS: YOUNGER AMERICAN PAINTERS FROM THE SAN FRANCISCO BAY AREA; LEFT TO RIGHT, WILLIAM MOREHOUSE, RICHARD DIEBENKORN, RICHARD WHITE, KYLE MORRIS, KARIM KHOSROVI, PAUL WONNER, SONIA GECHTOFF, KENNETH NACK, RALPH DU CASSE.

with who never says a word; and the movie heads for a happy ending like a loaded honey bee for home. . . . The lolloping French film, *Beauties of the Night*, slips into fantasy every other minute, with Gérard Philipe as a poor composer dreaming like some rococo Walter Mitty of gayer, richer lives. The movie, poking fun at his luscious dreams (one fully equipped with Gina Lollobrigida), directed by René Clair, shines brightest in scenes of the composer's waking world which is peopled by funny, good-hearted French workmen and their unworldly girls.

In art influences

When James Johnson Sweeney, one of the best known American art authorities took over The Solomon R. Guggenheim Museum in New York a year and a half ago, he stripped the tall narrow Fifth Avenue house to its bones, painted the walls stark white, snatched frames off all the paintings, dusted off modern masterpieces rolled up in the store room, hung small groups of paintings so brilliantly that sometimes the arrangements seem more worth examining than the pictures themselves, and started throwing off, like sparks, the influence of his own determined taste. His last winter's show, *Younger European Painters,* has begun a year-long cross-country tour. His new exhibition, *Younger American Painters,* including the row of young artists above, recently opened with about sixty artists, some familiar to art circles, some almost unknown.

Much of the most vigourous of the unsung talent came from the West Coast. In the Pacific Northwest he found a remarkably strong collector's market for new young art, and a correspondingly strong group of artists. In California, on the other hand, a large group of coming artists has grown out of nothing. With little general interest, little support, few galleries, young painters have collected there apparently in recognition of good university art schools, and of the creative friction on each other of their talents. The paintings in the show of the nine San Francisco Bay area painters—few of this group, above, came from California—have, for the most part, a wide-open flair, smashing colour or smashing line, an uninhibited vigour. Largely abstract to the innocent eye, these paintings stirred Mr. Sweeney to announce that he was surprised at how representational they were. Identifying a huge umbrous squiggle as a still-life, he added, "After all, they have to have been *something*."

GLAMOUR, JUNE, 1954

71

seemingly might supplant it at any moment is a key component of the works. Abstraction and figuration also were linked by the artist's working method, which consistently valued process, chance discoveries, and an unfinished appearance over preconceived ideas and definitive resolution. Diebenkorn's abstract and figurative modes also shared his conception of metamorphosis as an operating principle that not only generated new forms—and their subsequent permutations—but also endowed the resulting works with an animating energy.

Like most Abstract Expressionists of this era, Diebenkorn started out painting in a representational mode and only later developed a personal language of abstraction while studying and teaching at CSFA. As with his contemporaries, these outward shifts in style did not preclude his persistent incorporation of favored subjects and themes.[11] Indeed, the viewer's understanding of Diebenkorn's abstract Berkeley period is greatly enriched by an examination of comparably themed works from other periods, whether abstract or representational. In particular, the artist's earlier abstractions and later figurative works often are more legible to the viewer and thus more revealing of his creative process and possible intentions.

Moreover, while Diebenkorn's early Berkeley-period paintings certainly are abstract—or, more accurately, abstracted—they are not completely nonobjective, or lacking in references to imagery, real or imagined. As Diebenkorn noted:

> All paintings start out of a mood, out of a relationship with things or people, out of a complete visual impression. To call this expression abstract seems to me often to confuse the issue. Abstract means literally to draw from or separate. In this sense every artist is abstract . . . a realistic or nonobjective approach makes no difference. The result is what counts.[12]

Diebenkorn's three most persistent subjects—landscape, the figure, and still life—often served as initial sources of inspiration for the abstract paintings, even though the visible traces of these subjects typically were obscured or deleted in the final work. As the artist observed, both his subject and his style were variables that altered the very nature of the artistic equation:

> It interests me also that the different forms painters use, such as landscape, still life, or figure, bring out very different qualities. I see this in most painters of the past and certainly in myself. In this time there is one more option–that of not representing, which can bring out yet another set of things.[13]

While psychological content may seem more readily apparent in Diebenkorn's figurative paintings, his abstract paintings represent the culmination of a revelation that occurred while he was living in Albuquerque, when he "relaxed and began to think of natural forms in relation to my own feelings."[14] These feelings, eloquently embodied in Diebenkorn's representational landscapes, figures, and still lifes, are also among the defining elements of the abstract paintings, disrupting their tectonic planes and tracing calligraphic paths across their surfaces.

In 1956, just as he was completing the last of his abstract Berkeley paintings, Diebenkorn explicitly identified the emotional content of his work as its most salient quality. In response to the query "What is the good of painting?" he wrote,

> I would like to reply to this question by citing my friend, the painter Elmer Bischoff: "The painting may appear to us as a unique definition of a certain quality of feeling, or to use a stronger expression, of a certain quality of emotion. It can detach itself from any superficial correspondence and sink beyond our consciousness. We can then no longer distinguish forms and colors, the same way as while reading we are no longer conscious of the print on a page. What matters the most at this level *is the power the painting has to transcend through all generalities to reach a particularly poignant feeling*."[15]

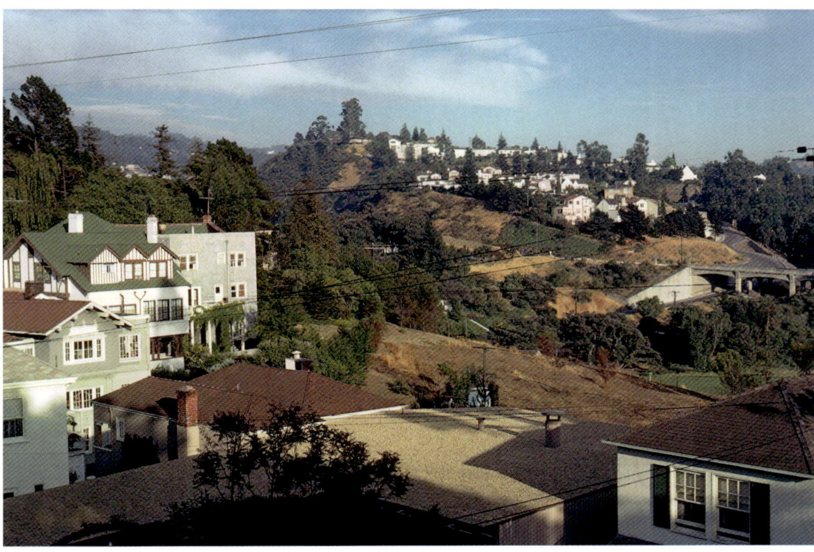

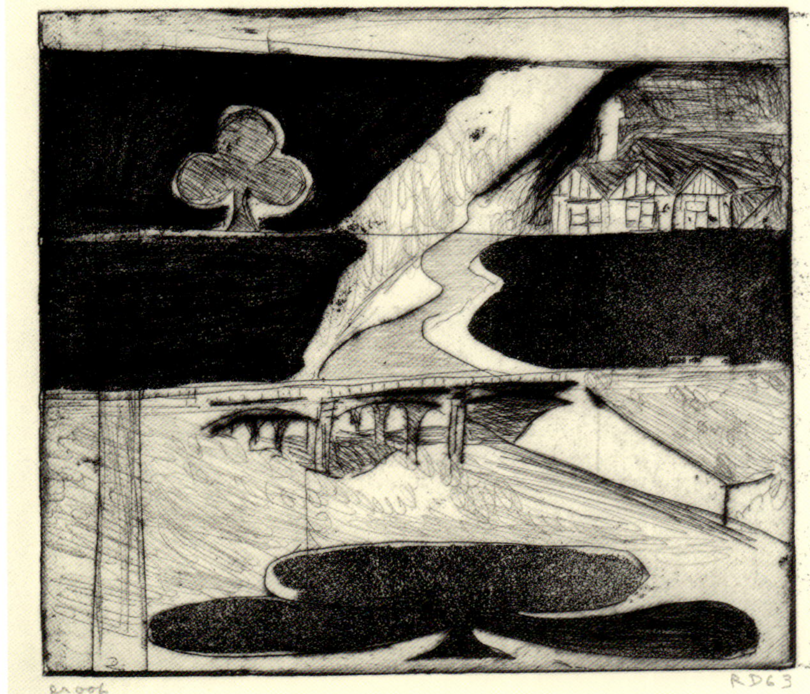

FIG 2
View from the Diebenkorn family's house at 217 Hillcrest Road, Berkeley, 1962

FIG 3
Richard Diebenkorn
Landscape with Clubs, 1963
Aquatint and drypoint
7 3/4 x 8 1/2 in. (19.7 x 21.6 cm)
Private collection
[1173]

LANDSCAPE—A SENSE OF PLACE

Berkeley (see fig. 2) was not merely the coincidental backdrop for Diebenkorn's life during this period; it also was a significant, if often indirect, influence in the works of an artist for whom place was paramount (see fig. 3). As his close friend William Brice observed, "I don't know of any artist who was more responsive to his physical environment than Dick. If he moves down the block, it changes everything. He absorbed the aura of a place."[16] In a similar vein, Diebenkorn noted, "Very often if you go to the locale where an artist works you'll suddenly really know that you're in that person's area. If you go to Arles, you feel the Van Gogh around you."[17] Diebenkorn's collective geographic designation for the numbered Berkeley paintings explicitly acknowledges that the surrounding environment played a significant role in shaping these works.[18]

The city of Berkeley, then as now with a population of approximately 100,000, sits on the eastern shore of San Francisco Bay, facing west toward the Golden Gate Bridge and the Pacific Ocean, some ten miles away. The terraced urban topography of San Francisco can be seen to the left, and Marin County, with its major geological landmark, Mount Tamalpais, is to the right. The presence of visible cross sections of geological strata that have been layered, twisted, and folded is a distinctive characteristic of the Bay Area's natural topography.

The gradual rise of the Berkeley hills up from the bay has the effect of creating a natural amphitheater for optimal viewing of the surrounding landscape. The shimmering surface of the bay can assume an astounding spectrum of colors from blue to green to gray, or, alternately, a silver or gold mirrorlike state at sunrise and sunset. The cyclical arrival and departure of the Bay Area's distinctive fog creates disorienting spatial effects, as when a narrow strip of land is visible between the low-lying mist above and the bay below, creating a form of tripartite stratification. The translucent haze often is backlit by sunlight that illuminates the suspended moisture, creating prismatic effects of extraordinary subtlety. The Abstract Expressionist Mark Rothko, who taught summer sessions at CSFA in 1947 and 1949, described the Bay Area landscape as "unspeakably beautiful."[19]

Like the works themselves, the origins of the numbered Berkeley paintings are many and multilayered. Collectively, their imagery is evocative of nature and the elemental encounter of earth, water, and sky—perceived through an atmospheric interplay of color, light, and shadow.[20] Yet none of the four studios that Diebenkorn occupied in Berkeley (including the one he built for himself) had a view of the bay.[21] Moreover, the Berkeley paintings, like his other geographically identified series of works (i.e., Sausalito, Urbana, Ocean Park), were created in a city. Just as they often seem to mediate between abstraction and figuration, these works also mediate between the alternating densities and complexities of natural and man-made environments.

Diebenkorn's first great revelation regarding the relationship of landscape to his painting occurred while living with his family in Albuquerque (1950–1952), where he enrolled in the Master of Fine Arts graduate program at the University of New Mexico. As occurred when he lived previously in Sausalito, and later in Berkeley, Diebenkorn found himself in a distinctive and inspiring natural environment that strongly influenced the forms and palette of his abstract work. He also felt liberated from his experience as both a student and a teacher at CSFA, where Clyfford Still and other advocates of abstraction rejected figuration in any form as retardataire, if not outright reactionary:

> I'd left all my influences in San Francisco. I left my mentors. I think I was saying to myself in Albuquerque that, OK , I'm going to damn well paint what I want. I'm not going to do this qualifying of my intuitive responses. . . . If grass green and sky blue and desert tan; if these associations come into the work that's part of my experience.[22]

The answer to the complex question of whether Diebenkorn's abstract Berkeley paintings also might be perceived as having landscape associations was posed by critics during his first one-person exhibition in New York in 1956.[23] Commenting specifically on the naming of his various series after the places where they were created (e.g., *Berkeley #1*), he later observed, "It's really the name of the place rather than the place itself."[24] More generally, Diebenkorn resisted interpretations of his abstract works as having specific landscape associations, and it would be impossible to identify a one-for-one correspondence with a precise geographic site. However, in a published statement of 1956, he acknowledged his persistent attraction to a landscape aesthetic, suggested that he might once have been or might once again be a landscape painter, and reserved the right not to describe his paintings with such limiting terms:

> What I paint often seems to pertain to landscape but I try to avoid any rationalization of this either in my painting or in later thinking about it. I'm not a landscape painter (at this time, at any rate) or I would paint landscape directly.
>
> I don't object to verbalizing about painting or feel that words damage it. I am simply aware of and (with my first paragraph in mind) wary of the scant and often absurd relationship between painters' works and their verbal stances and self-justifications.[25]

Berkeley #42 (fig. 4) of 1955 is perhaps one of the abstract Berkeley paintings Diebenkorn referenced that "seems to pertain to landscape." The aerial, bird's-eye perspective, influenced by the artist's 1951 airplane flight from Albuquerque to San Francisco, appears frequently in the abstract Berkeley

FIG 4
Richard Diebenkorn
***Berkeley #42*, 1955**
Oil on canvas
57 1/2 x 51 1/2 in. (146.1 x 130.8 cm)
Cleveland Museum of Art,
Contemporary Collection, 1968.95
[1139]

FIG 5
Henri Matisse
***Bay of Nice*, 1918**
Oil on canvas
35 1/8 x 28 in. (90 x 71 cm)
Private collection

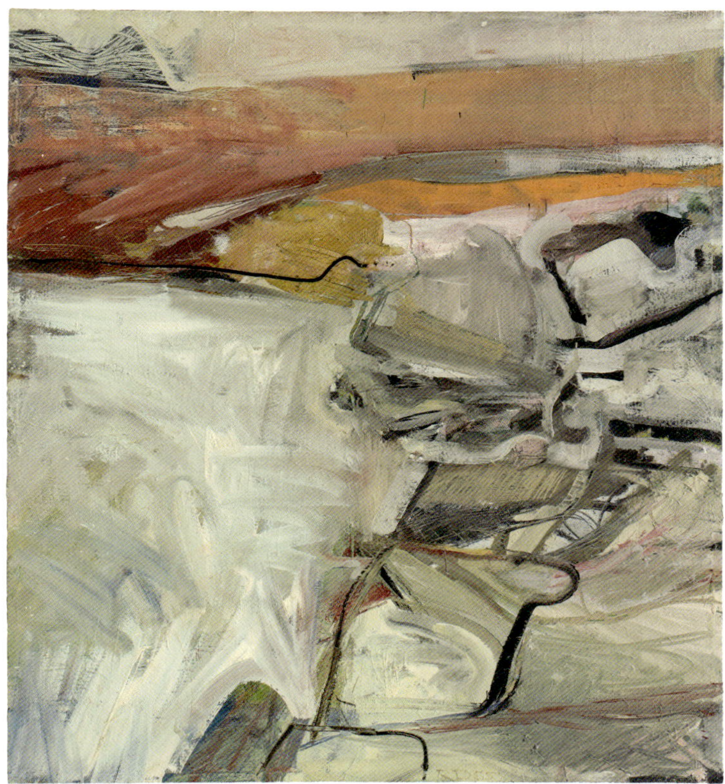

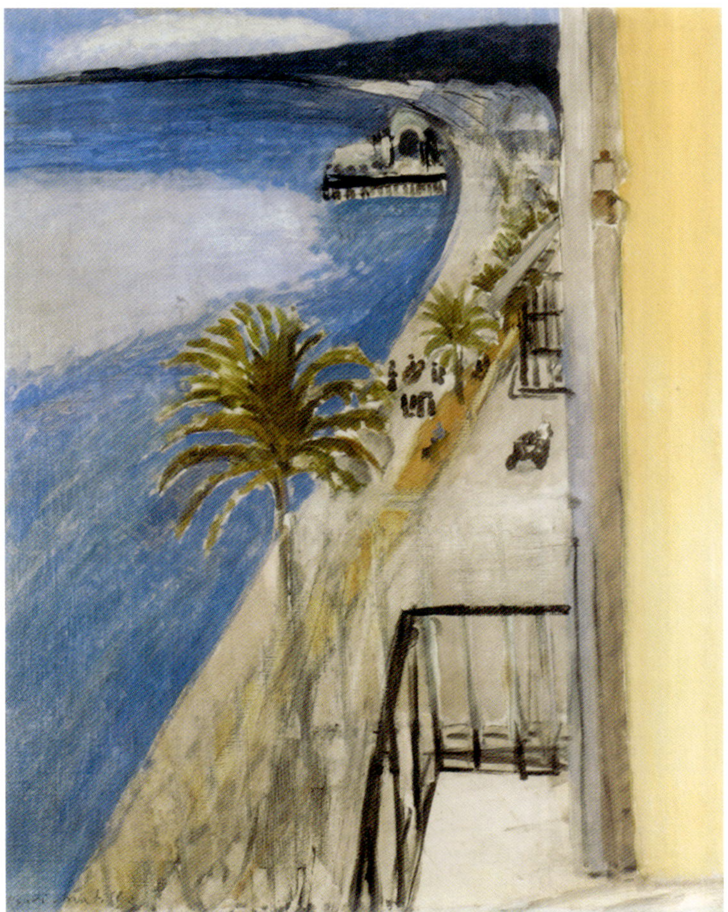

paintings, where it serves to compress three-dimensional objects and recessive space within the two-dimensional picture plane.[26] Recalling his revelatory experience, Diebenkorn observed, "The aerial view showed me a rich variety of ways of treating a flat plane—like flattened mud or paint. Forms operating in shallow depth reveal a huge range of possibilities available to the painter."[27] Noting the influence of the aerial perspective on his subsequent work, he recalled, "I was absolutely knocked out and thrilled, really taken. . . . It wasn't that I went right to the canvas and said I'm going to paint this but it just went right into the mill and started coming out strong."[28]

Berkeley #42 shares an aesthetic sensibility with an overt coastal landscape, Henri Matisse's *Bay of Nice* (fig. 5) of 1918, which Diebenkorn saw in 1943 at the Palo Alto home of Sarah Stein, whose extended family formed one of the greatest collections of modernist art.[29] Both paintings incorporate an aerial perspective in which the various compositional elements ascend the picture plane to a high horizon line that creates a sense of compression. The superimposed black lines emphasize the two-dimensional picture plane and counterbalance the deep recession into space. The translucent and transparent brushstrokes create a tangible, enveloping sense of atmosphere that heightens the spatial ambiguity of the compositions, in which elements alternately project outward or recede into space. Most significantly, the visibly reworked canvases embrace an aesthetic of seeming incompleteness as an essential component of the creative process. However, while Matisse's representation verges on abstraction, Diebenkorn's abstraction verges on representation, one of the distinctive characteristics of many of his numbered Berkeley paintings.

In Diebenkorn's abstract Berkeley paintings, "imagery that seems to pertain to landscape" is more or less visible on a sliding scale of legibility, but few seem to be entirely devoid of such references. Yet these same canvases simultaneously disorient the viewer with unrecognizable and impassable fields of paint that assert their autonomy as abstract works of art. These competing impulses are epitomized respectively by *Berkeley #42* and

Berkeley #42b (fig. 6), which appear to have commenced with similar compositions and palettes, but diverged to explore different means (e.g., vertical and horizontal formats; less abstract and more abstract) of achieving similar expressive ends. Ultimately, Diebenkorn's images, which do not depict nature, but aspire to be *like* nature, constitute an ongoing dialogue between the artist and the painting regarding the process of creation.

Artist and curator Kyle Morris, who included Diebenkorn's *Berkeley #52* and *Berkeley #53* in an exhibition at the Walker Art Center in Minneapolis in 1955, argued against reductive interpretations of Abstract Expressionist techniques and subject matter. He discerned an important distinction between means and ends that could be applied to Diebenkorn's work:

> The phrase "accidental discovery" has been bandied about a good deal, meaning that the artist did not begin with a preconceived idea of what his painting would be, but rather, by working directly upon the canvas, discovered his painting as it emerged. This phrase tends to imply that no controls governed the painting, but this situation has never existed, for the artist has always been present. . . . This type of painting does not start with nature and arrive at paint, but on the contrary, starts with paint and arrives at nature (although it can be of an unexpected kind).[30]

Diebenkorn's inclusion along with three other artists in the 1957 *Life* magazine article "Look of the West Inspires New Art" (see fig. 7) suggests that he may have become less resistant to landscape interpretations of his abstract paintings, perhaps because he had been making representational paintings since the previous year. Diebenkorn was photographed standing next to *Berkeley #44* (pl. 27) of 1955, whose composition is reminiscent of horizontal strata, rectilinear fields, and reservoirs of water. Under an adjacent caption, "Sweeping Patterns from California Fields," the text reads, "Painted with rough strokes, its broad forms recall the sweeping patterns of the fertile lands north of San Francisco."[31] While the writer erred in trying to associate

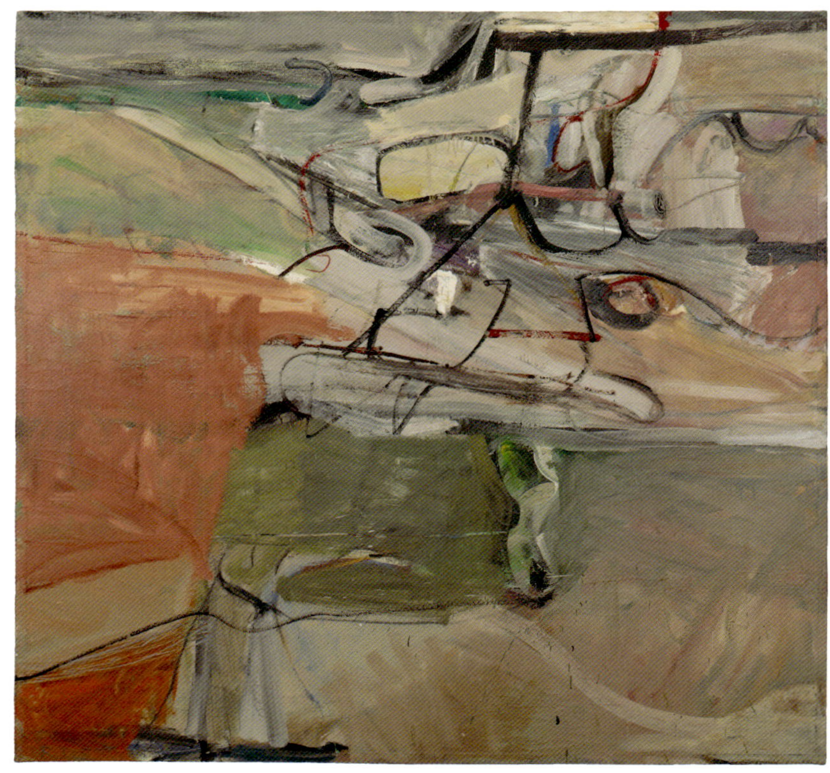

FIG 6
Richard Diebenkorn
***Berkeley #42b*, 1955**
Oil on linen
59 1/4 x 62 in. (150.5 x 157.5 cm)
Private collection
[221]

FIG 7
Richard Diebenkorn with *Berkeley #44*, in *Life* magazine, November 4, 1957

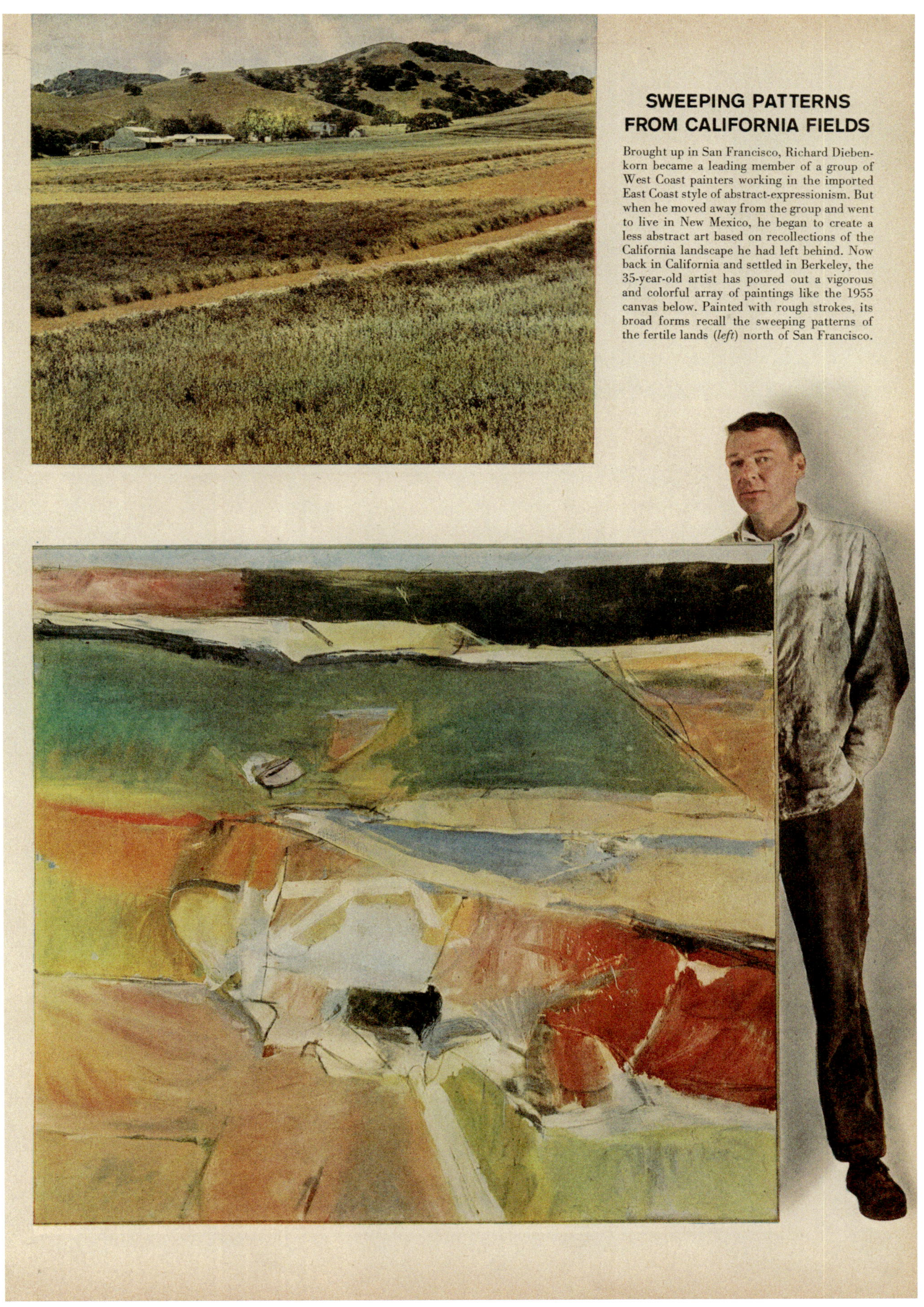

SWEEPING PATTERNS FROM CALIFORNIA FIELDS

Brought up in San Francisco, Richard Diebenkorn became a leading member of a group of West Coast painters working in the imported East Coast style of abstract-expressionism. But when he moved away from the group and went to live in New Mexico, he began to create a less abstract art based on recollections of the California landscape he had left behind. Now back in California and settled in Berkeley, the 35-year-old artist has poured out a vigorous and colorful array of paintings like the 1955 canvas below. Painted with rough strokes, its broad forms recall the sweeping patterns of the fertile lands (*left*) north of San Francisco.

Diebenkorn's painting with specific geographic locales, the impetus to perceive a landscape sensibility surely was not entirely misplaced.

The ultimate word on the landscape subject rightly belongs to Diebenkorn. In 1955 he declared, "I'm not a landscape painter (at this time, at any rate)."[32] In his *Self-Portrait* (fig. 8) of 1956, the year that he shifted his focus from abstraction to representation, he tellingly rendered his head silhouetted against a tripartite landscape comprising earth, water, and sky, implicitly suggesting a source of inspiration and identity. In 1957, the same year that the *Life* magazine article "Look of the West Inspires New Art" was published, Diebenkorn described a turning point regarding the relationship of his abstract work to the landscape that occurred while living in Albuquerque, New Mexico:

> Temperamentally, perhaps, I had always been a landscape painter but I was fighting the landscape feeling. For years I didn't have the color blue on my palette because it reminded me too much of the spatial qualities in conventional landscapes. But in Albuquerque I relaxed and began to think of natural forms in relation to my own feelings.[33]

Yet it is also unlikely that Diebenkorn ever painted a landscape motif directly from nature during his abstract Berkeley period. A clue to the resolution of this seeming contradiction may be found in the abstract painting *Inscape* (fig. 9) of 1953. Diebenkorn's evocative title explicitly suggests a correlation between the external appearance of his art and his imagination, a form of interior landscape. It is telling that the emphatically abstract and two-dimensional *Inscape*, while emanating color, light, and life, thwarts visual entry and thus appears both impenetrable and unknowable to the casual viewer.

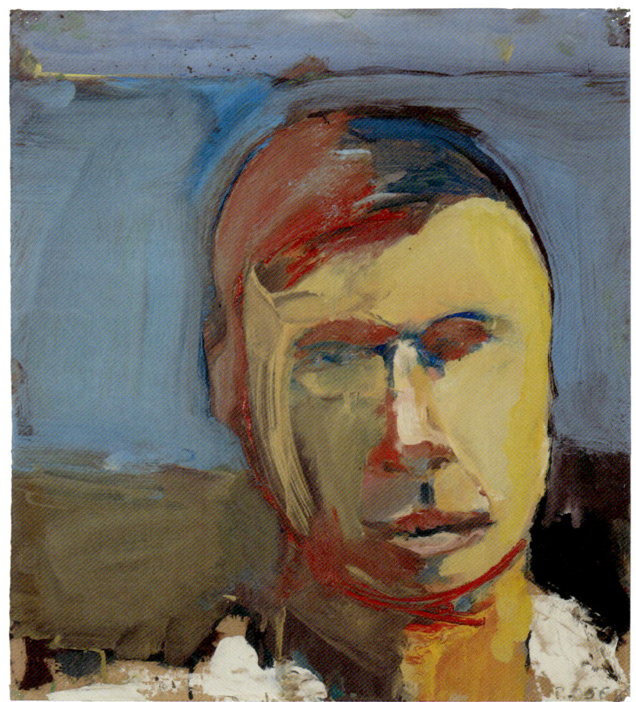

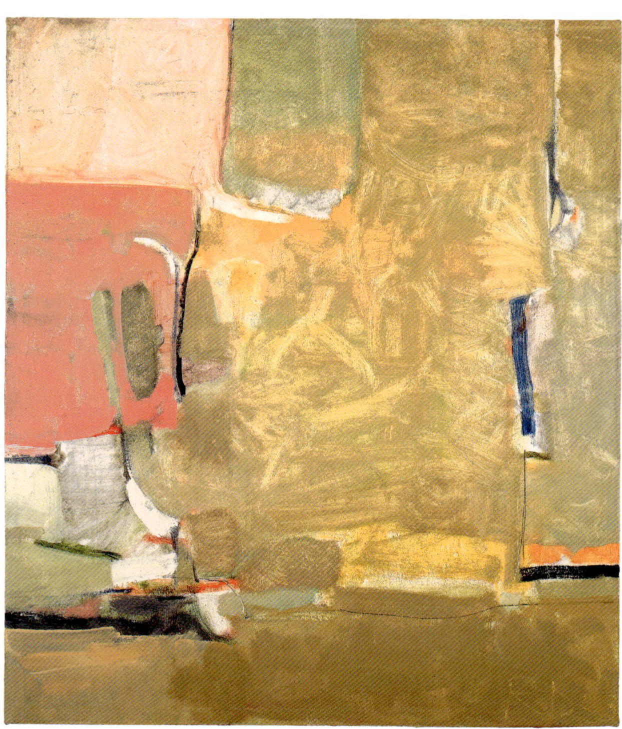

FIG 8
Richard Diebenkorn
***Self-Portrait*, 1956**
Oil on paper mounted on hardboard
19 x 17 in. (48.3 x 43.2 cm)
Private collection
[1192]

FIG 9
Richard Diebenkorn
***Inscape*, 1953**
Oil on canvas
37 3/4 x 32 1/8 in. (95.9 x 81.6 cm)
Private collection
[206]

FIG 10
Richard Diebenkorn
***Urbana #5 (Beach Town)*, 1953**
Oil on canvas
68 x 53 1/2 in. (172.7 x 135.9 cm)
Collection of Gifford and Joann Phillips
[1098]

FIG 11
Richard Diebenkorn
***Urbana*, 1953**
Oil on canvas
61 1/2 x 47 3/4 in. (156.2 x 121.3 cm)
Private collection
[1093]

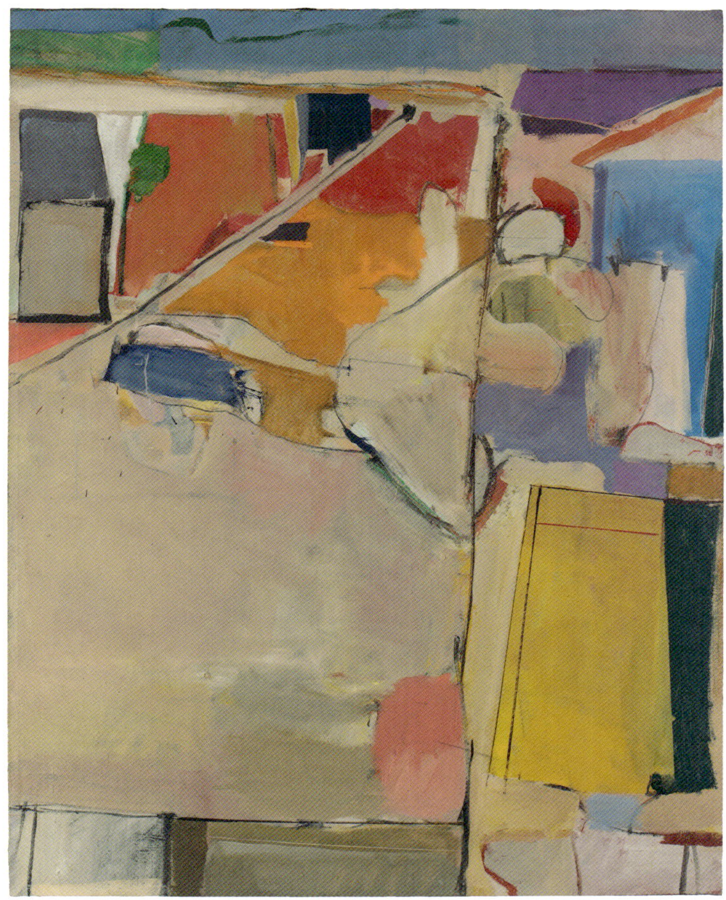

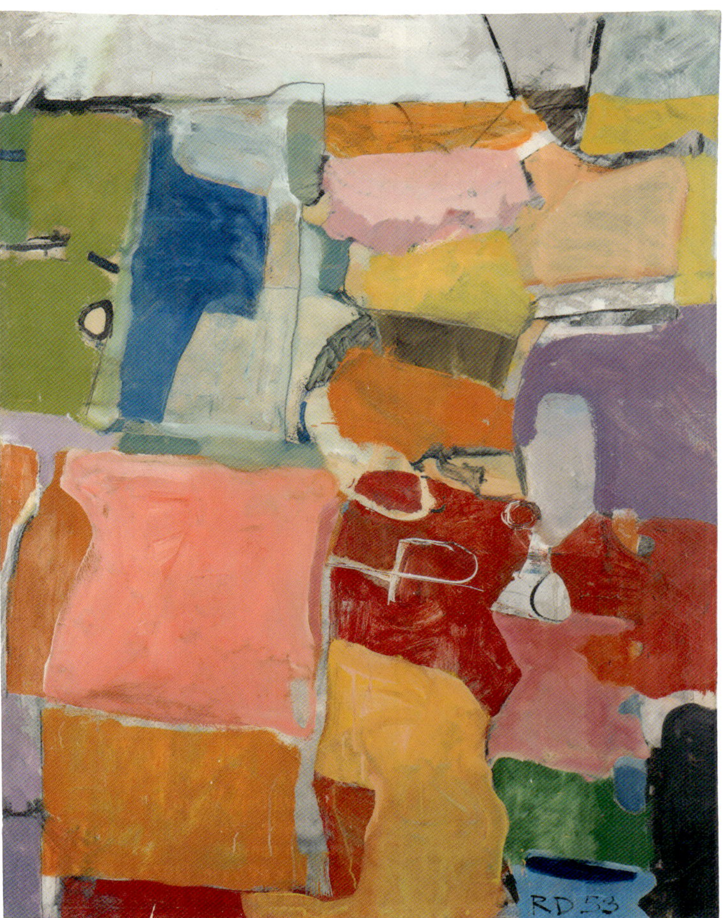

An examination of four paintings—variations on a theme rendered in semiabstract, abstract, and representational styles—illuminates some of the ways in which Diebenkorn's complex conceptions of landscape evolved over time. The first of these paintings, *Urbana #5 (Beach Town)* (fig. 10) of 1953, painted while he was teaching in Urbana, Illinois, is a rare instance in which Diebenkorn assigned a descriptive title to one of his abstract paintings.[34] The central street, flanked by planar and architectonic color blocks, is rendered with converging lines of perspective that rise up the picture plane to a high, broken horizon line, with a cliff or mesa form at the upper left and the sea and sky at the upper right. A blue house with an orange roofline is discernible on the upper right side of the street.

Painted shortly before the Berkeley period, *Beach Town* provides definitive proof of the artist's interest in landscape as both a source of inspiration and a point of departure for his work. Diebenkorn confirmed that it represents his conception of a coastal scene, albeit not one that he could see when he painted it in Illinois, two thousand miles from the California coast:

> [*Beach Town*] was done I think immediately after I left [Albuquerque]. There were colors like blue that I just knocked off my palette altogether because they were just spatial to me and yet they kept popping back and I'd scrape them off. There were landscape suggestions that kept coming in—I don't know, they had come in in New Mexico. Here I was in the Midwest, and I was pretty unhappy there because of all this ground and hay and stuff around, and then this painting occurred, I don't know, a suggestion of a street and buildings and perhaps an ocean on the other side of these things, kept coming, insisting. So, I thought well this is what I want to paint so I'm going to paint it. So, I did it. And then, I've always numbered pictures; I did this for some years afterwards, but this one I guess I identified because of the special feelings I had about it, and it was to me like a town near an ocean and just to remember it, I referred to it as *Beach Town*.[35]

While still in Urbana, Diebenkorn appears to have reprised the essential elements of *Beach Town* in the similarly scaled *Urbana* (fig. 11) of 1953, which also appears to incorporate a converging street running vertically up the surface to a high horizon line, as well as the blue house with a door at the middle right edge of the painting. Given Diebenkorn's recollection that *Beach Town* was created "immediately after I left [Albuquerque]," it seems likely that the relationship between this painting and *Urbana* is comparable to that between *Berkeley #42* (fig. 4) and *Berkeley #42b* (fig. 6). In both cases, Diebenkorn seems to have further abstracted his initial composition, distilling the essential elements and their relationships to achieve a more immersive form of expression.

Remarkably, *Beach Town*, which had its genesis in Diebenkorn's specific feelings about the city of Urbana, appears to have been reprised a third time—two thousand miles away and one year later—in the even more abstract *Berkeley #8* (fig. 12 and pl. 6) of 1954. Although the architectonic geometry of the buildings in *Beach Town* has been almost completely fused with the shifting tectonic planes in *Berkeley #8*, the defining elements of the diagonal street (now compressed); the blue building with a peaked roof (now tilting); the high, broken horizon line; and the distant ocean all appear to be present. Formally, the evolution from *Beach Town* to *Urbana* to *Berkeley #8* seems to epitomize Diebenkorn's observation that "abstract means literally to draw from or separate."[36] Thematically, if *Beach Town* originated as the external projection of an imaginary and longed-for landscape, *Berkeley #8* appears to represent the artistic attainment of this ideal.

Nine years later, the *Beach Town* composition resurfaced a fourth time in *Cityscape #1* (originally titled *Landscape #1*) (fig. 13 and pl. 99) of 1963, which also depicts an aerial view of a street flanked by buildings ascending toward the sky in the distance.[37] In some respects this representational painting seems more radical than the earlier semiabstract and abstract versions, as the viewer brings to it assumptions regarding the conventions of reality, perspective, and gravity. The tightly compressed buildings resemble vertically stacked building blocks that bulge toward the street like a dam about to burst. The narrow foreground street, devoid of cars or people, dead ends in a larger rectangular street that resembles a vertical drawbridge or roadblock. The sharp, bladelike elements of the landscape introduce a disquieting note. The painting seems to convey the inherent tension between nature and culture at the edge of urban development.

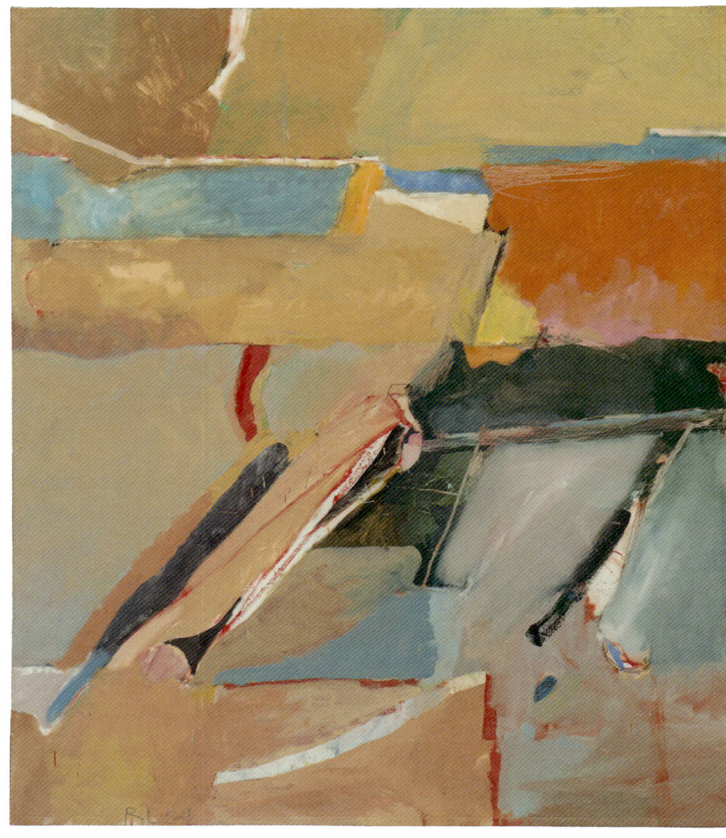

FIG 13
Richard Diebenkorn
***Cityscape #1*, 1963**
Oil on canvas
60 1/4 x 50 1/2 in. (153 x 128.3 cm)
San Francisco Museum of Modern Art, purchase with funds from Trustees and friends in memory of Hector Escobosa, Brayton Wilbur, and J. D. Zellerbach, 64.46
[1374]

FIG 12
Richard Diebenkorn
***Berkeley #8*, 1954**
Oil on canvas
69 1/8 x 59 1/8 in. (175.6 x 150.2 cm)
North Carolina Museum of Art, Raleigh, gift of W. R. Valentiner, G.57.34.3
[1109]

FIG 14
Richard Diebenkorn
***Ingleside*, 1963**
Oil on canvas
81 3/4 x 69 1/2 in. (207.6 x 176.5 cm)
Grand Rapids Art Museum, Michigan, Museum Purchase, 1967.1.1
[1383]

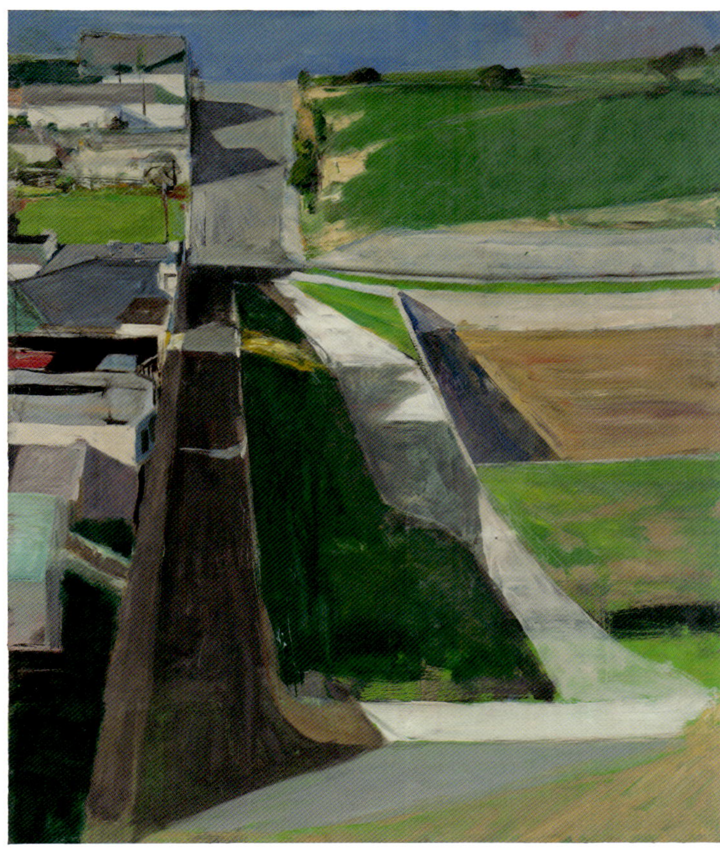

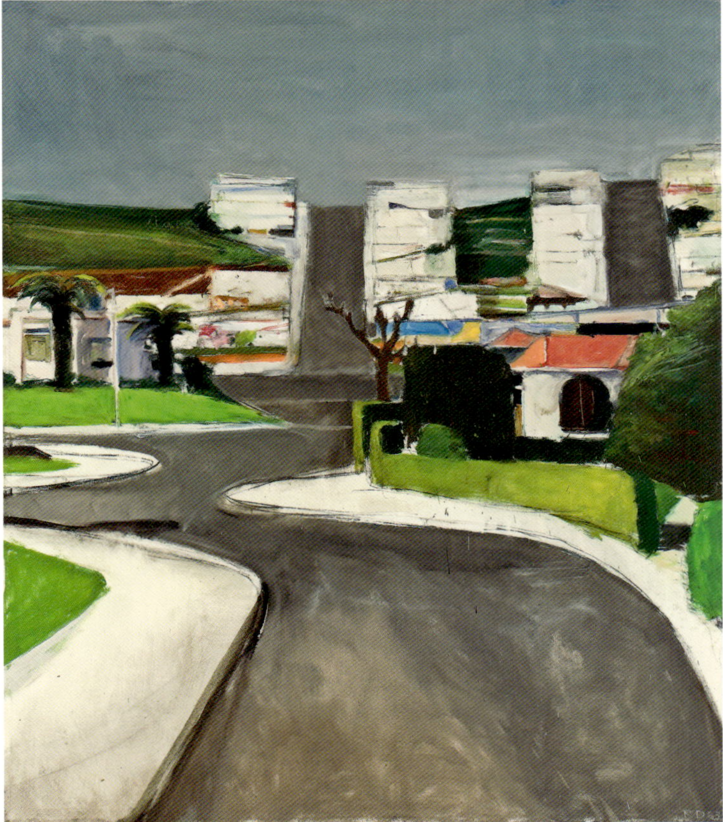

The various permutations of *Urbana #5 (Beach Town)*, including *Urbana*, *Berkeley #8*, and *Cityscape #1*, demonstrate that Diebenkorn's paintings ultimately relate as much to each other as they do to their varied sources of inspiration. This essential element of the artist's work accounts for his practice of working on several paintings simultaneously, making changes in individual works in order to enhance their resonance within the larger group. Diebenkorn explained this essential element of his working process to his New York art dealer Elinor Poindexter as early as 1955, and again in 1963:

> At worst what can happen when individual paintings, especially key works, slip out prematurely, is that I must start from scratch on each new painting. I can only blame myself for making exceptions to the way I know is right which is to hold tight to all the work until a kind of realization for the whole period is made.[38]

As Diebenkorn's remarks regarding the origins of the imaginary *Beach Town* composition suggest, his works could serve as external expressions of internal concerns. Similarly, his comments regarding *Ingleside* (fig. 14 and pl. 102) and *Ingleside II*, both from 1963, hint at the ways in which these paintings are—and are not—about Ingleside Terraces, the San Francisco neighborhood where Diebenkorn lived as a child:

> Visiting there [Ingleside Terraces] thirty years later provided me with a peculiarly concentrated subject matter, one which represented much that I had rejected in intervening years but which at the same time referred largely to what I am. A sense of place was built into my use of this material. I made on-the-spot sketches that were very brief, finding that when I painted from them in my Berkeley studio the relevant detail filled in easily. The pictures that came out of this don't refer to specific streets and houses but I believe are very much about the place, Ingleside. My sense of place is involved with particular pictures and subjects whereas my present environment has to do in a more general way with light, coloring, and configuration.[39]

Diebenkorn here makes a revealing distinction between his surrounding geographic "environment" and, alternately, "a sense of place," which was defined by his favored "pictures and subjects." In essence, he suggested that he physically inhabited his environment, while he traveled psychologically to his favored places through the medium of art. As a boy, Diebenkorn lived in Ingleside Terraces; as an adult he re-created an Ingleside Terraces that existed largely in his memories, which were tempered by time and experience—and by the necessities of art.

At least some of the "peculiarly concentrated subject matter" that had initially shaped Diebenkorn, but later had been rejected by him, may have involved the traditional values associated with suburban neighborhoods such as Ingleside Terraces. These values included the conventional career paths that he had rejected to pursue his true calling as an artist. As Diebenkorn recalled,

> My mother and father were super-bourgeois. My father was a good and honorable businessman but there was no imagination there. . . . As I got older and it was nearer to the time I would go to college, my father, who had turned down a fellowship to study medicine, wanted me to become a doctor or, if not, a lawyer. I wanted to be an artist. . . . But he didn't understand me really, and although my mother had a little more emotional understanding, she was with him.[40]

After revisiting his old neighborhood in the year prior to his father's death, Diebenkorn created paintings that captured the dual nature of suburbia, which can be beautiful or banal but, as in the idealized landscape of *Urbana #5 (Beach Town)*, also can proffer the promise of "an ocean on the other side of these things." The enduring resonance of this composition and theme for the artist is suggested by persistence of the imagery that first "kept coming, insisting" while he was living in Urbana, and remained with him in Berkeley. Sixteen years later, when Diebenkorn was working near an ocean in his Santa Monica studio, the familiar imagery of the *Beach Town* and Ingleside series paintings seems to have influenced the geometry of *Ocean Park #24* (fig. 15) of 1969, which evokes the presence of curvilinear pathways and geometric blocks, flanking a vertical red-orange passage that ascends to a blue-green expanse on the horizon.

Diebenkorn's Ingleside paintings reveal not only the intellectual component of the artist's works, but also his conception of a landscape or cityscape—or indeed any of his subjects—as a potential locus for the projection and expression of his thoughts and emotions. They serve as a reminder that Diebenkorn was both an abstract artist and an expressionist artist. As he observed, "I don't believe in the separation of intellect from emotion or intuition. To separate out one aspect, feeling for example, could lead to a hell of a mess."[41]

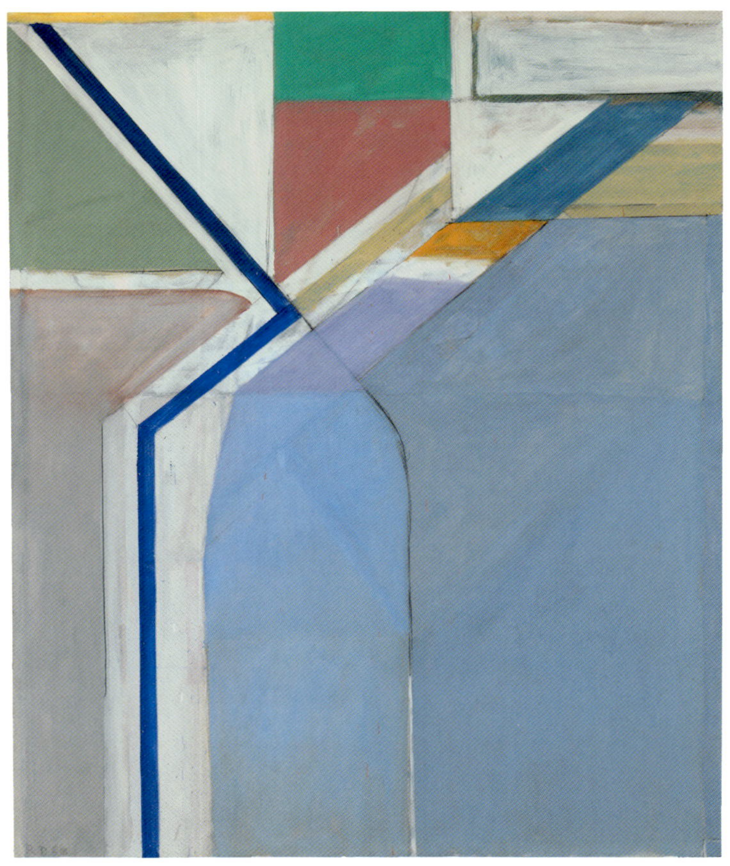

FIG 15
Richard Diebenkorn
***Ocean Park #24*, 1969**
Oil on canvas
93 3/4 x 77 1/2 in. (238.1 x 196.9 cm)
Yale University Art Gallery, New Haven, Connecticut, The Twigg-Smith Collection, gift of Laila and Thurston Twigg-Smith, B.E. 1942
[2414]

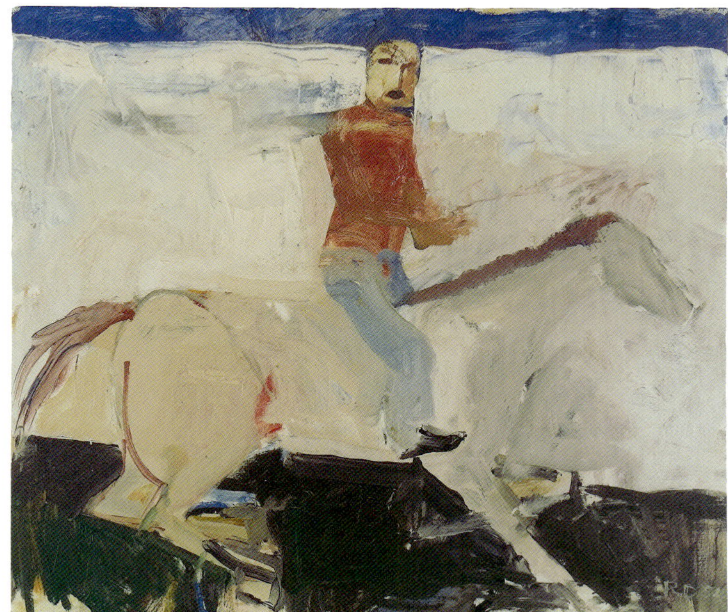

FIG 16
Richard Diebenkorn
Untitled (Horse and Rider), 1954
Oil on canvas
21 x 24 in. (53.3 x 61 cm)
The Grant Family Collection
[1122]

THE FIGURE—THE EMBODIMENT OF ART

Almost by definition, Diebenkorn's abstract Berkeley paintings typically were viewed as nonfigurative. The artist's own proscription against the identification of figurative imagery in these works was so strong that when the representational *Untitled (Horse and Rider)* (fig. 16) of 1954 first appeared in the family's home, at the height of his abstract period, his daughter was reluctant to verbally acknowledge the painting's figurative subject.[42]

Beyond the sympathetic audience of his family, one can empathize with Diebenkorn's dilemma regarding his abstract paintings. After having spent weeks or months forging an abstract vocabulary in a particular painting, the result often was reductively identified by viewers who perceived a figurative element. Diebenkorn spoke of his own apprehension regarding the persistent appearance of figurative elements in his abstract paintings:

> I thought I was being non-objective—absolutely non-figurative—and I would spoil so many canvases because I found a representational fragment, a Mickey Mouse . . . back it would go to be re-done. . . . It was impossible to imagine doing a picture without it being a landscape; to try to make a painting space, a pure painting space, but always end up with a figure against a ground.[43]

Paul Harris, a fellow graduate student at the University of New Mexico in Albuquerque in 1950–1951, recalled Diebenkorn's advocating "annihilating the image" and urging that "if you get an image, try to destroy it."[44] Diebenkorn's word choice is interesting as it acknowledges the occasional presence of an image that needed to be "annihilated" or "destroyed" (as opposed to simply covered or erased), a process that inherently could result in the presence of residual representational fragments and pentimenti in the final work.

Despite his admonitions to others, Diebenkorn acknowledged the presence of figurative animal elements in his otherwise abstract Albuquerque paintings. He explicitly identified such content in *The Disintegrating Pig* (fig. 17) of 1950; the title may serve as a metaphor for the artist's desire to "destroy" or abstract any conventional references to subject matter.[45] Diebenkorn also later recalled,

> Some of that animal imagery came about because . . . for the first year in Albuquerque we lived in a caretaker's small cottage on a kind of estate ranch on the outskirts of Albuquerque. . . . They raised both cattle and horses, so we might get up in the morning and go outside and find our house surrounded by animals. . . . Oh, and then another event there that related to some of the imagery; we went to a state fair in Albuquerque. And this was a total animal thing, and I just never had seen prize pigs and their humanoid aspects. They looked like big, hairy, fat men sitting around.[46]

At first glance, *Miller 22* (fig. 18) of 1951 seems to evoke a purely sensory experience of the pale, sun-bleached colors of Albuquerque's desert landscape. However, in the context of Diebenkorn's comments regarding the "animal imagery" in his works of this period, it is also possible to discern the schematic outline of a cow that has its head at the upper left, a nearly straight back that parallels the top of the painting, a single long blue-tipped leg at the left center, and pendant blue and brown udders/breasts at the right center. A possible second cow, represented by a trapezoidal head and a single, thick front leg, enters from the left and is only half visible.[47] Employing simple lines to distinguish form from space, Diebenkorn fused his "animal imagery" with the landscape ground to create a unified, two-dimensional pictorial field that resolved his tendency to "end up with a figure against a ground."

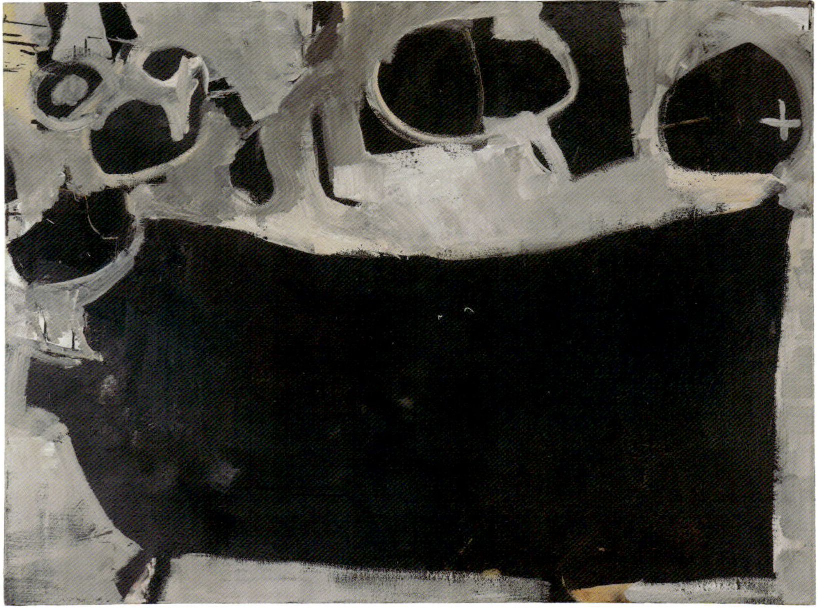

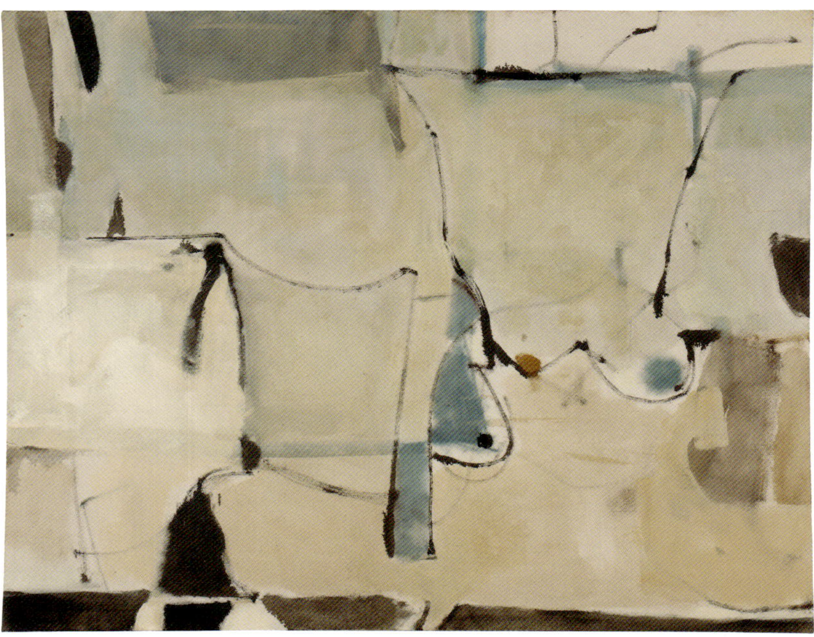

FIG 17
Richard Diebenkorn
***The Disintegrating Pig*, 1950**
Oil on canvas
36 1/2 x 47 1/4 in. (92.7 x 120 cm)
Iris and B. Gerald Cantor Center for Visual Arts at Stanford University, California, gift of Gretchen and Richard Grant, 1997.143
[573]

FIG 18
Richard Diebenkorn
***Miller 22*, 1951**
Oil on canvas
45 x 57 in. (114.3 x 144.8 cm)
Fine Arts Museums of San Francisco, bequest of Josephine Morris, 2003.25.1
[1070]

FIG 19
Richard Diebenkorn
***The Green Huntsman*, 1952**
Oil on canvas
42 3/4 x 69 1/2 in. (108.6 x 176.5 cm)
Private collection
[1091]

FIG 20
Richard Diebenkorn
***Urbana #2 (The Archer)*, 1953**
Oil on canvas
64 1/2 x 47 1/2 in. (163.8 x 120.7 cm)
Private collection
[1095]

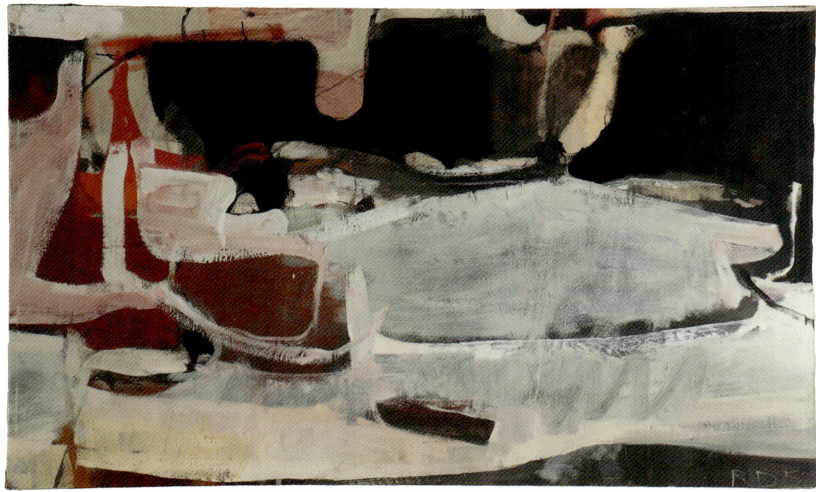

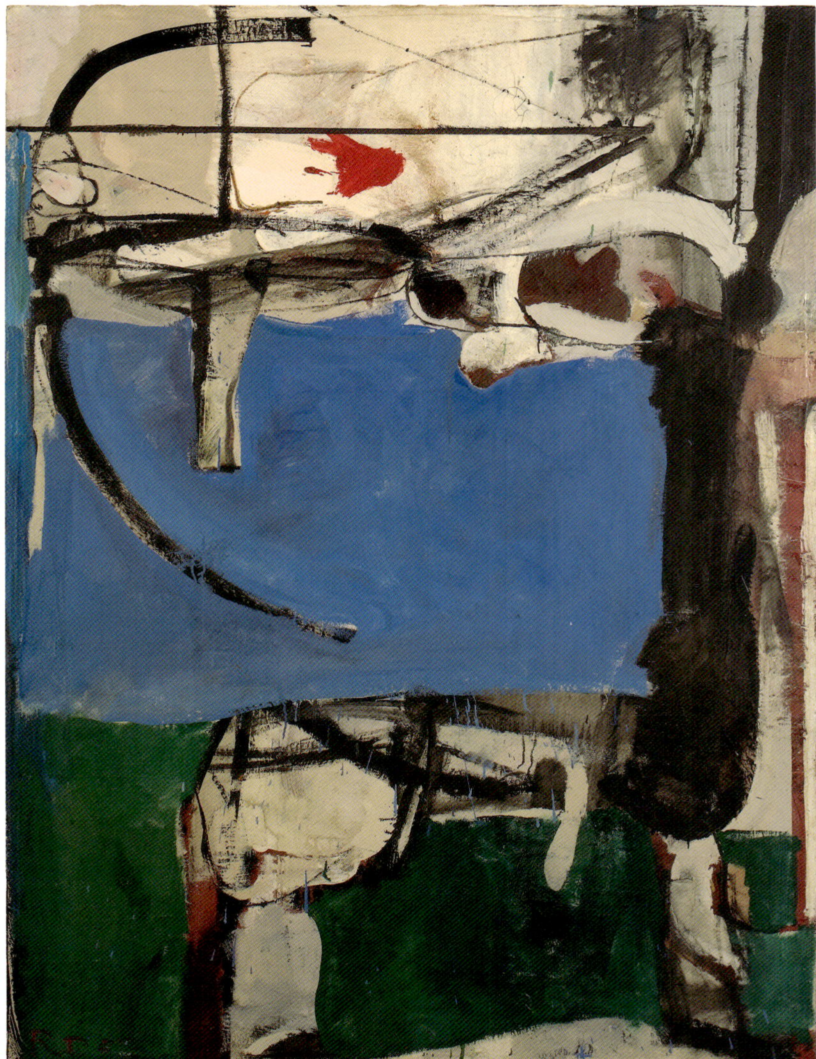

In *The Green Huntsman* (fig. 19) of 1952 Diebenkorn may have explored human figurative elements within a landscape setting.[48] The painting appears to depict a recumbent figure in profile, immersed in a red and black ground beneath a high horizon line. This enigmatic figure may evoke medieval precedents, such as a medieval tomb effigy or the dead soldiers that appear in the Bayeux Tapestry—an object much admired by the artist during his formative years.[49] Significantly, the painting may have provided a potential precedent for the artist's interest in embodying the landscape with the presence of an abstracted human figure.

Diebenkorn appears to have fused both human and animal imagery within a landscape setting in *Urbana #2 (The Archer)* (fig. 20) of 1953.[50] The black and white archer that dominates the composition holds a curved bow and is silhouetted against a banded landscape reminiscent of Mark Rothko's compositions. The shaft of the arrow doubles as a sight line, thus providing an apt metaphor for the archer's and the artist's intense focus. The upper third of the composition, which reads initially as a sky-like area, also may be seen as an animal form, with a short leg hanging down at the center left and anatomical elements that are conflated with those of the archer on the right.

Seemingly fusing a hunter with its prey at the critical moment of their intersection, *The Archer* reveals the influence of Viktor Lowenfeld's book *The Nature of Creative Activity* (1939), which Diebenkorn first read and admired in college.[51] Lowenfeld argued that there were two basic types of artists, visual and haptic, and he reproduced two drawings by children, both depicting the same subject—the picking of an apple from a tree—to explain the difference.[52] While the drawing by a "visual type" (fig. 21) depicts a relatively realistic view of this action, the drawing by a "haptic type" (fig. 22) accentuates the muscles/tendons in the upraised arm, enlarges the hand that reaches for the apple, and records the concerned expression of the man who makes the attempt.

Diebenkorn's vivid recollection of Lowenfeld's thesis nearly four decades later reveals his personal identification with the haptic or the "expressionist" type of artist, one who has an empathetic relationship with his subjects.[53] Works such as *The Archer* reveal Diebenkorn's interest in incorporating this sensibility—which emphasizes expressive, subjective, feeling, and sensing qualities over their representational, objective, thinking, and seeing counterparts—into his work. Reviewing various historical theories regarding styles of art that could be defined as representational and abstract, Lowenfeld offered a conclusion that elucidates an important distinction in Diebenkorn's own art:

> All these views have one thing in common: what is visually perceptible in the external universe is contrasted with what is seen with the inward "senses," with what is experienced. Art consists in depicting the relations of the artist to the world of his experiences, that is, in depicting his experience with objects and not the objects themselves. In other words, what is of final importance is the manner of experience which decisively determines the products of the artist.[54]

Diebenkorn's fusion of figurative forms within a landscape ground in *The Archer* reveals his interest in the metamorphosis of these varied elements as a component of his creative process, even if such elements are not readily visible in the abstract Berkeley paintings. Diebenkorn's desire to "destroy" or "annihilate" such imagery, often left incomplete during the Albuquerque and Urbana periods, typically was brought to greater resolution in the abstract Berkeley paintings, perhaps because of Diebenkorn's awareness that such hybrid images would be viewed with suspicion or hostility in the San Francisco Bay Area, where "abstract painting was a religion, and it didn't admit any backsliding to representational imagery."[55] Despite the artist's efforts to "destroy" any representational imagery, *The Archer* and other early works introduce the possibility that figurative elements occasionally might be present in otherwise abstract Berkeley-period works.

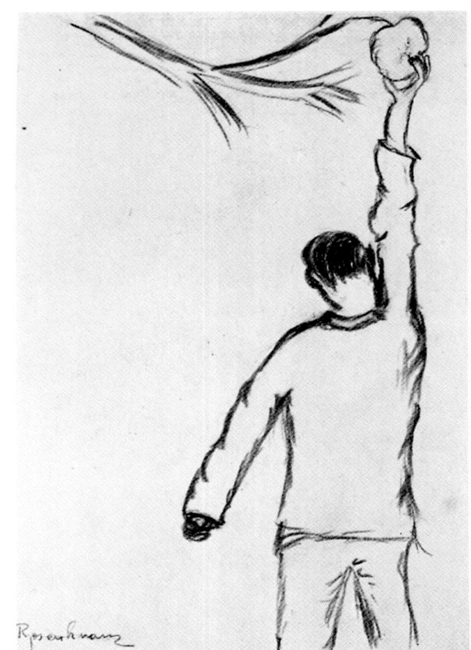

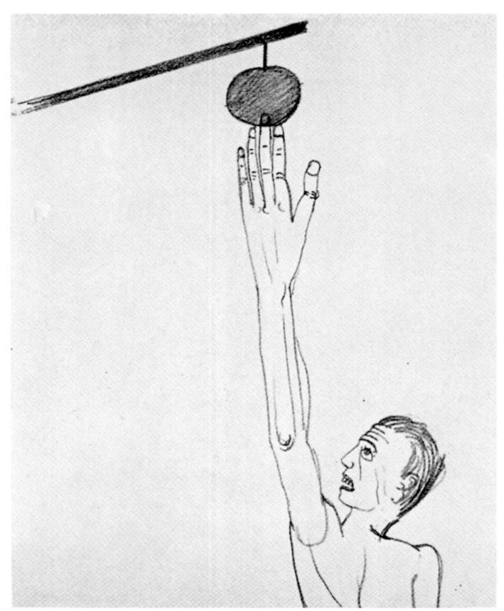

FIGS 21–22
Drawings of a man picking an apple by a "visual type" and a "haptic type," figs. 76a and 76b in Viktor Lowenfeld's *The Nature of Creative Activity*, 1939

FIG 23
Richard Diebenkorn
***Berkeley #3*, 1953**
Oil on canvas
54 1/8 x 68 in. (137.5 x 172.7 cm)
Fine Arts Museums of San Francisco, bequest of Josephine Morris, 2003.25.3
[1102]

FIG 24
Richard Diebenkorn
***Untitled*, 1953**
Ink on paper
19 x 24 in. (48.3 x 61 cm)
Private collection
[7811]

FIG 25
Richard Diebenkorn
***Untitled (Nude)*, 1954**
Oil on canvas
32 1/8 x 36 3/4 in. (81.6 x 93.3 cm)
Private collection
[2403]

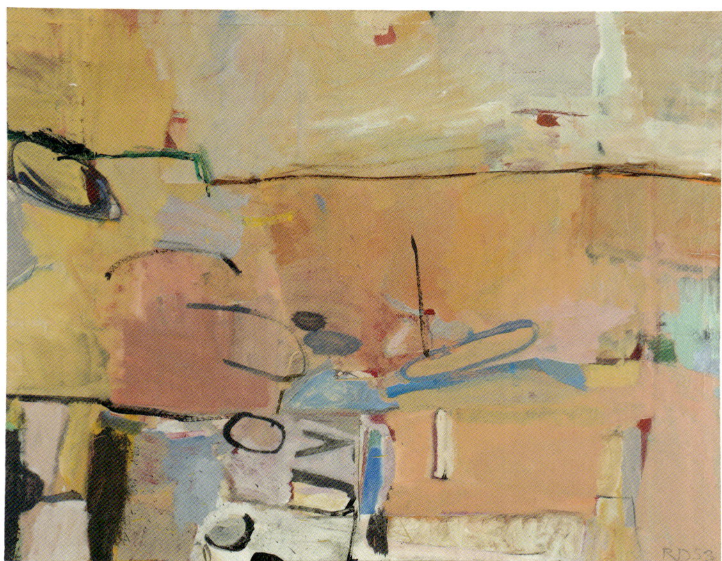

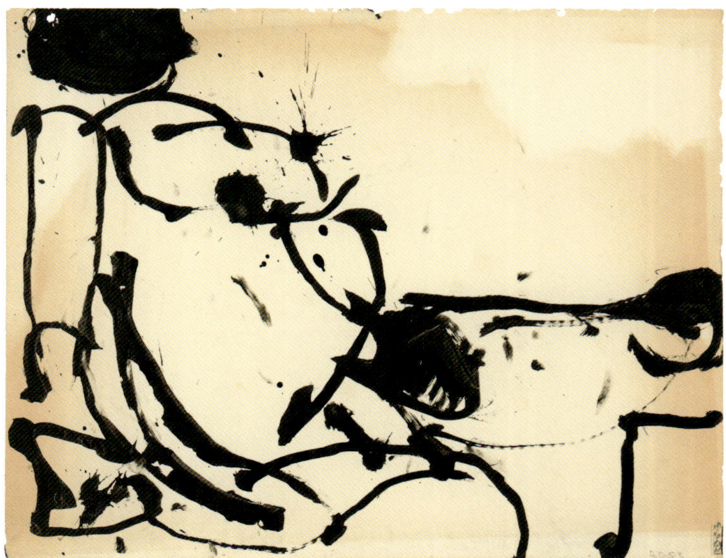

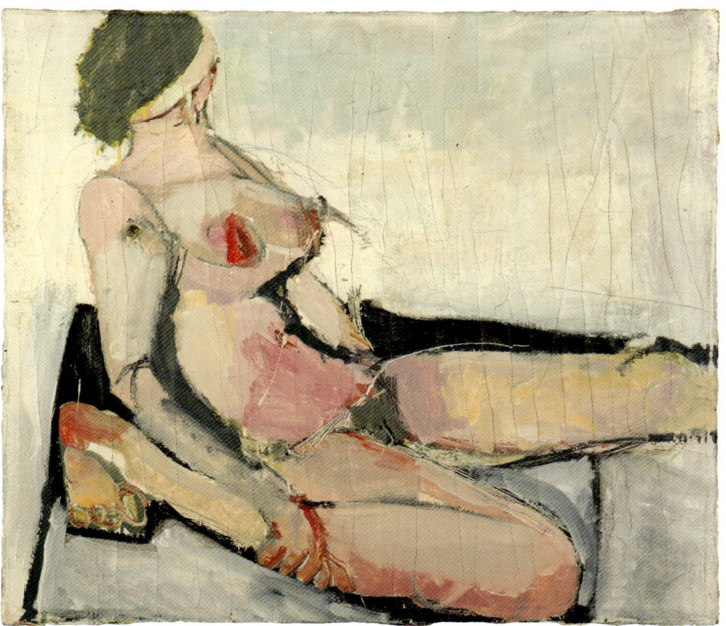

Berkeley #3 (fig. 23 and pl. 2) of 1953 appears to have been painted over an earlier Albuquerque or Urbana composition, and the stepped horizon line may be a reminiscence of a distinctive mesa that was visible from Diebenkorn's house in Albuquerque.[56] The tripartite division of the landscape is a defining characteristic of both Albuquerque, with its desert, distant mesa, and the sky, and Berkeley, which looks down on a flat shoreline, across San Francisco Bay, and up to the sky.[57] Diebenkorn's mingling of linear and aerial perspective cues has the effect of displacing normal conventions of seeing and thus disorienting the viewer. The implicit but unresolved presence of a landscape highlights the contrast between his abstract and representational inclinations.

Despite the abundance of landscape references in *Berkeley #3*, the painting's predominantly pink-hued palette also is evocative of human flesh. The painting thus bears comparison with a drawing of a nude, *Untitled* (fig. 24) of 1953, and the clearly related painting *Untitled (Nude)* (fig. 25) of 1954, a rare figurative work from this period that presages the artist's stylistic shift of the following year.[58] The female figures in both the drawing and the painting each have abstracted oval heads, prominent breasts, and awkward poses, each with one leg folded under her body and the other extended. Tellingly, the contours of their extended legs are suggestive of a shoreline or horizon line in a landscape.

Reexamining *Berkeley #3* in the context of these two related works, it is possible to perceive a similar semi-reclining figure, comprising a dark green and blue oval headlike form at the upper left, and two black and gray curvilinear breastlike forms below. This composition thus would seem to exemplify Diebenkorn's statement regarding his abstract works that "It was impossible to imagine doing a picture without it being a landscape; to try to make a painting space, a pure painting space, but always end up with a figure against a ground."[59] Yet, absent the context provided by the related drawing and oil study, the possible presence of vestigial figurative elements would be difficult to discern. In its final state, the complete integration of figure and ground in *Berkeley #3* seems to embody the artist's successful realization of his desire to create "a pure painting space."

Diebenkorn's interest in achieving a complete fusion of figure and ground in the abstract Berkeley works is apparent in a drawing, *Untitled (Berkeley)* (fig. 26 and pl. 18) of 1955. Spatially, the curvilinear imagery hints at three-dimensionality but is situated on an emphatically two-dimensional picture plane that can be viewed with equal emphasis from any of the four major orientations. Pictorially, the conventional rules of representation—not to mention the laws of gravity—have been suspended. Thematically, the viewer is confronted with what appears to be a disorienting array of flattened, flayed, and dismembered anatomical forms. Elements that resemble veins or organs, suggestive of connectivity or consummation, link these various fragments and underscore the universal nature of these life forces.

Untitled (Berkeley) records Diebenkorn's interest in the type of mutable biomorphic imagery associated with Surrealism and embraced for its pictorial potential by Abstract Expressionists such as Willem de Kooning. Seemingly initially derived from animal forms during the Albuquerque period, and then additionally from human forms during the Urbana period, this nascent figurative imagery may have served as a metaphor for artistic growth, a concept that animates the abstract Berkeley paintings, even—or perhaps especially—when such imagery was sublimated or suppressed.

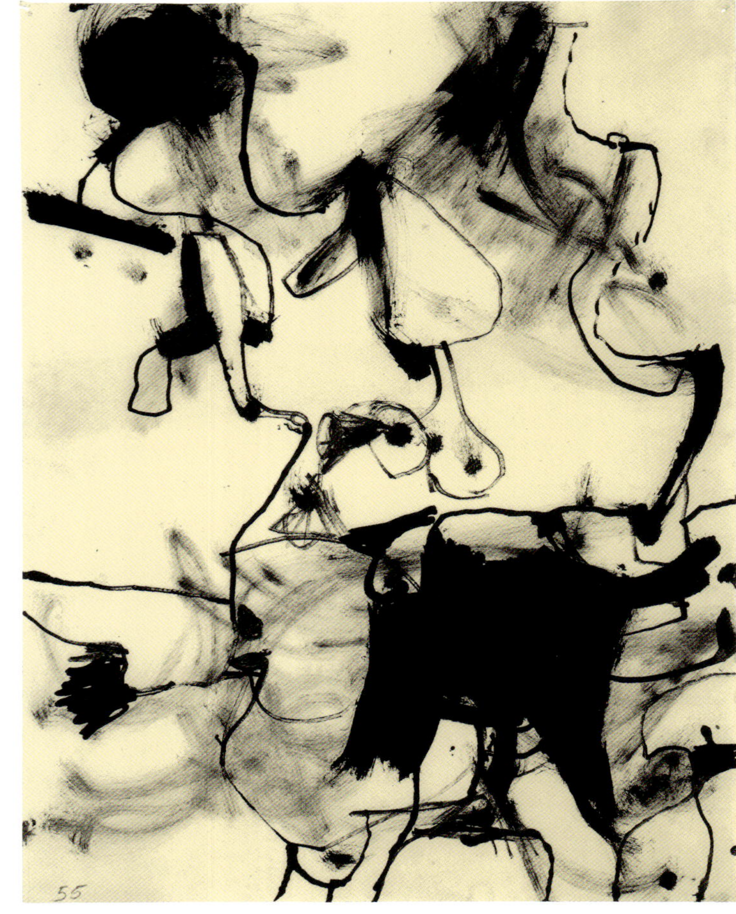

FIG 26
Richard Diebenkorn
***Untitled (Berkeley)*, 1955**
Ink and gouache on paper
11 x 8 1/2 in. (27.9 x 21.6 cm)
Private collection
[2149]

FIG 27
Richard Diebenkorn
***Berkeley #23* (first state painted over), 1954**
Oil on canvas
62 x 54 3/4 in. (157.5 x 139.1 cm)

FIG 28
Richard Diebenkorn
***Berkeley #23*, 1955**
Oil on canvas
62 x 54 3/4 in. (157.5 x 139.1 cm)
San Francisco Museum of Modern Art, gift of the Women's Board, 58.1729
[1125]

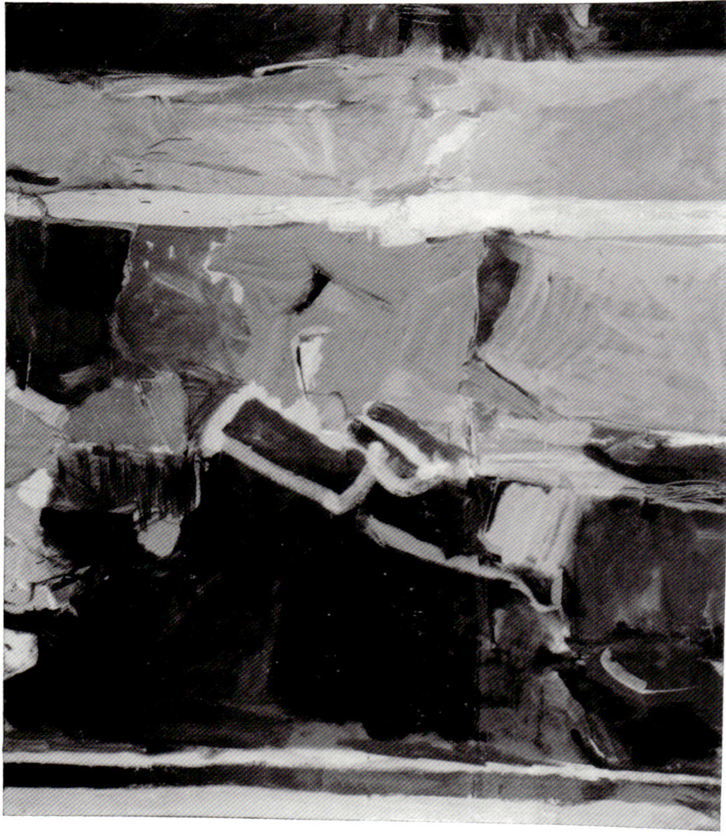

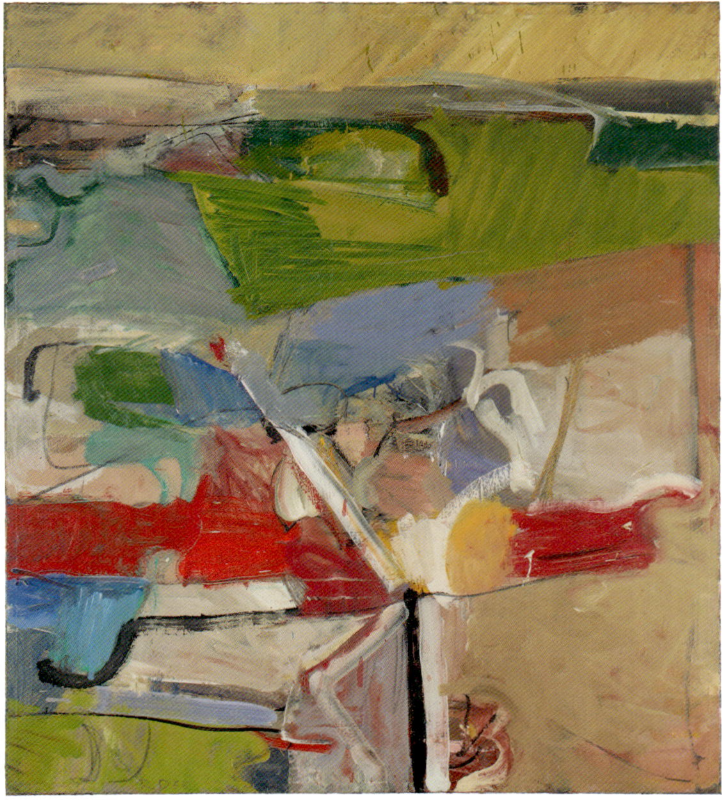

METAMORPHOSIS

Diebenkorn's first three years in Berkeley were distinguished by an array of exhibitions that identified him as a rising star in the art world. His critical and popular reputation was enhanced by Herschel B. Chipp's profile, "Diebenkorn Paints a Picture," published in *Art News* in May 1957.[60] Commissioned following the critical success of the artist's first major one-person exhibition of abstract works in New York, the article documents the creation of the figurative painting *Woman by the Ocean* (pl. 47) of 1956.[61] Rose Mandel's accompanying series of sequential photographs (see pp. 232–237) reveals the remarkable transformation of Diebenkorn's initial conception of a half-length figure of a seated man, posed at the lower right against an open field and distant hills, into a three-quarter-length image of a seated woman posed at the lower left on a covered porch with a distant view of a beach and ocean.

"Diebenkorn Paints a Picture" offers a rare glimpse of the artist's mature working method, in which subjects were not conceived a priori and then rendered, but rather were experienced visually, physically, and emotionally on the canvas, a hallmark of his Berkeley-period paintings. The article dramatically illustrates the degree to which every element in one of Diebenkorn's paintings was subject to a process of metamorphic mutation—one open to both chance and change.[62] Works such as *Landscape with Clubs* (fig. 3) also reveal the presence of a magical, alchemical component that mingles fact (e.g., the three peaks of the Tudor-style house next door to the artist's Berkeley home) and fantasy (e.g., the club-shaped tree and its massive shadow—a reminiscence of his childhood fascination with heraldic symbols in the Bayeux Tapestry).[63]

Despite the appearance of spontaneity that characterizes Dienbenkorn's abstract paintings, they typically required an extended creative effort. The artist's New York dealer Elinor Poindexter explained to an impatient client that "only he can decide when they are finished, and it is often involved in a reworking process covering several years."[64] The first state (fig. 27) of *Berkeley #23* was completed in 1954, but the final version (fig. 28 and pl. 8), completed in 1955, was so drastically reworked as to be unrecognizable. Diebenkorn's organic process of artistic metamorphosis underscored that he was not trying to realize a preconceived image, but rather sought to discover a compelling image through the painting process:

> I think that my necessity to work and rework a canvas in order to realize it becomes a process wherein my idea or ideas are externalized. I find that I can never conceive a painting idea, put it on canvas, and accept it. . . . Almost from the beginning, I looked forward with relief to being able to correct, to set things right. . . . It was as though I'd failed in my performance but somehow was able to steal this second chance and thereby come up with something that I could set out with the works of my peers (which were, of course, first crack). . . . Later yet I began to feel that what I was really up to in painting, what I enjoyed almost exclusively, was altering–changing what was before me–by way of subtracting or juxtaposition or superimposition of different ideas.[65]

Diebenkorn's paintings are distinguished by the accumulated physical traces of his reworking process, in which prior states are alternately amended, concealed, and revealed. Pictorial problems often are left suspended on the canvas, caught in a state of tension between further complication or final resolution. In a revealing verbal slip, Diebenkorn referred to the earlier marks or "pentimenti" in his works as "impedimenti."[66] Despite being finished, the works have an open-ended quality—the sense that their physical and emotional forces have been set in motion and, although momentarily achieving a state of realization on the canvas, might recommence at any time and continue to evolve.[67] Diebenkorn's reluctance to fix a definitive image was an affirmation of his belief in painting as a contingent process, rather than a finished product.[68] As his fellow artist and friend Wayne Thiebaud observed, "There's a systematic skepticism inherent in his paintings—they always seem complete, but never finished."[69]

THE SYNTHESIS OF ABSTRACTION AND REPRESENTATION

Ironically, as the recognition of Diebenkorn's work among critics, curators, and collectors increased, so, too, did the artist's doubts regarding his abstractions. Willem de Kooning's renewed interest in overtly figurative works, dramatically heralded by the publication of *Woman I* of 1950–1952 in *Art News* in 1953, deeply affected Diebenkorn, who recalled, "My faith in Abstract Expressionism had been shaken by de Kooning; so strong a man as he had changed."[70] Diebenkorn's undated drawing *Untitled* (fig. 29) was created at a time when Abstract Expressionism had taken on an aura of orthodoxy, with its leading practitioners canonized, while artists working in other—especially figurative—modes were condemned as reactionary:

> In the rush of painting that I did in 1954–1955, I had experienced my first kind of opposition. It was a struggle all along, but that is the story of being an artist! But in 1955 things started to slow down, and I was attributing this to my being in a stylistic straightjacket. I felt that perhaps I had too many rules, that there was too much Abstract Expressionism hanging over my head, and so . . . there was a need for change.[71]

Diebenkorn's caricature of an Abstract Expressionist recalls Clyfford Still's role as professor and proselytizer at CSFA in San Francisco. This figure is finger-painting a biomorphic form with red pigment—or perhaps even blood—on an unframed canvas, in a witty parody of the primal processes promoted by Abstract Expressionism. The cross in the upper right corner is a sign of the nearly religious zeal with which the dogma of the movement was preached and practiced by its masters and their acolytes. Rejecting these prescriptive practices, Diebenkorn argued through his work for aesthetic inclusivity and acceptance:

> Painting . . . art . . . has followed an exclusivity track which began with clearing out much false value which was brought to art in the 19th century. It continued with refining and simplifying of forms in the first one-third of this century. Then because this course had

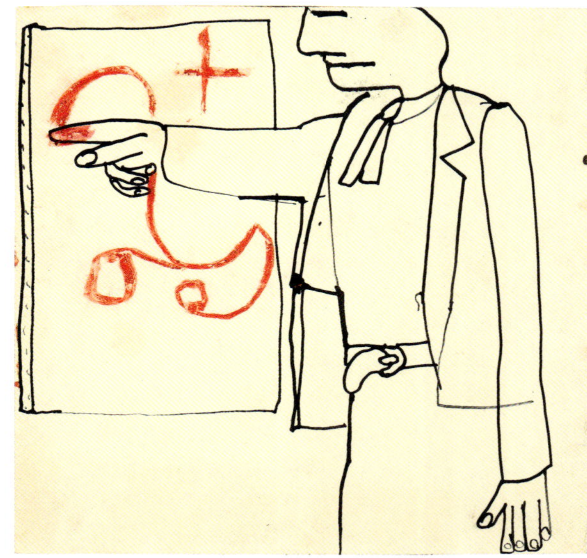

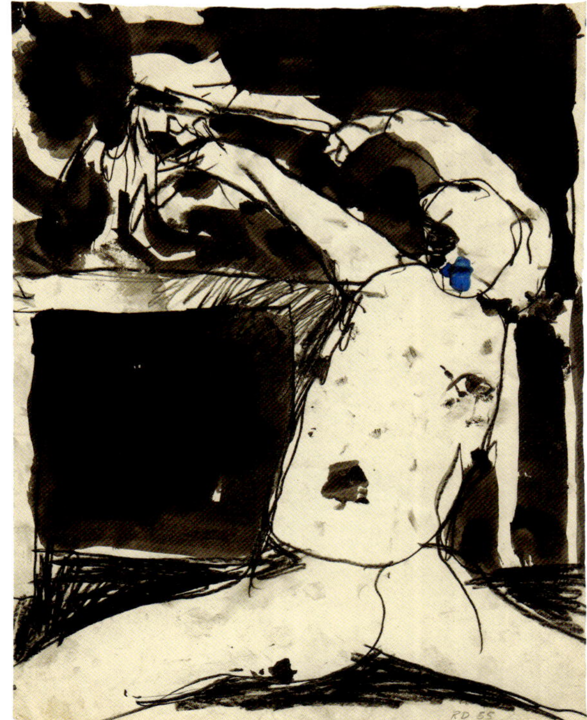

> been a right one for so long (50 or 60 years), it was continued. The point was not noticed when real and positive values were simplified and expunged, too.[72]

Diebenkorn's *Untitled (Abstract Expressionist Painter)* (fig. 30) of 1955 reveals that he was equally critical of his own identity as an Abstract Expressionist.[73] In a darkened room, presumably late at night, a paint-smudged artist is in a frenzy of creation, nearly collapsing under the weight of his exertions. He reaches with outstretched arms and, like a shaman, flings paint with abandon at his canvas. This overt parody of New York School "action painting," in which the artist commits his entire physical and psychological being to the work, embodied the excessive emotional content that Diebenkorn viewed with increasing misgivings in his own work. As he stated,

> I came to mistrust my desire to explode the picture and super-charge it in some way. At one time the common device of using the super-emotional to get "in gear" with a painting used to serve me for access to painting, too, but I mistrust that now. I think that what is more important is a feeling of strength in reserve—tension beneath calm. I don't want to be less violent or discordant or less shocking than before; but I think I can make my paintings more powerful this way.[74]

Diebenkorn's misgivings regarding his Abstract Expressionist works coalesced late in 1955, when he painted a small plein-air suburban landscape, *Chabot Valley* (pl. 36).[75] Although he often cited this as his first representational work, the actual sequence of events was more complicated. First, as we have seen, even while painting abstractly, figuration never completely disappeared from his art. Second, Diebenkorn already had created earlier representational paintings, including *Untitled (Pianist and Cellist)* of 1952–1953, *Untitled (Nude)* (fig. 25) of 1954, and *Untitled (Horse and Rider)* (fig. 16) of 1954.[76] Third, throughout the abstract period, Diebenkorn had created figurative drawings from live models during his drawing sessions with David Park and Elmer Bischoff, who preceded and influenced

FIG 29
Richard Diebenkorn
***Untitled*, n.d.**
Ink and crayon on paper
9 7/8 x 10 in. (25.1 x 25.4 cm)
Private collection
[5796]

FIG 30
Richard Diebenkorn
***Untitled (Abstract Expressionist Painter)*, 1955**
Charcoal, gouache, and ink on paper
15 1/2 x 12 in. (39.4 x 30.5 cm)
Private collection
[3541]

Diebenkorn's shift to figuration.[77] Finally, briefly wavering regarding his decision, in 1956 Diebenkorn created or completed additional abstract works (i.e., *Berkeley #59*, *#63*, *#65*, *#66* [pl. 39], *#67*) that postdate *Chabot Valley*.[78]

Describing the motivations for his dramatic shift to figuration, Diebenkorn commented,

> I can remember that when I stopped abstract painting and started figure painting it was as though a kind of constraint came in that was welcomed because I had felt that in the last of the abstract paintings around '55, it was almost as though I could do too much, too easily. There was nothing hard to come up against. And suddenly the figure painting furnished a lot of this.[79]

Diebenkorn's shift from abstraction to representation at the peak of his greatest critical acclaim shocked the art world, whose polarization made it nearly impossible for any artist to occupy a middle ground between the two aesthetic camps.[80] One private collector telephoned the artist to complain, "What have you done to the value of my paintings?"[81] Diebenkorn, however, stated emphatically, "I wasn't going to let considerations about career influence me as to whether I continued the figurative painting or not."[82] Perceiving the overlooked potential inherent in figuration, Diebenkorn defiantly declared, "Bad nonrepresentational painting isn't very bad. But representational painting can be so damned bad and so terrible that, perhaps, it can be that much better."[83]

Affirming his persistent interest in favored themes and subjects that transcended abstract or representational modes of expression, Diebenkorn observed, "I've simply taken somewhat different form to talk about the things I've always wanted to."[84] Unlike most of his contemporaries, who perceived the choice between representation and abstraction as an either/or proposition, Diebenkorn identified the continued oscillation between these two modes as ultimately more productive than their resolution:

> All paintings start out of a mood, out of a relationship with things or people, out of a complete visual impression. To call this expression abstract seems to me often to confuse the issue. Abstract means literally to draw from or separate. In this sense every artist is abstract . . . a realistic or non-objective approach makes no difference. The result is what counts. But I've been content to accept the label of Abstract-Expressionist because I do feel a kinship with the honest search of these painters. A forceful quality in art, truly representative of our modern situation, will rise above the labels of abstraction and realism . . . a painter is bound to reflect himself and his times.[85]

Diebenkorn's summary statement tellingly gives primacy to an emotional "mood"—his deeply personal relationship with his objects and subjects—as the protean force that generated and animated his images. Deliberately defining "abstract" as a verb rather than a noun, he also clearly stated his belief that the creation of every type of art involves a process of abstraction that is intrinsic to the very definition of art. While critics traditionally have viewed Diebenkorn's work through the prescriptive lenses of abstraction or figuration, he noted that their subjects—the artist and his work—are by nature resistant to such arbitrary categorizations.

In this regard, it might be more accurate to say that Diebenkorn did not so much reflect his times as struggle with them, affirming his kinship with the ideals of Abstract Expressionism, but ultimately rejecting the doctrinaire aspects of the movement in favor of a more encompassing definition of modernism that also embraced the human figure. Diebenkorn's struggle was embodied in the gradual synthesis of his "super emotional" abstract mode with a figurative mode characterized by a "strength in reserve—tension beneath calm." This symbiotic synthesis was explored during the pre-Berkeley years, obscured or obliterated in the Berkeley abstractions, and then openly expressed and fully realized in the subsequent figurative works (see fig. 31). The catalytic combination of these ostensibly opposing forces, abstraction and figuration, closely paralleled by emotion and intellect, endow the resulting artworks with a physical and psychological resonance that is exponentially greater than they could achieve in isolation.

FIG 31
Richard Diebenkorn in his Hillcrest studio with *Berkeley #41* (1955) and *Man and Woman Seated* (1958), Berkeley. Photographed by Fred Lyon, 1958

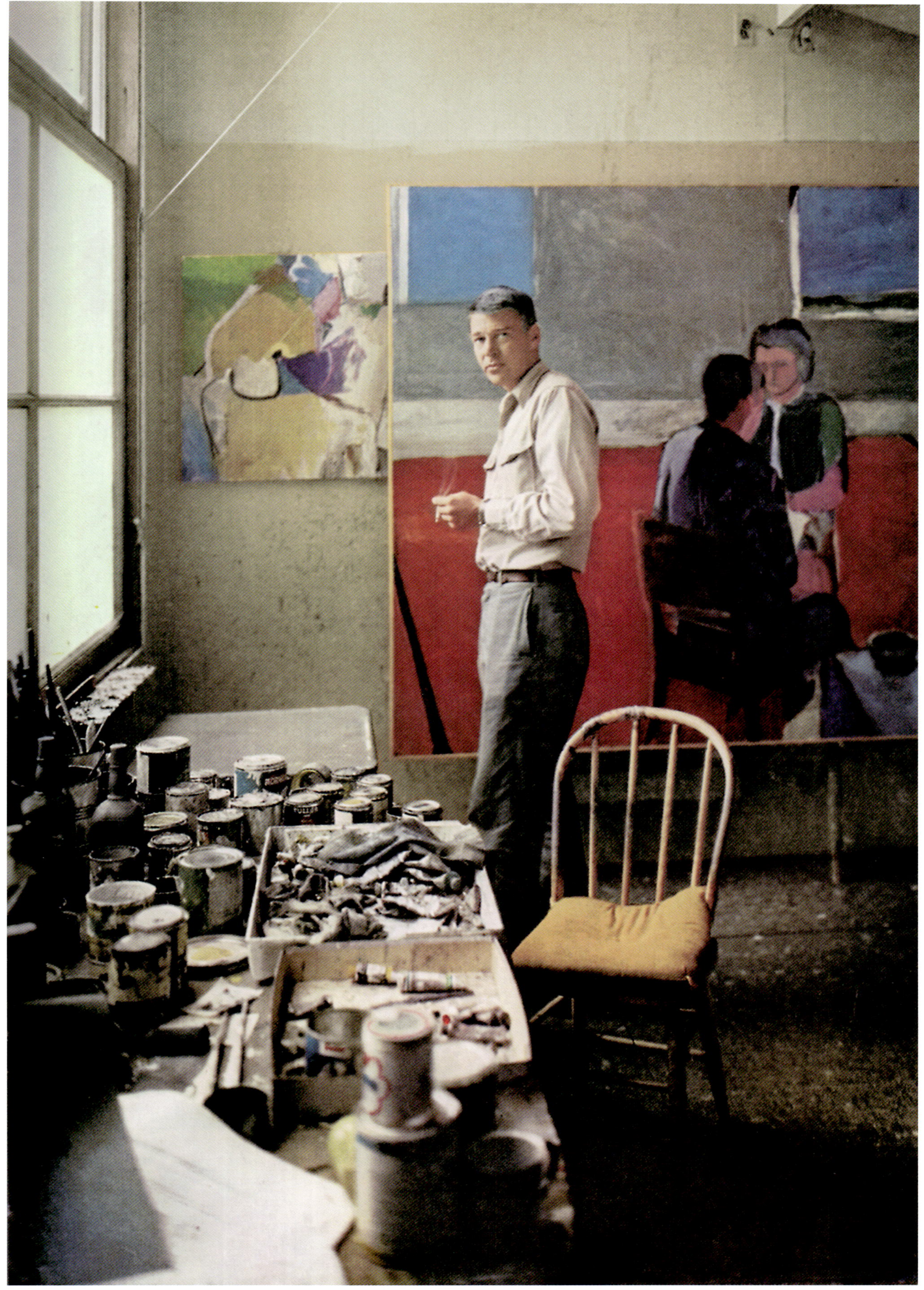

1 Herschel B. Chipp, "Diebenkorn Paints a Picture," *Art News* 56, no. 3 (May 1957): 45–47, 54–55.

2 Manuel Neri, quoted in Beth Coffelt, "Doomsday in the Bright Sun," *San Francisco Sunday Examiner and Chronicle: California Living Magazine*, October 16, 1977.

3 Richard Diebenkorn, quoted by sculptor Paul Harris, cited in Maurice Tuchman, "Diebenkorn's Early Years," in Robert T. Buck, Jr., Linda L. Cathcart, Gerald Nordland, and Maurice Tuchman, *Richard Diebenkorn: Paintings and Drawings, 1943–1976*, exh. cat. (Buffalo, NY: Albright-Knox Art Gallery, 1976), 13.

4 The Abraham Rosenberg Fellowship was "awarded to mature artists to carry out approved projects in the fields of painting or sculpture." The jury included the painters David Park, Karl Kasten, and Ward Lockwood; director of the San Francisco Museum of Art Dr. Grace L. McCann Morley; and critic Alfred Frankenstein. See "Richard Diebenkorn Wins Rosenberg Fellowship," *San Francisco Art Association Bulletin* 20, nos. 2–3 (February–March 1954): n.p.

5 Eleven additional numbered Berkeley canvases were either painted over or are missing and presumed destroyed by the artist. Diebenkorn's sequential numbers often document when the works were commenced but, given his propensity for reworking canvases, do not necessarily indicate the date of completion. Thus, *Berkeley #25*, *#26* (pl. 23), and *#33* (fig. 65) are dated 1954, even though every other painting numbered *#23* or higher is dated 1955 or 1956. Documentation for the abstract Berkeley paintings provided by Andrea Liguori, Director of Research and Associate Editor for the Diebenkorn catalogue raisonné project, in an e-mail to the author, July 17, 2012.

6 The works of Mark Rothko (whom Diebenkorn knew when the New York School artist taught summer sessions at CSFA in 1947 and 1949) would have provided a precedent for numbered painting titles. Critiquing his own system, Diebenkorn noted, "It was an extremely unsatisfactory system of naming paintings—number this and that; I haven't any idea which was which." Ellen Johnson, "Diebenkorn's 'Woman by a Large Window,'" *Allen Memorial Art Museum Bulletin* 16, no. 1 (Fall 1958): 19. In 1955, the year Diebenkorn shifted from abstraction to figuration, artist Kyle Morris, curator of an exhibition that included Diebenkorn's work, observed, "A few years back it was almost *démodé* to suggest that one's painting referred to something outside of itself, that it was less than pure art. This attitude has changed somewhat, and fewer painters title their work by numbers." Kyle Morris, *Vanguard 1955: A Painter's Selection of New American Paintings*, exh. cat. (Minneapolis: Walker Art Center, 1955), n.p.

7 Regarding her husband's switch from abstraction to representation, Phyllis Diebenkorn told him, "There'd been unmistakable feints in that direction, but, then, there'd been so many feints before. So it did sort of shake me up. Some people were terribly shocked. . . . As for me, I was just sitting there. I had taken a lot of time just getting used to what you were doing before you switched, and then you totally changed course. I was so puzzled. And probably a bit disappointed, too, though I never said so. What you'd started doing seemed a little square, and you'd trained me so carefully not to be square." Dan Hofstadter, "Profiles: Almost Free of the Mirror," *The New Yorker*, September 7, 1987, 54.

8 Nearly two decades later, Diebenkorn offered his own perspective: "There is something that I want to say here about the 'ability to move back and forth.' It's true that I've done this—three times in my life—into abstraction from representation, back to representation, then back to abstraction. So apparently I have this capacity—but putting it that way makes it sound like 'I know how to do it,' and this is very far from the case. It has been done with the utmost trepidation and great difficulty. In my experience abstraction and reality are totally different worlds—different laws—different methodology." Richard Diebenkorn, quoted in Jan Butterfield, "Pentimenti: Seeing and Then Seeing Again" in *Resource/Response/Reservoir—Richard Diebenkorn: Paintings 1948–1983*, exh. brochure (San Francisco: San Francisco Museum of Modern Art, May 1983), n.p.

9 Hofstadter, "Profiles," 55, 58.

10 In a lecture on September 26, 2011, in conjunction with the exhibition *Richard Diebenkorn: The Ocean Park Series* (September 24, 2011–January 15, 2012) at the Modern Art Museum of Fort Worth, Texas, the artist's daughter, Gretchen Diebenkorn Grant, noted that "nearly all of his representational landscapes and interiors are from his mind."

11 Jorge Goya-Lukich, whose studies (1947–1950) at CSFA overlapped with Diebenkorn's, described the complex yet surprisingly consistent ways that an artist's concerns could find expression in both abstract and representational modes: "So whether I was painting in a studio with Clyfford Still, which you might call refining an interior experience, or painting landscapes with Hassel [Smith], which would be refining an exterior experience, didn't make any difference." Mary Fuller McChesney, *A Period of Exploration: San Francisco 1945–1950*, exh. cat. (Oakland, CA: Oakland Museum Art Department, 1973), 53.

12 James Schevill, "Art: Richard Diebenkorn," *Frontier: The Voice of the New West* 8, no. 3 (January 1957): 21.

13 Richard Diebenkorn, quoted in Gail R. Scott, *New Paintings by Richard Diebenkorn*, exh. brochure (Los Angeles: Los Angeles County Museum of Art, 1969), n.p.

14 Gerald Nordland, *Richard Diebenkorn* (New York: Rizzoli, 1987), 38.

15 Richard Diebenkorn, translated from the original French text in Alain Jouffroy and K. A. Jelenski, "Une grande enquête: Tendances de la jeune peinture," *Preuves* 68 (October 1956): 36.

16 William Brice, quoted in Jane Livingston, "The Art of Richard Diebenkorn," in Jane Livingston, John Elderfield, and Ruth E. Fine, *The Art of Richard Diebenkorn*, exh. cat. (New York: Whitney Museum of American Art in association with University of California Press, 1997), 75.

17 Richard Diebenkorn, quoted in the film *Richard Diebenkorn*, directed by Tom McGuire (Los Angeles: Los Angeles County Museum of Art and TV, 1977). Videocassette (VHS), 22:40 min.

18 Despite their landscape referents, only a few abstract Berkeley canvases (e.g., *Berkeley #3* [fig. 23 and pl. 2], *#25*, and *#56* [pl. 33]) have emphatically horizontal landscape proportions. Far more (e.g., *Berkeley #17*, *#22* [pl. 24], and *#39*) are perceived by the viewer as horizontal due to the artist's use of stratification and horizon lines as prominent compositional elements.

19 Mark Rothko, letter to Herbert Ferber, ca. fall 1947, in Miguel López-Remiro, *Mark Rothko: Writings in Art* (New Haven, CT: Yale University Press, 2006), 53.

20 Edward Corbett, a friend and fellow teacher (1947–1951) at CSFA who also painted in New Mexico, articulated views regarding the relevance of place to an artist's work that seem sympathetic with Diebenkorn's own perspective: "I am quite aware of my surroundings and I know damned well that they do influence the painting. I never have believed that any painter has escaped this kind of effect on his work, that is, of his visual experience. That's limiting it pretty closely to the visual experience but everything else—the way things smell, the way things are ordered in an abstract way, the seasons, the days, the hours—all of these things enter into it. I think it is not to be simplified. It is complex by its nature." Edward Corbett, quoted in McChesney, *A Period of Exploration*, 55.

21 Diebenkorn's four Berkeley studios: in the family's apartment at 2837 Webster Street (1953–1954), in the "VW studio" at 2751 Shattuck Avenue (1954–1956), in the backyard of the family's house at 217 Hillcrest Road (1956–1966), and in the "Triangle studio" at the intersection of Ashby Avenue and Adeline Streets (1958–1964).

22 Richard Diebenkorn, quoted in interview with Mark Lavatelli, November 1978, cited in Lavatelli, "Diebenkorn's Albuquerque Years," in Gerald Nordland, Mark Lavatelli, and Charles Strong, *Richard Diebenkorn in New Mexico*, exh. cat. (Santa Fe: Museum of New Mexico Press, 2007), 29.

23 Dore Ashton, in a review of Diebenkorn's first one-person exhibition at the Poindexter Gallery in New York in 1956, deemed landscape to be Diebenkorn's point of departure: "The Western landscape too has worked undeniable magic in the soul of this young painter who was born in Oregon in 1922, and spent painting time both in California and New Mexico. I think that if Diebenkorn had never lived in the volatile deserts, if he had never experienced Pacific scale, his painting would have been very different. Diebenkorn's motif has always been landscape." Dore Ashton, "First One-Man Show in New York at Poindexter Gallery," *Arts & Architecture* 73, no. 4 (April 1956): 11.

24 Susan Larsen interviews with Richard Diebenkorn, 1977, 1985, 1987, Archives of American Art, Smithsonian Institution, Washington, DC. Cited here, December 15, 1987, 73.

25 Richard Diebenkorn, quoted in Samuel Heavenrich and Grace L. McCann Morley, *California Painting: 40 Painters*, exh. cat. (Long Beach, CA: Municipal Art Center in collaboration with the San Francisco Museum of Art, 1956), n.p.

26 Diebenkorn recalled, "One thing that I know has influenced me a lot is looking at landscape from the air. I was first struck by aerial views when I was flying back to California from Albuquerque in 1951. . . . I guess it was the combination of desert and agriculture that really turned me on, because it had so many things I wanted in my paintings. Of course, the earth's skin itself had 'presence'. . . . It was all like a flat design—and everything was usually in the form of an irregular grid. . . . I think the many paths, or lathlike bands, in my paintings may have something to do with this experience, especially in that wherever there was agriculture going on you could see process—ghosts of former tilled fields, patches of land being eroded." Hofstadter, "Profiles," 60–61. See also Acker essay, this volume.

27 Richard Diebenkorn, quoted in an interview with Gerald Nordland, May 1986, cited in Nordland, *Richard Diebenkorn*, 43.

28 Mark Lavatelli, "The Berkeley Paintings of Richard Diebenkorn," unpublished manuscript, 1985, 21, note 6; and Mark Lavatelli, "Diebenkorn's Albuquerque Years," in Nordland et al., *Richard Diebenkorn in New Mexico*, 32.

29 Tuchman, "Diebenkorn's Early Years," in Buck, Jr. et al., *Richard Diebenkorn: Paintings and Drawings*, 5. Sarah Stein was the widow of Michael Stein, the brother of Gertrude Stein. For the Michael and Sarah Stein Collection, see Janet Bishop et al., *The Steins Collect: Matisse, Picasso, and the Parisian Avant-Garde*, exh. cat. (New Haven, CT: San Francisco Museum of Modern Art in association with Yale University Press, 2011), 126–219.

30 Morris, *Vanguard 1955*, n.p. John Elderfield has argued for the autonomy of Diebenkorn's work from any potential subject source: "Very occasionally, Diebenkorn does abstract from his environment. . . . The decipherable elements exist in relationships that are clearly more important to the artist than what they are made from. . . . If they allude to external reality, it is to a version of external reality—a rearrangement of its relationships—that the artist has made under his control." John Elderfield, *The Drawings of Richard Diebenkorn*, exh. cat. (New York: Museum of Modern Art, 1988), 42.

31 "Look of the West Inspires New Art," *Life*, November 4, 1957, 67.

32 Heavenrich and Morley, *California Painting*, n.p.

33 Schevill, "Art: Richard Diebenkorn," 22.

34 The compositions of *Berkeley #13* (1954) and *Berkeley #23* (1955) (pls. 7 and 8) also are reminiscent of *Urbana #5 (Beach Town)*.

35 Frederick Wight, "The Phillips Collection—Diebenkorn, Woelffer, Mullican: A Discussion," *Artforum* 1, no. 10 (April 1963): 27.

36 Schevill, "Art: Richard Diebenkorn," 21.

37 Before Diebenkorn removed the buildings that originally lined the right side of the painting, *Cityscape #1* even more closely resembled *Beach Town*. Gerald Nordland, in a phone conversation with Emma Acker, Assistant Curator of American Art, Fine Arts Museums of San Francisco, April 10, 2012.

38 Richard Diebenkorn, letter to Elinor Poindexter, March 18, 1963, Poindexter Gallery records, Archives of American Art, Smithsonian Institution, Washington, DC. Cf. Richard Diebenkorn letter to Elinor Poindexter, October 2, [1955], in which the artist writes, "My primary concern is that all my work over a given period be seen as one group."

39 Richard Diebenkorn, quoted in Alan Gussow, *A Sense of Place: The Artist and the American Land* (Washington, DC: Island Press, 1972), 143.

40 Richard Diebenkorn, quoted in Michael Kimmelman, "A Life Outside," *New York Times Magazine*, September 13, 1992, 62.

41 Gordon J. Hazlitt, "Problem Solving in Solitude," *Art News* 76, no. 1 (January 1977): 77.

42 Diebenkorn's daughter, Gretchen Grant, recalled: "My father didn't like it when we said, 'I think I see a cow, a car, a. . . .' I think he wanted to be able to see in a less restricted way. Also, I think in retrospect it had to do with identifying ways of looking at something that he wasn't focused on when working, and which could permanently alter his perception." E-mail from Gretchen Grant to the author, September 2, 2012.

43 Maurice Tuchman, "Richard Diebenkorn: The Early Years," *Art Journal* 36, no. 3 (Spring 1977): 211; and Nordland, *Richard Diebenkorn*, 26. In some notes he made, Diebenkorn wrote, "I am mistrustful of extra-painting allusions and would ordinarily end up painting them out." See Gerald Nordland, "The Figurative Works of Richard Diebenkorn," in Buck, Jr. et al., *Richard Diebenkorn: Paintings and Drawings*, 35. Peter Shoemaker, who was a student (1947–1950) at CSFA, remembered Mark Rothko as sharing a similar aesthetic: "I remember that in *Tiger's Eye*, which was a little magazine of the time, there was an excerpt from a statement of Rothko's in which he said that (I'm pretty sure I'm remembering it accurately) as soon as he found a subject that had some meaning for him in his painting, he tried to eliminate it. In other words, he didn't want anything having any reference outside of the painting itself." Peter Shoemaker, quoted in McChesney, *A Period of Exploration*, 34.

44 Tuchman, "Richard Diebenkorn: The Early Years," 213.

45 Diebenkorn destroyed at least one Albuquerque painting because it rendered an animal—a bull—too literally. See Tuchman, "Diebenkorn's Early Years," in Buck, Jr. et al., *Richard Diebenkorn: Paintings and Drawings*, 16, 17 (illustrated).

46 Larsen interview, May 1, 1985, 29.

47 For other paintings in which cows may be perceived, see *Albuquerque* (1951), which includes the front half of a cow in profile, and *Albuquerque* (1952), which incorporates a cow viewed from a three-quarter perspective, both in Nordland et al., *Richard Diebenkorn in New Mexico*, plates 71 and 72.

48 Phyllis Diebenkorn suggested the title *The Green Huntsman*, derived from Stendhal's novel *Lucien Leuwen* (1832): "Dick asked me what I thought it should be called. I knew that he was reading Stendhal's *The Green Huntsman* at the time, so that's what I suggested and he took it." Andrea Liguori interview with Phyllis Diebenkorn, August 14, 2012. Diebenkorn's decision to use the suggested title leaves the painting open to possible figurative associations.

49 For Diebenkorn's interest in the Bayeux Tapestry, see Larsen interview, June 2, 1977, 30.

50 Diebenkorn observed of *Urbana #2 (The Archer)*, "That was the only one that was intentionally representational. . . . It does represent the archer." Larsen interview, May 2, 1985, 32.

51 For Diebenkorn's early interest in Viktor Lowenfeld, see Larsen interview, May 24, 1977, 8. See Viktor Lowenfeld, *The Nature of Creative Activity: Experimental and Comparative Studies of Visual and Non-Visual Sources of Drawing, Painting, and Sculpture by Means of the Artistic Products of Weak Sighted and Blind Subjects and the Art of Different Cultures and Epochs* (London: Kegan Paul, Trench, Trubner & Co., 1939).

52 For the two drawings, see Lowenfeld, *The Nature of Creative Activity*, 204, figs. 76a and 76b. Lowenfeld wrote, "Through his drawings the visual type wants to bring the outer world closer to himself, whilst the haptic type is above all concerned with projecting his inner world into the picture" (89).

53 Diebenkorn recalled, "There was a psychologist who wrote a book that interested me. I saw it in 1941 or something. I've always remembered this book, and I can't remember the psychologist's name. . . . His theory was that among artists there were . . . two categories of artists: the visual type and the haptic type . . . the visual was strictly working from visual image and with, logically in terms of that image in a sense, naturalistically, realistically. One automatically draws a hand in terms of what a hand appears to be. . . . With the haptic there would be a real close empathy. The person is involved with the hand. And, if it were holding something, well, one would feel the holding of it. And this would be where the emphasis was. So roughly, it would be a kind of expressionist, naturally gravitating to that kind of image." Richard Diebenkorn, Larsen interview, May 24, 1977, 8.

54 Lowenfeld, *The Nature of Creative Activity*, 132.

55 See John Gruen, "Richard Diebenkorn: The Idea Is to Get Everything Right," *Art News* 85, no. 9 (November 1986): 85.

56 The upper edge of *Berkeley #3* appears to have been a tacking margin, unfolded when the canvas was restretched, perhaps after the move to Berkeley in fall 1953. Dried paint drips run in each of the four possible orientations, and paint appears to have been added over and into previously existing cracks, perhaps created when the painting was rolled for transport. For Diebenkorn's depiction of the mesa in Albuquerque, see Tuchman, "Diebenkorn's Early Years," in Buck, Jr. et al., *Richard Diebenkorn: Paintings and Drawings*, 16, 23. Discussing his Albuquerque paintings Diebenkorn recalled, "The flat line of the western mesa of Albuquerque . . . influenced my work." Nordland, 38.

57 This type of landscape division, rendered more explicitly, appears frequently in paintings of the late 1950s and early '60s that depict a lower foreground porch, an intermediary field of greater activity (e.g., a landscape or townscape), and an upper register with water and/or sky. See, for example, *View from the Porch* (1959, pl. 70), *Figure on a Porch* (1959, pl. 73), *Woman on a Porch* (1958, pl. 74), *Ocean from a Window* (1959, pl. 76), *Yellow Porch* (1961, pl. 79), and *Interior with View of Buildings* (1962, pl. 80).

58 For two additional related drawings, see RD 7810 and RD 5347.

59 Tuchman, "Richard Diebenkorn: The Early Years," 211.

60 Chipp, "Diebenkorn Paints a Picture," 45–47, 54–55. Perhaps because of the inevitable celebrity component of the article, Diebenkorn was uncomfortable with the project and its reception. Larsen interview, May 7, 1985.

61 Diebenkorn's first formal one-person exhibition, *Richard Diebenkorn: Paintings*, was held at Poindexter Gallery in New York, February 28–March 24, 1956. The gallery owner, Elinor Poindexter, represented Diebenkorn's work until 1971.

62 Diebenkorn: "A premeditated scheme or system is out of the question. Search for a mutation in a sequence that is sensible, inevitable, perhaps predictable. One is enough. The mutation, too, is sensible and inevitable but it is so in violation of the system of forces that called it up." Nordland, "The Figurative Works of Richard Diebenkorn," in Buck, Jr. et al., *Richard Diebenkorn: Paintings and Drawings*, 34. Diebenkorn was also fascinated by random visual occurrences: "I am interested in those arrangements and configurations made by people when the look of what they produce is incidental to their intentions. . . . Personal discoveries often are made in what appears to be a chance way when changes are made in the picture. I can grasp and predict only a few of them—perhaps only the main consequences of altering the relationships of a painting. . . . The unforeseen consequences that occur, when they are in favor of the main idea of the painting, often seem to quicken my perceptions and produce insights and a deeper involvement. The most 'real' look for me in painting is where one of the most interesting aspects of my own seeing is represented—the way things are endlessly out of place—sometimes delightfully, sometimes tragically." Chipp, "Diebenkorn Paints a Picture," 45–46.

63 For Diebenkorn's interest in heraldry, see Livingston, "The Art of Richard Diebenkorn," in Livingston et al., *The Art of Richard Diebenkorn*, 19.

64 Elinor Poindexter letter to Mrs. James E. Pollak, May 23, 1960, Poindexter Gallery records.

65 Livingston, "The Art of Richard Diebenkorn," in Livingston et al., *The Art of Richard Diebenkorn*, 72.

66 Diebenkorn observed: "I'm always afraid of this word—impediment—or is it pentimenti?" Larsen interview, May 24, 1977, 16. Responding to the presence of "time-lapse phenomenon" created by pentimenti, Diebenkorn mused: "You see, I have picked up something in the process of the corrections and erasures—something positive—and I think that's fine. I figure that when I have done something that's not quite right, and I want to take it out—it isn't all wrong either, so it is just as well that some of it remain. You see, I'm quite good at rationalizing but, also, I like to see pentimenti." Diebenkorn, quoted in Butterfield, "Pentimenti," n.p.

67 Diebenkorn reflected: "I think one of the best things that has happened to me a few times—maybe quite a few times—in looking back in completing a picture . . . that necessarily there is plenty of action of sorts—maybe not overt—but then the feeling, along with things coming together, that . . . it really is still . . . and it has been for me a very exciting kind of stillness. . . . The word isn't quite right. If one action arrested or stopped . . . like a photographer doing a broad jumper or something like that. . . . Silence—there is another good word." Larsen interview, June 2, 1977.

68 Wayne Thiebaud observed of Diebenkorn's work, "It isn't 'comfortable' painting. It skirts after the ugliness with a kind of delicate ineptness. He refuses to let out too much 'ingratiation,' let it get too 'pretty.' It's full of intelligent hesitations. That's what makes it so interesting to other painters. It shows a struggle. The picture and its problems are always being confronted. Like Cézanne, Matisse—he allows the *process* of formation to be visibly included at the end. . . . He has more to do with questions than answers. He insists on a kind of provocation. It becomes a symbolic record of pursuing how these things might be perceived from as wide a dimension and series of variables as possible. He puts down something, wipes it out, re-establishes it, destroys it again. Form considered under duress and doubt." Coffelt, "Doomsday in the Bright Sun," 27–28.

69 Adam Gopnik, "Diebenkorn Redux," *The New Yorker*, May 24, 1993, 100. Wayne Thiebaud recalled, "Dick discussed 'crudities' with me. This is something like 'ineptitudes' or 'awkwardnesses,' which are retained in one's work in order to avoid the slick, the ingratiating. It is a redirection to avoid getting easy. . . . Diebenkorn retains the stumbling. . . . It becomes crucial to the character of his work." Nordland, *Richard Diebenkorn*, 199. In response to an inquiry from art historian Ellen Johnson at Oberlin College, Diebenkorn wrote in 1958: "Concerning unfinish that you speak of. Years ago I learned that I couldn't say about a painting, 'Yes—this is it—this is what I'm after—except I've got to tidy up this area, un-muddy that, make another look decisive.'. . . Following out these words I would find that the qualities that were to me rare and involved with the kind of meaning I wanted depended on every part of the whole I was responding to—the negative features, that is, awkwardness, mistakes, undeveloped parts, etc., as well as the positive ones. I think that a *realization* can come about in the crudest terms as well as the most refined, in the most overworked terms as well as underworked, etc., etc., and for me what looks like realization is such a rare, tenuous state that I take it where I find it." Richard Diebenkorn, letter dated July 20, 1958, to Ellen Johnson, Allen Memorial Art Museum files, Oberlin College.

70 Richard Diebenkorn comments on Paul Mills's third version of his thesis, June 27 and July 5, 1962, Paul C. Mills Archives of California Art, Oakland Museum of California, cited in Nancy Boas, *David Park: A Painter's Life* (Berkeley: University of California Press, 2012), 173.

71 Richard Diebenkorn, quoted in Butterfield, "Pentimenti," n.p.

72 Richard Diebenkorn, "Miscellaneous Notes," Poindexter Gallery records.

73 See the related untitled drawings RD 4384, 4386, 3546, and 5704, all dated 1955.

74 Richard Diebenkorn, quoted in Paul Mills, *Contemporary Bay Area Figurative Painting*, exh. cat. (Oakland, CA: Oakland Art Museum, 1957), 12.

75 Larsen interview, May 2, 1985, 39–40. "But, in November of 1955 Diebenkorn abruptly decided that in abstraction he had come to the end of the road." "Edging Away from Abstraction," *Time*, March 17, 1958, 64.

76 For the painting *Untitled (Pianist and Cellist)* of 1952–1953, see RD 5527.

77 Describing his turn toward figuration, Diebenkorn recalled, "At one point in an interview, when *he* was asked why he changed to figurative work, Elmer Bischoff said, 'Well, David Park was having so much fun, so I thought I would get in on it!' I am paraphrasing him, but the meaning was very much like that. So, that was an element, too. David and Elmer had already been drawing from the figure in the evenings off and on, and then when I came back to the Bay Area that made three of us so the model was cheaper, and we could draw every week. Also, in 1953, 1954, 1955, I was drawing figuratively all of the time that I was doing abstract painting. I would draw the figure at night, not taking it all that seriously, but as a sort of exercise in seeing. And, so, I think that had a great influence on me, too." Butterfield, "Pentimenti," n.p.

78 Recalling his moments of doubt regarding his new figurative work, Diebenkorn observed: "I had all sorts of moments and days and weeks when I would go back to abstract painting. I would think I had made a very bad and hasty decision and decide, let's go back to abstract painting." Elderfield, *The Drawings of Richard Diebenkorn*, 29.

79 Richard Diebenkorn, quoted in Scott, *New Paintings*. Cf. "One of the reasons I got into figurative or representational painting in the *first* place was that I wanted my ideas to be `worked on,' changed, altered, by what was `out there.' I felt that I had been putting things together too much in accord with how I thought painting *ought* to be, and that can be fine but, at the same time, it can start to be a `fixed' or `static' image of painting." Butterfield, "Pentimenti," n.p. Cf. Diebenkorn: "In abstract painting one can't deal with a kind of entity, like an object or person, a concentration of psychology which a person is—as opposed to where the figure isn't in the painting. . . . And, that's one thing that's always missing for me in abstract painting, that I don't have this kind of dialogue between elements that can be wildly different and can be at war, or in extreme conflict. . . . So, that's the major sacrifice for me in doing abstract painting." Larsen interview, May 2, 1985, 41.

80 Critic Anita Ventura was an exception in discussing Diebenkorn's turn to figuration in terms of personal necessity, rather than art-world trends: "For it is inevitable that the figurative paintings of an ex-Expressionist of any sort will be used in some quarters as pawns in a battle for the recapture of American realism. But a 'return' for Diebenkorn is a particular journey of his talent and his nature to a mode of painterly expression that he finds most viable; the qualities that distinguish him make his destination a private one, not part of a general crusade." Anita Ventura, "In the Galleries: Richard Diebenkorn," *Art* 32, no. 6 (March 1958): 56.

81 Hofstadter, "Profiles," 54.

82 Richard Diebenkorn, quoted in an interview with Gerald Nordland, July 2, 1985, cited in Nordland, *Richard Diebenkorn*, 86.

83 "Edging Away from Abstraction," 64, 67.

84 Luther Meyer, "Abstractionist Back on Track," *San Francisco Call-Bulletin*, March 28, 1958, 16.

85 Schevill, "Art: Richard Diebenkorn," 21.

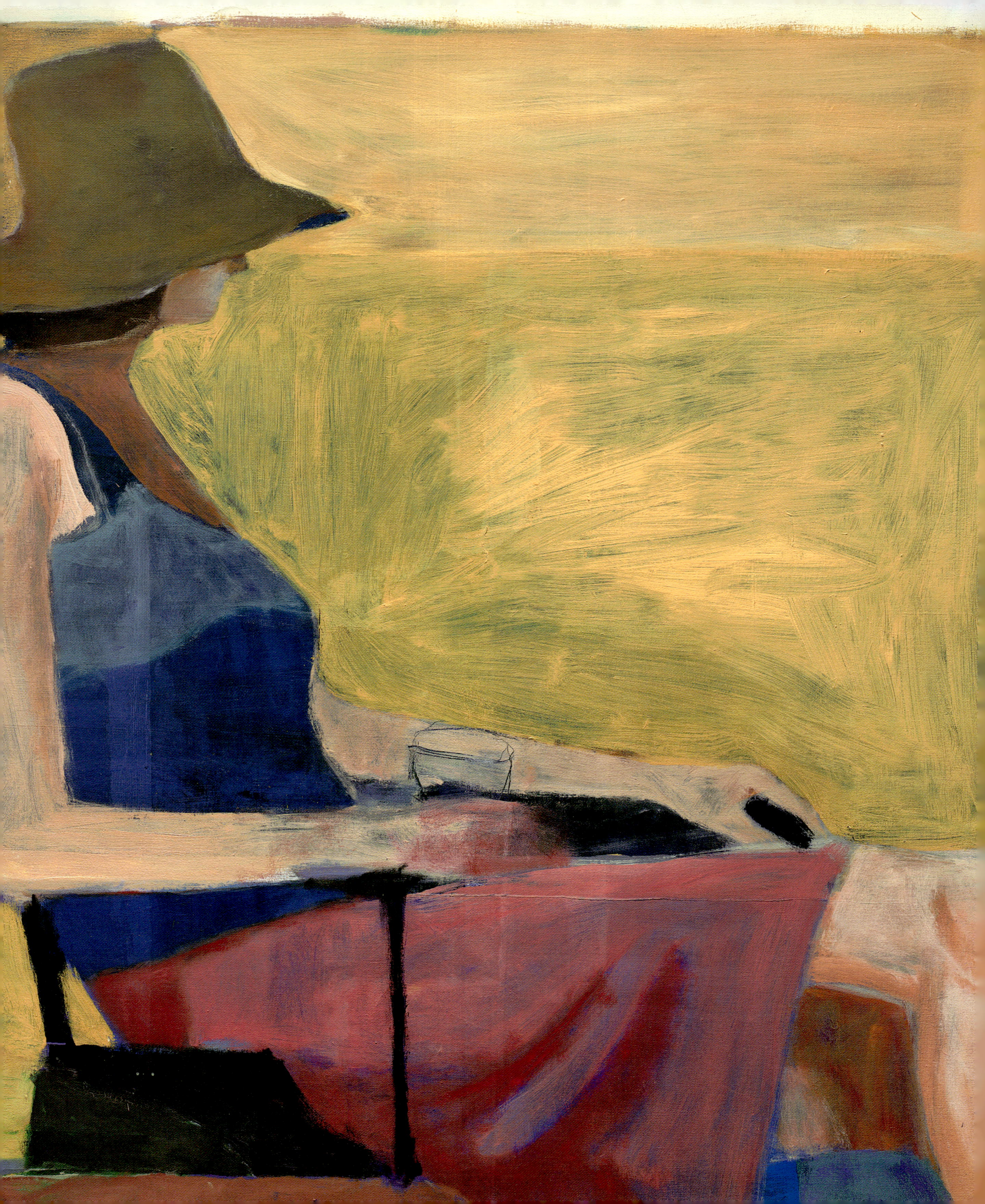

Tension beneath Calm

Richard Diebenkorn's Figurative Work

STEVEN A. NASH

In Richard Diebenkorn's long and productive career, which began and ended with celebrated periods of abstract work, his dedication to representational imagery from 1955 to 1967 may seem a non sequitur. Even today, after more than half a century, his seemingly abrupt abandonment around 1955 of the abstract style that yielded such powerful and increasingly acclaimed work during his early Berkeley years can be difficult to understand. To some observers at the time, it was shocking. Certain critics who had come to view his abstractions as a compelling West Coast response to the New York School's aesthetic primacy quickly shifted gears and condemned his new figurative work as a heretical rejection of Abstract Expressionist doctrine. Epithets such as "traitor" were hurled at him, and he once declared, "You would not believe what people called me."[1] The figurative chapter in his development nevertheless resulted in some of his most iconic and widely respected paintings and drawings, works that continue to play a key role in the history of figuration in post–World War II American art. But then, barely more than ten years after this conversion, he again changed course and began his radiant Ocean Park abstractions, once more surprising his closest friends and followers as he initiated a body of work that would continue for the rest of his life.

One historian has written that Diebenkorn's "elective figurative-abstract shifts became a stamp of identity from which he could not escape,"[2] but it could be argued that, rather than a critical liability, these shifts signal key values underlying all of Diebenkorn's art. On the one hand, they show the integrity and independence with which he pursued his career, ignoring the siren call of contemporary trends and following instead his own instincts and aesthetic needs. It took a fierce sense of independence to recalibrate those needs around 1955 and, under the glare of national opinion, essentially start over. On the other hand, this push–pull relationship in his work of the 1950s and 1960s is only the most dramatic example of a phenomenon basic to his art in general, the invigorating interchange across permeable borders between abstraction and representation. Key examples of this dynamic are found in his Berkeley abstractions from the years 1953–1956 and his Ocean Park paintings and drawings from 1967 onward, namely, the underlying importance of landscape and its topographical and climatological conditions as sources of inspiration in both of these series. Diebenkorn himself was quick to underscore the differences for him between the two realms of seeing and working: "In my experience, abstraction and representation are totally different worlds—different laws—different methodology."[3] He rankled when critics interpreted his abstractions too much as landscapes—"I'm not a landscape painter (at this time, at any rate) or I would paint landscapes directly"[4]—or, conversely, saw his figurative works "as a peg on which to hang my [abstract] conceptions of painting."[5] Nevertheless, throughout his work there is an undeniable dialogue between these opposing principles, even when his stylistic balance shifted strongly in one direction or the other, as it did in the figurative period.[6]

This chapter of Diebenkorn's development is indeed a clear "stamp of identity." During his lifetime and in studies since his death in 1993, it has become the most frequently examined aspect of his entire career, yet there remains much about it to explore and discuss. Questions persist, for example, about the nature and course of his conversions from abstraction to figuration and back again. The historic sources he drew upon in this period and the personal meanings embedded in his figurative work need clarification. Also, attention to the features that help distinguish Diebenkorn's figurative work from that of his close friends and associates can help answer two basic questions: (1) What did figuration give him as an expressive vehicle that abstraction could not? (2) How did these two opposing forces find resolution in representational imagery?

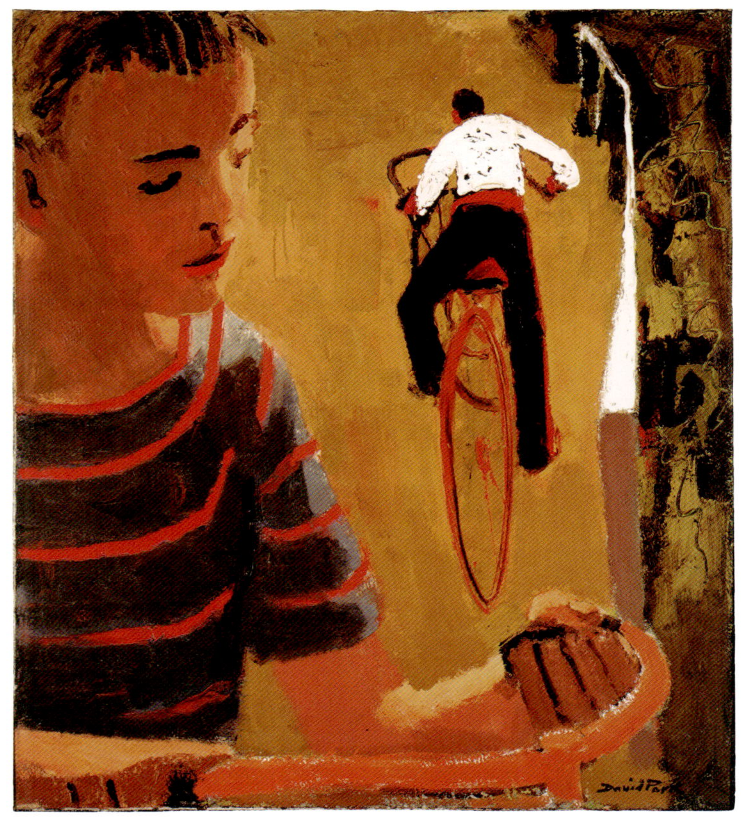

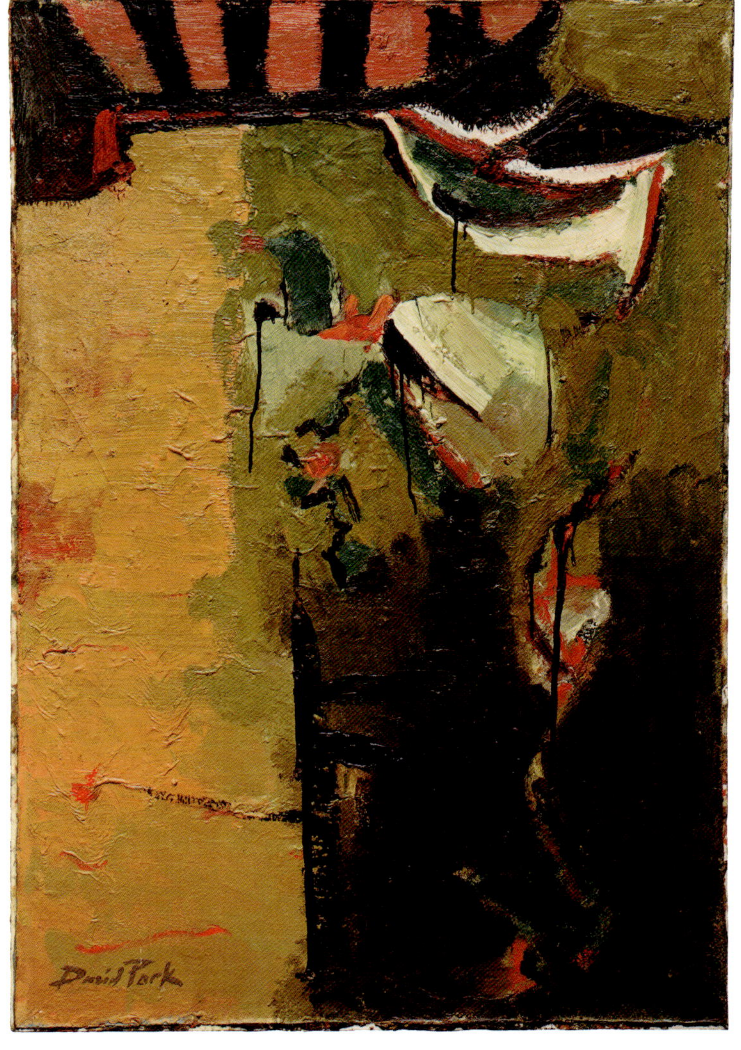

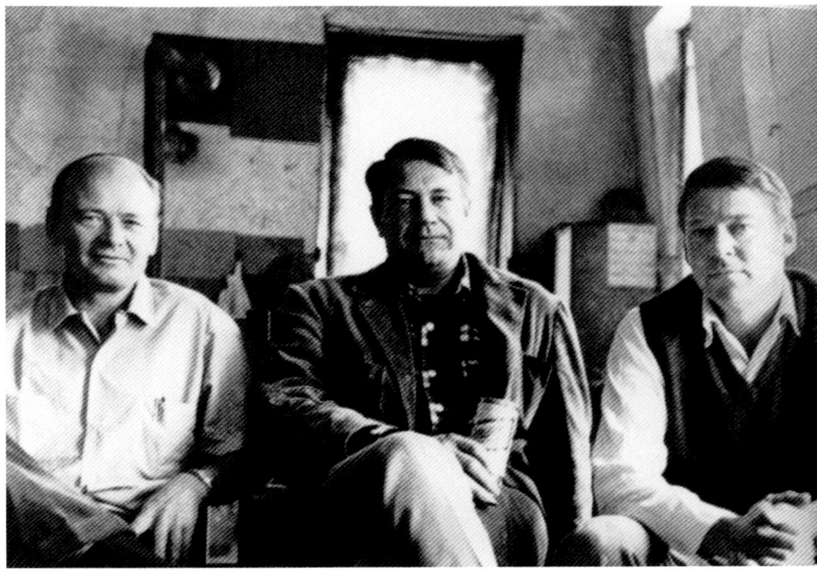

INTO FIGURATION

The creative vitality of the Bay Area as an art center in the late 1940s and 1950s is now well documented in studies of the period, and the emergence of figurative art as a rebellious counterinfluence to the prevailing norms of Abstract Expressionism has become an especially fabled chapter in the history of California art.[7] Within this history, it is also well known that Diebenkorn was a relative latecomer to figuration compared to his two friends David Park and Elmer Bischoff. All three taught in the late 1940s at the California School of Fine Arts in San Francisco (CSFA, later named the San Francisco Art Institute [SFAI]), and each developed personal idioms of abstraction. The work of such artists as Clyfford Still and Mark Rothko, both of whom taught for periods at CSFA, as well as Willem de Kooning and Franz Kline, became particularly important influences in San Francisco art circles at the time, resulting in the ascendency of Abstract Expressionist ideals. So strong were these prevailing trends that Park's denunciation of his earlier abstract work (see fig. 33) around 1949 and his move to figuration created a shock wave that resonated for years. Diebenkorn first learned of this development while working toward his master's degree at the University of New Mexico in Albuquerque in 1950. He saw an illustration of Park's *Kids on Bikes* (fig. 32) in the bulletin of the San Francisco Art Association and reacted famously with both curiosity and surprise: "My God, what's happened to David?"[8] Soon Bischoff followed Park's aesthetic lead. When Diebenkorn returned to the Bay Area in September of 1953, after having moved from Albuquerque to Urbana, Illinois, and then to New York, he encountered firsthand the gathering force of this new figurative movement.

Diebenkorn's own transformation was not as sudden as often assumed; in fact, it had a rather lengthy gestation. After settling in a house in the Berkeley hills in 1953, and

FIG 32
David Park
Kids on Bikes, 1950
Oil on canvas
48 x 42 in. (121.9 x 106.7 cm)
Curtis Galleries, Minneapolis

FIG 33
David Park
Untitled, 1948–1949
Oil on canvas
50 x 38 in. (127 x 96.5 cm)
Private collection, courtesy of John Berggruen Gallery

FIG 34
Elmer Bischoff, Frank Lobdell, and Richard Diebenkorn at Lobdell's 9 Mission Street studio, San Francisco, 1959

while he was working so successfully on his Berkeley abstractions, he participated regularly with Park and Bischoff in drawing sessions with models.[9] He later noted about these experiences:

> David and Elmer had already been drawing from the figure in the evenings off and on, and then when I came back to the Bay Area that made three of us so the model was cheaper, and we could draw every week. Also, in 1953, 1954, 1955, I was drawing figuratively all of the time that I was doing abstract painting. I would draw the figure at night, not taking it all that seriously, but as a sort of exercise in seeing. And, so, I think that had a great influence on me, too.[10]

He also concluded, "The seeds of . . . what was to happen to me were in . . . those figure-drawing sessions."[11]

During the Berkeley period Diebenkorn made hundreds of figure drawings in a wide variety of media, the vast majority of which are undated and bear no inscriptions that could assist with chronological placement. Some certainly derive from the earliest years of his work from models (i.e., 1954–1955), but it is difficult to separate these from the ones that came later. Just a handful of drawings are actually dated to this early period, an indication of the nonchalant, experimental nature of these "exercise[s] in seeing." One landscape with a date of 1954, a watercolor of a scene in Ensenada (fig. 35), helps document Diebenkorn's awakening interest in representational imagery.[12] It is both an essay in fluid brushwork and a straightforward account of direct observation. Essentially a "portrait" of architecture, the study recalls in its strong light and focus on a central cubic form the influence of Edward Hopper (see fig. 58), which had been an important force in Diebenkorn's work during his college years as clearly seen in his *Palo Alto Circle* (fig. 36) of 1943. A small group of figure drawings with

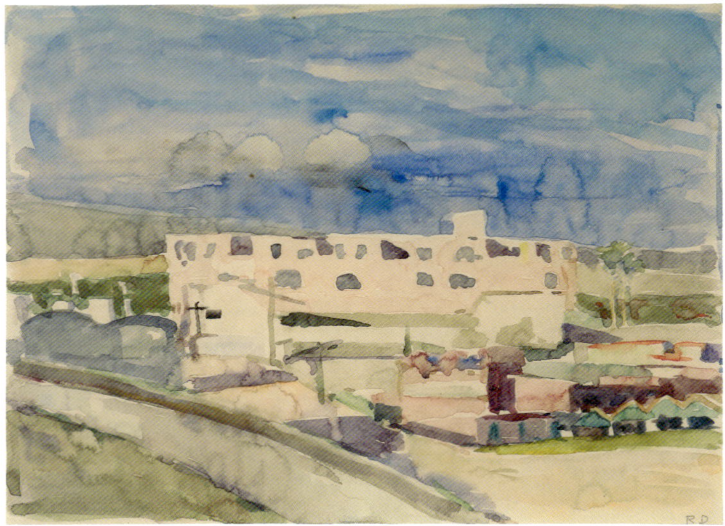

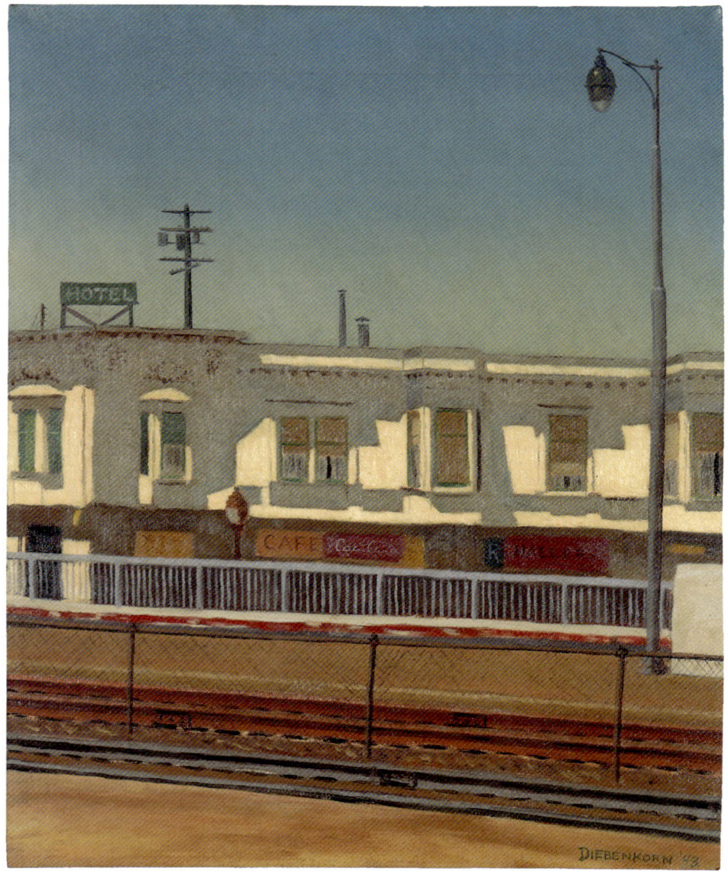

FIG 35
Richard Diebenkorn
***Ensenada–1954*, 1954**
Watercolor on paper
8 3/4 x 11 3/4 in. (22.2 x 29.8 cm)
Private collection
[2111]

FIG 36
Richard Diebenkorn
***Palo Alto Circle*, 1943**
Oil on canvas
20 1/8 x 16 1/8 in. (51.1 x 41 cm)
Santa Cruz Island Foundation,
Carpinteria, California
[1015]

dates of 1954 and 1955 provide at least an introductory idea of the stylistic nature of other figurative pieces from these years.[13] The subjects are rendered with linear, sketchy outlines and very little interior modeling, with the exception of one work in which the model's body is more volumetrically expressed with the shading of highlights and shadows. We see in all of these drawings evidence of insecurity in transposing three-dimensional form onto a flat ground. This quality is also detectable in some of his earliest representational paintings, signaling the transitional character of his work at the time. A different, more expressionistic side of Diebenkorn's sensibility appears in a number of shadowy drawings of figures in dimly lit interiors.[14] Heavy washes of dark ink or gouache create a mysterious, nocturnal mood, and the figures are sometimes strangely distorted, a manner that resurfaces occasionally in his later work, but with greater refinement.

Diebenkorn's movement into representational art, at least in the world of drawings, came at first as a speculative effort, not a very pressing pursuit. But by 1955, when he had completed more than sixty of his Berkeley abstractions, he felt the need to embrace figuration more resolutely. He was asked many times about the motivations for this change. He later explained that it was a complicated issue with no single clear answer: "I don't know how many times I have said to interviewers, 'If I tell you *one* thing, that becomes *the* thing, it becomes a distortion right away. If I can't tell you the *whole story*, well, there is just no point in it.'"[15] Certainly, his drawing sessions with Park and Bischoff and the motivating influence of their paintings, along with their regular discussions concerning the principles of art, must have influenced his ways of thinking. Sometime afterward he revealed that he had begun to feel a sense of frustration with his abstractions, having difficulty finding the inspiration to carry them forward. By 1955 Abstract Expressionism in the Bay Area had become increasingly academic through its dominance at CSFA and its widespread practice, and increasingly it reflected a stylized manner rather than an urgent personal search. For Diebenkorn, "things started to slow down, and I was attributing this to my being in a stylistic straightjacket. I felt that perhaps I had too many rules, that there was too much Abstract Expressionism hanging over my head, and so . . . there was a need for change."[16]

Like Park before him, Diebenkorn thought that abstraction was no longer "troublesome" enough,[17] that there was not enough to "come up against,"[18] and he found it increasingly difficult to "super-charge" his paintings through reliance strictly on the internal promptings of emotion and intuition.[19] Figuration, by contrast, offered not only an external construction basic to a picture's composition but also a cue to painterly and emotional response. There was something to push against—the demands of a perceptual truth to natural forms married to the demands of a different truth, the subjective process of making a painting. The expressive handling of light, color, and brushwork inherent in his abstractions found new application in the service of representation. It is important to remember that Diebenkorn rarely worked from models or direct observation of nature in his larger paintings, relying instead on the freedom of memory and spontaneous invention. In this duality of nature and intuition, he found within his new style the "tension beneath calm" he had sought.[20]

It is impossible now to trace the exact course of Diebenkorn's earliest experimentation with figuration in his paintings, partly because very few dated paintings survive from 1954 and 1955 and partly because his development did not follow a linear course. In the last stages of his Berkeley abstractions he also began to work with the figure, and as his figurative style took shape, he would revert occasionally to abstraction. A later work that seems to encapsulate this conflicted position is the fascinating *Landscape with Figure* of 1956 (pl. 40), which combines elements of the Berkeley abstractions with a clear landscape format and figurative motifs. Through exhibitions in a number of cities from San Francisco and Los Angeles to

New York, as well as the increased awareness and appreciation of his work in the art press, Diebenkorn had begun to build a national reputation based on his abstractions. The momentum of this success plus admonitions from dealers and collectors to "stay the course" would have been a powerful incentive to resist any changes,[21] and Diebenkorn admitted, despite strong convictions to move forward into figuration, that he sometimes feared he might be making "a very bad and hasty decision."[22]

The earliest examples we have of this new style show the difficulties Diebenkorn encountered. Bruce Conner, a younger Bay Area artist who was an admirer, paid Diebenkorn a visit at his studio in 1955 and was shown a small figure painting that he found to be "really grotesque."[23] We do not know which painting was involved, but an untitled study of a nude dated 1954 (fig. 25) may give an idea of the type of work Conner saw; it clearly manifests an attempt by the artist at something new and still unnatural for him. *Untitled (Horse and Rider)* (fig. 16) of 1954 is another transitional study, both sketchy in form and strange in subject matter.[24] A much greater degree of resolution is seen, however, in the small landscape entitled *Chabot Valley* (fig. 37 and pl. 36) of 1955, later identified by Diebenkorn as the first of his figurative paintings, by which we can assume he meant the first satisfyingly accomplished work in this genre. Diebenkorn related that he was driving around Berkeley in his car looking for suitable landscape subjects when he spotted this view not far from the house on Hillcrest Road the Diebenkorns would buy in 1956 (for a similar view of the surrounding topography, see fig. 38).[25] It is an urban scene, looking across small houses toward San Francisco Bay in the distance. Its strongly brushed blocks of paint and rich coloration create in a small format a vivid impression that seems to capture the firm determination of Diebenkorn's recent conversion.

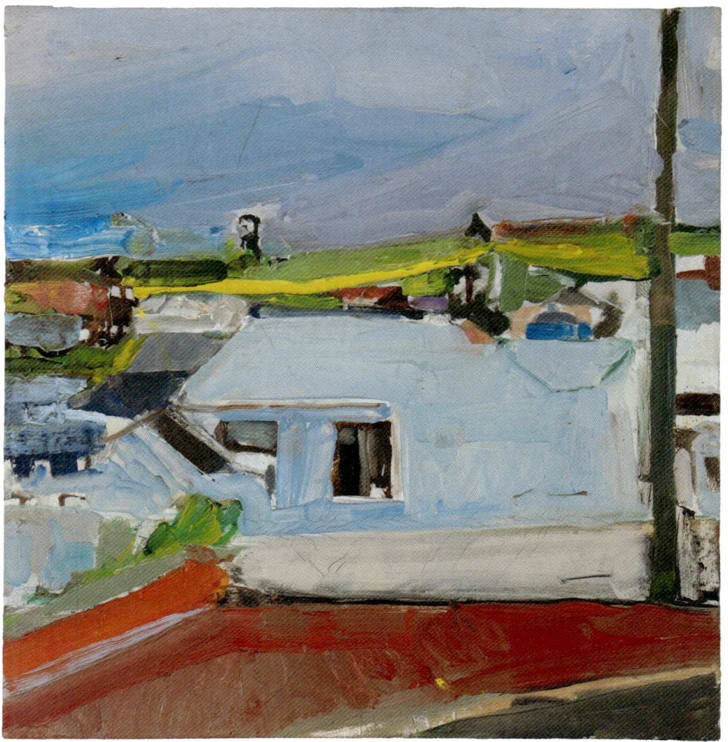

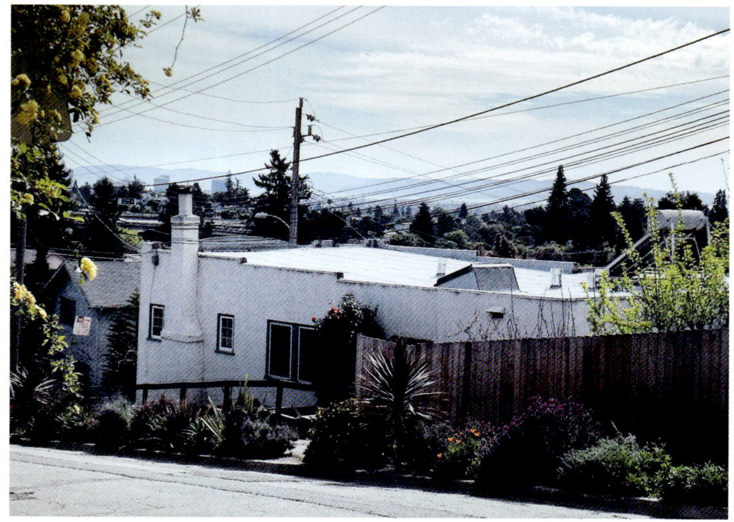

FIG 37
Richard Diebenkorn
***Chabot Valley*, 1955**
Oil on canvas
19 1/2 x 18 3/4 in. (49.5 x 47.6 cm)
Collection of Christopher Diebenkorn
[1154]

FIG 38
View in the vicinity of Chabot Valley, 2012

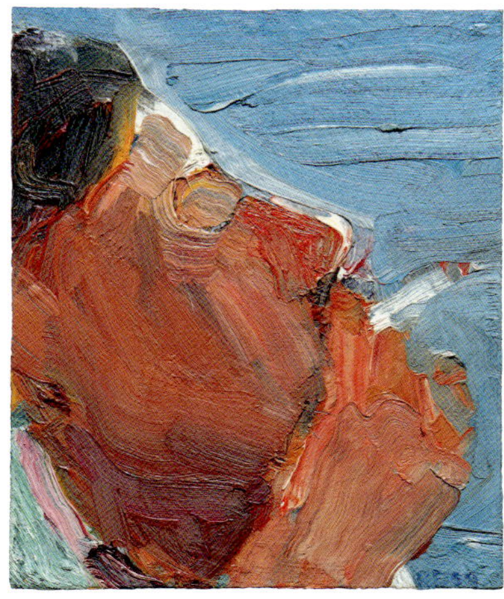

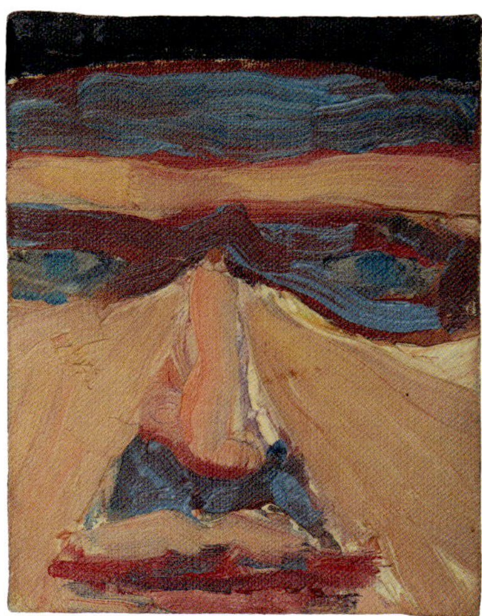

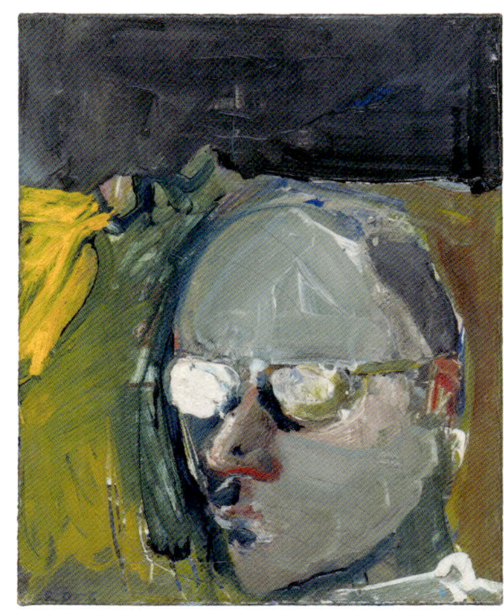

FIG 39
Richard Diebenkorn
***Man Smoking*, 1959**
Oil on wood panel
9 3/4 x 8 1/8 in. (24.8 x 20.6 cm)
Private collection
[1266]

FIG 40
Richard Diebenkorn
***Face*, 1956**
Oil on canvas
6 5/8 x 5 1/8 in. (16.8 x 13 cm)
Private collection
[1183]

FIG 41
Richard Diebenkorn
***Man with Glasses*, 1956**
Oil on canvas
16 1/2 x 13 in. (41.9 x 33 cm)
Private collection
[1189]

Once Diebenkorn committed himself fully, his progress from small but strong works such as *Chabot Valley* to his first large-scale figure paintings was remarkably fast and confident. Two powerfully composed works from 1956, *Girl on a Terrace* and *Woman by the Ocean* (pls. 46 and 47), show the distance he had traveled. In both cases he placed women in architectural settings, one on a terrace and one in a glassed-in or tented room, in front of wide expanses of landscape. Both figures are truncated at the knees and pushed outward to the picture plane, making dramatic the first visual steps into the paintings. The abrupt juxtapositions of interior and exterior spaces create forceful contrasts between near and far, observers and their fields of vision, culture and nature. As is common in Diebenkorn's large figurative works, however, an underlying geometry of architectural elements and broad bands of color provides a unifying structure and a formal scaffolding upon which Diebenkorn animated each entire canvas with his typically dynamic brushwork and vivid palette.

The lengthy compositional history of *Woman by the Ocean* has long been familiar through a revealing series of photographs taken by Rose Mandel in Diebenkorn's studio as he worked on the painting, but numerous other recently discovered photographs from the same sessions expand that history considerably (see pp. 232–237). Through these works it is possible to trace the evolutionary progress of the composition, involving among other changes the transformation of a seated male figure on the right side of the painting into the seated female on the left. Several photographs show the canvas installed upside down on its easel, dramatizing just how abstractly Diebenkorn could view his works as they evolved. From this early stage in his figurative development, the dialogue between abstraction and representation was in full force and would remain a stylistic hallmark, provoking both negative and positive criticism.

The brushwork in paintings such as this has a freedom and exuberance familiar from Diebenkorn's earlier Berkeley abstractions, emphasizing again his debts to Abstract Expressionism. Compared to the fluidity of surface treatment in those works, however, his manipulation of paint in the figurative pictures, while retaining his delight in thick impasto, is more varied in touch, speed, and directionality. In *Woman by the Ocean*, for example, several blue tonalities in the center of the sky are clustered in bold strokes, extending forward to engulf one of the vertical architectural supports and confound our sense of foreground and background. The colors defining forms behind the seated figure are pushed up brusquely against, and sometimes over, her contours. Splintery strokes invade smooth biomorphic forms along the right edge, and the green vertical plane of the foreground is a patchwork of dashing strokes of different widths and densities. Diebenkorn's challenge, and one reason for the lengthy process for many of his paintings, was to balance these disparate patterns, the dissonance of which he actually cultivated. His imagery exists partway between ocular experience and pure painterly invention, and his ability to hold these opposites in suspension contributes much to his work's pictorial energy.

As Diebenkorn's career progressed, he worked alternately, and sometimes simultaneously, on several different themes, including figures, interiors, landscapes, and still lifes, in both paintings and drawings. If scale of presentation were any gauge of the ambitions behind different categories of work, then the large figure, landscape, and interior scenes would hold primary standing. Nevertheless, some of Diebenkorn's greatest work comes in small formats, and many intimate still-life, landscape, and figure paintings have a power that belies their diminutive scale. They provide ample testimony for the reputation that Diebenkorn always had as "a painter's painter" (see fig. 41 and pls. 93 and 94) and could sometimes be startlingly experimental (see figs. 39 and 40).

FIGURES, INTERIORS, AND THE EMOTIONS OF SILENCE

The human figure in various contexts—alone, coupled with one other figure (but seldom more), seated or standing in an interior, occasionally shown out-of-doors, and sometimes referenced only by a symbol or empty chair—is the dominant theme throughout this period of Diebenkorn's work. It also includes portraits, although he made only a few other than the many studies of his wife, Phyllis, and studies of anonymous models. The stylistic terms of this engagement changed somewhat, particularly in the last years of their development, but there is nevertheless a dedicated continuity of investigation here that is consistent with the serial nature of his work in other segments of his career.

Girl on a Terrace and *Woman by the Ocean* suggest a prominent theme in Diebenkorn's representational work—the presentation of figures in architectural settings, often with windows opening onto a landscape view. Several works in this exhibition (including pls. 50, 60, and 61) show different formulations of this leitmotif. *Girl with Cups* from the Yale University Art Gallery, for example (pl. 63), shows a woman in the quotidian act of tending to the preparation of cups of coffee, with two loosely stacked books adding to the nonchalant nature of the subject. It seems an especially humble theme for a large-scale, highly developed composition, particularly when compared to the heated emotionalism of the artist's earlier abstractions. But the mood of quiet solitude is central in Diebenkorn's representational imagery, perhaps as an imagined relief from the emotional strains of modern life. He repeatedly gives such subjects a quality of monumentality, achieved here through the pyramidal form of the figure, the solid blocking out of the composition with rectangular zones, and the sensuously rich and free handling of paint and color.

Diebenkorn's figurative paintings are not often discussed in terms of their iconographic dimension, yet this is an important aspect of the work that enriches its personal expressiveness.[26] With *Girl with Cups*, he was responding, whether consciously

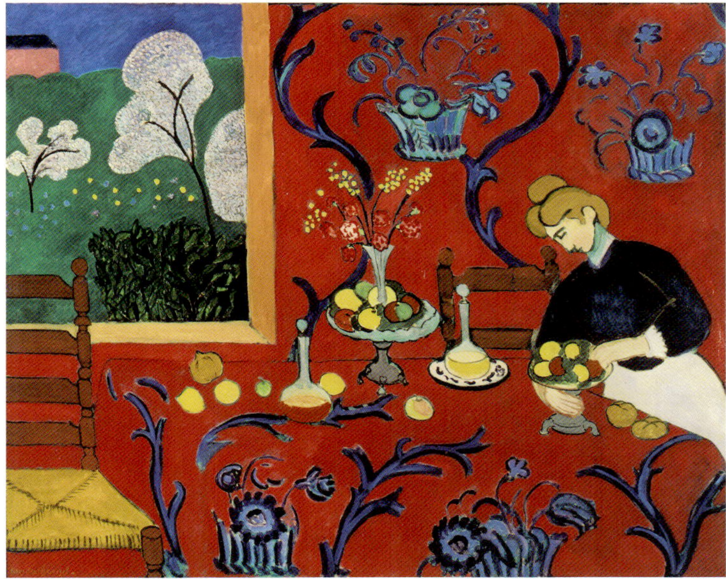

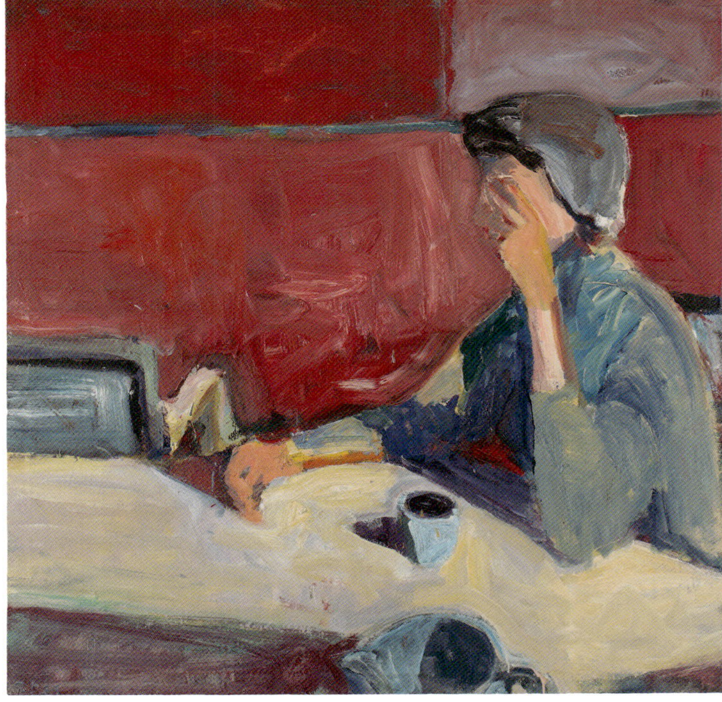

FIG 42
Henri Matisse
***Harmony in Red*, 1908**
Oil on canvas
71 1/16 x 87 in. (180.5 x 221 cm)
The State Hermitage Museum, Saint Petersburg

FIG 43
Richard Diebenkorn
***Woman at Table in Strong Light*, 1959**
Oil on canvas
48 1/2 x 48 1/2 in. (123.2 x 123.2 cm)
Private collection
[1279]

or subconsciously, to an intimist tradition in early modern art made famous by the Nabi painters Édouard Vuillard and Pierre Bonnard, and also in works by Henri Matisse. It is well known that Diebenkorn became closely familiar with outstanding examples of the art of these masters through visits to The Phillips Collection in Washington, DC, while stationed with the Marine Corps in 1944 at Quantico, Virginia.[27] Their influence surfaced in strength much later as important sources for his figurative work and possibly as part of the motivation to return to figuration in general. A precursor of *Girl with Cups* is found, for example, in Matisse's *Harmony in Red* (fig. 42) of 1908, which, in its depiction of a woman arranging a tabletop still life in a decorative interior, projects a general sense of comfort and middle-class luxury. A similar relationship exists in the painting *Woman at Table in Strong Light* (fig. 43) of 1959. The domestic interior becomes a locale for solitude, serenity, and pleasure. Not just Matisse and Bonnard are invoked, but even Dutch masters such as Johannes Vermeer. Numerous works by Edward Hopper also come to mind; one of his favored expressive motifs involved figures isolated in interiors with large windows opening to the world beyond.

A different thematic and compositional format is found in *Woman in a Window* (fig. 44) and *Girl Looking at Landscape* (pl. 50). Both use the device of a large-scale figure in the foreground gazing out a window. The windows serve as strong geometric elements that structure the compositions and also contrast with the irregular, organic forms of the figures. In this case, the thematic and psychological referent lies in the tradition of Northern European Romanticism and its frequently repeated motif of the open window, as most famously represented by Caspar David Friedrich's *Woman at the Window* from 1822 (fig. 46).[28] And while it is questionable whether Diebenkorn had direct knowledge of any examples of this tradition, he knew very well its modern reincarnation in works by Matisse and Bonnard. The latter's contribution to this genealogy is seen, for example, in *Dining Room on the Garden* in the Solomon R. Guggenheim Museum (fig. 45) (although here, and in similar works by Bonnard, the girl is depicted looking inward). In Friedrich's *Woman at the Window*, as in Diebenkorn's treatments of the same theme, the woman's gaze psychologically links the interior realm of human existence, confinement, and culture with the outdoor spaces of expansive nature and freedom. It is a juxtaposition that implies an outward projection of thought, even longing, or at least an act of quiet contemplation.

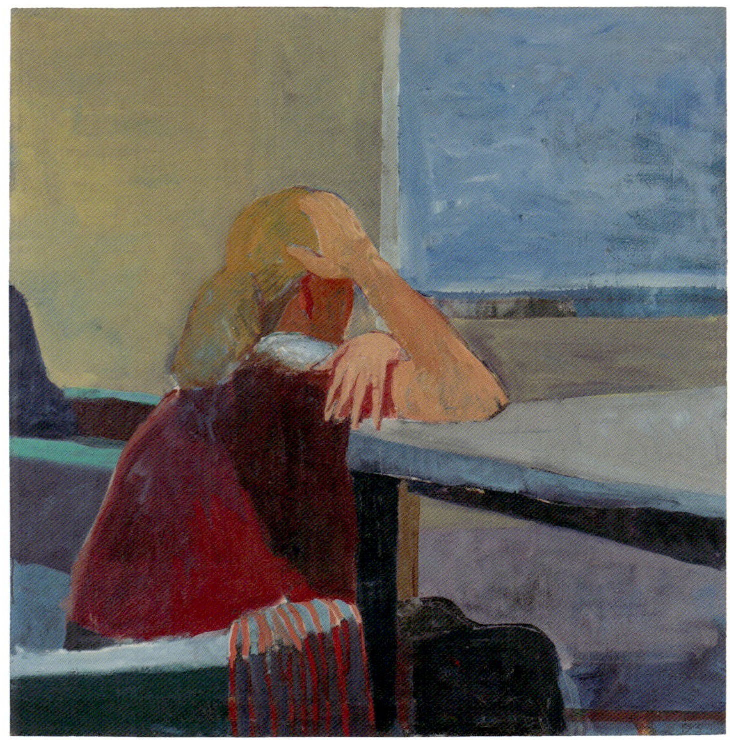

A still different variation on the theme of figures in an interior is seen in *Man and Woman in a Large Room* (pl. 52) and *Man and Woman Seated* (fig. 31 and pl. 49), in which two figures face one another but stand or sit in silence. In both cases, a male artist is intently drawing or painting from a female model. There are no gestures or signs of communication, and the face of one of the models is, in fact, totally obliterated. The result is a psychological isolation of each of the individual figures that borders on a sense of ennui. Here we are reminded of themes of tense self-containment and noncommunication that arose in late nineteenth-century French art, for example, in such works by Edgar Degas as *Intérior (Le viol)*, *Bouderie*, and *Édouard Manet et Mme. Manet*.[29]

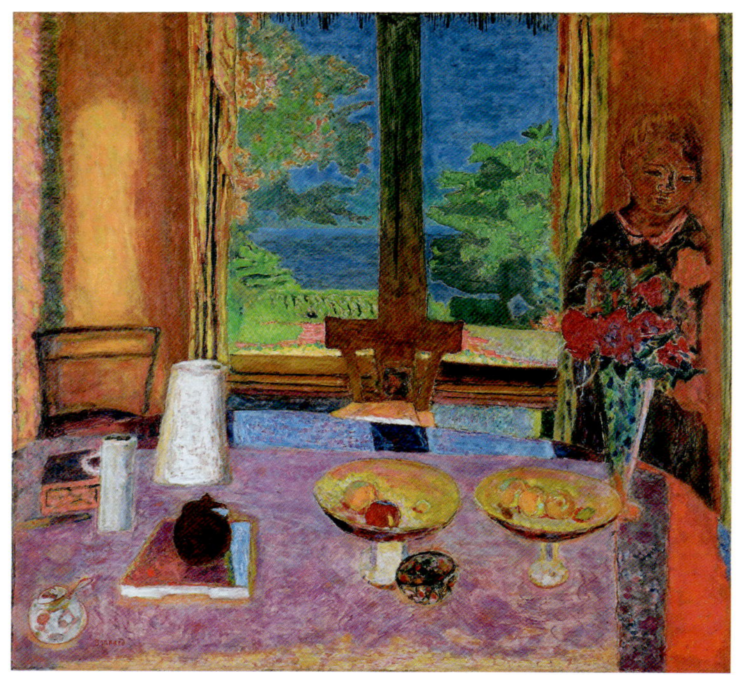

So central to Diebenkorn's thematic imagination during these years was the concept of figures in an interior that he explored it even without actual figures, using empty chairs and other symbols as stand-ins for the missing subjects. *Interior with Doorway* and *Window* (pls. 78 and 146) both capture the loneliness of an interior without its inhabitant, and *Interior with View of Buildings* (pl. 80) includes both an empty chair and a small painting showing the back of a woman's head (facing, figuratively speaking, toward the distant view of buildings) to represent the missing person. The "presence" of the figure is strongly invoked through its absence.

To some degree, all of these interior scenes involve elements of human emotion or psychological interaction, a consideration within Diebenkorn's figurative work more important than

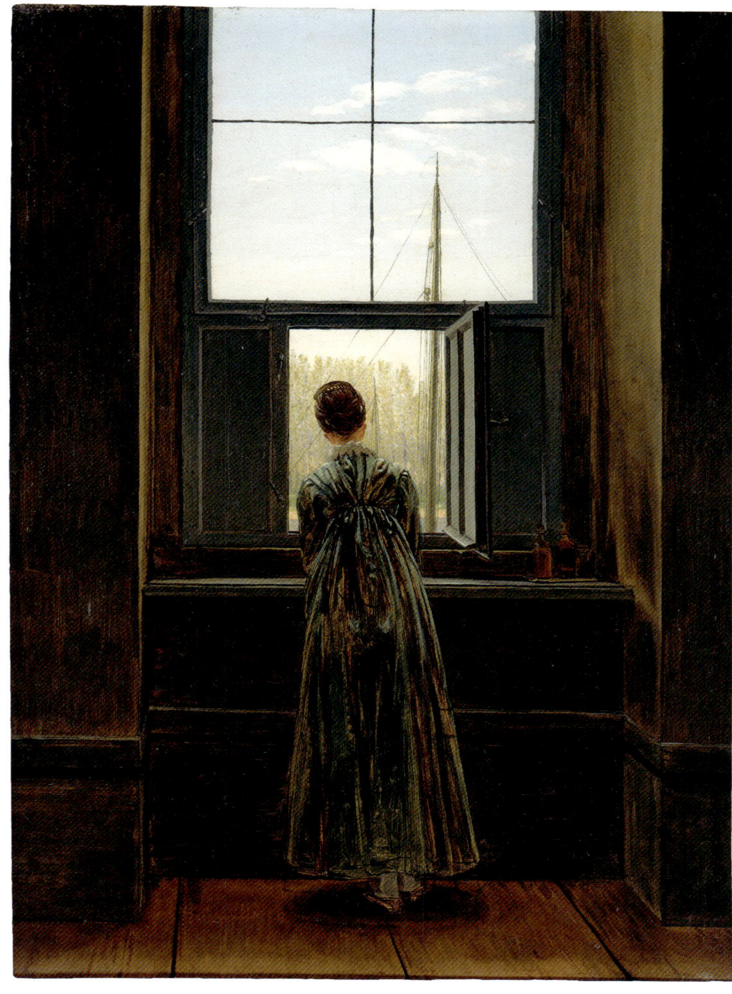

is generally acknowledged. In his move from abstraction to representational imagery, a quest for psychological balance between the various components of a painting became a strong driving force. As he explained in regard to one work, the evolutionary process behind its composition (which typically was quite protracted) could not be considered finished until "the relationship of the figure and the setting seem psychologically right."[30] And he declared at another point that his "represented forms are loaded with psychological feeling. And it can't ever just be *painting*."[31] Critics have noted the sense of reverie or even melancholy in his paintings, and Irving Sandler, for instance, wrote in his review of Diebenkorn's exhibition at the Poindexter Gallery in New York in 1961 that the figures are "introspective and lonely, affected by the vastness of the settings in which they are placed."[32]

Diebenkorn and other members of the Bay Area Figurative movement were generally reluctant to speak of any narrative quality in their work, insisting instead that it was all about getting the figure "right" in its pictorial context. They assiduously avoided the sentimental or anecdotal, but even a fast review of Diebenkorn's figure paintings reveals a distinctive undercurrent of human feeling. He dealt with human experience and inner states of being, seeking always to keep the psychological relationships in his paintings both balanced and true. This was a key value he found in figurative work versus abstraction, and the particular climates of feeling he created help distinguish his work from that of fellow Bay Area Figurative painters just as much as the singularity of his compositional structures and the "handwriting" of his brushwork.

Of course, the most direct and unmediated aspect of Diebenkorn's work with the figure is represented by his many drawings from models (see fig. 47). He made literally thousands of such works, ranging from sketchy "snapshots" of the model intended only for personal study, to highly finished and sometimes laboriously reworked drawings meant potentially

FIG 44
Richard Diebenkorn
***Woman in a Window*, 1957**
Oil on canvas
59 x 56 in. (149.9 x 142.2 cm)
Albright-Knox Art Gallery, Buffalo, New York, gift of Seymour H. Knox, Jr., 1958, K1958:32
[1225]

FIG 45
Pierre Bonnard
***Dining Room on the Garden*, 1934–1935**
Oil on canvas
50 x 53 1/4 in. (127 x 135.3 cm)
Solomon R. Guggenheim Museum, New York, Solomon R. Guggenheim Founding Collection, by gift, 38.432

FIG 46
Caspar David Friedrich
***Woman at the Window*, 1822**
Oil on canvas
17 3/4 x 12 7/8 in. (45 x 32.7 cm)
Staatliche Museen zu Berlin, Alte Nationalgalerie

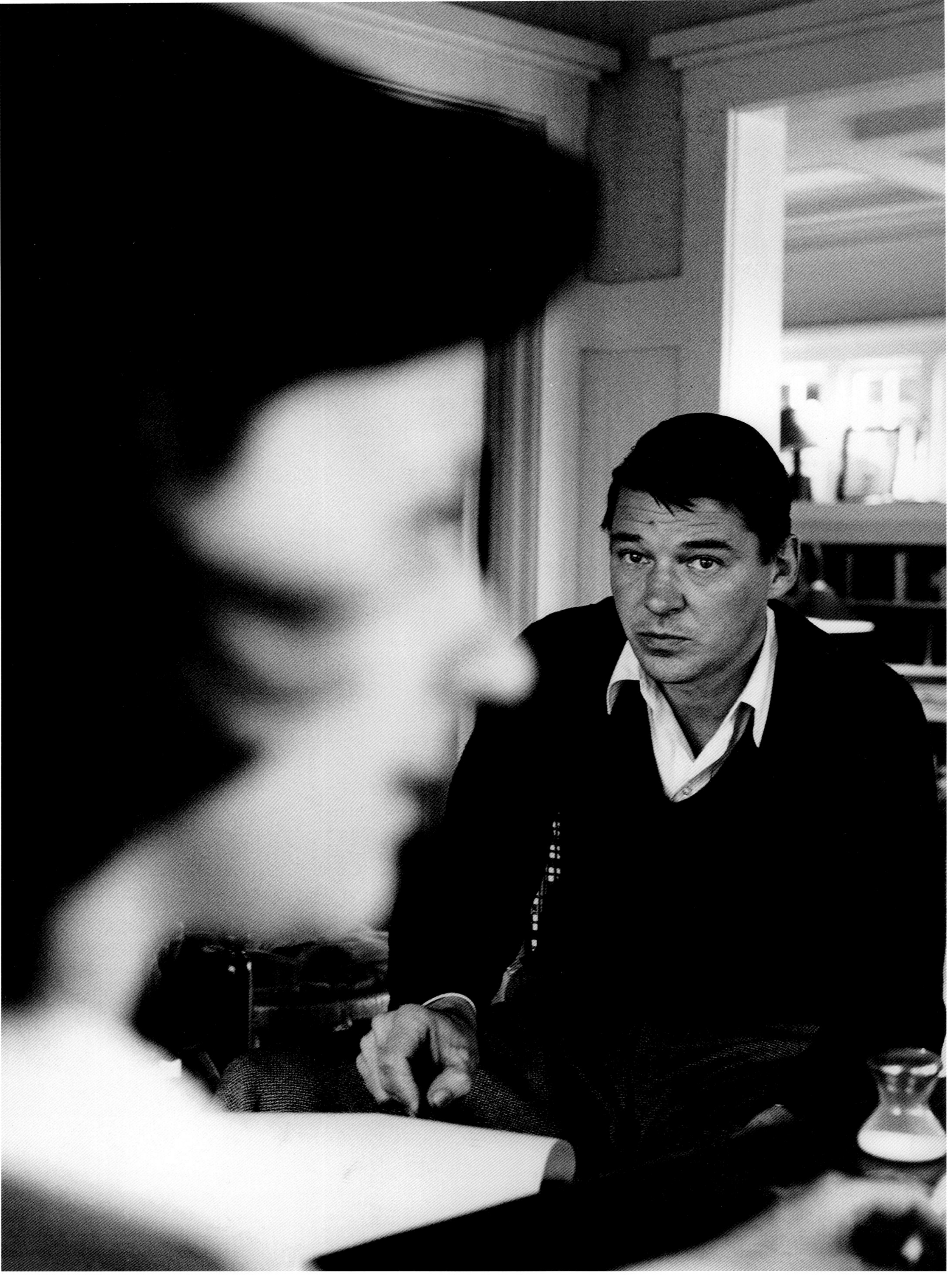

Richard Diebenkorn

for public display. This aspect of his figurative work, and of his drawings in general, comprises a large subject unto itself, but a few key points should be made here. Most important, Diebenkorn loved to draw. In addition to the abundant evidence from his studio sessions with models, a great many still-life drawings, landscapes, interiors, architectural studies, and a few portraits are prominent in collections around the country. The catalogue raisonné of his work will include more than four thousand drawings in a wide variety of media, and this number represents only a fraction of his total output. He drew during all phases of his career, and although drawings are often quite independent of paintings, connections during the figurative period existed in regard to subject matter, composition, and also stylistic handling. For example, many of the figurative drawings are heavily worked with washes of ink or gouache, or dense shadings with conté crayon, producing painterly effects suggestive of the bold handling of oils in the paintings (see pls. 43, 125, and 130). Light and dark passages in these works create strong contrasts. Contours are never sharp but rather waver and dissolve as if the subjects themselves were fluid. It is a vision of light, space, and form controlled by suggestion, nuance, flux, and purposeful emphasis on the action of the hand.

At the other end of the spectrum are lean linear drawings that represent form through a distilled tracking of contours (see pls. 119 and 120). These works are far more minimal. The contour lines are not continuous and precise, as in neoclassical drawings. They have movement and irregularity, and while lines sometimes gather or thicken into denser patterns, most of the surface of the paper is left blank. It is a testimony to Diebenkorn's skill as a draftsman that he was able to suggest convincingly through the play of contours a physical presence of plastic form, although he could also emphasize flatness so that the linear pattern reads more abstractly. These works in general have a particularly "old master" quality that links him, again, to the traditions of Bonnard and Matisse.

Very few drawings, however, can be identified as preparatory works for paintings.[33] Diebenkorn's many hundreds of drawings of nudes seem to have provided a way to study poses and anatomy, remember them better, exercise his powers of looking and coordination of eye and hand, and simply enjoy the pure act of drawing. His drawing sessions with other artists were as much sources of camaraderie and discussions of art as laboratories for the development of figurative compositions. But this is not to discount the fact that many of the works emerging from these sessions rank among Diebenkorn's greatest, and among the most accomplished figure drawings of the century. Several larger-scale drawings from around 1966 in the present exhibition exemplify this high standard (see pls. 135–140). In almost all of these works, the figure is truncated at top and bottom to completely fill the space of the drawing, emphasizing its monumentality. It seems to press outward into the space of the viewer, dominating the whole field of vision. Faces often are left blank or hidden by a turn of the head, as if to say that anonymity reigns over identity, and it is the whole body that counts. Outlines of the figures are dark and definite, so strongly placed in charcoal that they suggest a sculptural carving of the contours. Against and beneath these contours swarm patterns of pentimenti, rubbings, and half-effaced, ghostly images, making palpable a deep and visually rich pictorial space. Such works strike an unusually powerful balance between monumental stasis and vibrant visual activity.

FIG 47
Richard Diebenkorn drawing his wife, Phyllis, in the living room of their home on Hillcrest Road, Berkeley. Photographed by Hans Namuth, 1958

OTHER SIDES OF FIGURATION

Diebenkorn's figurative work first came to public attention in 1956 and 1957 through a number of Bay Area exhibitions and a key article in a national publication. He showed eleven figurative paintings and thirteen drawings and watercolors in *Richard Diebenkorn: Guest of Honor* at the Oakland Art Museum (now part of the Oakland Museum of California) in September 1956; two figurative paintings at the members' exhibition of the San Francisco Art Association in February–March 1957; and five paintings in the groundbreaking exhibition *Contemporary Bay Area Figurative Painting*, organized by Paul Mills in September 1957, also at the Oakland Art Museum. Herschel B. Chipp's article in the May 1957 issue of *Art News* on the working process behind Diebenkorn's *Woman by the Ocean* elevated recognition of his new work from a regional to a national plane. Already apparent in these developments was the balance in Diebenkorn's representational imagery between still-life subjects, landscapes, and the figure, a combination of interests that continued throughout the figurative period.

Still-life paintings and drawings play a role related to that of the interior domestic scenes. They explore personal worlds of familiar objects in interior settings, emphasizing quiet pleasure and the rewards of up-close, careful looking. They also provided an endlessly variable field for compositional invention as Diebenkorn focused on different types of groupings of objects and experimented with lighting and the angle and depth of perspective. He generally chose objects that had a certain resonance for him. He later noted, "I've been very conscious in a lot of my paintings with things, that I select them because they're simply there in a way that gets to me, and to say things beyond that would negate the nice simplicity of the thereness."[34] Through the still-life paintings and drawings we are admitted into the privacy of the artist's studio and the intimacy of sensation generated for him by these different objects and their relational dialogues. We have a sense in many of the still-life groupings of a very casual placement, as if objects were "found" in their respective locations, but the tension between them suggests an *adjusted* casualness that is reminiscent of Paul Cézanne's relativity of still-life objects.[35] Over

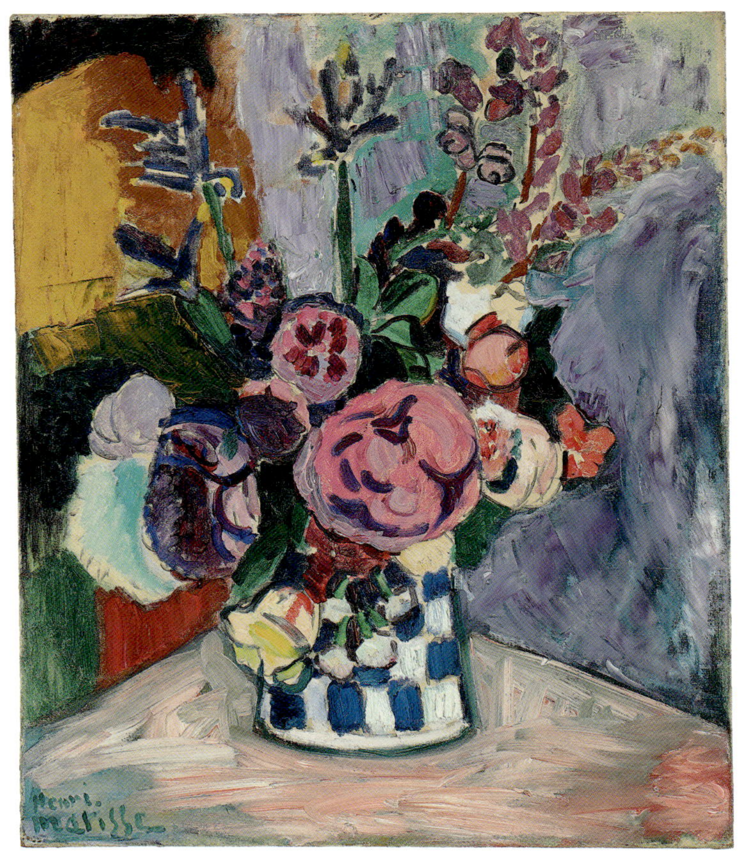

FIG 48
Henri Matisse
***Les pivoines*, 1907**
Oil on canvas
25 1/2 x 21 1/4 in. (65 x 54.6 cm)
Private collection

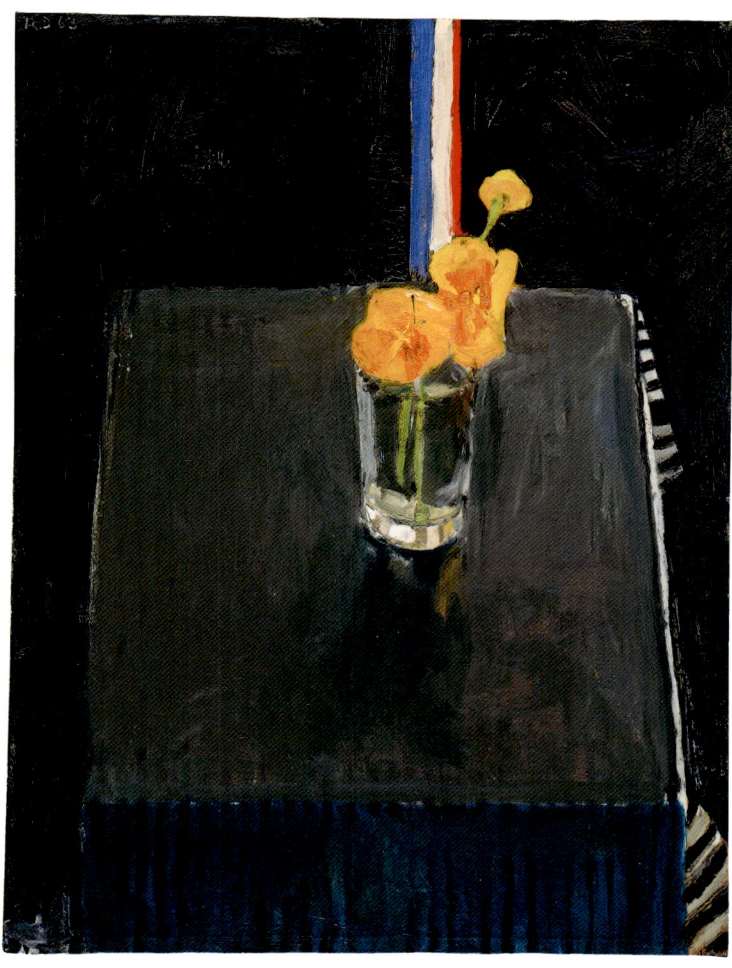

the course of many works, certain studio paraphernalia—such as printed textiles, a French ashtray, pens and ink bottles, coffee cups, books, and the artist's glasses—appear and reappear like old friends. Especially in his drawings, the illumination is often dimmed, giving even more the sense of an enclosed, solitary space for contemplation, removed from nature's sunlight.

In these works Diebenkorn frequently followed the lead of Matisse and Bonnard in composition and even mood (see fig. 49). An untitled drawing from 1964 (pl. 105) is particularly Matisse-like. The view more or less straight down onto the tabletop, the winding floral pattern of the tablecloth that engulfs the objects, and the mood of pleasurable leisure are all reminiscent of various Matisse drawings and paintings. *Flowers and Cigar Box* (pl. 41) of 1956, with its vase of flowers set against a bright background and its sense of bursting color, relates closely, for example, to Matisses's *Les pivoines* (fig. 48) from 1907, whereas the sharply angled perspective in an untitled gouache from ca. 1961 (pl. 90), with cup, ashtray, and bottle all clinging improbably to a tipped-up table, shows devices found frequently in Bonnard's still-life compositions.[36] A link with Édouard Manet's small and richly brushed still-life paintings is apparent in some of Diebenkorn's smaller works such as the succulent *Scissors and Lemon, II* of 1959 and *Knife in a Glass* of 1963 (pls. 88 and 94), in which the artist's sheer pleasure in the application of paint and color is readily apparent. Such sensuality of handling, made more intense by its concentration in small formats, reinvigorates in a personal way Diebenkorn's historical sources. It is also interesting that such works dare to explore erotic content in a manner that is not employed in the larger paintings. The juxtaposition of knives and scissors with round fruits is particularly suggestive.

A fine example of his large-scale still-life paintings is provided by *Interior with Flowers* (pl. 96) of 1961. Again we find a memory of the work of Matisse, especially with the motif of a table with curved corners breaking into the composition from the right and setting up a major visual chord that is echoed in the curves of the silver tray, a play on round and oval forms similar to Matisse's use of curved tables and trays. We look into a dim interior with what seems to be a dark shade pulled down across a window at

FIG 49
Richard Diebenkorn
Poppies, 1963
Oil on canvas
40 x 30 in. (101.6 x 76.2 cm)
Private collection
[1391]

the rear, but with bright bursts of color in the flowers, the blue rug, and the red bedcover. In terms of abstract pattern, zones of color are established as planes in space, interspersed with the heavy dark sections. But Diebenkorn's dashing brushwork opens up even the monolithic areas of dark brown and black to admit subtle patches of light and space, and underlying brighter tones. First reading the painting as a restful interior, the viewer is quickly swept up in the curving lines, dramatic contrasts, and strong tracks of the brush that animate the entire canvas.

Landscapes are another subject Diebenkorn explored throughout his figurative period, working in a variety of media and formats from drawings and watercolors to oil sketches and large-scale canvases. Landscapes were among the very first works in his figurative development, and at least some of these were made directly from nature, including *Chabot Valley* (fig. 37 and pl. 36) of 1955 and the watercolor landscape views he produced on trips to Santa Cruz Island off the coast of Santa Barbara in 1958 (pls. 67 and 68). Larger works were painted in the studio, although the vividness of color and convincing sense of natural light in such paintings as *Seawall* and *View from the Porch* (pls. 66 and 70) show how effectively Diebenkorn could transport indoors his memories and impressions of natural experiences.[37]

In both of these works, the artist imposes even on the raw organic forms of landscape his propensity to build compositions on a geometric scaffolding. In *View from the Porch*, the outlines of the porch in the foreground set a major theme that is answered in the loosely geometric divisions of landscape in the distance. In *Seawall*, with no architectural referent, Diebenkorn still crystallizes various shapes, including a green hillside, ocher cliffs, and dark shadows, into shards of form tightly interspersed across a basically flat plane under the dark blue horizontal band of sky.

Within the resulting compositional subdivisions, Diebenkorn worked up his surfaces with characteristic brio, producing vigorous patchworks of directional brushwork and layers of color that move the eye around rapidly, tracing the tactile, almost sculptural management of paint and virtuoso passages in which description gives way to

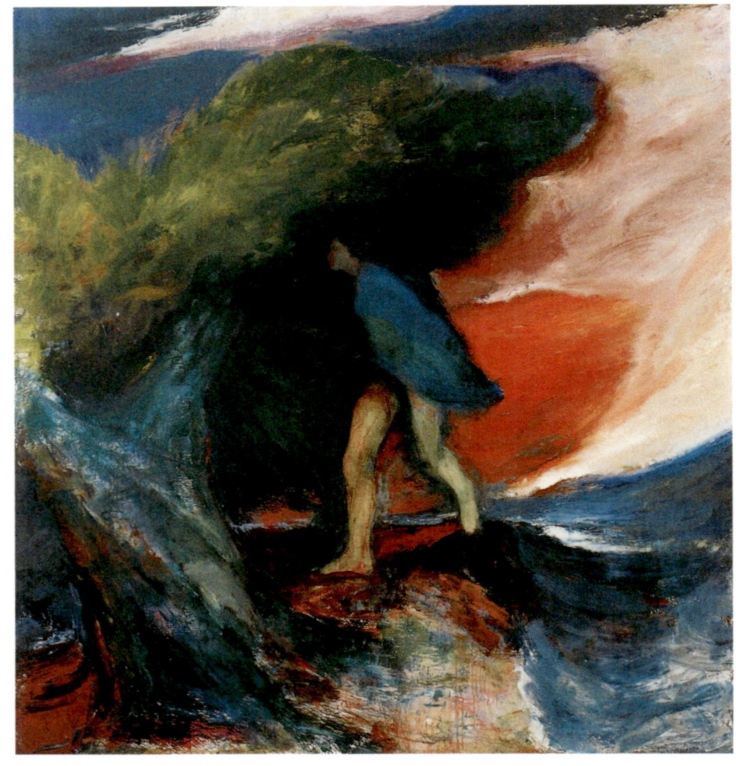

FIG 50
Elmer Bischoff
Figure with Tree, 1972
Oil on canvas
86 1/2 x 80 in. (219.7 x 203.2 cm)
Collection of Adelie Landis Bischoff, courtesy of John Berggruen Gallery

FIG 51
Richard Diebenkorn
Landscape with Freeway, 1961
Oil on canvas
36 1/8 x 29 7/8 in. (91.8 x 75.9 cm)
Private collection, New York
[1319]

FIG 52
Richard Diebenkorn
Cityscape #3 (Landscape #2), 1963
Oil on canvas
47 x 50 1/4 in. (119.4 x 127.6 cm)
Collection of Donald and Barbara Zucker
[1375]

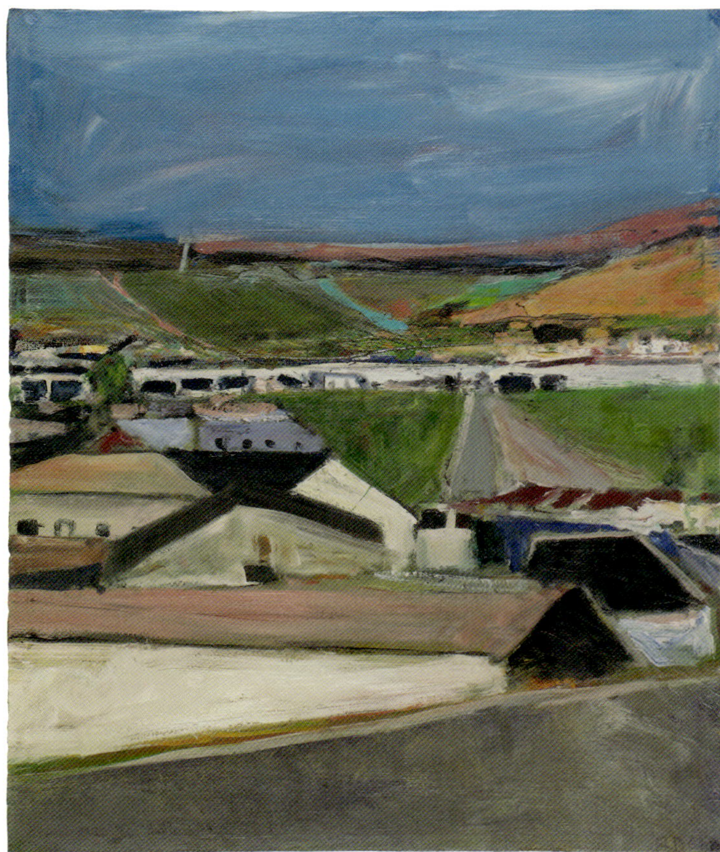

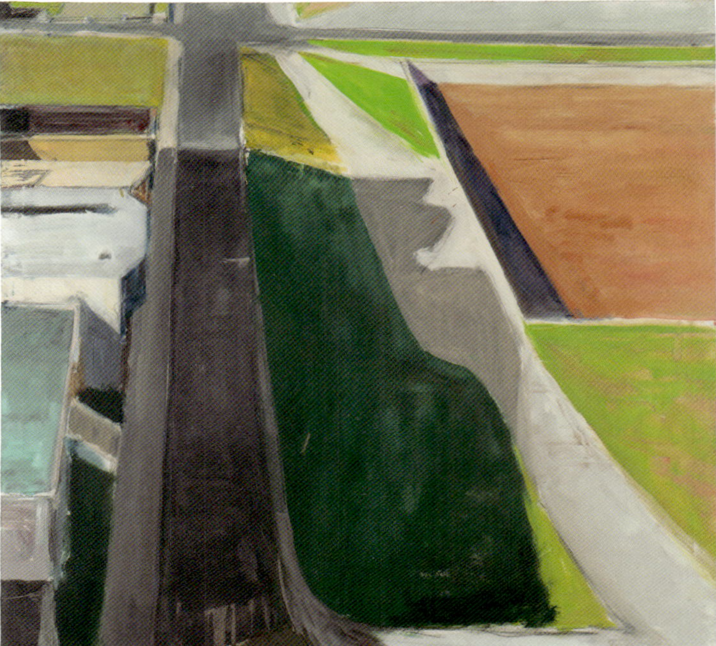

enjoyment of pure painterly values. It is this expressive handling, of course, that led certain critics to claim that Diebenkorn was still an abstract artist, but one who painted figures and landscapes.[38] He did allow that "much of what had been learned in the previous abstract work was retained [in my figuration]," but insisted that it functioned differently and that surfaces in the representational work were "dense and *responsibly* realized."[39] In the case of the two landscapes under discussion, this meant in *response* to the natural environment.

In these and similar landscape paintings, Diebenkorn almost never inserted humans, a trait markedly different from the work of both Park and Bischoff, who frequently populated their outdoor scenes with bathers or other figures communing with nature. This contrast in approach also signals a contrast of meanings. For Diebenkorn, his representational landscapes were essentially celebrations of nature, a signature element also in the abstract landscapes of his early Berkeley period. They are lyrical in feeling and full of the sensory richness so typical of the California coastal environment. In the art of Park and Bischoff, with their emphasis on human relationships with nature, there is less of a local and more of a universal quality. In Park's many bathing and boating scenes, for example, figures are completely suspended in nature, engulfed by dazzling passages of water, light, reflections, and landscape.[40] We feel in his work and in Bischoff's a sense of pantheistic integration with nature, sometimes involving human awe of nature's forces, sometimes a contemplative reverence, and occasionally even an Edvard Munch–like trepidation (see fig. 50). In this way Diebenkorn was more a painter of direct landscape experience than were either of the others.

A landscape subcategory that Diebenkorn appears to have invented, but which other artists since then have explored, is the urban or suburban streetscape with steeply rising roadways, all treated semiabstractly (see fig. 52 and pl. 100). It is an imagery born, naturally, of San Francisco's strikingly vertical topography. Having grown up there, Diebenkorn had this landscape embedded in his memory. A group of paintings, drawings, and prints, dating mostly from 1963, examine variations on this theme (see pls. 99–102).

The urban landscape presented Diebenkorn with a different spatial problem to solve. In order to conform to his technique of condensing imagery onto the picture plane, in his other landscapes featuring long views over land toward a distant horizon he employed dramatic foreshortening and eliminated atmospheric perspective. With the urban views, the hills and streets rise up to meet the picture plane and provide a natural flattening of pictorial space. Diebenkorn sometimes eliminated any trace of horizon lines, reducing still more all reference to perspective or depth. Within this format the vertical streets act as a kind of trunk from which architectural and landscape imagery fan out to either side. The majority of works treating this particular theme came from a one-year span during which he introduced and then quickly concluded his investigations.

Yet another subcategory of Diebenkorn's work with landscape is the coastal view, featuring a perspective from land, vegetation, and/or architecture across a broad sweep of water toward a horizon topped by a flat band of blue sky. Deep space and the issues of structuring that space pictorially are again a primary concern. Matisse had treated similar themes earlier, but Diebenkorn's most direct source of inspiration was the great nineteenth-century master Paul Cézanne, and especially the series of paintings he produced around 1882 to 1886 on the intersection of land, sea, and sky at L'Estaque, on the Mediterranean coast of France. Cézanne concentrated particularly on the cupping of the Gulf of Marseilles by natural landscape and man-made architecture (see fig. 53). His customary layering of form—and flattening of space—achieved through a foreground triangle of land, with its contrasts of color and directional brushwork, topped by a flatly painted triangle of water, and then a block of blue sky, is essentially the same approach seen in Diebenkorn's *Santa Cruz I* (pl. 75). Even the pacing of brushwork from zone to zone is similar. Although the influence of Cézanne on Diebenkorn's still-life paintings was constantly filtered through the work of Matisse and Bonnard, the coastal landscapes show how pure some of his debts to this nineteenth-century predecessor could be.

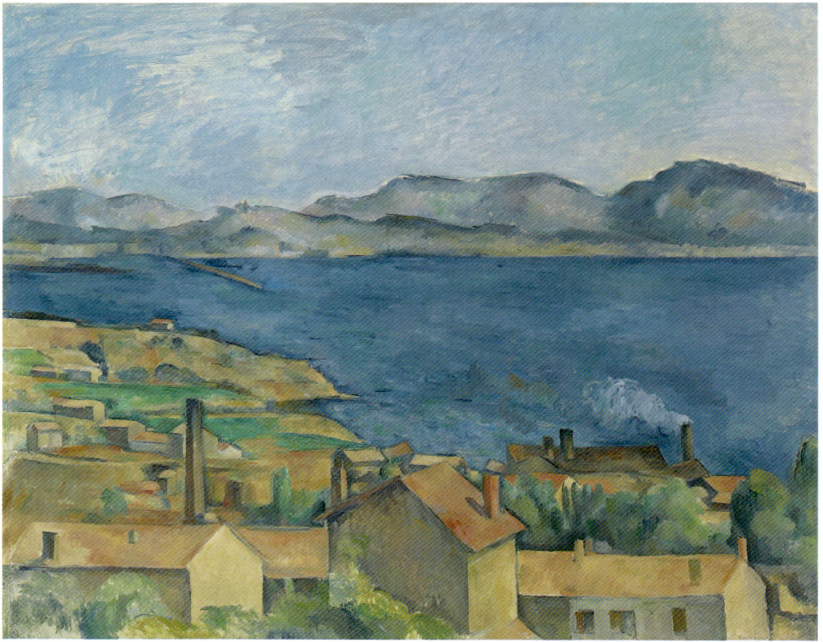

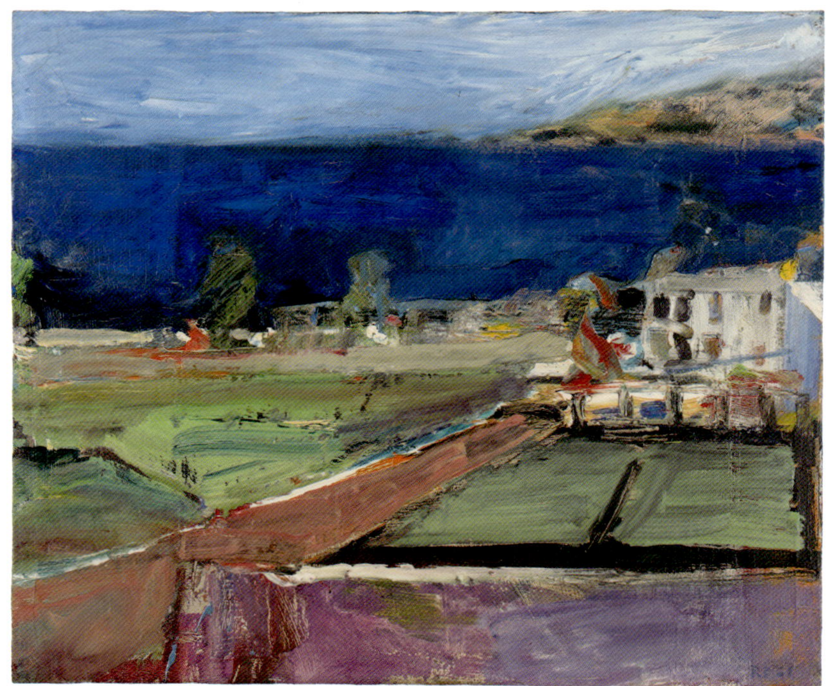

FIG 53
Paul Cézanne
The Bay of Marseilles, Seen from L'Estaque, ca. 1885
Oil on canvas
31 5/8 x 39 5/8 in. (80.2 x 100.6 cm)
Art Institute of Chicago, Mr. and Mrs. Martin A. Ryerson Collection, 1933.1116

FIG 54
Richard Diebenkorn
Prisoners' Harbor, Santa Cruz Island, 1961
Oil on canvas, 21 1/2 x 25 in. (54.6 x 63.5 cm)
Santa Cruz Island Foundation, Carpinteria, California, 1988.23
[1322]

TOWARD ABSTRACTION

Starting in 1965 a trend that would eventually lead to Diebenkorn's return to abstraction became apparent in his art. It involved increased flatness of imagery, greater saturation of colors, and a tendency to fill flattened spaces with large geometric forms and decorative panels. Several works in the current exhibition manifest these changes, including *Large Still Life* and *Nude on Blue Ground* from 1966, and *Window* and *Seated Figure with Hat* from 1967 (pls. 141, 145, 146, and 143). *Recollections of a Visit to Leningrad* from 1965 (pl. 142) signals the key turning point in this evolution.

The governing force behind these changes was Diebenkorn's resurgent interest in the work of Matisse, occasioned by the visit he and Phyllis made in 1964 to the stunning collections of Matisse paintings at the Pushkin Museum in Moscow and the Hermitage Museum in Saint Petersburg. Although a steady factor in his figurative work from the very beginning, and later reinforced by a visit to the Matisse retrospective at the University of California Los Angeles Art Galleries in 1966, this interest took a giant leap with his introduction to masterpieces that had rarely been seen by Westerners since the time of the Russian Revolution.

Recollections of a Visit to Leningrad, completed just a little more than a year after the Diebenkorns returned from Russia, is alive with fresh impressions of the art seen there. It is a joyous painting dominated by deep and vivid blues and greens that celebrate Matisse's sensuous coloration. The paint application is thinner and less gestural than in past years, which reinforces the overall flatness of design, with colors gathered together into compartmentalized zones. In contrast to the simplification of form in the landscape view to the right, the brightly printed floral pattern on the textile hanging over the window to the left (a bedspread that Diebenkorn had kept in his studio over many years)[41] provides a luxuriously decorative passage highly reminiscent of similar motifs in works by Matisse. The rug on the floor of the interior, its light blue band reflecting light from the window above, climbs straight upward to merge with the vertical wall to the rear. All in all, the painting amounts to a visual manifesto of new principles in Diebenkorn's figurative work, and if one mentally removes the patterned textile and the tree on the right, the geometric composition that emerges anticipates the early abstract Ocean Park paintings that Diebenkorn began to produce around 1967–1968.

Elements of this painting are repeated and elaborated on in the four works from 1966 and 1967 noted above. In *Large Still Life*, for example, a similar floral pattern appears in the wallpaper behind the desk. In *Seated Figure with Hat*, which started as a drawing of Phyllis sitting in their backyard in Santa Monica, the wall behind the figure is abstracted into a design that is a direct antecedent of the Ocean Park series. *Nude on Blue Ground* presents, on an intense lapis lazuli background that harks back to Matisse, a monumental and strikingly simplified nude recalling that master's figure style from around 1907 to 1910. It could be a response specifically to one of the two versions of *Dance* from 1909 and 1910,[42] with large, flattened nudes disporting against deep blue backgrounds. With the well-known *Window* from 1967, we see a work conceived at a transitional moment that looks in two directions at once. The theme of an interior with a lonely chair situated in front of a window looking out onto architecture and sky is one that continues throughout the figurative period. But the relatively thinner paint surface and the simplified compositional armature and the decorative iron railing to the left are all a part of Diebenkorn's new stylistic direction.

Window also embodies a signature trait that prevails throughout the figurative works but carries over into the Ocean Park series with even greater effect, that is, the gradual and episodic reworking of compositions with pentimenti revealed in the final surfaces. In this work the chair has been moved around several times; the upper contour of the window ledge in front of the chair was adjusted, as were other elements of the architecture; and the surfaces of the green interior space were repainted probably several times. This thoughtful and prolonged evolution of paintings and also certain drawings, often recorded in the final work through revealed sublayers and pentimenti, is a trademark of Diebenkorn's working method documented in the 1957 article on his *Woman by the Ocean* in *Art News*[43] and given visual evidence in *Window*, among many other pieces. Regarding his tendency to work and rework compositions repeatedly, and often radically, Diebenkorn reported that once he started a composition, "I keep plastering it until it comes around to what I want. . . ."[44] He also noted that the resulting pentimenti were not left visible in order to record the passage of time: "The *pentimenti*, which trace earlier activity, are simply *allowed.* They are truly part of the process . . . nor am I trying to make it a diary of the activity either. . . . I have *picked up* something in the process of the corrections and erasures—something positive. . . . I *like to see pentimenti.*"[45]

In the fall of 1966 Diebenkorn moved with his family to Southern California, first renting a home and later buying one in Santa Monica Canyon, to take a teaching position at the University of California, Los Angeles. He established his first studio in the neighborhood south of Santa Monica called Ocean Park, which would also become the name of the series of abstractions he was soon to commence. Later he rented a studio in the same building as the painter Sam Francis. At first Diebenkorn continued to work on both figurative paintings and drawings, completing several of his large-scale compositions there.[46] But then, fairly abruptly, he dropped figuration altogether.

This move was unhesitating and, to most observers, surprising and even more abrupt than his original switch *to* figuration around 1955. Concerning his drawings, he recounted, "In 1967, just before I began my abstract work, I drew from a model in my studio. I also drew in the evenings with friends. But in 1967 I just cut that off—*completely.* I didn't have any interest in it at that point, and it wasn't relevant to what I wanted to do."[47] Diebenkorn's drawings from this period reveal both his representational interests (see pl. 125) and as his nascent interest in abstraction (see pls. 113 and 114).

Had he explored figuration to the point that it no longer offered anything new or important? Occasionally in later years he would revert to representational modes, but not very often. Undoubtedly, the changes in both cultural milieu—different traditions and different artist friends—and physical environment had an influence. Aspects of his new surroundings, such as a more suffused quality of light, softer landscape colors, and constant ocean views, definitely influenced his art. But the pendulum of the abstract-figurative dynamic in his work had swung again, as he embarked on an amazingly productive period of abstraction that essentially filled the remainder of his career.

CRITICAL FORTUNES

The critical responses to Diebenkorn's work from the mid-fifties to the mid-sixties provide a mixed history. Reactions to his new figuration from critics, art historians, and museum directors around the Bay Area were, from the beginning, largely sympathetic. The responses of critics on the East Coast, however, sometimes bordered on astonishment, if not hostility. An anonymous review of the exhibition *Contemporary Bay Area Figurative Painting* in *Arts Magazine* in 1957 set the tone for much of what was to follow in the abstraction-figuration battles of the period by asking whether the show "represents a new pictorial strength or, as its adversaries have argued . . . is merely a new failure of nerve in the challenge which the so-called 'heroic' period of American abstract painting laid before a younger generation."[48]

The most sustained and intensive examination of Diebenkorn's figurative work on the national level came in reviews of his one-person exhibitions of new paintings at the Poindexter Gallery in New York in 1958, 1961, and 1963. These shows, plus solo exhibitions for Park and Bischoff at the Staempfli Gallery in 1959 and 1960 and various group exhibitions (including *New Images of Man* at The Museum of Modern Art in 1959, which included works by Diebenkorn and Nathan Oliveira), brought to the East greater familiarity with West Coast developments. Critical response ran the gamut from positive to severely negative.[49] Particularly harsh reviews came from Hilton Kramer and Dore Ashton, both of whom had been admirers of Diebenkorn's abstractions. Kramer wrote of Park's work that it contained "crude cartoons of the human figure . . . completely devoid of pictorial expression,"[50] and Ashton found his exhibition "a great disappointment" that did not live up to the perceived ambition of justifying the resurgence of figurative art.[51] Their reviews of Diebenkorn's work were less astringent but nevertheless condemning.

Diebenkorn's first one-man exhibition of figurative work at the Poindexter Gallery in 1958 was a remarkable success commercially; museums including the Albright-Knox Art Gallery and

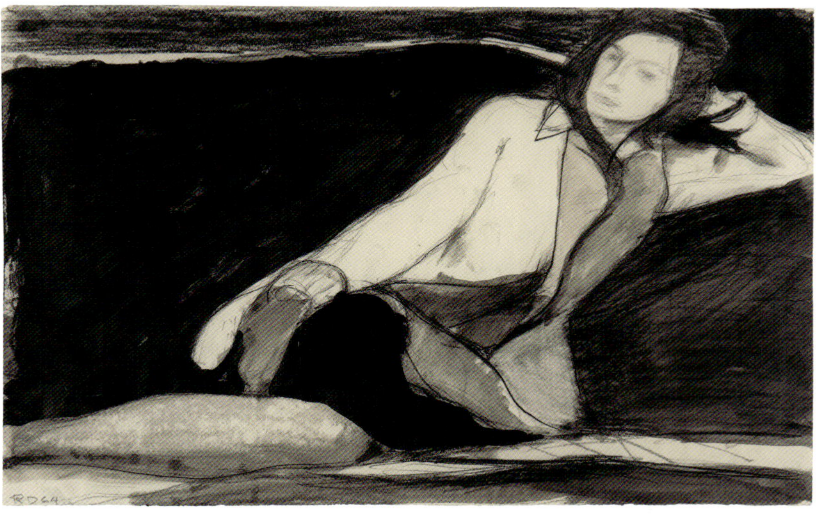

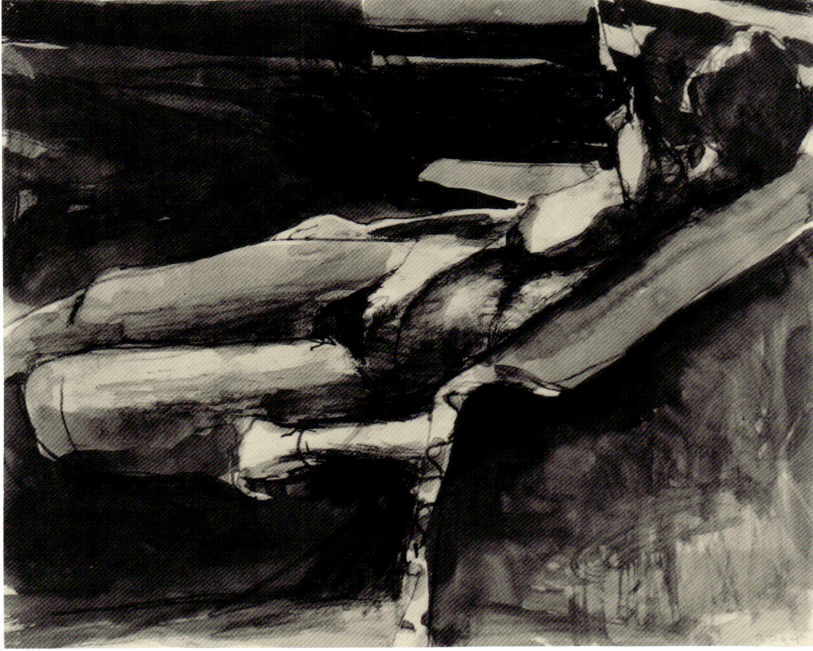

The Phillips Collection purchased works, as did such leading collectors as Richard Brown Baker, Joseph Hirshhorn, Roy Neuberger, and Giuseppe Panza di Biumo. A number of favorable notices appeared in publications as diverse as *Time* and *Arts Magazine*,[52] but Ashton's review, while thoughtful, clearly expressed disappointment. For her, the "inherent problems in the new style . . . remained troubling throughout [the] exhibition." Her admiration for the earlier abstractions still in mind, she felt that the figures, with their "touching clumsiness," had forced Diebenkorn to "pull in his imagination and submit to the dictates of real perspective."[53] In other words, the figurative style cramped his inventiveness.

Kramer's review of the Poindexter exhibition of 1963 went considerably further, and in fact remains a touchstone in the critical literature on Diebenkorn.[54] He gave clear and definite voice to the old criticism that Diebenkorn (and, by implication, others in the Bay Area Figurative group) remained, in his figurative work, merely an Abstract Expressionist manqué. Diebenkorn's representational style, "if no longer abstract in a strict sense, remained Abstract Expressionist in taste, physical deportment, and all-over aesthetic loyalty. . . . Diebenkorn was an abstract painter who now painted figures and landscapes." He thought that the ambitions of the figurative paintings to justify their existence with an integration of serious themes and with the techniques used to express them were not realized. These ambitions were not only unfulfilled by the works themselves but were "clearly unfulfillable by the very terms in which the pictures were conceived." He perceived an "existential weakness" in the paintings, with their supposed reliance strictly on the aesthetic experience of the paint handling. And Diebenkorn's admittedly masterful but nevertheless backward-looking emulation of such painters as Manet isolated an "aesthetic atavism."

Kramer knew how to make a point and managed to codify thinking about Diebenkorn and his work that was hard to shed, stretching in the hands of certain critics even into the 1990s.[55] (Kramer himself eventually came around to a much different and more celebratory view of Diebenkorn's work.)[56] The weakness

FIG 55
Richard Diebenkorn
***Untitled*, 1964**
Ink and conté crayon on paper
11 1/8 x 17 1/2 in. (28.3 x 44.5 cm)
Collection of Gretchen and John Berggruen
[312]

FIG 56
Richard Diebenkorn
***Untitled (Reclining Nude, Side View)*, 1964**
Ink and conté crayon on paper
13 3/4 x 16 3/4 in. (34.9 x 42.5 cm)
Fleming Museum of Art, University of Vermont, Burlington, Museum Purchase, 1966.12 [340]

underlying such thought was the assumption that Diebenkorn's turn to figuration was a more or less random development without concrete meaning to his art. The artist himself was later at pains to refute such views. His shift from abstraction to figuration around 1955, although seemingly facile and rapid, was actually the result of heavy soul searching and a relatively protracted and fitful evolution in both his thinking and practice. It grew out of genuine dissatisfaction with the state of his work in abstract modes, followed by clear choices that offered a fresh and exciting start for his art. While making definite distinctions in his own mind between abstraction and representation, he (and others in the figurative group) never denied that they carried over from their previous work important lessons and habits.[57] The basic message was that the techniques of painting abstractly were put to new and very different purposes, and that the *content* of figurative art, that is, its underlying themes and meanings and their urgency for the very *conception* of the works, existed, whether or not it was readily apparent to different observers, especially those with a strong intellectual or aesthetic investment in abstraction.

In response specifically to Kramer's claim that he, Park, and Bischoff had "taken up the painting of the figure in a serious way without any real decision about its meaning," Diebenkorn replied, "One can simply disagree. I know that David Park made as serious a decision as anybody I've known or heard about in regard to a choice between abstract painting and figurative painting. . . . I don't think this criticism has held up objectively."[58] And more directly to the point, when asked if it mattered whether he was painting a woman or an abstract shape, he responded,

> Absolutely yes. *It mattered.* And when I was doing representational painting, I was often offended when critics or writers would say that I was really only *using* representational material as a peg on which to hang my conceptions of painting. That offended me *mightily* because it was *absolutely not true*! One of the reasons I got into figurative or representational painting in the *first* place was that I wanted my ideas to be "worked on," changed, altered, by what was "out there."[59]

This was the visual reality that offered him something to "come up against."[60] And the ways that he "came up against" it were far from simple or purely visual. There abides in his figurative work a rich life of memories or impressions from earlier artists, from Degas and Bonnard to Matisse and beyond to Hopper, that either consciously or subconsciously influenced his thematic decisions. He was finely attuned to the subtleties of mood and psychological interaction in his paintings, and was fastidious in his efforts to get the compositional and emotional balances just right. Throughout his figurative phase, he returned to drawing, and most often drawing from models, for information, relaxation, and encouragement. And while he may have believed along with Bischoff and Park in "finding the painting through the painting,"[61] he also believed that process, and the abstract values of pure painting, needed to be resolved in tension with nature. If others worried about his seemingly heretical switches between abstraction and figuration, he took heart in similar oscillations in the work of one of his favorite painters, Willem de Kooning.[62] During Diebenkorn's figurative trajectory, he was fully committed to the proposition that imagination and observation could merge completely, and that the materiality of abstract work and the "presentness" of natural form could coexist as one. It was an idea that served him very well for more than a decade, until he came to feel that his imagination had to be more fully unleashed.

1 John Gruen, "Richard Diebenkorn: The Idea Is to Get Everything Right," *Art News* 85, no. 9 (November 1986): 85.

2 Jane Livingston, John Elderfield, and Ruth E. Fine, *The Art of Richard Diebenkorn*, exh. cat. (New York: Whitney Museum of American Art in association with University of California Press, 1997), 17.

3 Jan Butterfield, "Pentimenti: Seeing and Then Seeing Again" in *Resource/Response/Reservoir—Richard Diebenkorn: Paintings 1848–1983*, exh. brochure (San Francisco: San Francisco Museum of Modern Art, May 1983), n.p.

4 From Diebenkorn's studio notes, Diebenkorn estate; quoted in Livingston et al., *The Art of Richard Diebenkorn*, 46.

5 Butterfield, "Pentimenti," n.p.

6 John Elderfield has commented on this underlying characteristic of Diebenkorn's work: "Diebenkorn's art, both as a whole and in its parts, suggests discussion in terms of the relationship between abstraction (and the formalizing imagination of the artist) on the one hand, and representation (and the external reality that comprises his subject) on the other. It seems not only to exhibit such a relationship, as all pictorial art to some degree must do. It seems also to depend on such a relationship." John Elderfield, *The Drawings of Richard Diebenkorn*, exh. cat. (New York: Museum of Modern Art, 1988), 16–17. In a generally related vein, Henry Moore stated concisely, "I see no reason why realistic art and purely abstract art can't exist in the world side by side . . . even in one artist at the same time." Interview with Moore by Donald Hall, *Horizon: A Magazine of the Arts* 3, no. 2 (November 1960): 102.

7 The best general sources on this subject remain Thomas Albright, *Art in the San Francisco Bay Area, 1945–1980: An Illustrated History* (Berkeley: University of California Press, 1985), and Caroline A. Jones, *Bay Area Figurative Art: 1950–1965*, exh. cat. (San Francisco: San Francisco Museum of Modern Art in association with University of California Press, 1990), augmented by studies of individual artists including Gerald Nordland, *Richard Diebenkorn* (New York: Rizzoli, 1987); Paul Mills, *The New Figurative Art of David Park* (Santa Barbara: Capra Press, 1988); Livingston et al., *The Art of Richard Diebenkorn*; Susan Landauer, *Elmer Bischoff: The Ethics of Paint*, exh. cat. (Berkeley: University of California Press in association with Oakland Museum of California, 2001); Peter Selz, *Nathan Oliveira*, exh. cat. (Berkeley: University of California Press in collaboration with San Jose Museum of Art, 2002); and Nancy Boas, *David Park: A Painter's Life* (Berkeley: University of California Press, 2012).

8 See Mills, *The New Figurative Art*, 70, and Butterfield, "Pentimenti," n.p.

9 Later on Diebenkorn also worked in drawing sessions with Theophilus Brown, Paul Wonner, Frank Lobdell, and others, including Nathan Oliveira. For information on these sessions, see Boas, *David Park*, 172–173, 189–195; and Bruce Guenther, "Every Thursday Night," in *Frank Lobdell: Figure Drawings*, exh. cat. (Stanford, CA: Cantor Center for Visual Arts, Stanford University, 2009), 13f.

10 Butterfield, "Pentimenti," n.p.

11 See Susan Larsen interviews with Richard Diebenkorn, May 1, 2, 7, 1985, and December 15, 1987, Archives of American Art, Smithsonian Institution, Washington, DC.

12 RD 2111, inscribed "RD" at lower right and "Ensenada—1954" on reverse.

13 RD 961, 1758, 3019, 6474.

14 RD 3541 (fig. 42), 3545, 3546, 3696. One such drawing is illustrated in Elderfield, *The Drawings of Richard Diebenkorn*, fig. 4.

15 Butterfield, "Pentimenti," n.p.

16 Butterfield, "Pentimenti," n.p.

17 Mills, *The New Figurative Art*, 35, quoted from Paul Mills, *Contemporary American Painting*, exh. cat. (Urbana: University of Illinois/Urbana, 1952), 220.

18 Gail R. Scott, *New Paintings by Richard Diebenkorn*, exh. brochure (Los Angeles: Los Angeles County Museum of Art, 1969), n.p.

19 "I came to mistrust my desire to explode the picture and supercharge it in some way. At one time the common device of using the super emotional to get 'in gear' with a painting used to serve me for access to painting, but I mistrust that now." Quoted in Paul Mills, *Contemporary Bay Area Figurative Painting*, exh. cat. (Oakland, CA: Oakland Art Museum, 1957), 12.

20 Mills, *Contemporary Bay Area Figurative Painting*, 12.

21 For example, Nancy Boas recounts how the Los Angeles dealer Paul Kantor, who had supported Diebenkorn's work during his early Berkeley period, lost interest when he began to painting figuratively. Boas, *David Park*, 167.

22 Gruen, "Richard Diebenkorn," 85.

23 Bruce Conner interview conducted by Paul Cummings, April 16, 1973, Archives of American Art, Smithsonian Institution, Washington, DC, ms.19.

24 RD 1122.

25 Larsen interview, May 2, 1985.

26 For brief remarks on the iconographical elements found in Diebenkorn's work, see Steven A. Nash, *Abstract and Figurative: Highlights of Bay Area Painting*, exh. cat. (San Francisco: John Berggruen Gallery, 2008), 4–9.

27 Diebenkorn's earliest firsthand familiarity with work by Matisse came through a visit to the collection of Michael and Sarah Stein in Palo Alto when he was a student at Stanford University. See Janet Bishop et al., *The Steins Collect: Matisse, Picasso, and the Parisian Avant-Garde*, exh. cat. (New Haven, CT: San Francisco Museum of Modern Art in association with Yale University Press, 2011), 146, 148n64; and Nordland, *Richard Diebenkorn*, 12.

28 For a recent scholarly study of this tradition, see Sabine Rewald, *Rooms with a View: The Open Window in the 19th Century*, exh. cat. (New Haven, CT: The Metropolitan Museum of Art in association with Yale University Press, 2011).

29 See P. A. Lemoisne, *Degas et son oeuvre* (Paris: Paul Brame and C.M. De Hauke, 1946), vol. 2, nos. 348, 335, 127.

30 Herschel B. Chipp, "Diebenkorn Paints a Picture," *Art News* 56, no. 3 (May 1957): 45. He quotes Diebenkorn further: "It is the opposition and interrelation of environment . . . and the figure with its distinct and concentrated psychology which concerns me at present" (46).

31 John Elderfield, *Richard Diebenkorn*, exh. cat. (London: Whitechapel Art Gallery, 1991), 31.

32 Irving Hershel Sandler, "New York Letter," *Art International* 5, no. 4 (May 1, 1961): 54.

33 Exceptions include a watercolor study for *Seated Figure with Hat* (reproduced in Livingston et al., *The Art of Richard Diebenkorn*, pl. 146); a sketch for *Nude on Blue Ground* (Livingston et al., *The Art of Richard Diebenkorn*, pl. 28); a study for *Woman in a Window* (RD 5071V); and the drawing of a seated man (reportedly a self-portrait) that served as the basis for the figure in the first state of *Woman by the Ocean* (Chipp, "Diebenkorn Paints a Picture," 45). Diebenkorn used a number of drawings in the production of prints during this period. See in particular the etchings and drypoints printed at Crown Point Press in 1964 and 1965 and released as *41 Etchings Drypoints* in 1965. Kathan Brown, ed., *Richard Diebenkorn: Etchings and Drypoints 1949–1980*, exh. cat. (Houston: Houston Fine Art Press, 1981), 7–14.

34 Scott, *New Paintings by Richard Diebenkorn*, 2.

35 When asked if the artist, for his still-life paintings and drawings, consciously arranged objects for the compositions, Phyllis Diebenkorn replied, "I really don't know. He was usually in the studio alone. He maybe sometimes grouped things, or spotted a grouping that appealed to him, or maybe a little of both." Interview with the author, May 14, 2012.

36 Elmer Bischoff told Nancy Boas that he, Park, and Diebenkorn always spoke with enthusiasm for Bonnard, particularly "the color and light, and in his best work, the very strong presence [of flattened space]." Boas, *David Park*, 203.

37 Phyllis Diebenkorn confirmed that *Seawall* was painted in the studio. See Steven A. Nash, *Facing Eden: 100 Years of Landscape Art in the Bay Area*, exh. cat. (San Francisco: Fine Arts Museums of San Francisco in association with University of California Press, 1995), 100.

38 Hilton Kramer, "Pure and Impure Diebenkorn," *Arts Magazine* 38, no. 3 (December 1963): 46.

39 Butterfield, "Pentimenti," n.p.

40 For an introductory discussion of these aspects of Park's and Bischoff's work, see Nash, *Abstract and Figurative*, 4–9.

41 What seems to be the same textile appears, for example, in a drawing from ca. 1963–1964. See Lorenz Eitner, *Drawings by Richard Diebenkorn*, exh. cat. (Stanford, CA: Department of Art and Architecture, Stanford University, 1964), no. 26. Phyllis Diebenkorn recalls that she and Richard bought several similar Indian bedspreads very inexpensively and used them for various purposes around their house. As the textiles began to wear, they found their way into the artist's studio. Interview with the author, May 14, 2012.

42 John Elderfield, *Henri Matisse: A Retrospective*, exh. cat. (New York: Museum of Modern Art, 1992), pls. 112, 125.

43 Chipp, "Diebenkorn Paints a Picture," passim. In this article photographs by Rose Mandel document various stages in the evolution of the composition and illustrate dramatically how radical these changes could be. Additional unpublished photographs by Mandel from this same series have recently come to light and will be shown at the de Young Museum in June–October 2013. These show how much more extensive this evolutionary process was than previously understood, and how many more distinct stages it passed through. Another radical compositional change recently discovered involves *Woman in Profile* from 1958 (pl. 61). See Janet Bishop et al., "Bay Area Figurative Painting and the San Francisco Art Association," in Janet Bishop, Corey Keller, and Sarah Roberts, eds., *75 Years of Looking Forward*, exh. cat. (San Francisco: San Francisco Museum of Modern Art, 2009), 166. And yet another good example of how extensively Diebenkorn could sometimes rework his canvases is provided by a frontispiece photograph in Livingston et al., *The Art of Richard Diebenkorn*, 16, which shows the artist at work on his *Interior with View of Buildings* (pl. 80). In the center of the canvas appear the ghostly remains of a large figure that eventually would be completely painted out.

44 Mills, *Contemporary Bay Area Figurative Painting*, 12.

45 Butterfield, "Pentimenti," n.p.

46 These include *Large Woman* and *Seated Figure with Hat* from 1967 (Livingston et al., *The Art of Richard Diebenkorn*, pls. 144, 145).

47 Butterfield, "Pentimenti," n.p. He also noted about the suddenness of this change, "One day, I made the decision to return to abstraction."

48 "Figurative Painters in California," *Arts* 32, no. 3 (December 1957): 26.

49 Laudatory reviews of Park's work, for example, are found in Bennett Schiff, "In the Art Galleries," *New York Post*, Sunday, October 11, 1959, M12; and Irving Sandler, "Reviews and Previews: New Names This Month," *Art News* 58, no. 6 (September 1959): 12.

50 Hilton Kramer, "Month in Review," *Arts* 34, no. 4 (January 1960): 42, 45.

51 Dore Ashton, *Arts & Architecture* 76, no. 12 (December 1959): 7–8.

52 On the positive side, see, for example Anita Ventura, "In the Galleries: Richard Diebenkorn," *Art* 32, no. 6 (March 1958): 56; and "Edging Away from Abstraction," *Time*, March 17, 1958, 64–65, 67.

53 Dore Ashton, "Art," *Arts & Architecture* 75, no. 5 (May 1958): 29.

54 Kramer, "Pure and Impure Diebenkorn," 46–53.

55 Gay Morris, "Report from San Francisco: Figures by the Bay," *Art in America* 78, no. 11 (November 1990): 92f.

56 For Diebenkorn's remarks on Kramer's changing views of his art, see Joan Bossart, interview with Diebenkorn, 1981, quoted in Boas, *David Park*, 310n74, and also Butterfield, "Pentimenti," n.p.

57 Bischoff told Nancy Boas that his figurative art as well as Diebenkorn's and Park's was "derived from the abstract expressionist approach," and that they discussed this work "always in terms of abstract expressionism," an instructive if perhaps exaggerated statement. Boas, *David Park*, 174. Diebenkorn also observed that "much of what had been learned in the previous abstract work was retained." Butterfield, "Pentimenti," n.p.

58 Bossart, interview with Diebenkorn, in Boas, *David Park*, 310n74.

59 Butterfield, "Pentimenti," n.p.

60 Scott, *New Paintings*, 5.

61 Boas, *David Park*, 174.

62 Diebenkorn told Paul Mills, "My faith in abstract expressionism had been shaken by de Kooning; so strong a man as he had changed." Quoted in Boas, *David Park*, 173.

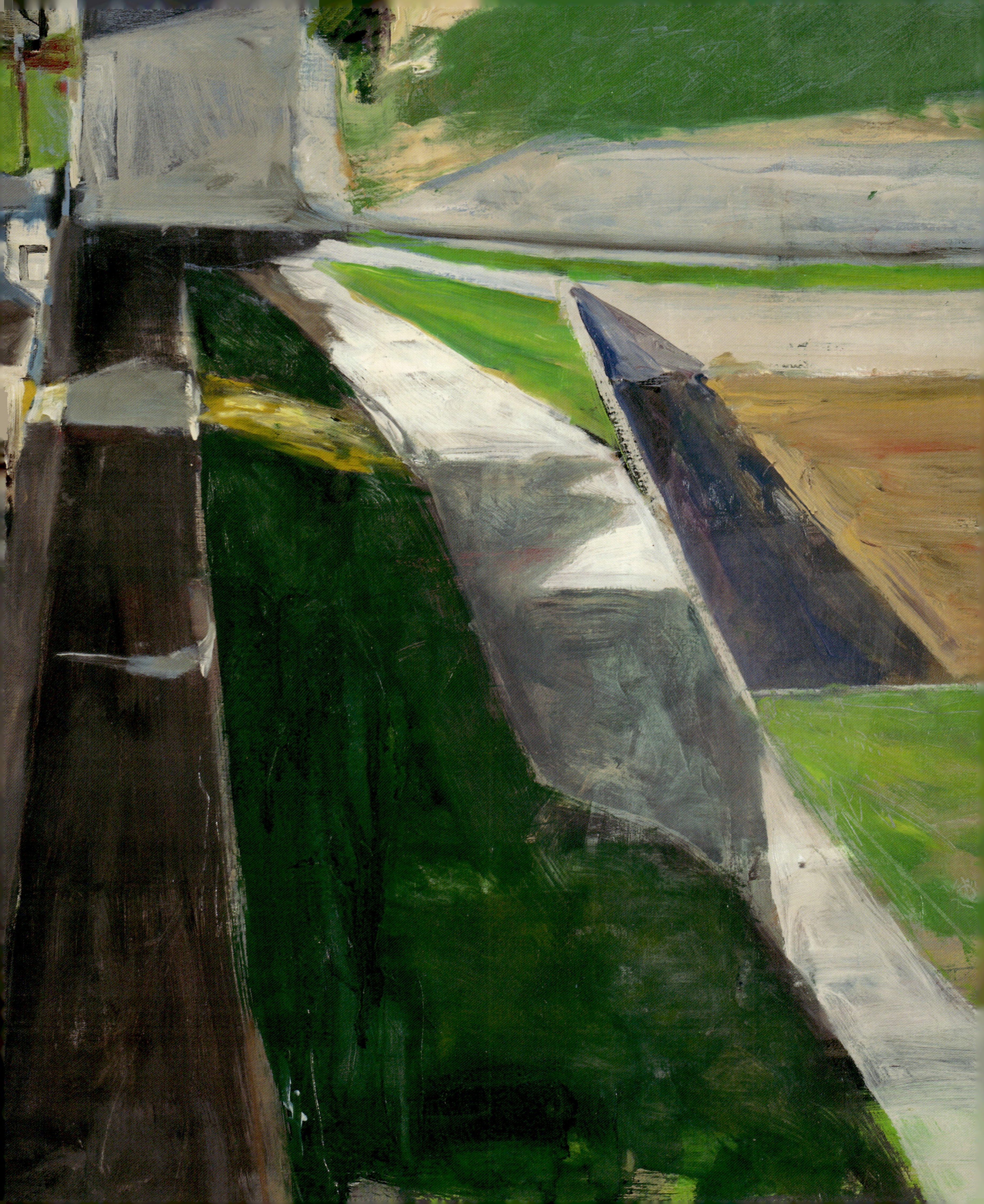

A Sense of Place

Richard Diebenkorn and the Aerial View

EMMA ACKER

The works from Richard Diebenkorn's Berkeley period show him grappling with what it meant to be a painter working in the mid-twentieth century, absorbing and synthesizing the dominant artistic influence of Abstract Expressionism, while striving to translate onto canvas his own particular aesthetic and emotional responses to his surroundings. The open structure and sweeping brushwork of his Berkeley-period works stem not only from the vocabulary of modernist abstraction but also from the elevated vantages and new visual terrain that he experienced in 1951 during his first flight across the desert.

Diebenkorn had a lifelong interest in the aerial view, but its influence on his work varied according to the stylistic and conceptual issues that he was addressing at different phases of his career. With its shallow space and emphasis on flattened planes of color and pattern, this perspective aligned with the aesthetic principles of Abstract Expressionism—the predominant influence on Diebenkorn's work from the mid-1940s until his shift to representation in 1955. A bird's-eye viewpoint is suggested in many of the works from Diebenkorn's numbered Berkeley series (1953–1956), in which he combined the gestural energies and formal rigors of Abstract Expressionism with his sensory experiences of his environment. Following his turn to figuration, Diebenkorn continued to use an aerial perspective in works such as *Seawall* of 1957 (pl. 66) and *Cityscape #1* (originally titled *Landscape #1*) of 1963 (pl. 99), and the elevated vantages in these compositions simultaneously abstract the depicted scenes and heighten their phenomenological and psychological intensity.[1]

The Berkeley-period work reflects the influence of a landscape and a culture in which Diebenkorn was deeply rooted, having spent significant portions of both his childhood and adult life in the Bay Area. Enrolled at Stanford University in 1940, he studied art with Professors Victor Arnautoff and Daniel Mendelowitz. With the latter Diebenkorn shared a passion for the art of Edward Hopper, whose influence can be seen in works from this period such as *Palo Alto Circle* (1943) (fig. 36). Diebenkorn's praise for the formal and psychological qualities of Hopper's landscapes and cityscapes reveals an early fascination with the poetic evocation of place: "And I think with Hopper, the use of light and shade and the atmosphere, that kind of drenched, saturated with mood, and its kind of austerity, it was the kind of work that just seemed made for me."[2] An early untitled drawing by Diebenkorn (fig. 57) of ca. 1944–1945 presents a nocturnal view of a deserted street and the rooftop and facade of a rectangular, low-lying building,[3] which, in its unusual perspective, strong chiaroscuro, and desolate subject matter, is reminiscent of Hopper's *Night Shadows* (1921) (fig. 58). Although the vantage in *Night Shadows* is more dramatically vertiginous, in both works the elevated viewpoints lend the scenes a surreal, mysterious, and even slightly foreboding quality.

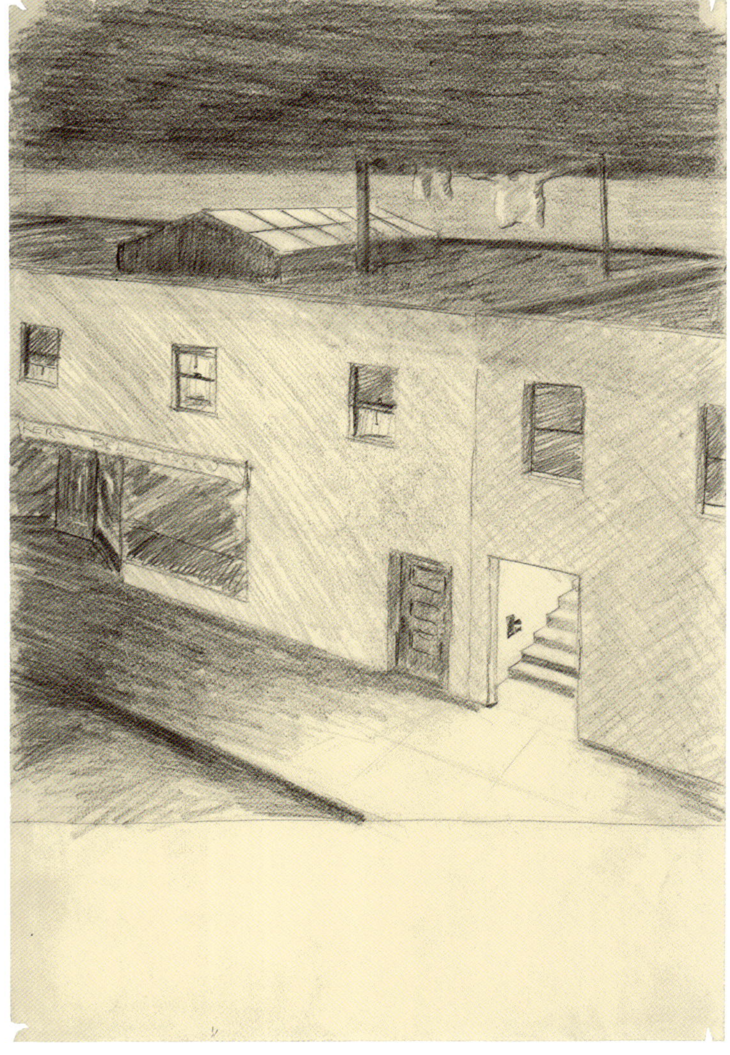

Mendelowitz also introduced his student to the works of early twentieth-century masters, notably Paul Cézanne, Henri Matisse, and Pablo Picasso. In 1943 they visited the art collection of Sarah and the late Michael Stein in Palo Alto,[4] where Diebenkorn encountered Matisse's *Bay of Nice* of 1918 (fig. 5), which features a distinctive aerial perspective. During the summer of that year Diebenkorn was further exposed to the formalist modernism of these painters through his studies in art under Erle Loran, Worth Ryder, and Eugen Neuhaus at the University of California, Berkeley.[5]

Soon after completing his undergraduate studies, Diebenkorn had another experience that may have reinforced his innate attunement to the abstract possibilities of landscape—he found himself working as a cartographer. Diebenkorn enlisted in the United States Marine Corps shortly after the Japanese attack on Pearl Harbor. After attending basic training, he was sent in the summer of 1944 to Officer Candidates School (OCS) in Quantico, Virginia, where he made a number of what he described as "[Hans] Holbein–derived" portrait drawings of officers and sergeants, which greatly impressed his colleagues. Recognizing Diebenkorn's talents, one of the sergeants recommended to the Commanding Officer that, following his dismissal from OCS, he should be reassigned to the photographic section (Marine Photographic Unit) at Quantico. The staff consisted of Walt Disney–trained animators, cartographers, and graphic artists who deployed their skills to create expansive colored washes delineating geographical areas and military positions.

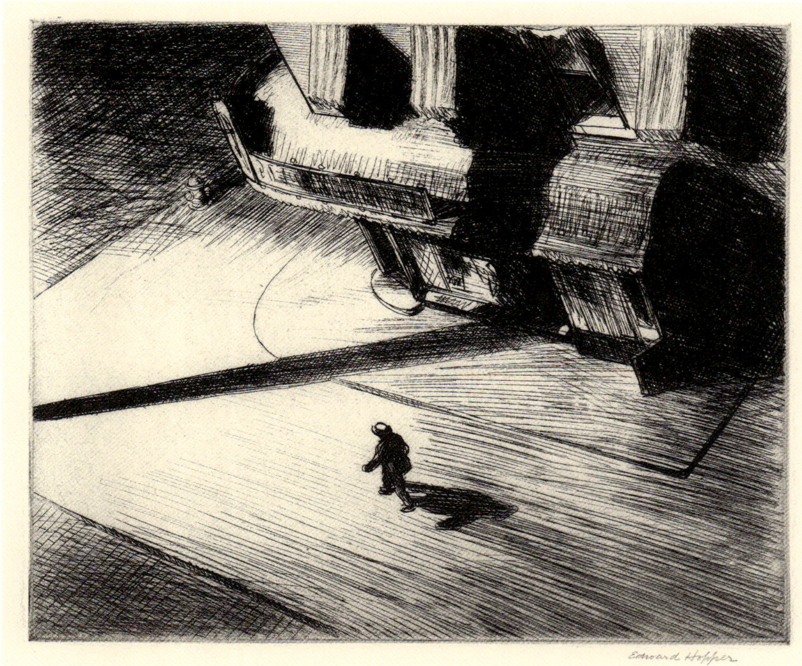

Diebenkorn recalled,

> So these were training films, and [I] played with an animated map to show how positions were taken. So that's what I was assigned to do. And so I made some friends there, right away. It was a jolly group. And I didn't have their kind of skills at all. . . . So I got less and less to do. Each big map wash that I tried to make . . . there'd be a big bubble or blob in it every time, and I just couldn't do that kind of thing.[6]

Diebenkorn's shortcomings as a mapmaker served him well as a painter, for he was given fewer and fewer assignments and, with time and materials at his disposal, could focus on his own art. As he noted, "I was a big flop. . . . Consequently I could do my own work."[7] Whether or not he was suitable for the profession, Diebenkorn gained experiences considering and depicting vast swaths of terrain in the flattened, abstracted manner of a cartographer that seem highly relevant to the development of the landscape abstractions in his Berkeley series, which are characterized by the interplay of large fields of color and demarcated linear elements.

In 1947, while living in the small town of Sausalito on San Francisco Bay, Diebenkorn began teaching at the California School of Fine Arts (CSFA, now the San Francisco Art Institute [SFAI]), where he was a student the year prior. The school had become a center for Abstract Expressionism on the West Coast with faculty including Clyfford Still, Mark Rothko, David Park, Elmer Bischoff, Edward Corbett, Hassel Smith, and Clay Spohn.[8] The formalist creed of art critic Clement Greenberg, the reigning advocate of Abstract Expressionism, dictates that a work of art should visually assert the elements of its own construction—in the case of painting, by emphasizing the two-dimensional surface of the picture plane.[9] Greenberg maintained that the importance painters placed on revealing the "limitations that constitute the medium of painting—the flat surface, the shape of the support, the properties of pigment . . . remained . . . more fundamental than anything else to the processes by which pictorial art criticized and defined itself under Modernism."[10] While Diebenkorn

FIG 57
Richard Diebenkorn
***Untitled*, ca. 1944–1945**
Graphite on paper
17 7/8 x 11 7/8 in. (45.4 x 30.2 cm)
Private collection
[5828]

FIG 58
Edward Hopper
***Night Shadows*, 1921**
Etching
6 7/8 x 8 5/16 in. (17.6 x 21 cm)
Fine Arts Museums of San Francisco, Museum Purchase, Achenbach Foundation for Graphic Arts Endowment Fund, 1970.25.16

was keenly aware of and interested in Greenberg's theories, he resisted the rigid orthodoxy of his pronouncements.[11] Indeed, of all the Abstract Expressionists, Diebenkorn eventually came to most admire Willem de Kooning, whose references to the external world in his work contravened the dictates of pure non-objectivism espoused by Greenberg.[12]

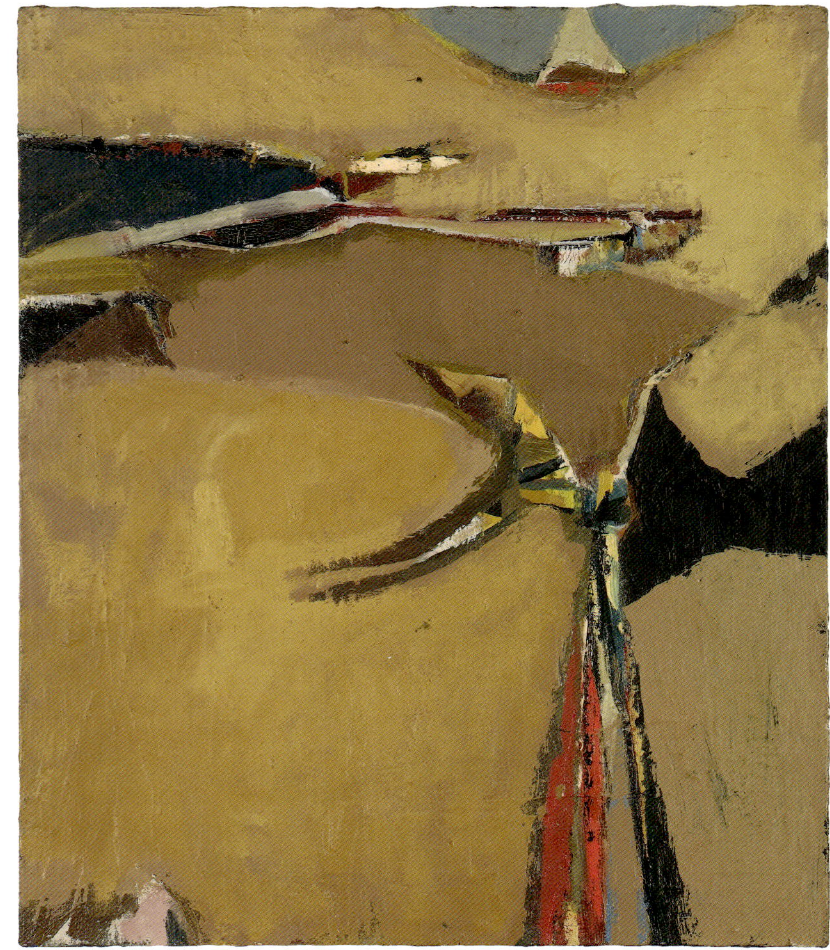

Diebenkorn's seemingly improvised but in fact carefully structured paintings of the Sausalito period incorporate cubist divisions of space; softened, organic forms; and gestural, painterly brushwork. They reflect the influence of early twentieth-century modernists, such as Picasso and Joan Miró, as well as Abstract Expressionists, particularly Still, Rothko, and de Kooning. They also manifest Diebenkorn's emergent interest in the aerial view; the landscape references and maplike qualities of works such as *Untitled (Sausalito)* of 1949 (fig. 59) not only reflect his response to the coastal topography of Northern California but also may stem from his earlier Marine Corps experiences with cartography.

The works from Diebenkorn's Albuquerque period (1950–1952) clearly reflect his interest in surveying and abstracting the landscape. In 1950 Diebenkorn enrolled through the GI Bill in the master's program in art at the University of New Mexico in Albuquerque. He has stated that his fondness for the landscape of New Mexico formed a large part of his decision to move there. Of an early train trip through the Southwest, he recalled that he "had strong memories of an interesting landscape, a special light, and sharp blue skies."[13] Although he and his wife, Phyllis, were apprehensive that they "couldn't really live away from the water, the sea, too long," they found that in New Mexico "the sky took the place of the ocean."[14] The vast desert landscape and brilliant light had an immediate impact on his work:

> I think I was saying to myself in Albuquerque that, OK, I'm going to damn well paint what I want. I'm not going to do this qualifying of my intuitive responses. . . . If grass green and sky blue and desert tan; if these associations come into the work that's part of my experience.[15]

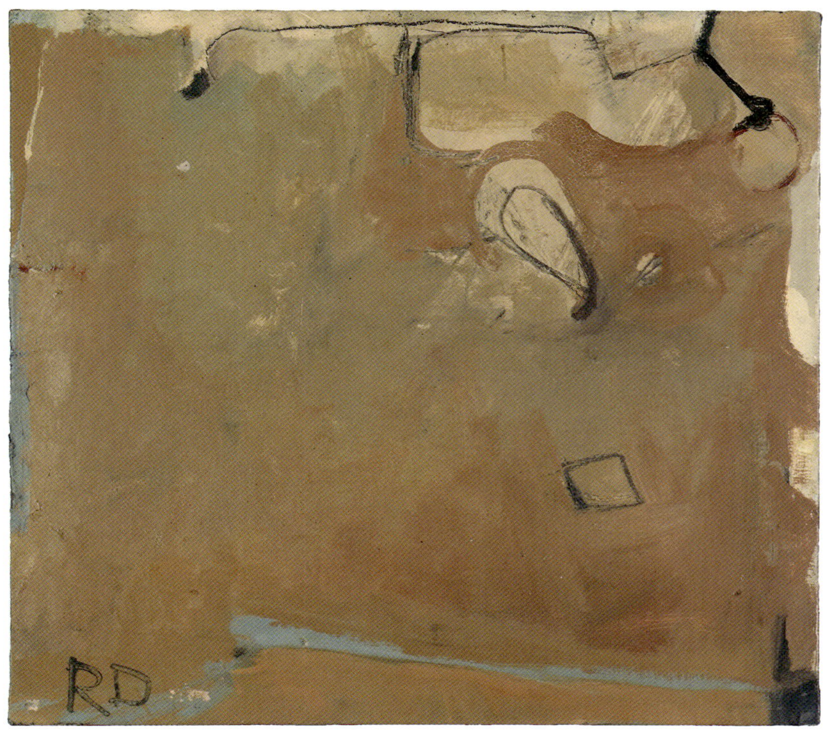

The slightly defiant tone Diebenkorn strikes here may reflect the liberation he felt once he was at a safe remove from the rigid aesthetic dogma propounded by adherents of abstraction such as Still at CSFA. He recalled,

> I lived in Albuquerque and it was a fine situation for painting. . . . Somehow the flat line of the western mesa of Albuquerque may have influenced my work. Temperamentally, perhaps, I had always been a landscape painter but I was fighting the landscape feeling. For years I didn't have the color blue on my palette because it reminded me too much of the spatial qualities in conventional landscapes. But in Albuquerque I relaxed and began to think of natural forms in relation to my own feelings.[16]

Perhaps inspired by the vistas Diebenkorn could have experienced from Albuquerque's West Mesa, paintings such as *Untitled (Albuquerque)* of 1950–1951 (fig. 60) and *#22 (Albuquerque)* of 1951 appear to be abstractions of landscapes viewed from on high. The predominantly earth-toned palettes of both works evoke the dry, dusty terrain of the New Mexico desert—punctuated, in the case of *Untitled (Albuquerque)*, by brilliant bursts of blue that could refer to a sliver of sky or water, and a series of pale boulder-like outcroppings that hug the top and right-hand edges of the painting. In these works, Diebenkorn's incorporation of flat fields of color and irregular, almost calligraphic lines reflects the influence of Abstract Expressionist contemporaries such as de Kooning, but it also suggests a topographic survey.[17]

Diebenkorn's perspective on the landscape was forever altered in the late spring or summer of 1951, when he took his first daytime civilian flight, traveling from Albuquerque to San Francisco. Shortly after mounting his master's degree exhibition at the University of New Mexico,[18] Diebenkorn flew to the Bay Area to see the Whitney Museum of American Art's traveling exhibition of the work of Arshile Gorky, which was on view at the San Francisco Museum of Art from May 9 to July 9. For Diebenkorn, the views he saw from the plane were a kind of artistic epiphany:

FIG 59
Richard Diebenkorn
***Untitled (Sausalito)*, 1949**
Oil on canvas
28 7/8 x 24 in. (73.3 x 61 cm)
Private collection
[1050]

FIG 60
Richard Diebenkorn
***Untitled (Albuquerque)*, 1950–1951**
Oil on canvas
16 1/4 x 17 5/8 in. (41.3 x 44.8 cm)
Private collection
[1072]

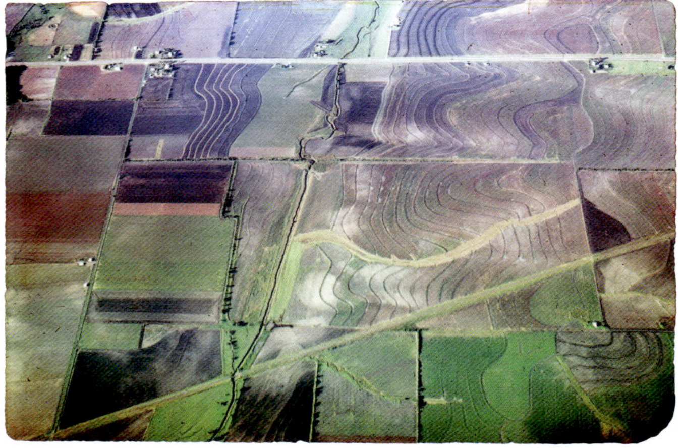

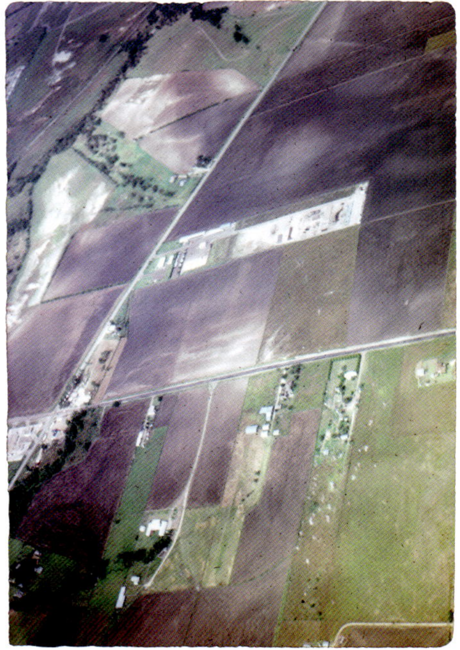

> The airplane was a prop plane, and it flew very low by today's standards. The pilot actually dipped down into the Grand Canyon so we could get a look at the scenery—and this was during a scheduled flight of a national airline! I guess it was the combination of desert and agriculture that really turned me on, because it has so many things I wanted in my paintings. Of course, the earth's skin itself had "presence"—I mean. . . . It was all like a flat design—and everything was usually in the form of an irregular grid. A bit later, I started photographing through airplane windows, and actually got quite good results [figs. 61 and 62]. [19]

From the air, the landscape appeared to Diebenkorn as a series of patchwork patterns—a network of linear contours shaping and delineating two-dimensional fields of color. This view revealed to him "a rich variety of ways of treating a flat plane—like flattened mud or paint. Forms operating in shallow depth reveal a huge range of possibilities."[20] Describing the exhilaration he experienced during the 1951 flight and its impact on his work, he recalled, "I was absolutely knocked out and thrilled, really taken. . . . It wasn't that I went right to the canvas and said I'm going to paint but it just went right into the mill and started coming out strong."[21]

Diebenkorn's ensuing painterly, improvisational, edge-to-edge compositions incorporated these aerial impressions of fields, mesas, mountains, towns, and rivers. The tensions between geometry and organicism in *Albuquerque #3* (fig. 63) and *Albuquerque #4* (fig. 64), both from 1951, may stem in large part from the interplay of natural and man-made landscape elements Diebenkorn observed from a bird's-eye vantage. *Urbana #5 (Beach Town)* of 1953 (fig. 10), which Diebenkorn produced during the year he lived in Urbana, Illinois,[22] evokes the sense of a built environment viewed from above.

The influence of an aerial perspective is evident in many of the works in Diebenkorn's Berkeley series, in which he used the language of modernist abstraction to convey the atmospheric and visual qualities of the Bay Area climate and topography. Produced between the fall of 1953 and early 1956, the fifty-eight extant paintings in the series arguably represent Diebenkorn's greatest achievement in assimilating his own landscape tendencies with the stylistic innovations of Abstract Expressionism.

FIG 61
Richard Diebenkorn
35mm color slide, ca. 1962

FIG 62
Richard Diebenkorn
35mm color slide, ca. 1962

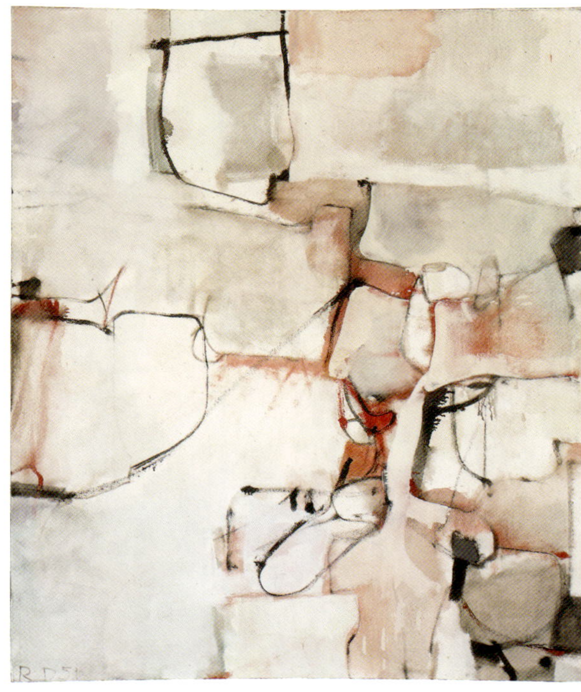

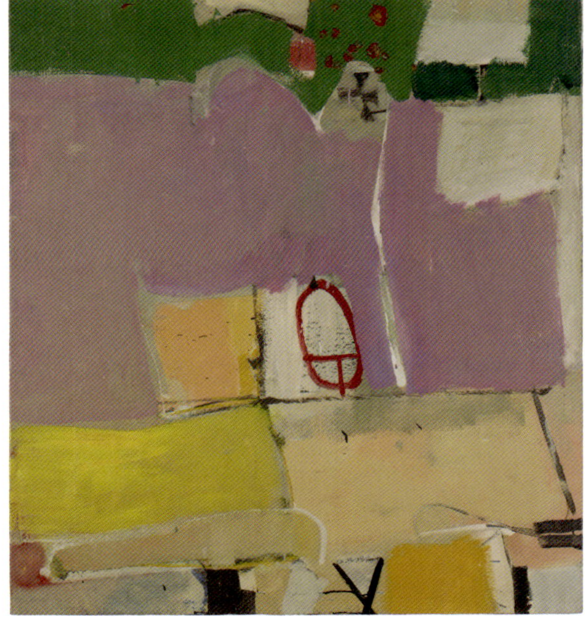

FIG 63
Richard Diebenkorn
Albuquerque #3, 1951
Oil on canvas
56 x 46 in. (142.2 x 116.8 cm)
The Shidler Family Collection
[1079]

FIG 64
Richard Diebenkorn
Albuquerque #4, 1951
Oil on canvas
50 1/2 x 45 7/8 in. (128.3 x 116.5 cm)
Saint Louis Art Museum, gift of Joseph Pulitzer, Jr., 117:1969
[1080]

In September 1953, after spending the year in Urbana and a summer in New York, Diebenkorn and his family moved back to the Bay Area.[23] In his painting, the move is reflected in the shift from the more somber palette of many of his Urbana pieces to the typically warmer tonal range, looser structure, and expressive, at times even frenzied, paint handling in the works in his Berkeley series. As is the case with the works Diebenkorn produced in Sausalito, Albuquerque, and Urbana, the paintings in the Berkeley series were deeply influenced by the gestural abstraction of the New York School. Nonetheless, the references to the natural world they contain connected him to local artistic traditions such as the Bay Area Figurative movement, which stood outside the mainstream narrative of Greenbergian modernism.[24]

Although at the time he produced them, Diebenkorn characterized the works in his Berkeley series as being "purely abstract,"[25] by titling them as he did, he explicitly associated them with the place where they were produced. In a 1983 interview he acknowledged the links between the palette of his Berkeley abstracts and the lush topography of the Bay Area:

> I was shocked when I was up in the San Francisco area a month ago. It had been raining a lot, and the hills were green, and driving through Northern California on the way home I couldn't *believe* a lot of the color! Then I started to think, 'God, that is the color *I* used to *use*, when I *lived up here*!'[26]

Early works in the series, such as *Berkeley #1* (pl. 1), *#3* (pl. 2), and *#4*, all from 1953, reflect the beige tonalities of the arid New Mexico landscape, but Diebenkorn's palette becomes increasingly vibrant as the series progresses. The brilliant jewel tones of paintings such as *Berkeley #13* of 1954, and *Berkeley #23*, *#32*, *#38*, and *#56*, all from 1955 (pls. 7, 8, 28, 31, and 33), evoke the verdancy and luminosity of Northern California.[27]

The sense of landscape that pervades these and many other works in the Berkeley series is enhanced by Diebenkorn's use of an elevated perspective. Of the paintings exhibited at the Poindexter Gallery in New York in the winter of 1956, one reviewer wrote that "they resemble aerial photographs of a big varied landscape with shore-line, mountains, cliffs and fields, the contours, perhaps, of California."[28] In a 1957 article in *Life* magazine (fig. 7), Diebenkorn's *Berkeley #44* of 1955 (pl. 27)—in which the influence of an aerial perspective is particularly strong—is described as recalling "the sweeping patterns of the fertile lands . . . north of San Francisco."[29]

The richly painted and intimately scaled *Berkeley #33* (fig. 65) of 1954 strongly alludes to an aerial view of a landscape. The painting is composed of three distinct horizontal zones, each sloping slightly downward. The broad band in the lower foreground features densely clustered, irregularly shaped forms, their mostly gray and white tonalities interrupted by bursts of orange, pink, and yellow. This visually charged area of tilting, often trapezoidal, forms predominates in later compositions such as *Berkeley #57* (1955) (pl. 32). In *Berkeley #33*, however, it is juxtaposed with the far more simplified expanses of heavily stroked, lush greens and blues in the middle and upper registers of the composition, which suggest a bird's-eye vantage on a field bounded by a horizon or sea. The allusions to an aerial view of a grassy ground with a slivered glimpse of ocean or sky in *Berkeley #33* are even more overt in an untitled work on paper from 1954 (fig. 66), which is similar to the painting in both its vibrant, atmospheric palette and its horizontally banded composition.

The elevated vantage in *Berkeley #33* creates a push-pull sensation between surface and depth, enhancing the formal resonance of the composition. Layers of color and form evoke a sense of spatial recession, yet the visible facture of the painting emphasizes its two-dimensionality. Expressive scumblings and linear scrawls—such as the inexplicable vertical line that Diebenkorn scraped down the center of the composition, allowing the ground of the canvas to show through—are contrasted with heavily impastoed areas, for instance, the thick daubs of blue paint encrusted on the surface of the picture at the upper right. By adopting an aerial view in this and other works from the Berkeley series, Diebenkorn could incorporate the formalist principles of Abstract Expressionism, such as its emphasis on the flatness of the picture plane, while still conveying his experience of landscape.

In 1955, in spite of the critical acclaim growing around the abstract works in his Berkeley series, Diebenkorn became increasingly disenchanted with Abstract Expressionism. Viewing it as a "stylistic straightjacket," he began searching for ways for his "ideas to be 'worked on,' changed, altered, by what was 'out there.'"[30] Rekindling a practice begun in 1953, he participated in weekly drawing sessions with David Park and Elmer Bischoff.[31] In addition to sketching figures from the model, Diebenkorn made drawings featuring still lifes, interior scenes, and landscapes. Yet it was not until the late fall of 1955 that he painted what he identified as his first representational landscape, the small oil on canvas *Chabot Valley* (pl. 36).[32]

Two years later Diebenkorn produced a tour de force of his figurative period, *Seawall* (pl. 66), which, like *Chabot Valley*, demonstrates his ability to seamlessly integrate representation with the raw, gestural brushwork, surface richness, and emphasis on the formal properties of paint and canvas that form the hallmarks of Abstract Expressionism. Small, compact, and self-contained, but bursting with tightly coiled energy, the painting has a magnetic power—its visual impact felt both upon close contemplation and from afar—and is perhaps the most dramatic example of Diebenkorn's use of an aerial perspective in his figurative work. *Seawall* depicts a bird's-eye view inspired by the Northern California coastline—including a lush green hillside that drops precipitously to an expanse of shore and ocean below.[33] The saturated jewel tones of Diebenkorn's palette evoke a sense of the verdancy of the Bay Area on a clear day. The intimate scale of the work contrasts with the majestically sweeping scene it presents, giving the viewer the surreal sense of soaring above the landscape. From this lofty vantage, the earth below resembles a patchwork of abstract forms, just as the desert terrain Diebenkorn saw as he flew from Albuquerque to San Francisco seemed to him "like a flat design."[34]

While the image in *Seawall* is clearly a landscape, the painting can also be seen as a series of abstract forms, planes of color, and contrasting textures. The sensuous and variegated paint handling both emphasizes the flat surface of the picture plane and records the artist's process, reflecting Diebenkorn's assertion that "one wants to see the artifice of the thing as well as the subject. Reality has to be digested, it has to be transmuted by paint. It has to be given a twist of some kind."[35] Phyllis Diebenkorn confirmed that her husband painted

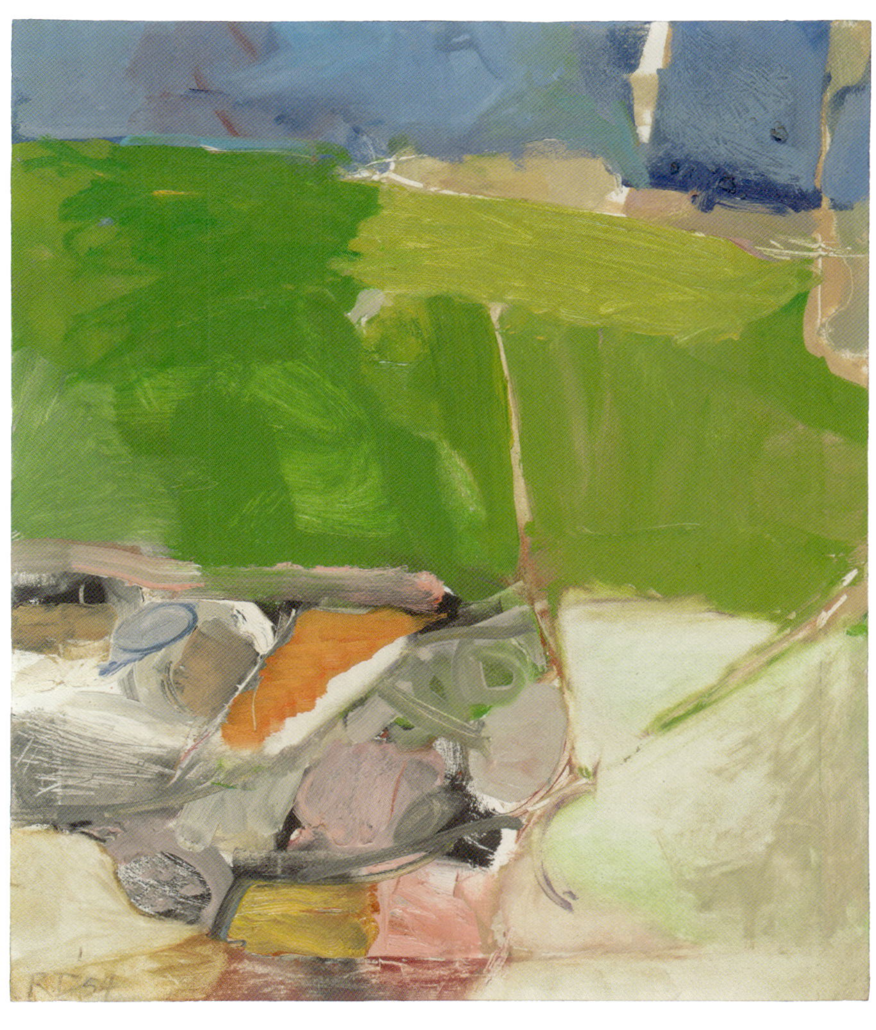

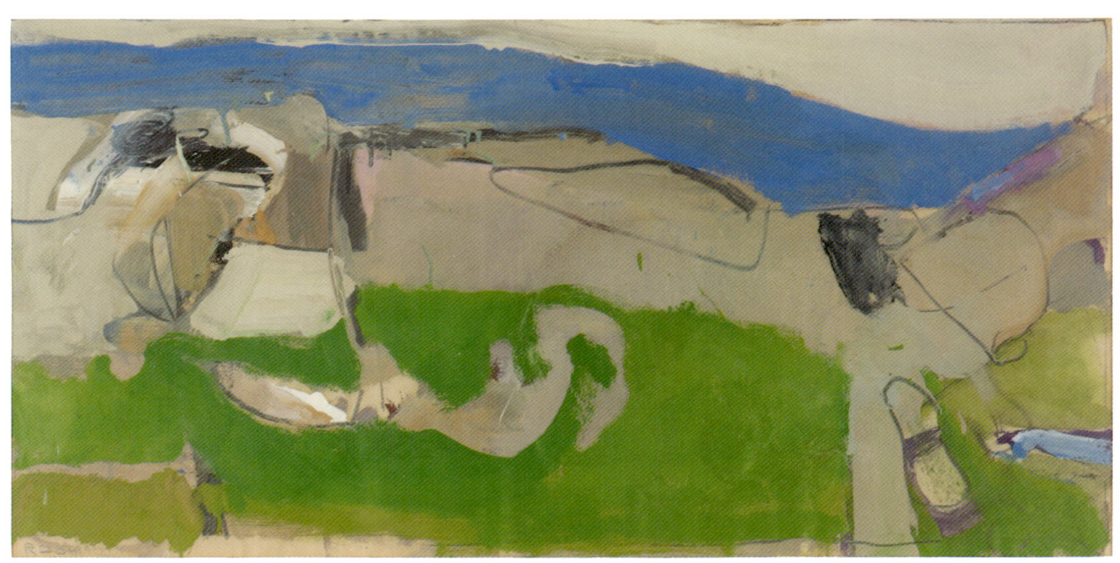

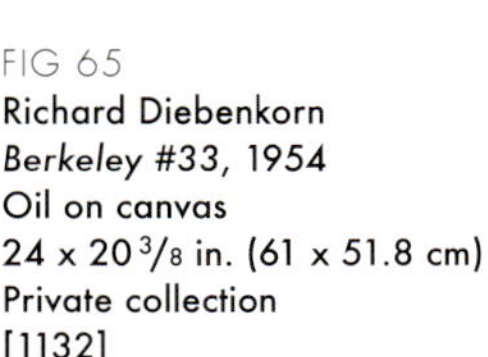

FIG 65
Richard Diebenkorn
Berkeley #33, 1954
Oil on canvas
24 x 20 3/8 in. (61 x 51.8 cm)
Private collection
[1132]

FIG 66
Richard Diebenkorn
Untitled, 1954
Oil on paper
17 3/4 x 35 1/2 in. (45.1 x 90.2 cm)
Private collection
[3226]

Seawall in his studio. Nonetheless, the work conveys the atmosphere of the outdoors with an immediacy characteristic of plein-air painting—and moves far beyond a purely visual transcription of the subject to capture the artist's sensory impressions of a landscape, based perhaps on both memory and imagination.[36]

The sky—in which a nebular oblong of light blue at the upper left hovers in Rothko-esque fashion over a slightly darker blue ground—incorporates the broad, open paint handling characteristic of Abstract Expressionism. Similarly painterly brushwork describes the swaths of land and sea below, such as the densely clustered daubs of black paint applied over a white ground in the center of the composition. Sharp tonal contrasts both evoke a semblance of three-dimensionality—as with the dramatically angled wedges of color that describe the sloping coastline—and create a complex, jigsaw-like pattern of interlocking, flat fields of color.

Contrasting with these geometries, the loose, sketchy brushstrokes with which Diebenkorn depicts a wide swath of scribbled green grass at right lend the field an animated, even agitated, air. The white ground of the canvas shows through his thin brushwork—in some instances he may have used a sgraffito technique, perhaps scraping away layers of pigment with a palette knife—calling attention to the painting's facture. Resembling a path or a trail, the track of two white parallel lines the artist has roughly scratched in at the lower right leads the viewer's eye diagonally upward and outside the confines of the picture plane. Diebenkorn embraced what he termed the "awkwardness" of "unfinished" passages such as this, stating, "I think that a *realization* can come about in the crudest terms as well as the most refined, in the most overworked terms as well as underworked . . . and for me what looks like realization is such a rare, tenuous state that I take it where I can find it."[37]

The rich contrasts in *Seawall* between passages marked by a loose, painterly organicism and those that contain sharper, more hard-edged forms contribute to the vibrancy and dynamism of the work.[38] Yet despite the opposing forces of the dichotomous colors and textures that activate its surface, the painting is imbued with a pervading sense of calm. This compositional resolution—what the art historian Gerald Nordland has described as a "logical totality"[39] in Diebenkorn's work—relies upon the fragile and tentative balance held by the disparate components of the picture.

In *Cityscape #1* (pl. 99),[40] Diebenkorn similarly relies upon an elevated viewpoint to abstract his subject—a hilly, residential street in San Francisco, fronted on one side by a series of squat buildings and on the other by verdant open fields and vacant lots. *Cityscape #1* is dated October 31, 1963, indicating that Diebenkorn finished the painting in his studio on the campus of Stanford University in Palo Alto, more than a month after beginning an academic-year residency at the school.[41] However, Diebenkorn probably began this, as he did other works in a series of urban landscapes from that year (including the paintings *Ingleside* [pl. 102], *Ingleside II*, *Cityscape #2*, *Cityscape #3 (Landscape #2)* [pl. 100], and *Cityscape #4* [pl. 101]), while still living in Berkeley.[42]

In a conversation he had with Nordland in the mid-1980s, Diebenkorn stated that in an earlier version of *Cityscape #1* he included a row of houses along the upper right-hand side of the paved road, which he subsequently eliminated and replaced with the grassy field, thus simplifying and flattening the composition.[43] Diebenkorn claimed to have struggled with the painting over a protracted period of more than three or four months, but viewed the finished work as being representative of an artistic breakthrough of sorts.[44] His powerful juxtapositions of color and form—such as the contrast between the compact masses of tightly clustered buildings at the left and the broad planes of color that describe the geometrically divided fields at the right—contribute to the painting's dynamism. The work is further imbued with a sense of energy and movement by the forceful diagonals and dramatic chiaroscuro created by the shadows that sweep across vast segments of the landscape.

Like *Seawall*, *Cityscape #1* can be experienced as a highly formal arrangement of contrasting patterns and tones—a series of self-contained, painterly abstractions—but it also coheres into a clearly legible depiction of a scene. Yet while Diebenkorn's paint application in *Seawall* is charged and expressive, by comparison, his brushwork in *Cityscape #1*, though sketchy and impastoed in areas, is

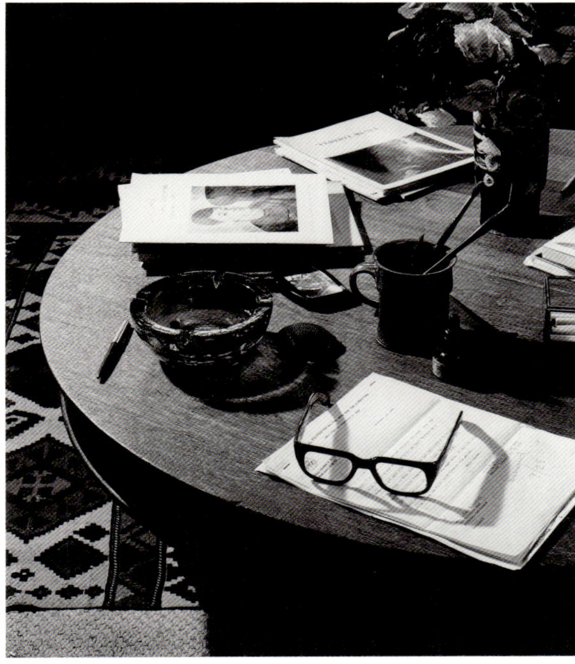

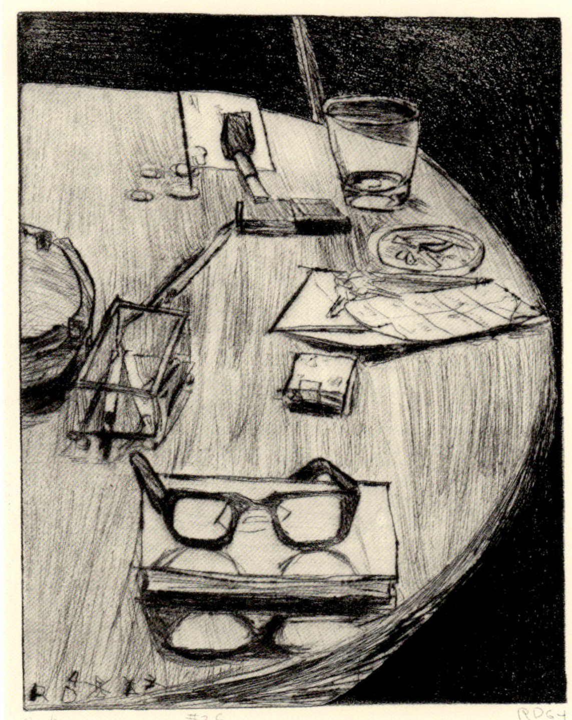

FIG 67
Tabletop at 217 Hillcrest Road, Berkeley. Photographed by Morley Baer, 1966

FIG 68
Richard Diebenkorn
#26 from *41 Etchings Drypoints*, 1964
Aquatint, drypoint, and hard-ground etching
10 7/8 x 8 3/8 in. (27.6 x 21.3 cm)
Printed by Kathan Brown
Published by Crown Point Press, Berkeley (now San Francisco)
Fine Arts Museums of San Francisco, Crown Point Press Archive, Museum Purchase, Earthquake Fund, 1991.28.357
[3000.#26]

restrained—smoother and more uniform. A sense of cool rationalism pervades the image. Ironically, the more detached manner with which Diebenkorn depicts the subject of *Cityscape #1* increases the emotional resonance of the scene. The painting evokes the desolate, solitary feel of an unpopulated street bathed in raking sunlight—recalling the bleak existentialism of Hopper's urban landscapes. Furthermore, by virtue of the painting's large scale and incorporation of various perspectives—some more classically topographic and others more frontal—the viewer has the sense of being thrust into the foreground of the scene while concurrently surveying swaths of the landscape from above, heightening the picture's moody atmospherics.[45]

In *Cityscape #3* Diebenkorn further removes the urban landscape from any familiar context. By eliminating the upper third of the composition that appears in *Cityscape #1* and enlarging and simplifying the remaining two-thirds of the view, Diebenkorn produces a sparer, highly abstracted artwork in which he more overtly emphasizes formal properties over the particularized representation of a site. As in *Cityscape #1*, Diebenkorn's use of an aerial perspective here facilitates his transformation of a quotidian street scene into a strikingly beautiful geometric composition in which a patchwork of forms and colors is superimposed on a flat, two-dimensional plane. In its radically reduced and streamlined geometries, *Cityscape #3* foreshadows the minimalist and architectonic aesthetic of the works in the Ocean Park series.

Many of Diebenkorn's still lifes incorporate an aerial view, relating to the bird's-eye vantages in his abstract and figurative landscapes. These works also reflect the dramatic flattening of objects in the Persian and Rajput Indian miniatures he so admired, as well as in still lifes by European modernists such as Cézanne, Matisse, and Paul Gauguin.[46] The utilitarian objects Diebenkorn portrays—many of which appear in photographs such as those taken by Morley Baer in Diebenkorn's Triangle studio in Berkeley, which he began using in 1958, and in his house at 217 Hillcrest Road (fig. 67)—are dispersed across dramatically tilted tabletops, resembling actors on a stage, or landscape elements spread across a flat terrain. In paintings such as *Untitled*, 1955 (pl. 37); *Still Life with Matches*, 1955 (pl. 38); *Scissors and Lemon, II*, 1959 (pl. 88); *Pliers and Match*, 1961 (pl. 87); *Still Life with Letter*, 1961 (pl. 91); *Poppies*, 1963 (pl. 95); and *Large Still Life*, 1966 (pl. 141); and drawings such as *Untitled*, ca. 1961 (pl. 90); *Untitled*, 1964 (pl. 105); *#26* from *41 Etchings Drypoints*, 1964 (fig. 68); *Untitled*, 1965 (pl. 108); and *Still Life, Cigarette Butts and Glasses*, 1967 (pl. 112), a bird's-eye vantage diminishes spatial depth by eliminating the obvious distinctions between foreground and background. As he does with the abstract works in his Berkeley series and with his representational cityscapes, in these still lifes Diebenkorn bridges the divide between abstraction and figuration by emphasizing the interplay between two-dimensional patterning and the depiction of forms in shallow, recessive space.

Diebenkorn's preoccupation with the aerial view persisted throughout his lifetime.[47] The most direct, documented link between his work and specific aerial views appears in his Lower Colorado series from 1969 to 1970, abstractions that are clearly based on photographs he took of the Western landscape from a helicopter.[48] The series was commissioned in 1969 by John DeWitt, Director of Art Programs for the Bureau of Reclamation, an agency of the Department of the Interior responsible for water conservation in the arid regions of the American West. Under the direction of DeWitt and Lloyd Goodrich, former director of the Whitney Museum of American Art, some forty artists—including Diebenkorn, Peter Hurd, Jack Tworkov, Ralston Crawford, and Norman Rockwell—were invited to depict images of water projects in the American West. The artists were given free rein to choose any scene in an assigned territory and use any medium as long as the subject matter pertained (however loosely) to the Bureau of Reclamation's program.[49]

For the commission, Diebenkorn was given the task of depicting the Salt River and Lower Colorado River basins in Arizona.[50] Diebenkorn traveled to these areas and looked at the landscape from a high mesa as well as from a helicopter, and aerial photographs he took during the trips contain the same abstracted geometries and strong diagonals that appear in many of the works from the series (see figs. 69 and 70).[51] He recalled,

> We spent five days in a helicopter surveying [the Salt River Canyon]. . . . I did some drawings—or, rather, paintings on

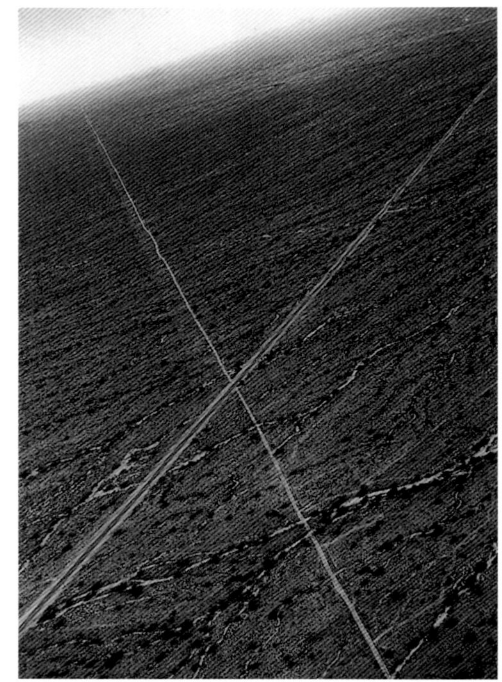

FIG 69
Richard Diebenkorn
Aerial photograph, Arizona, 1970
[3141]

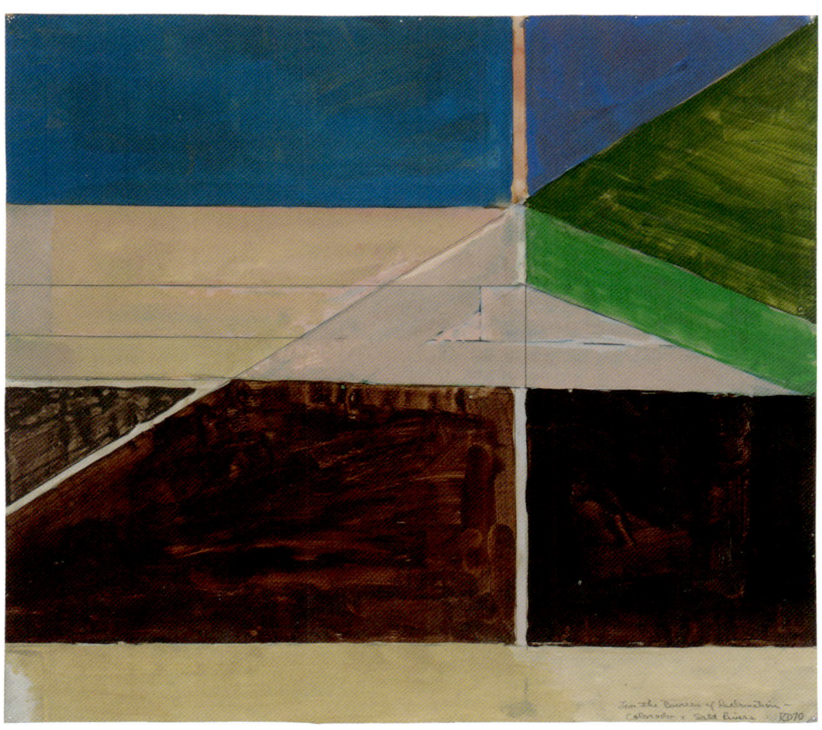

> paper—there; we were supposed to do documentary drawings but mine came out as abstract interpretations. I think the many paths, or pathlike bands, in my paintings may have something to do with this experience, especially in that wherever there was agriculture going on you could see process—ghosts of former tilled fields, patches of land being eroded.[52]

Through his use of varied paint application and contrasting textures, Diebenkorn created a sense of the shifting terrain of landscape in the Lower Colorado works. Mirroring the patched and patterned impression of a landscape viewed from on high, some areas of the compositions are matte, while others have a mottled surface akin to marbled paper, or incorporate rough-edged, collaged elements.[53] The contrasts between linear demarcations and variegated fields of color in these works recall the tensions between geometry and organicism in Diebenkorn's earlier Berkeley-period works, as well as in his Ocean Park series.[54] Given how directly they are tied to specific sites because of their subject and the context in which they were commissioned, the works in the Lower Colorado series clearly demonstrate the ways in which Diebenkorn looked to landscape and the aerial view as the inspiration for his abstractions.[55]

Diebenkorn, who once stated that it sometimes took him more than ninety days to become fully acclimated to the light and space of a new environment,[56] remarked in a 1992 interview, "I'm a very impressionable person and I think the landscape will sometimes lead me to something. It usually has."[57] The rigid non-objectivism of Abstract Expressionism could be limiting for an artist so sensitively attuned to his surroundings, and for whom the moody landscapes and interiors of artistic predecessors such as Cézanne, Matisse, and Hopper held such appeal. The aerial view provided Diebenkorn with a means of expressing his responses to landscape—visual, sensory, emotional—while incorporating into his art many of the formalist principles and the calligraphic gesturalism of modernist abstraction. Reconciling as it does the seemingly oppositional poles of abstraction and figuration, Diebenkorn's work from the Berkeley period—and from his oeuvre as a whole—is a testament to his assertion that "a forceful quality in art, truly representative of our modern times, will rise above the labels of abstraction and realism."[58]

FIG 70
Richard Diebenkorn
***Lower Colorado #4*, 1970**
Acrylic and graphite on paper
20 5/8 x 23 in. (52.4 x 58.4 cm)
Department of the Interior, Bureau of Reclamation, DO.3
[1610]

1 Although the fascination with unusual perspectives in art is not unique to the modern era, the aerial view gained artistic currency in the twentieth century due in part to the advent of mechanized flight and aerial photography, and it dramatically affected the stylistic and conceptual direction of modern and contemporary art. This is reflected in the work and writings of the early twentieth-century European avant-garde such as the Russian Suprematist artist Kazimir Malevich, the Swiss architect Le Corbusier (Charles-Édouard Jeanneret), and the Italian Futurists (movement founded in 1909). In the United States the aerial view was similarly embraced in avant-garde circles, particularly by artists associated with photographer Alfred Stieglitz and his 291 Gallery, among them Charles Sheeler, Georgia O'Keeffe, and Paul Strand. The elevated vantages in the work of realists such as Edward Hopper and Edwin Wolfe express a heightened psychological sense of menace, unease, and isolation, giving the viewer an omniscient, almost voyeuristic perspective on the artists' subjects. Many artists working after the Second World War, including Wayne Thiebaud, Yvonne Jacquette, Emmet Gowin, William Garnett, and Ed Ruscha, also adopted distinctive aerial perspectives in their work. In addition to being visually compelling, their dizzyingly surreal vantages reflect some of the anxieties of the modern age and convey a sense of the precariousness, fragility, and absurdity of human existence. The ubiquity of the aerial view persists in contemporary art and culture, thanks in part to the widespread availability of digital technologies such as Google Earth.

2 Susan Larsen interviews with Richard Diebenkorn, 1977, 1985, 1987, Archives of American Art, Smithsonian Institution, Washington, DC. Cited here May 1 and 2, 1985.

3 The view could depict one of the barracks at either Quantico, Virginia, or Camp Pendleton, California, where Diebenkorn was transferred as a member of the United States Marine Corps between 1944 and 1945.

4 Sarah Stein was the sister-in-law of the writer and art collector Gertrude Stein.

5 In 1943, after enlisting in the United States Marine Corps, Diebenkorn spent part of his military training studying physics and art for a summer semester at University of California, Berkeley (UC Berkeley).

6 Larsen interview, May 1, 1985.

7 Jerry Tallmer, "Diebenkorn: Painter Against the Grain," *New York Post*, June 11, 1977, 20.

8 Rothko was a visiting professor at CSFA during the summers of 1947 and 1949. Diebenkorn first encountered the Abstract Expressionist paintings of the New York School in the November 1944 issue of *Dyn* magazine, which included reproductions of work by Robert Motherwell, William Baziotes, Georges Braque, Stanley William Hayter, Roberto Matta, Jackson Pollock, and David Smith. Diebenkorn later described the tremendous impact of this discovery: "There was a new flavor. . . . Something very fresh and compelling. . . . Within five years . . . it became Abstract Expressionism." Jane Livingston, John Elderfield, and Ruth E. Fine, *The Art of Richard Diebenkorn*, exh. cat. (New York: Whitney Museum of American Art in association with University of California Press, 1997), 25. Two years later Diebenkorn experienced his "first contact with Abstract Expressionism in the flesh" when, during a fall and winter spent living in Woodstock, New York, and traveling frequently to Manhattan, he met artists such as Bradley Walker Tomlin and Baziotes, and visited galleries in Manhattan such as The Museum of Modern Art and the Kootz Gallery. Jan Butterfield, "Pentimenti: Seeing and Then Seeing Again" in *Resource/Response/Reservoir—Richard Diebenkorn: Paintings 1948–1983*, exh. brochure (San Francisco: San Francisco Museum of Modern Art, May 1983), n.p.

9 Clement Greenberg is considered the architect of twentieth-century American modernist criticism. The articles he published in prestigious journals such as *Partisan Review, The Nation, Commentary, Art News*, and *Art in America* brought intellectual rigor to the formerly journalistic genre of art criticism, and his influence on artists' careers and the art market is unparalleled in the history of modern art.

10 Clement Greenberg, "Modernist Painting" (1960), repr. in *Clement Greenberg: The Collected Essays and Criticism*, ed. John O'Brian, vol. 4, *Modernism with a Vengeance, 1957–1969* (Chicago and London: University of Chicago Press, 1993), 85.

11 By the early 1950s Diebenkorn was hailed as the West Coast's leading abstractionist, a characterization he qualified but did not entirely eschew—see quote in James Schevill, "Art: Richard Diebenkorn," *Frontier: The Voice of the New West* 8, no. 3 (January 1957): 21.

12 Diebenkorn first saw examples of de Kooning's work in the April 1948 issue of *Partisan Review*: "Seeing de Kooning's work reproduced at that time showed me in a glance what I somehow knew painting could be and what I was flailing around trying to do." Quoted in Herman Cherry et al., "Willem de Kooning on His Eighty-Fifth Birthday," *Art Journal* 48, no. 3 (Autumn 1989): 231. For one of the works reproduced in the publication, *Painting* (1948), de Kooning transferred segments of figurative drawings to the canvas with tracing paper, over which he applied layers of paint. De Kooning's figurative references increased in his Woman series (1950–1953) and in later landscape abstractions such as *Merritt Parkway* (1959).

13 Gerald Nordland, "Richard Diebenkorn: Routes to New Mexico," in Gerald Nordland, Mark Lavatelli, and Charles Strong, *Richard Diebenkorn in New Mexico*, exh. cat. (Santa Fe: Museum of New Mexico Press, 2007), 17.

14 Larsen interview, May 2, 1985.

15 Mark Lavatelli, "Diebenkorn's Albuquerque Years," in Nordland et al., *Richard Diebenkorn in New Mexico*, 29.

16 Schevill, "Art: Richard Diebenkorn," 22. Diebenkorn also ascribed the increase in the size of his paintings from this period to the "physicality" of New Mexico, stating, "I think that has a lot to do with the Southwest, because the scale . . . is something that really is kind of overwhelming and most immediately apparent [when] one is there, I think." Larsen interview, May 2, 1985.

17 Maurice Tuchman discusses another influence from this period, Diebenkorn's "affection for poetic cartoonist George Herriman's Krazy Kat comics, an anthology of which he bought in Albuquerque. This classically imaginative strip set in the desert contains whimsical depictions of the terrain—sagebrush and tumbleweed, mesas and bluffs, rocks and trees—that often parallel Diebenkorn's forms." Maurice Tuchman, "Richard Diebenkorn: The Early Years," *Art Journal* 36, no. 3 (Spring 1977): 214.

18 Diebenkorn's master's degree exhibition, April 29–May 5, 1951, University Art Museum of New Mexico, Albuquerque.

19 Dan Hofstadter, "Profiles: Almost Free of the Mirror," *The New Yorker*, September 7, 1987, 60.

The Diebenkorn Foundation holds uncatalogued slides, which include these aerial views. Another slide in the collection of the Foundation depicts a view of Santa Cruz Island, where Diebenkorn's college friend Carey Stanton had a home, and to which the Diebenkorn family made frequent visits from 1958 on. An airstrip constructed on the island in 1961 enabled Diebenkorn to travel there by helicopter.

20 Gerald Nordland, *Richard Diebenkorn*, rev. ed. (New York: Rizzoli, 2001), 43.

21 Lavatelli, "Diebenkorn's Albuquerque Years," in Nordland et al., *Richard Diebenkorn in New Mexico*, 32.

22 Diebenkorn and his family spent the 1952–1953 academic year in Urbana; he taught drawing and painting to architecture students at the University of Illinois.

23 The Diebenkorns rented an apartment at 2837 Webster Street in the Elmwood district of Berkeley, a residential neighborhood a few blocks away from the shops and restaurants along College Avenue and about a mile from the main campus of UC Berkeley. In 1954 the family moved half a block away to a rented house at 2947 Magnolia Street.

24 This movement was boldly inaugurated in late 1949 or early 1950 when David Park, then a young instructor at CSFA, deposited all his Abstract Expressionist canvases at the Berkeley dump and abruptly shifted to painting in a representational mode. At a time when abstraction reigned supreme in both New York and San Francisco and was associated with artists' ethical commitments to and seriousness about their work, Park's move to figuration was viewed as a radical—even treasonous—defection. Yet for Park the shift was liberating—a rejection of the rigid nonobjectivism espoused by Clyfford Still and his disciples at CSFA—and he became the first of several Bay Area artists (followed by Elmer Bischoff, James Weeks, and Diebenkorn) to reconcile the gestural brushwork of Abstract Expressionism with figurative subjects. For further discussion, see also Nash essay, this volume.

25 Diebenkorn wrote in 1955, "What I paint often seems to pertain to landscape but I try to avoid any rationalization of this either in my painting or in later thinking about it. I'm not a landscape painter (at this time, at any rate), or I would paint landscape directly." Richard Diebenkorn, quoted in Samuel Heavenrich and Grace L. McCann Morley, *California Painting: 40 Painters*, exh. cat. (Long Beach, CA: Municipal Art Center, in conjunction with the San Francisco Museum of Art, 1955), n.p.

26 Butterfield, "Pentimenti," n.p.

27 In addition to incorporating environmentally influenced color into the works in his Berkeley series, Diebenkorn employed "systems" to pack "every hue and every variation into the picture. With six basic hues, and at least one variant for each—that's twelve—plus black and white and grays, I would get the ball rolling. I would ask, how much further can I go, what further break in the color system can I make?" Tuchman, "Richard Diebenkorn: The Early Years," 219–220.

28 "[Diebenkorn's] compositions are vast and stratified irregularly, bedecked with lumps of pigment and run through with snake-like lines. In short they resemble aerial photographs of a big varied landscape with shore-line, mountains, cliffs and fields, the contours, perhaps, of California, where this painter lives and has made his reputation." Stuart Preston, "Painting on View," *New York Times*, March 4, 1956, X14.

Dore Ashton wrote, "All of Diebenkorn's forms are kept in horizontal bands. Depth is suggested by the tilting trapezoidal forms below, like ploughed fields seen from a fairly high vantage point. (Many of his landscapes are approached from an aerial perspective, some even border on a classical use of perspective)." Dore Ashton, "First One-Man Show in New York at Poindexter Gallery," *Arts & Architecture* 73, no. 4 (April 1956): 11.

29 "Look of the West Inspires New Art," *Life*, November 4, 1957, 67.

30 Butterfield, "Pentimenti," n.p.

31 Park and Bischoff had begun working in a figurative mode in 1950 and 1952, respectively.

32 Diebenkorn's first representational painting of the Berkeley period appears to be the small-scale *Untitled (Horse and Rider)* (1954, fig. 16). A small oil on canvas, *Untitled (Nude)* (fig. 25) also dates to this year.

33 The title of *Seawall* refers to a form of coastal defense intended to protect areas of human habitation, conservation, and leisure activities from the action of tides and waves.

34 Hofstadter, "Profiles," 60–61.

35 Paul Mills, *Contemporary Bay Area Figurative Painting*, exh. cat. (Oakland, CA: Oakland Art Museum, 1957), 12.

36 As Ruth E. Fine discusses, for his representational paintings Diebenkorn frequently relied on a "storehouse of forms in his memory; forms that had become part of that memory through the process of looking and drawing." Ruth E. Fine, "Reality: Digested, Transmuted, and Twisted," in Livingston et al., *The Art of Richard Diebenkorn*, 96. According to Phyllis Diebenkorn, *Seawall* may or may not have been based on an actual scene, but she recalls that it was painted shortly after a trip she and her husband took up the north coast of California. Carl Schmitz, e-mail to author, March 8, 2012.

37 Diebenkorn in a letter to Ellen Johnson dated July 20, 1958, Allen Memorial Art Museum files, Oberlin College.

38 Robert Hughes praised the artist for his "breezy lyricism of feeling . . . an exhilaration at the material fullness of the world, translated into terms of pigment." Robert Hughes, "God Is in the Vectors," *Time*, December 8, 1997, 100.

39 Nordland, *Richard Diebenkorn*, 43.

40 The painting was formerly known as *Landscape #1*, but Diebenkorn wrote, "I don't think *Cityscape I* was my title but I think I prefer it." Letter to museum archivist Louis Grachos, December 16, 1981, object file for *Cityscape #1*, San Francisco Museum of Modern Art Archives.

41 Diebenkorn inscribed the painting in the upper right quadrant of the back of the painting's support: "10–31–63/ R. Diebenkorn/ Landscape #1–1963." In 1963 Stanford University's academic year began on September 25. Photographs taken of Diebenkorn in his studio in the old Union building on Stanford's campus in the winter of 1963 depict him posing with a finished version of *Cityscape #1*.

42 Diebenkorn produced a few smaller urban scenes beginning in 1962, such as *Mission Landscape* (1962), *Street II* (1962), and *Untitled (View from Triangle)* (ca. 1963). A series of rooftop views undertaken around this time—including the painting *View of Oakland* (1962), two related (untitled) works on paper from 1962 and 1963, and the paintings *Santa Cruz* and *Santa Cruz I* (1962, pl. 75)—show him experimenting with an elevated perspective.

Diebenkorn discussed working on his Ingleside series from his Berkeley studio: "Ingleside is a residential area west of Twin Peaks in San Francisco, where I lived as a boy. Visiting there thirty years later provided me with a peculiarly concentrated subject matter, one which represented much that I had rejected in intervening years but which at the same time referred largely to what I am. A sense of place was built into my use of this material. I made on-the-spot sketches that were very brief, finding that when I painted them from my Berkeley studio the relevant detail filled in easily." Alan Gussow, *A Sense of Place: The Artist and the American Land* (Washington, DC: Island Press, 1972), 143. For further discussion, see Burgard essay, this volume.

43 Gerald Nordland, in phone conversation with the author, April 10, 2012.

Diebenkorn's articulation of this often tortuous process of revision and refinement was quoted in a 1963 article published in *Artforum*: "[A painting] came about by putting down what I felt in terms of some overall image at the moment today, and perhaps being terribly disappointed with it tomorrow, and trying to make it better and then despairing and destroying partially or wholly and getting back into it and just kind of frantically trying to pull something into this rectangle which made some sense to me." Frederick Wight, "The Phillips Collection—Diebenkorn, Woelffer, Mullican: A Discussion," *Artforum* 1, no. 10 (April 1963): 27.

44 Nordland phone conversation with the author, April 10, 2012. That the painting was viewed in the same light by the art world is reflected in its provenance—the San Francisco Museum of Art purchased *Cityscape #1* from the Poindexter Gallery in 1964, just one year after it was painted.

45 The drypoint *Athene Palace* (1964)—likely made while Diebenkorn was visiting Bucharest, during an extended tour of the Soviet Union and Europe—incorporates an even more vertiginous perspective, recalling the bold angles of vision and crude, graphic lines in the urban views of George Grosz.

46 See John Elderfield, *The Drawings of Richard Diebenkorn*, exh. cat. (New York: Museum of Modern Art, 1988), 47, 200.

47 In 1973 Diebenkorn accompanied the painter James Doolin on a helicopter ride over West Los Angeles, during which Doolin made studies for *Shopping Mall* (1973–1977), his large-scale aerial depiction of a busy intersection in Santa Monica.

48 The author's research into Richard Diebenkorn's Lower Colorado series was generously funded by a 2010 Wilhelmina Barns-Graham Research Support Grant, administered by the Paul Mellon Centre at Yale University.

49 Those artists who accepted the commission were offered a small stipend (around $800, including travel and living expenses) to visit the Bureau of Reclamation projects and record their visual impressions in styles ranging from super-realism to nonobjective painting. The exhibition *The American Artist and Water Reclamation: A Selection of Paintings from the Bureau of Reclamation*, which opened at the National Gallery of Art in 1972 (where it was on view March 25–May 28) and then toured the country in a traveling exhibition sponsored by the Smithsonian Institution, featured more than sixty-five paintings, watercolors, and drawings chosen from the 360-plus pictures commissioned by the Bureau of Reclamation. Installation shots of the exhibition reveal the diversity of styles—ranging from realism to surrealism to pure abstraction—displayed side by side in the newly refurbished cafeteria corridor of the National Gallery. Uniting these disparate works, however, is their subject—the landscapes of the West—and in his introductory essay for the exhibition catalogue, Douglas MacAgy extols the "vital sense of place that only artists seem able to transmit." Douglas MacAgy, *The American Artist and Water Reclamation*, exh. cat. (Washington, DC: Bureau of Reclamation, United States Department of the Interior, 1973), 6.

50 The exhibition file for *The American Artist and Water Reclamation* held in the archives of the National Gallery of Art includes a 1969 map drafted by the Bureau of Reclamation titled *Western United States Showing the Federal Reclamation Dams (Completed and Under Construction)*. The map presents a useful overview of the projects and territories that were covered by the Bureau's programs and includes handwritten notations indicating the location to which each artist involved in the commission was assigned.

51 Three of the photographs were exhibited and reproduced in the catalogue for *Private Images: Photographs by Painters*, Los Angeles County Museum of Art, January 18–March 27, 1977.

52 Hofstadter, "Profiles," 60–61.

53 Ranging from 23 ½ x 17 ½ inches to 29 x 23 inches, the works are intimate in scale, each presenting a self-contained world evocative of landscape that the viewer can grasp on a human level. There is a real sense of dynamism, experimentation, and play—each varies in terms of tonal range, compositional format, and mood, but when viewed as a group the works appear as variations on a theme, like improvisational jazz riffs.

54 Sarah C. Bancroft discusses the relationships between the works from the Lower Colorado and the Ocean Park series in her essay "A View of Ocean Park," in Sarah C. Bancroft, Susan Landauer, Peter Levitt, and Anna Brouwer, *Richard Diebenkorn: The Ocean Park Series*, exh. cat. (Newport Beach, CA: Orange County Museum of Art in association with Prestel, 2011), 22–23.

55 The three works from the Lower Colorado series that were displayed and reproduced in the catalogue for the Smithsonian Institution's traveling exhibition *The American Artist and Water Reclamation* (nos. 2, 7, and 8) are described as "Patterns of irrigated lands and canals in the Lower Colorado River Basin from a helicopter." MacAgy, *The American Artist and Water Reclamation*, 19.

56 Nordland, recalling a conversation with Diebenkorn in the mid-1980s. Nordland phone conversation with the author, April 10, 2012.

57 Julian Machin, "Richard Diebenkorn: A Rare Interview," *San Francisco Chronicle*, November 17, 1992, D3.

58 Diebenkorn, quoted in entry by Joseph Pulitzer, Jr. in Charles Scott Chetham and Joseph Pulitzer, Jr., *Modern Painting, Drawing & Sculpture: Collected by Louise and Joseph Pulitzer, Jr.* (Cambridge, MA: Fogg Art Museum, 1957), 31.

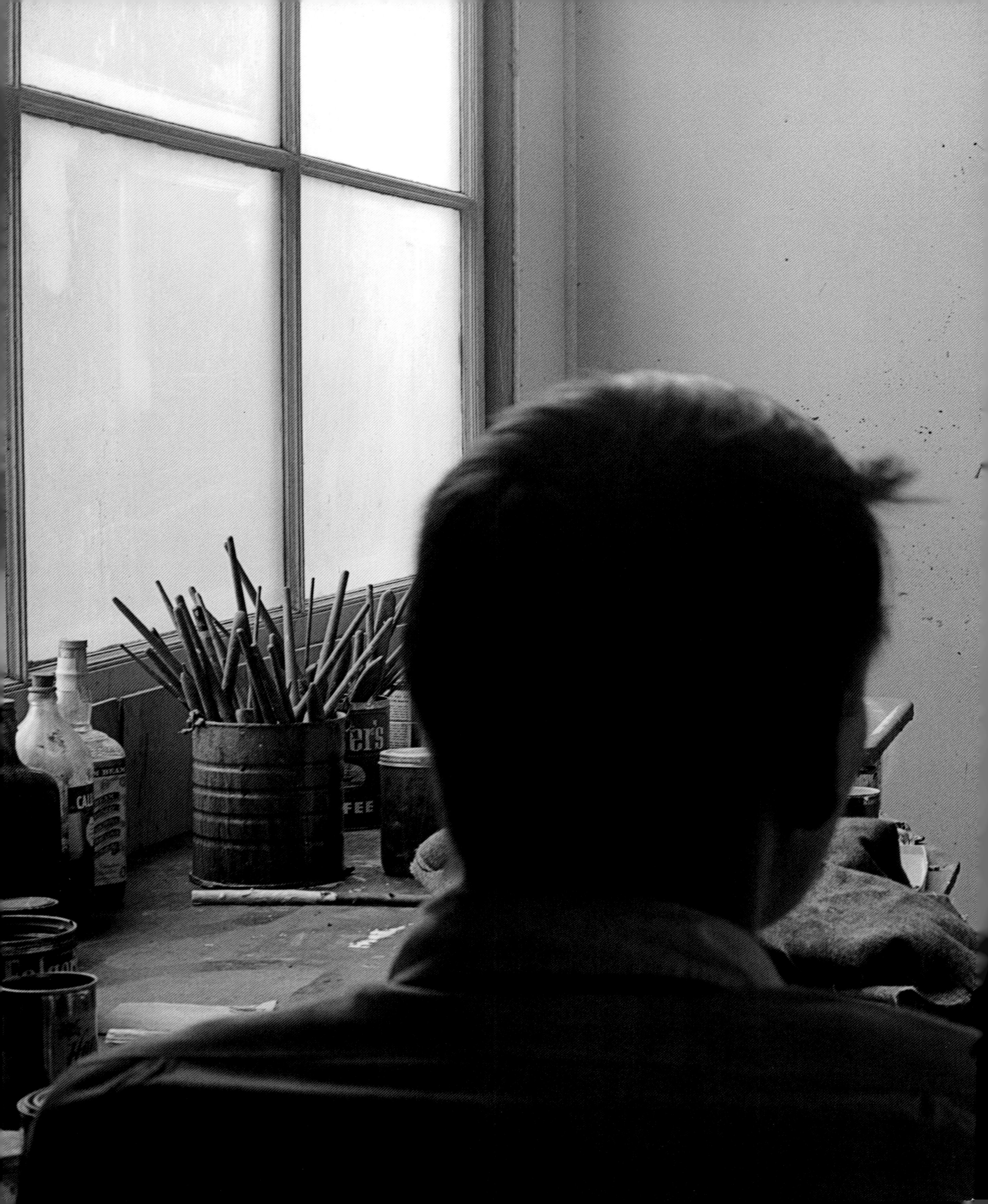

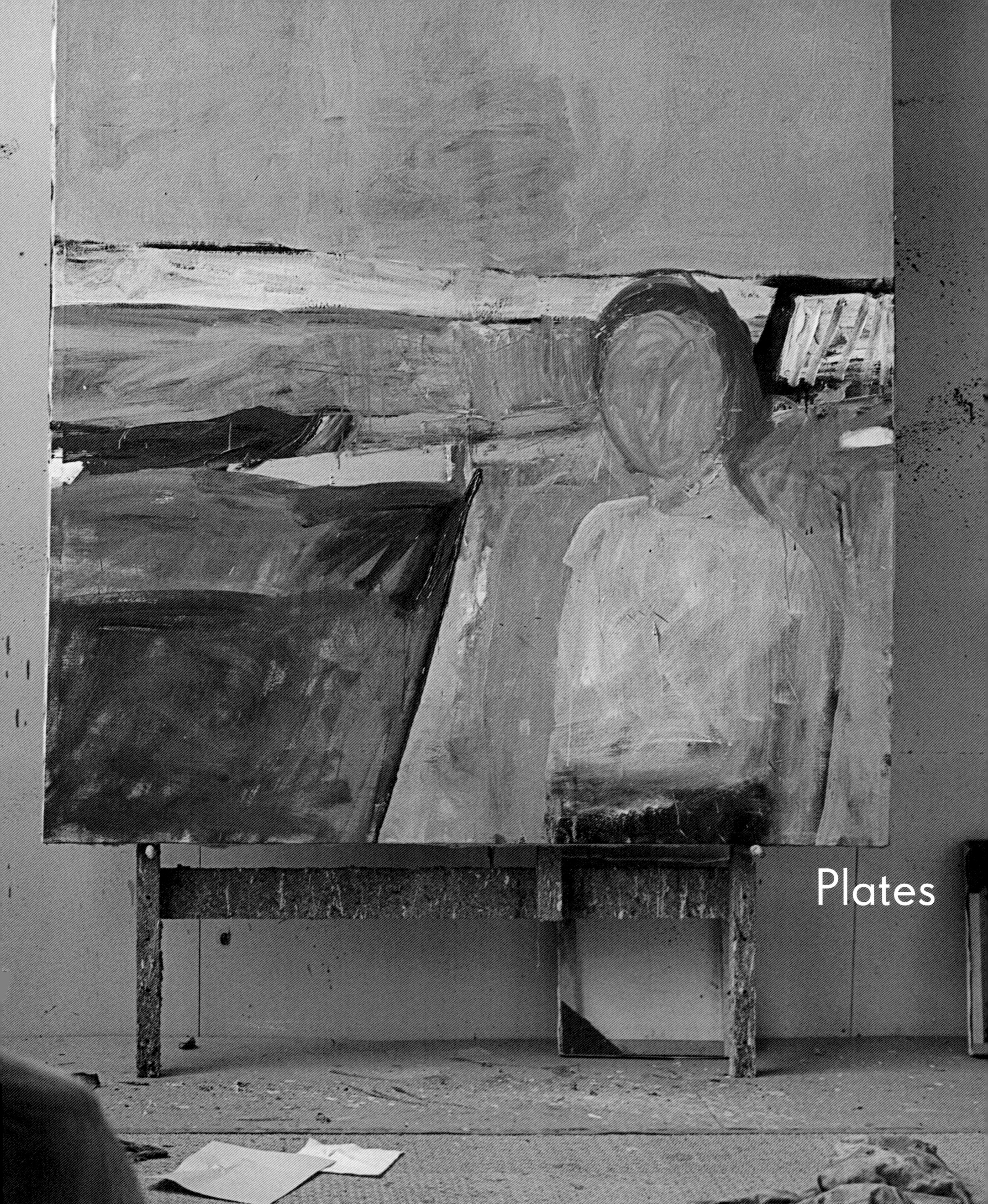

Plates

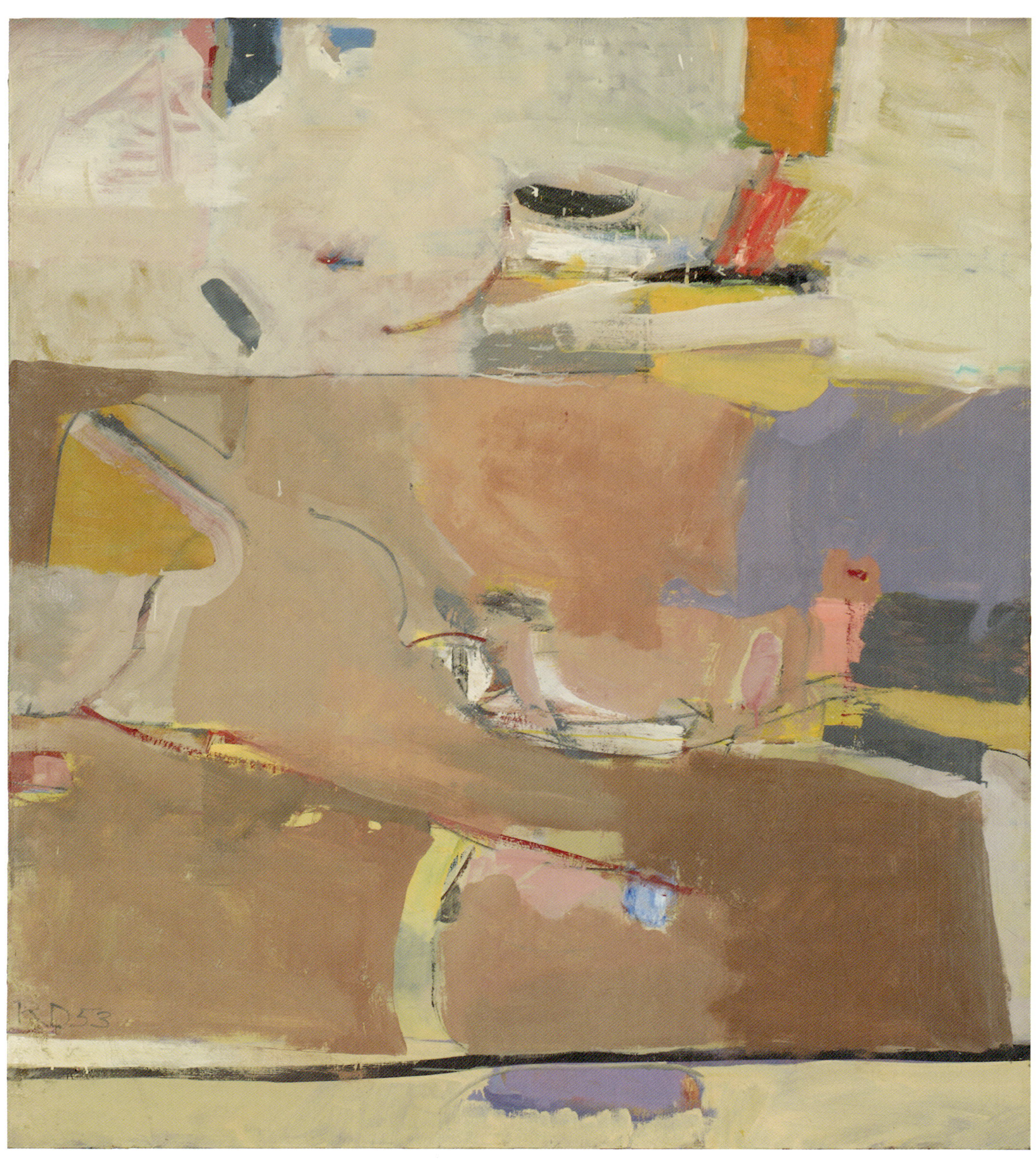
RD53

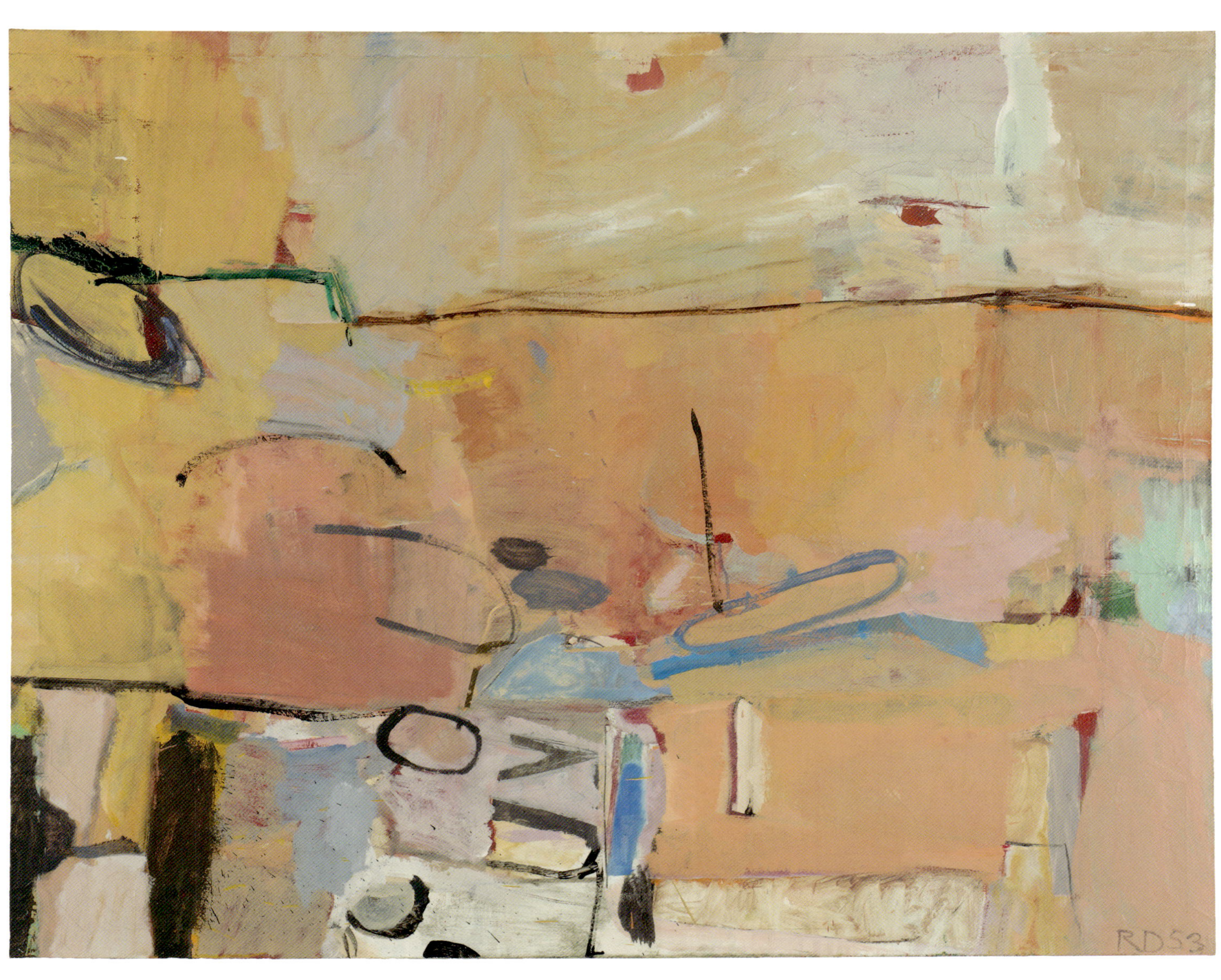

1. *Berkeley #1*, 1953
Oil on canvas, 60 1/4 x 52 3/4 in. (153 x 134 cm)
The Phillips Collection, Washington, DC, gift of Mr. and Mrs. Gifford Phillips, 1977, 0518 [1100]

2. *Berkeley #3*, 1953
Oil on canvas, 54 1/8 x 68 in. (137.5 x 172.7 cm)
Fine Arts Museums of San Francisco, bequest of Josephine Morris, 2003.25.3 [1102]

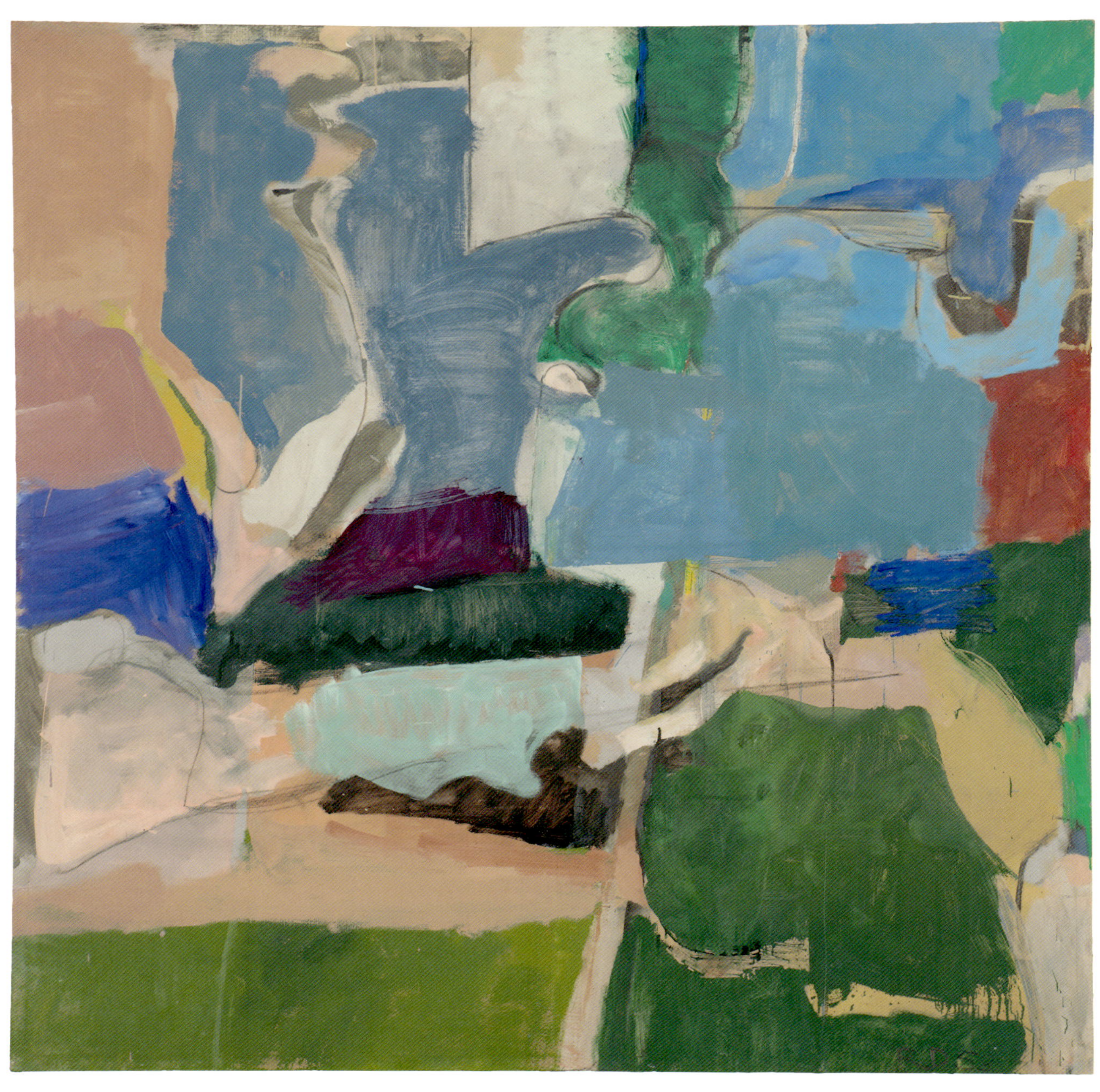

3. *Berkeley #5*, 1953
Oil on canvas, 53 x 53 in. (134.6 x 134.6 cm)
Private collection [1104]

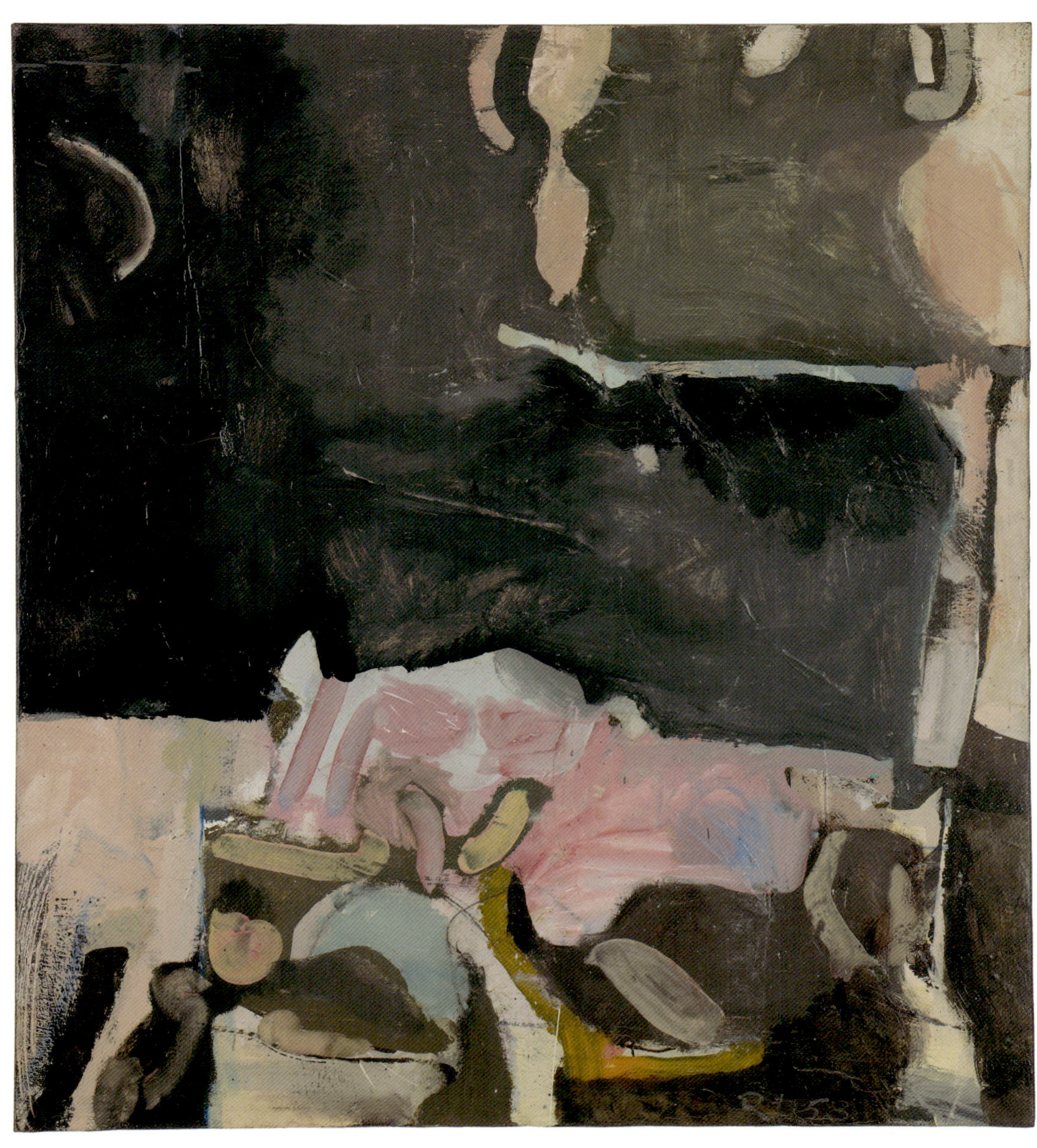

4. *Berkeley #7*, 1953
Oil on canvas, 47 3/4 x 43 in. (121.3 x 109.2 cm)
Mildred Lane Kemper Art Museum, Saint Louis, Missouri, gift of Joseph Pulitzer, Jr., WU 4019 [1106]

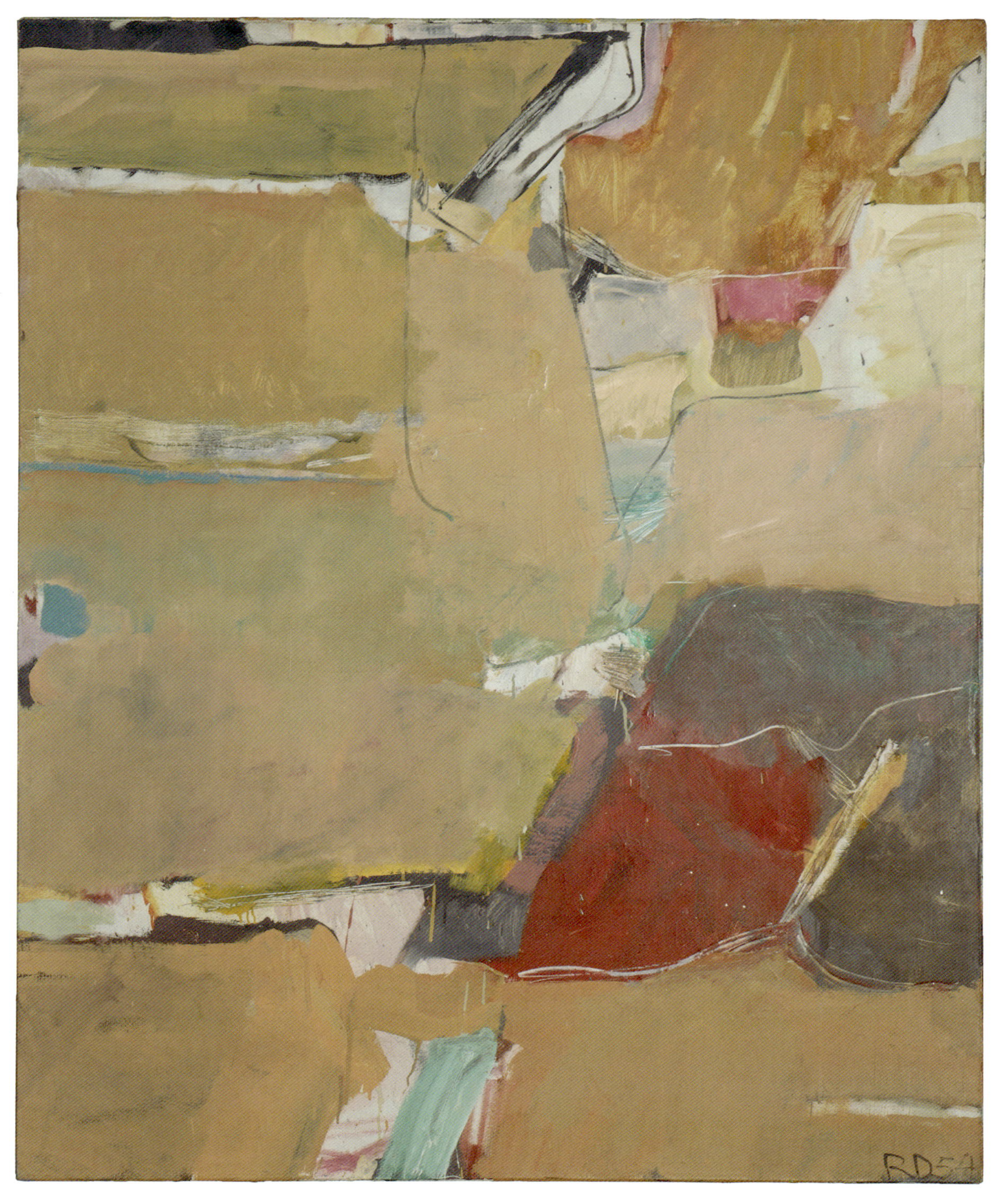

5. *Berkeley #12*, 1954
Oil on canvas, 53 1/4 x 43 1/4 in. (135.3 x 109.9 cm)
The Phillips Collection, Washington, DC, gift of Judith H. Miller, 1990.006.0005 [1111]

6. *Berkeley #8*, 1954
Oil on canvas, 69 1/8 x 59 1/8 in. (175.6 x 150.2 cm)
North Carolina Museum of Art, Raleigh, gift of W. R. Valentiner, G.57.34.3 [1109]

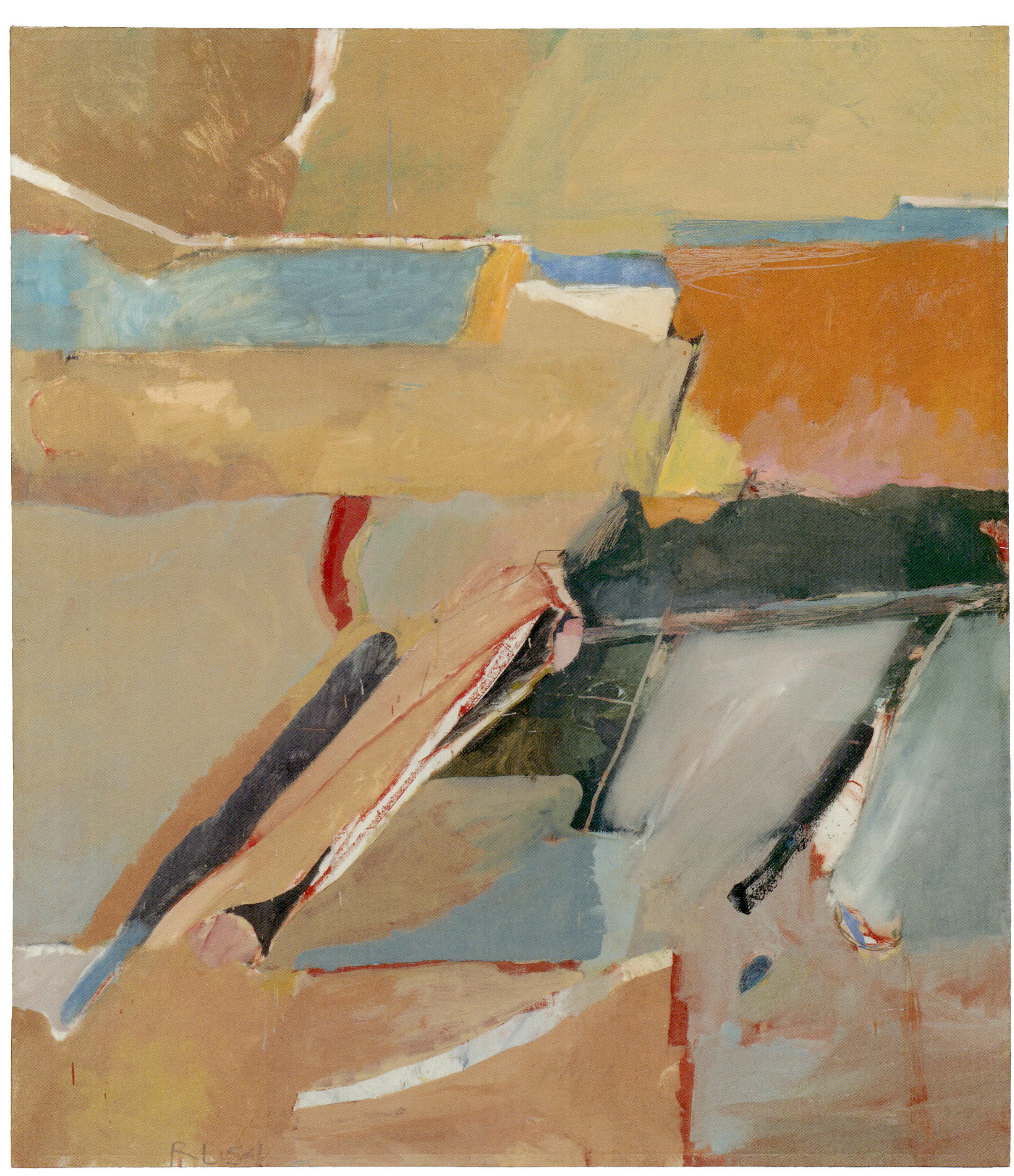

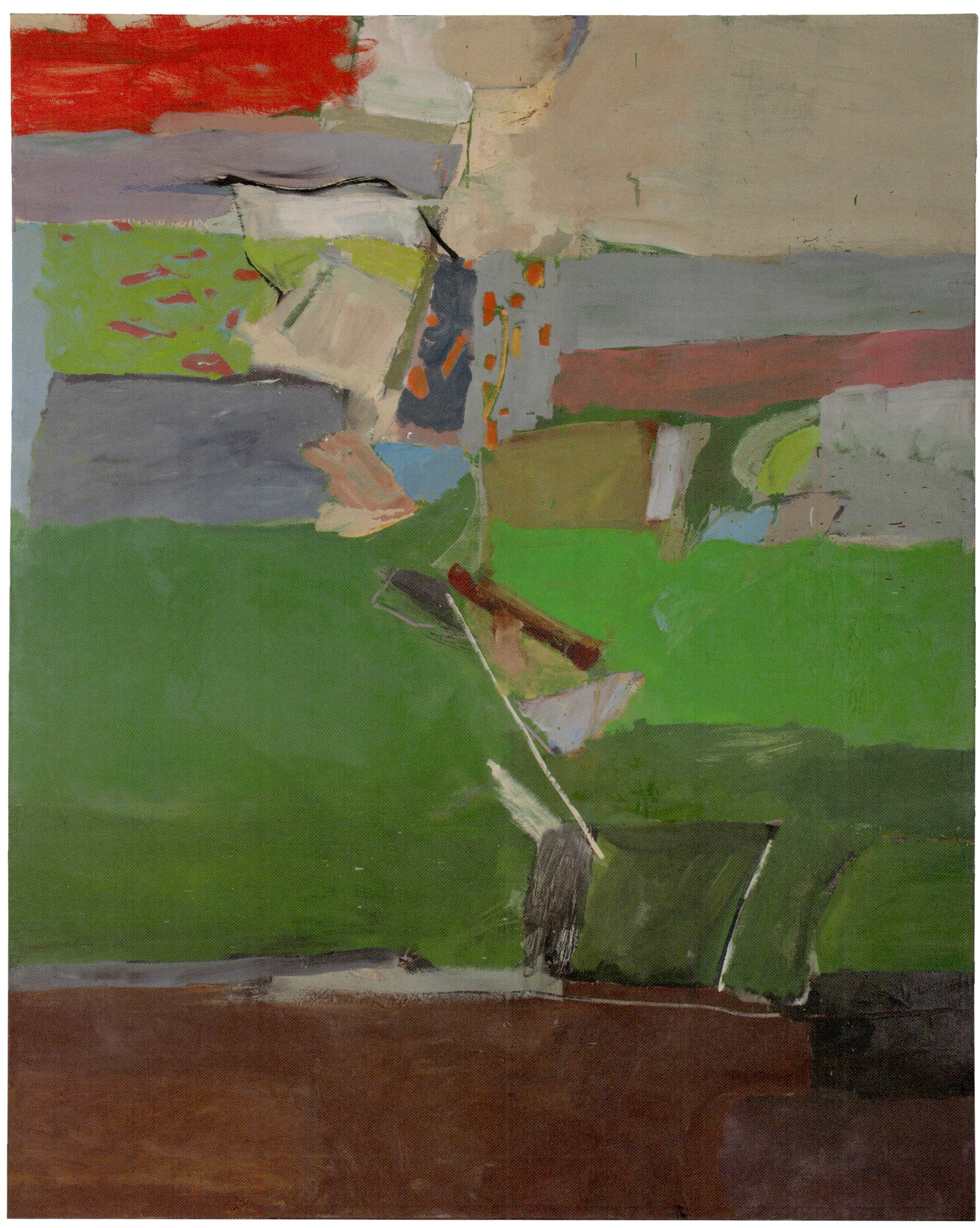

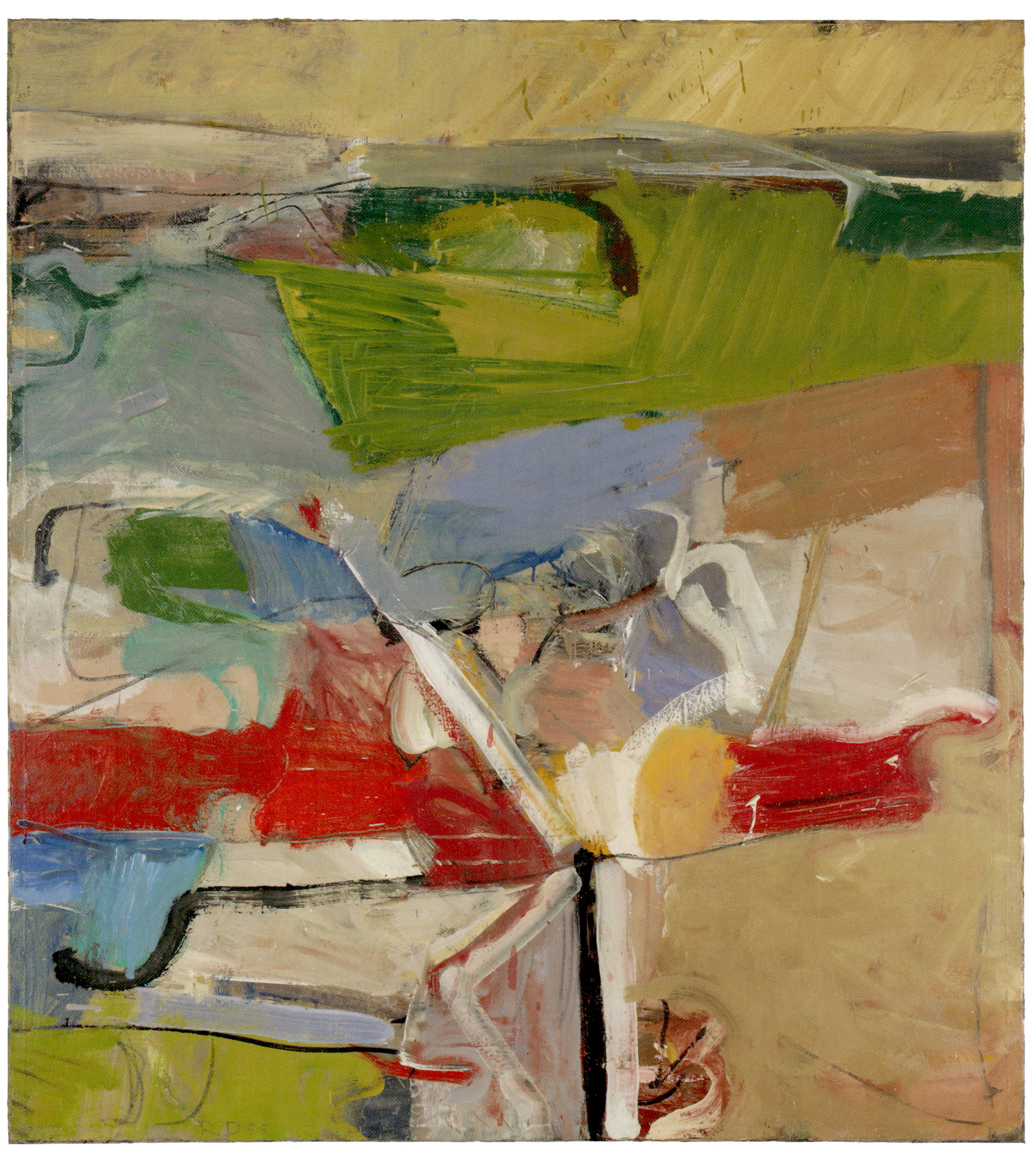

7. *Berkeley #13*, 1954
Oil on canvas, 69 5/8 x 54 1/2 in. (176.8 x 138.4 cm)
Private collection [1112]

8. *Berkeley #23*, 1955
Oil on canvas, 62 x 54 3/4 in. (157.5 x 139.1 cm)
San Francisco Museum of Modern Art, gift of the Women's Board, 58.1729 [1125]

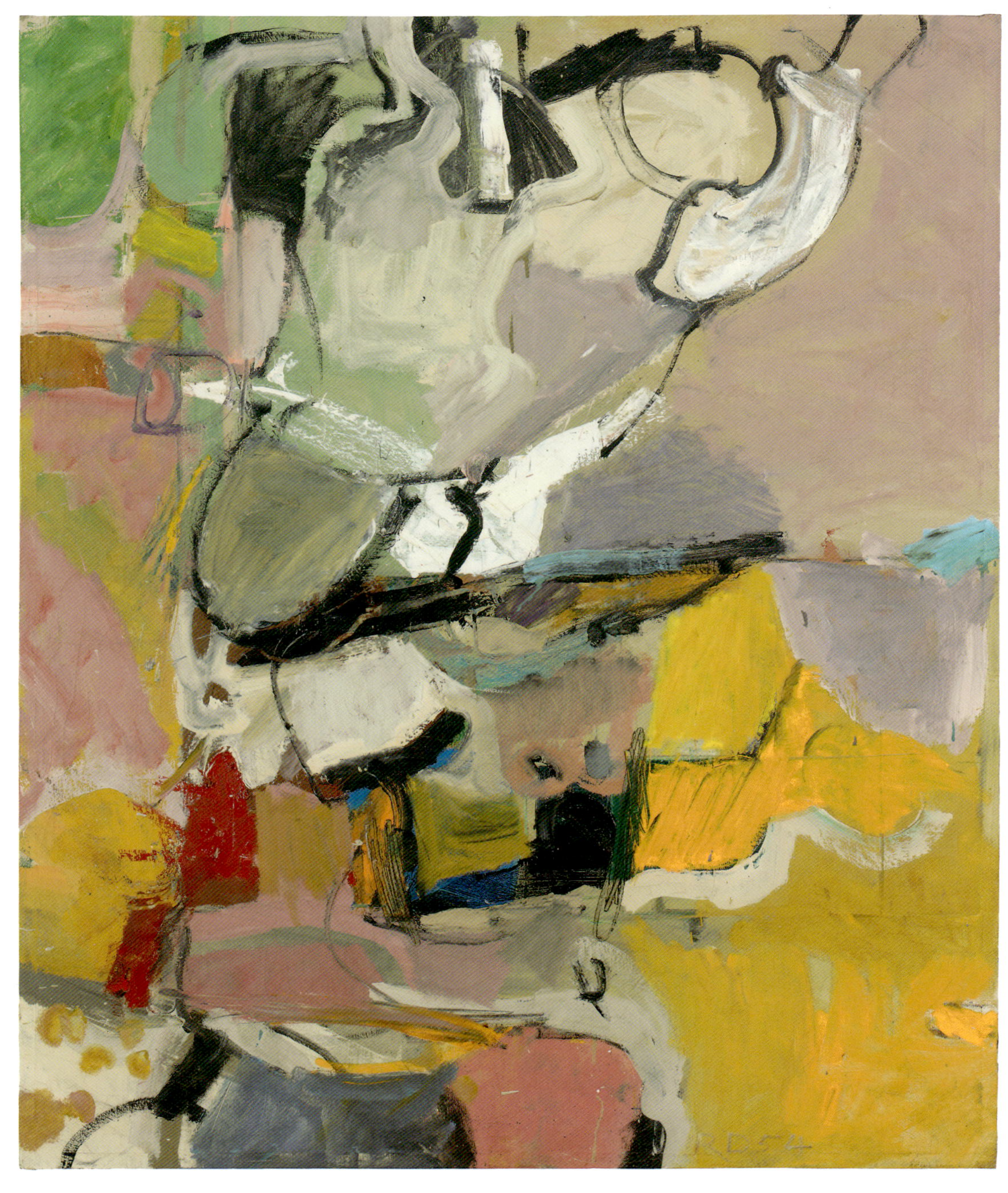

9. *Berkeley #16*, 1954
Oil on canvas, 56 x 46 1/4 in. (142.2 x 117.5 cm)
Private collection [1114]

10. *Berkeley #15*, 1954
Oil on canvas, 64 1/4 x 53 in. (163.2 x 134.6 cm)
New Mexico Museum of Art, Santa Fe, gift of Mr. and Mrs. Gifford Phillips, 4565.23P [1113]

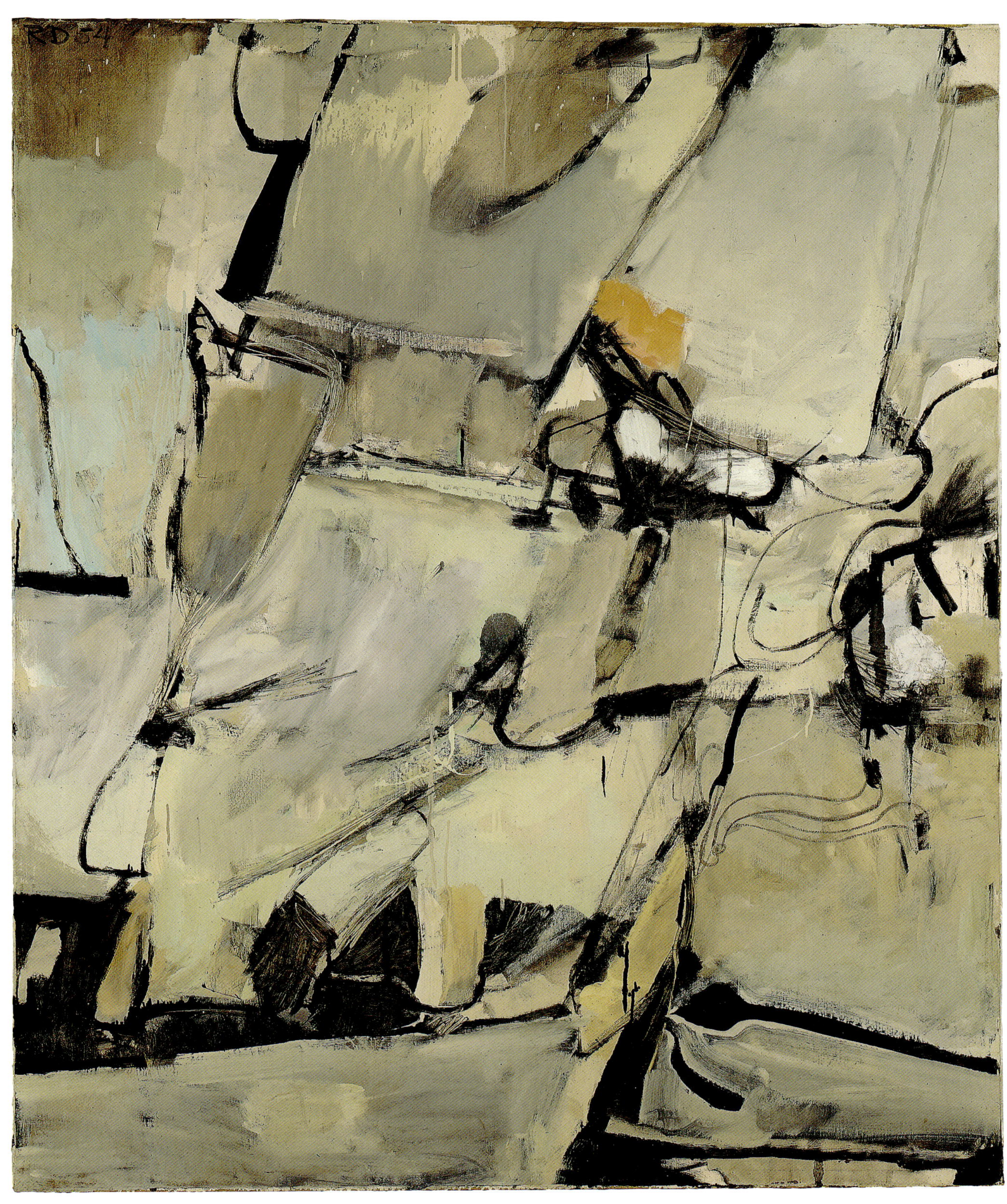

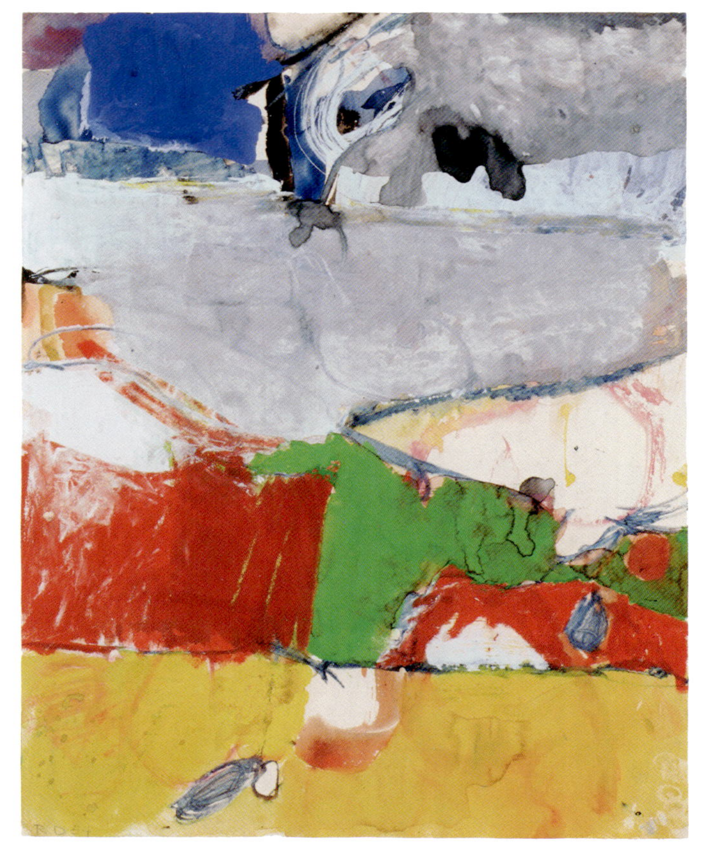

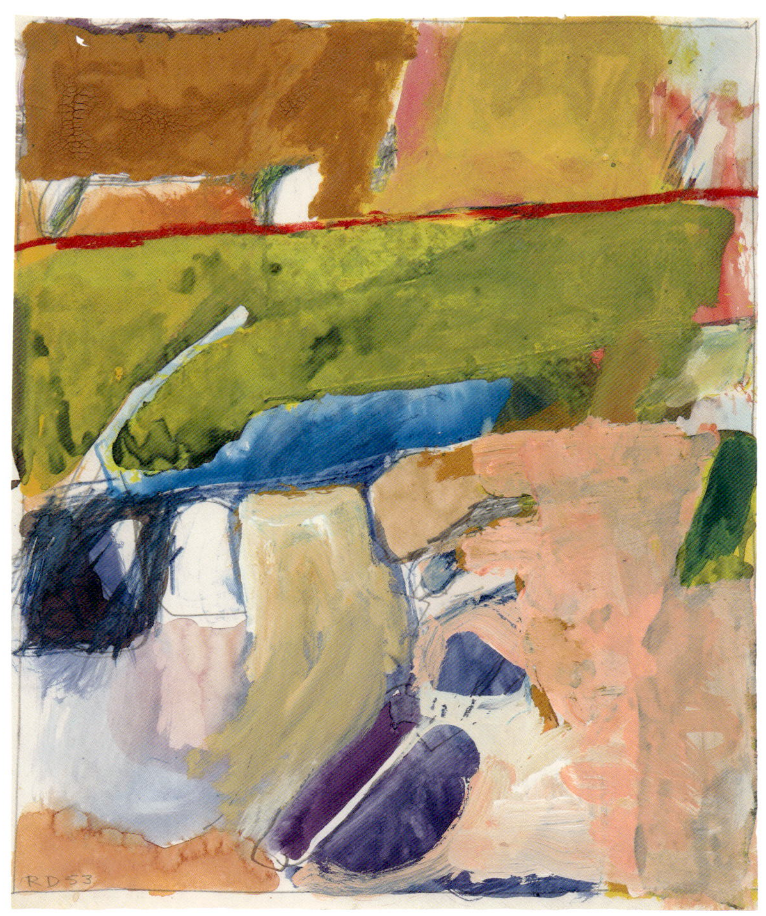

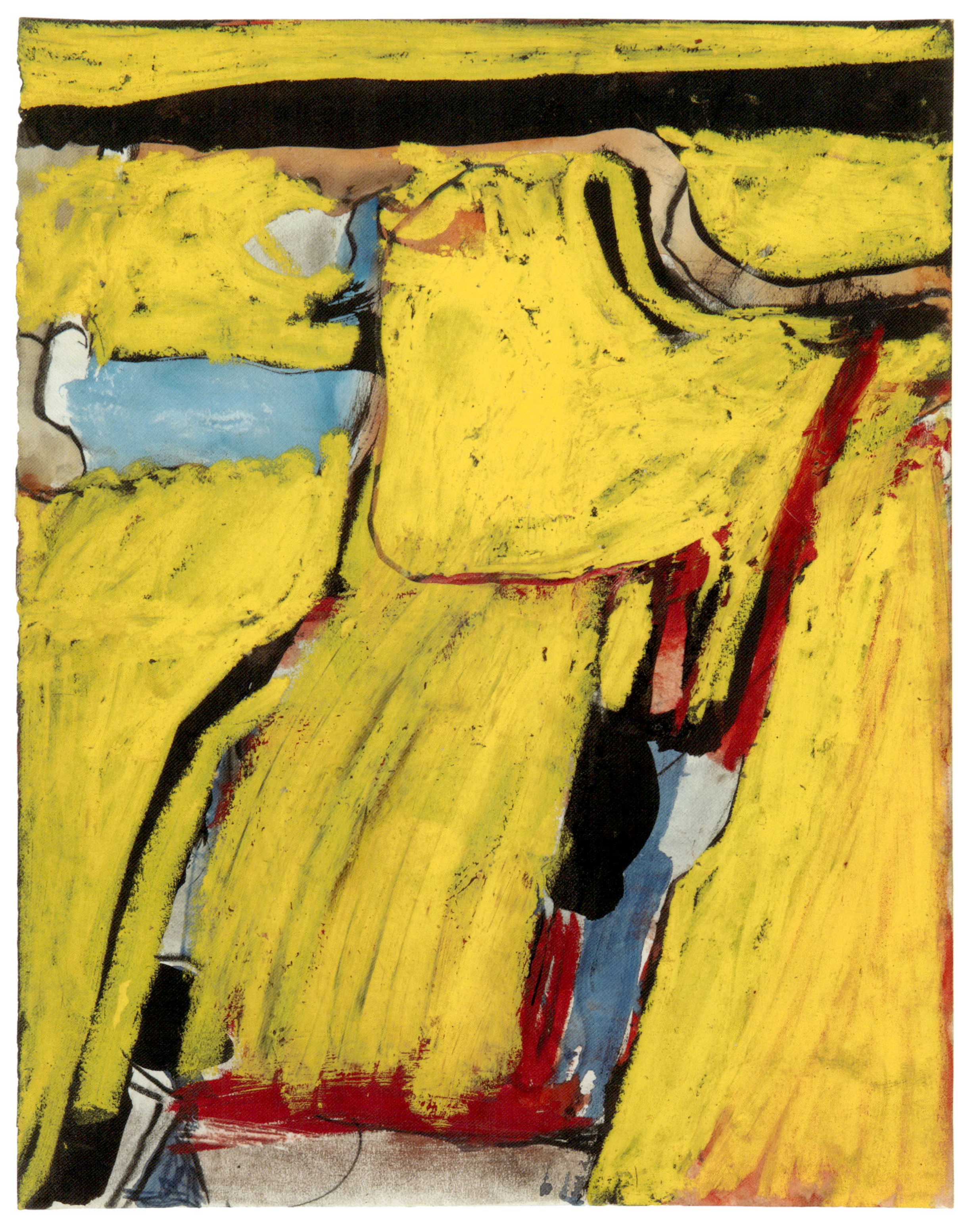

11. *Untitled*, 1954
Watercolor, crayon, and colored pencil on paper, 14 1/2 x 11 1/2 in. (36.8 x 29.2 cm)
Allen Memorial Art Museum, Oberlin College, Ohio, transferred from the rental collection to the permanent collection via Art Museum Gift Fund, AMAM 1994.27 [4166]

12. *Untitled*, 1953–1955
Gouache, pencil, and colored pencil on paper, 16 x 13 in. (40.6 x 33 cm)
Collection of Leslie A. Feely [3289]

13. *Untitled (Berkeley)*, ca. 1953–1954
Oil, ink, gouache, and crayon on paper, 13 7/8 x 10 7/8 in. (35.2 x 27.6 cm)
Collection of John and Sally Van Doren, courtesy of Van Doren Waxter [2154]

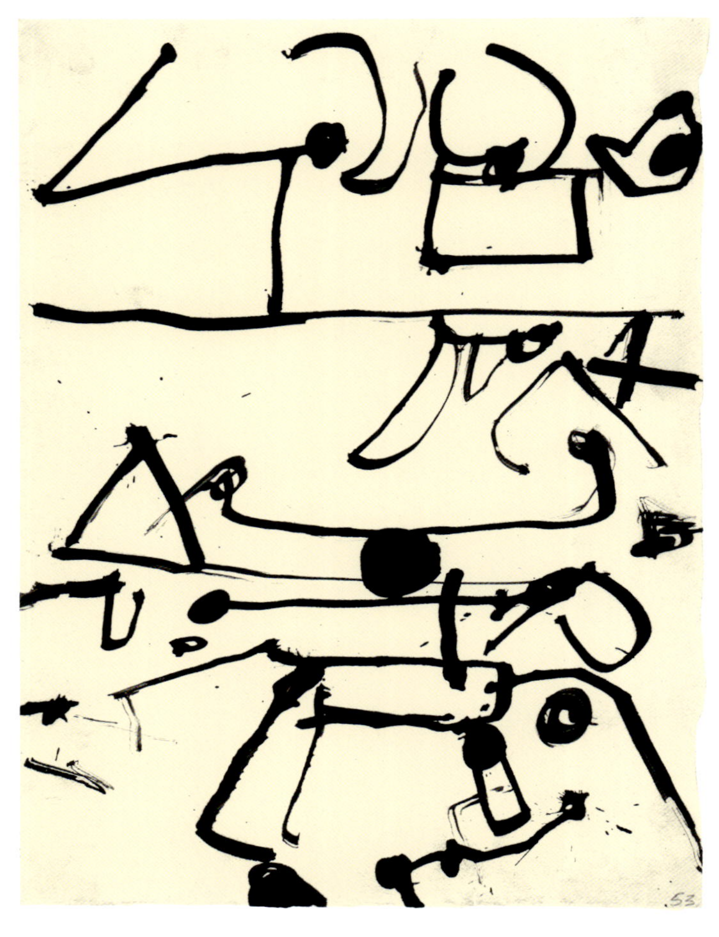

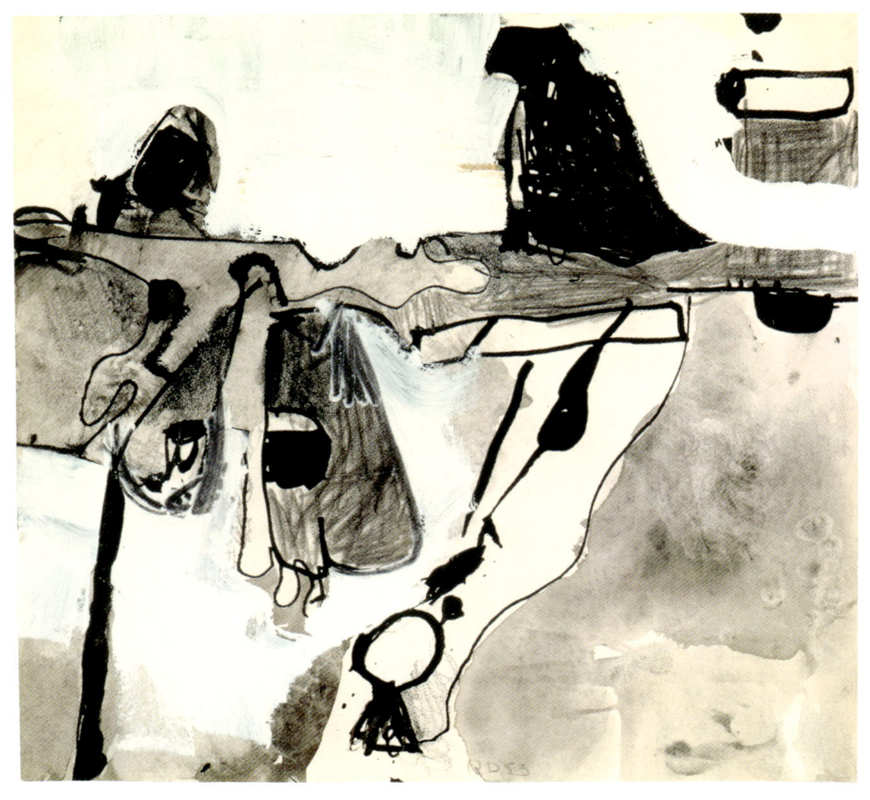

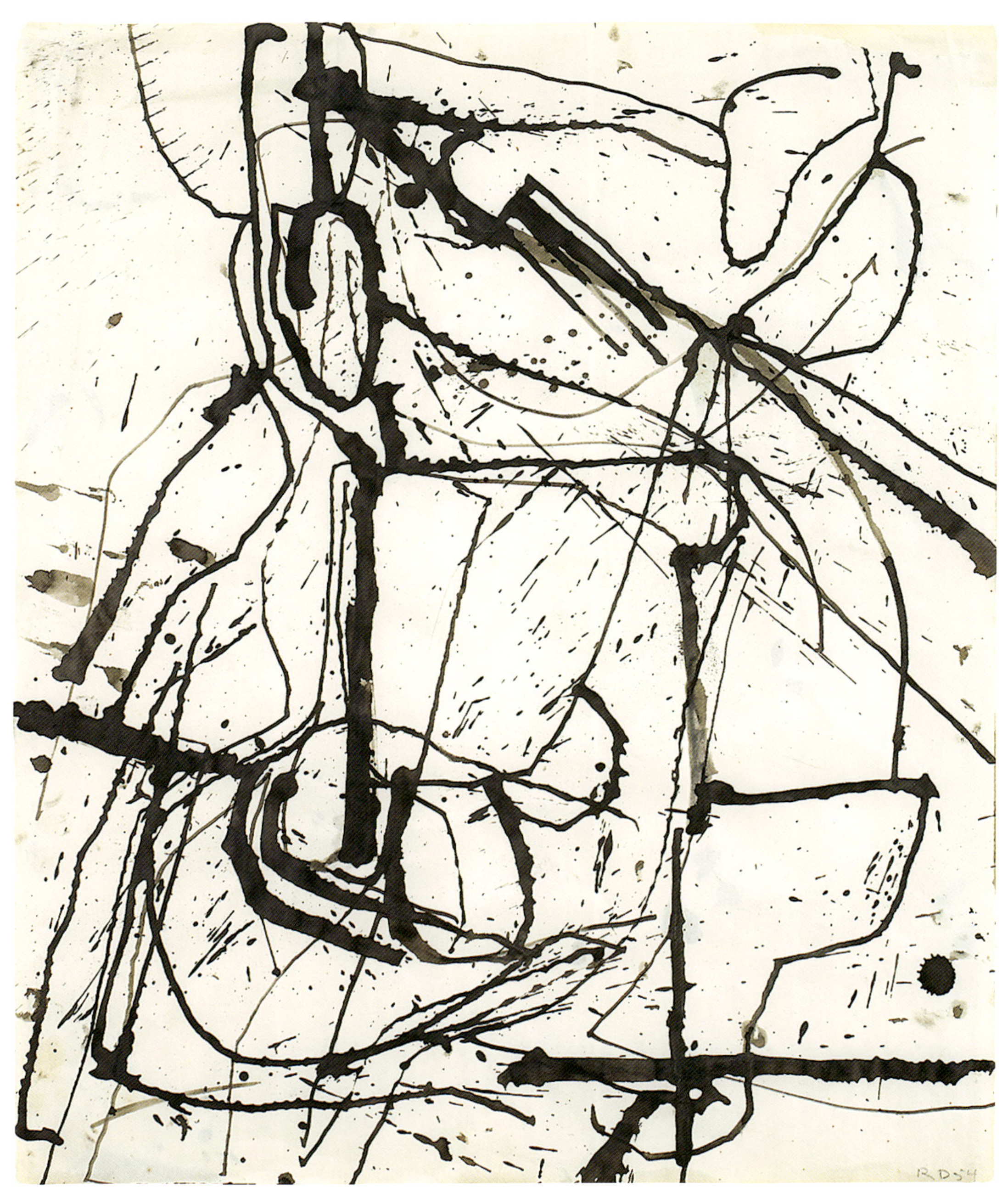

14. *Untitled*, 1953
Ink on paper, 12 x 9 1/8 in. (30.5 x 23.2 cm)
Private collection [5319]

15. *Untitled (Berkeley)*, 1953
Ink, gouache, and graphite on paper, 10 1/2 x 11 1/4 in. (26.7 x 28.6 cm)
Collection of Ann and Robert L. Freedman, New York [58]

16. *Untitled (Berkeley)*, 1954
Ink on paper, 16 7/8 x 13 7/8 in. (42.9 x 35.2 cm)
Private collection, San Antonio, Texas [333]

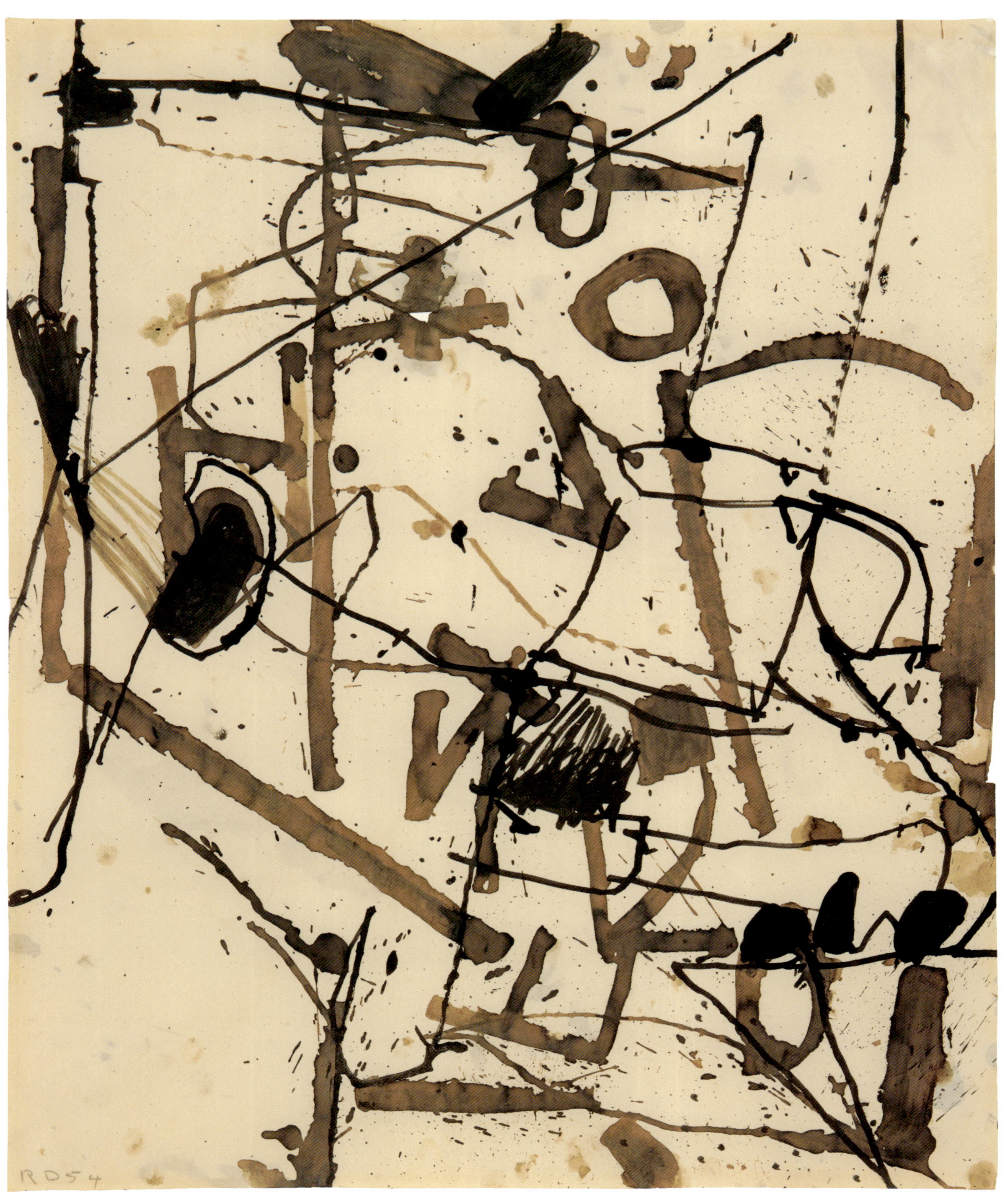
RD54

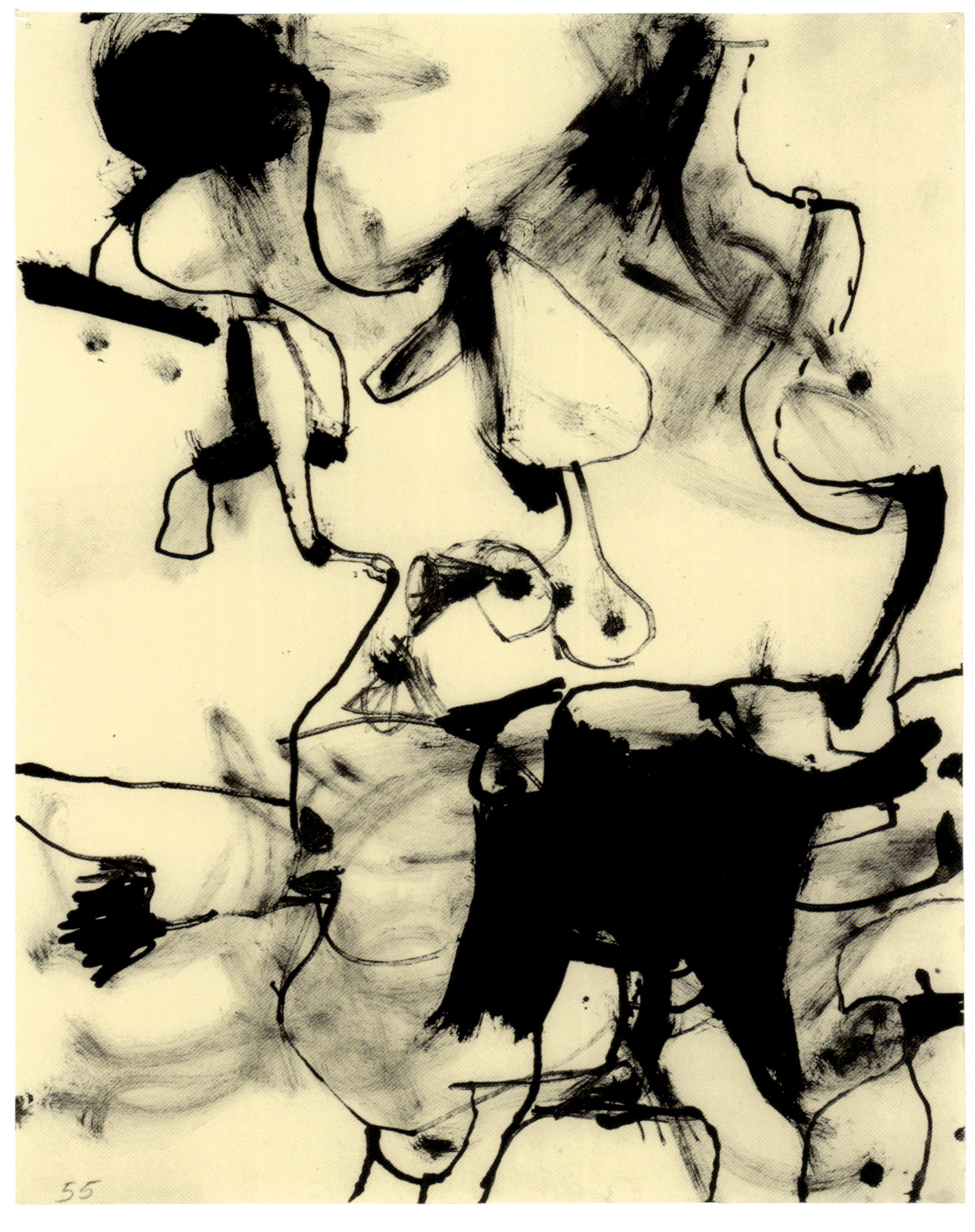

17. *Untitled (Berkeley)*, 1954
Ink on paper, 16 3/4 x 13 3/4 in. (42.5 x 34.9 cm)
Collection of Hackett | Mill, San Francisco [335]

18. *Untitled (Berkeley)*, 1955
Ink and gouache on paper, 11 x 8 1/2 in. (27.9 x 21.6 cm)
Private collection [2149]

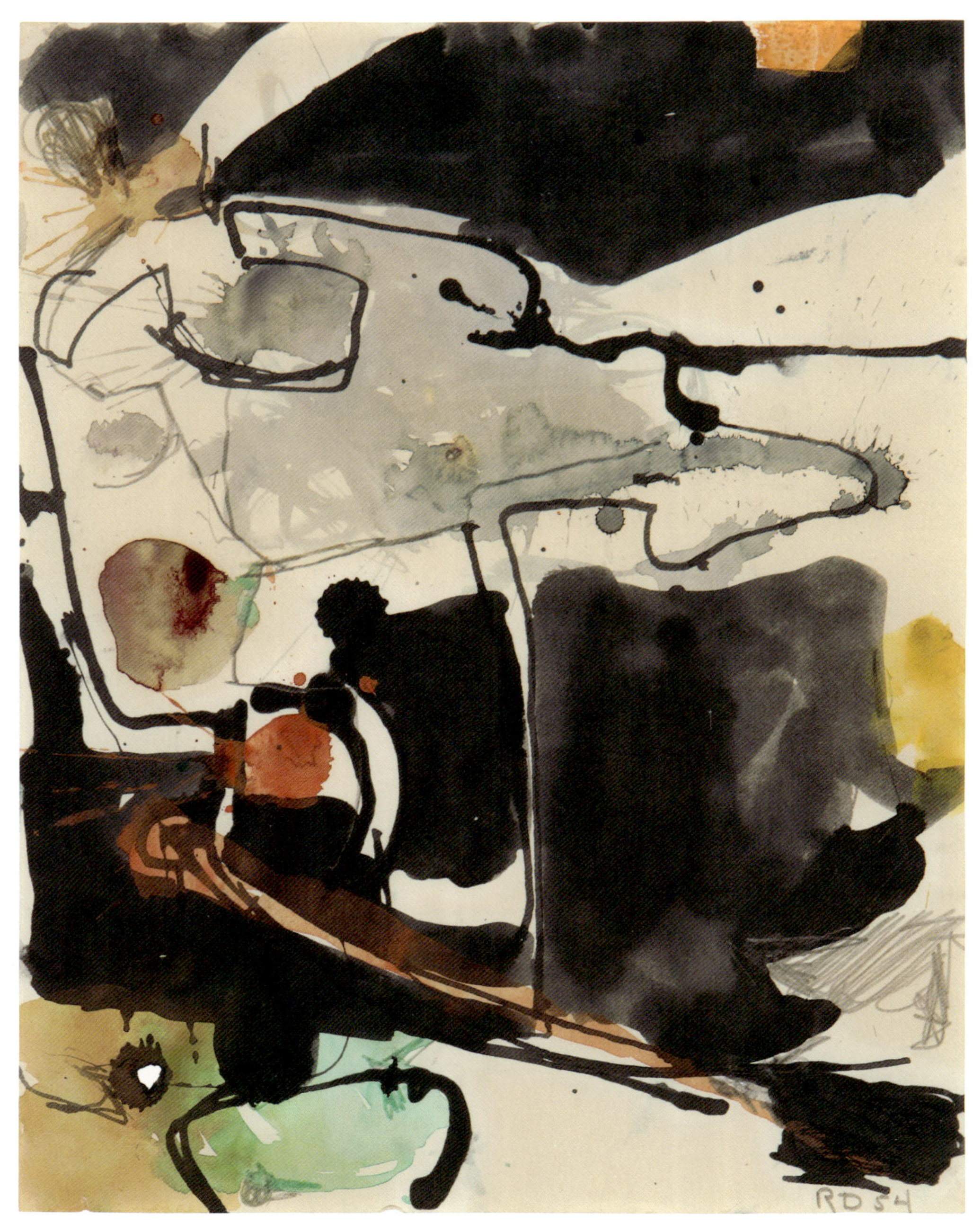

19. *Untitled*, 1954
Watercolor and graphite on paper, 10 7/8 x 8 3/8 in. (27.6 x 21.3 cm)
Private collection [595]

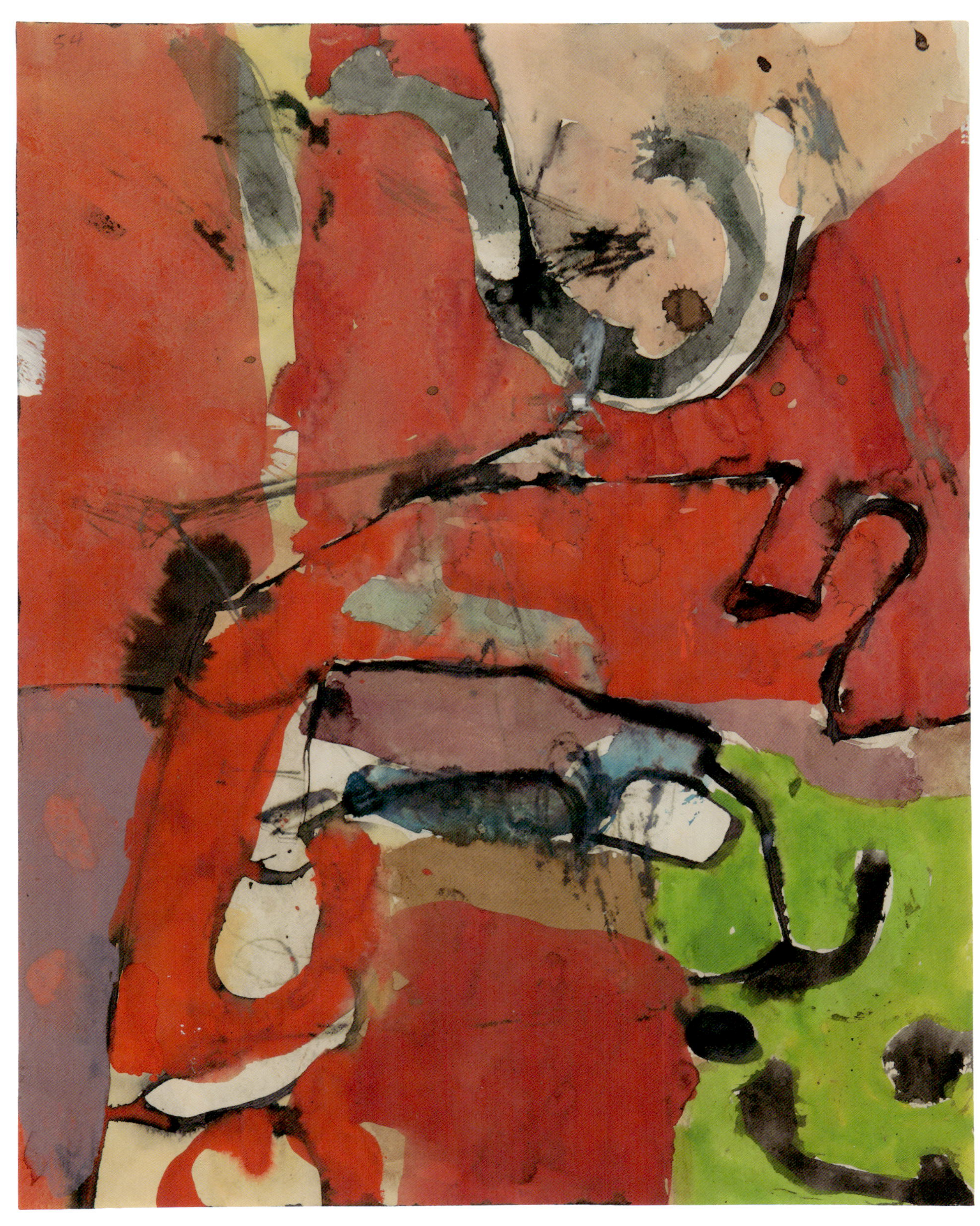

20. *Untitled (Berkeley)*, 1954
Watercolor, ink, and charcoal on paper, 14 1/2 x 11 1/2 in. (36.8 x 29.2 cm)
Private collection [2159]

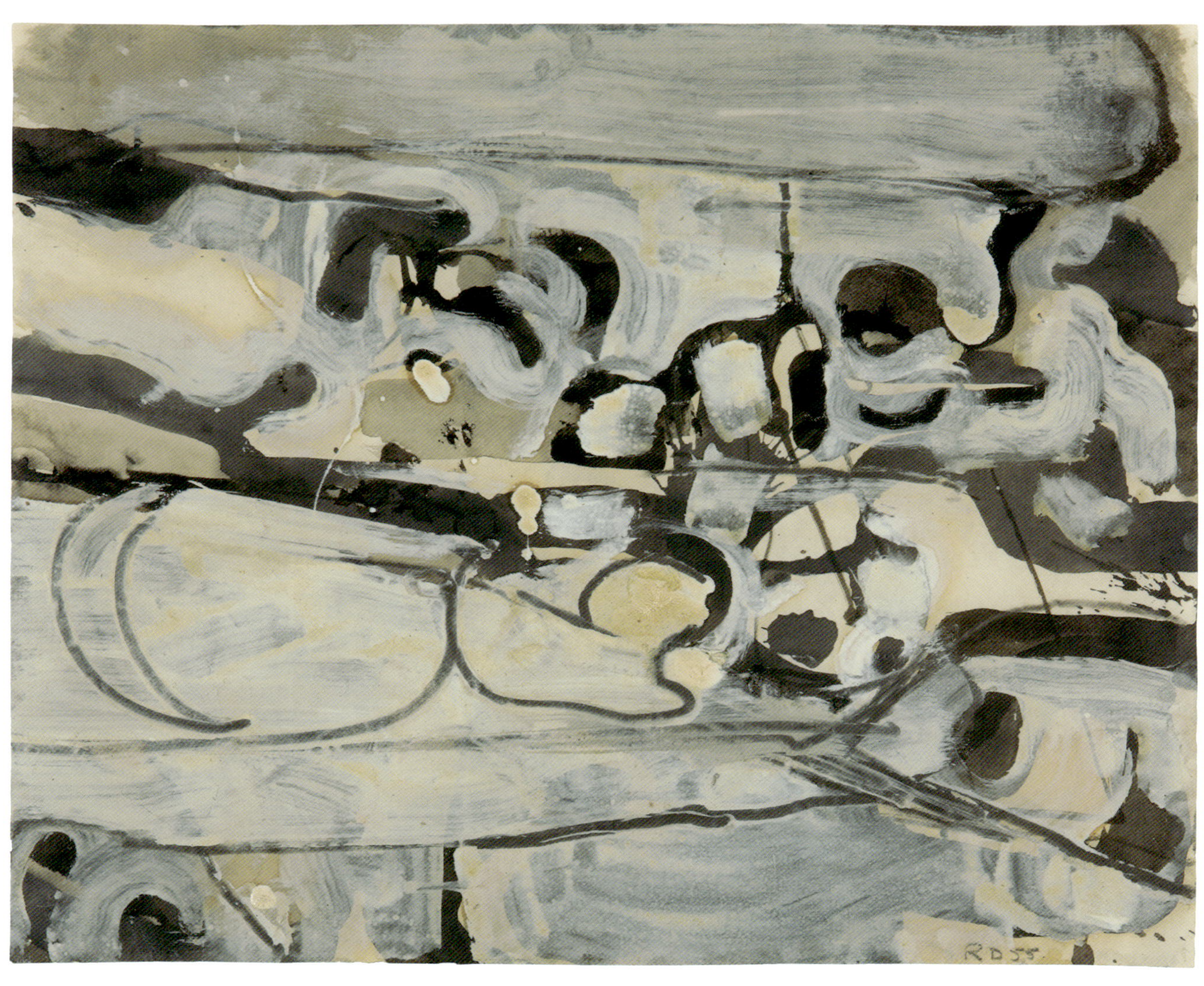

21. *Untitled (Berkeley)*, 1955
Oil, ink, and gouache on paper, 14 x 17 in. (35.6 x 43.2 cm)
Private collection [602]

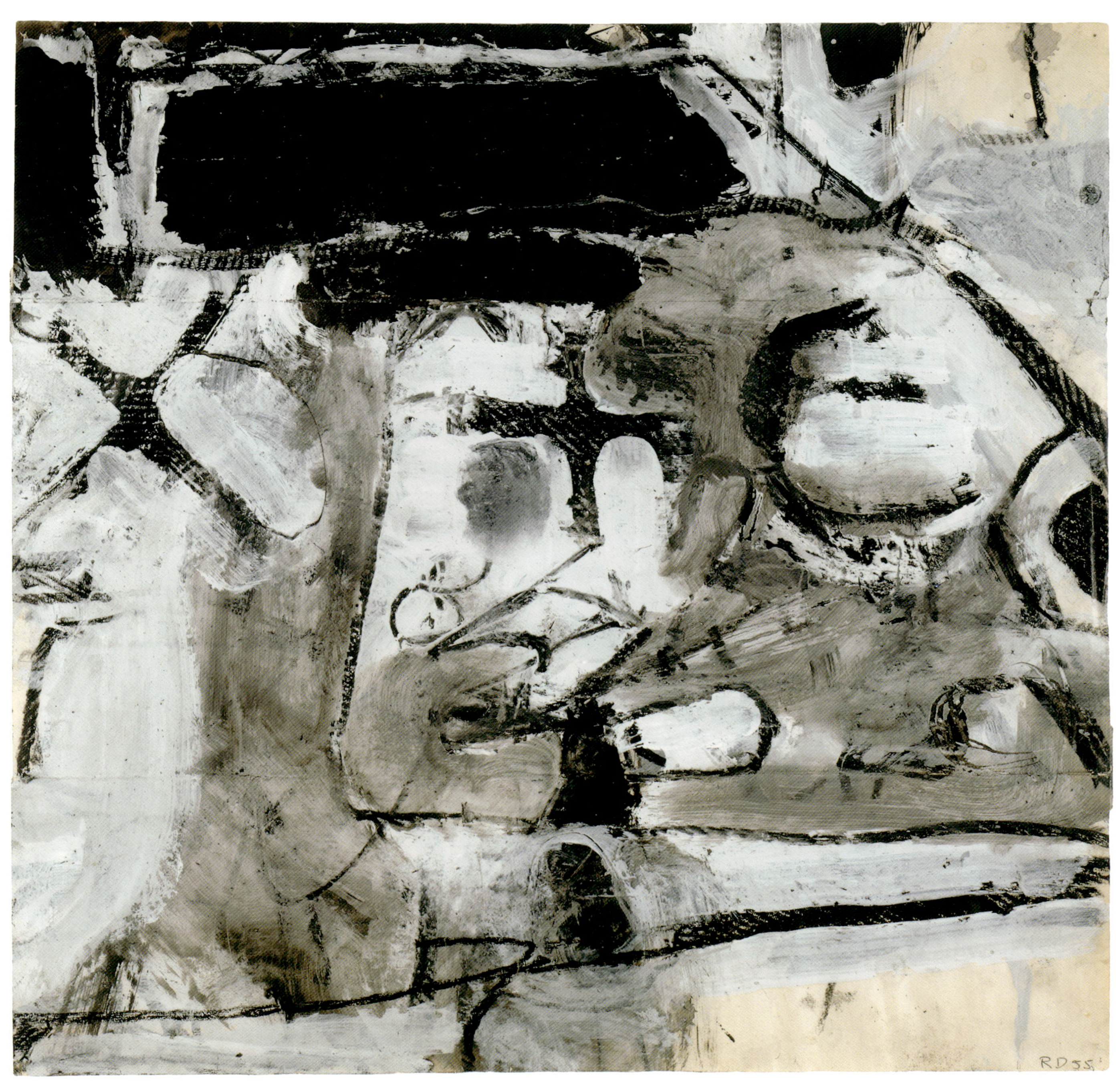

22. *Untitled (Berkeley)*, 1955
Gouache, ink, and oil stick on joined paper, 18 3/4 x 19 in. (47.6 x 48.3 cm)
Art Institute of Chicago, gift of the Diebenkorn Family, restricted gift of Adele and William Gidwitz, 1996.615 [2152]

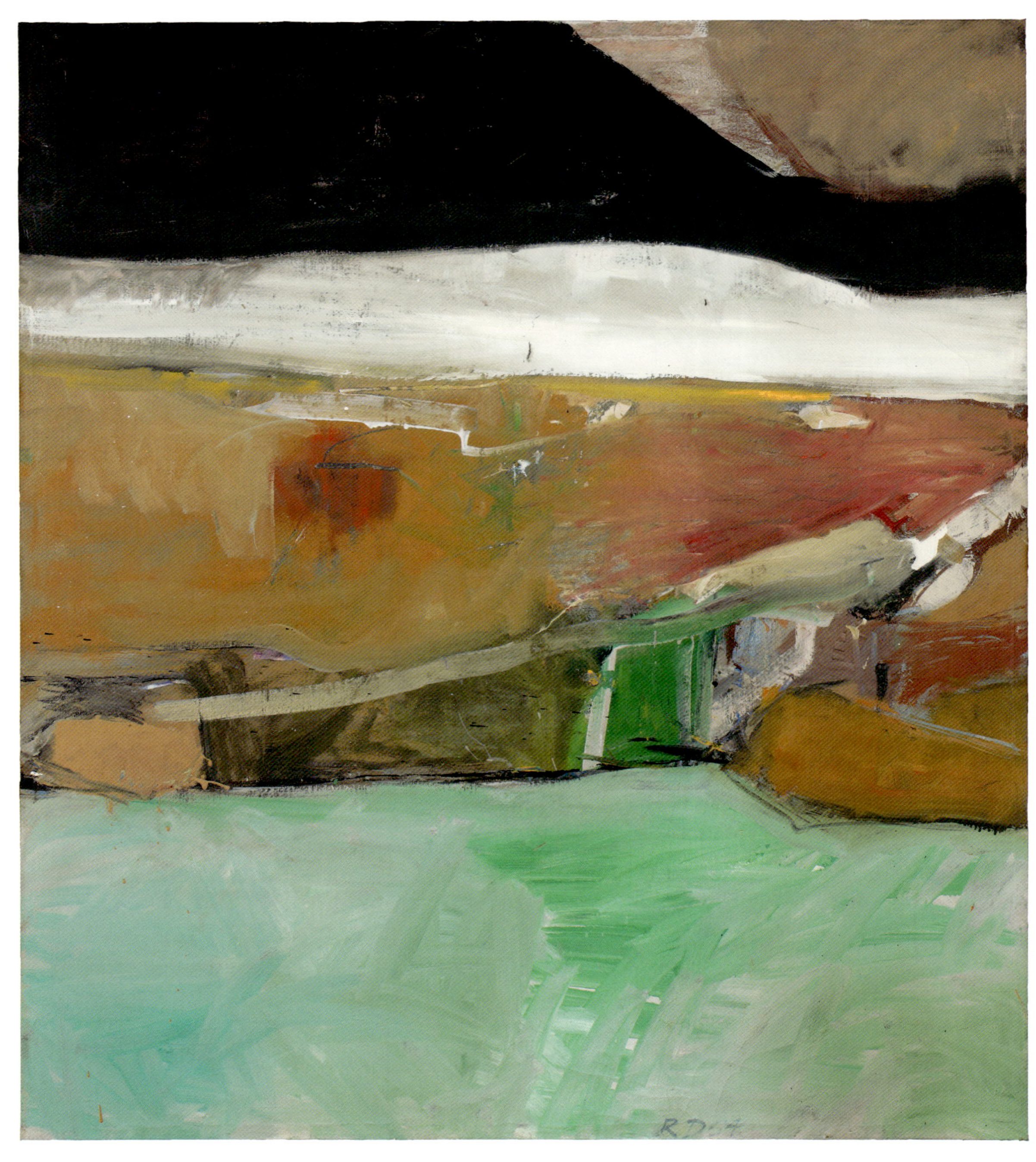

23. *Berkeley #26*, 1954
Oil on canvas, 56 1/4 x 49 1/4 in. (142.9 x 125.1 cm)
Collection of Harry W. and Mary Margaret Anderson, 1969.013 [1121]

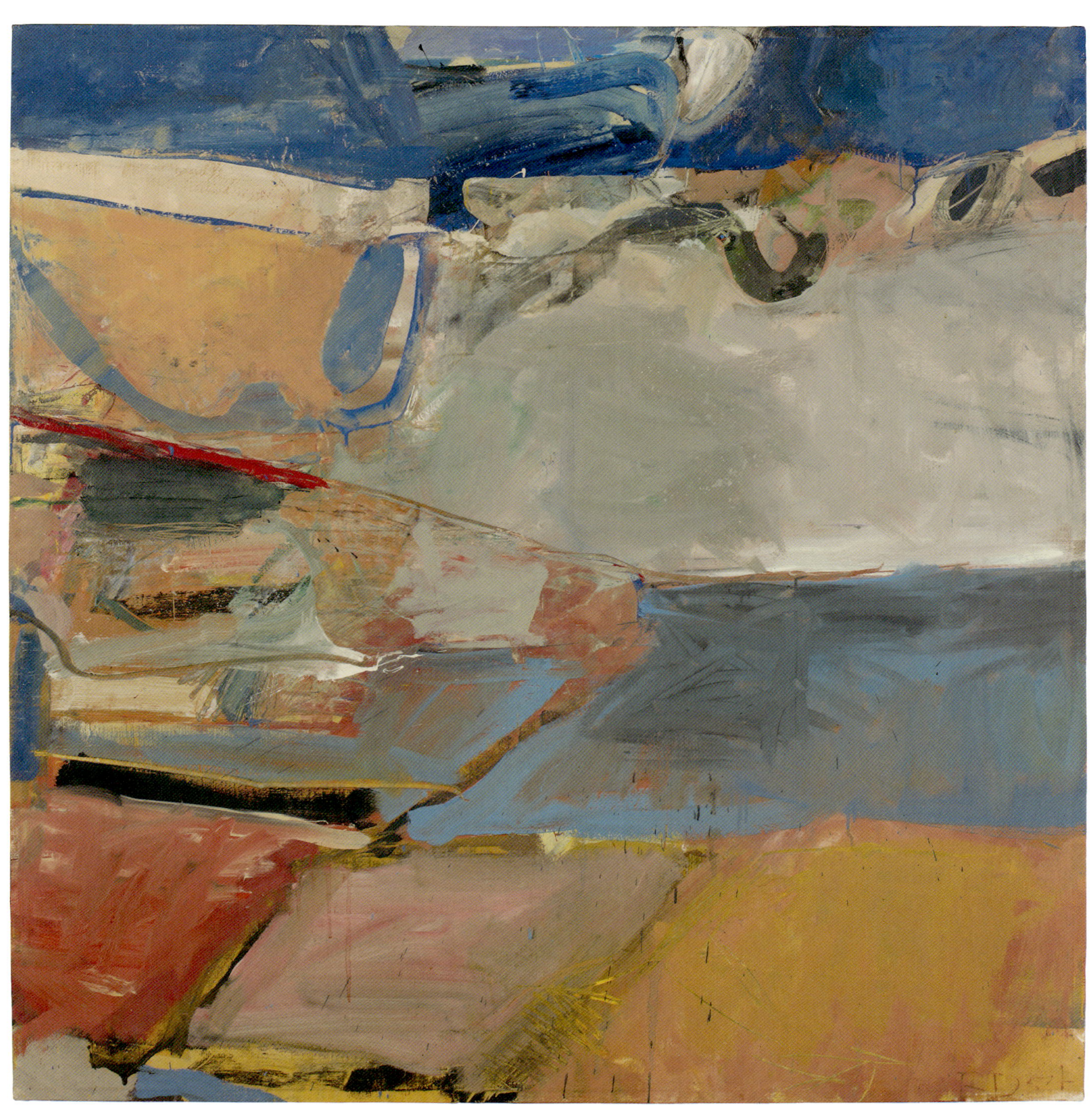

24. *Berkeley #22*, 1954
Oil on canvas, 59 x 57 in. (149.9 x 144.8 cm)
Hirshhorn Museum and Sculpture Garden, Smithsonian Institution, Washington, DC, Regents Collections Acquisition Program, 1986, 86.5886 [1119]

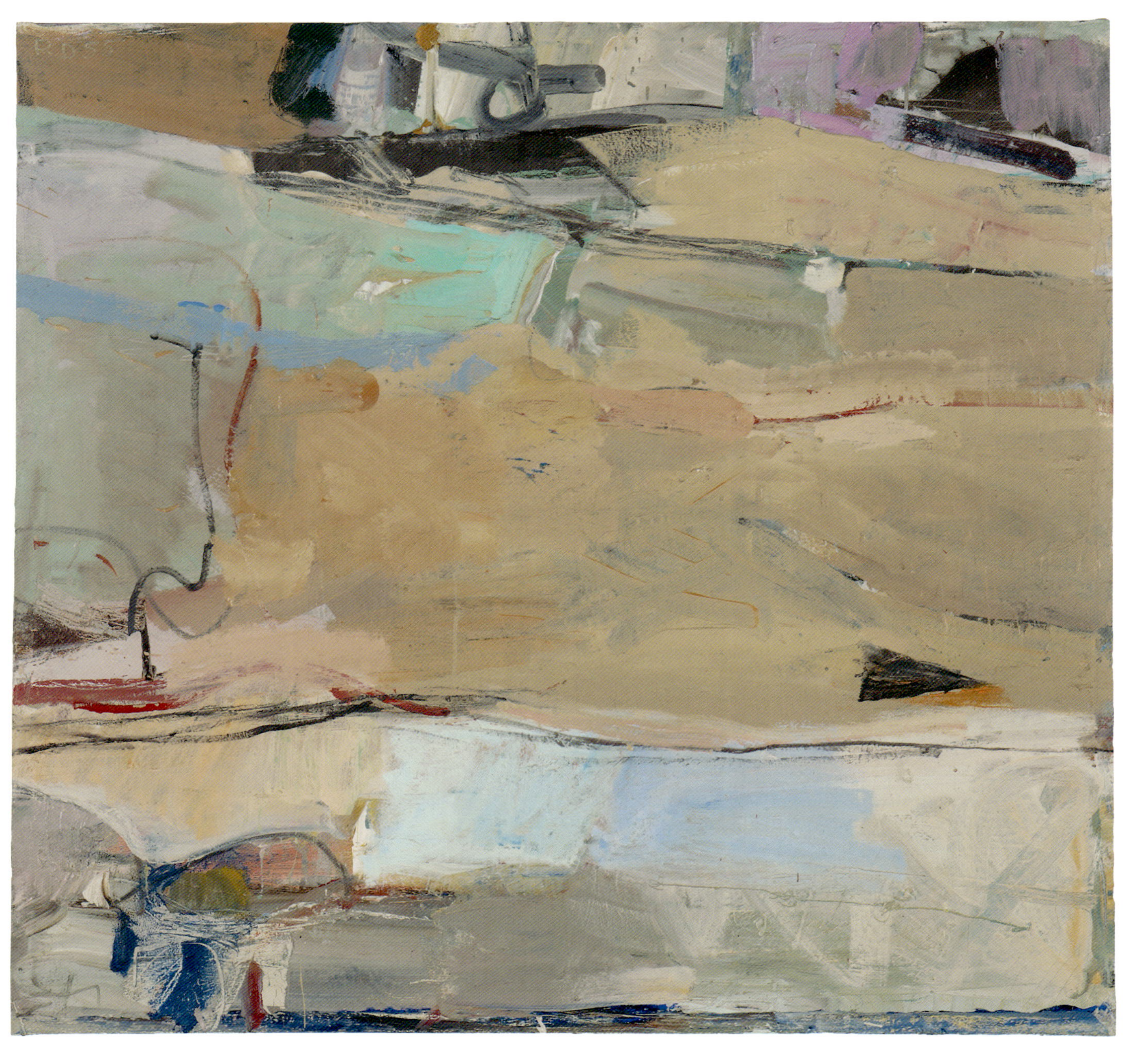

25. *Berkeley #27*, 1955
Oil on canvas, 41 3/4 x 44 1/8 in. (106 x 112.1 cm)
Private collection [1127]

26. *Berkeley #31*, 1955
Oil on canvas, 58 7/8 x 53 1/4 in. (149.5 x 135.3 cm)
Collection of Marguerite and Robert Hoffman [1130]

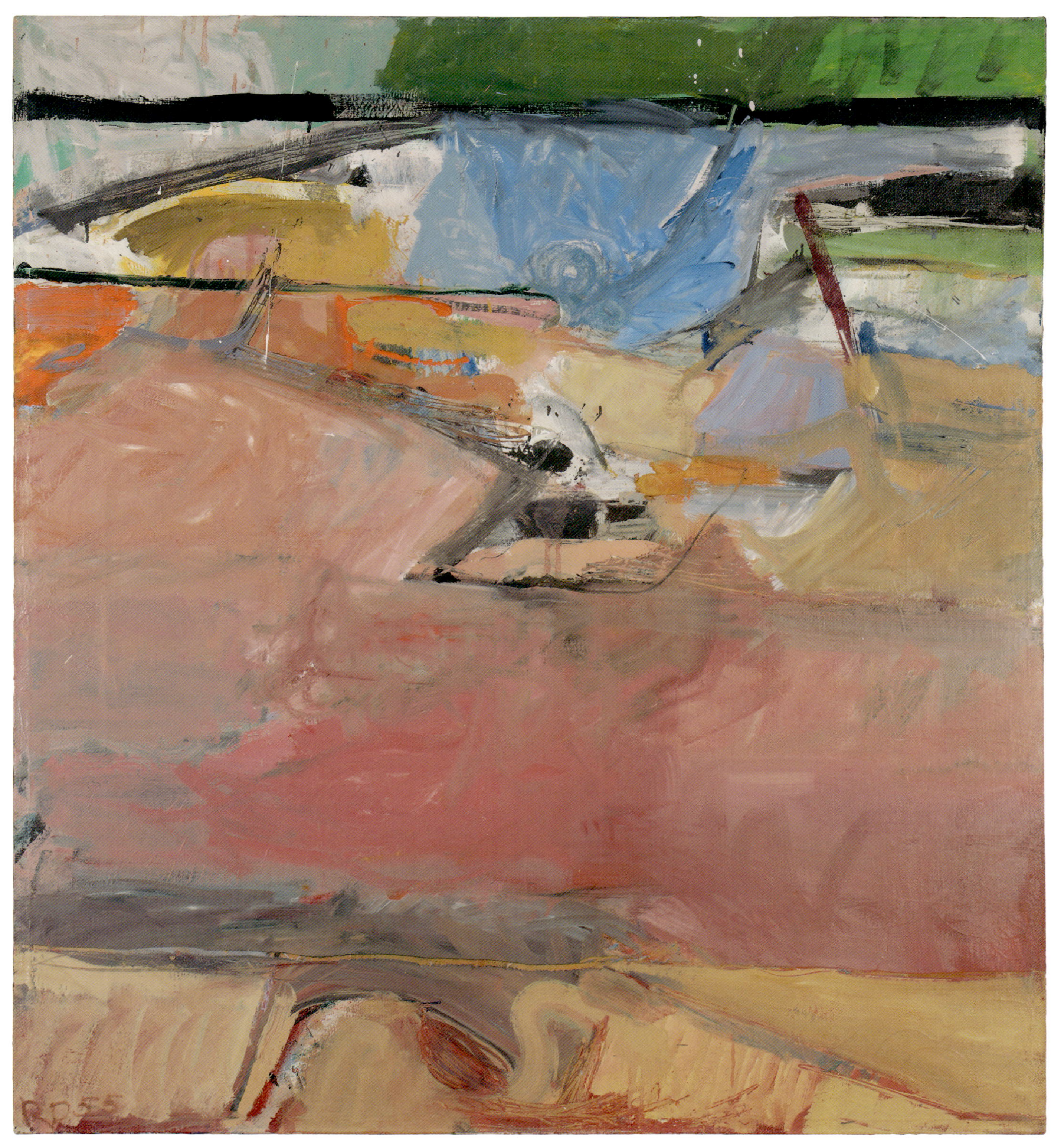

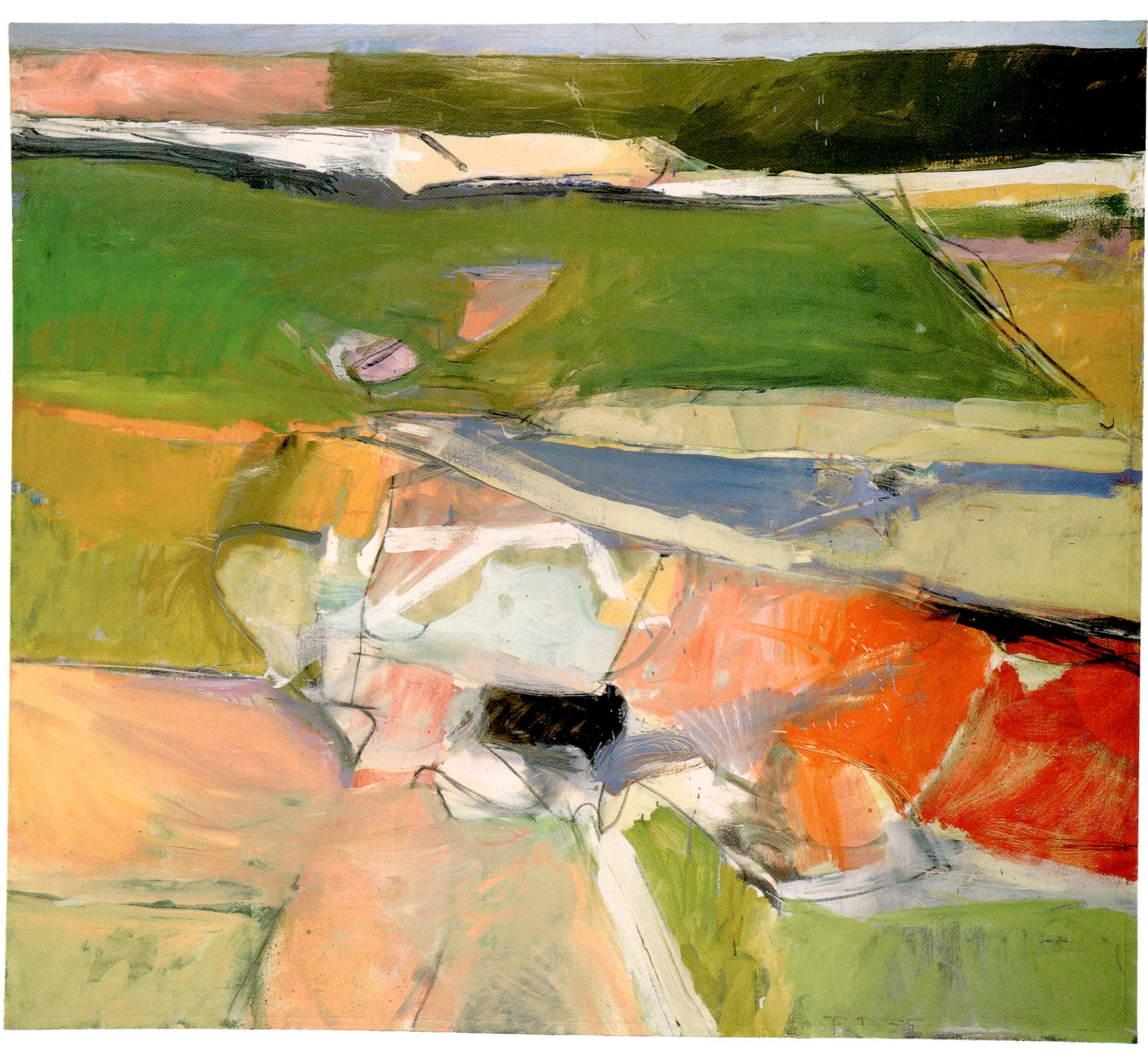

27. *Berkeley #44*, 1955
Oil on canvas, 59 x 64 in. (149.9 x 162.6 cm)
Private collection [1124]

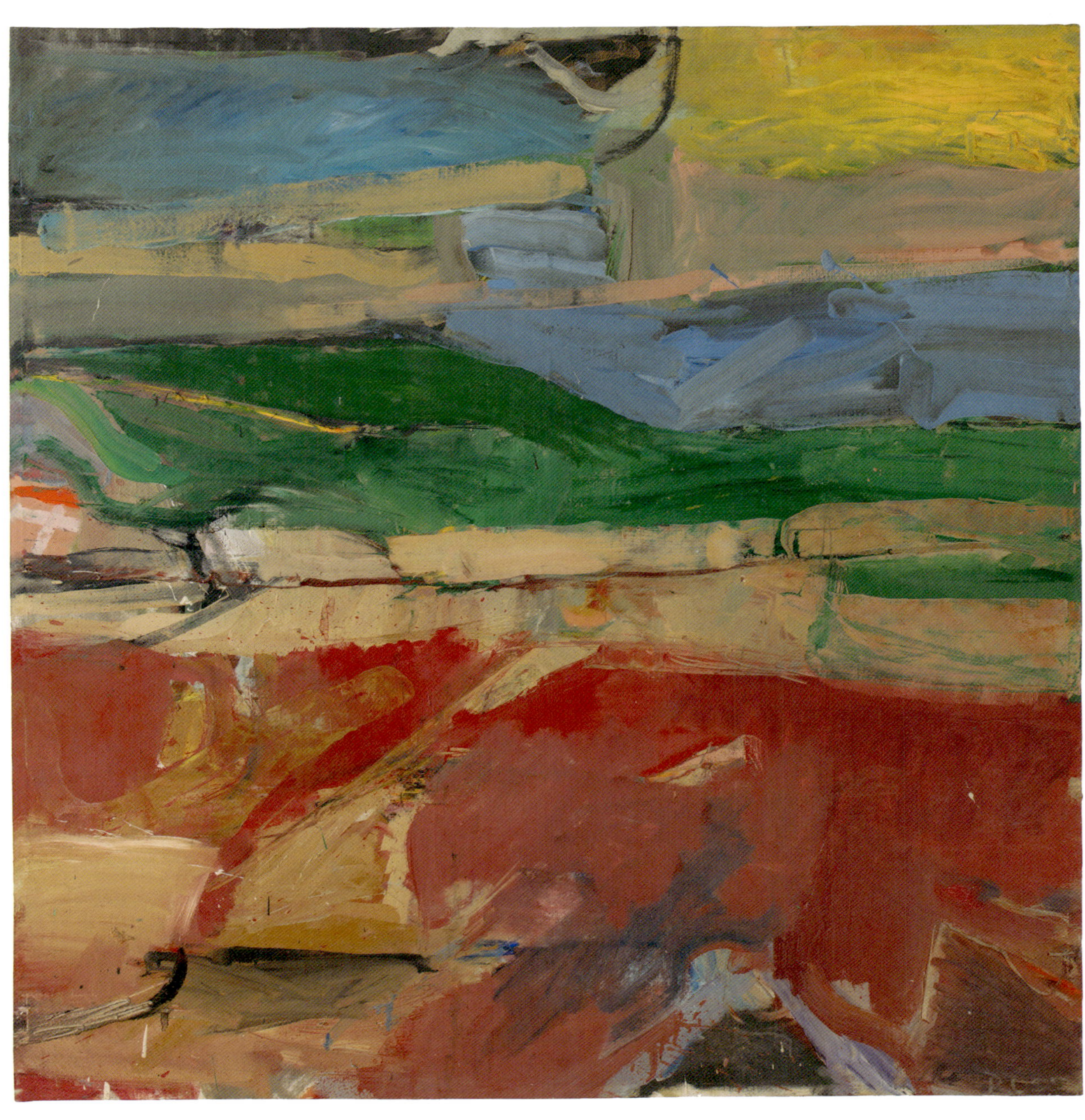

28. *Berkeley #32*, 1955
Oil on canvas, 59 x 57 in. (149.9 x 144.8 cm)
Private collection [1131]

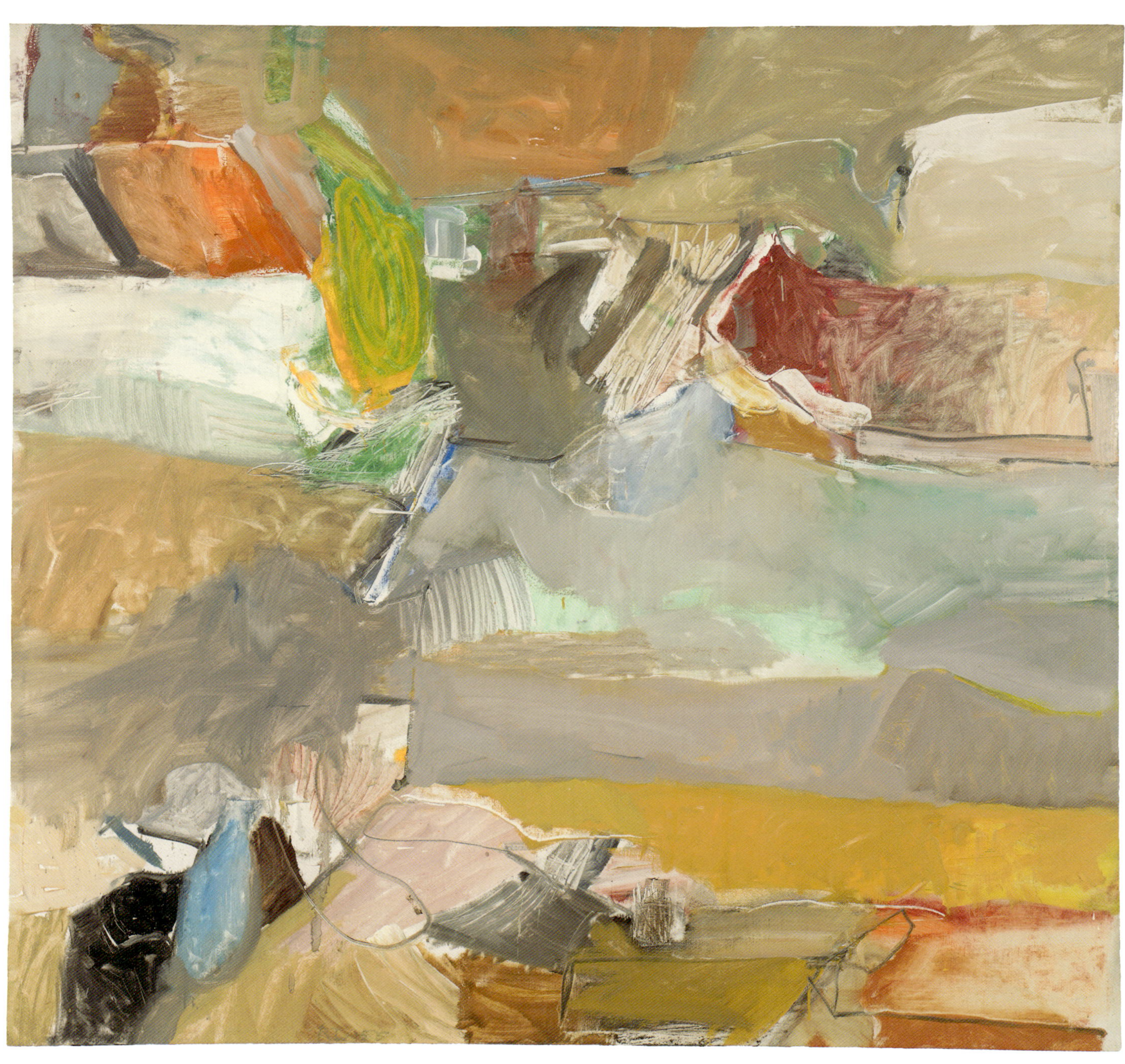

29. *Berkeley #46*, 1955
Oil on canvas, 58 7/8 x 61 7/8 in. (149.5 x 157.2 cm)
The Museum of Modern Art, New York, gift of Mr. and Mrs. Gifford Phillips, 188.1973 [1142]

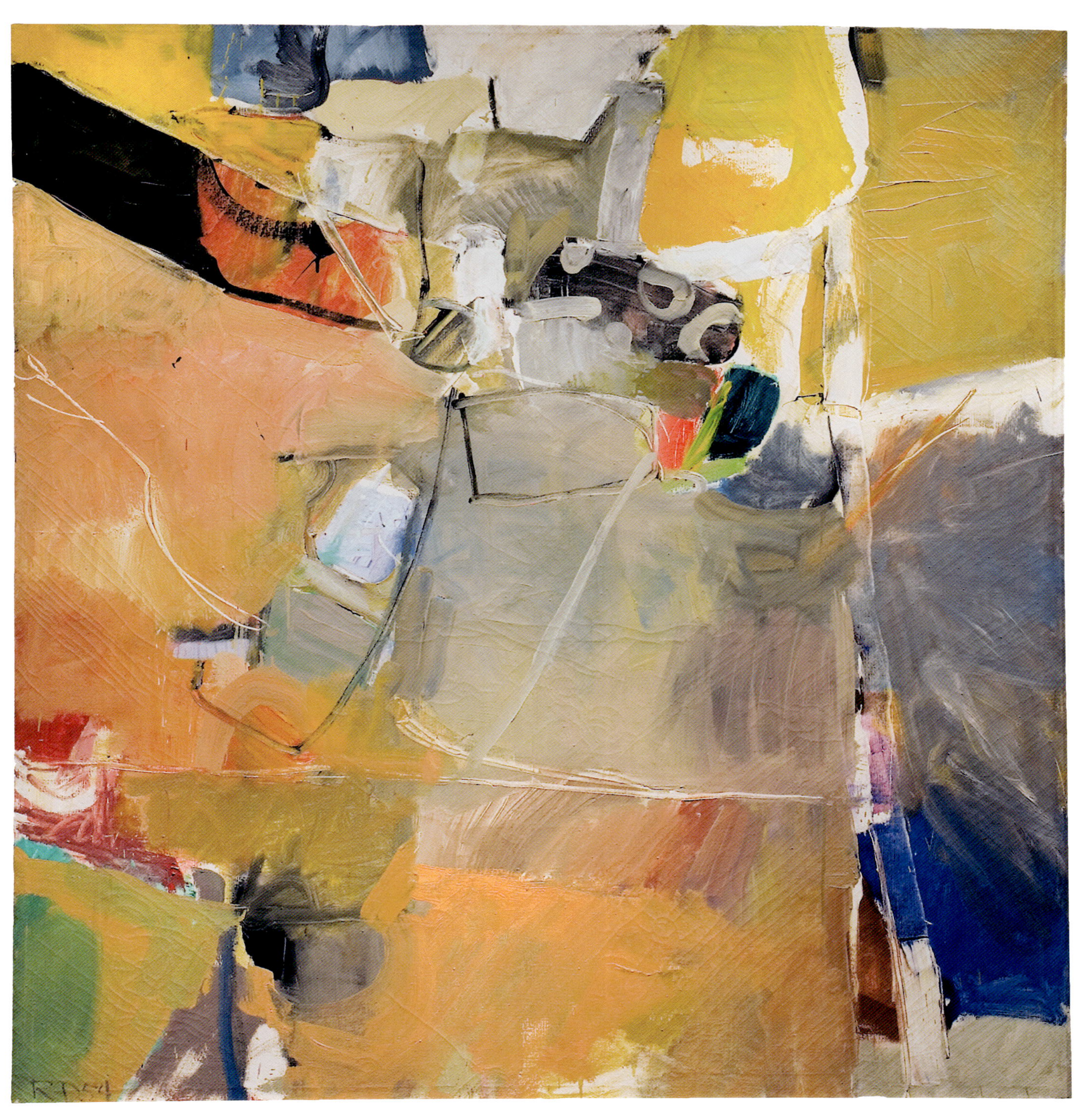

30. *Berkeley #19*, 1954
Oil on canvas, $59\ ^1/_2$ x 57 in. (151.1 x 144.8 cm)
University of Arizona Museum of Art, Tucson, gift of Gloria Vanderbilt, American Federation of Arts, 1962.16.1 [1116]

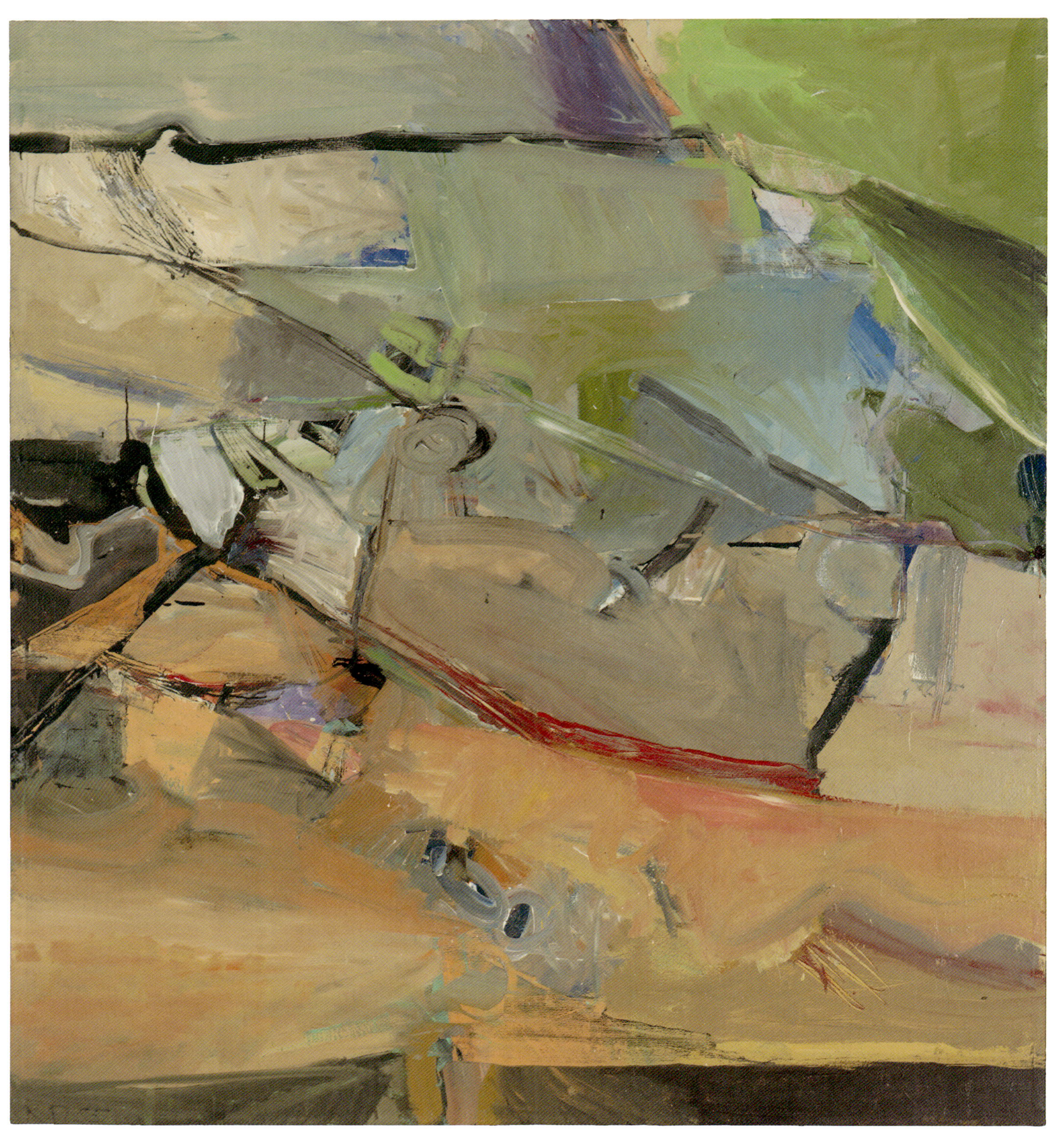

31. *Berkeley #38*, 1955
Oil on canvas, 63 ¾ x 58 ¾ in. (161.9 x 149.2 cm)
Carnegie Museum of Art, Pittsburgh, gift of Mr. and Mrs. Sidney M. Feldman, 64.9 [1136]

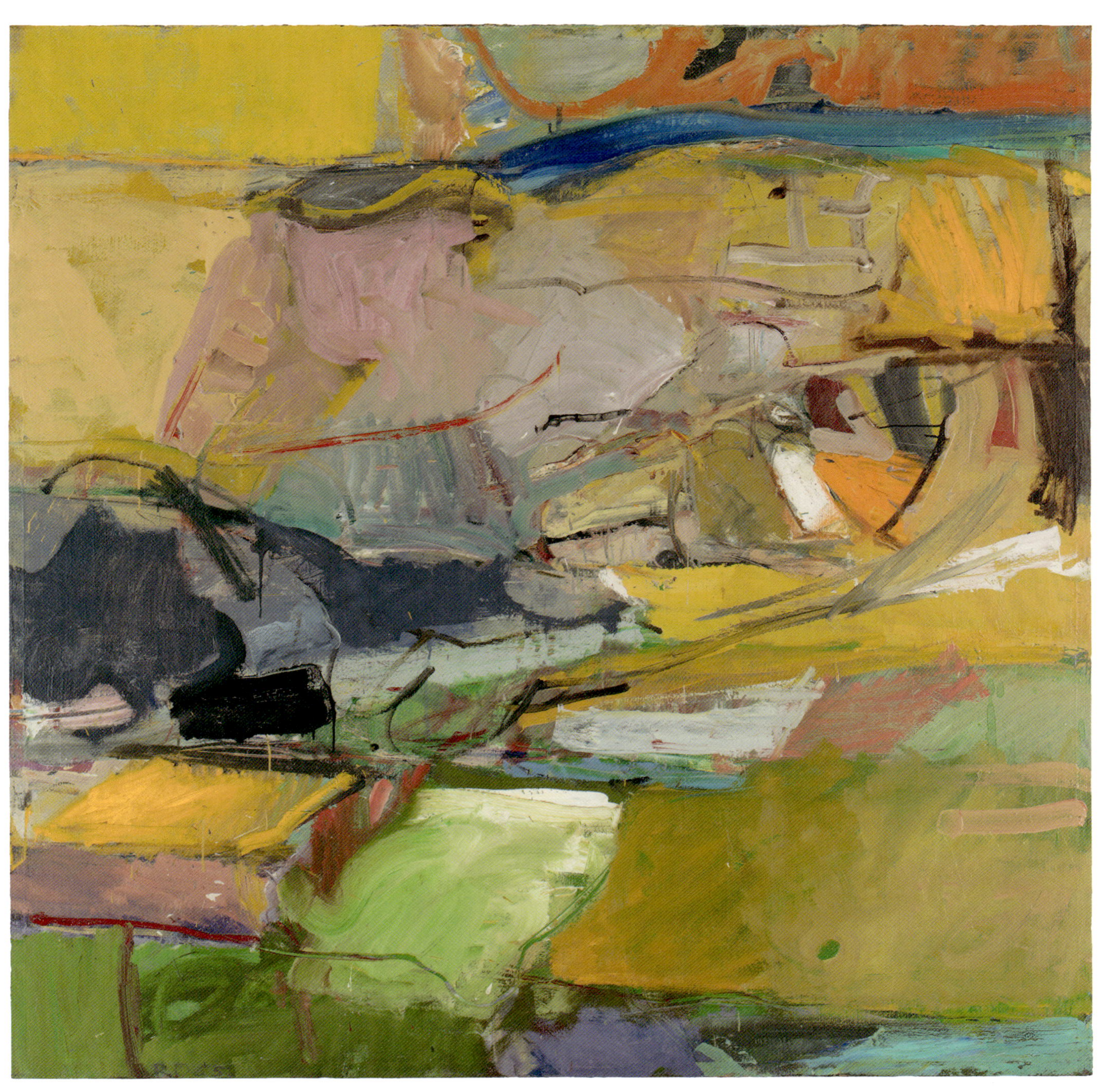

32. *Berkeley #57*, 1955
Oil on canvas, 58 3/4 x 58 3/4 in. (149.2 x 149.2 cm)
San Francisco Museum of Modern Art, bequest of Joseph M. Bransten in memory of Ellen Hart Bransten, 80.423 [1149]

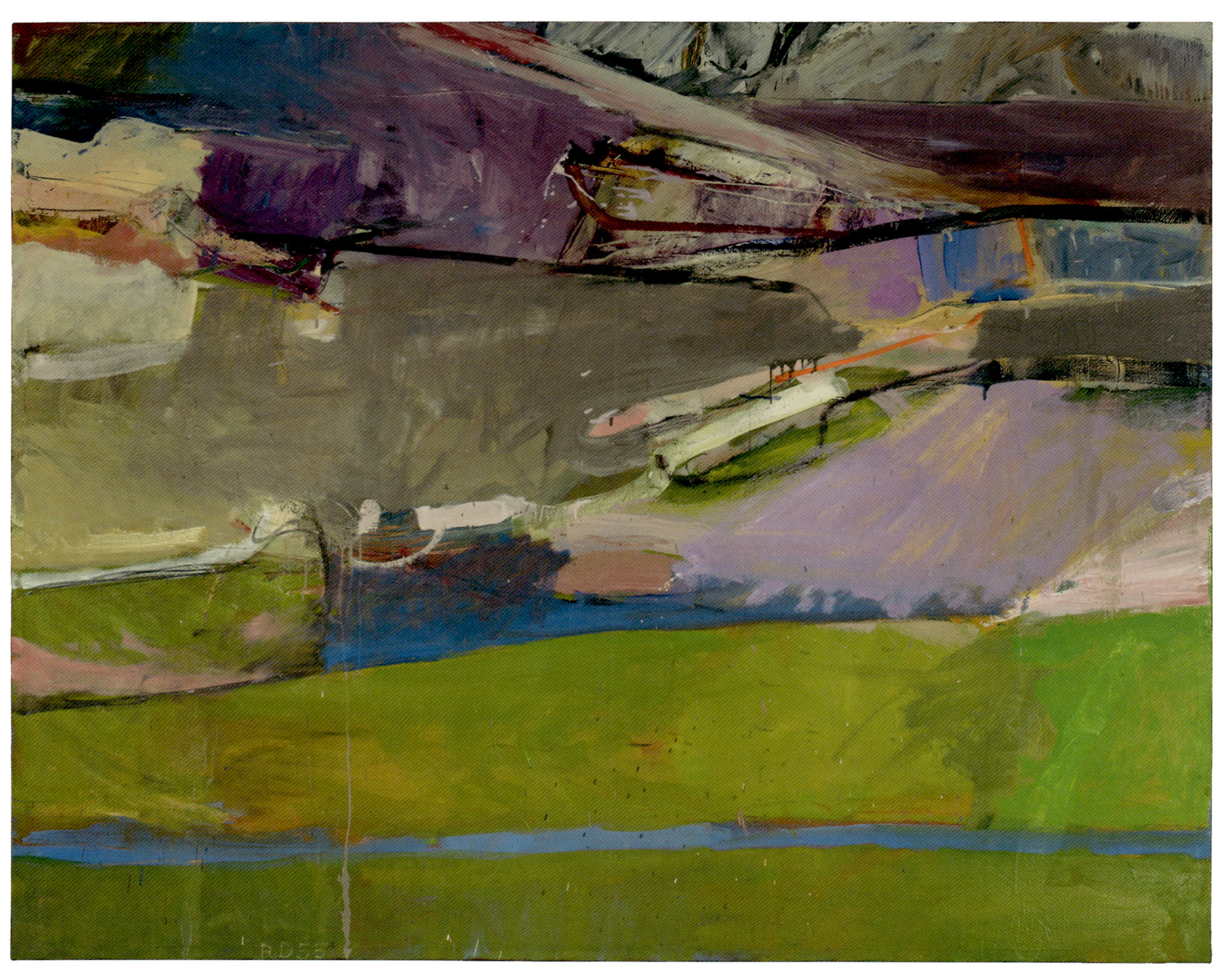

33. *Berkeley #56*, 1955
Oil on canvas, 58 x 72 in. (147.3 x 182.9 cm)
Private collection [4092]

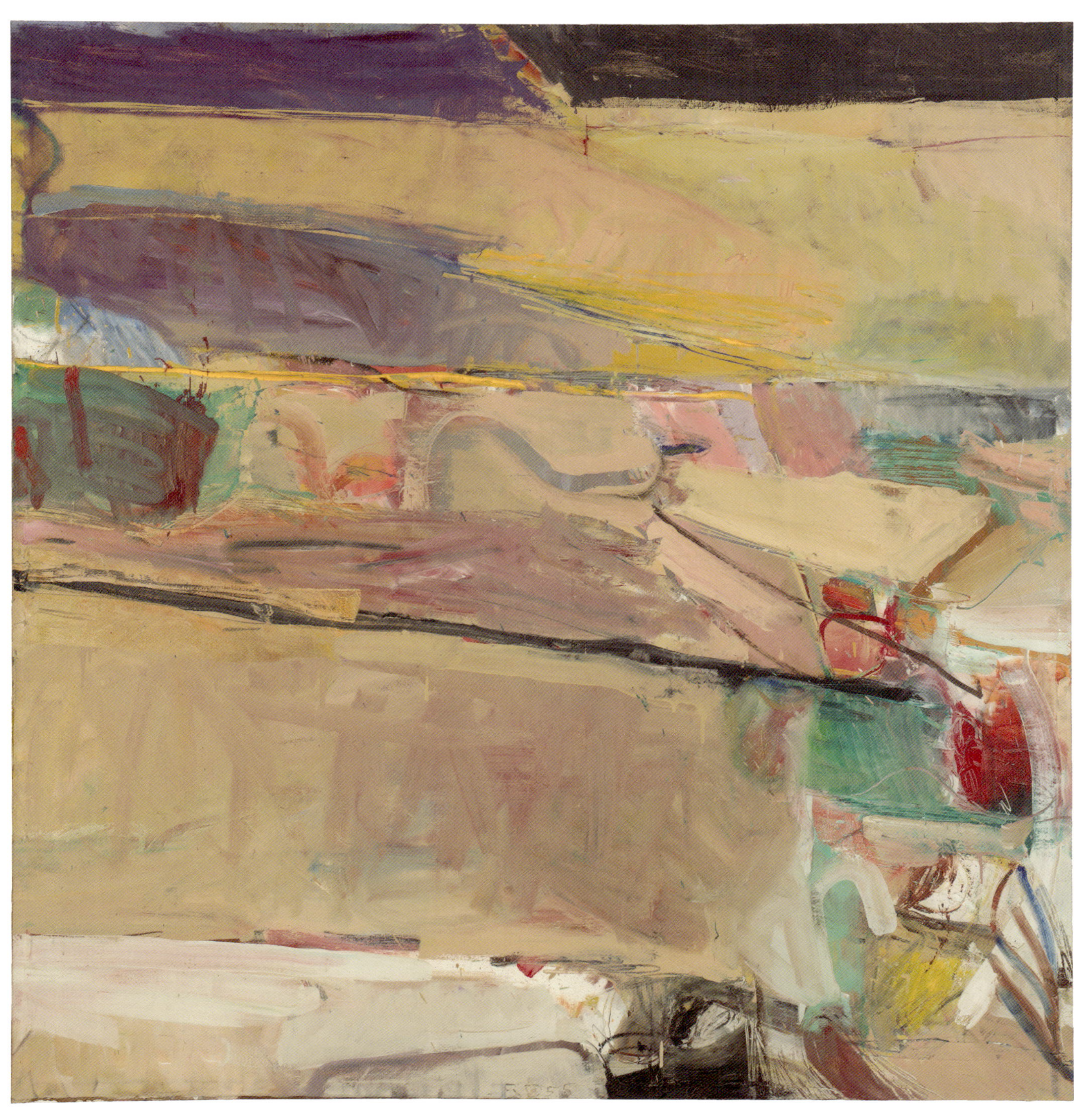

34. *Berkeley #54*, 1955
Oil on canvas, 61 1/4 x 58 5/8 in. (155.6 x 148.9 cm)
Albright-Knox Art Gallery, Buffalo, New York, gift of Mr. and Mrs. David K. Anderson to The Martha Jackson Collection, 1977, 1977:8 [1147]

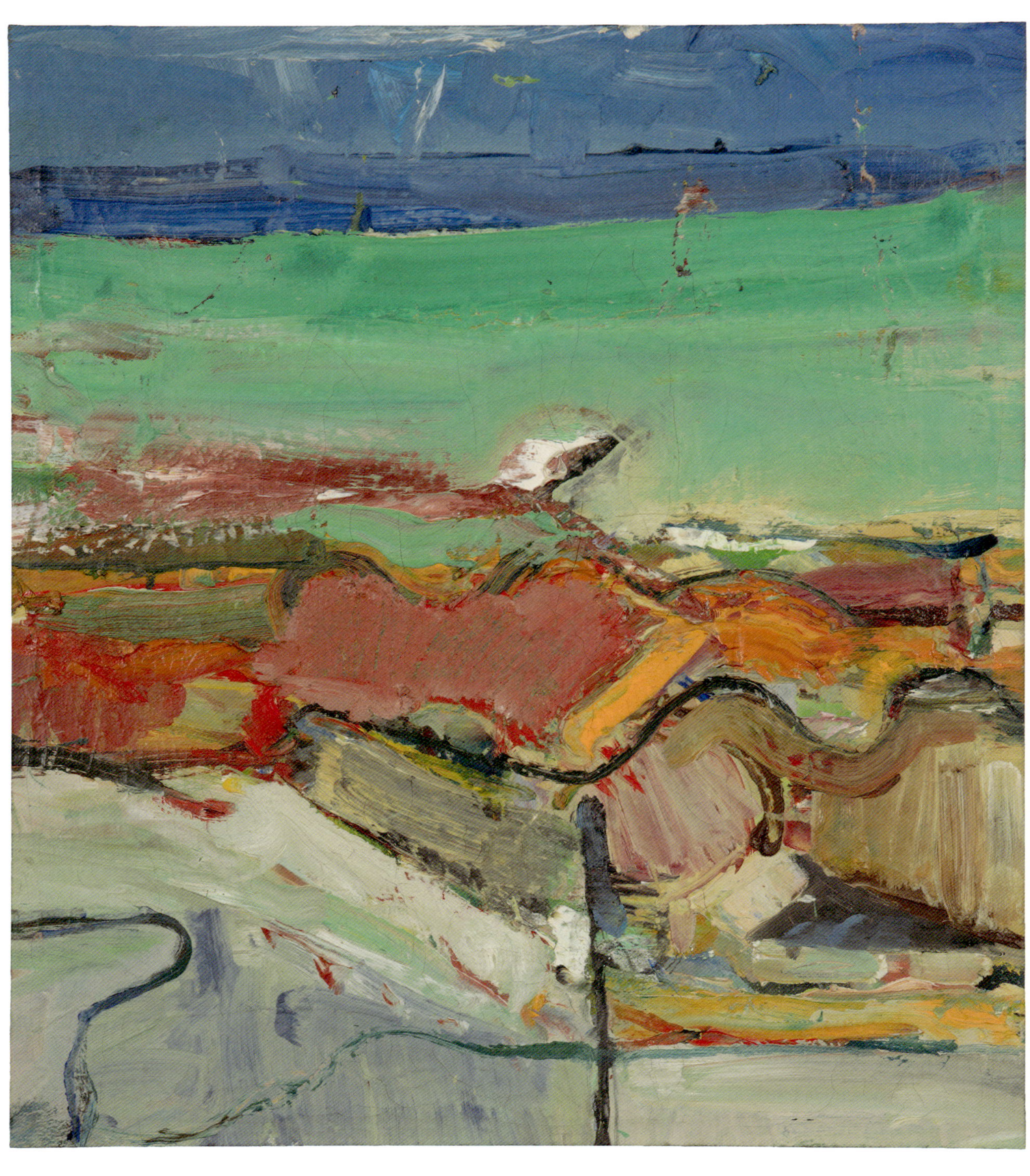

35. *Berkeley*, 1955
Oil on canvas, 24 1/8 x 21 1/8 in. (61.3 x 53.7 cm)
Private collection [1123]

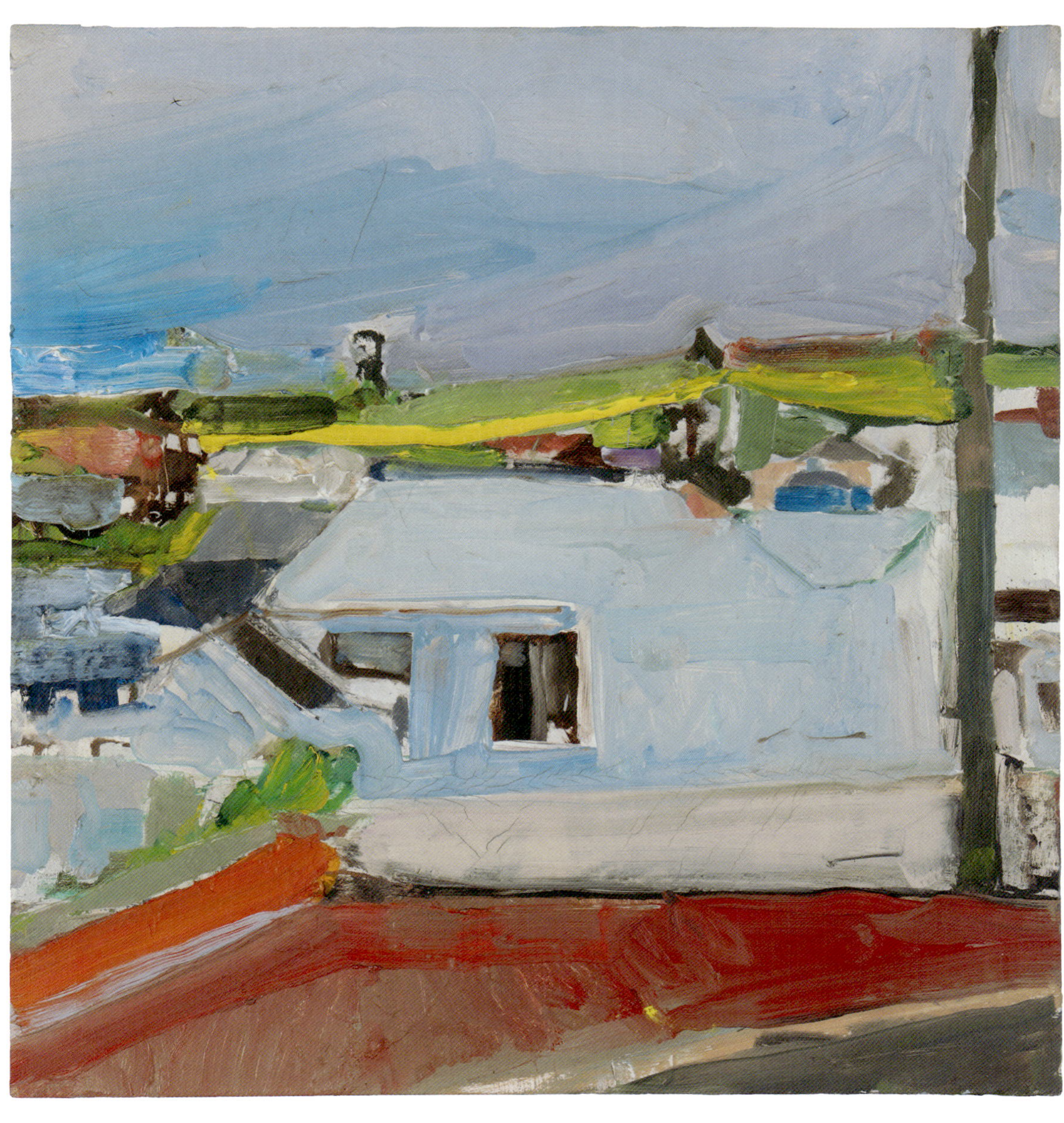

36. *Chabot Valley*, 1955
Oil on canvas, 19 1/2 x 18 3/4 in. (49.5 x 47.6 cm)
Collection of Christopher Diebenkorn [1154]

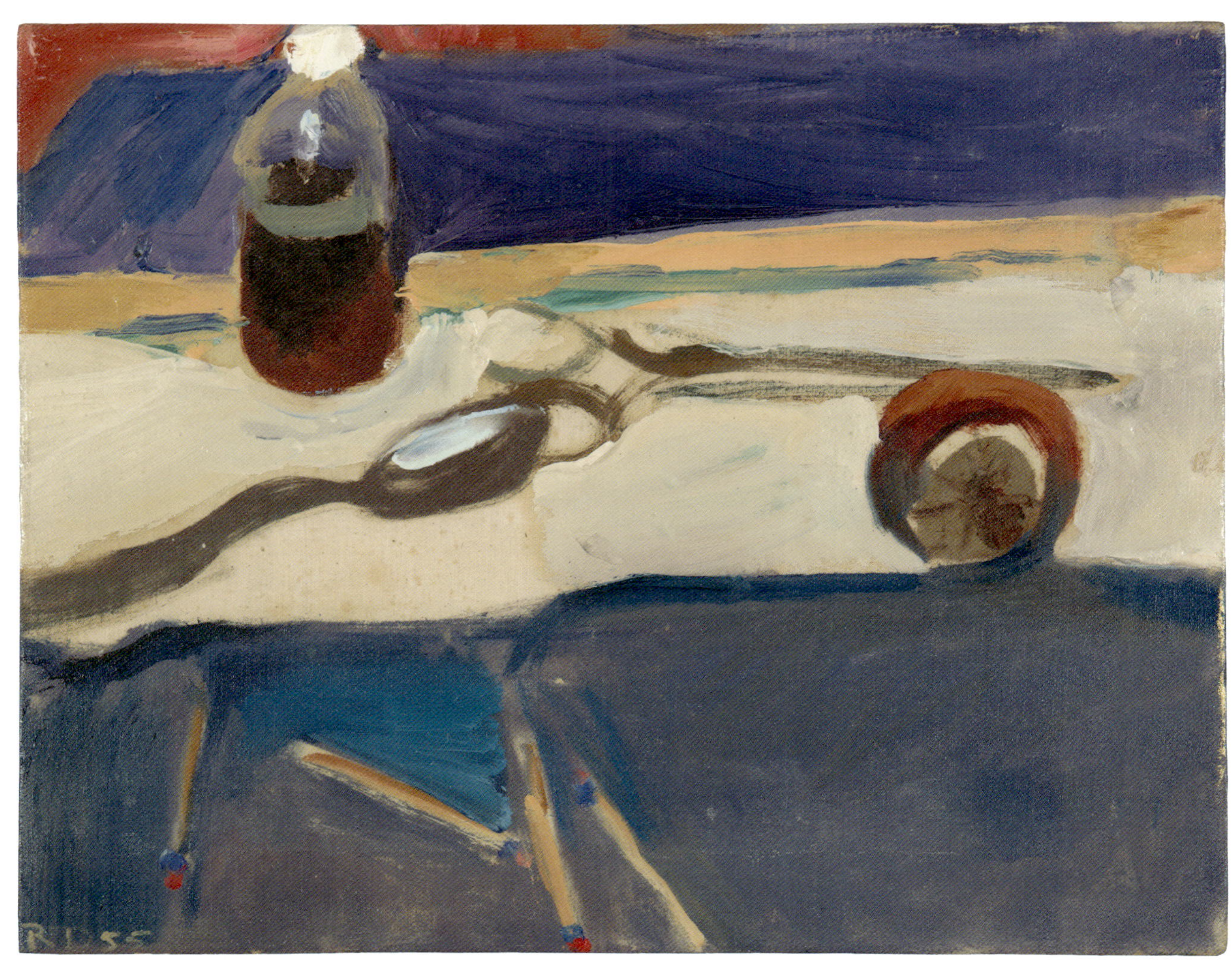

37. *Untitled*, 1955
Oil on canvas, 12 5/8 x 16 in. (32.1 x 40.6 cm)
The Thiebaud Family Collection [3795]

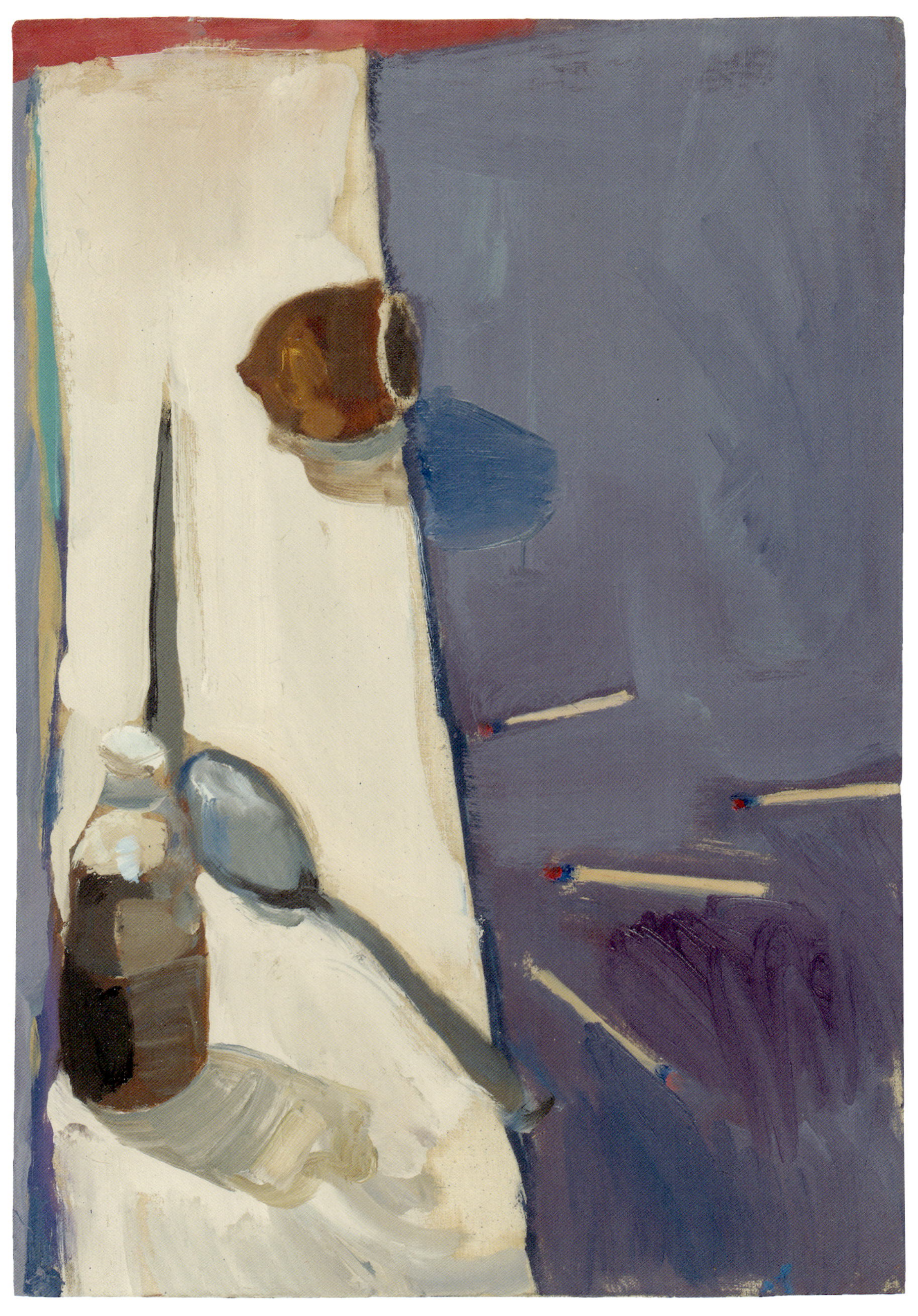

38. *Still Life with Matches*, 1955
Oil on canvas, 20 1/2 x 14 1/4 in. (52.1 x 36.2 cm)
Private collection [2394]

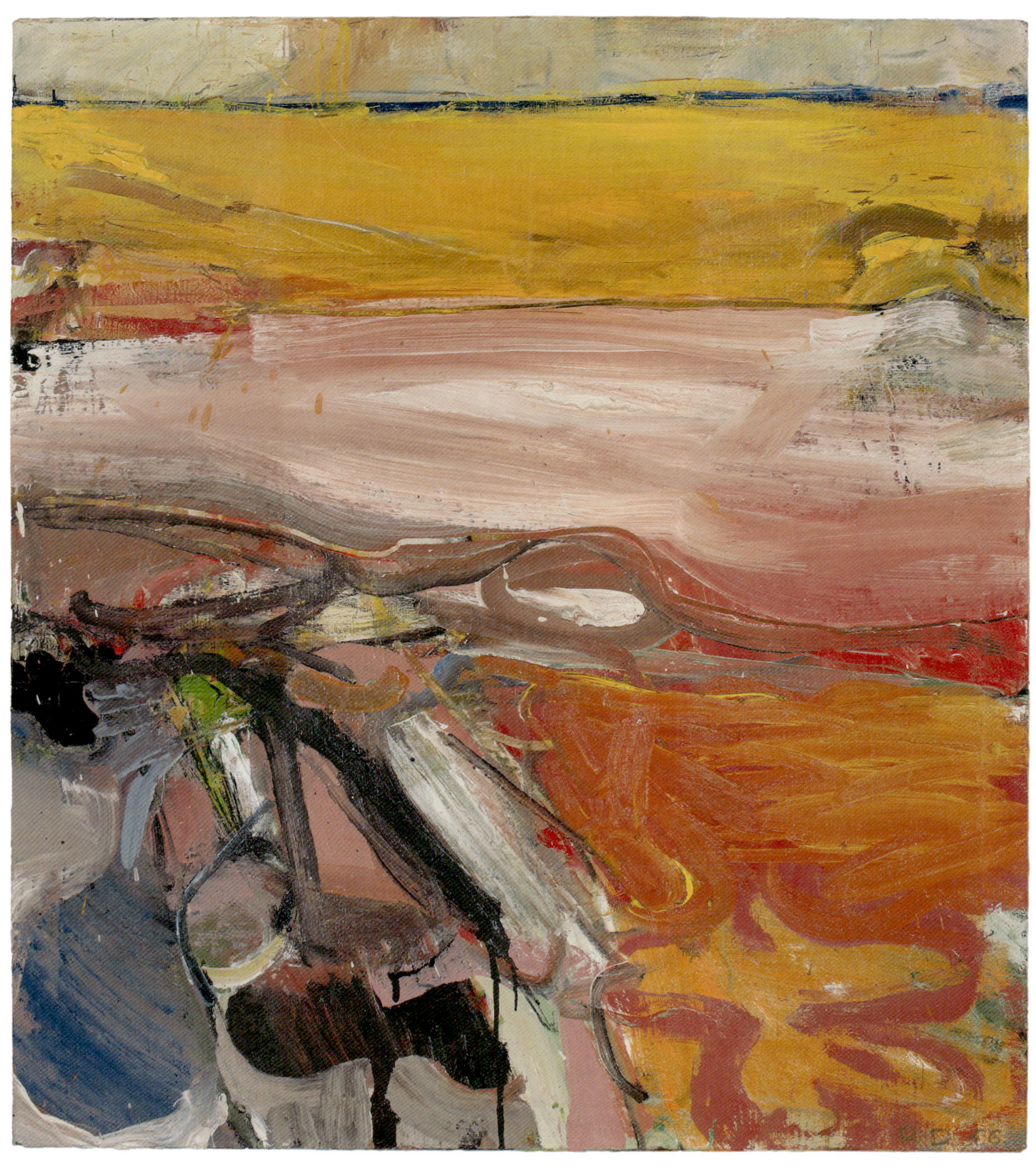

39. *Berkeley #66*, 1956
Oil on canvas, 41 3/4 x 36 1/2 in. (106 x 92.7 cm)
Collection of Jack and Frances Levy [1153]

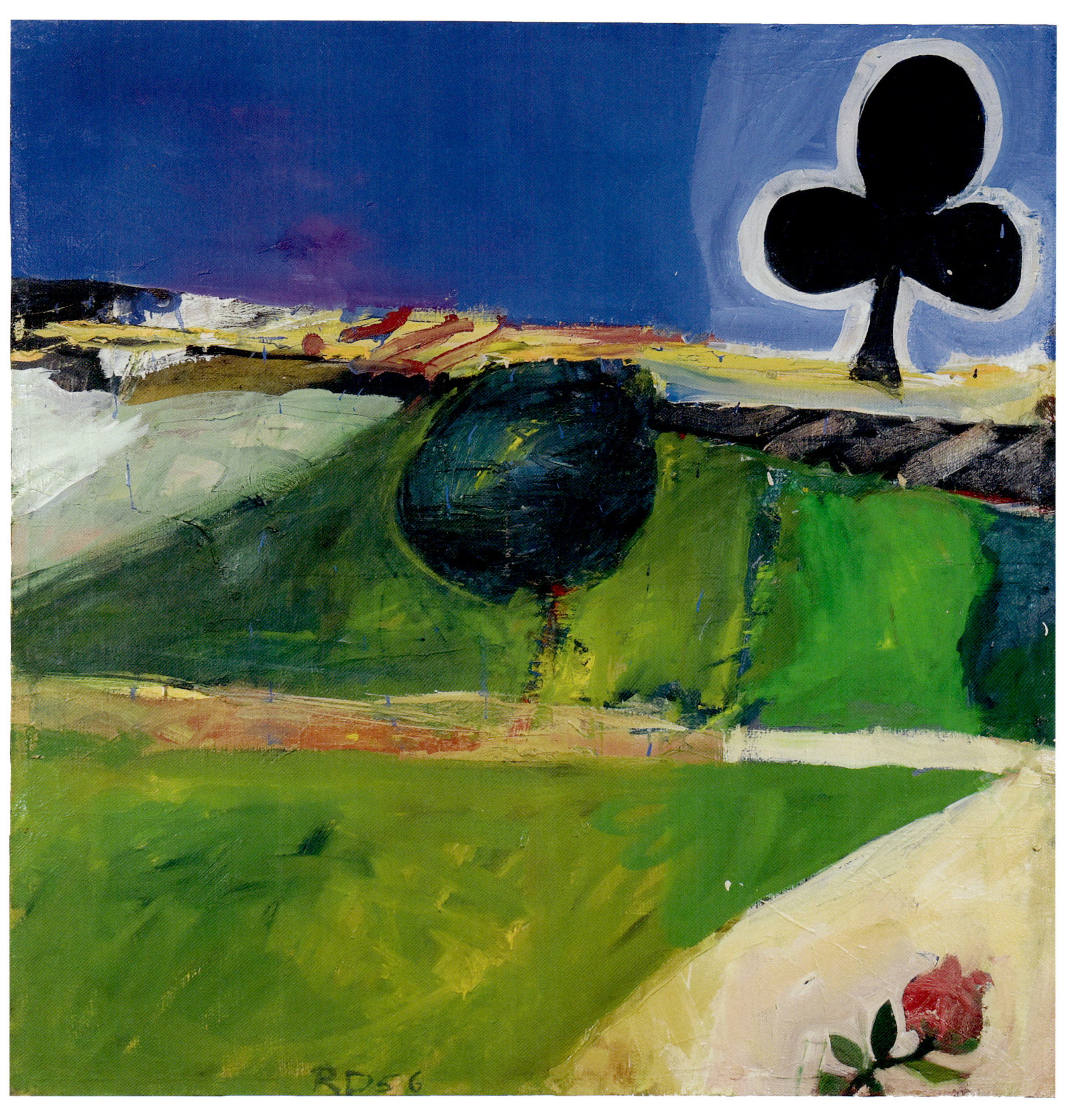

40. *Landscape with Figure*, 1956
Oil on canvas, 50 1/4 x 47 5/8 in. (127.6 x 121 cm)
Private collection [1186]

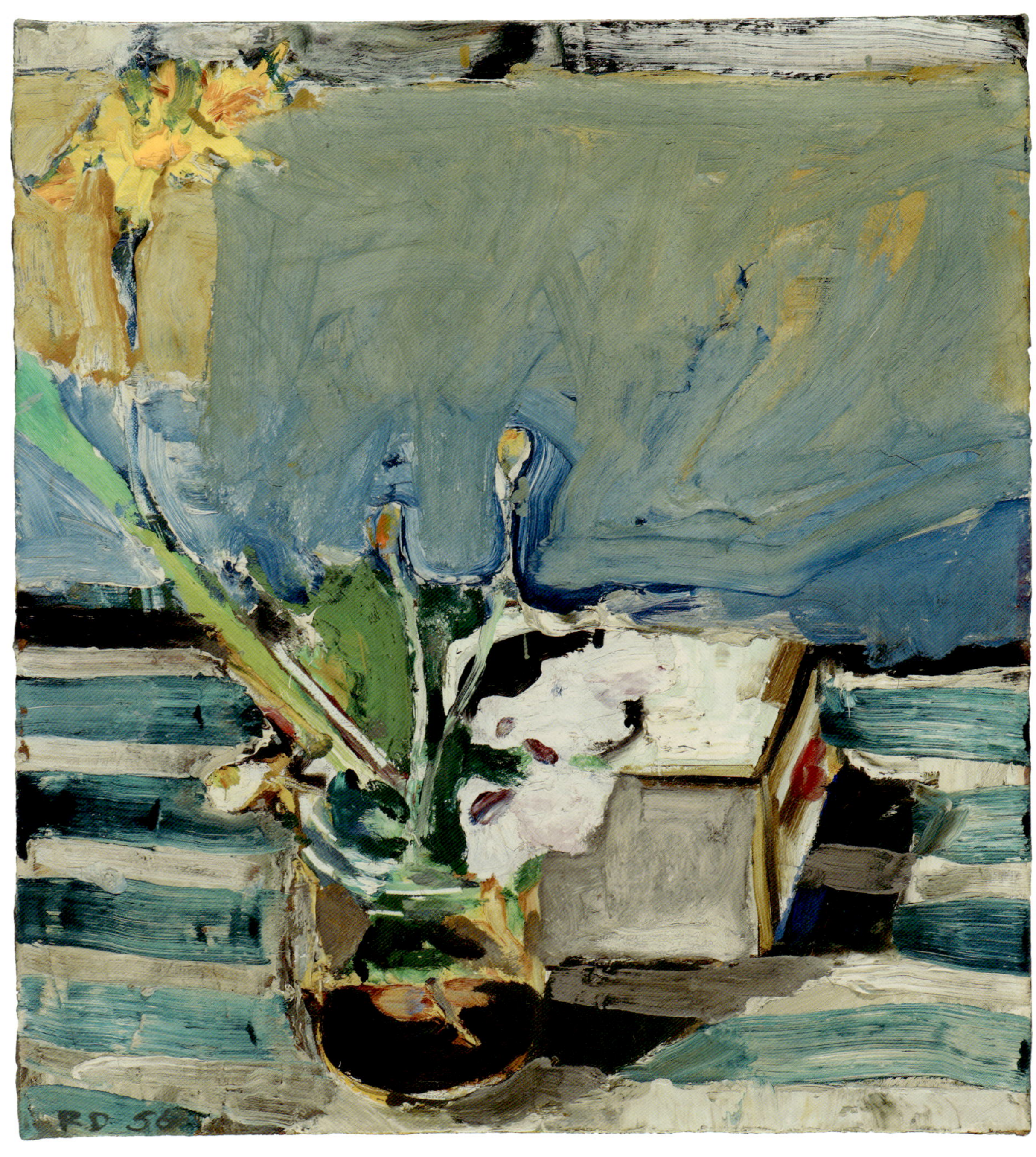

41. *Flowers and Cigar Box*, 1956
Oil on canvas, 17 3/4 x 15 5/8 in. (45.1 x 39.7 cm)
Private collection [1184]

42. *Bottles*, 1960
Oil on canvas, 34 x 26 in. (86.4 x 66 cm)
Norton Simon Museum, Pasadena, California, gift of the artist, P.1961.27 [1285]

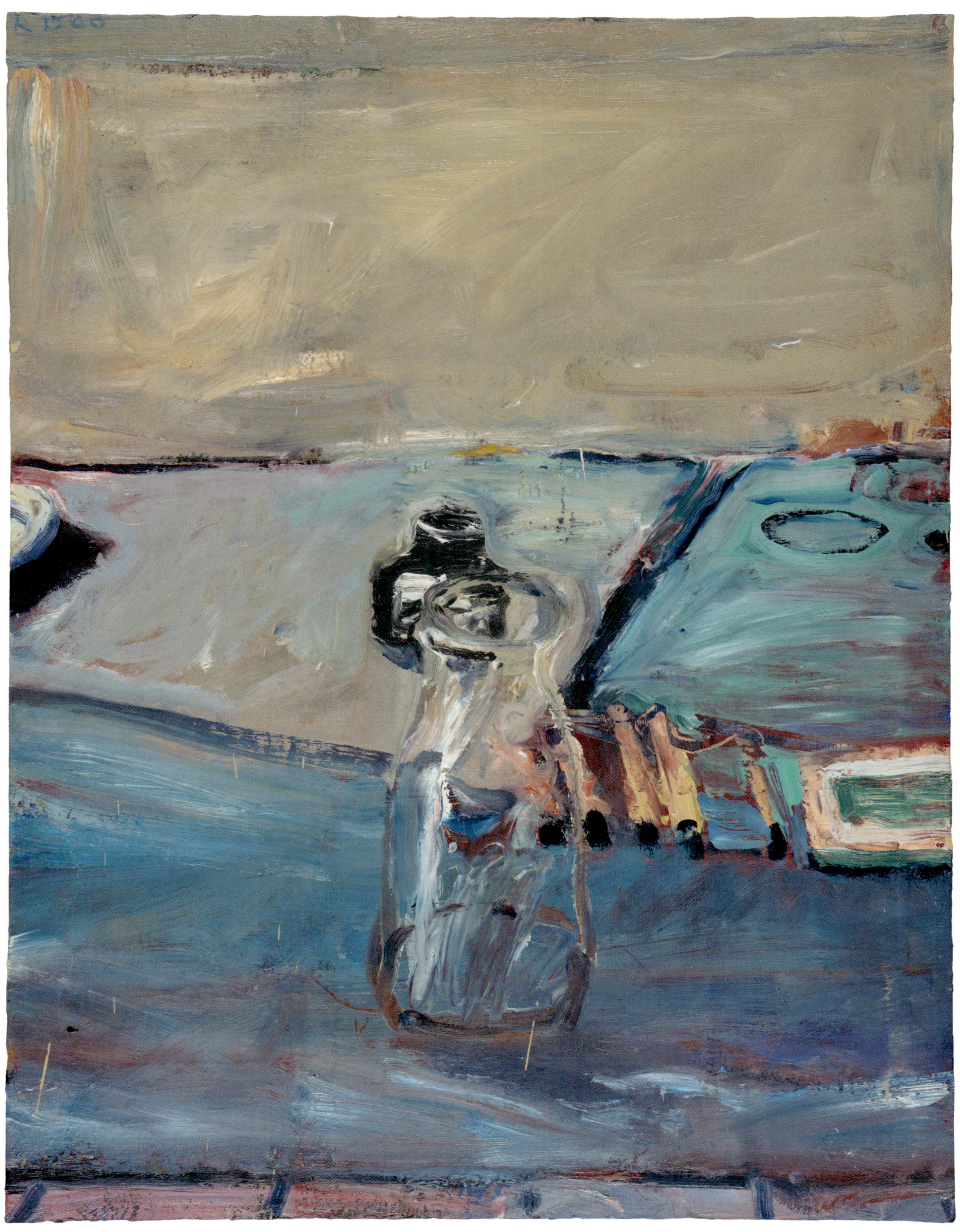

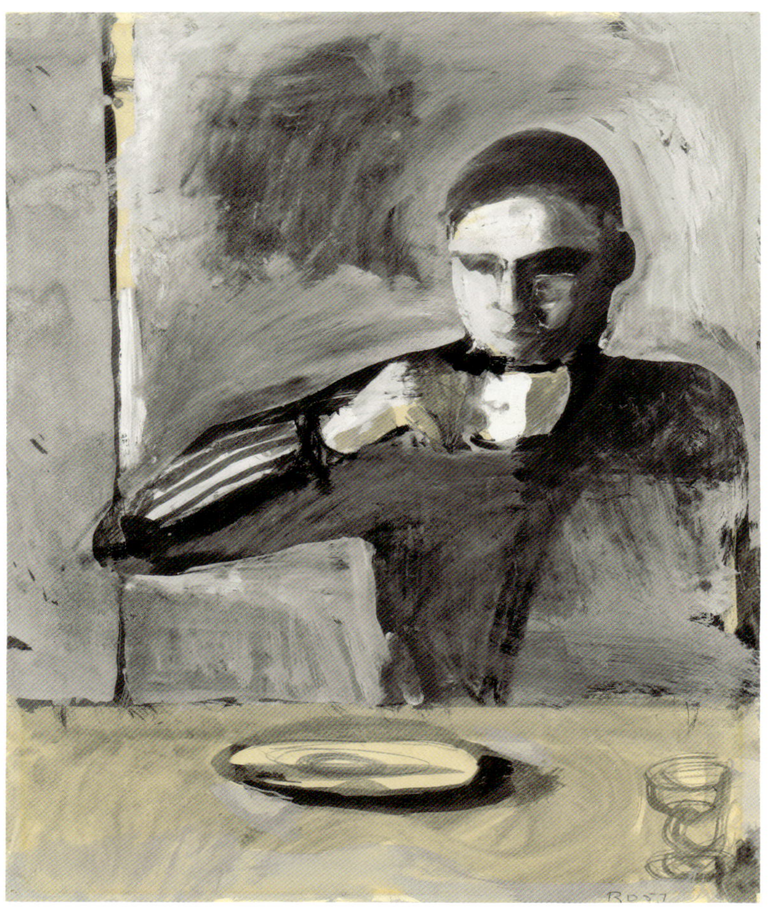

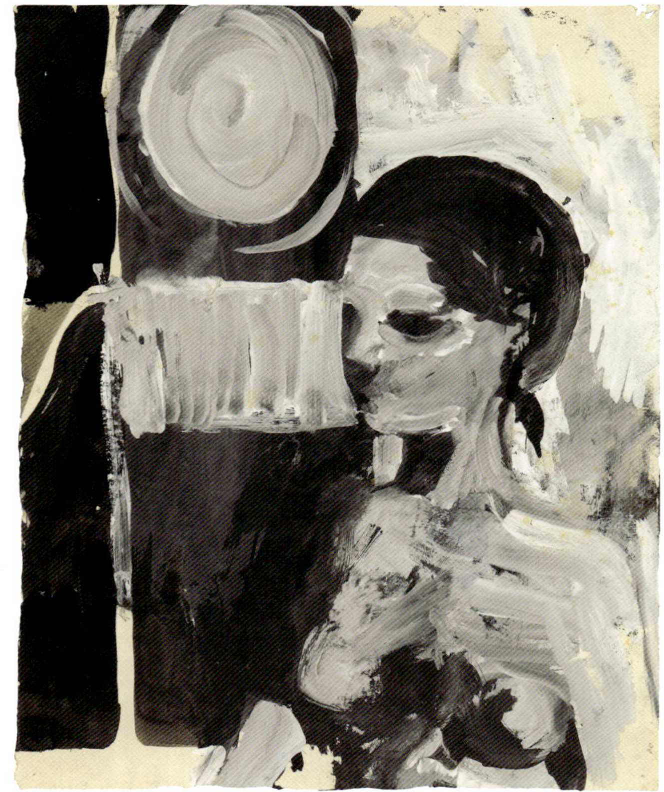

43. *The Drinker*, 1957
Gouache and graphite on paper, 16 3/4 x 14 in. (42.5 x 35.6 cm)
Yale University Art Gallery, New Haven, Connecticut, Katharine Ordway Collection, 1980.12.44 [336]

44. *Untitled*, ca. 1956–1957
Gouache and ink on paper, 12 1/2 x 9 3/4 in. (31.8 x 24.8 cm)
Private collection [738]

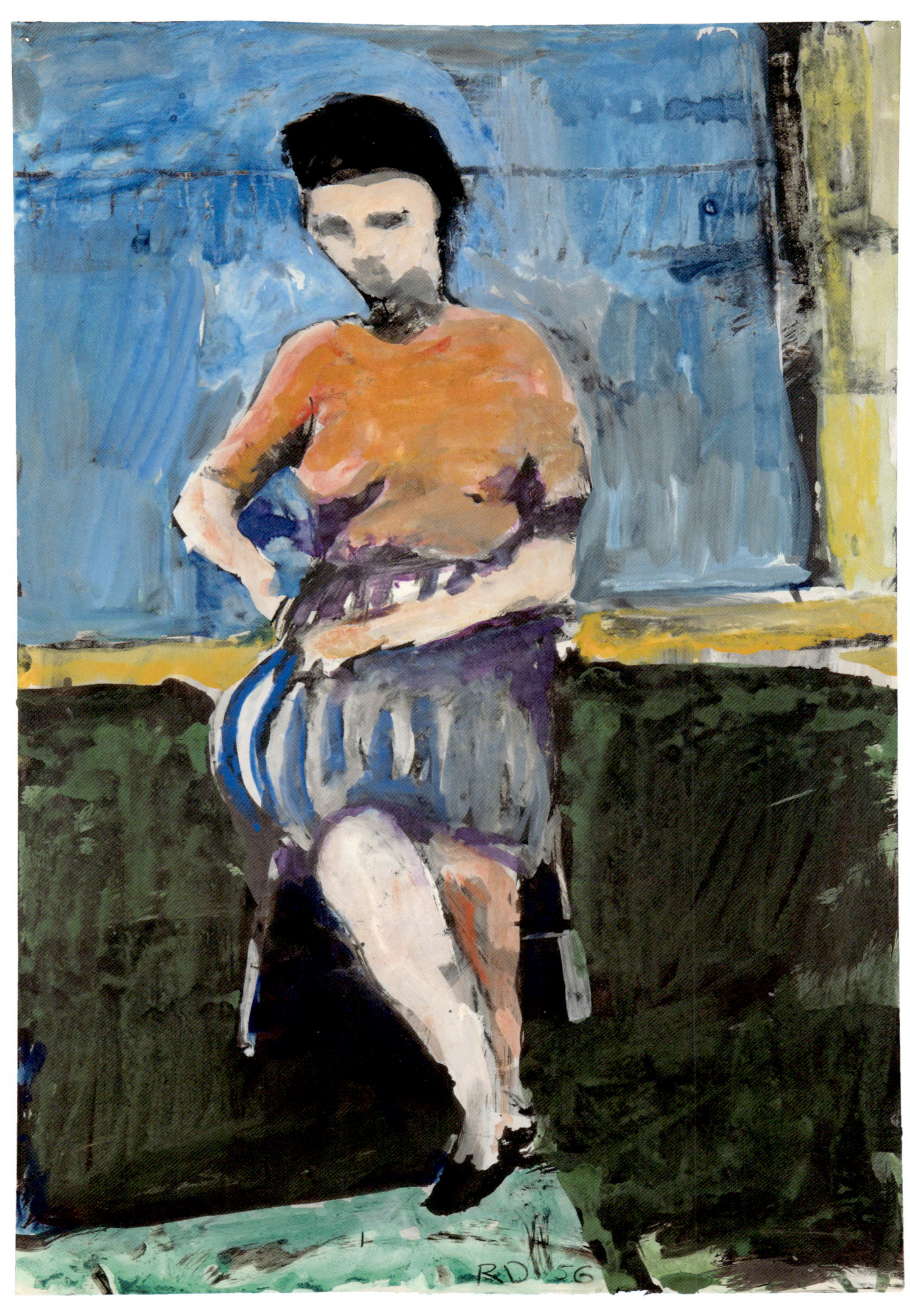

45. *Untitled*, 1956
Gouache and ink on paper, 16 x 10 7/8 in. (40.6 x 27.6 cm)
Private collection, courtesy of Acquavella Galleries [5907]

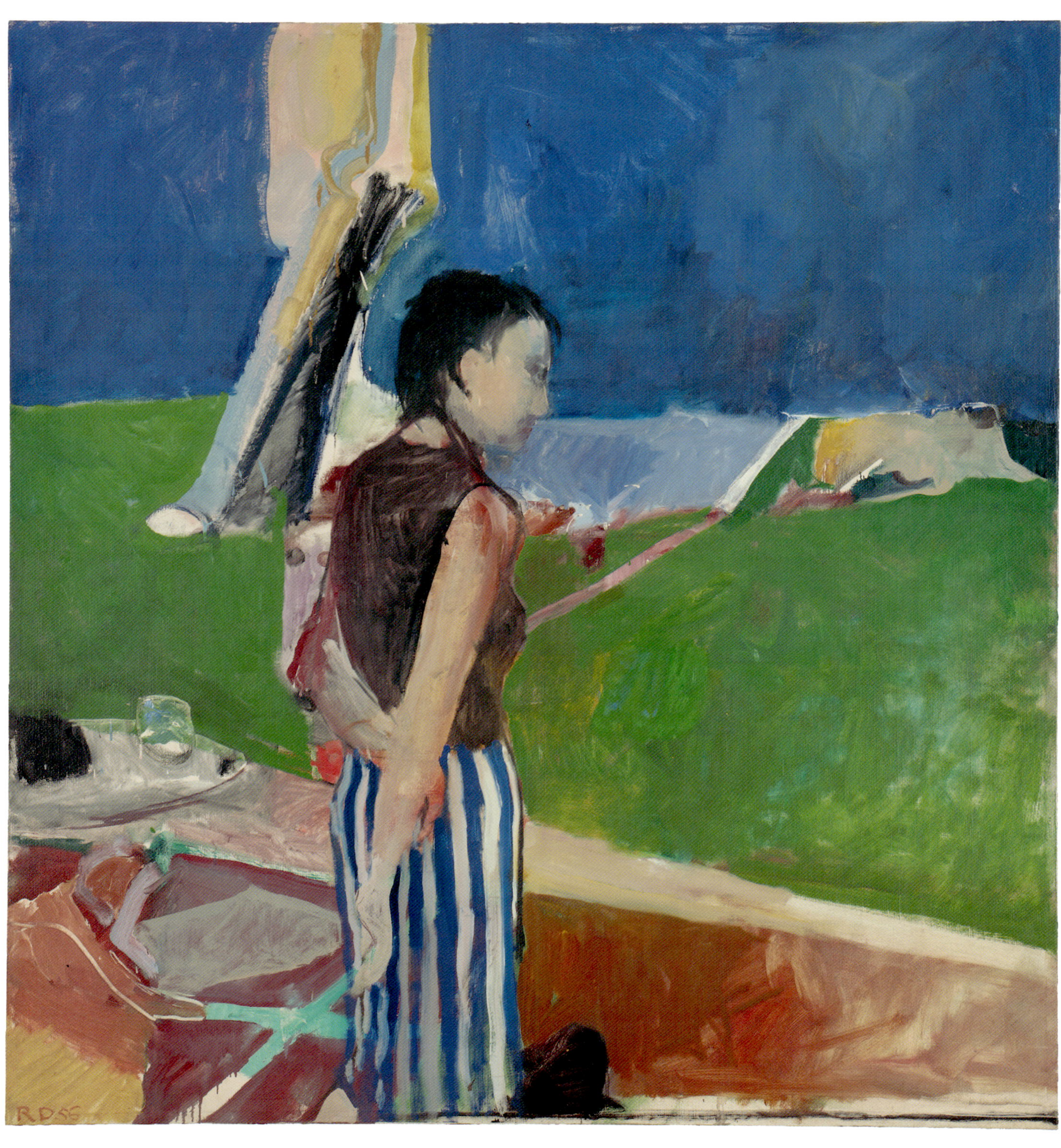

46. *Girl on a Terrace*, 1956
Oil on canvas, 70 1/2 x 65 3/8 in. (179.1 x 166.1 cm)
Neuberger Museum of Art, Purchase College, State University of New York, gift of Roy R. Neuberger, 1975.16.09 [1185]

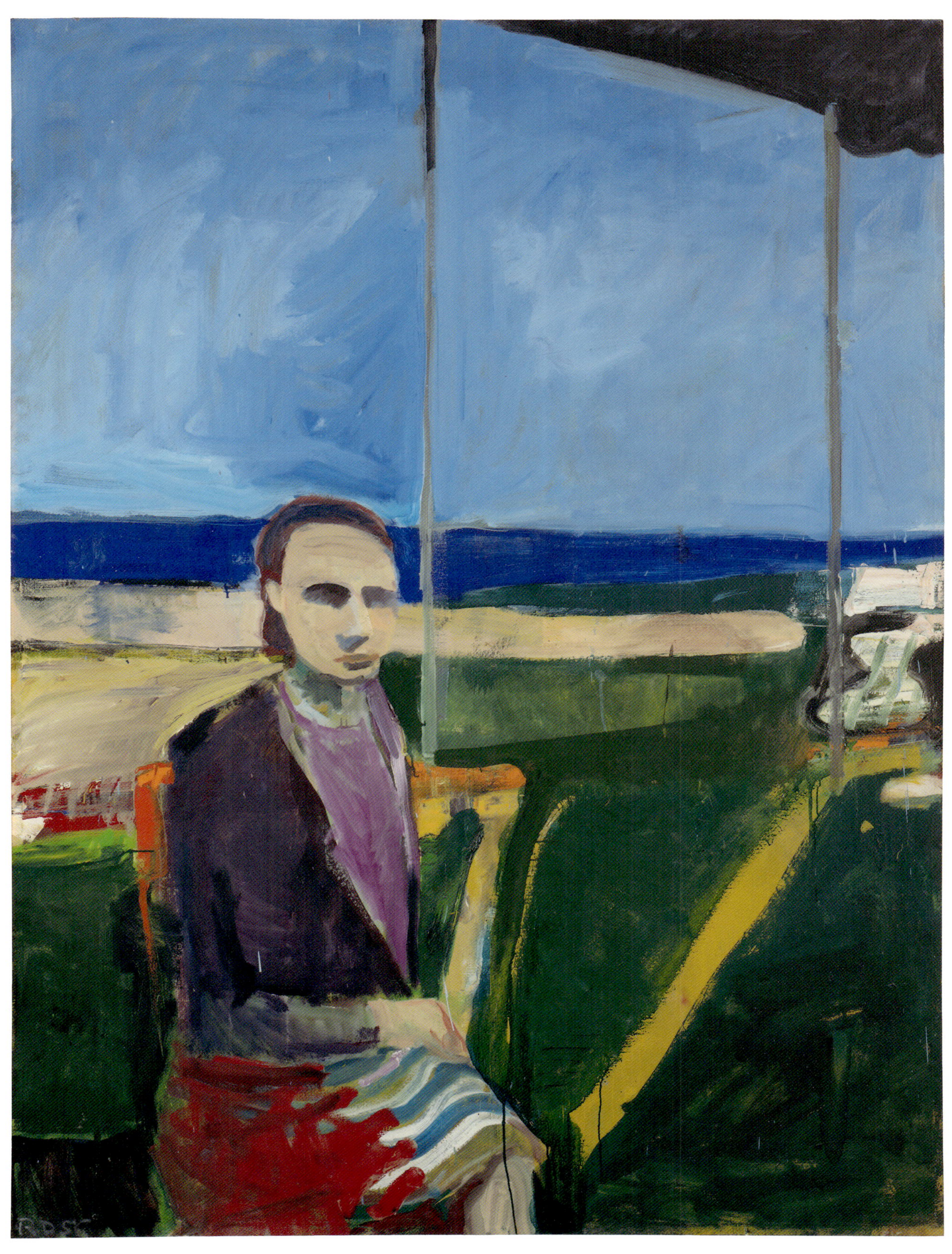

47. *Woman by the Ocean*, 1956
Oil on canvas, 79 x 59 in. (200.7 x 149.9 cm)
Collection of the Lisa and Douglas E. Goldman Family [1196]

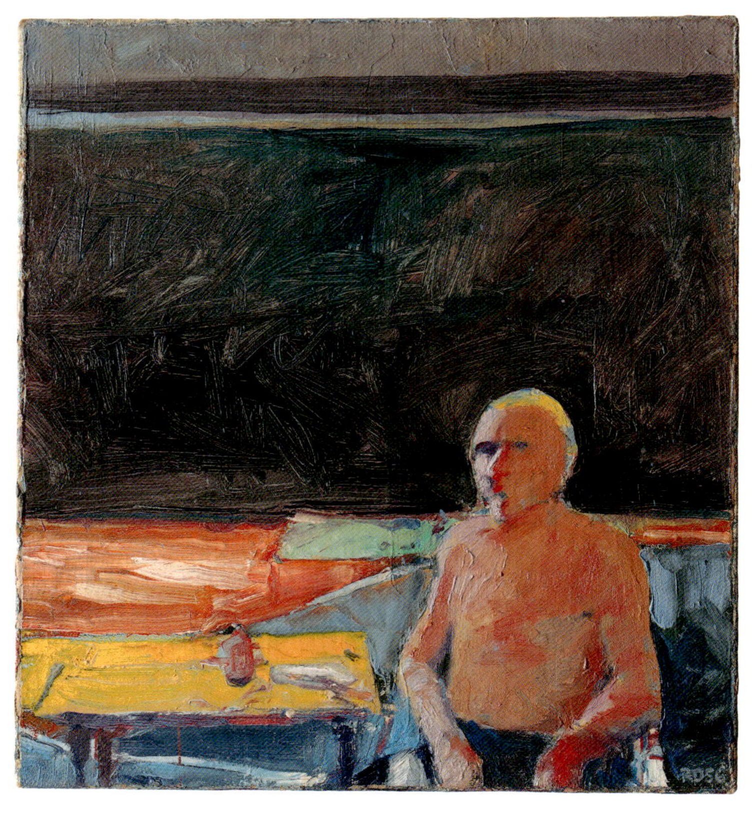
RD56

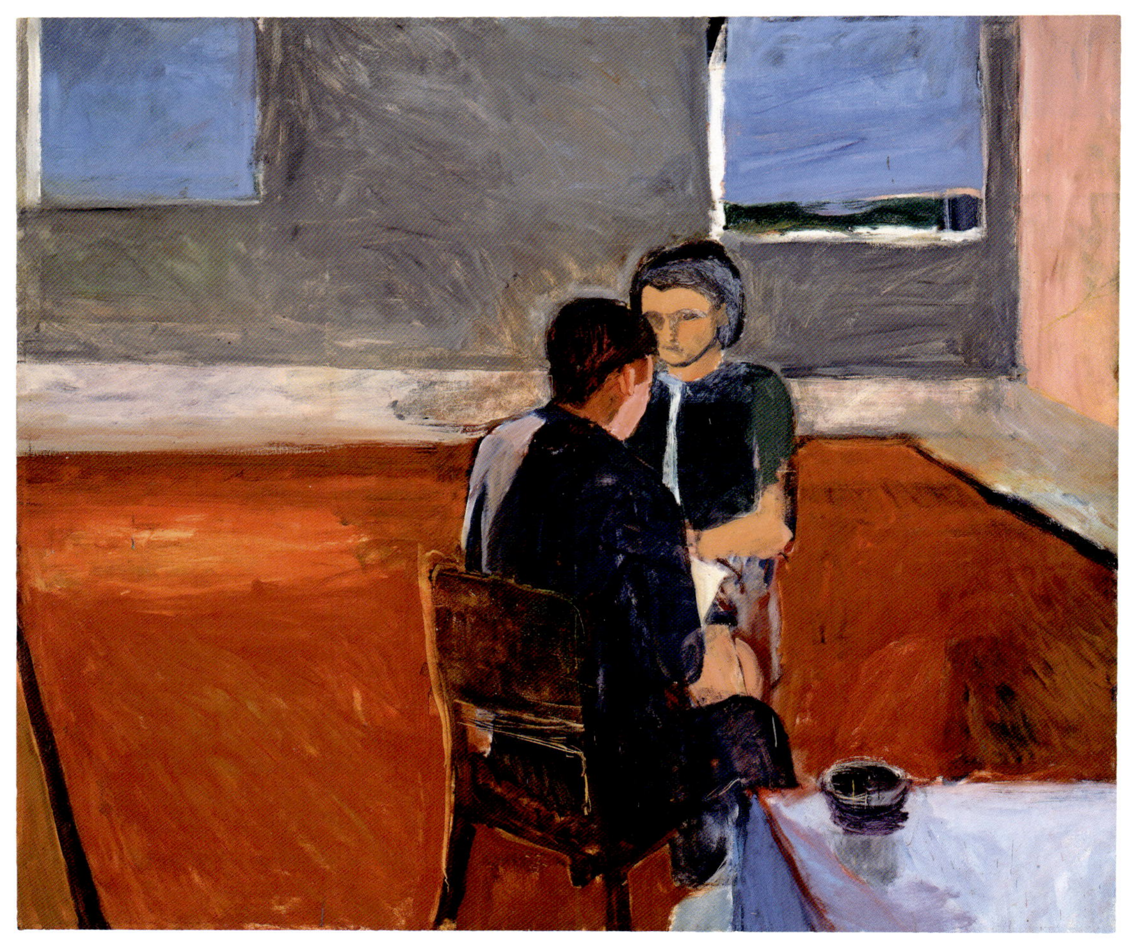

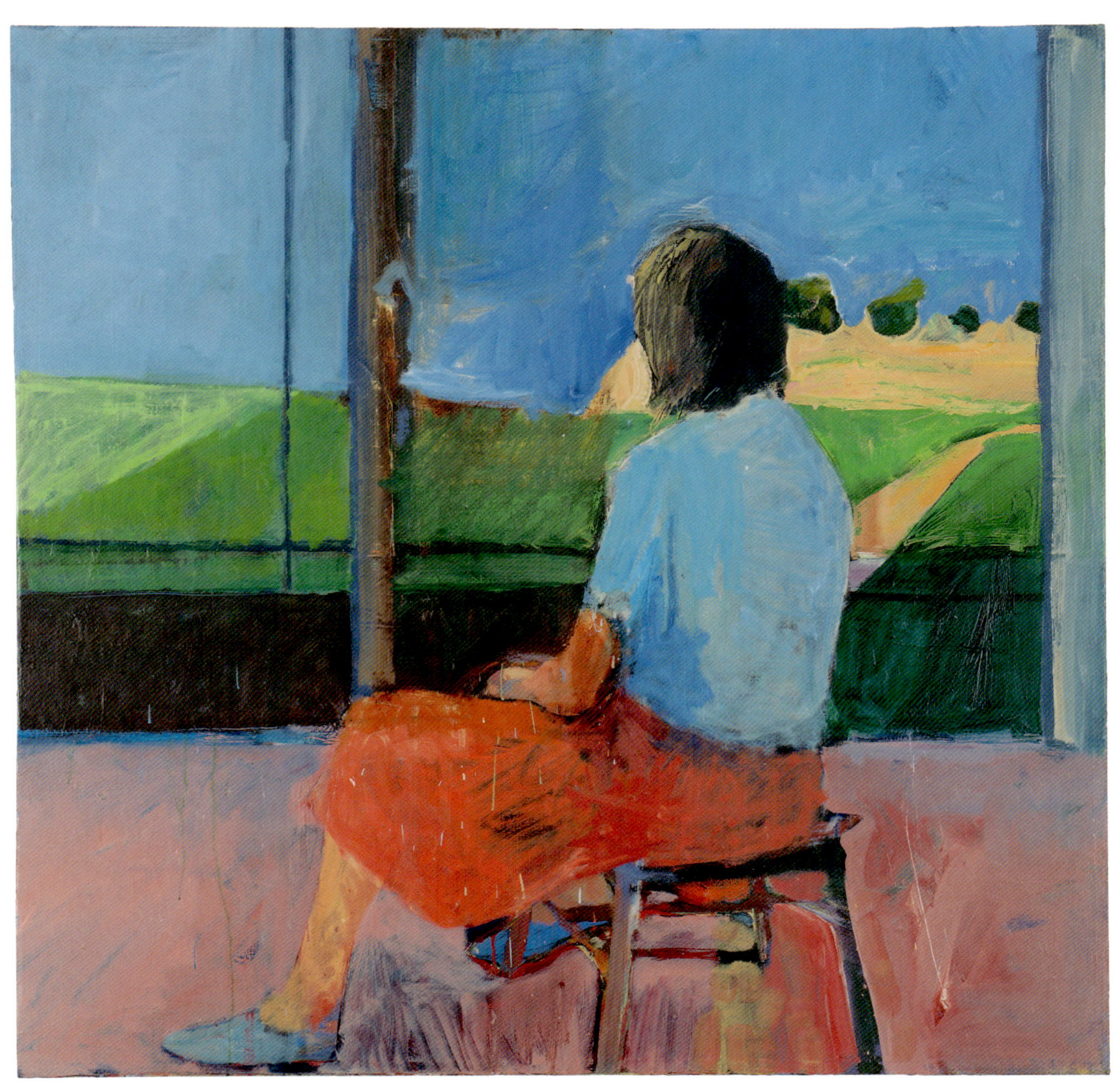

48. *Seated Man*, 1956
Oil on canvas, 22 1/8 x 20 in. (56.2 x 50.8 cm)
Collection of Gretchen and John Berggruen [1644]

49. *Man and Woman Seated*, 1958
Oil on canvas, 70 3/4 x 83 1/2 in. (179.7 x 212.1 cm)
Palmer Museum of Art of The Pennsylvania State University, University Park, 76.6 [1237]

50. *Girl Looking at Landscape*, 1957
Oil on canvas, 59 x 60 3/8 in. (149.9 x 153.4 cm)
Whitney Museum of American Art, New York, gift of Mr. and Mrs. Alan H. Temple, 61.49 [1203]

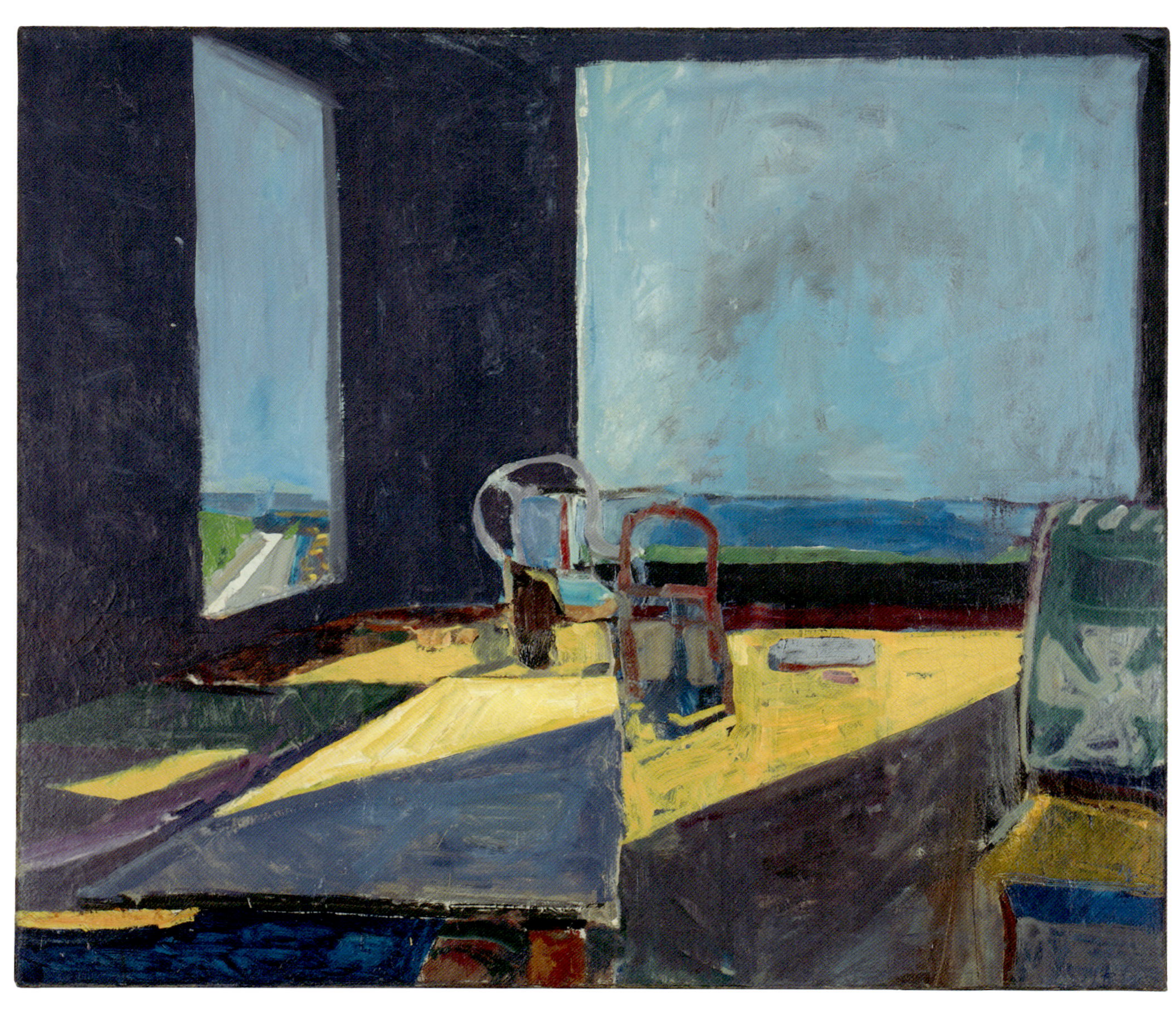

51. *Interior with View of the Ocean*, 1957
Oil on canvas, 49 1/2 x 57 7/8 in. (125.7 x 147 cm)
The Phillips Collection, Washington, DC, acquired 1958, 0520 [1210]

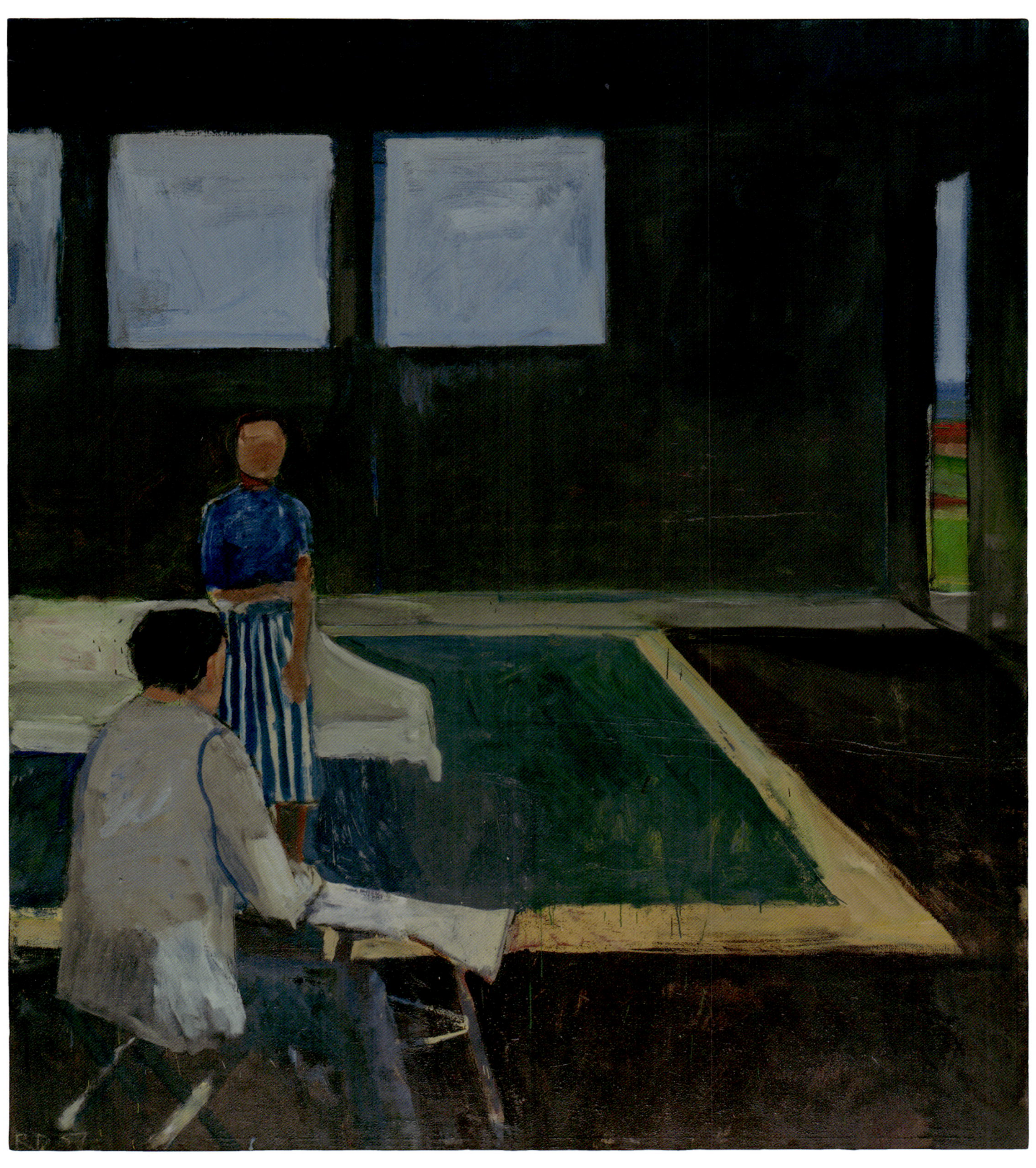

52. *Man and Woman in a Large Room*, 1957
Oil on canvas, 71 1/8 x 62 1/2 in. (180.7 x 158.8 cm)
Hirshhorn Museum and Sculpture Garden, Smithsonian Institution, Washington, DC, gift of the Joseph H. Hirshhorn Foundation, 1966, 66.1371 [1214]

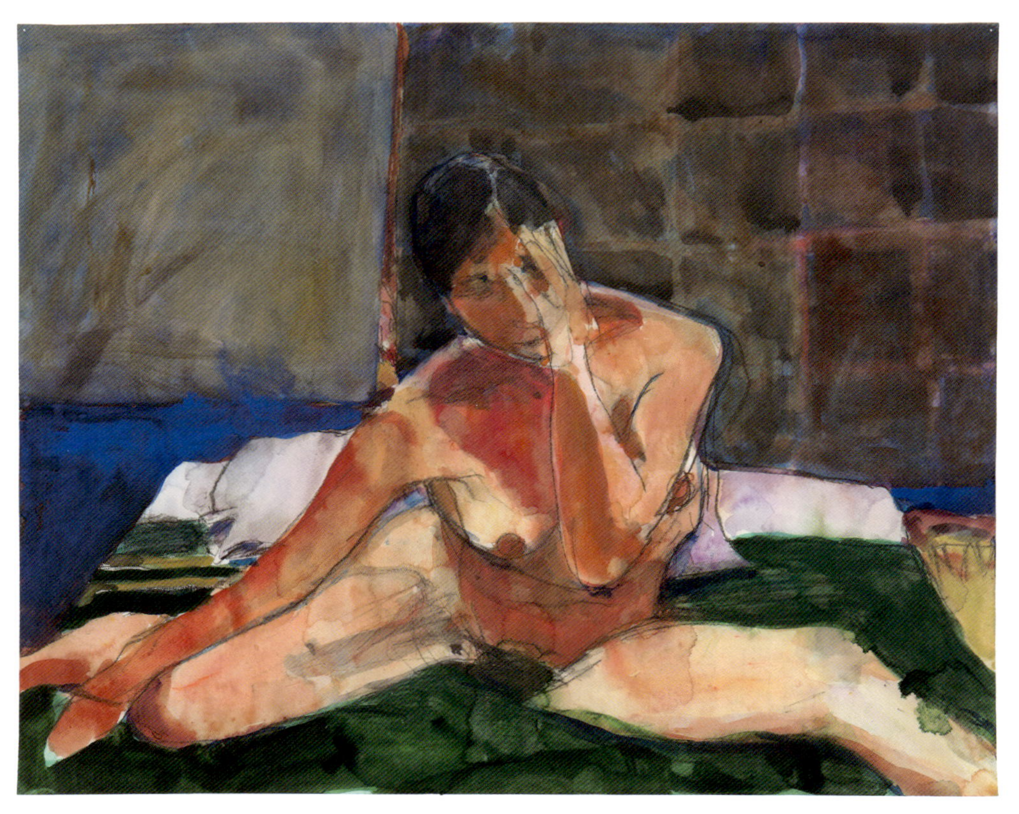

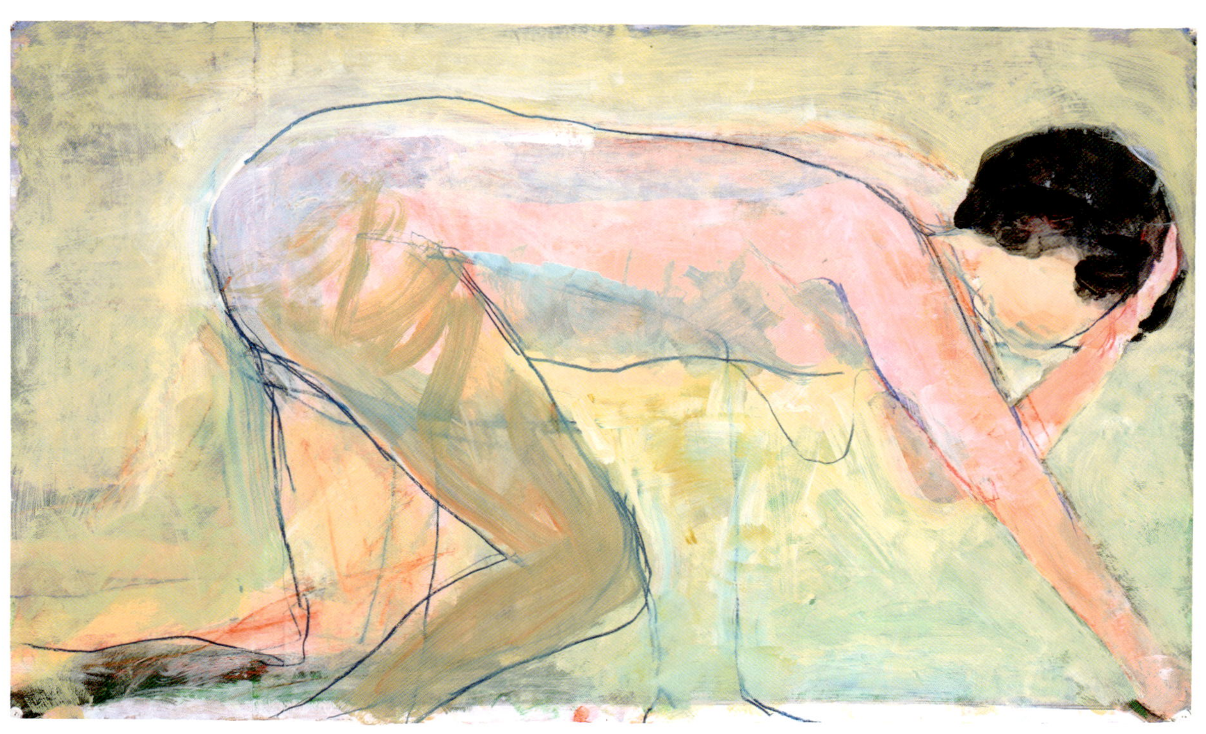

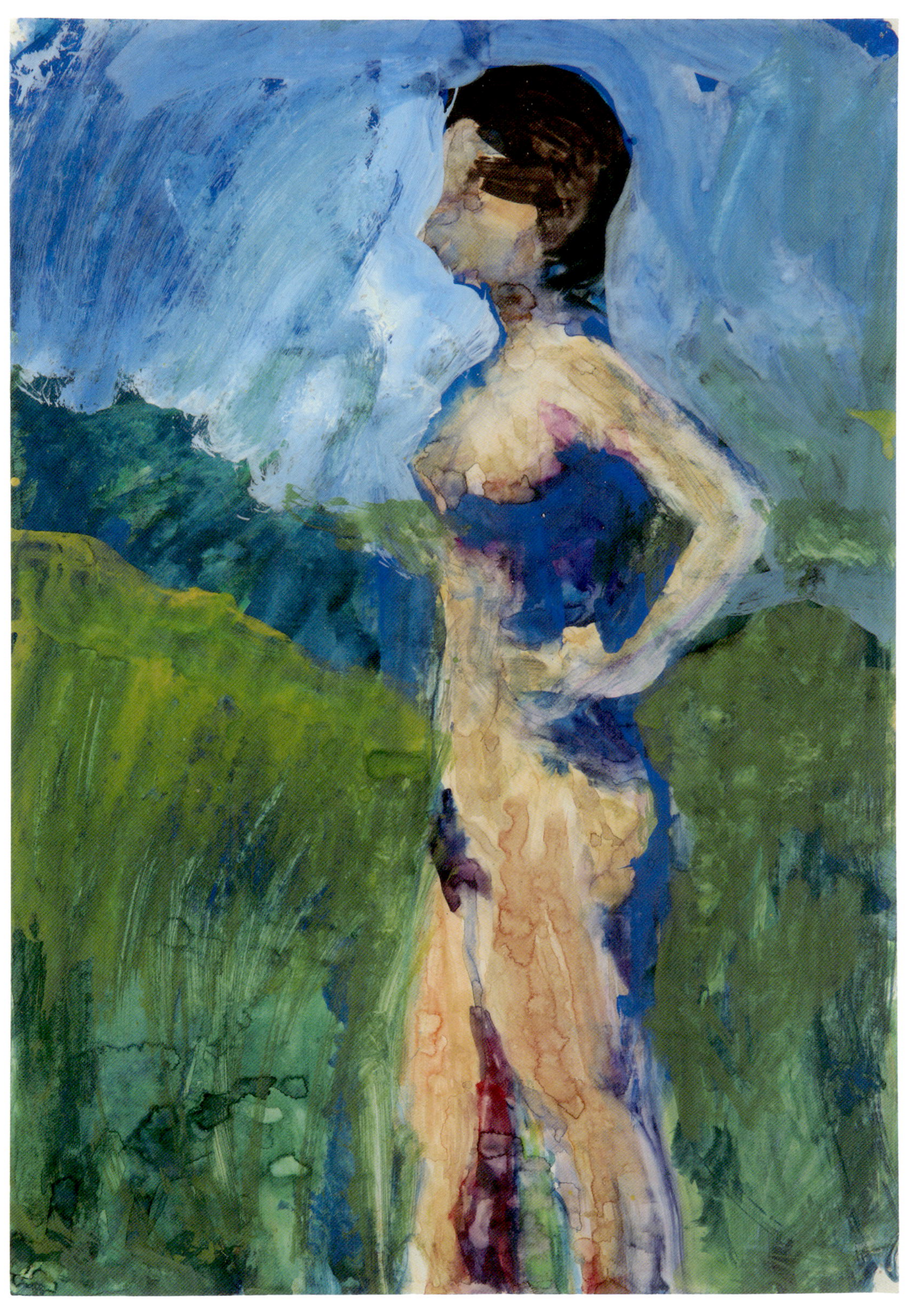

53. *Untitled*, ca. 1960–1966
Gouache, crayon, and graphite on paper, 14 x 17 in. (35.6 x 43.2 cm)
Collection of Marguerite Steed Hoffman [2094]

54. *Untitled*, ca. 1955–1966
Gouache, oil, and crayon on joined paper, 19 x 31 1/2 in. (48.3 x 80 cm)
Private collection [2192]

55. *Untitled*, ca. 1957–1958
Watercolor on paper, 16 x 10 7/8 in. (40.6 x 27.6 cm)
Collection of Richard Nagler and Sheila Sosnow, courtesy of John Berggruen Gallery [751]

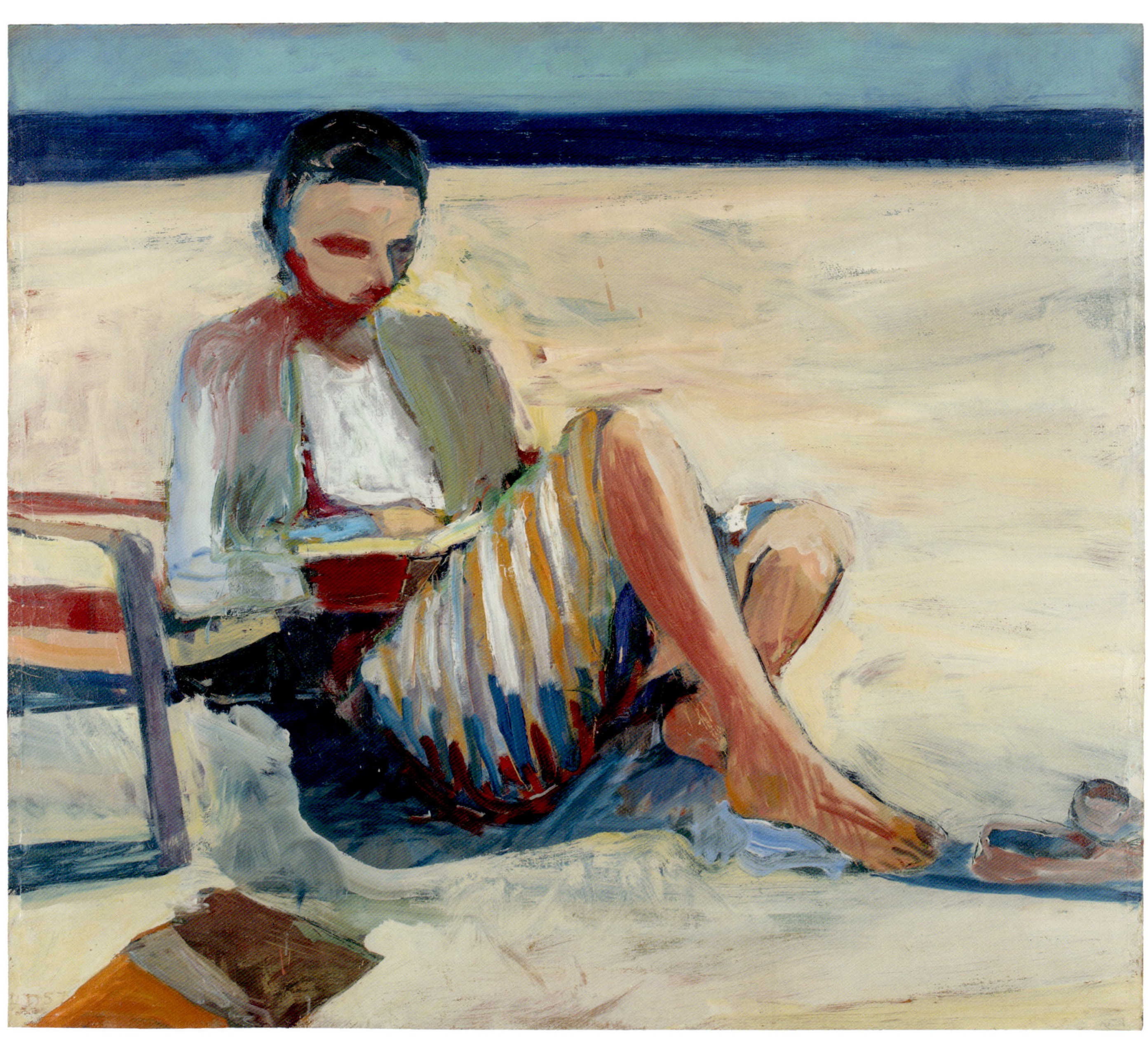

56. *Girl on the Beach*, 1957
Oil on canvas, 52 1/8 x 57 1/4 in. (132.4 x 145.4 cm)
Collection of Harry W. and Mary Margaret Anderson, 1969.023 [1206]

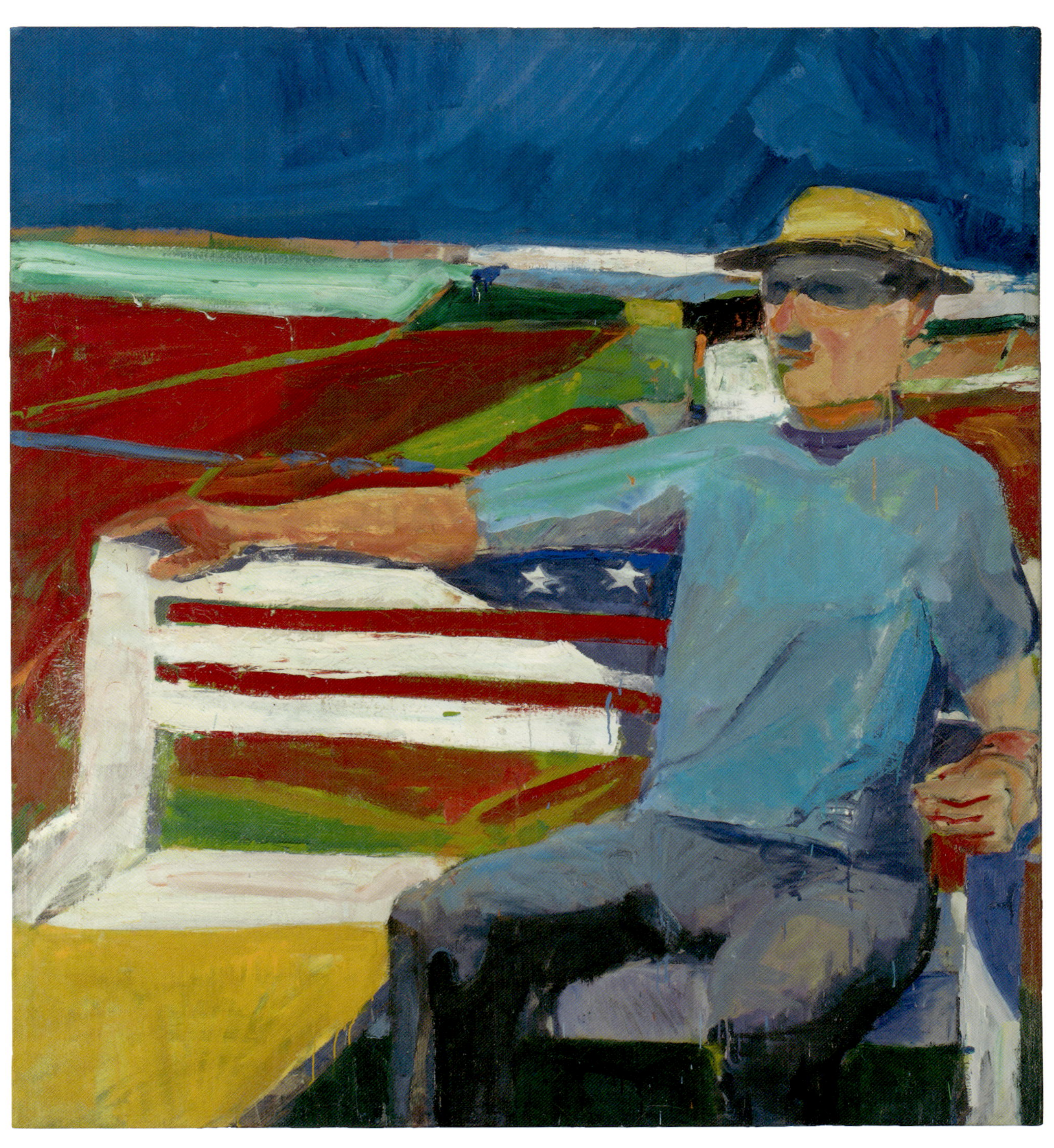

57. July, 1957
Oil on canvas, 58 1/2 x 53 1/4 in. (148.6 x 135.3 cm)
Private collection [1211]

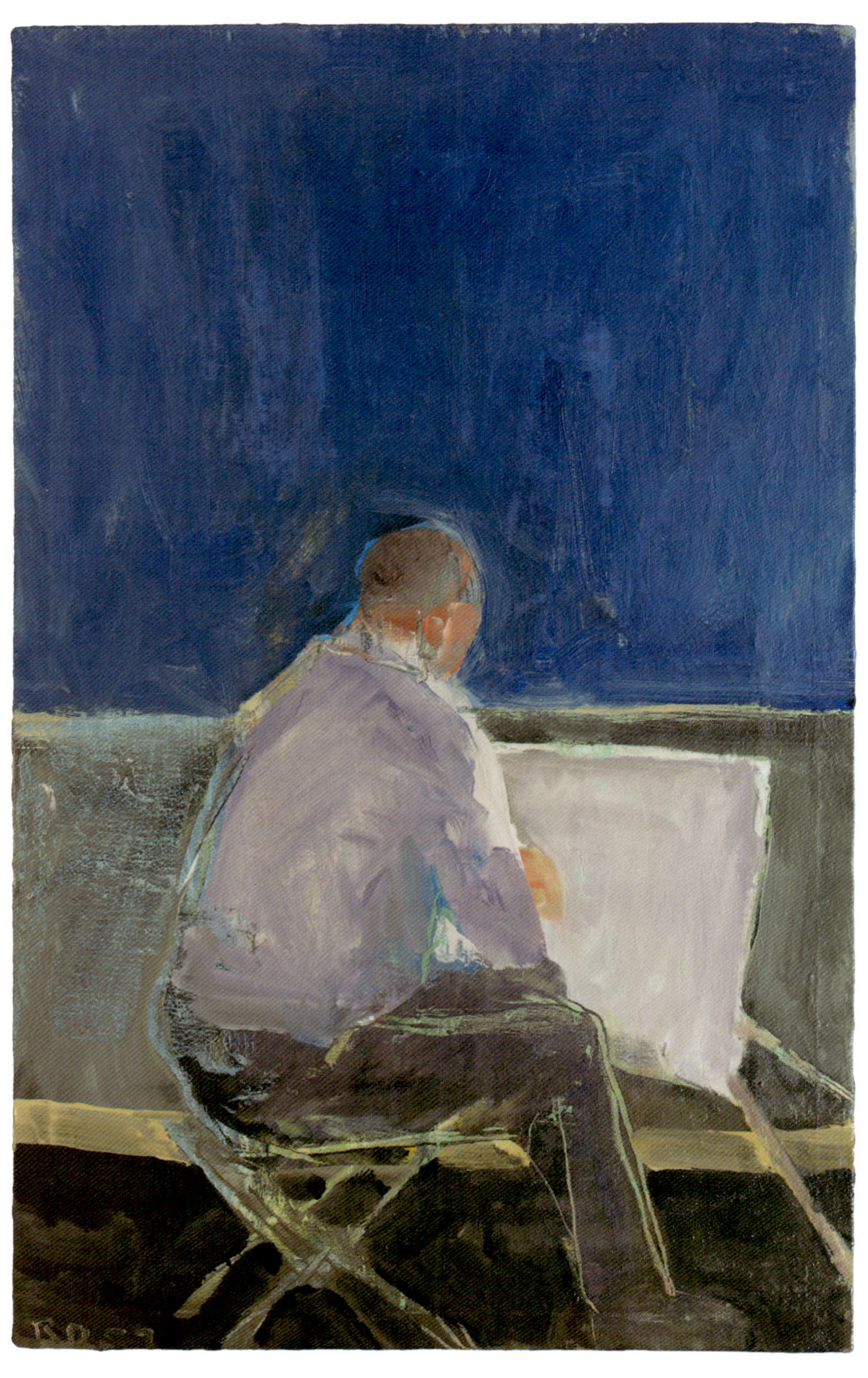

58. *Painter*, 1957
Oil on canvas, 27 3/4 x 17 1/8 in. (70.5 x 43.5 cm)
Private collection [1217]

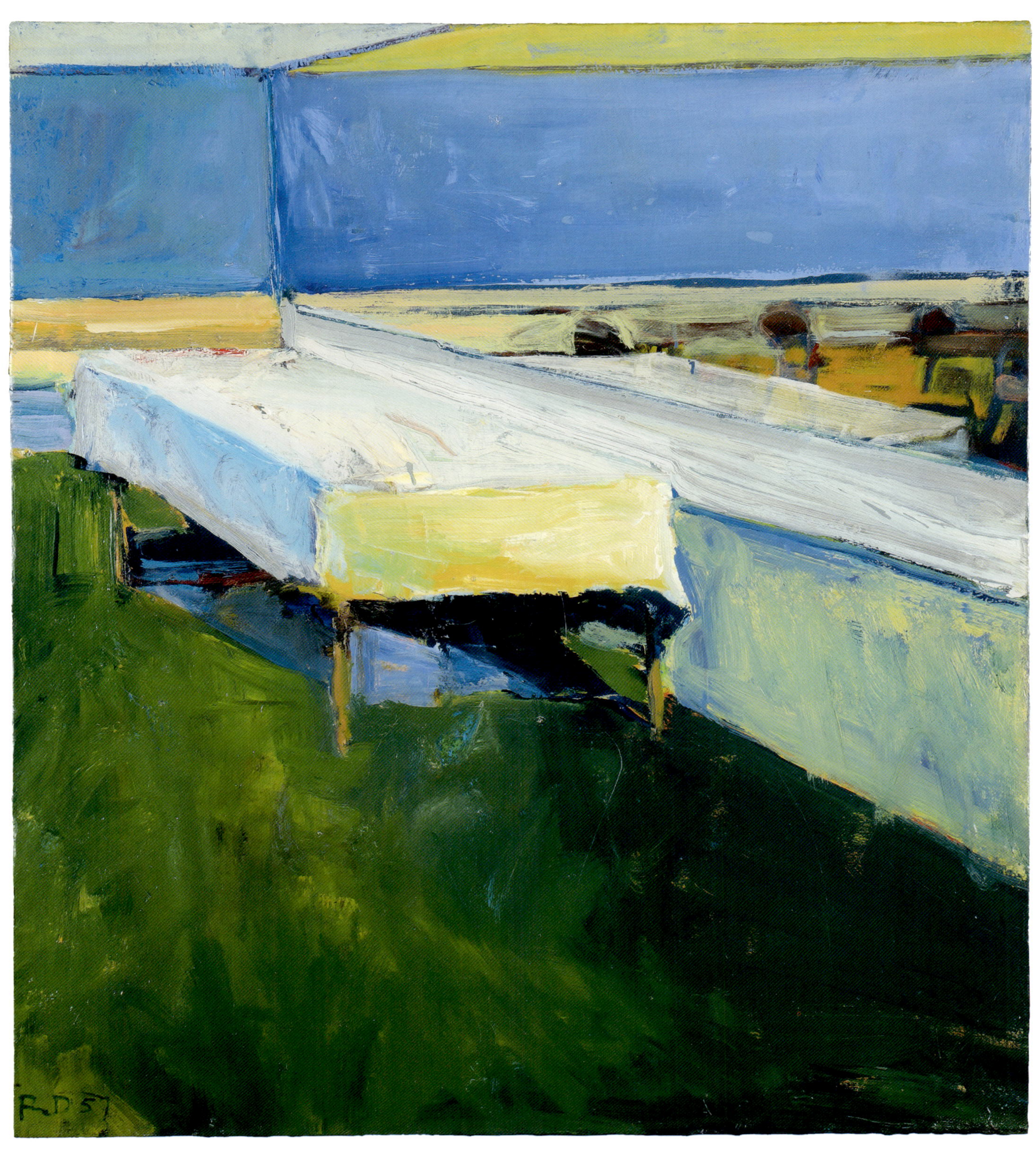

59. *The Table*, 1957
Oil on canvas, 30 x $26\frac{7}{8}$ in. (76.2 x 68.3 cm)
Des Moines Art Center Permanent Collections, Iowa, gift of James S. and Dorothy Schramm, 1961.49 [1223]

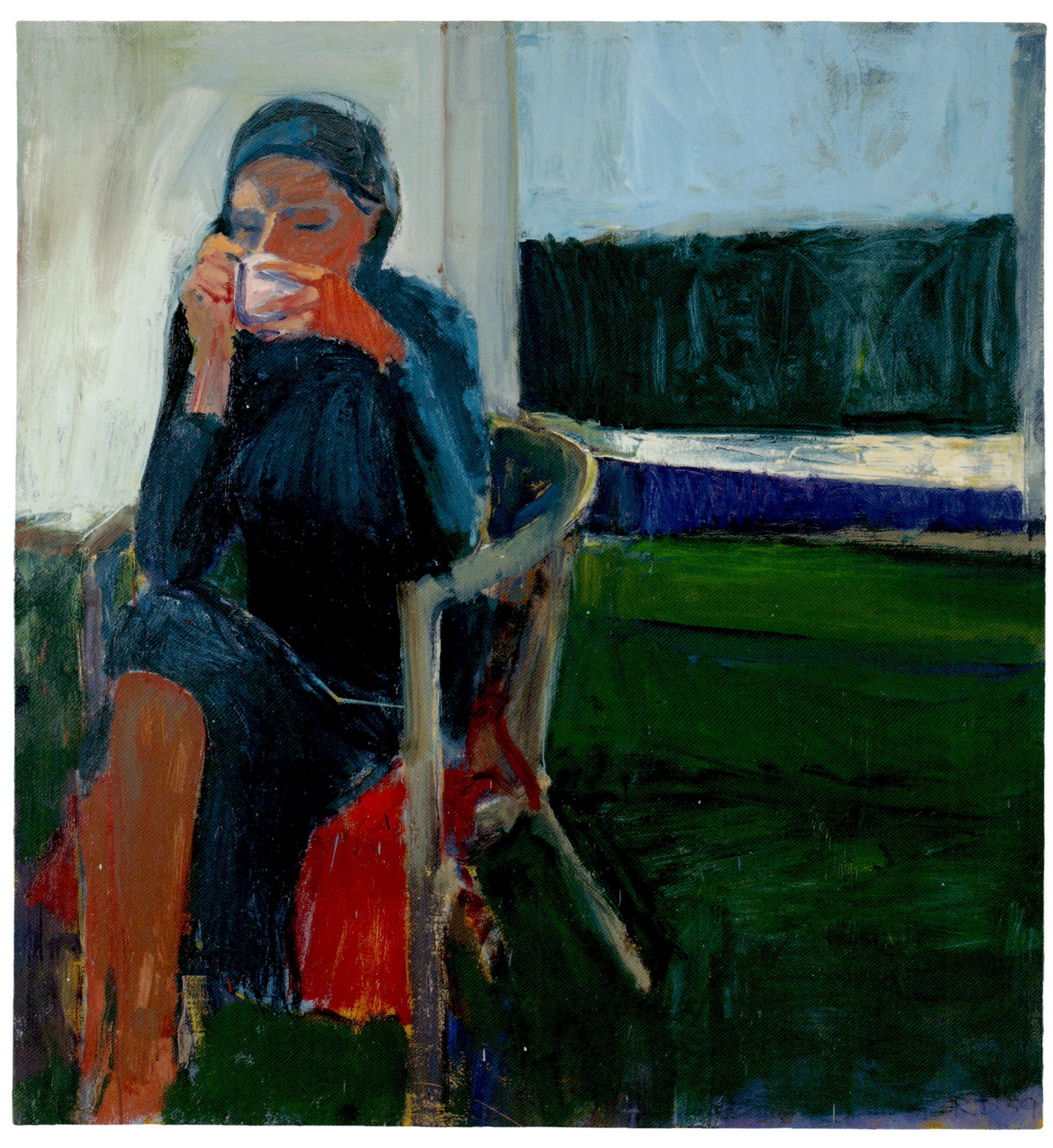

60. *Coffee*, 1959
Oil on canvas, 57 1/2 x 52 1/4 in. (146.1 x 132.7 cm)
San Francisco Museum of Modern Art, fractional gift of Barbara and Gerson Bakar, 94.428 [1253]

61. *Woman in Profile*, 1958
Oil on canvas, 68 1/8 x 59 in. (173 x 149.9 cm)
San Francisco Museum of Modern Art, bequest of Howard E. Johnson, 84.196 [1246]

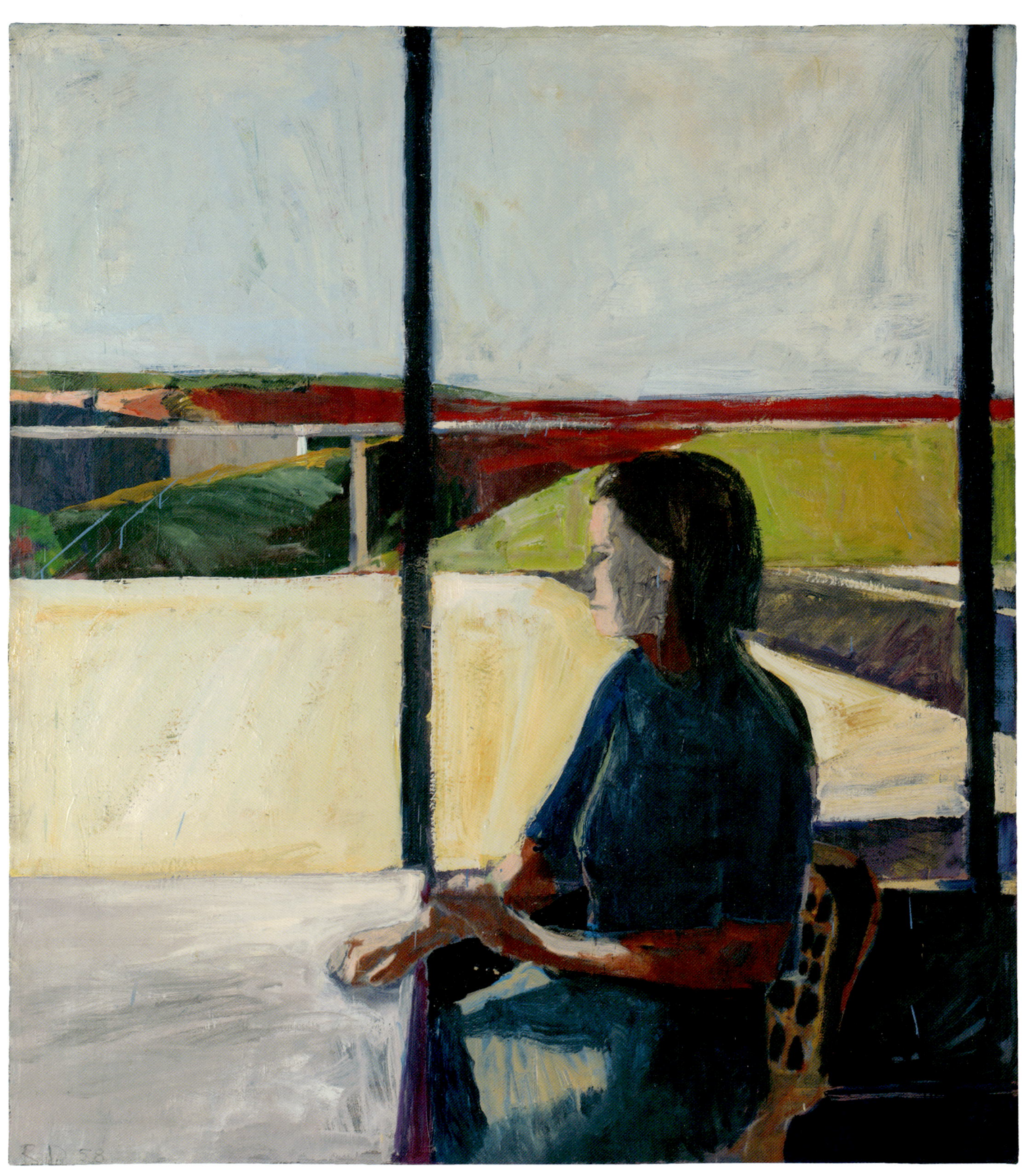

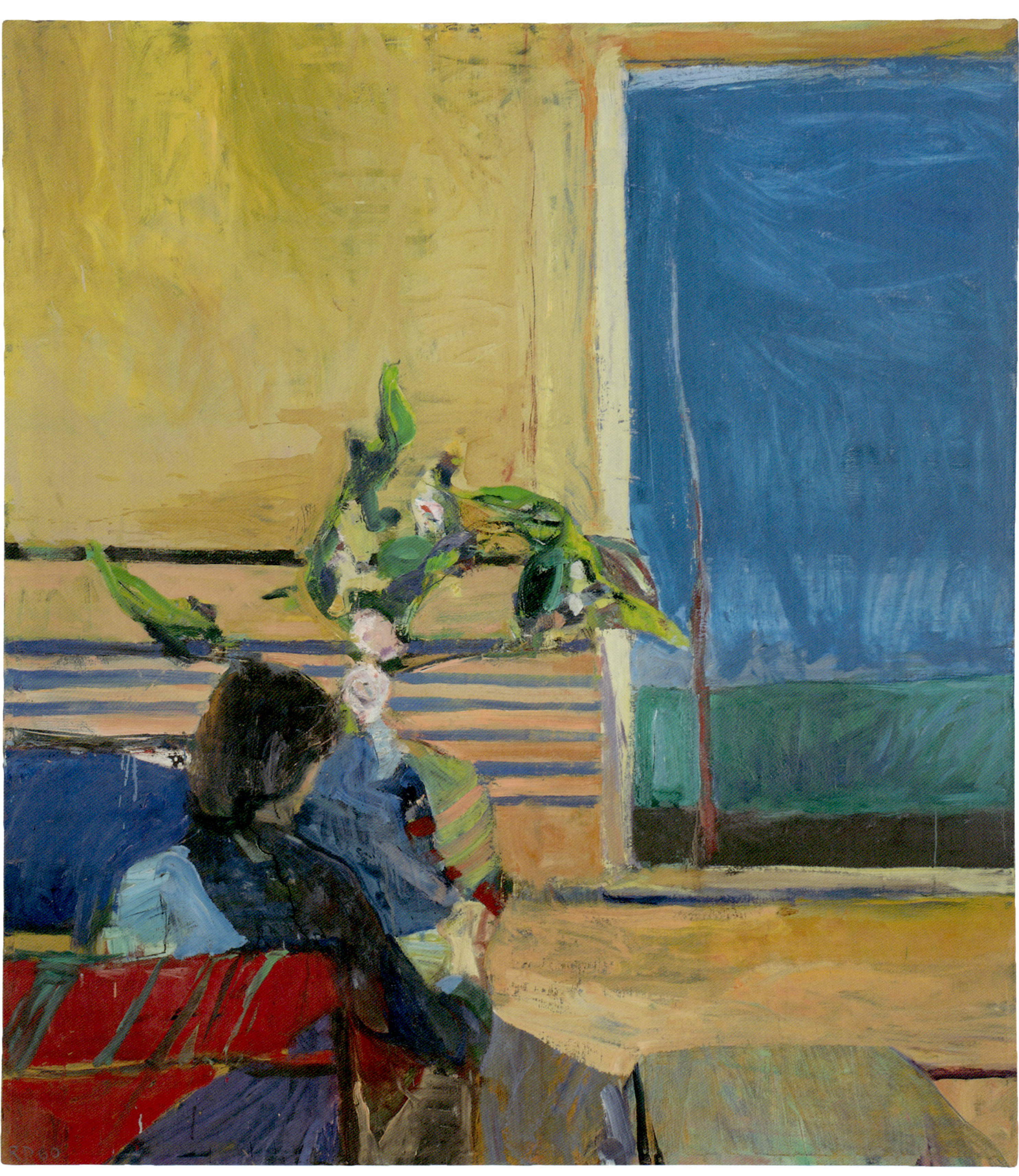

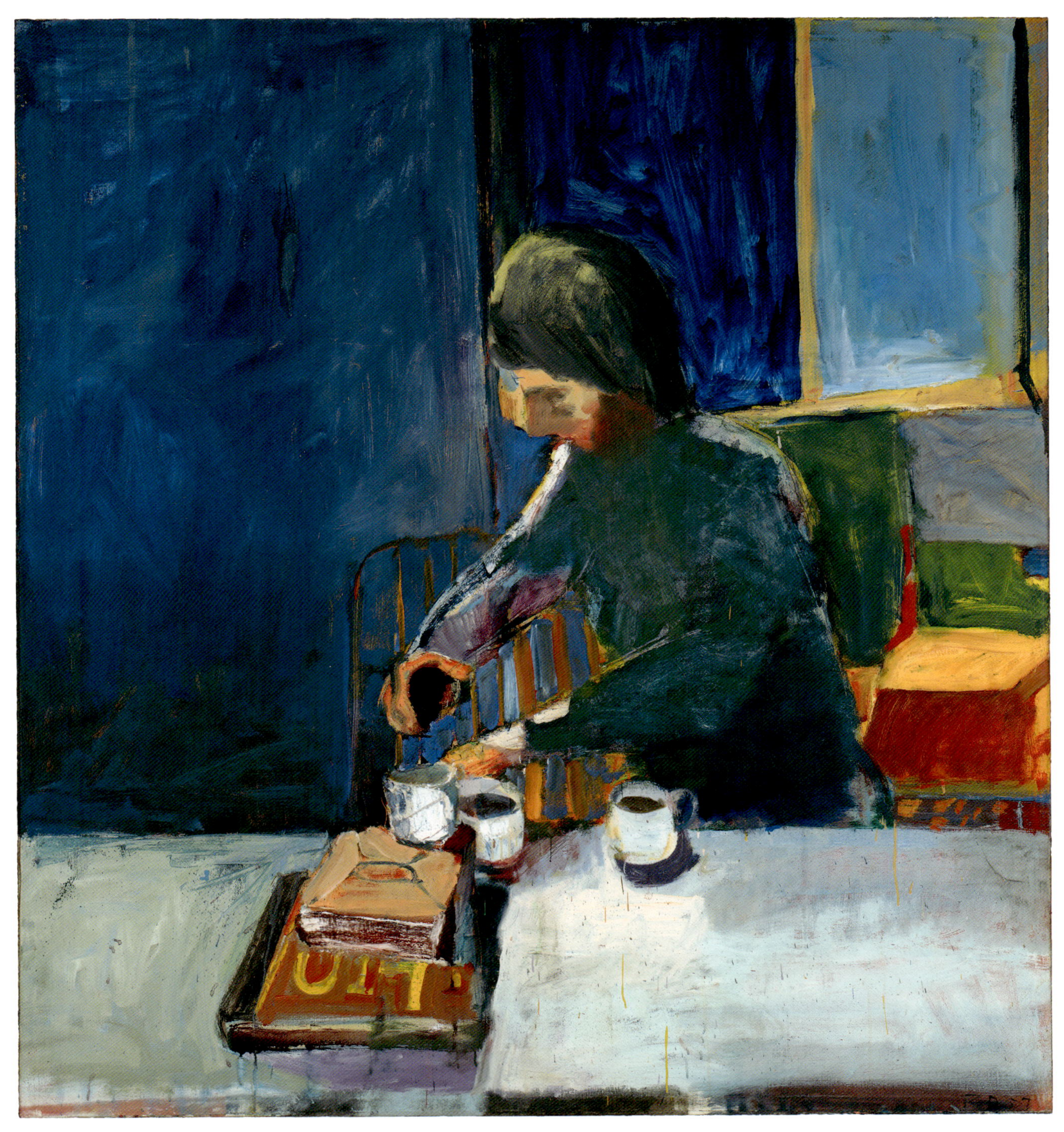

62. *Girl with Plant*, 1960
Oil on canvas, 80 x 69 1/2 in. (203.2 x 176.5 cm)
The Phillips Collection, Washington, DC, acquired 1961, 0519 [1293]

63. *Girl with Cups*, 1957
Oil on canvas, 59 x 54 in. (149.9 x 137.2 cm)
Yale University Art Gallery, New Haven, Connecticut, gift of Richard Brown Baker, B.A. 1935, 1975.110.1 [1202]

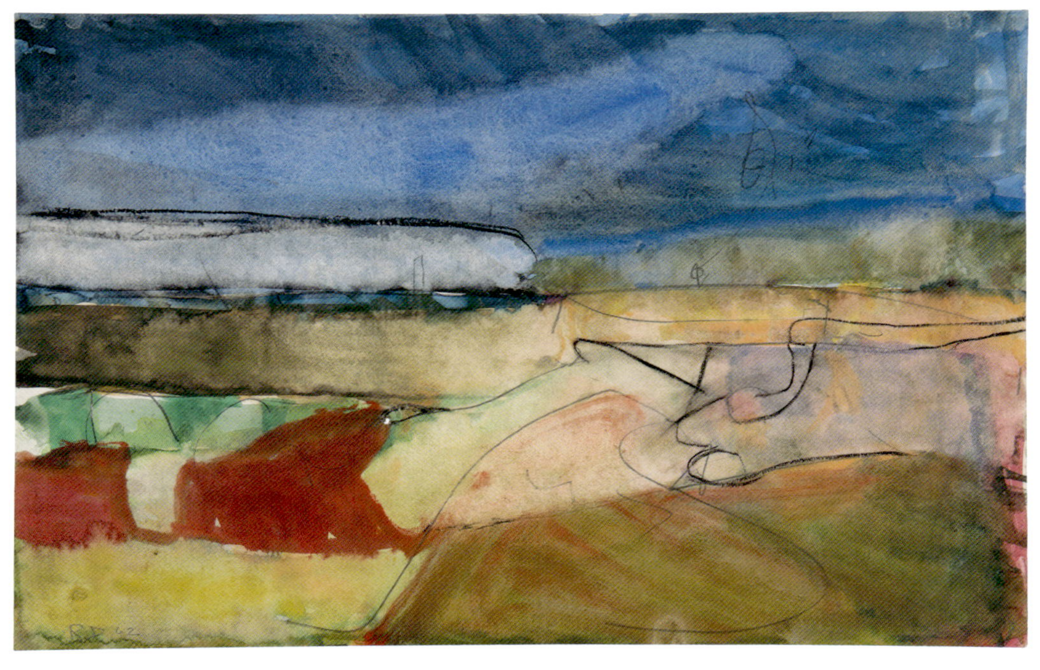

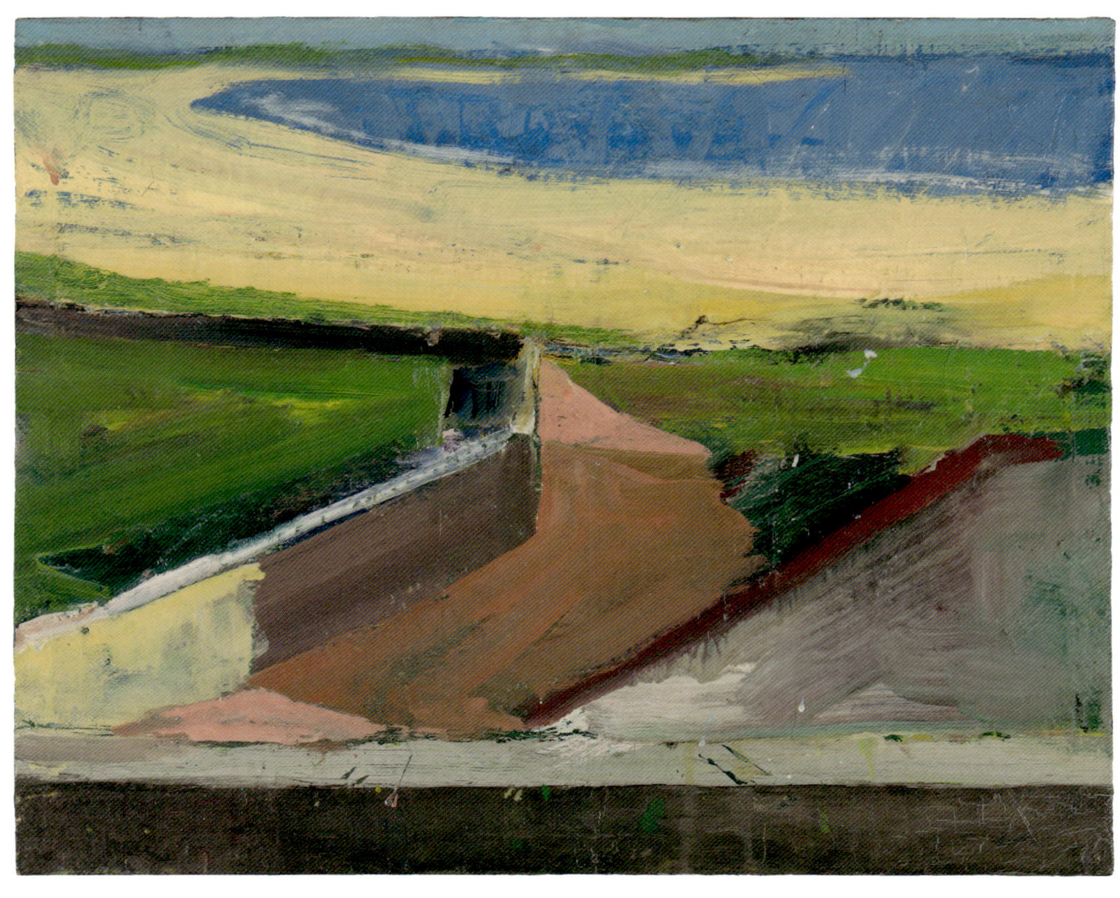

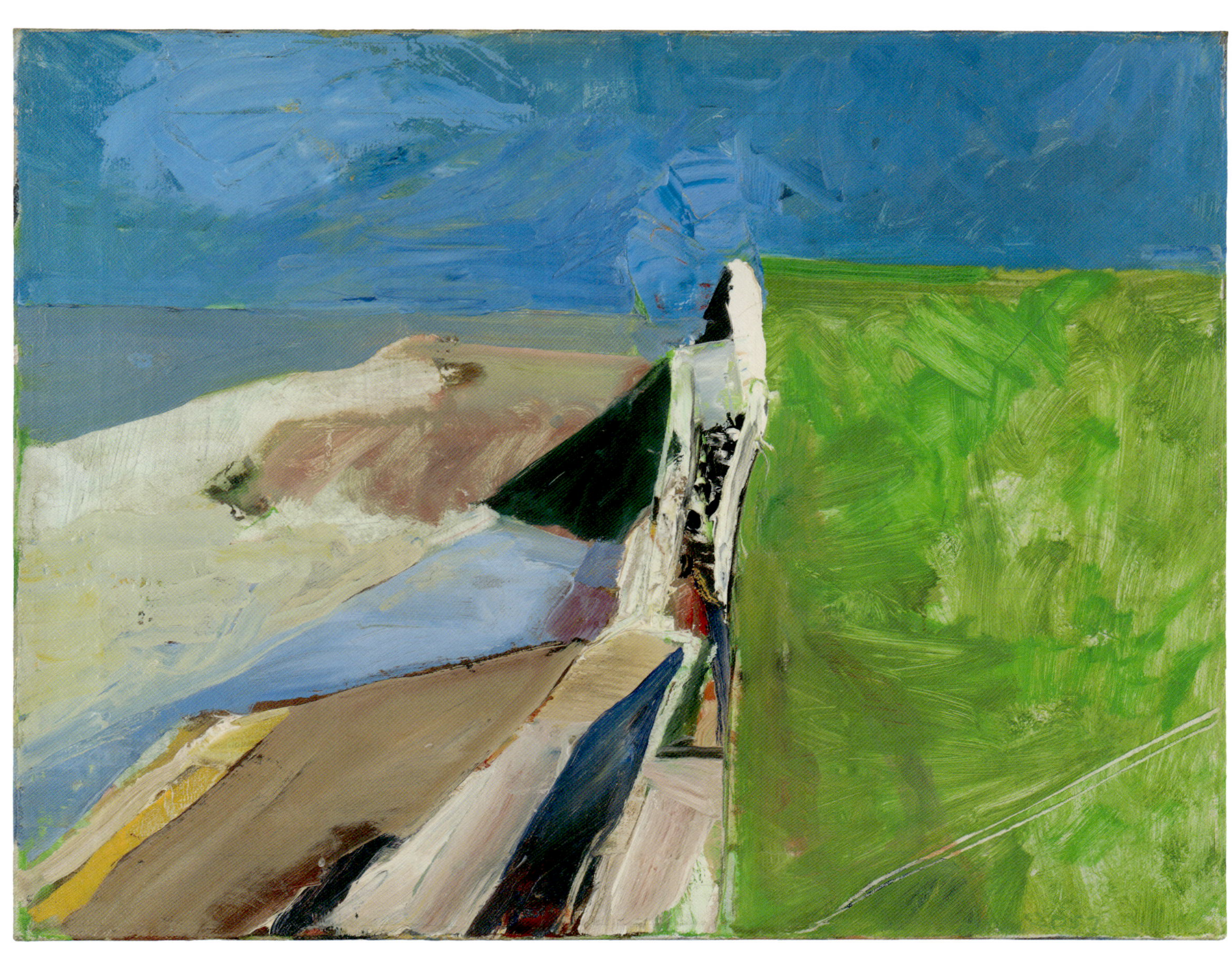

64. *Untitled*, 1962
Gouache, graphite, and charcoal on paper, 11 x 17 in. (27.9 x 43.2 cm)
Richard Diebenkorn Foundation [922]

65. *Beach*, 1957
Oil on canvas, 17 5/8 x 22 in. (44.8 x 55.9 cm)
Collection of Gretchen and John Berggruen [125]

66. *Seawall*, 1957
Oil on canvas, 20 x 26 in. (50.8 x 66 cm)
Fine Arts Museums of San Francisco, gift of Phyllis G. Diebenkorn, 1995.96 [1220]

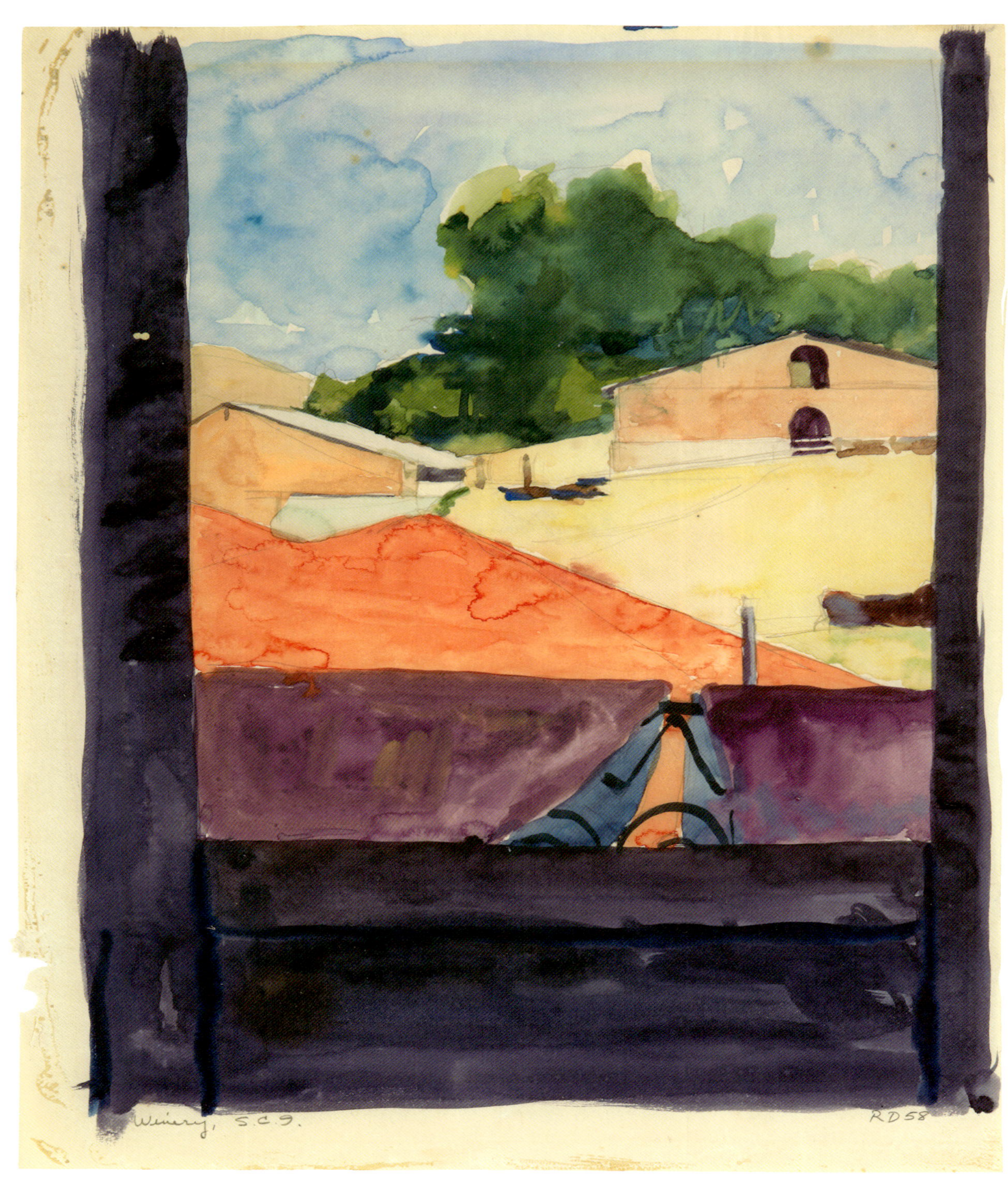

67. *Winery, S.C.I.*, 1958
Watercolor and graphite on paper, 16 3/4 x 13 7/8 in. (42.5 x 35.2 cm)
Santa Cruz Island Foundation, Carpinteria, California, 1988.5 [2534]

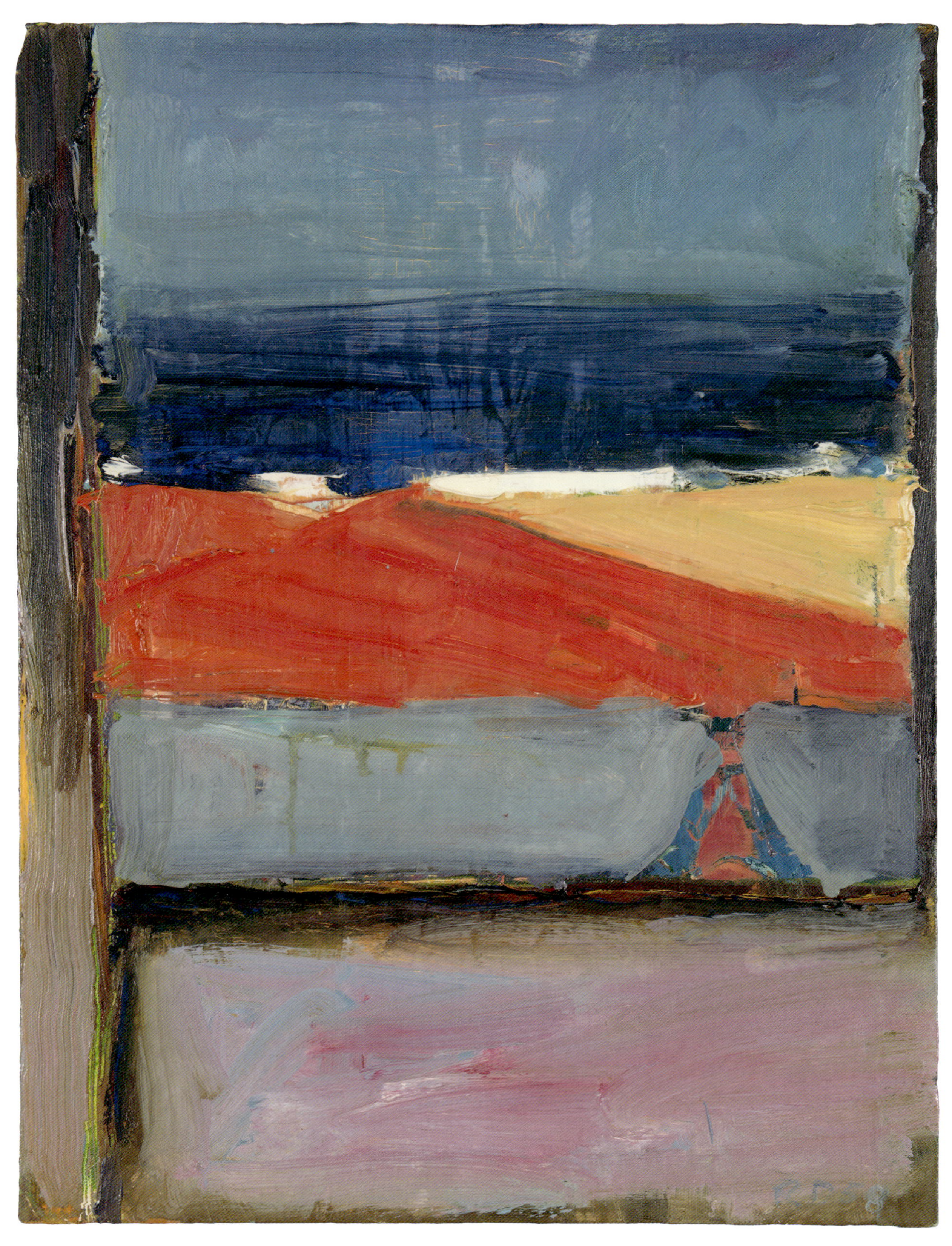

68. *View of the Ocean, Santa Cruz Island*, 1958
Oil on canvas, 19 1/8 x 14 3/8 in. (48.6 x 36.5 cm)
Santa Cruz Island Foundation, Carpinteria, California, 1988.6 [2538]

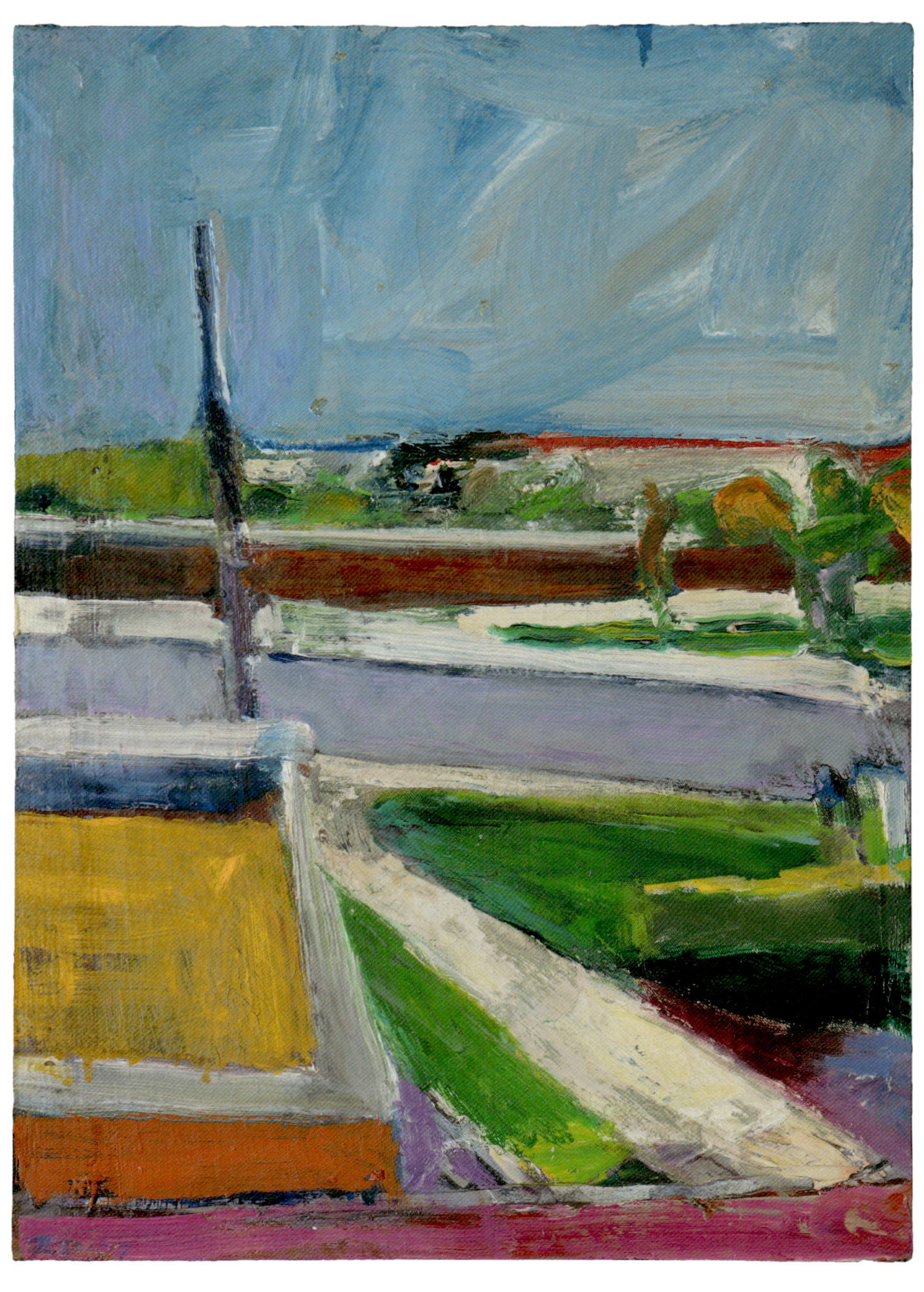

69. *Untitled Landscape*, 1957
Oil on canvas, 18 1/2 x 13 1/8 in. (47 x 33.3 cm)
Private collection [1212]

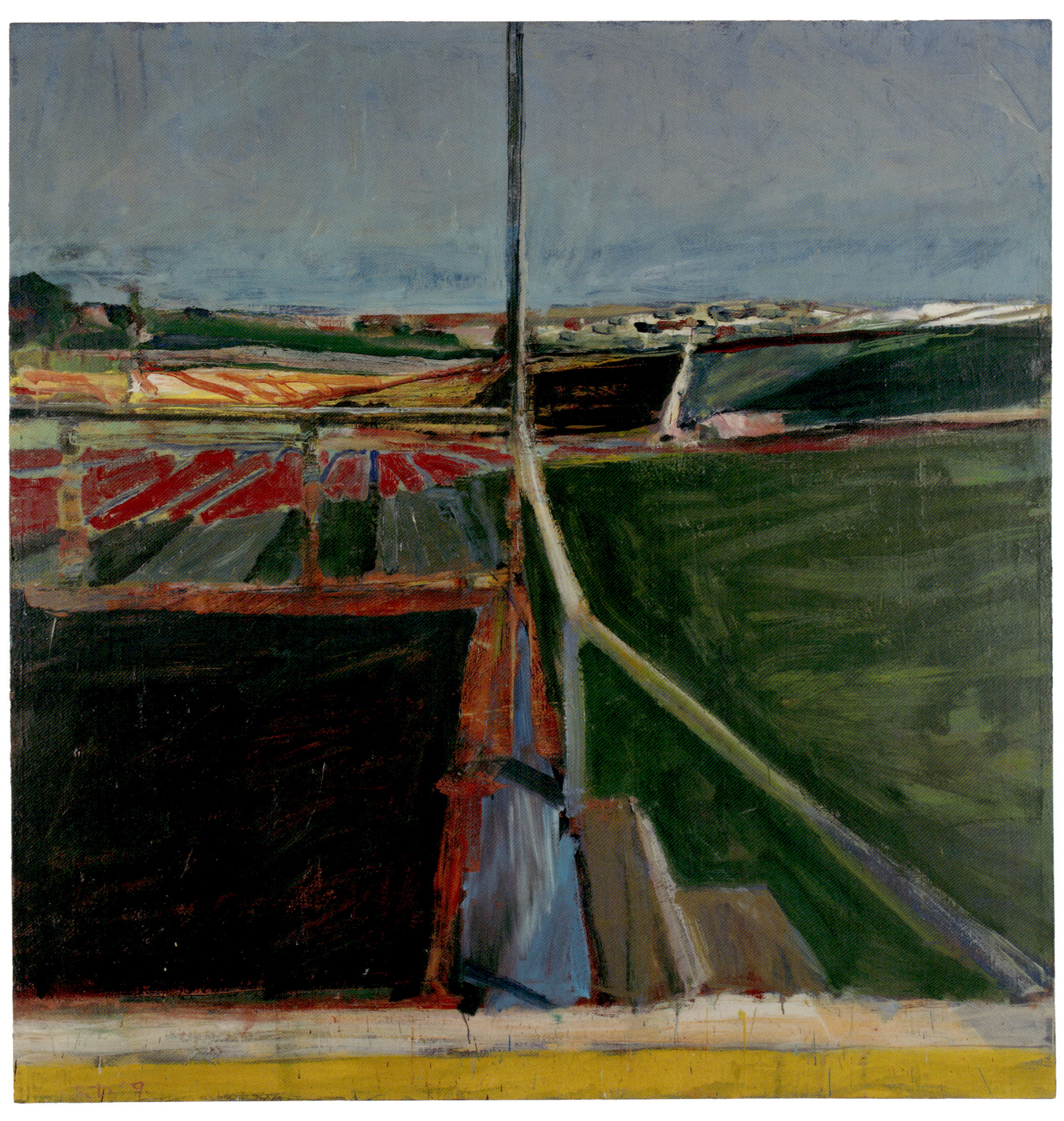

70. *View from the Porch*, 1959
Oil on canvas, 70 x 66 in. (177.8 x 167.6 cm)
Collection of Harry W. and Mary Margaret Anderson, 1970.018 [1277]

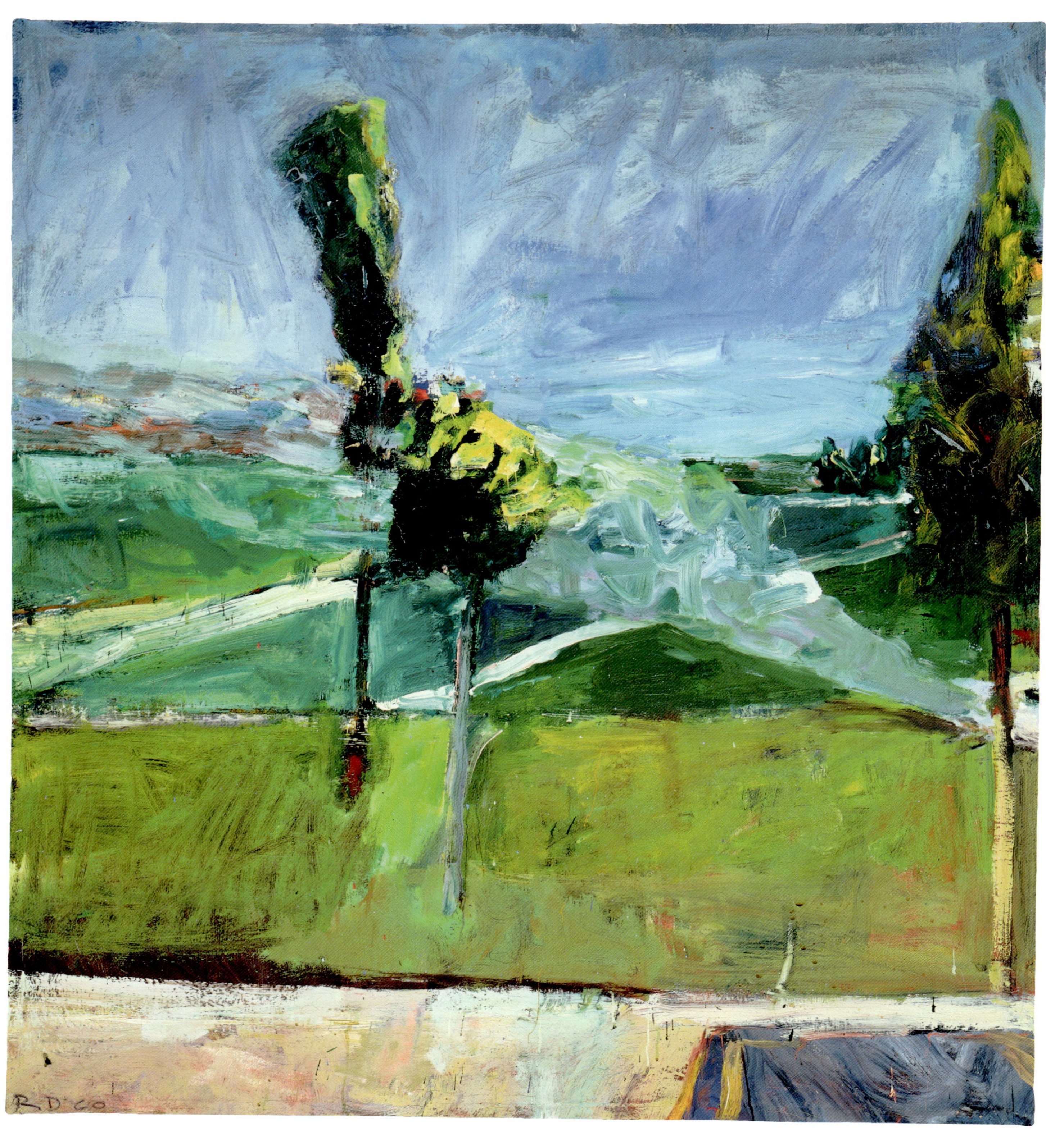

71. *Landscape with Smoke*, 1960
Oil on canvas, 54 3/4 x 49 3/4 in. (139.1 x 126.4 cm)
Private collection [1295]

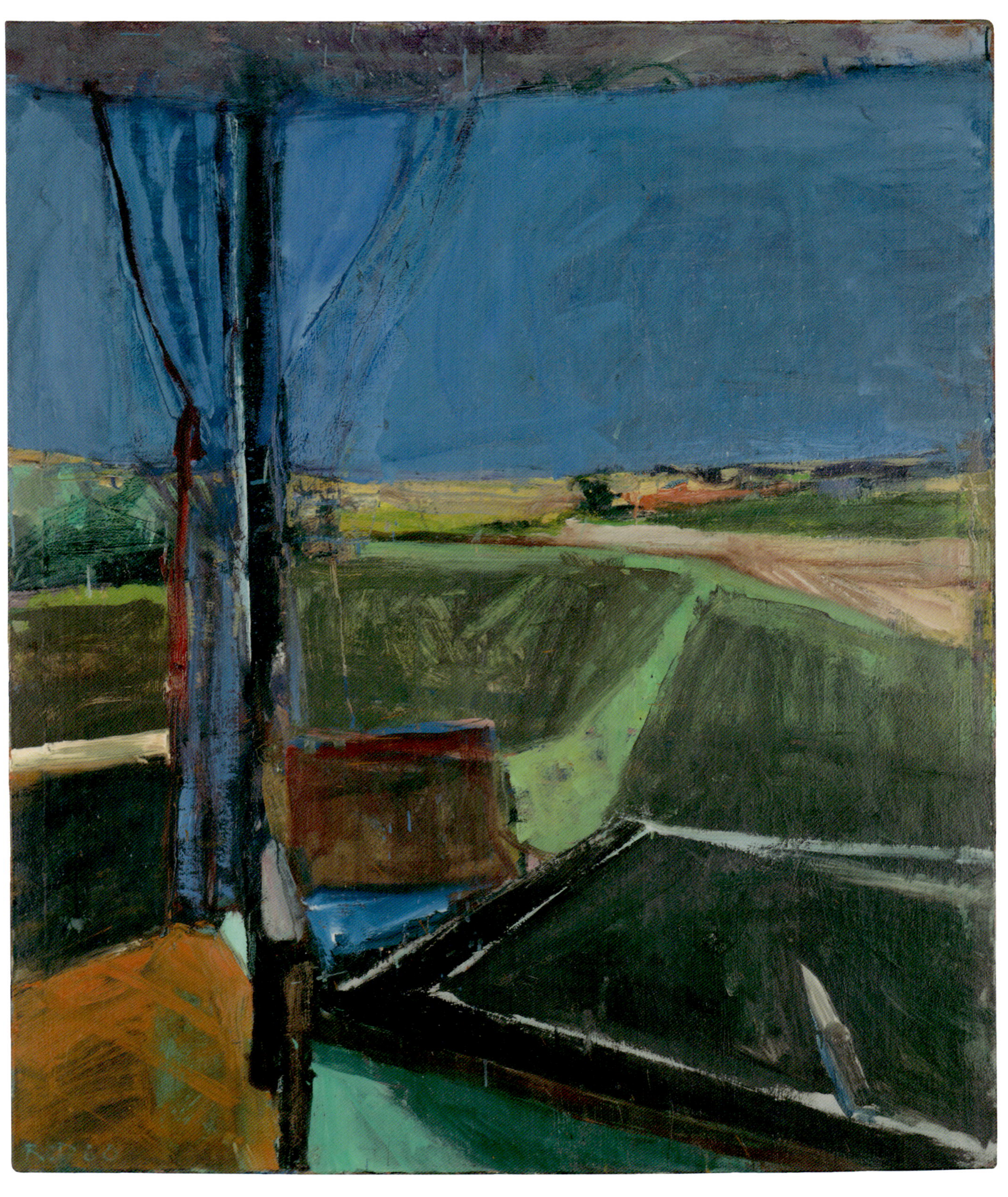

72. *Black Table*, 1960
Oil on canvas, 55 1/2 x 47 in. (141 x 119.4 cm)
Carnegie Museum of Art, Pittsburgh, gift of Mr. and Mrs. Charles Denby, 70.54.2 [1284]

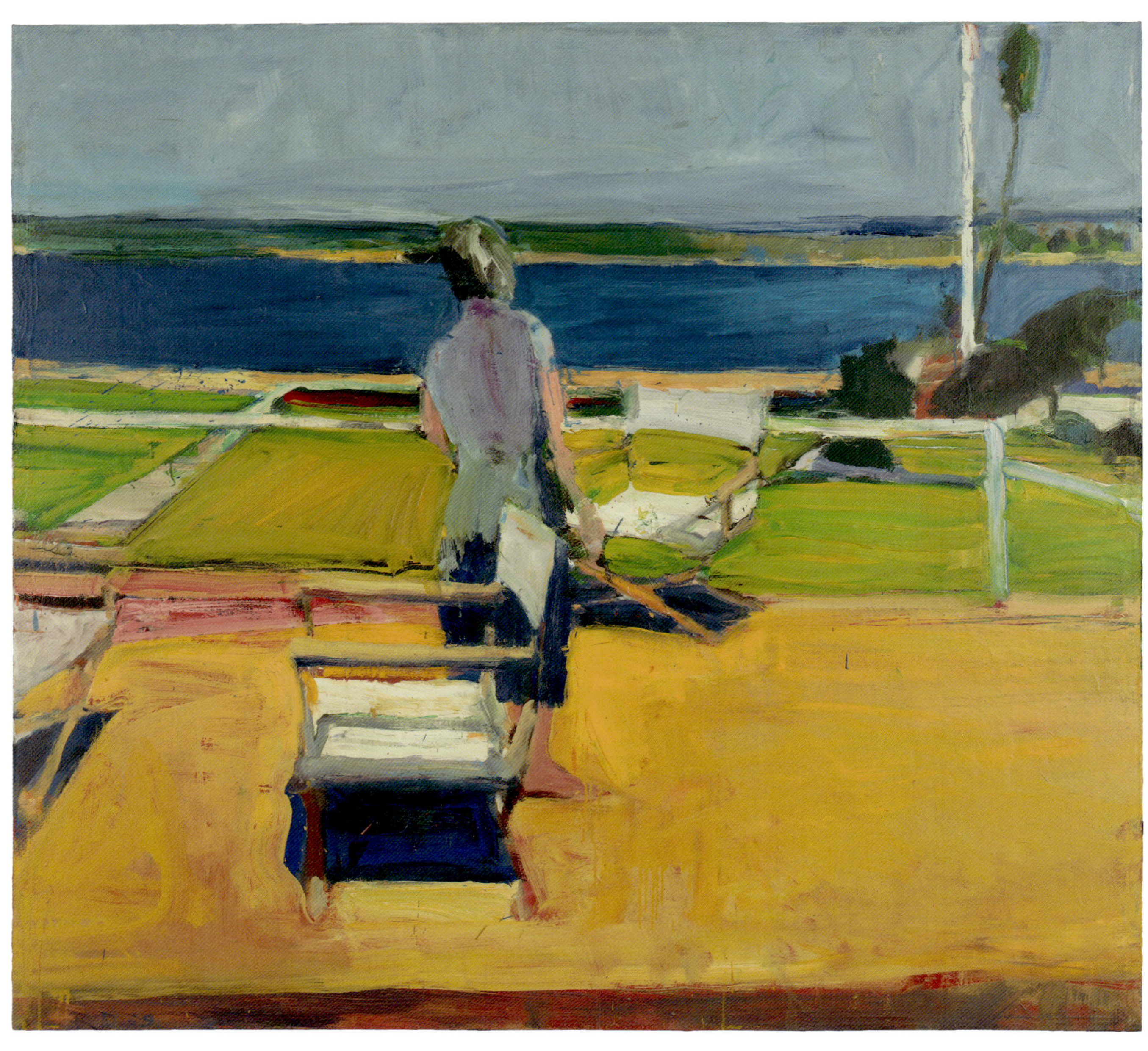

73. *Figure on a Porch*, 1959
Oil on canvas, 57 x 62 in. (144.8 x 157.5 cm)
Oakland Museum of California, gift of the Anonymous Donor Program of the American Federation of the Arts, A60.35.5 [1254]

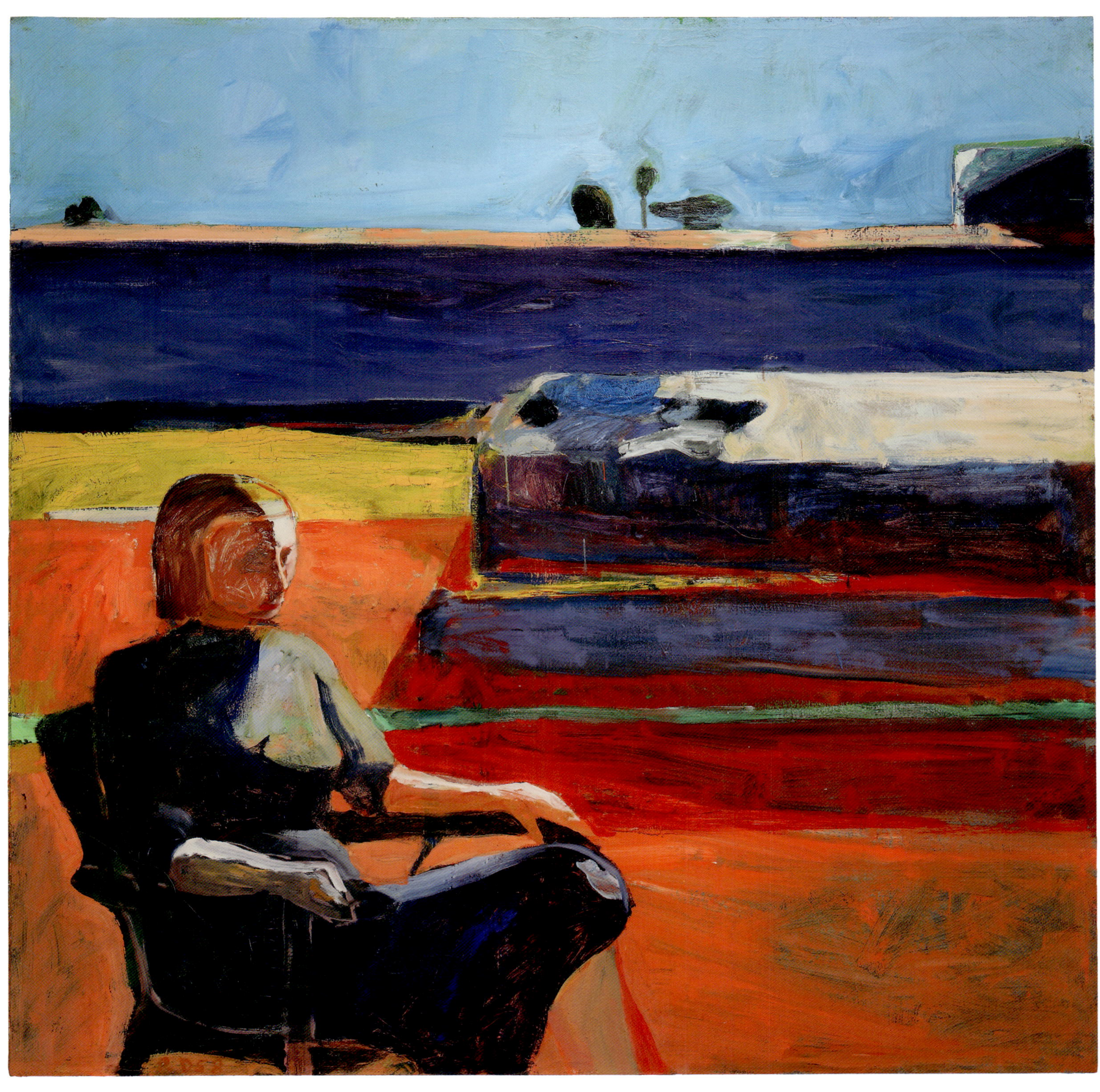

74. *Woman on a Porch*, 1958
Oil on canvas, 72 x 72 in. (182.9 x 182.9 cm)
New Orleans Museum of Art, Louisiana, museum purchase through the National Endowment for the Arts Matching Grant, 77.64 [1248]

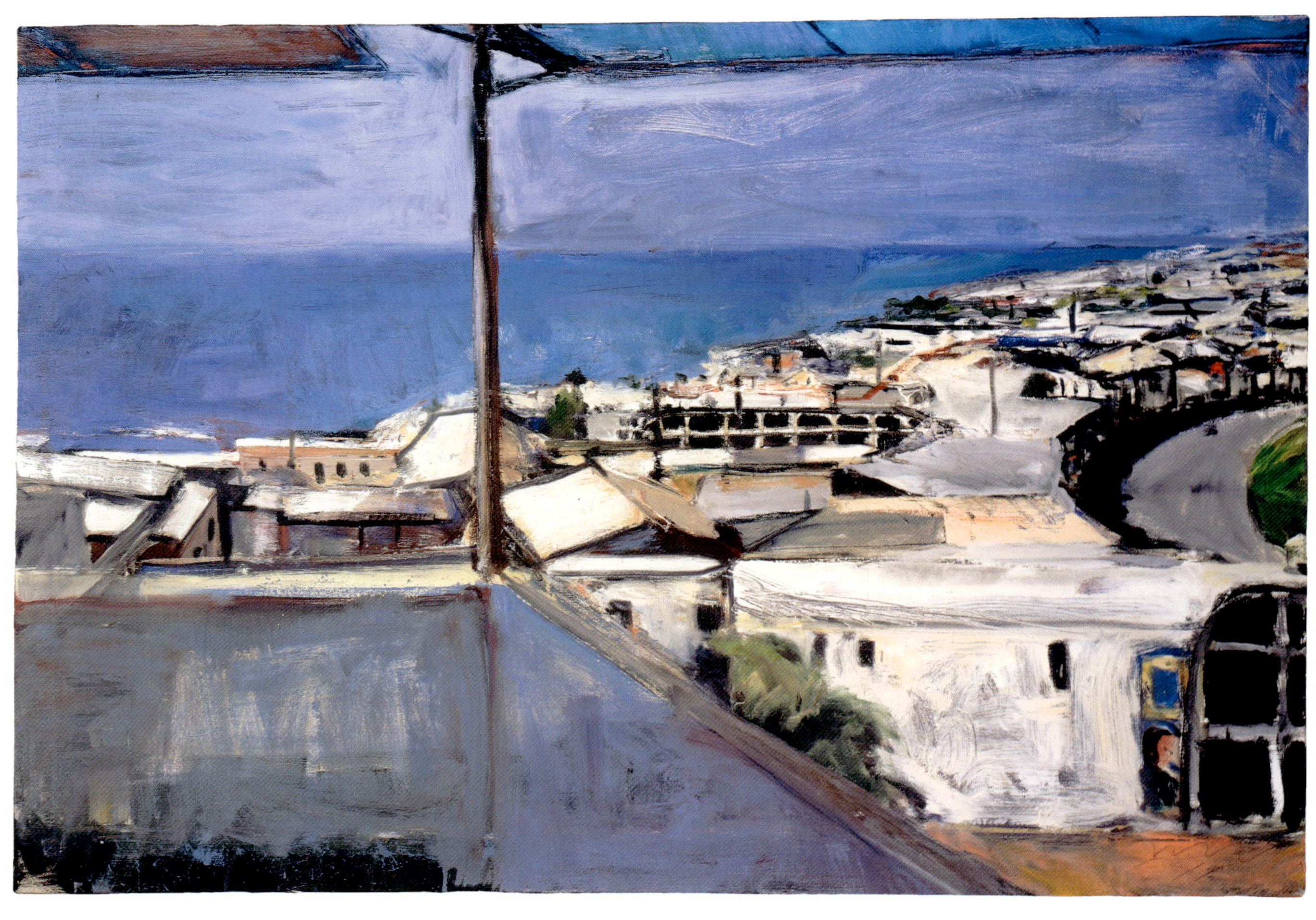

75. Santa Cruz I, 1962
Oil on canvas, 36 x 52 in. (91.4 x 132.1 cm)
Private collection [1355]

76. Ocean from a Window, 1959
Oil on canvas, 70 x 64 in. (177.8 x 162.6 cm)
Private collection [1267]

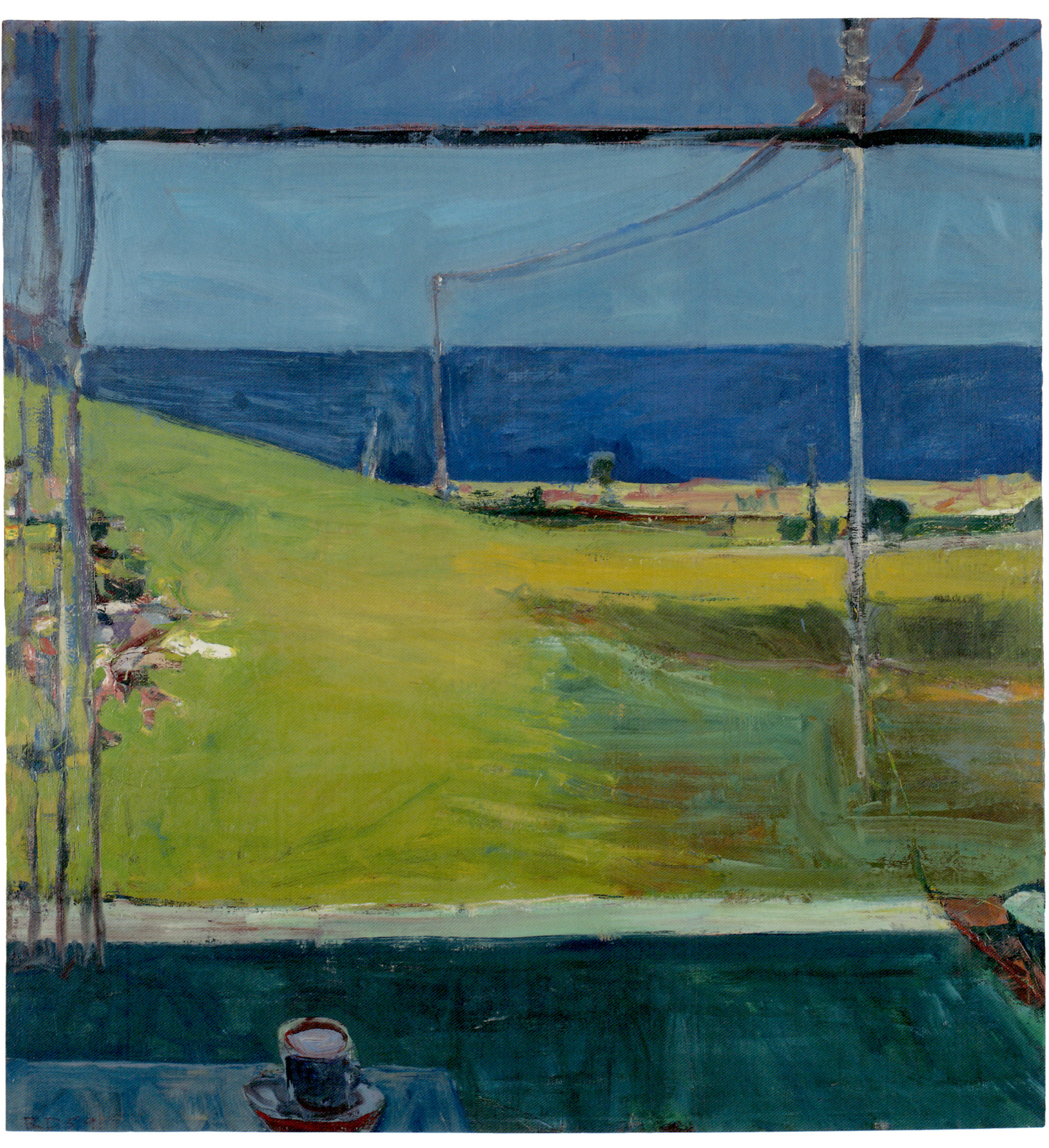

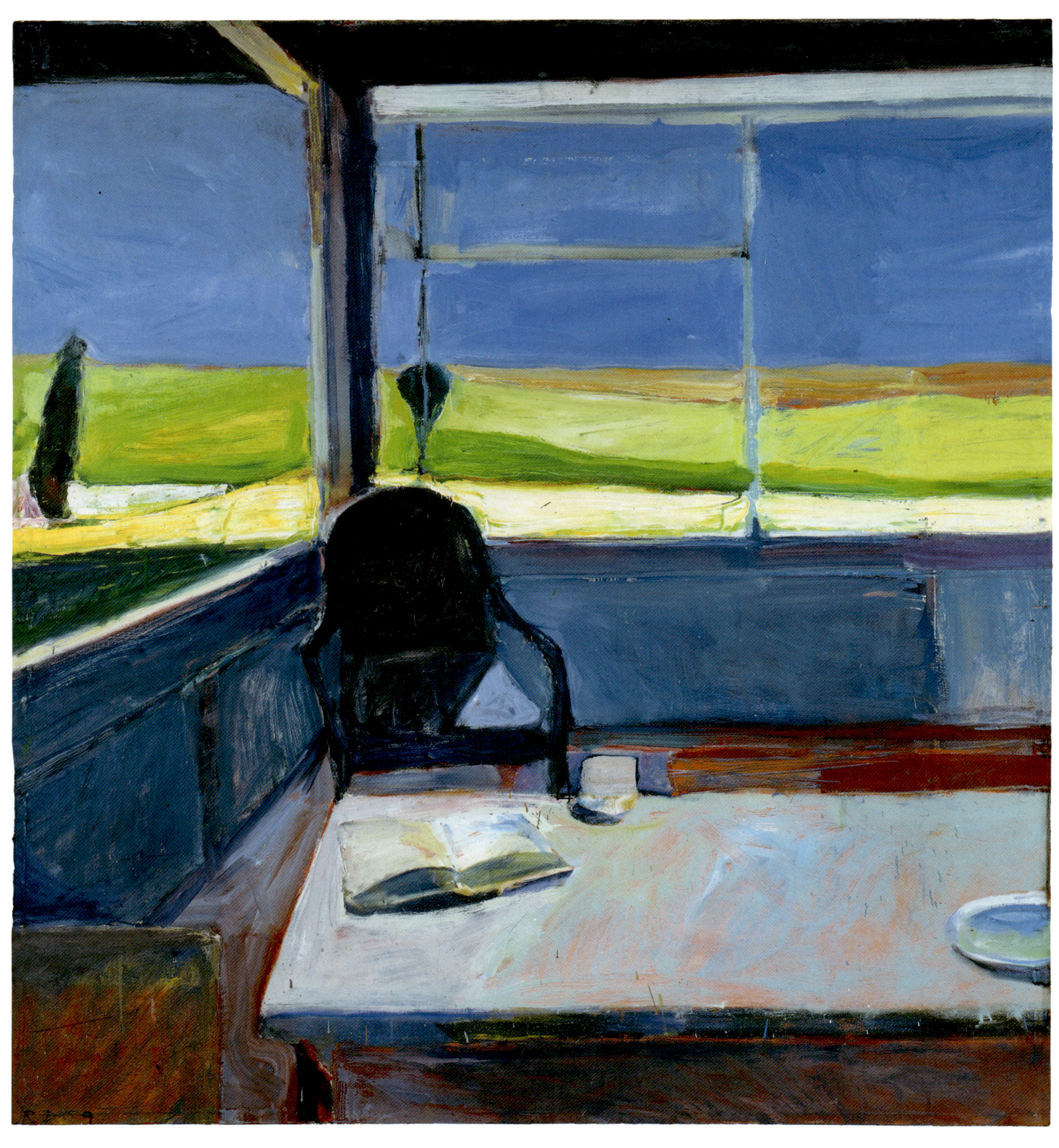

77. Interior with Book, 1959
Oil on canvas, 70 x 64 in. (177.8 x 162.6 cm)
Nelson-Atkins Museum of Art, Kansas City, Missouri, gift of the Friends of Art, F63-15 [1264]

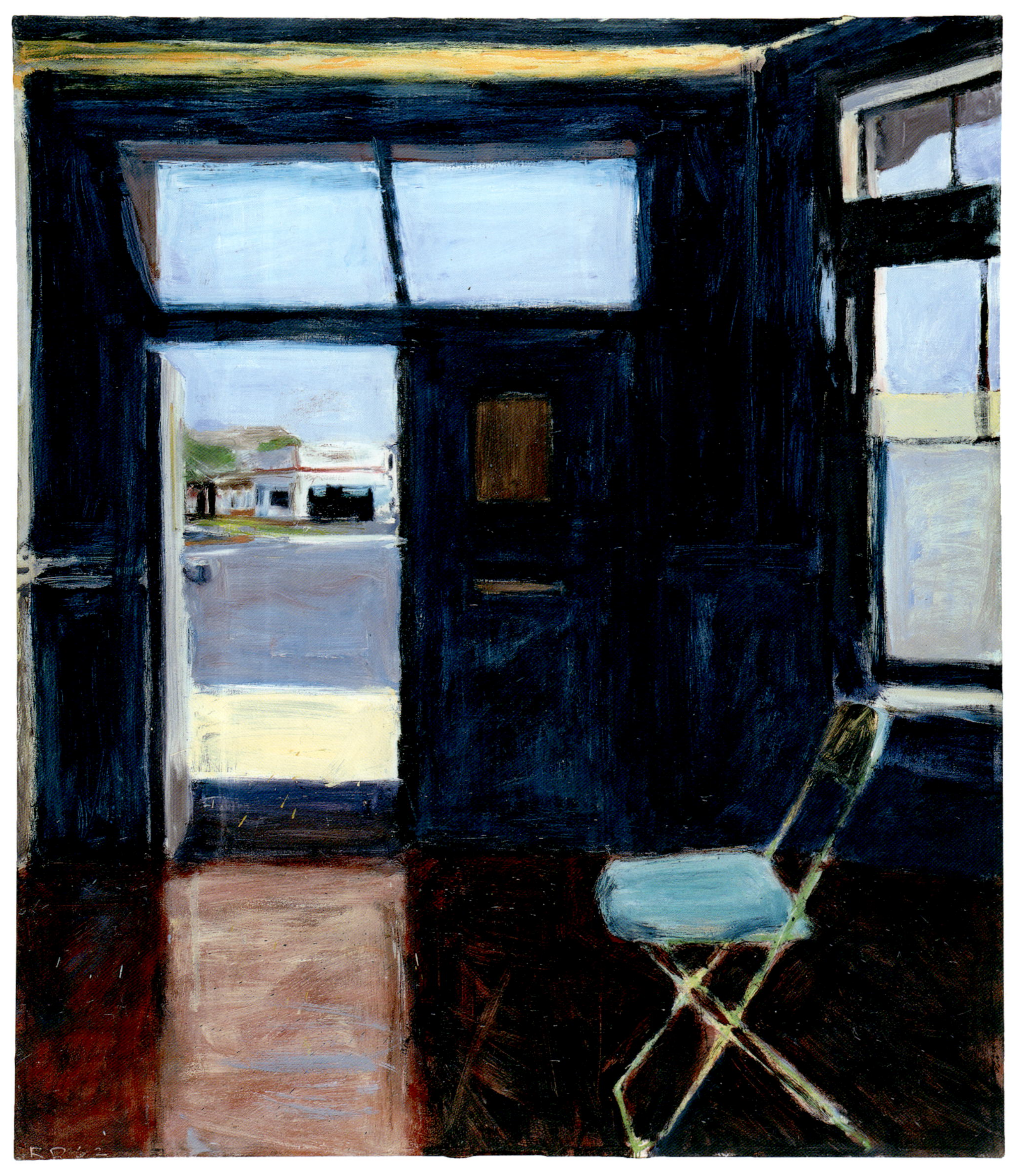

78. *Interior with Doorway*, 1962
Oil on canvas, 70 3/8 x 59 1/2 in. (178.8 x 151.1 cm)
Pennsylvania Academy of the Fine Arts, Philadelphia, Henry D. Gilpin Fund, 1964.3 [1347]

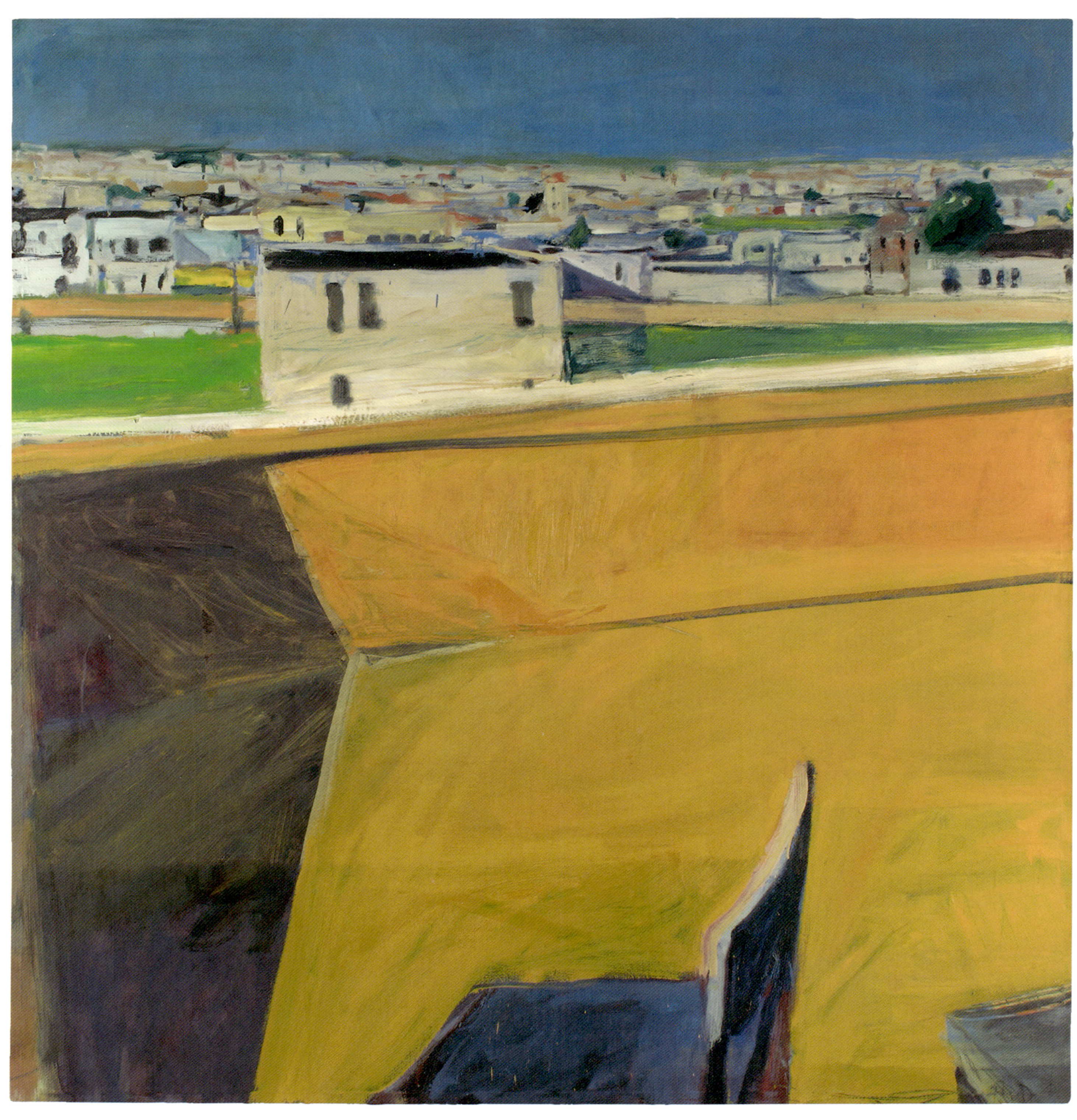

79. *Yellow Porch*, 1961
Oil on canvas, 69 7/8 x 66 7/8 in. (177.5 x 169.9 cm)
Private collection [1334]

80. *Interior with View of Buildings*, 1962
Oil on canvas, 84 x 67 in. (213.4 x 170.2 cm)
Cincinnati Art Museum, Ohio, The Edwin and Virginia Irwin Memorial, 1964.68 [1346]

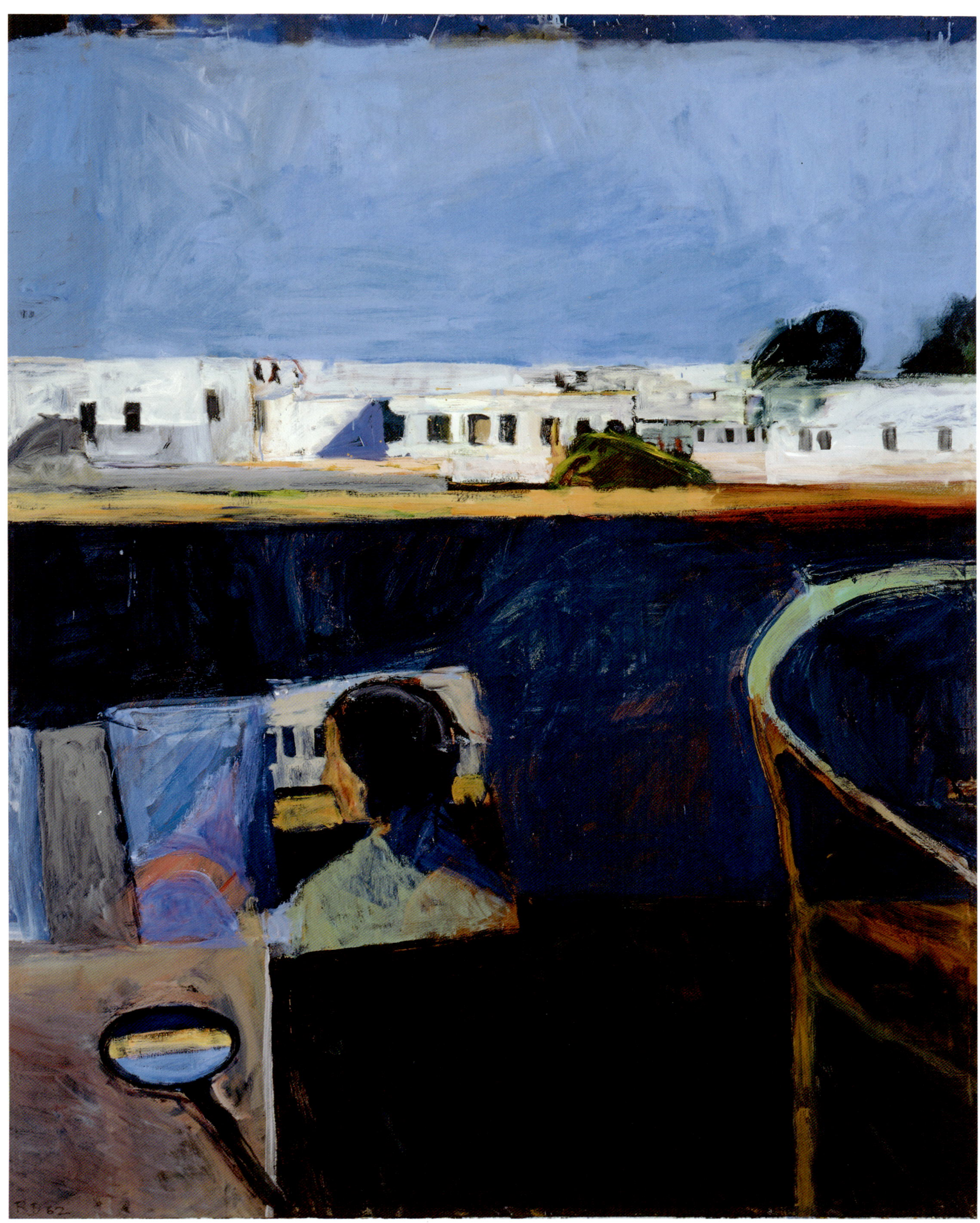

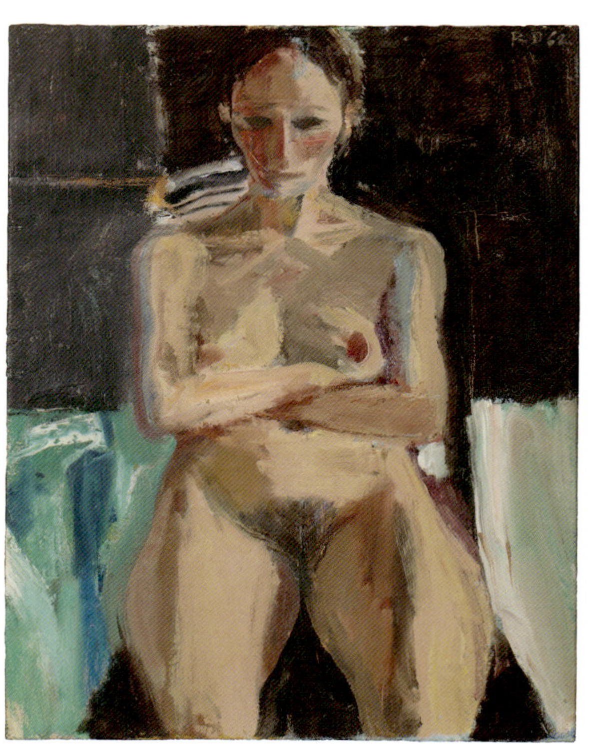

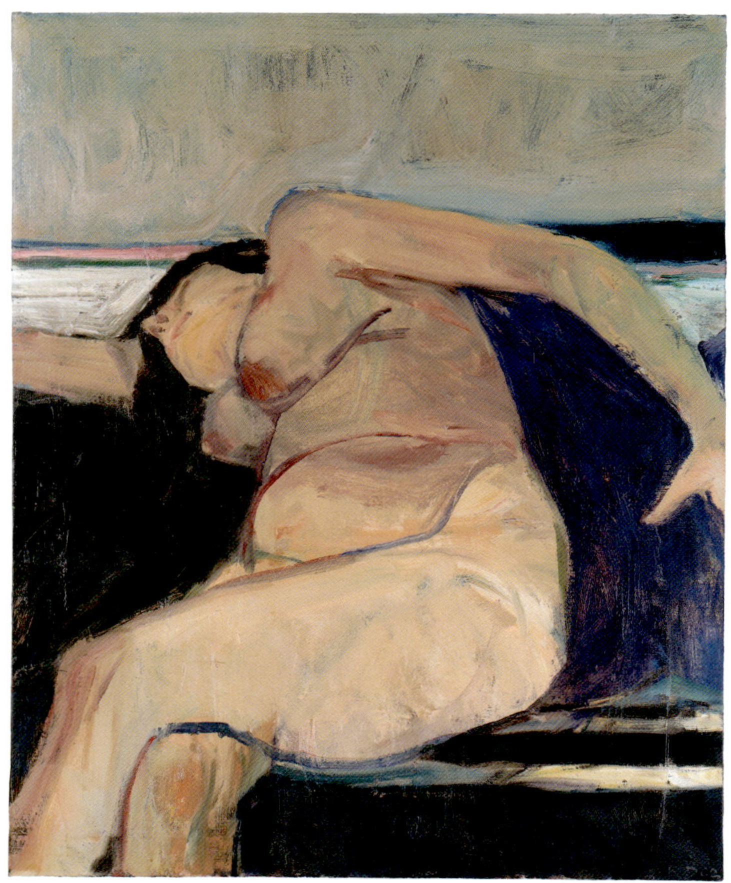

81. *Nude–Arms Folded*, 1962
Oil on canvas, 26 3/4 x 20 7/8 in. (67.9 x 53 cm)
Collection of John McEnroe [1350]

82. *Reclining Nude, Pink Stripe*, 1962
Oil on canvas, 30 3/4 x 24 3/4 in. (78.1 x 62.9 cm)
The Metropolitan Museum of Art, New York, purchase, Lila Acheson Wallace Gift, 2001, 2001.664 [1352]

83. *Seated Nude, Black Background*, 1961
Oil on canvas, 84 x 54 in. (213.4 x 137.2 cm)
Private collection [1641]

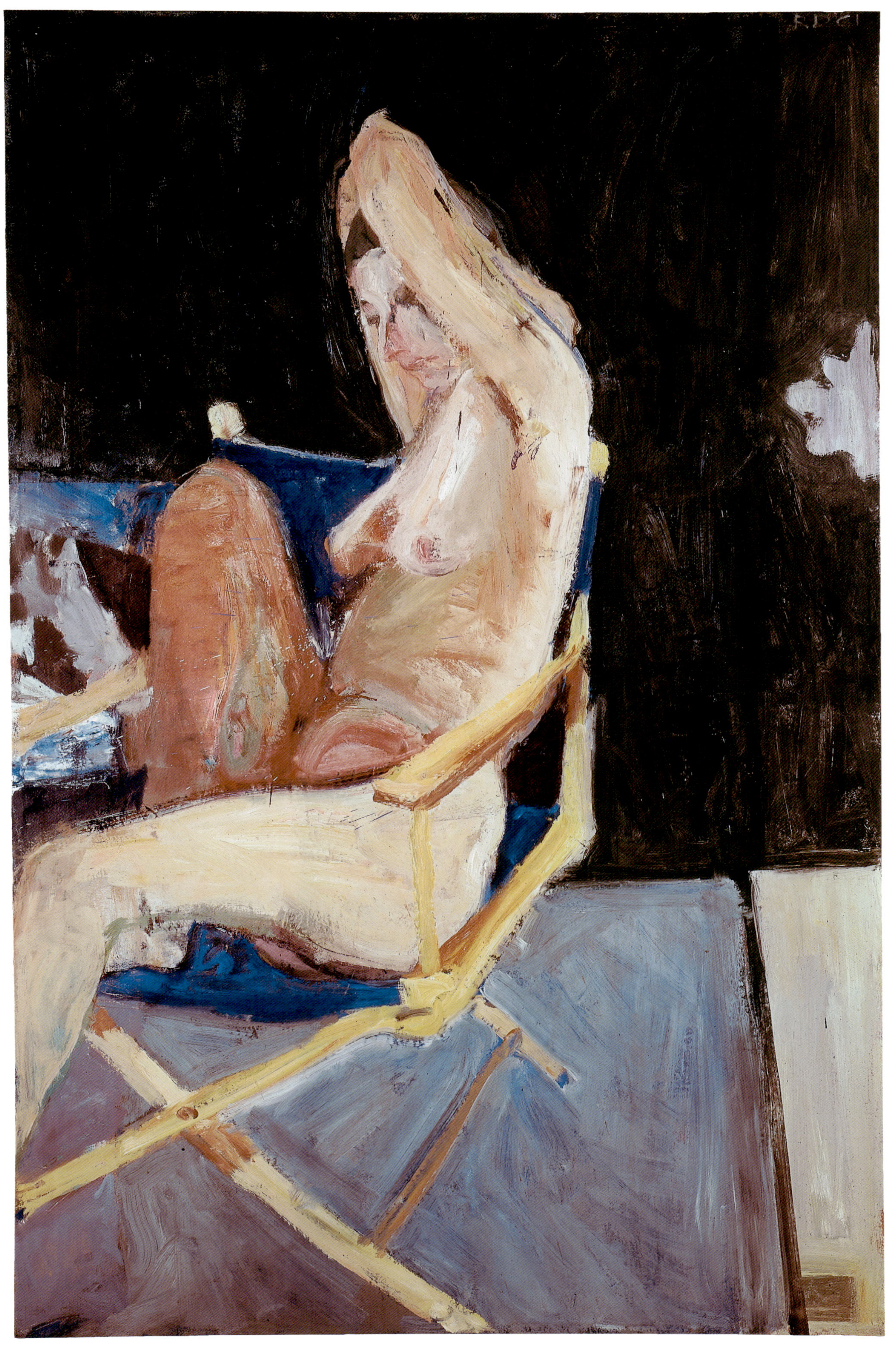

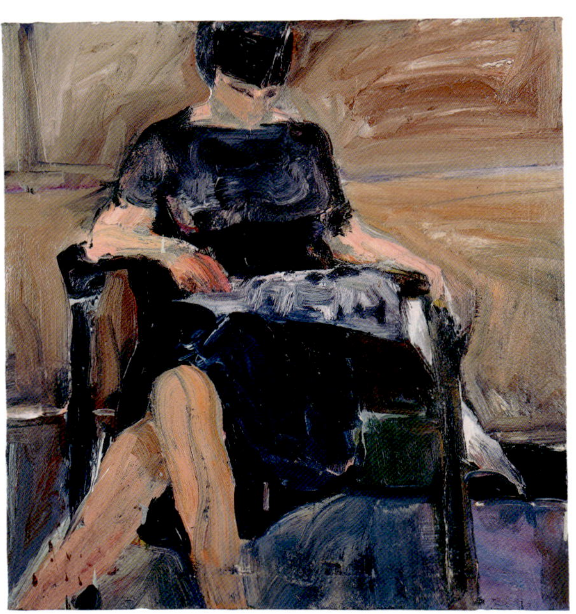

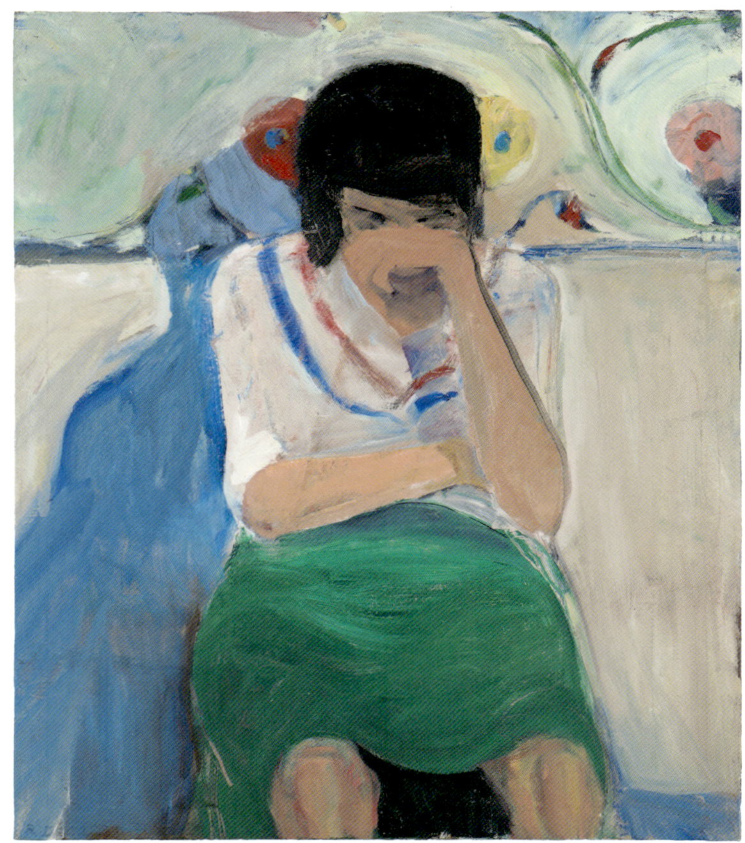

84. *Untitled*, 1961
Oil on canvas, 24 x 22 in. (61 x 55.9 cm)
Private collection [1333]

85. *Girl with Flowered Background*, 1962
Oil on canvas, 40 x 34 in. (101.6 x 86.4 cm)
Modern Art Museum of Fort Worth, Texas, Museum Purchase, Sid W. Richardson Foundation Endowment Fund, 1991.11.P.P [1342]

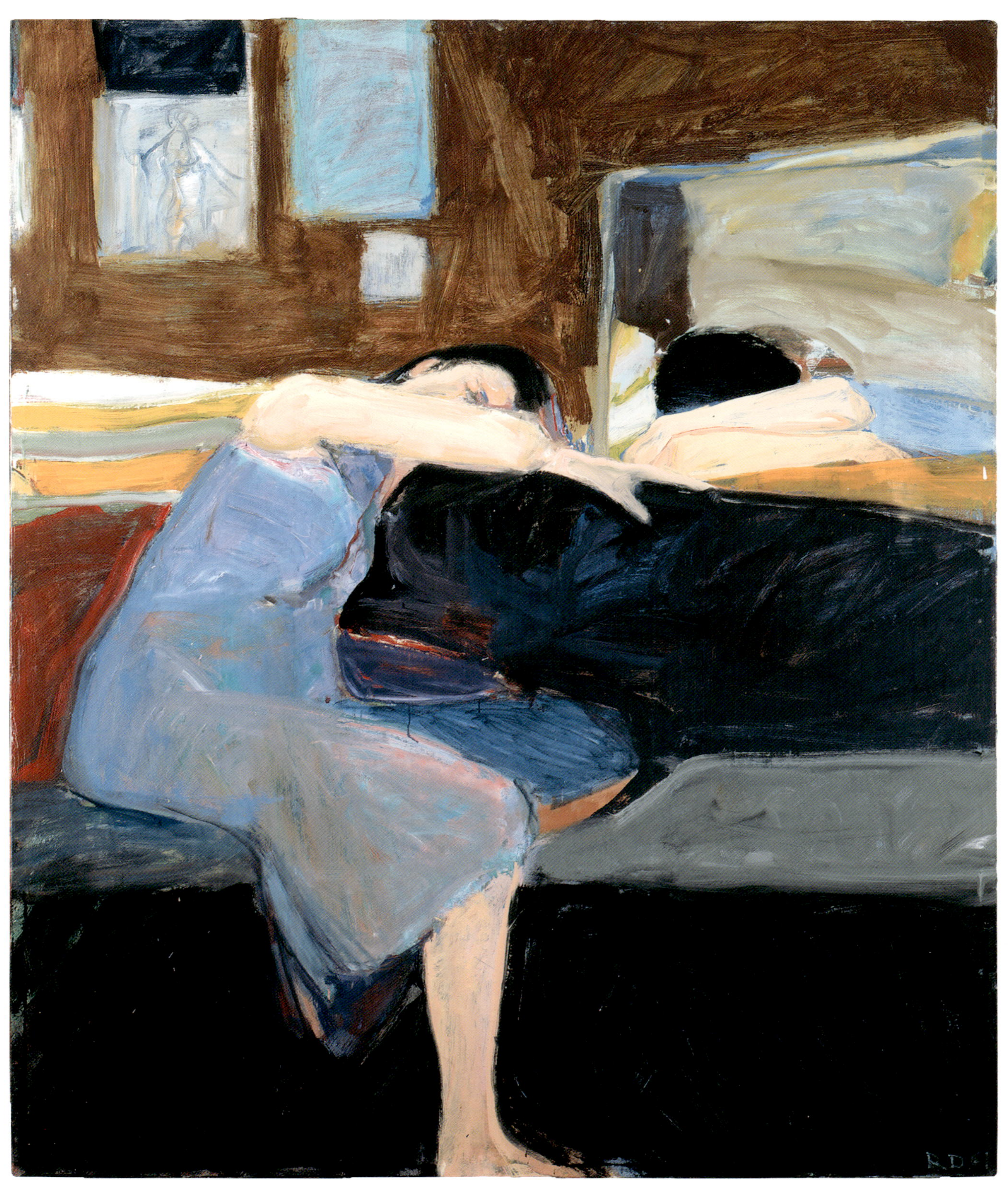

86. *Sleeping Woman*, 1961
Oil on canvas, 70 x 58 in. (177.8 x 147.3 cm)
Kalamazoo Institute of Arts, Michigan [1328]

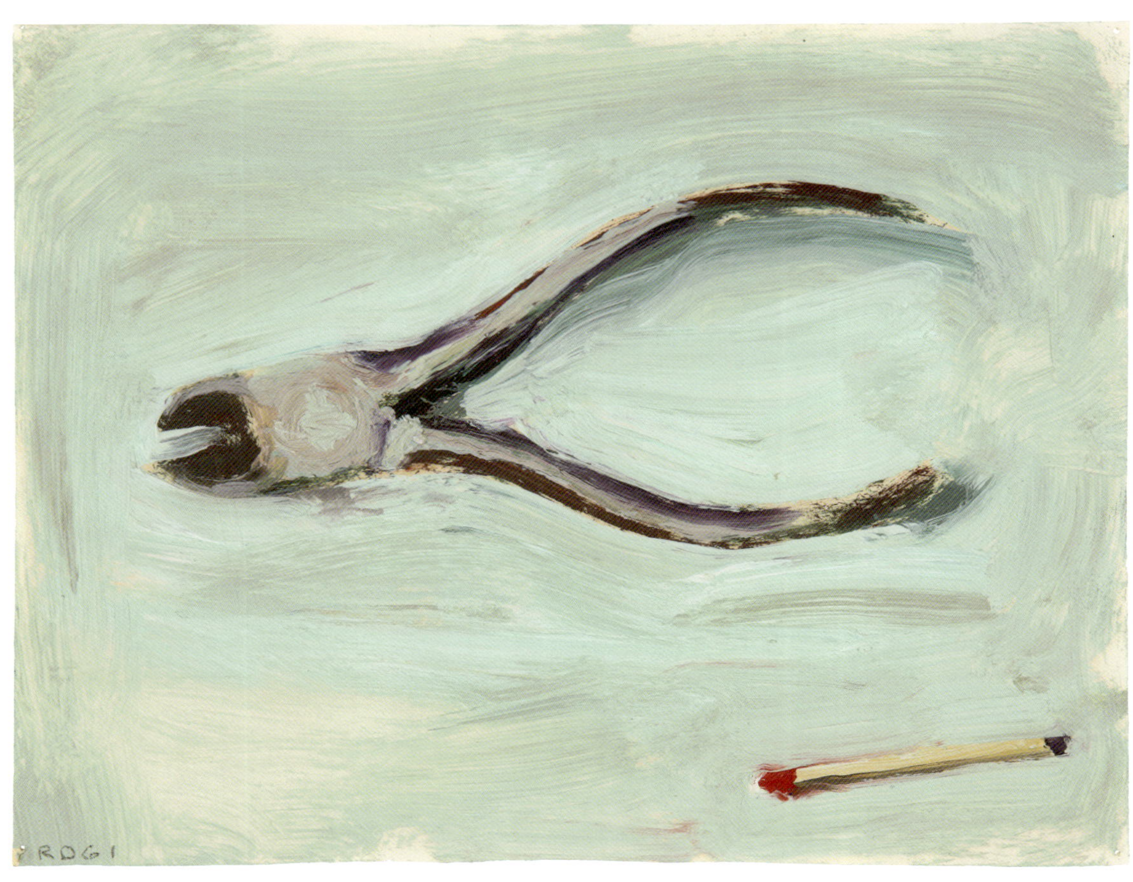

87. *Pliers and Match*, 1961
Oil on paper, 8 1/2 x 10 7/8 in. (21.6 x 27.6 cm)
The Grant Family Collection [2110]

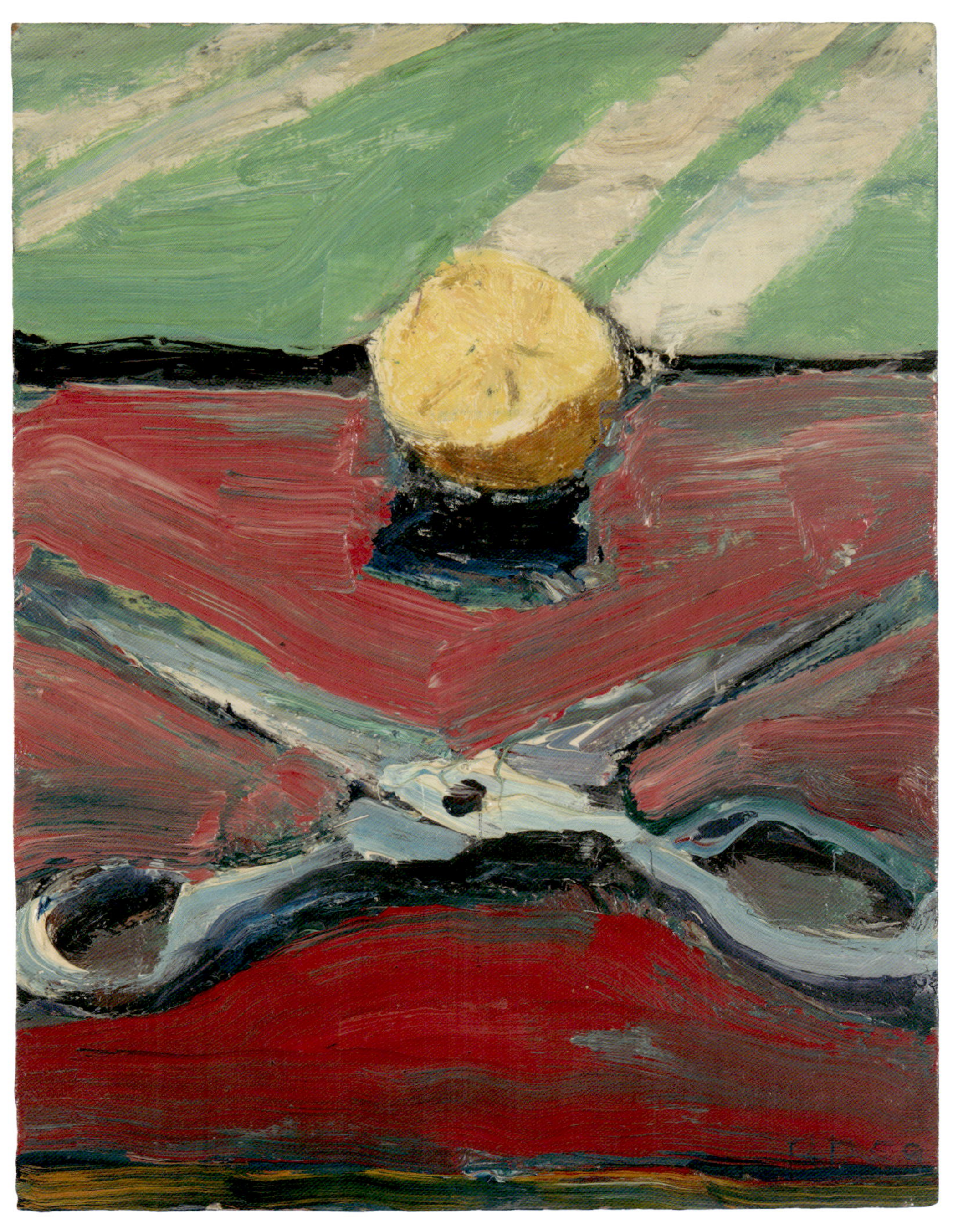

88. *Scissors and Lemon, II*, 1959
Oil on hardboard, 13 1/4 x 10 in. (33.7 x 25.4 cm)
Santa Cruz Island Foundation, Carpinteria, California, 1988.17 [1276]

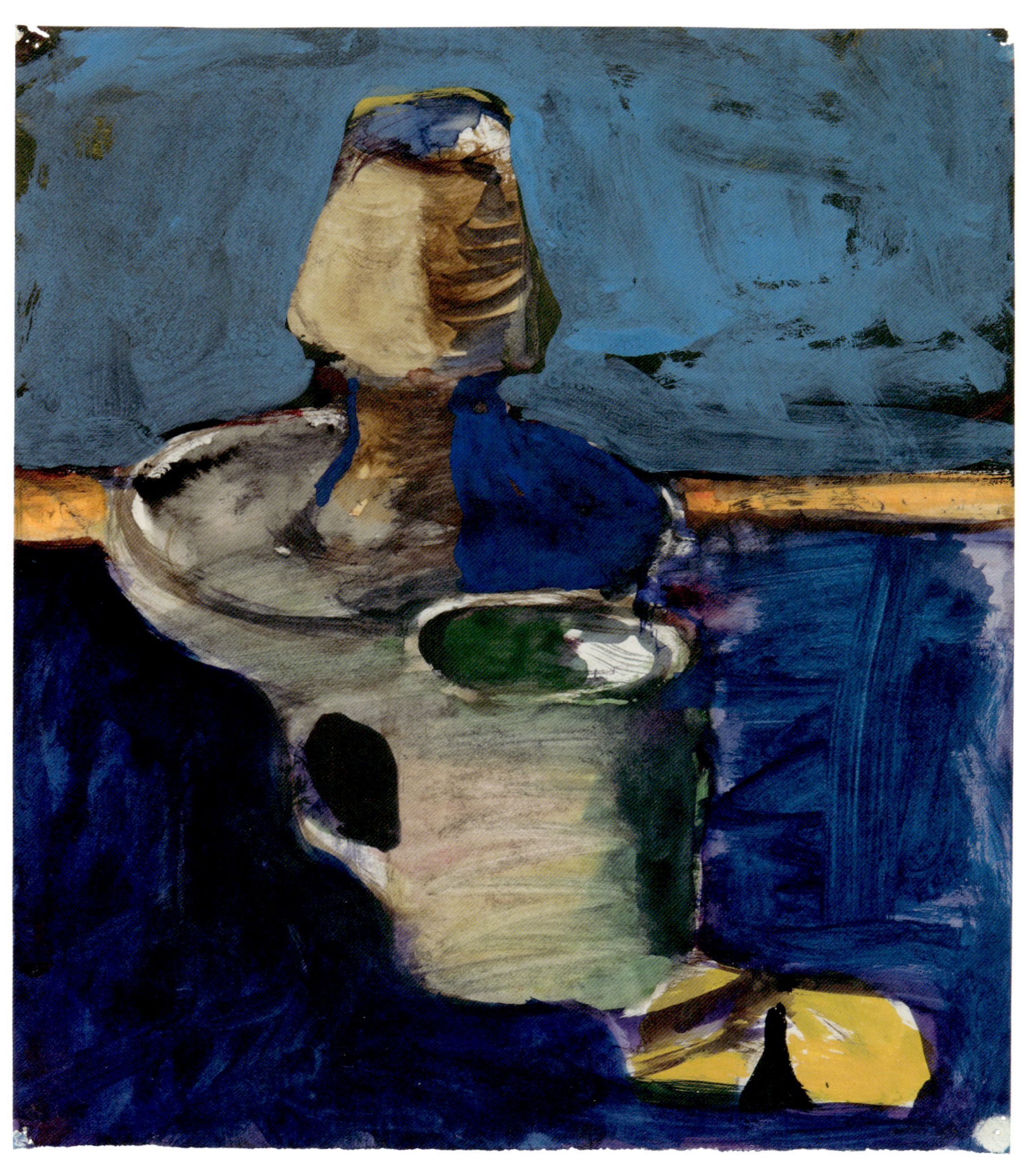

89. *Untitled*, ca. 1964
Gouache on paper, 12 3/4 x 10 7/8 in. (32.4 x 27.6 cm)
Private collection [655]

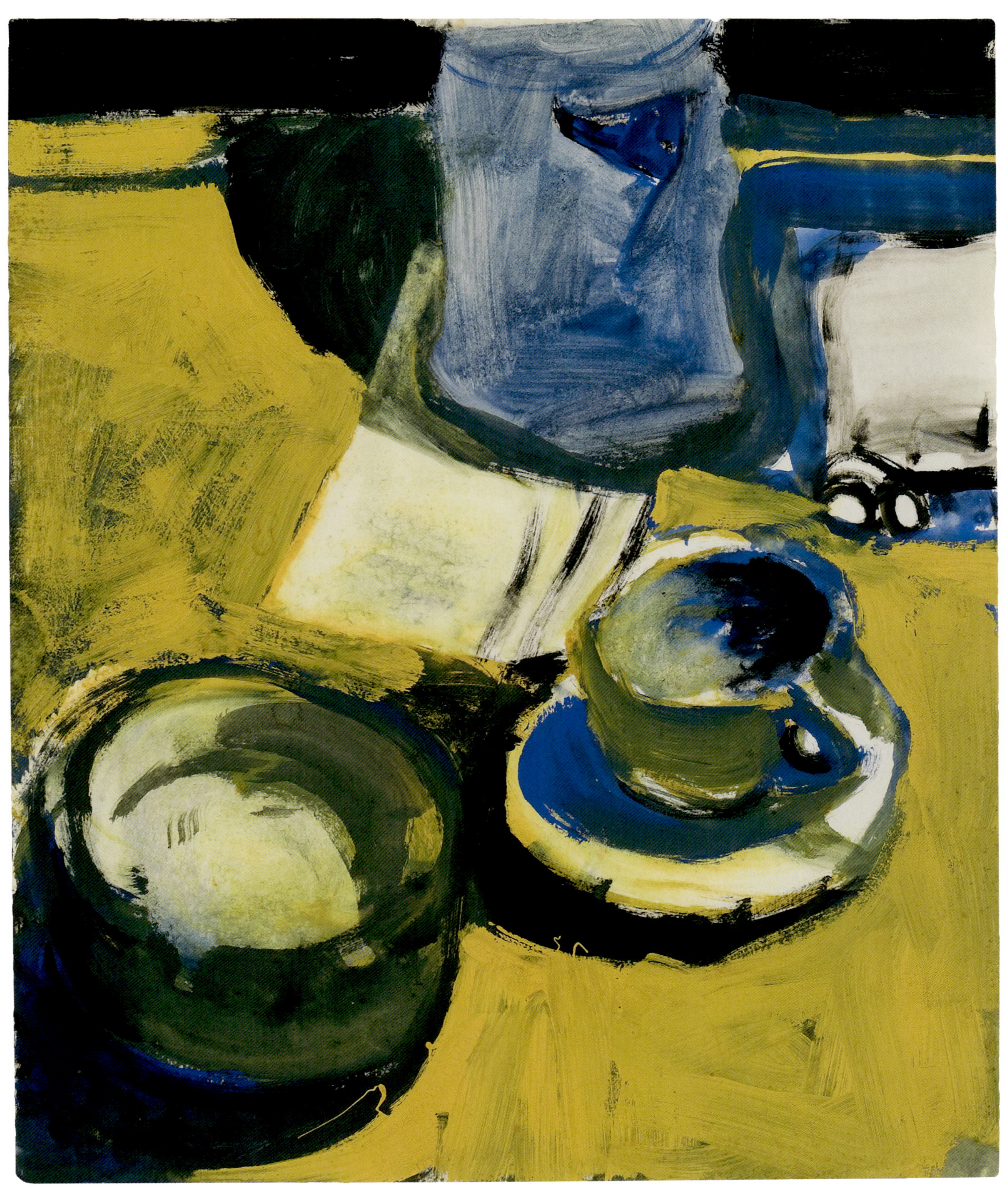

90. *Untitled*, ca. 1961
Gouache on paper, 17 x 14 in. (43.2 x 35.6 cm)
Collection of Christopher Diebenkorn [2513]

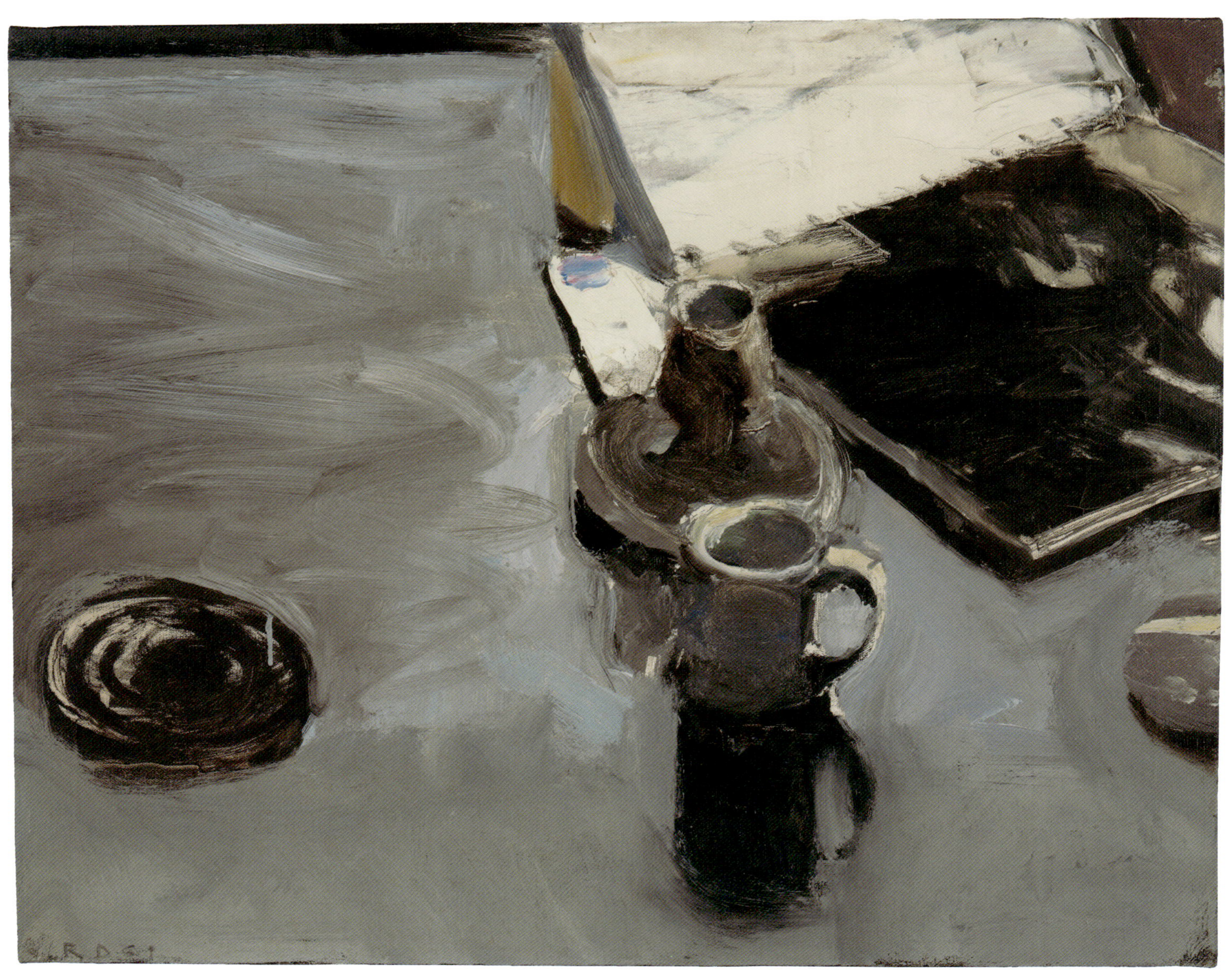

91. *Still Life with Letter*, 1961
Oil on canvas, 20 5/8 x 25 5/8 in. (52.4 x 65.1 cm)
Collection of the City and County of San Francisco, purchased by the San Francisco Arts Commission for the Hall of Justice, 1967.31 [1329]

92. *Ashtray and Doors*, 1962
Oil on canvas, 29 x 20 3/8 in. (73.7 x 51.8 cm)
Private collection [1335]

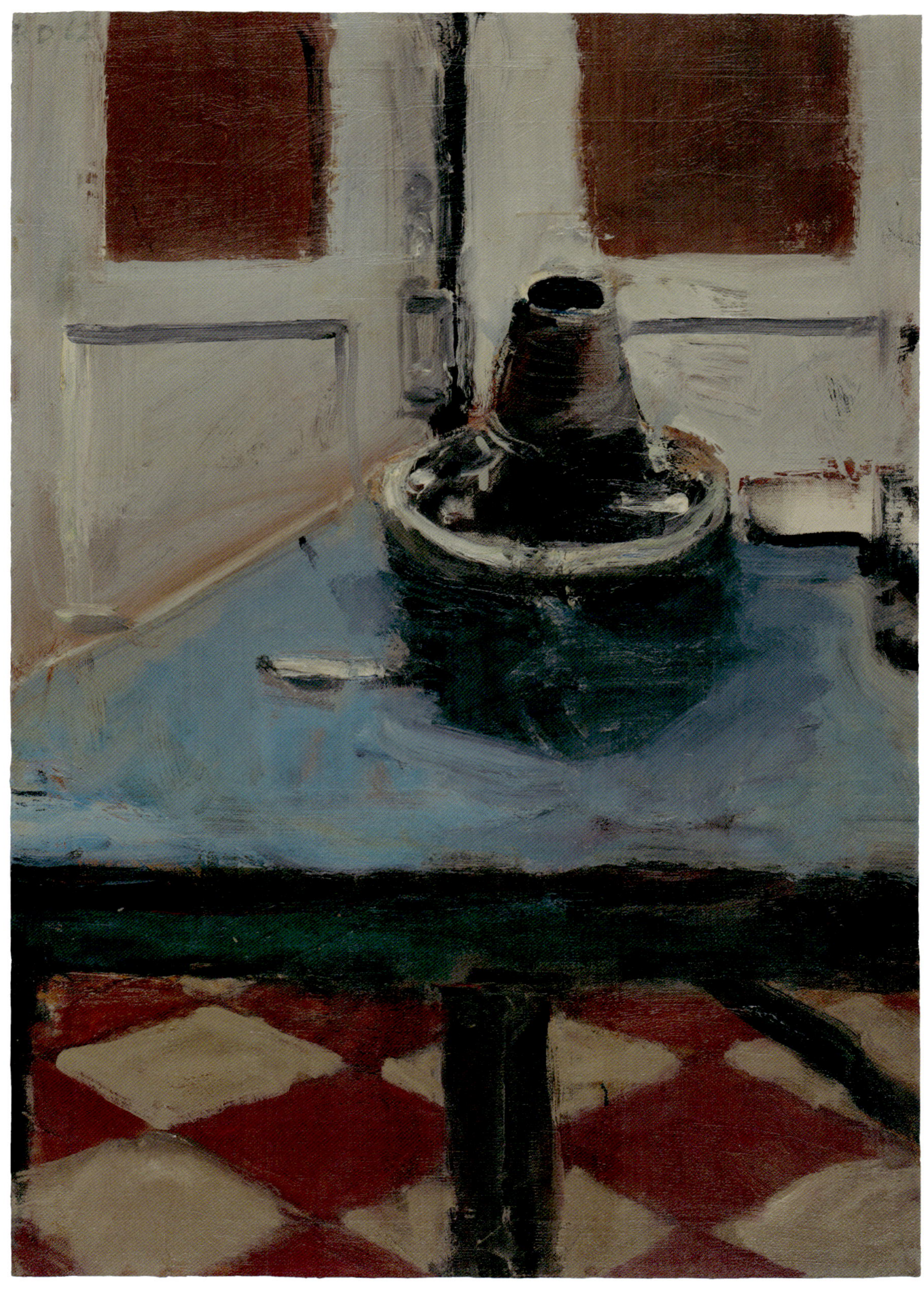

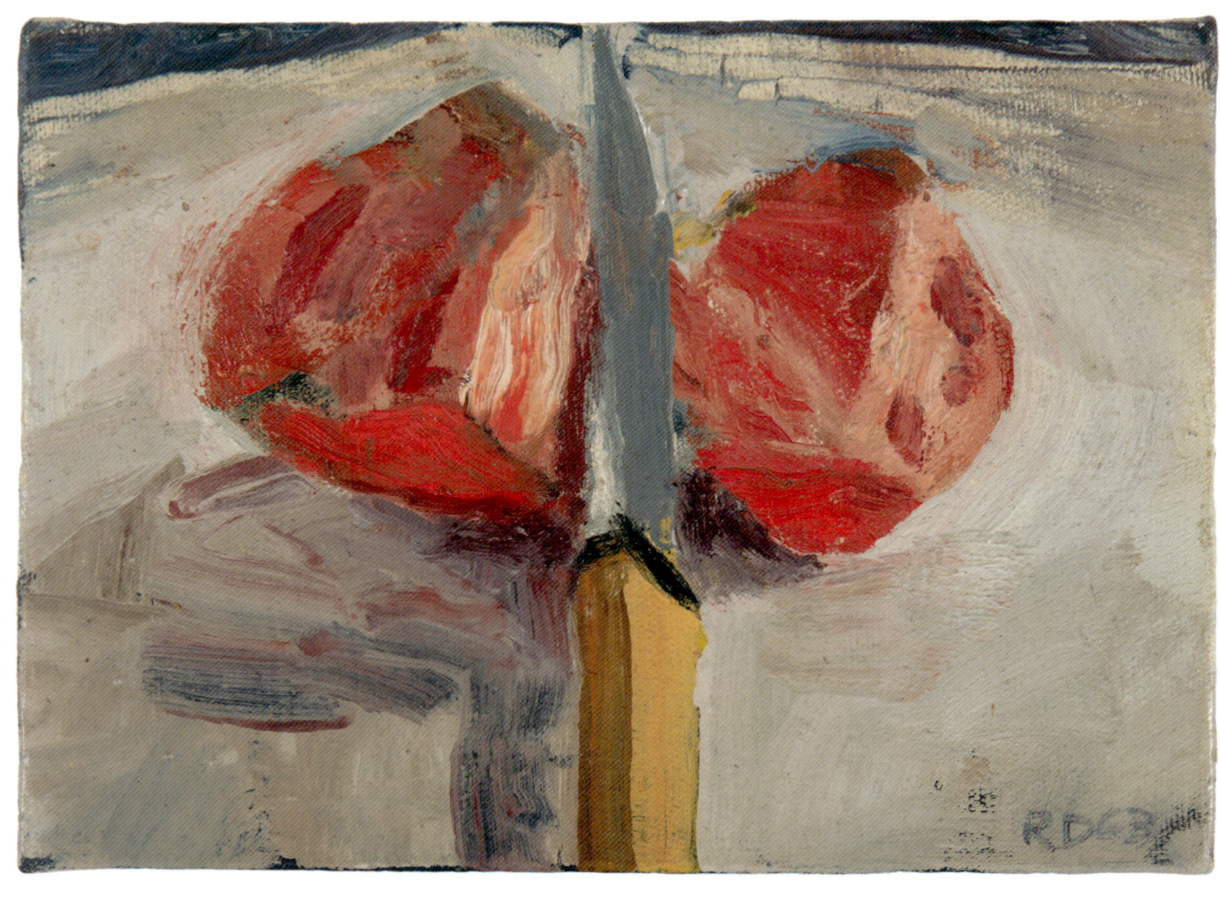

93. *Untitled (Tomato and Knife)*, 1963
Oil on canvas mounted on board, 5 5/8 x 7 7/8 in. (14.3 x 20 cm)
Santa Cruz Island Foundation, Carpinteria, California, 1988.27 [1396]

94. *Knife in a Glass*, 1963
Oil on hardboard, 14 5/8 x 10 3/4 in. (37.1 x 27.3 cm)
Collection of Nancy and Roger Boas [1386]

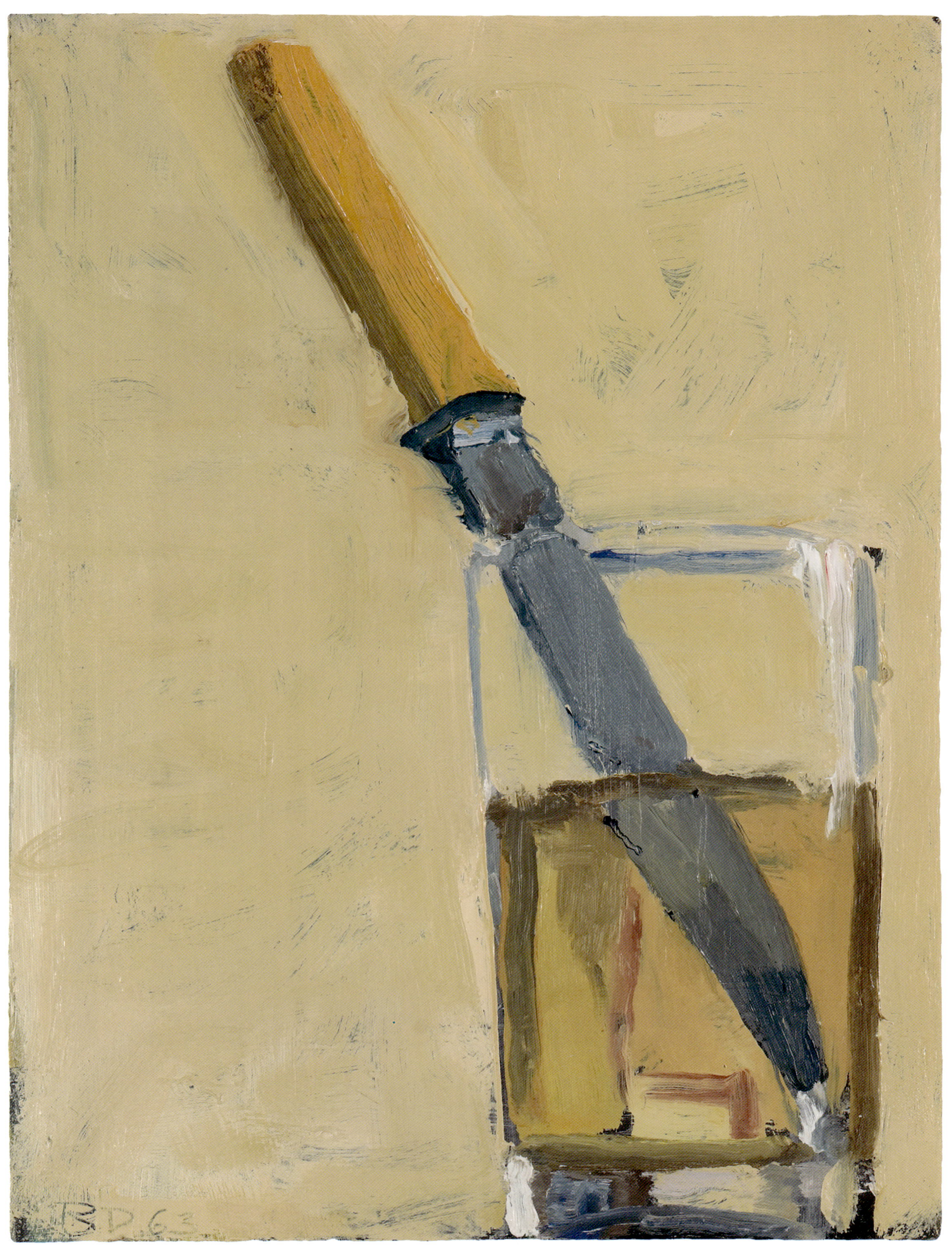

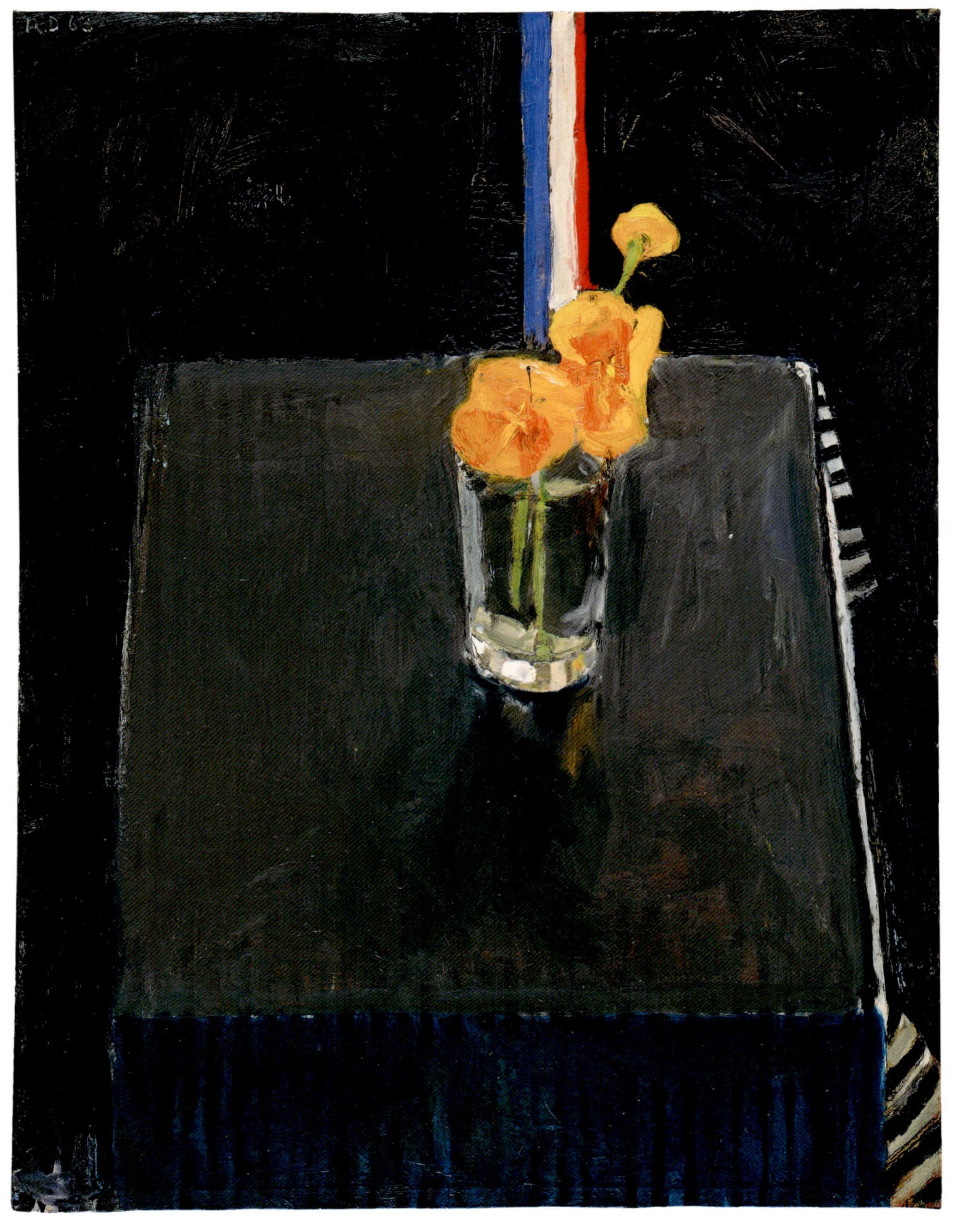

95. *Poppies*, 1963
Oil on canvas, 40 x 30 in. (101.6 x 76.2 cm)
Private collection [1391]

96. *Interior with Flowers*, 1961
Oil on canvas, 57 x 38 3/4 in. (144.8 x 98.4 cm)
Collection of Gretchen and John Berggruen [1316]

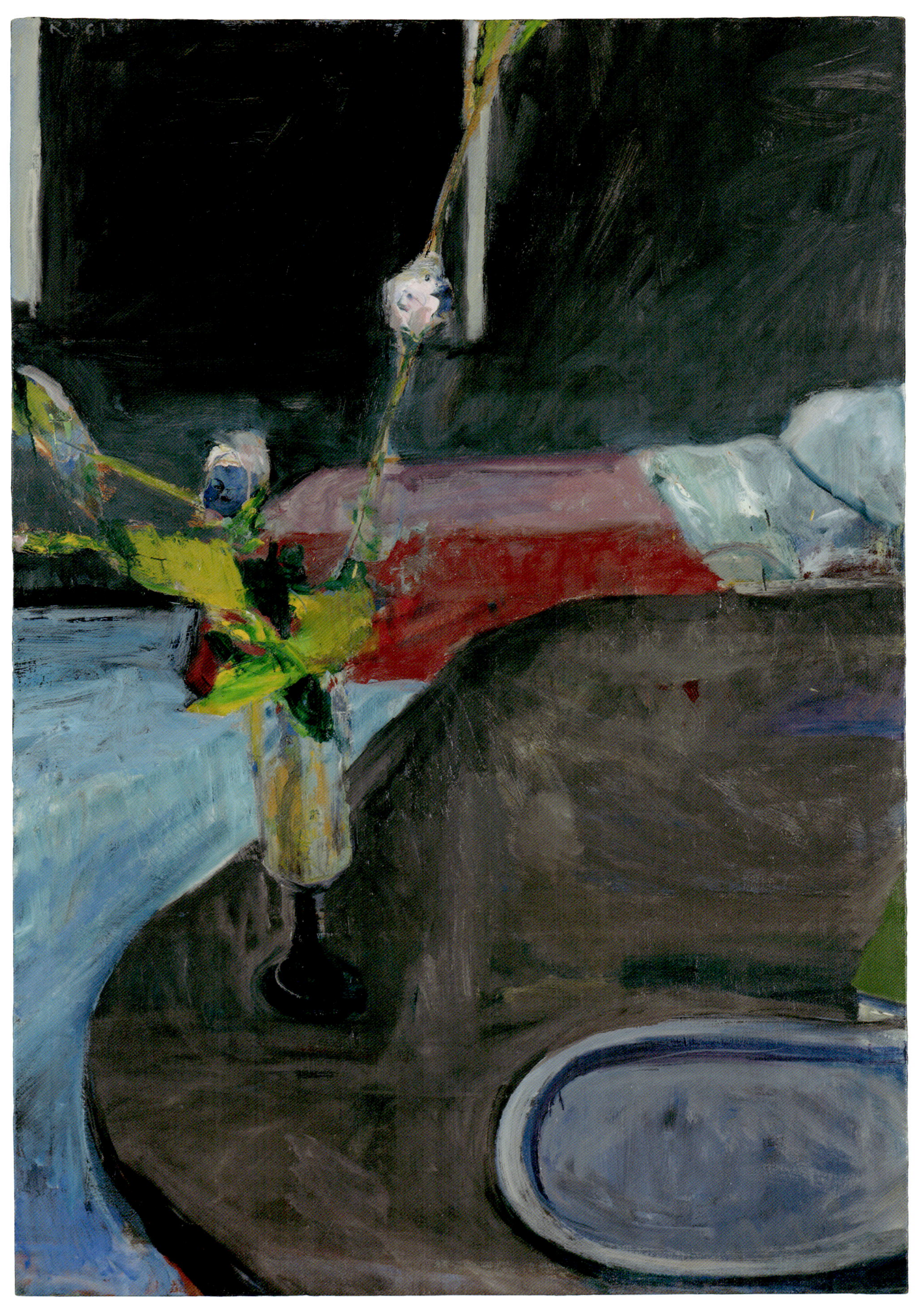

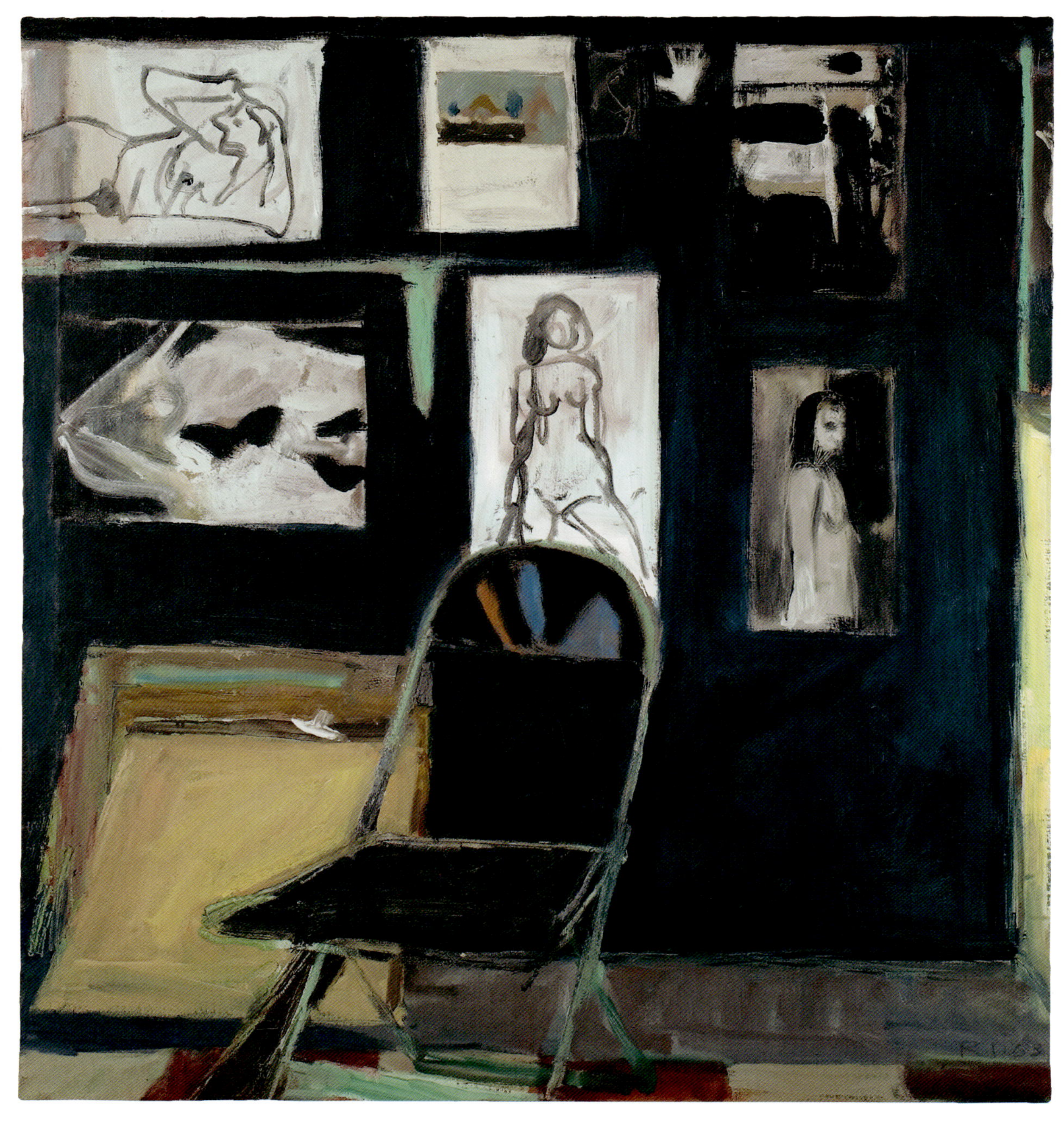

97. *Studio Wall*, 1963
Oil on canvas, 45 3/8 x 42 1/2 in. (115.3 x 108 cm)
Private collection [1395]

98. *Corner of Studio—Sink*, 1963
Oil on canvas, 76 3/4 x 70 in. (194.9 x 177.8 cm)
Private collection [1378]

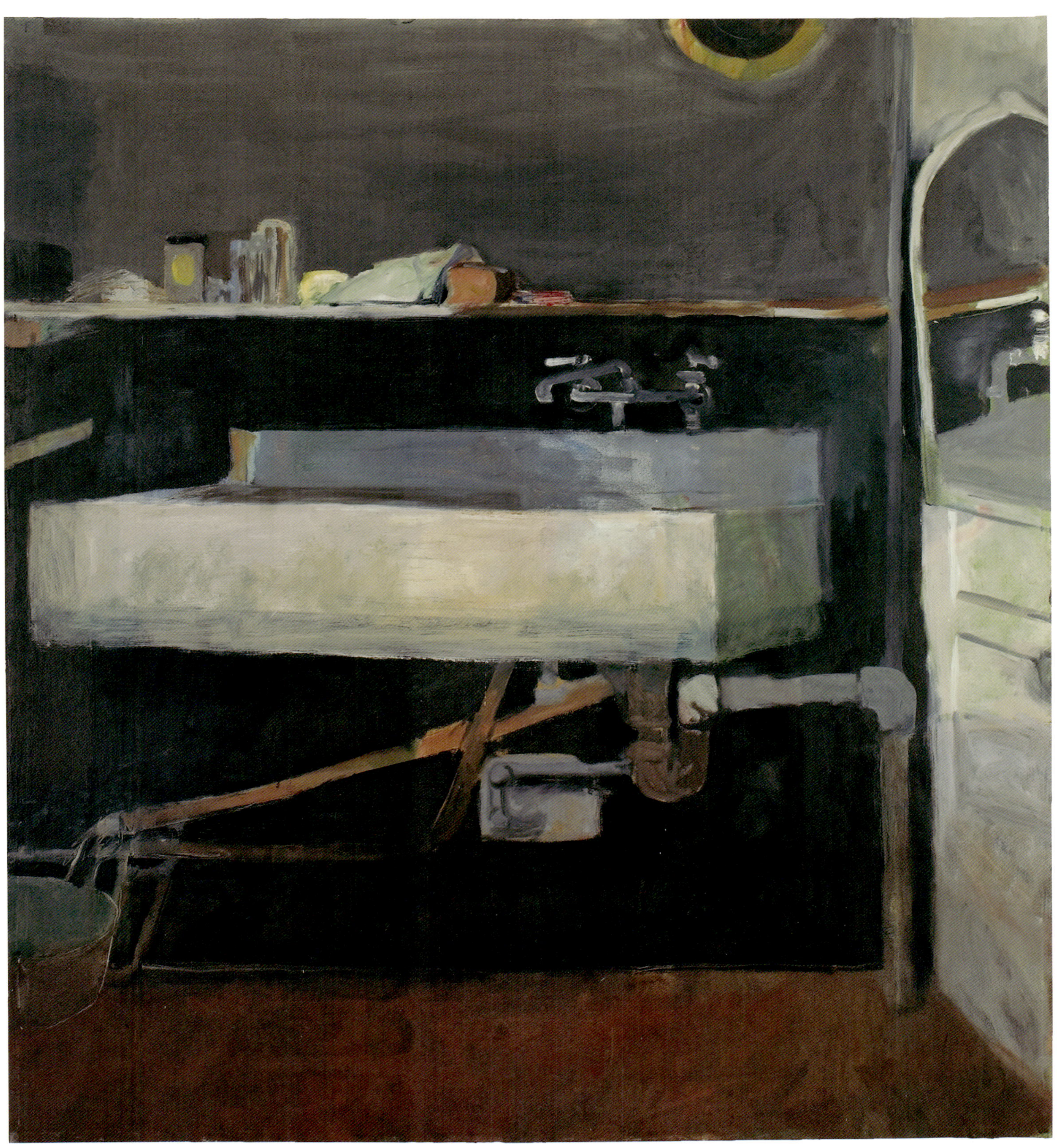

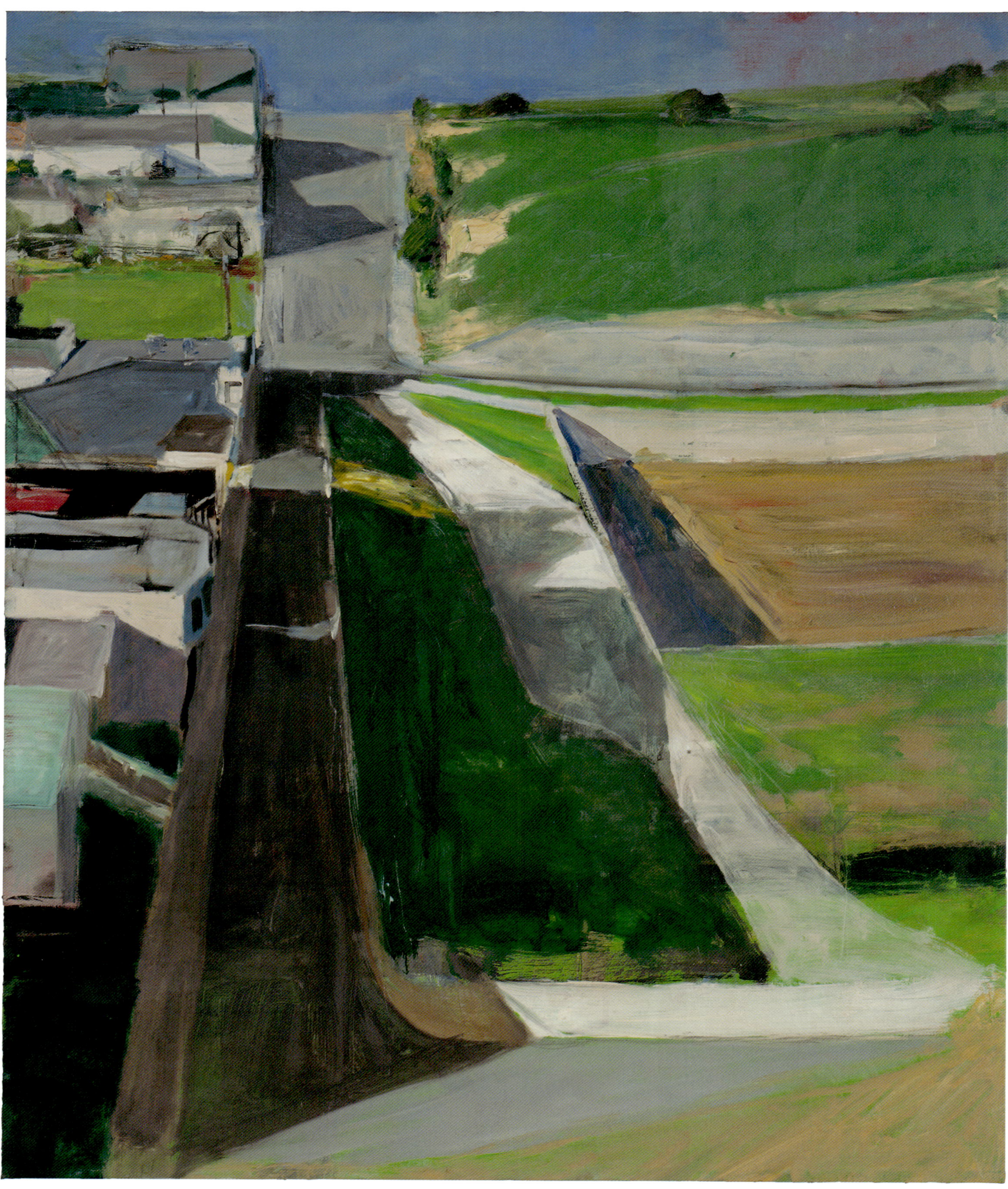

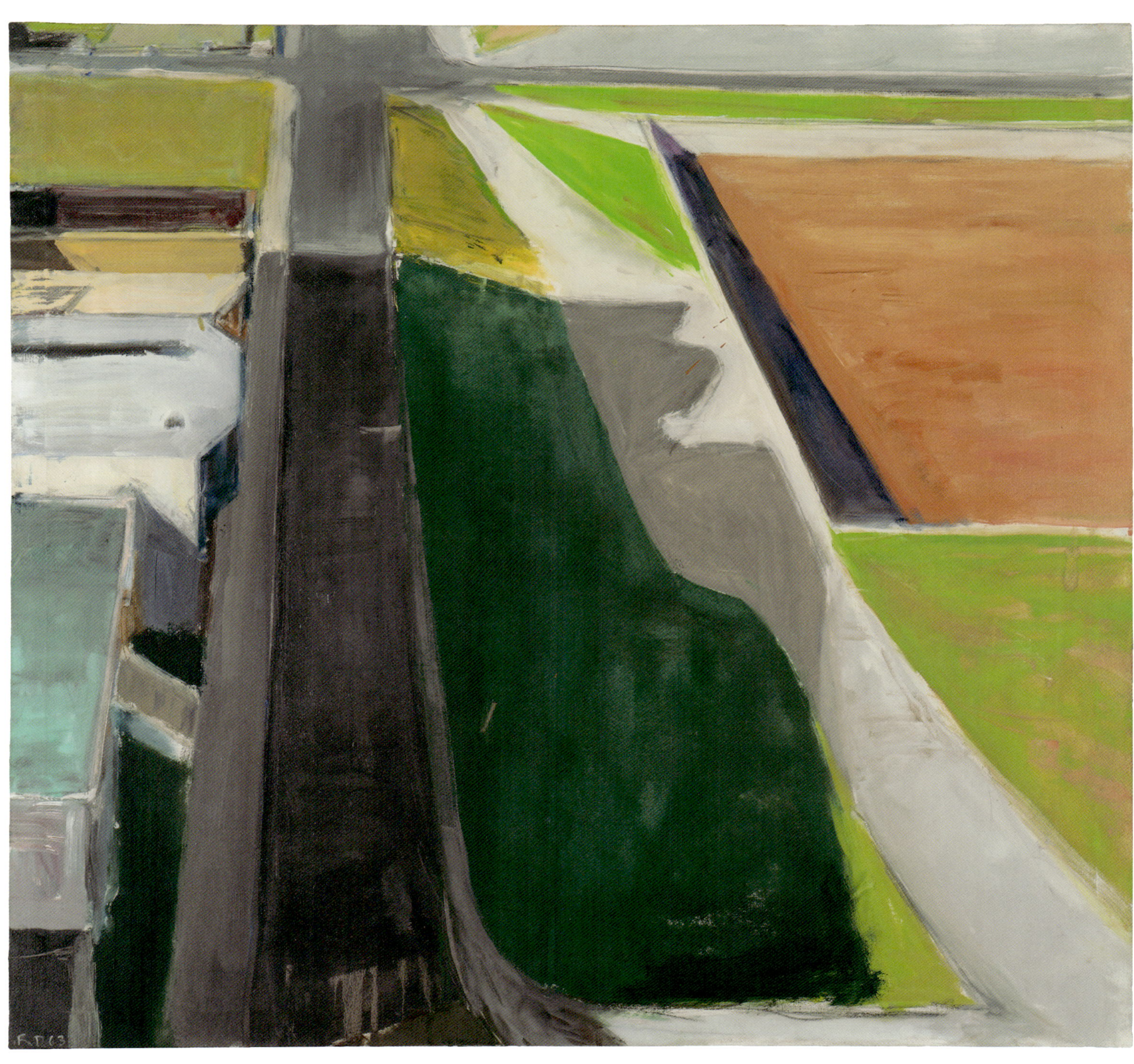

99. *Cityscape #1*, 1963
Oil on canvas, 60 1/4 x 50 1/2 in. (153 x 128.3 cm)
San Francisco Museum of Modern Art, purchase with funds from Trustees and friends in memory of Hector Escobosa, Brayton Wilbur, and J. D. Zellerbach, 64.46 [1374]

100. *Cityscape #3 (Landscape #2)*, 1963
Oil on canvas, 47 x 50 1/4 in. (119.4 x 127.6 cm)
Collection of Donald and Barbara Zucker [1375]

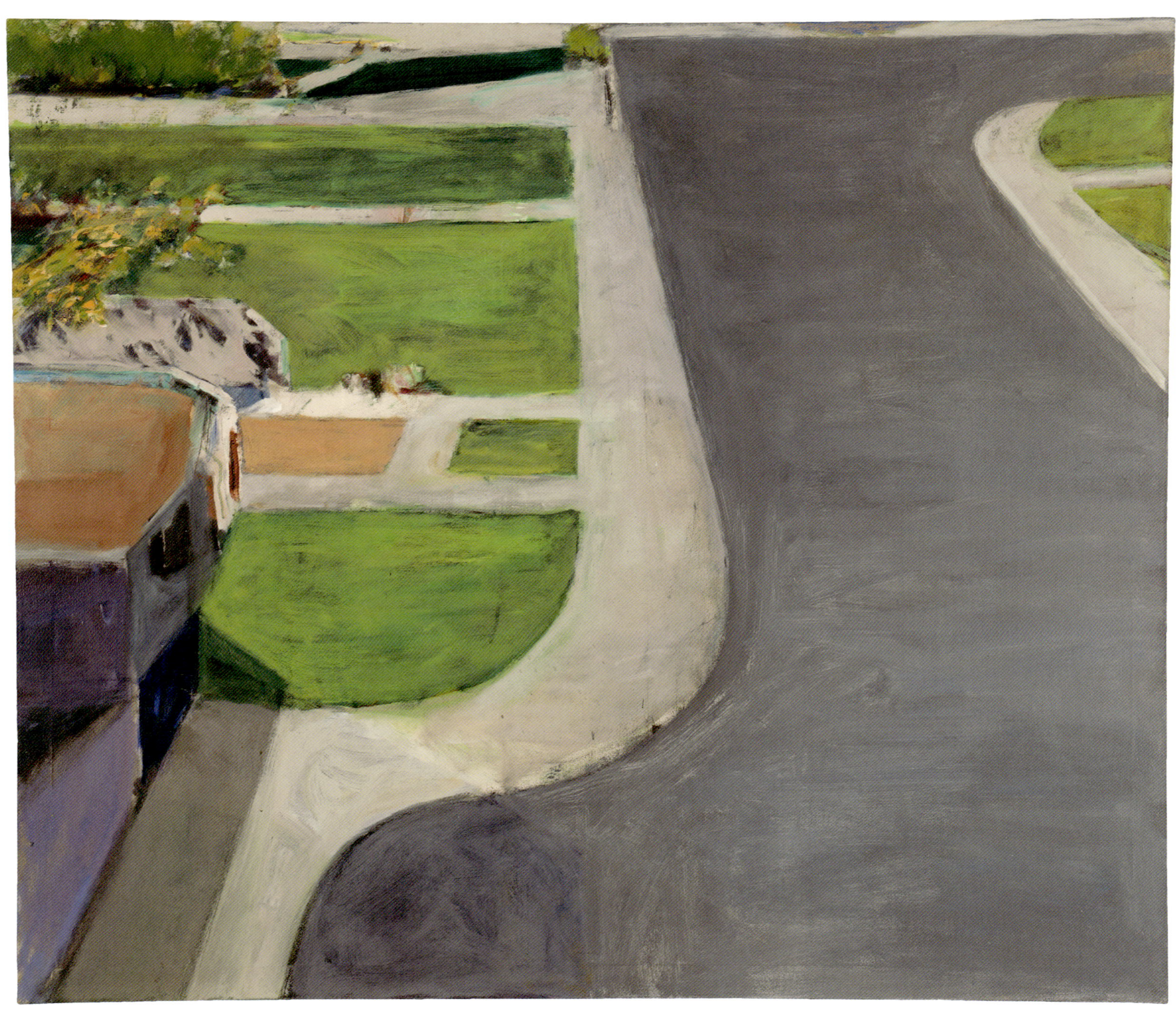

101. *Cityscape #4*, 1963–1966
Oil on canvas, 47 x 53 3/4 in. (119.4 x 136.5 cm)
Collection of Christopher Diebenkorn [1377]

102. *Ingleside*, 1963
Oil on canvas, 81 3/4 x 69 1/2 in. (207.6 x 176.5 cm)
Grand Rapids Art Museum, Michigan, Museum Purchase, 1967.1.1 [1383]

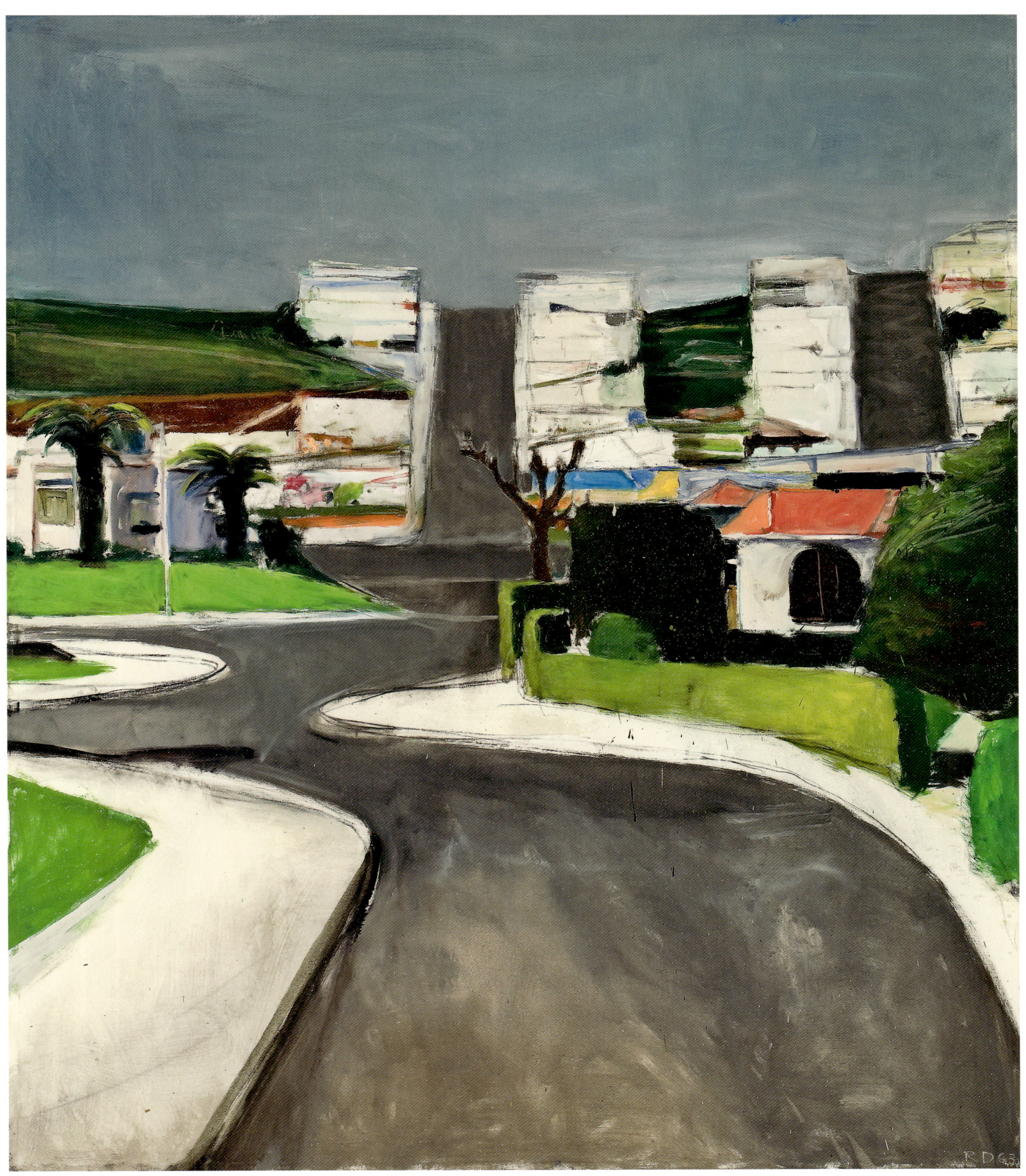

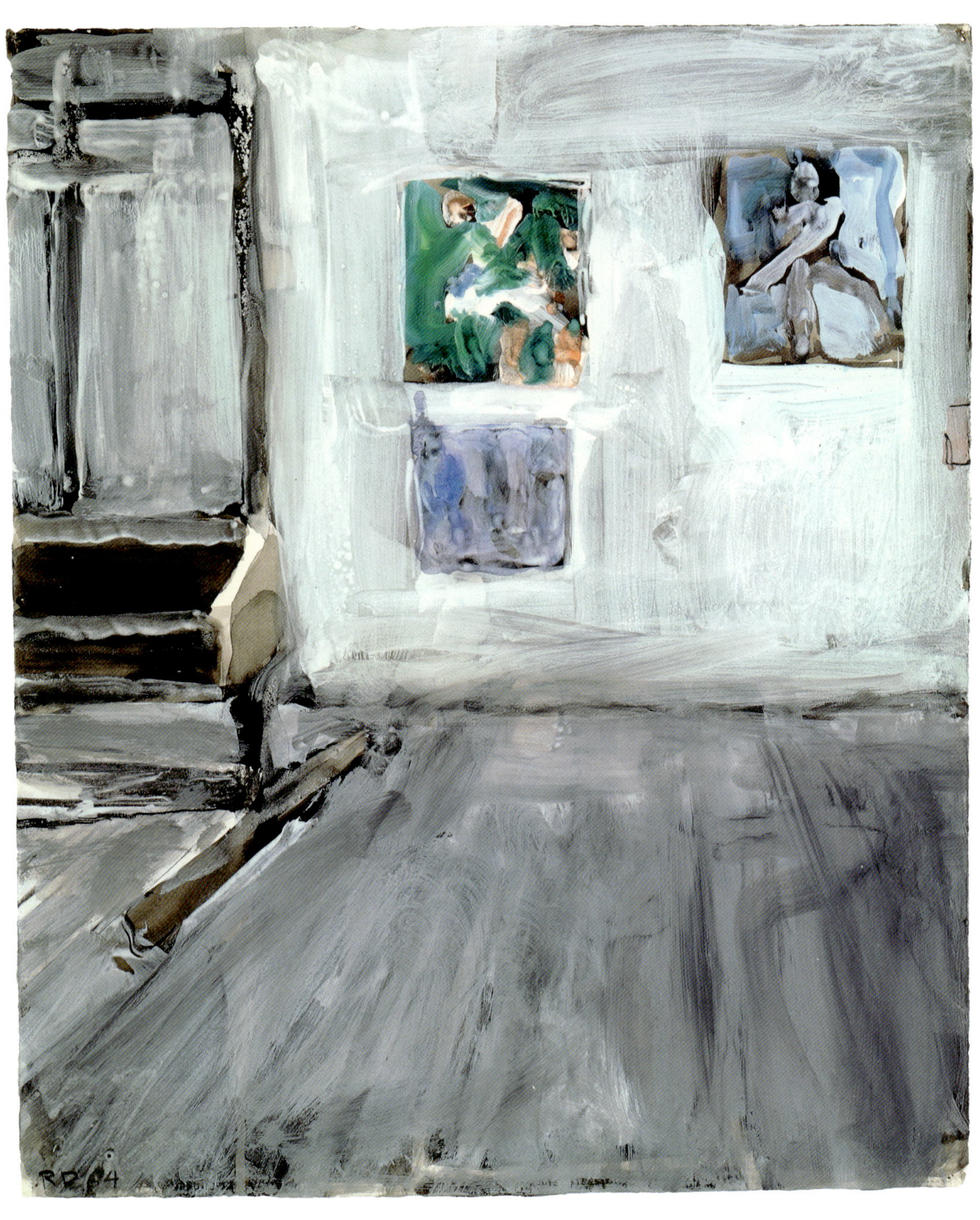

103. *Studio Interior*, 1964
Watercolor on paper, 14 1/2 x 11 1/2 in. (36.8 x 29.2 cm)
Private collection [468]

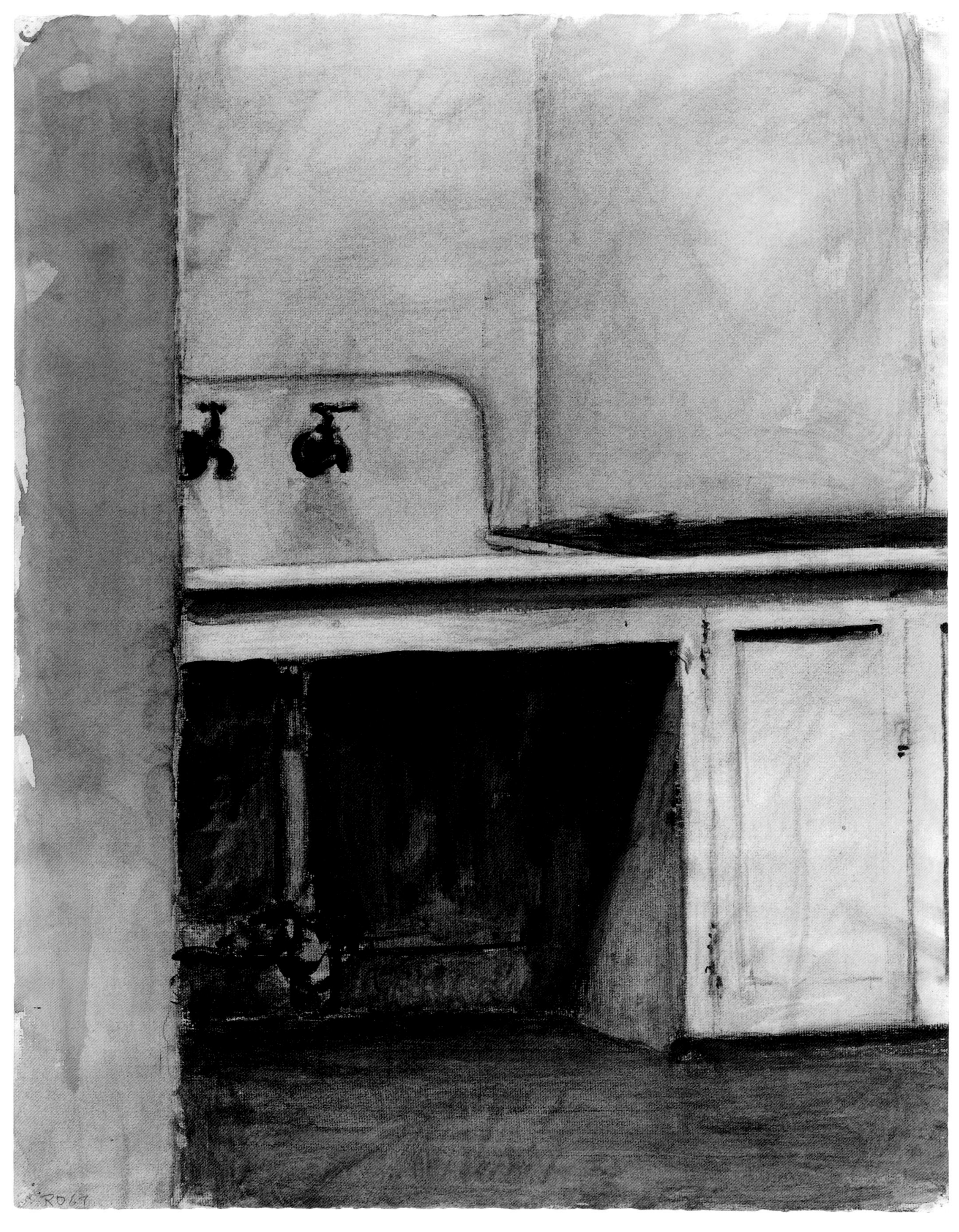

104. *Sink*, 1967
Ink, charcoal, and watercolor on paper, 24 3/4 x 18 3/4 in. (62.9 x 47.6 cm)
Baltimore Museum of Art, Thomas E. Benesch Memorial Collection, BMA 1969.2 [342]

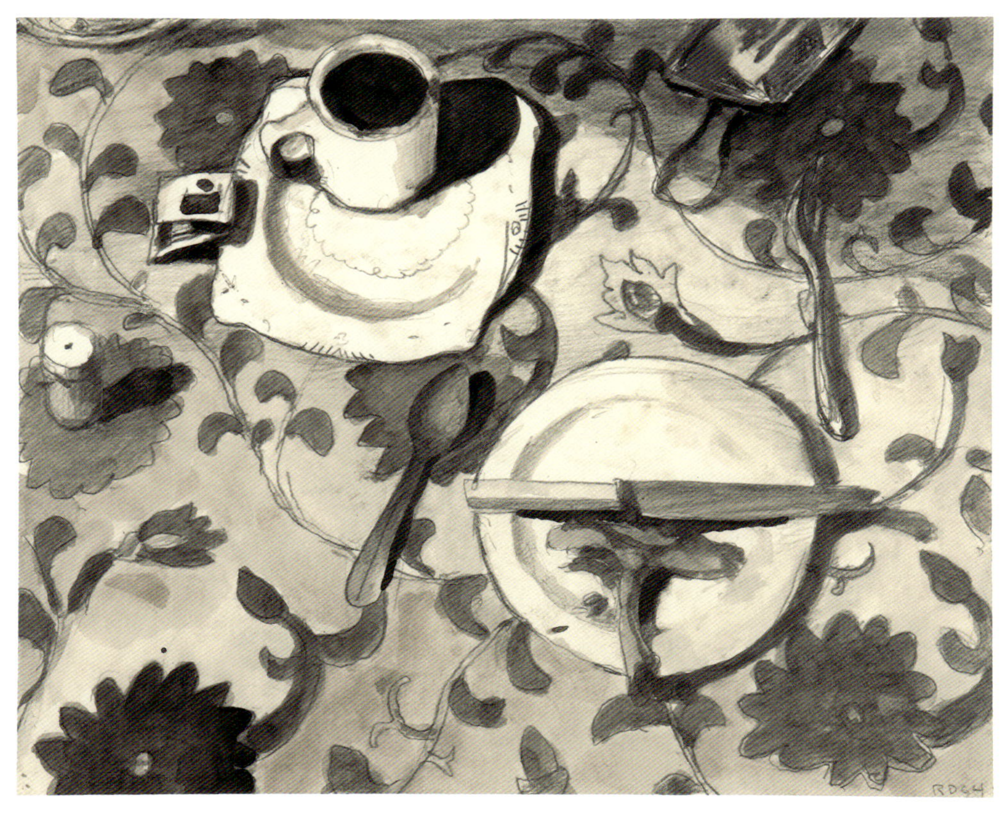
RD64

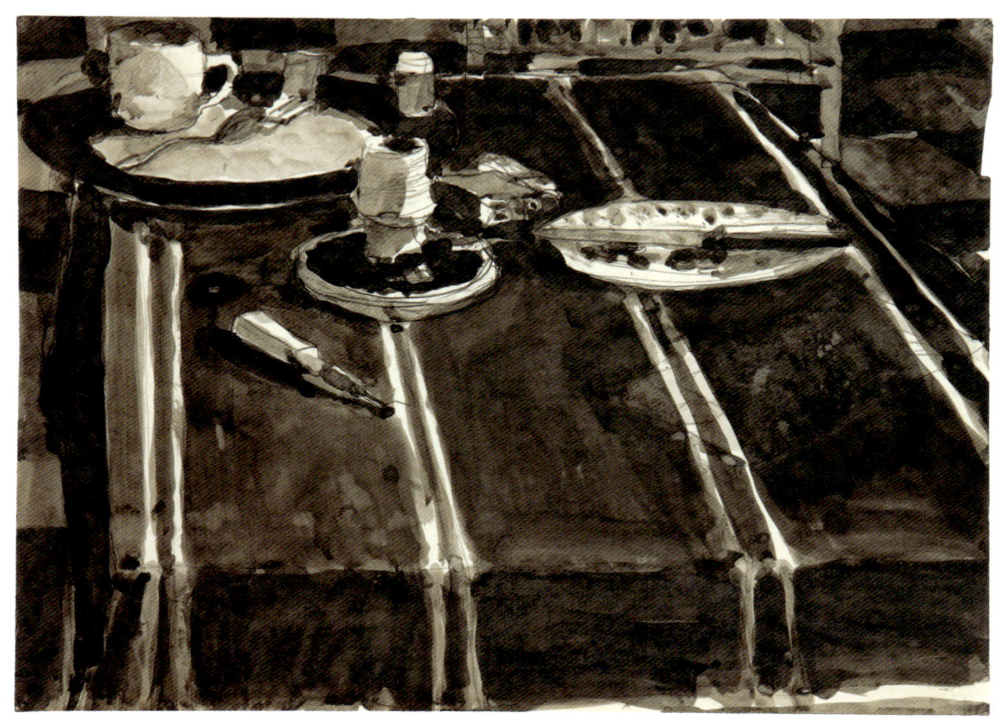

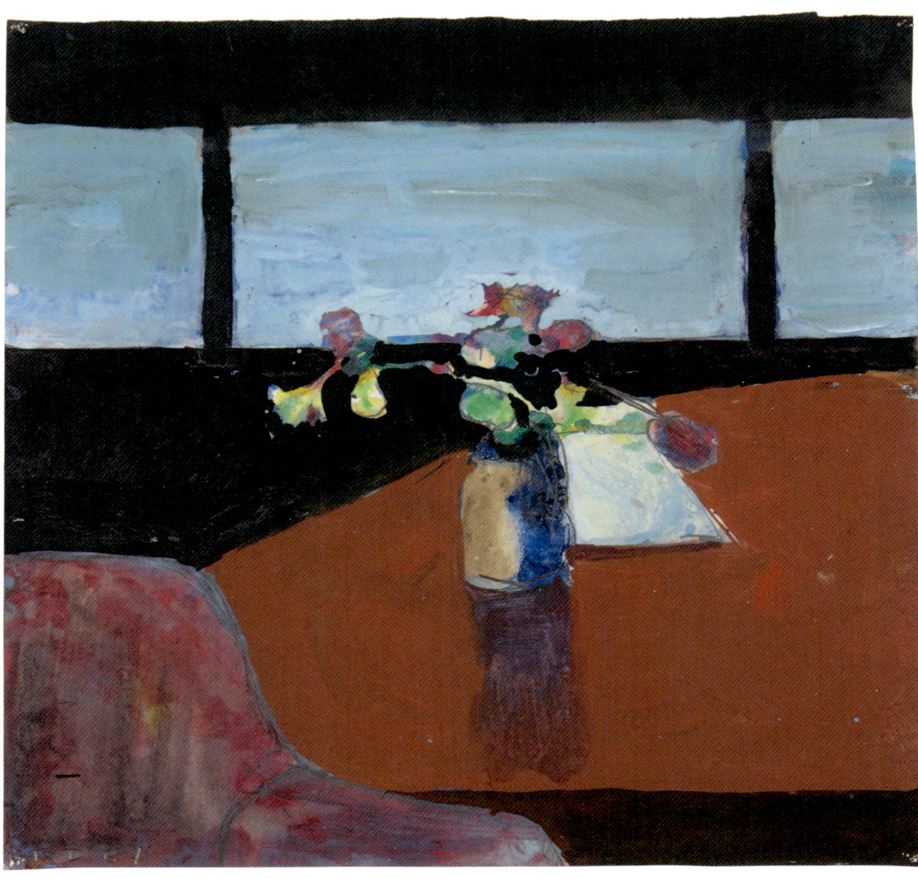

105. *Untitled*, 1964
Graphite and ink on paper, 13 7/8 x 16 7/8 in. (35.2 x 42.9 cm)
Collection of Leslie A. Feely [410]

106. *Untitled*, 1964
Ink, charcoal, and graphite on paper, 12 1/2 x 17 in. (31.8 x 43.2 cm)
Collection of Christopher Diebenkorn [688]

107. *Untitled*, 1964
Gouache and graphite on paper, 13 3/8 x 13 7/8 in. (34 x 35.2 cm)
Collection of John and Sally Van Doren, courtesy of Van Doren Waxter [665]

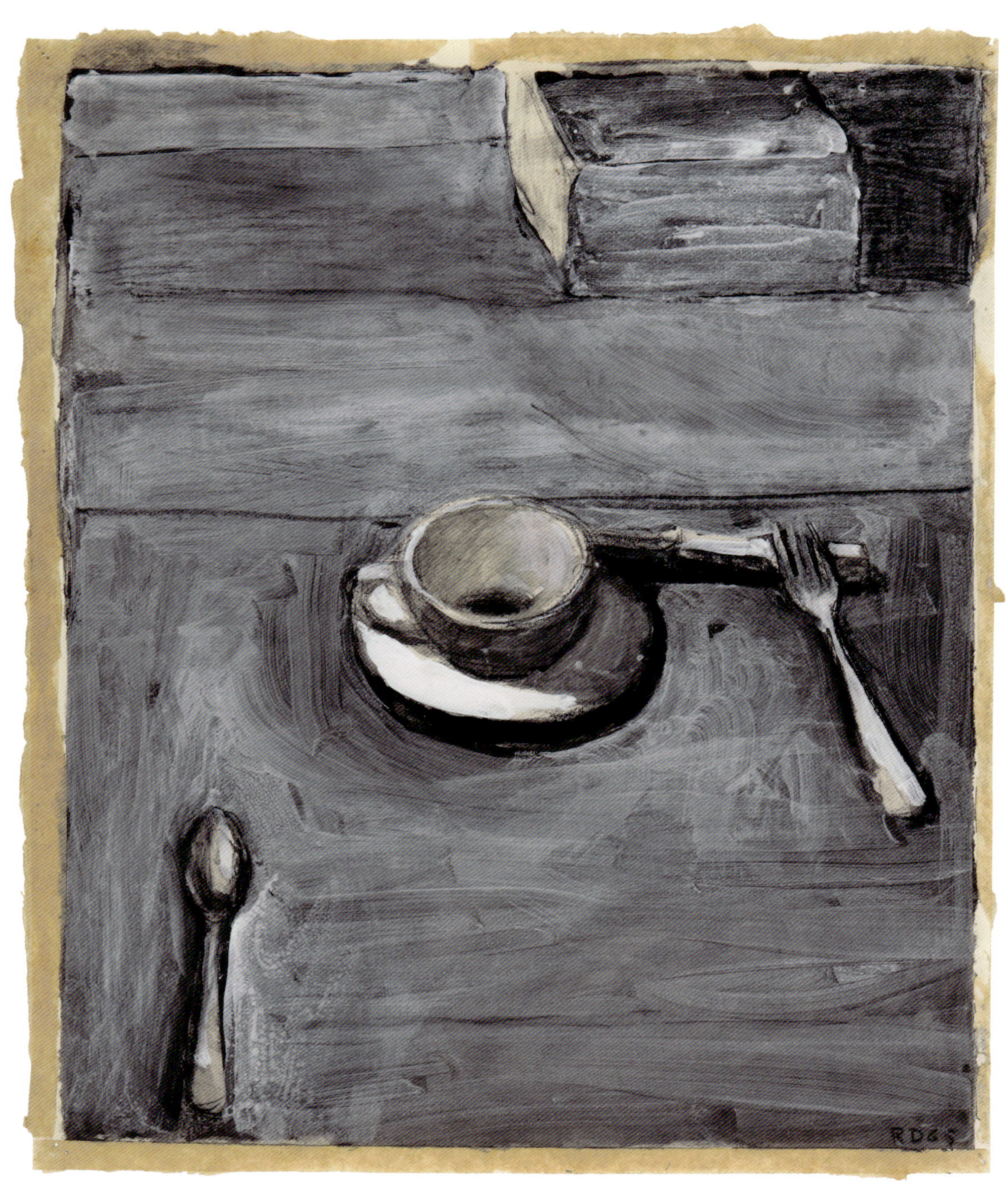

108. *Untitled*, 1965
Gouache, crayon, and ink on paper, 17 1/8 x 14 1/4 in. (43.5 x 36.2 cm)
Private collection, courtesy of the Greenberg Gallery, Saint Louis [672]

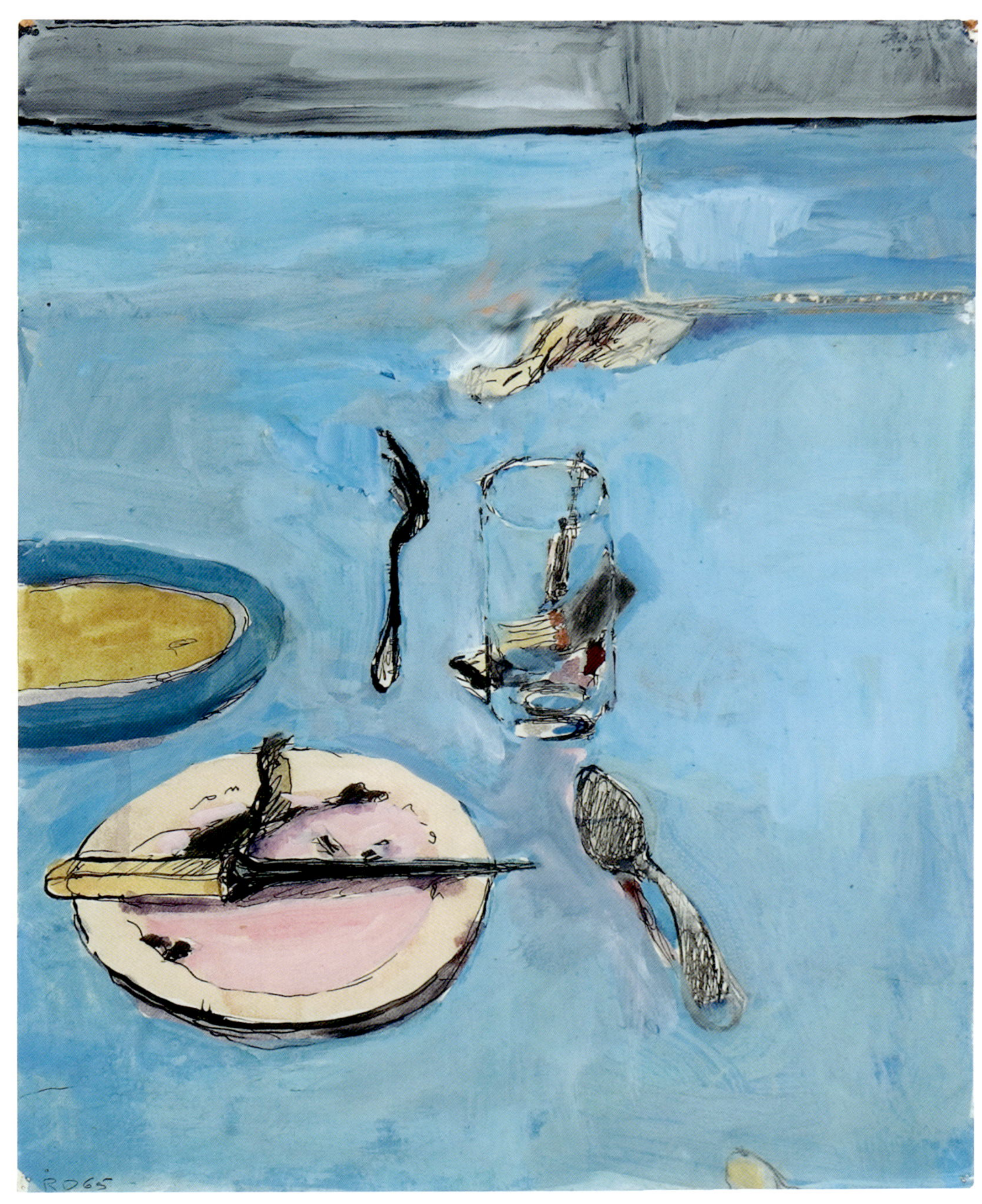

109. *Untitled*, 1965
Gouache and ink on paper, 13 3/4 x 10 3/4 in. (34.9 x 27.3 cm)
Collection of Thelma and Melvin Lenkin [4536]

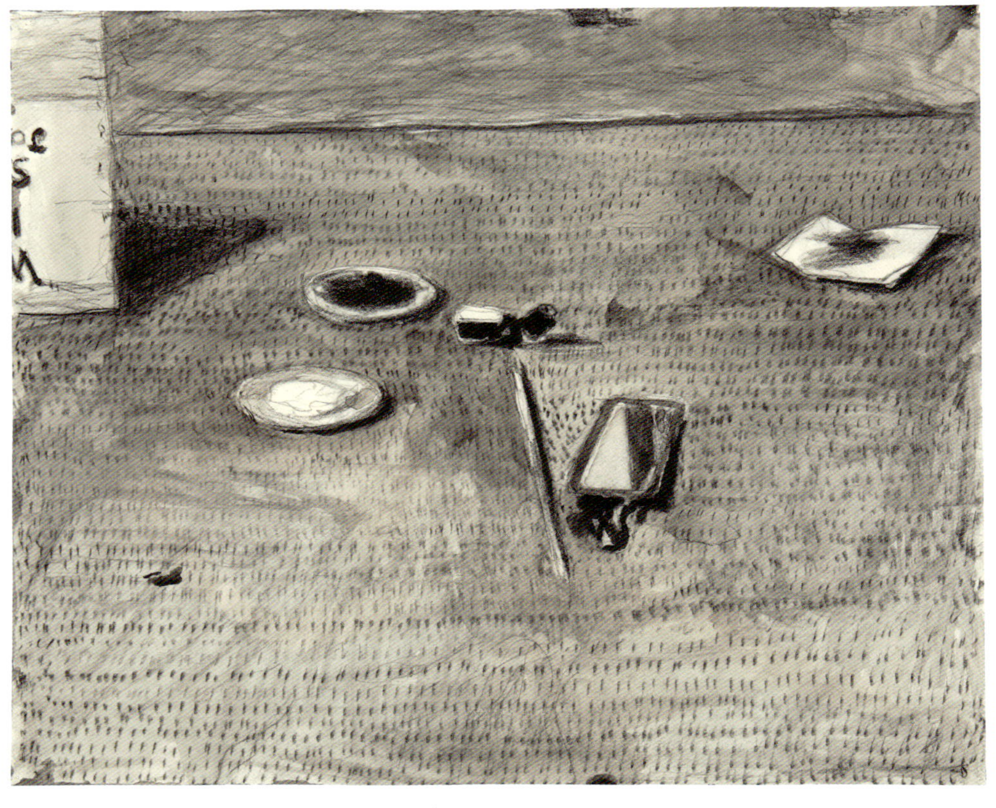

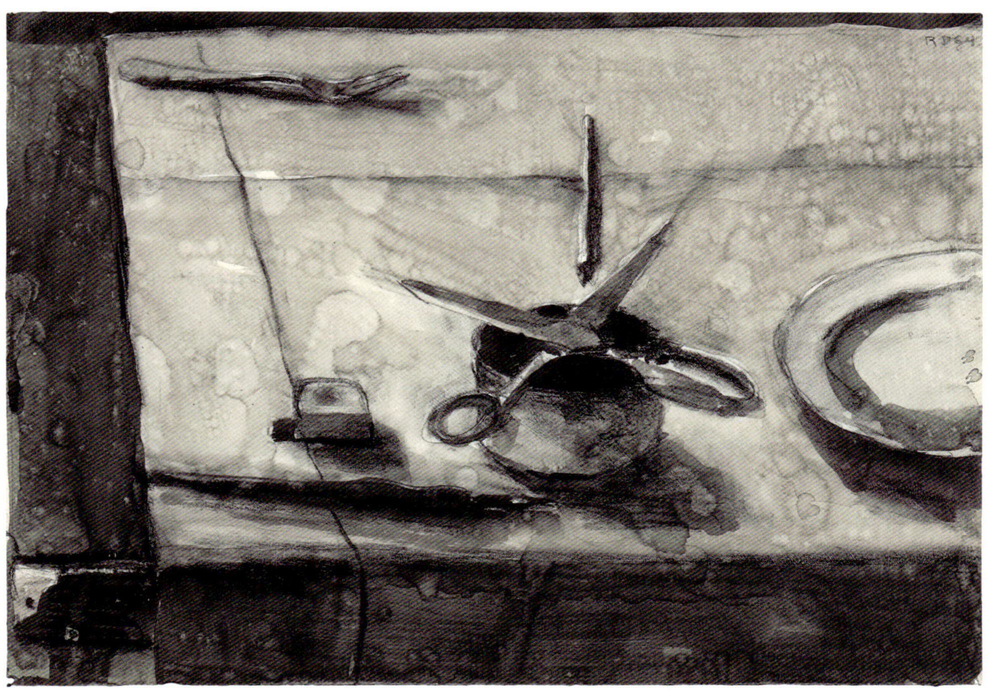

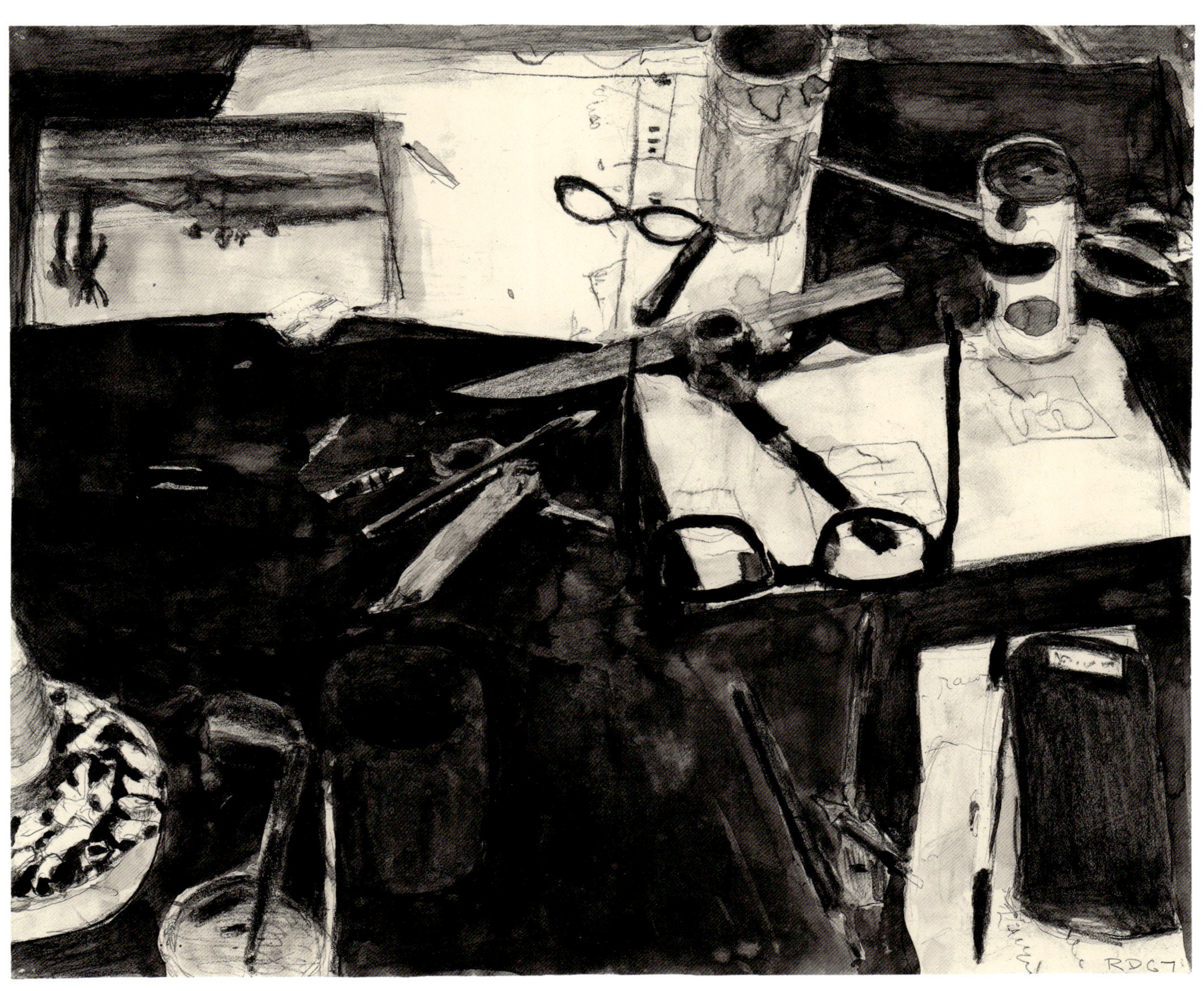

110. *Untitled (Still Life with Textured Cloth)*, 1965
Ink and charcoal on paper, 13 7/8 x 16 7/8 in. (35.2 x 42.9 cm)
Collection of John and Sally Van Doren, courtesy of Van Doren Waxter [27]

111. *Untitled (Scissors on Cup)*, 1964
Ink, gouache, graphite, and charcoal on paper, 11 7/8 x 17 in. (30.2 x 43.2 cm)
Collection of Christopher Diebenkorn [581]

112. *Still Life, Cigarette Butts and Glasses*, 1967
Ink, conté crayon, charcoal, and ballpoint pen on paper, 13 7/8 x 16 3/4 in. (35.2 x 42.5 cm)
National Gallery of Art, Washington, DC, gift of Mr. and Mrs. Richard Diebenkorn, in Honor of the Fiftieth Anniversary of the National Gallery of Art, 1990.101.1 [2347]

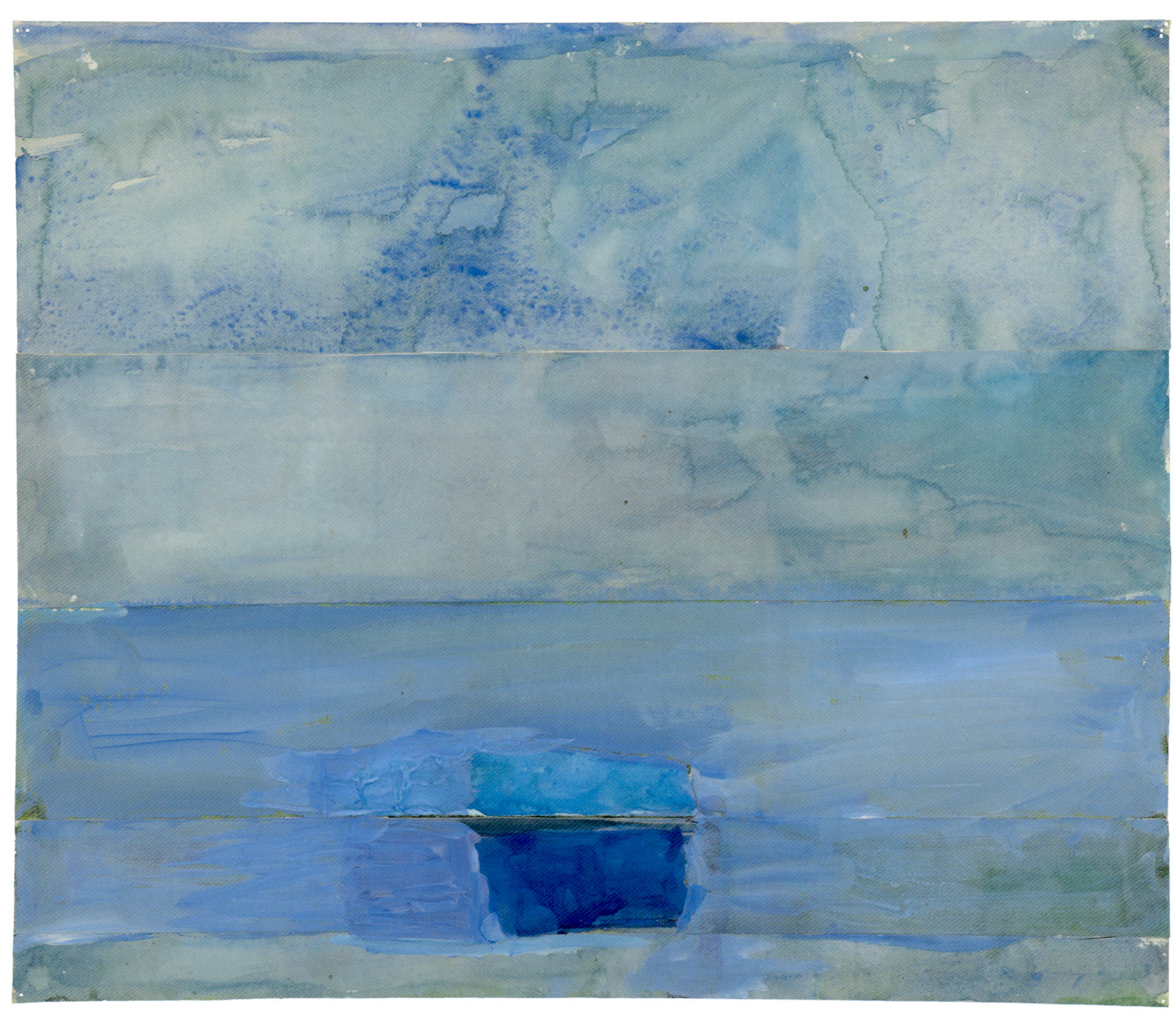

113. *Untitled*, ca. 1956–1966
Watercolor, ink, and torn-and-pasted paper on joined paper, 15 3/4 x 18 in. (40 x 45.7 cm)
Private collection [65]

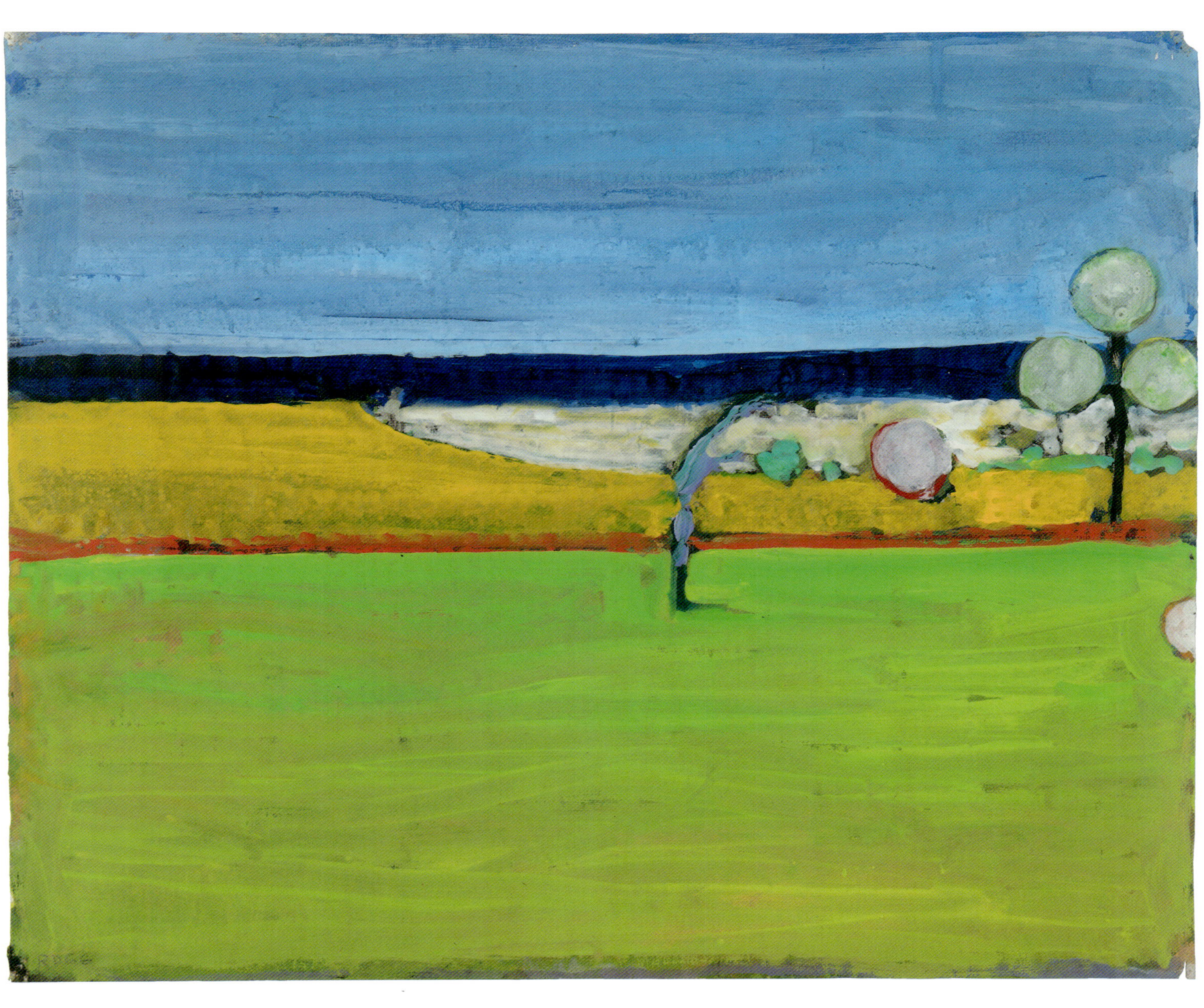

114. *Invented Landscape*, 1966
Acrylic on paper, 18 x 23 in. (45.7 x 58.4 cm)
Oakland Museum of California, gift of the Estate of Howard E. Johnson, A84.45.6 [2549]

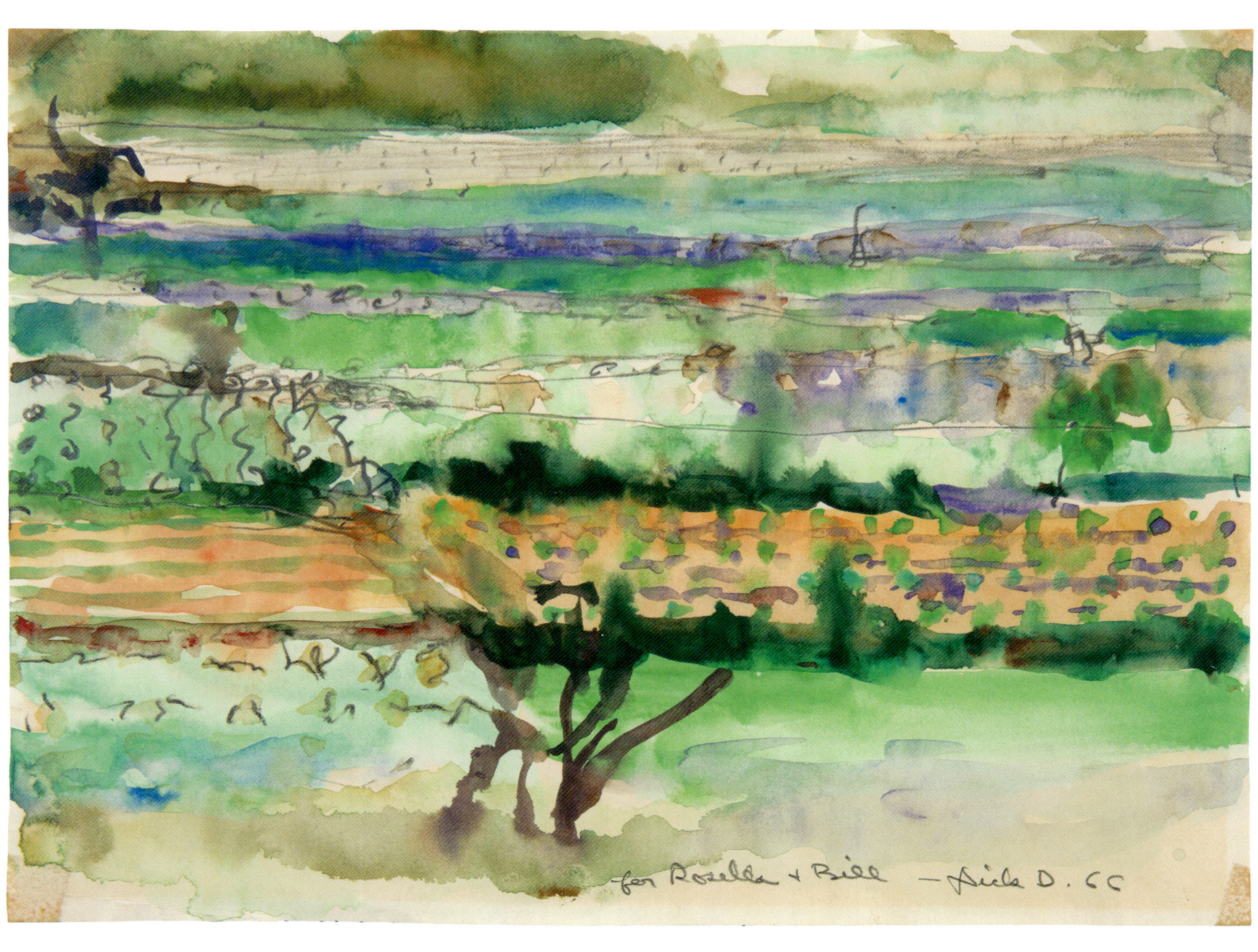

115. *Untitled*, 1966
Watercolor and graphite on paper, 8 x 10 7/8 in. (20.3 x 27.6 cm)
Private collection [5892]

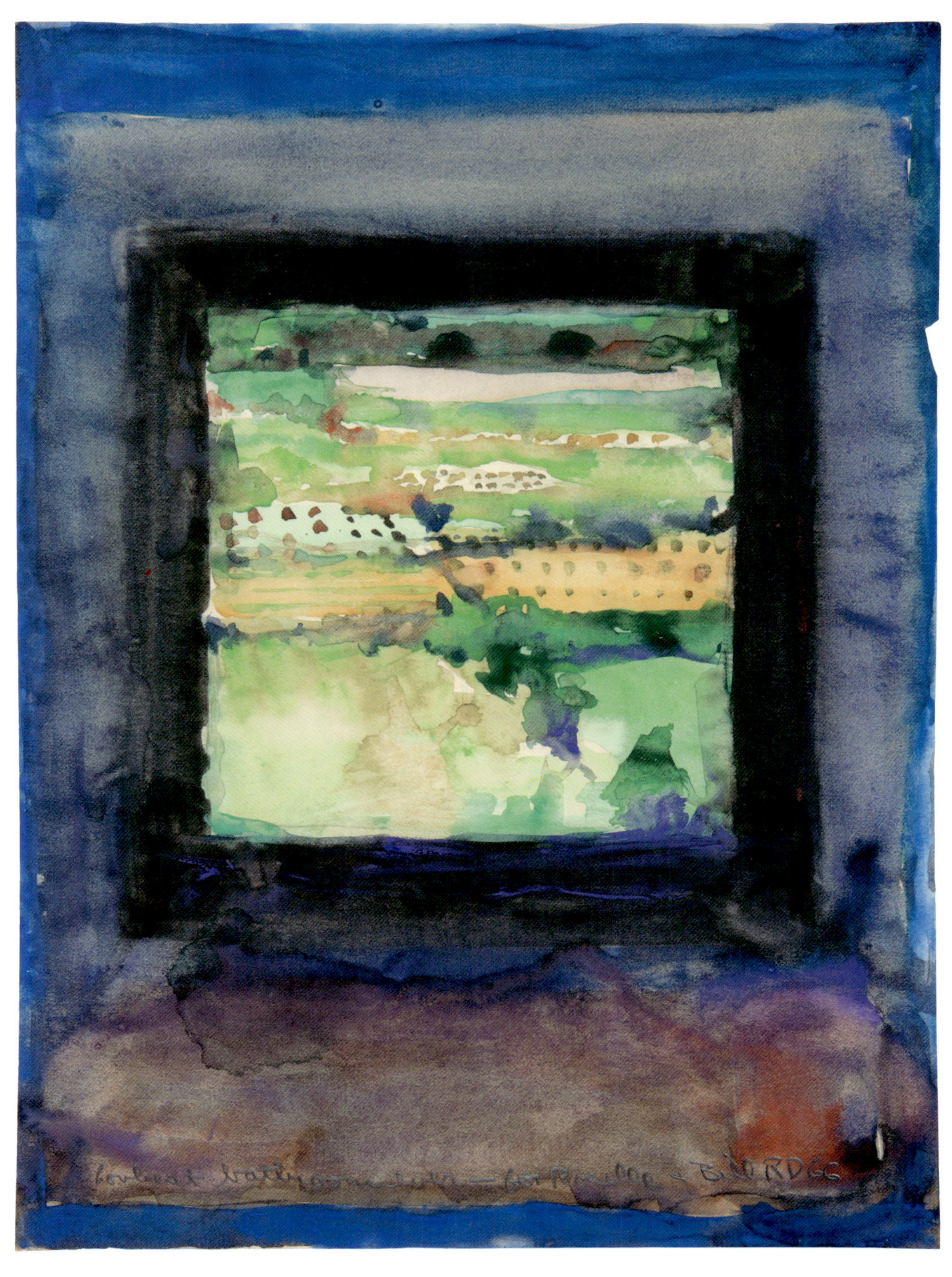

116. *Untitled*, 1966
Watercolor and graphite on paper, $10^{7}/_{8}$ x 8 in. (27.6 x 20.3 cm)
Private collection [5893]

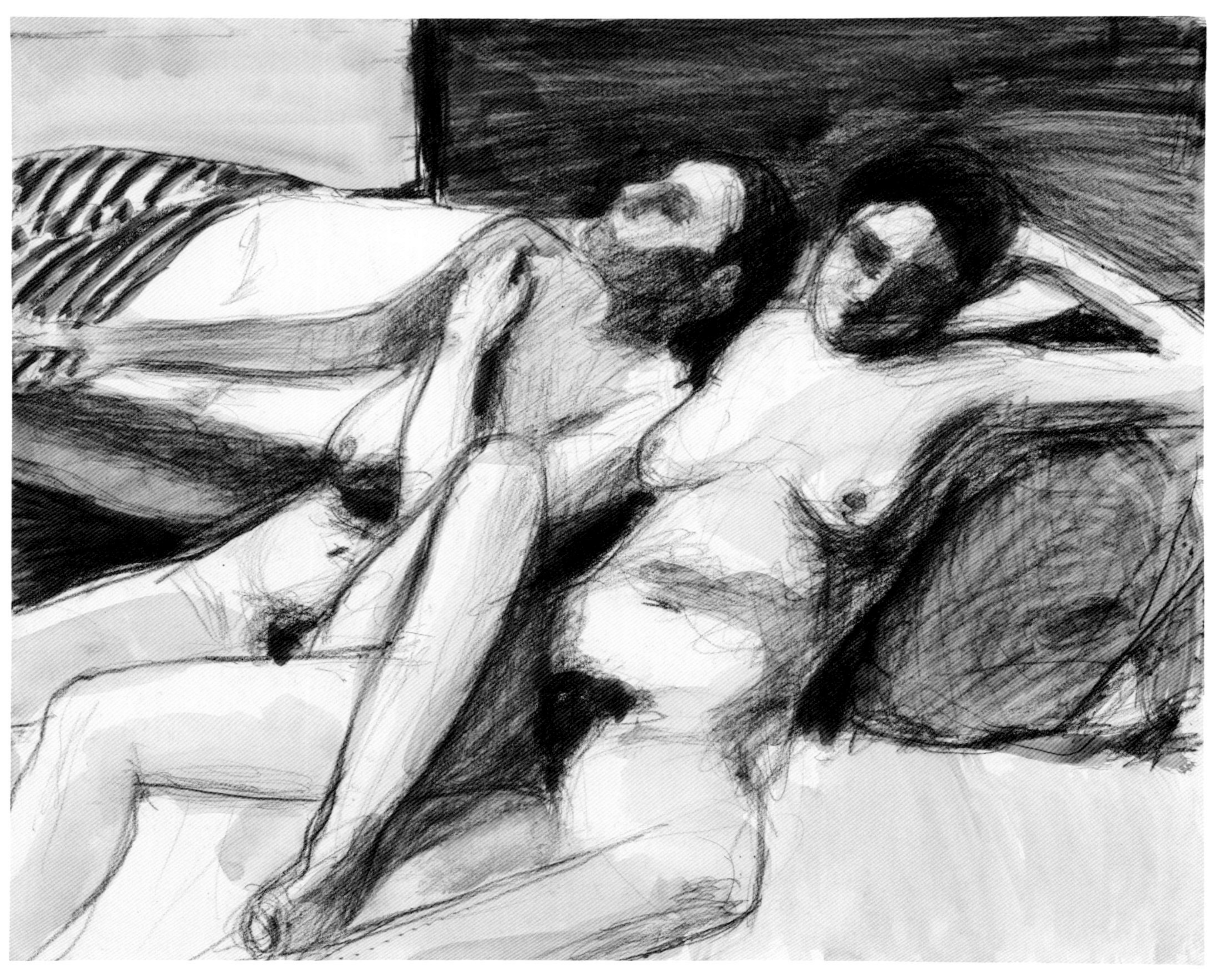

117. *Untitled*, ca. 1960–1966
Charcoal and ink on paper, 13 7/8 x 17 in. (35.2 x 43.2 cm)
Richard Diebenkorn Foundation [4305]

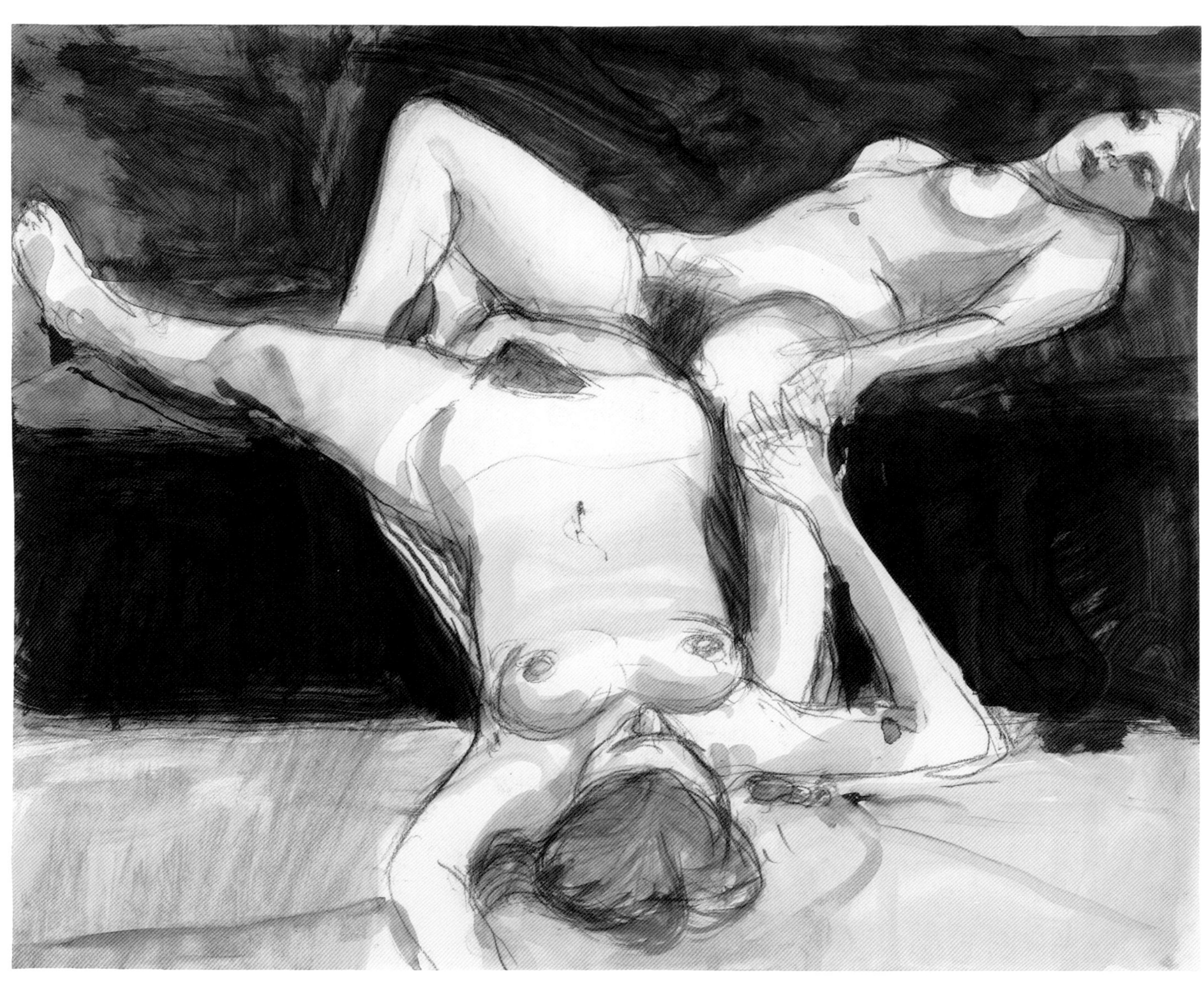

118. *Untitled*, ca. 1961–1962
Charcoal and ink on paper, 13 3/4 x 16 7/8 in. (34.9 x 42.9 cm)
Private collection [2031]

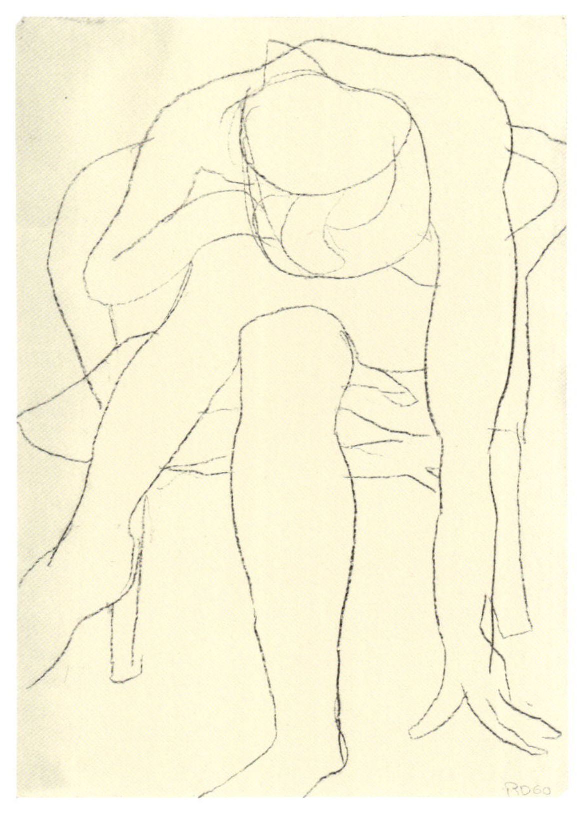
RD60

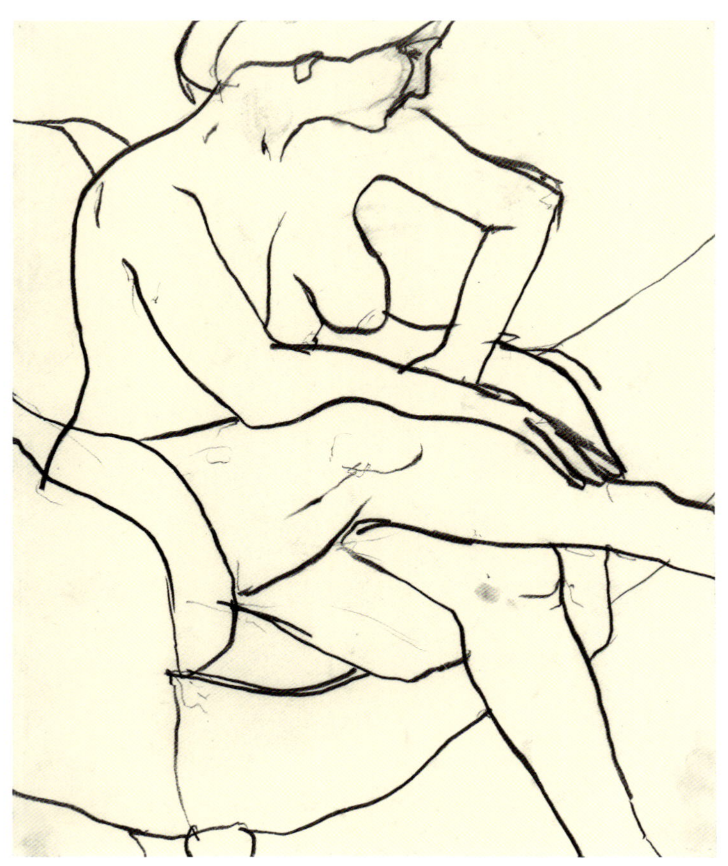

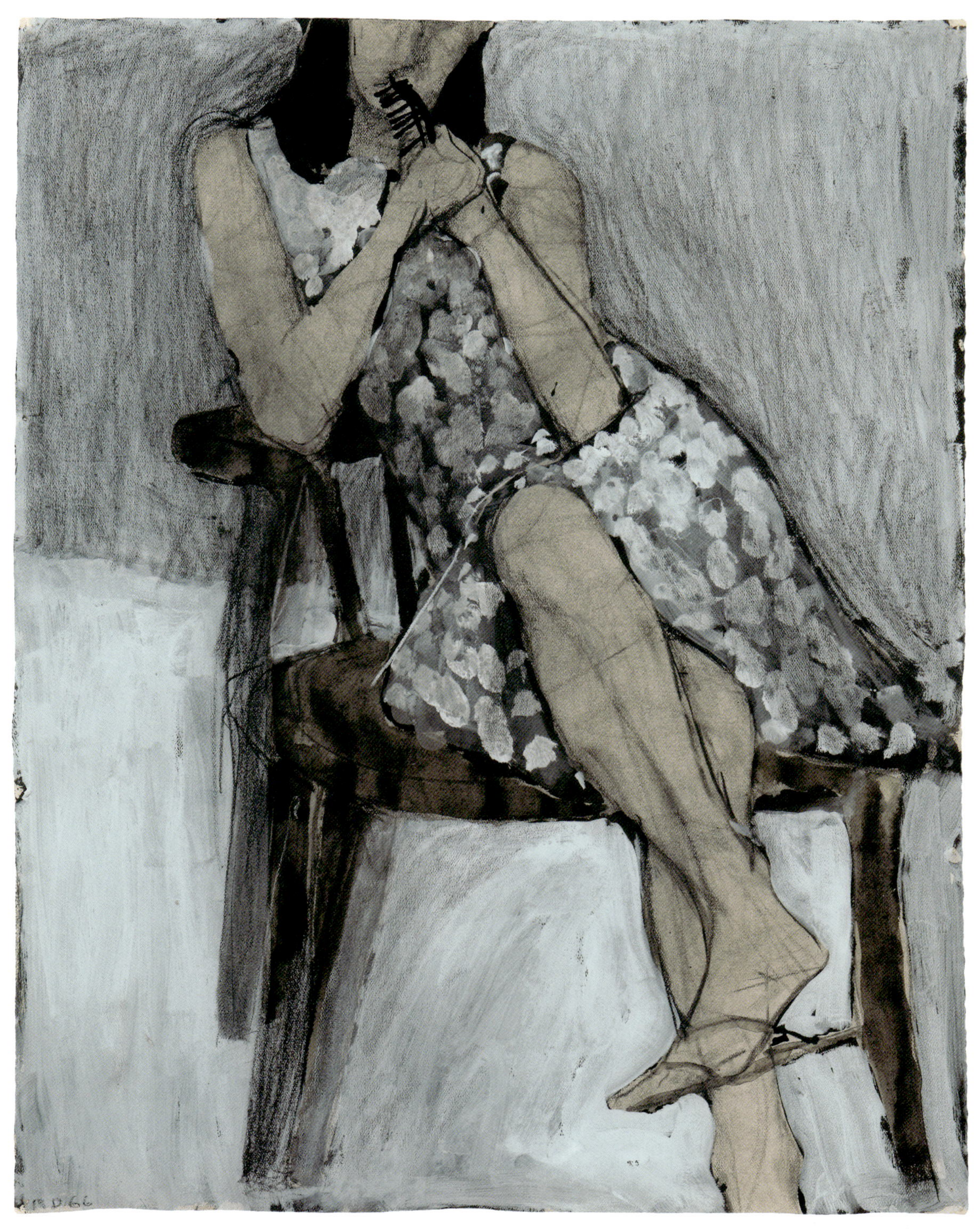

119. *Untitled (Seated Woman, Reaching Down)*, 1960
Charcoal on paper, 15 3/4 x 11 in. (40 x 27.9 cm)
Private collection [2176]

120. *Untitled*, ca. 1964
Charcoal on paper, 17 x 14 in. (43.2 x 35.6 cm)
Private collection [582]

121. *Seated Woman*, 1966
Gouache, crayon, and ink on paper, 30 1/4 x 23 1/4 in. (76.8 x 59.1 cm)
University Art Museum, The State University of New York, Albany, 1970:0049 [18]

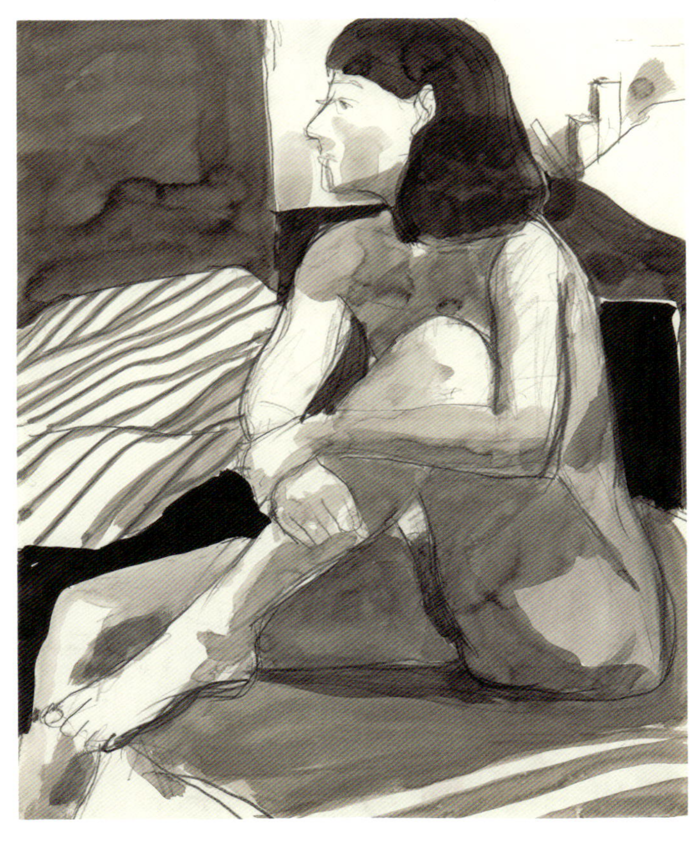

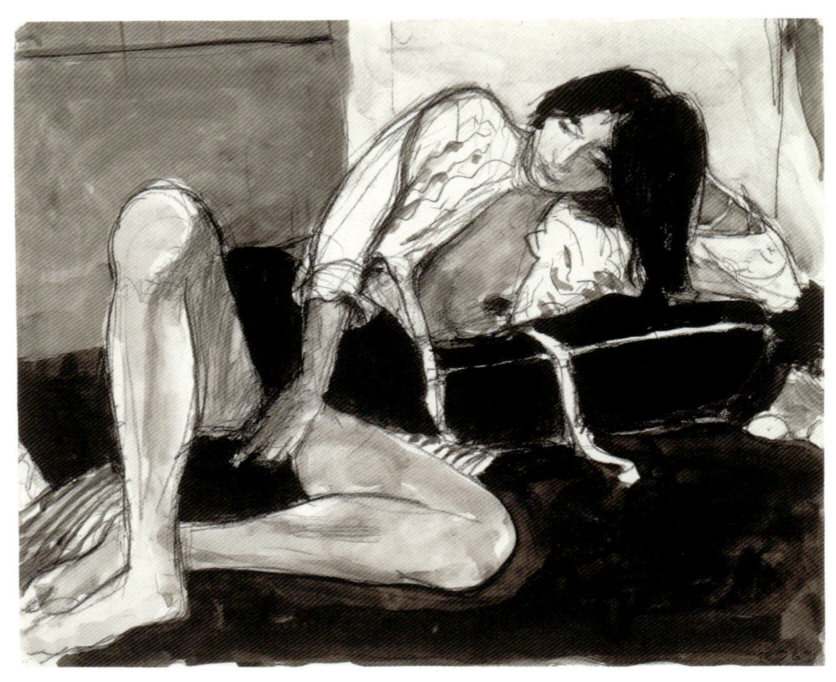

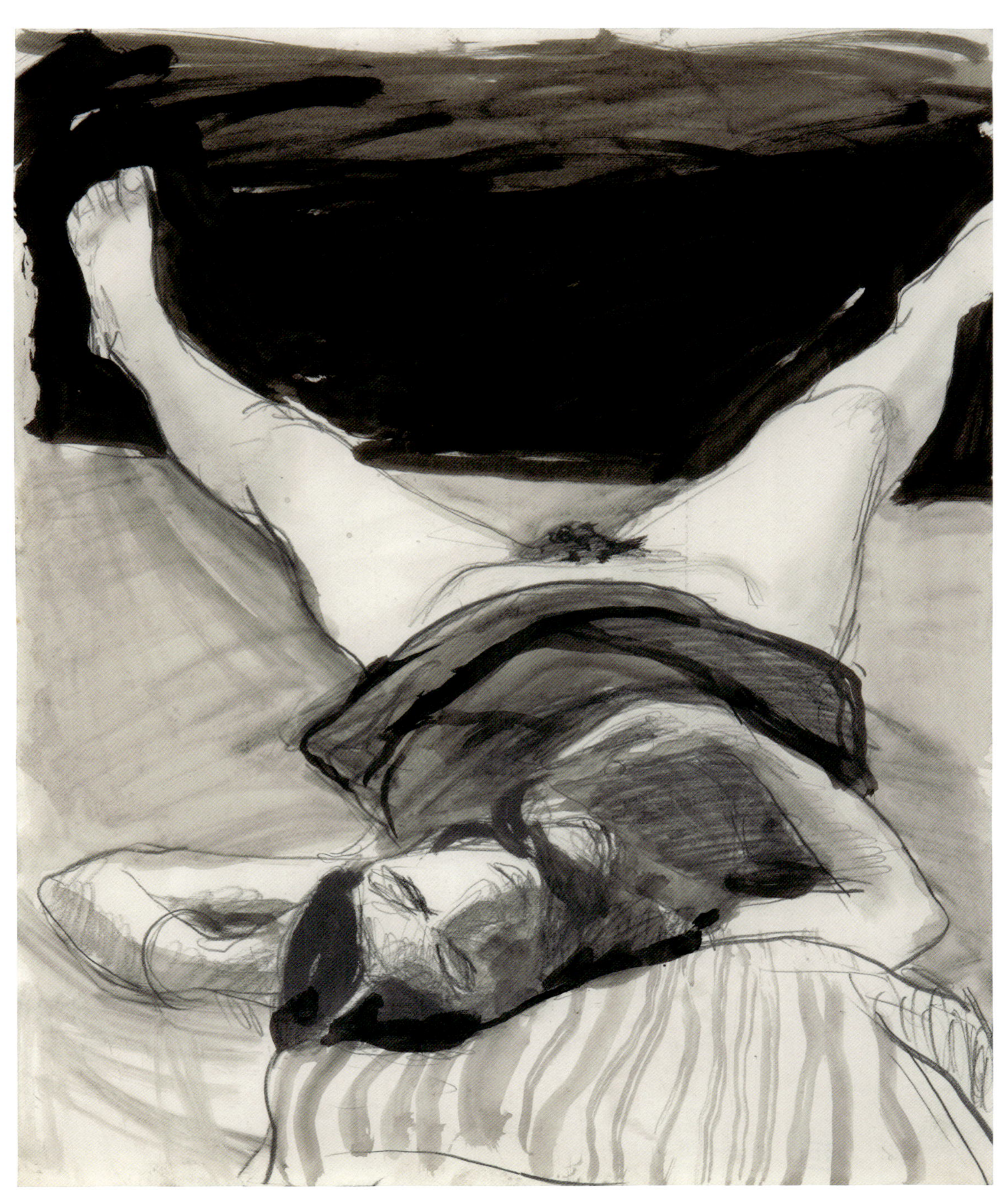

122. *Untitled*, ca. 1960–1966
Graphite and ink on paper, 17 x 13 7/8 in. (43.2 x 35.2 cm)
Private collection [533]

123. *Reclining Woman*, 1967
Ink and crayon on paper, 14 x 17 in. (35.6 x 43.2 cm)
Collection of John and Sally Van Doren, courtesy of Van Doren Waxter [2173]

124. *Untitled*, ca. 1962
Ink and graphite on paper, 17 x 14 in. (43.2 x 35.6 cm)
Private collection, courtesy of Gerald Peters Gallery, New York [2032]

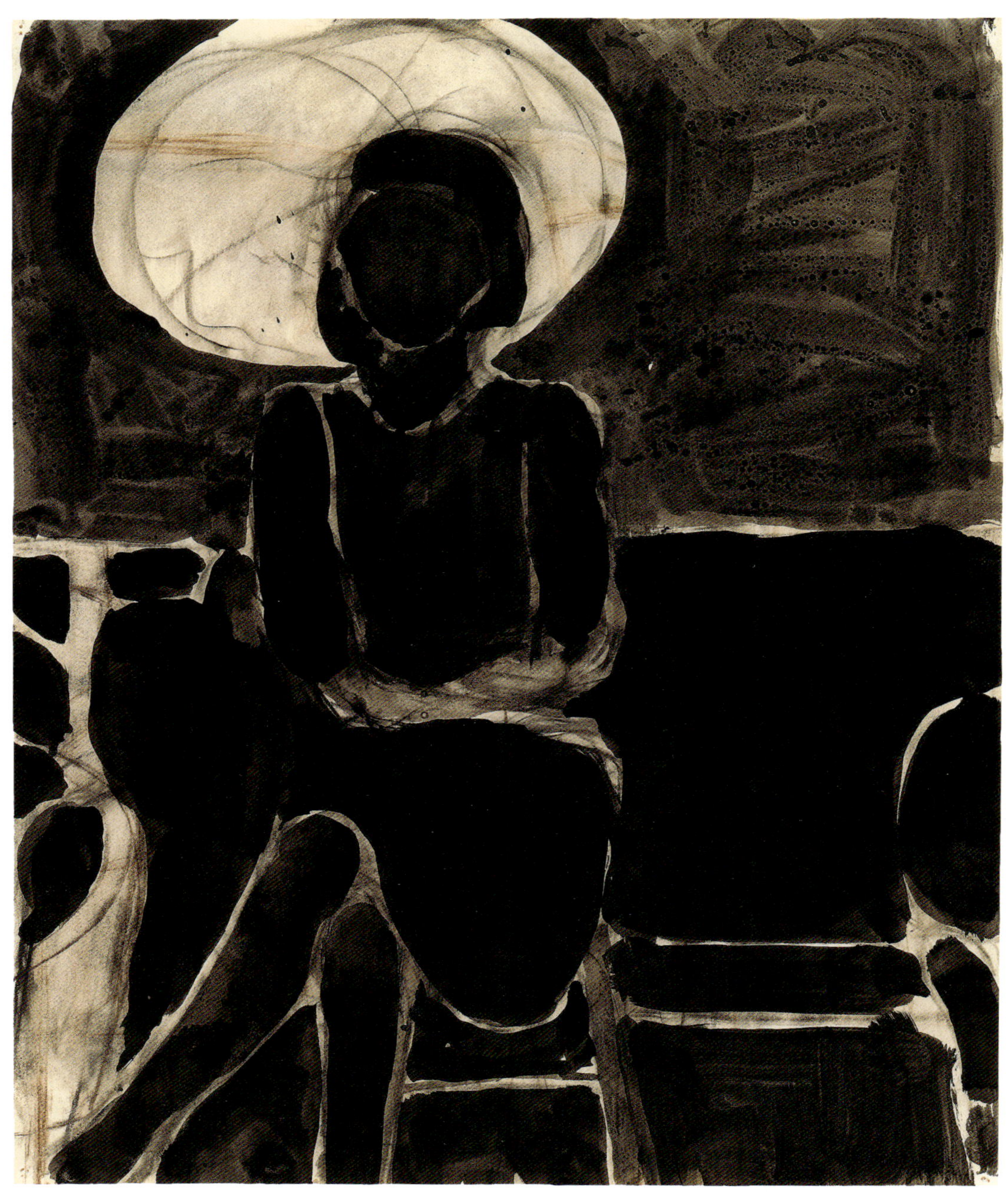

125. *Seated Woman, Umbrella*, 1967
Ink and charcoal on paper, 17 x 13 7/8 in. (43.2 x 35.2 cm)
National Gallery of Art, Washington, DC, gift of Phyllis Diebenkorn, 2000.141.2 [2168]

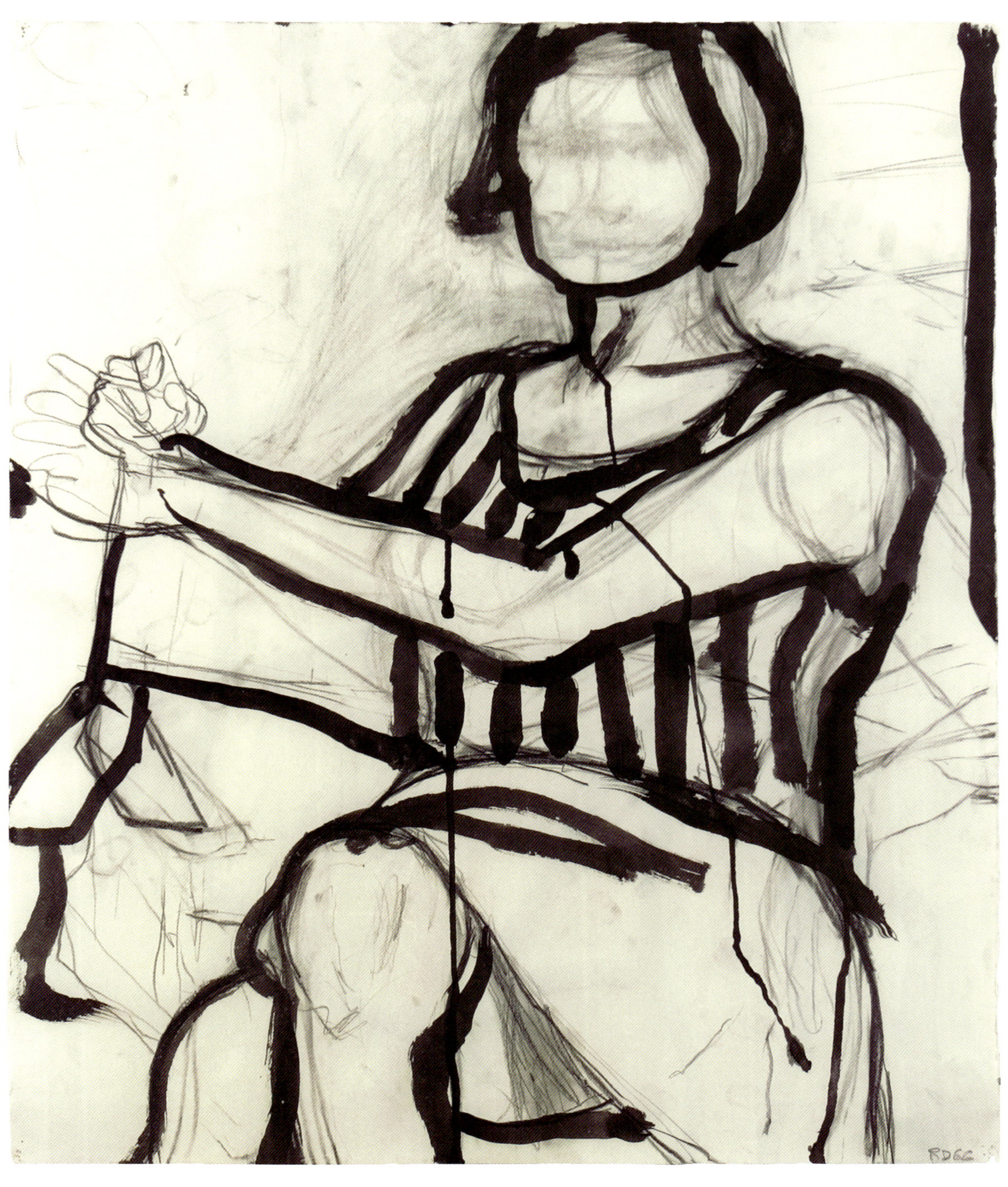

126. *Untitled (Striped Blouse)*, 1966
Ink and graphite on paper, 27 1/8 x 22 5/8 in. (68.9 x 57.5 cm)
The Grant Family Collection [1601]

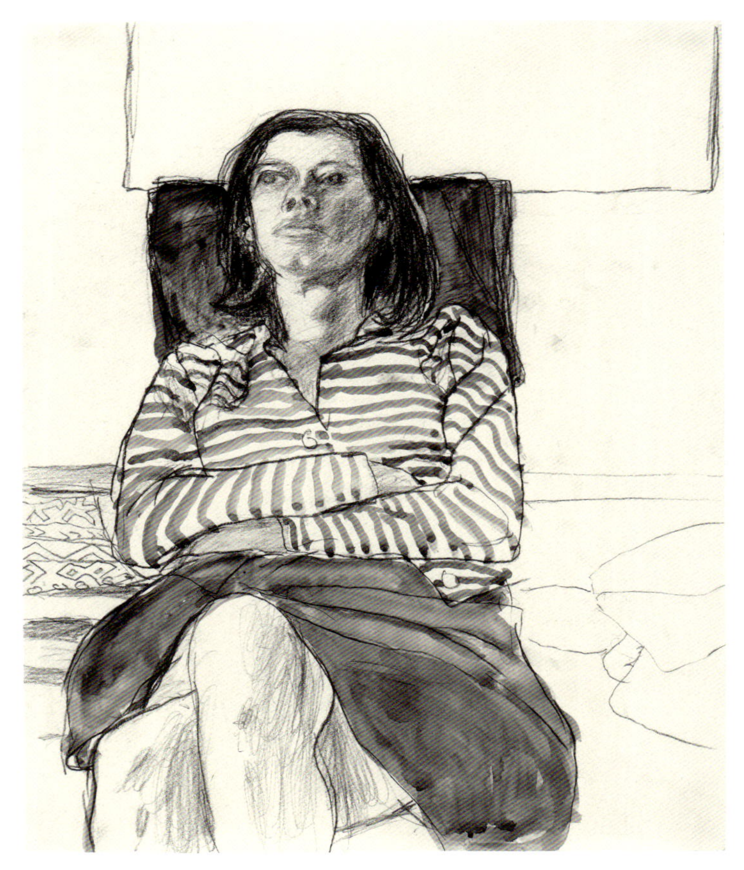

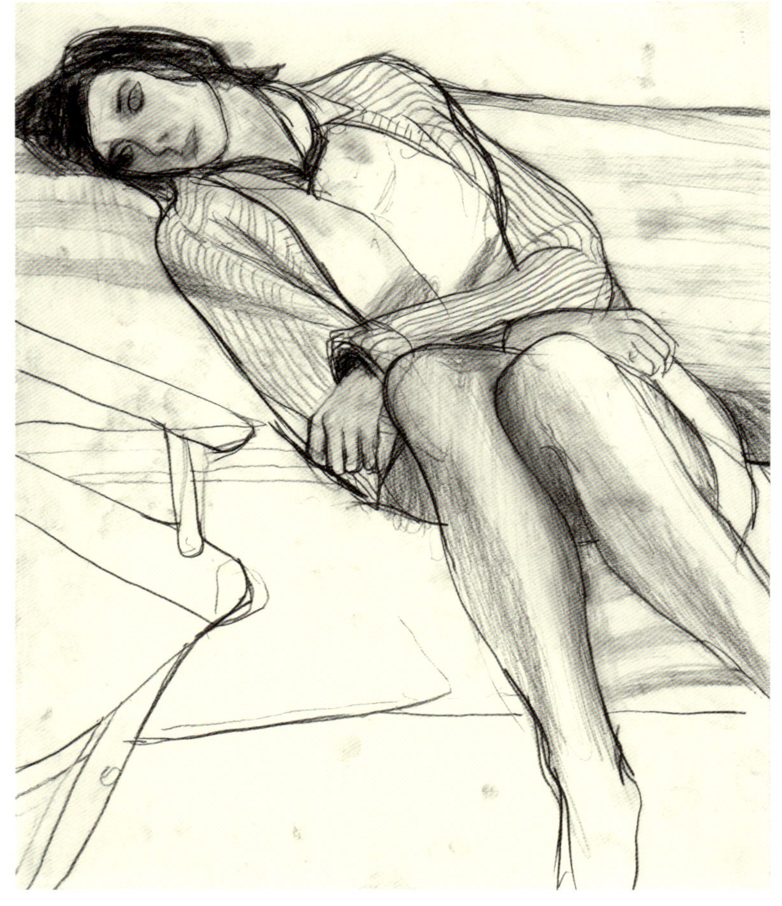

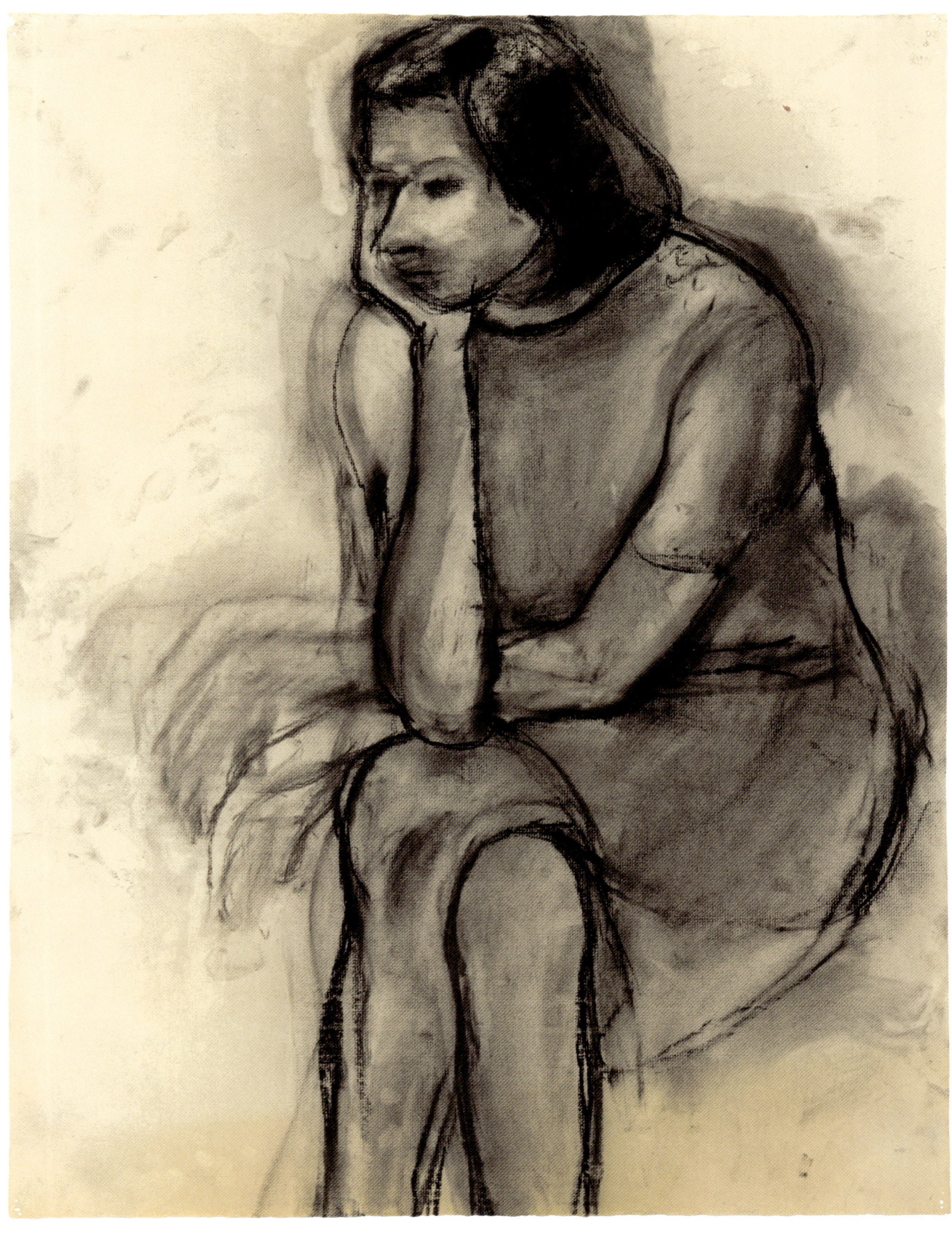

127. *Untitled*, ca. 1955–1967
Charcoal, chalk, and ink on paper, 17 x 14 in. (43.2 x 35.6 cm)
Richard and Mary L. Gray and the Gray Collection Trust [2050]

128. *Untitled*, ca. 1963–1964
Charcoal on paper, 17 5/8 x 14 3/8 in. (44.8 x 36.5 cm)
Collection of Gretchen and John Berggruen [928]

129. *Seated Woman, Head in Hand*, 1966
Charcoal on paper, 25 x 19 in. (63.5 x 48.3 cm)
Collection of Christopher Diebenkorn [2561]

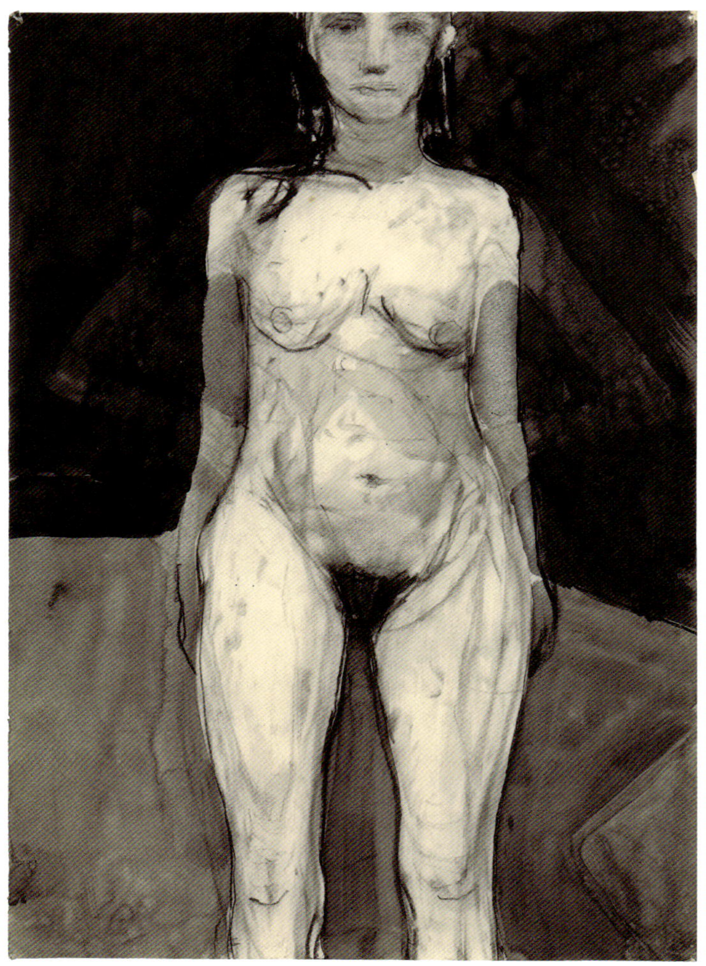

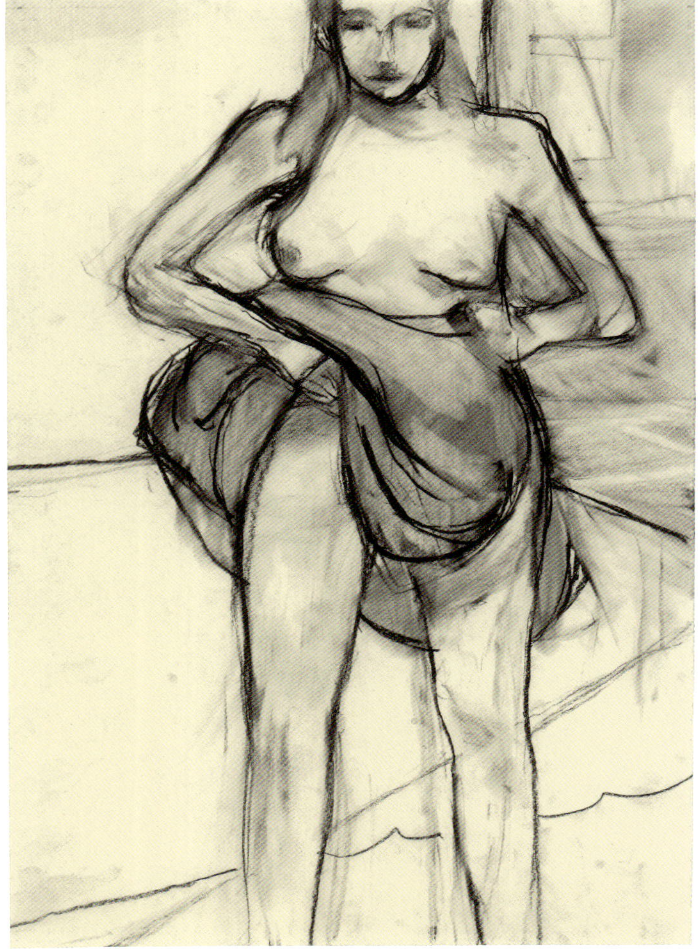

130. *Standing Nude*, ca. 1965–1966
Ink, watercolor, and charcoal on paper, 17 x 12 in. (43.2 x 30.5 cm)
The Grant Family Collection [344]

131. *Untitled*, ca. 1965
Charcoal on paper, 17 x 11 3/4 in. (43.2 x 29.8 cm)
Private collection [579]

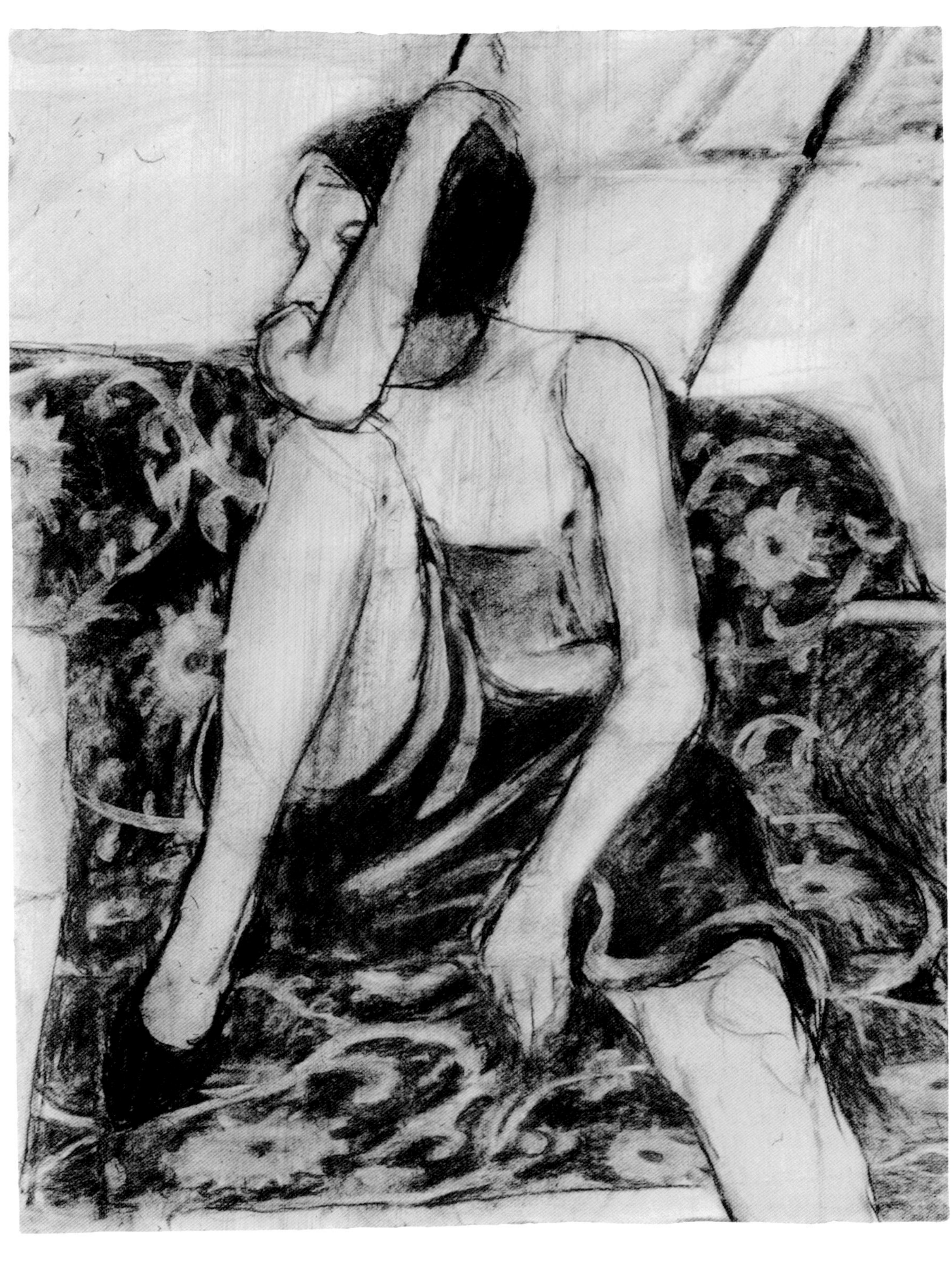

132. *Untitled (Seated Woman on Flowered Sofa)*, 1966
Charcoal on paper, 24 3/4 x 18 3/4 in. (62.9 x 47.6 cm)
Private collection [9]

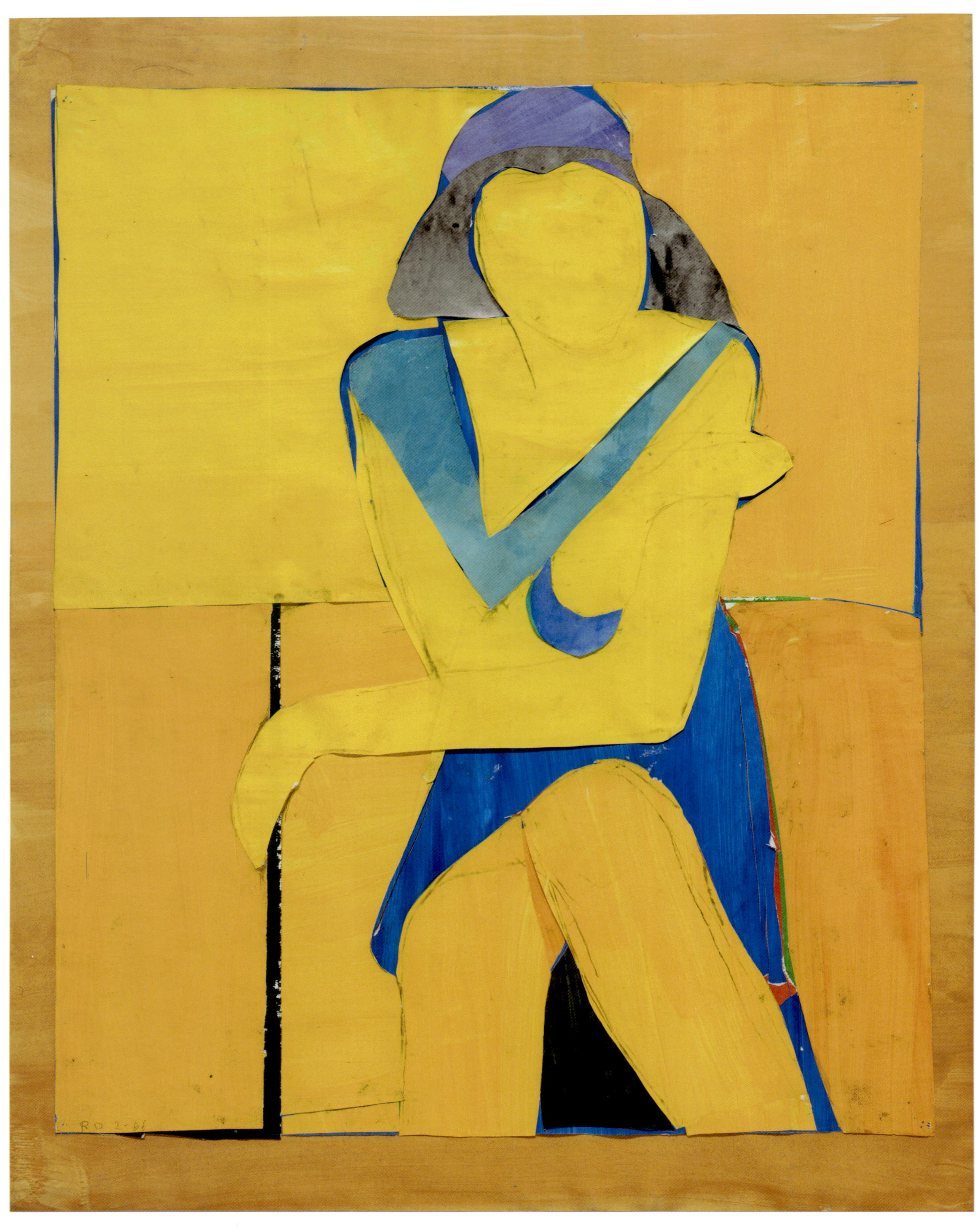

133. *Untitled (Yellow Collage)*, 1966
Cut-and-pasted paper, gouache, and ink on paper, $28\frac{3}{4}$ x 22 in. (73 x 55.9 cm)
The Grant Family Collection [11]

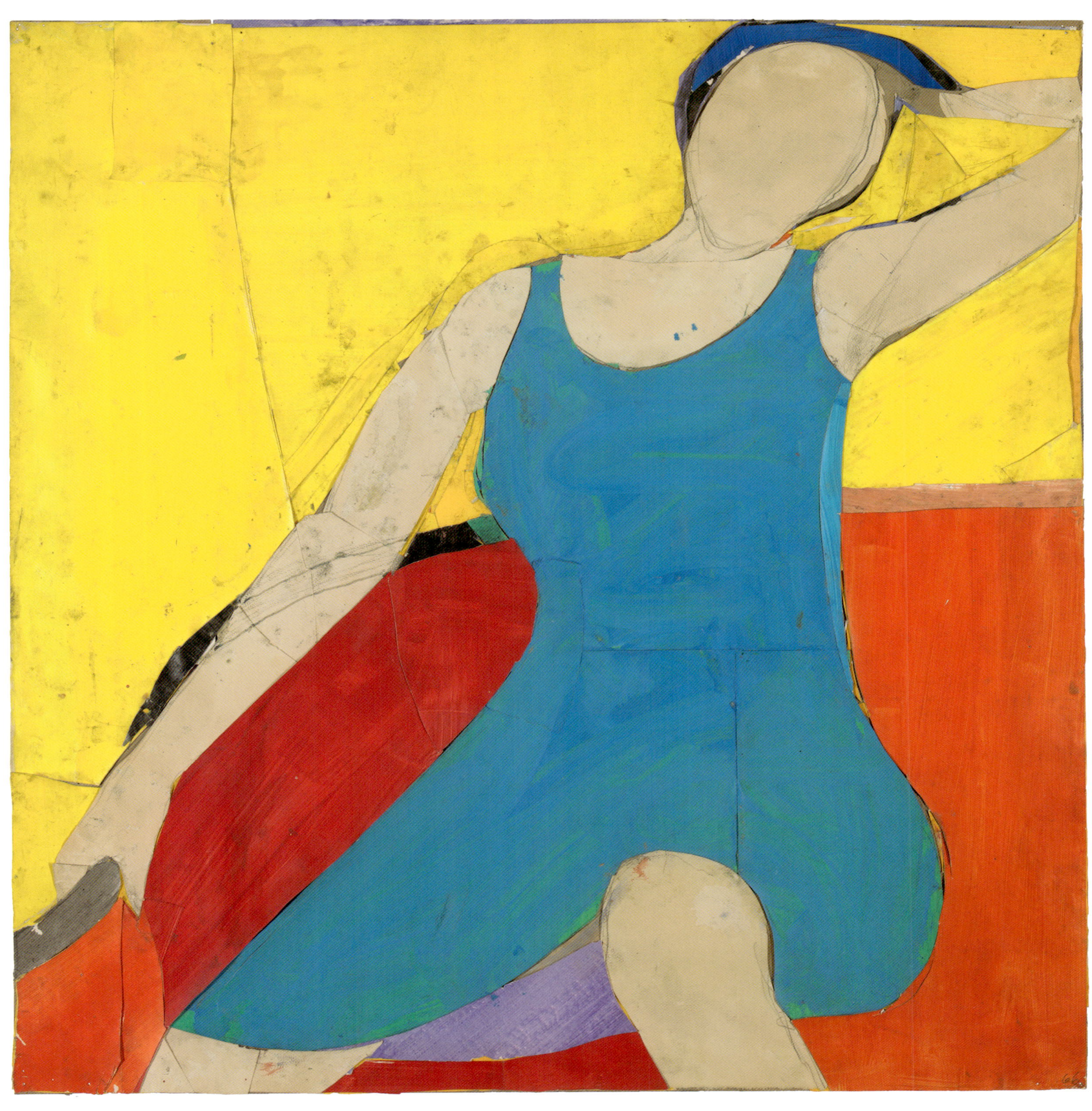

134. *Untitled (Collage—Woman in a Blue Dress)*, 1966
Cut-and-pasted paper, construction paper, graphite, and ink on joined cardboard, 25 1/2 x 24 7/8 in. (64.8 x 63.2 cm)
Private collection [2195]

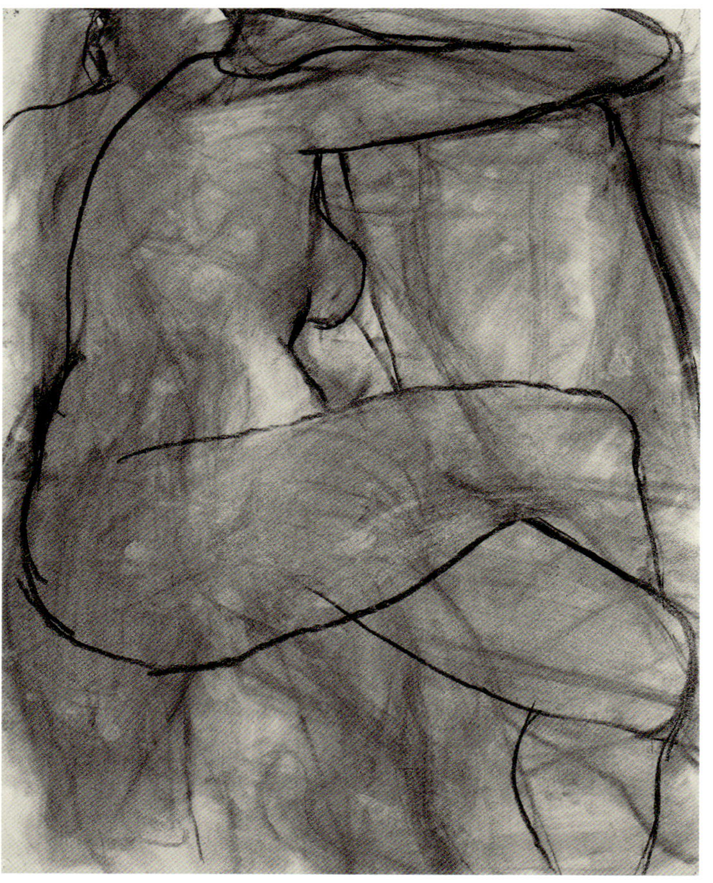

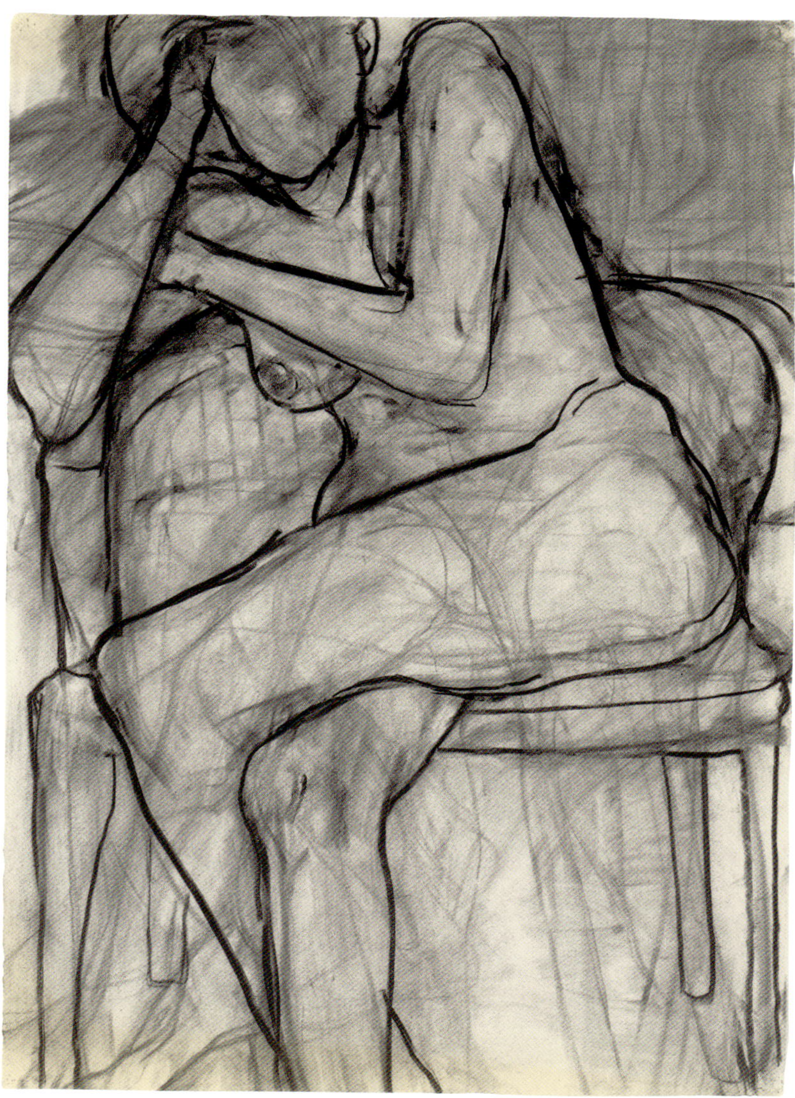

135. *Seated Nude, Profile*, 1966
Charcoal on paper, 24 x 19 in. (60.9 x 48.2 cm)
Art Institute of Chicago, gift of the Diebenkorn Family, restricted gift of Adele and William Gidwitz, 1998.80 [2179]

136. *Untitled (Seated Nude)*, 1966
Charcoal on paper, 33 x 23 1/2 in. (83.8 x 59.7 cm)
San Francisco Museum of Modern Art, gift of the Diebenkorn Family and purchase through a gift of Leanne B. Roberts, Thomas W. Weisel, and the Mnuchin Foundation, 96.435 [2181]

137. *Seated Woman*, 1966
Acrylic and charcoal on board, 31 x 20 in. (78.7 x 50.8 cm)
The Museum of Modern Art, New York, gift of the artist, 253.1990 [599]

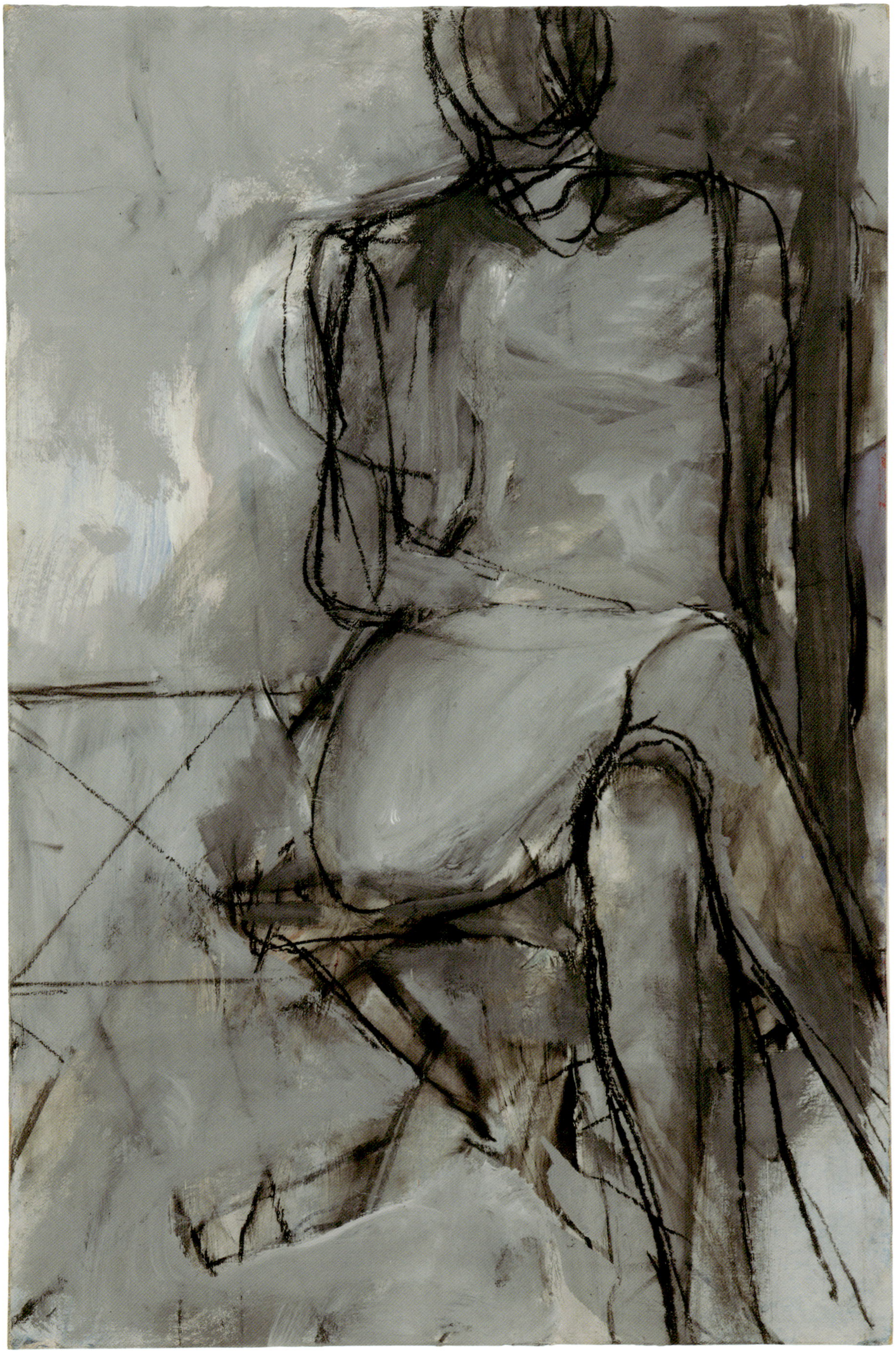

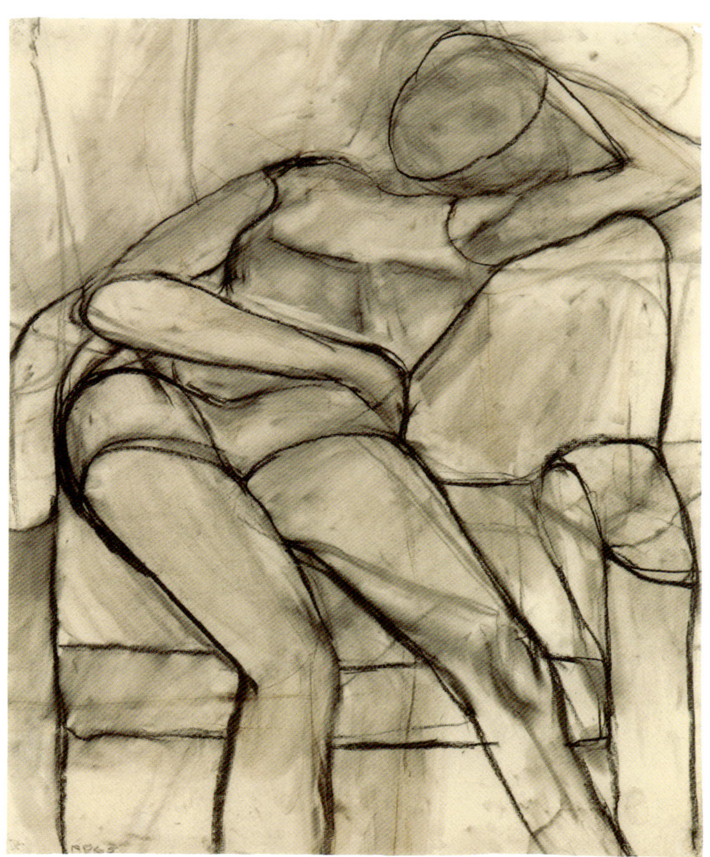

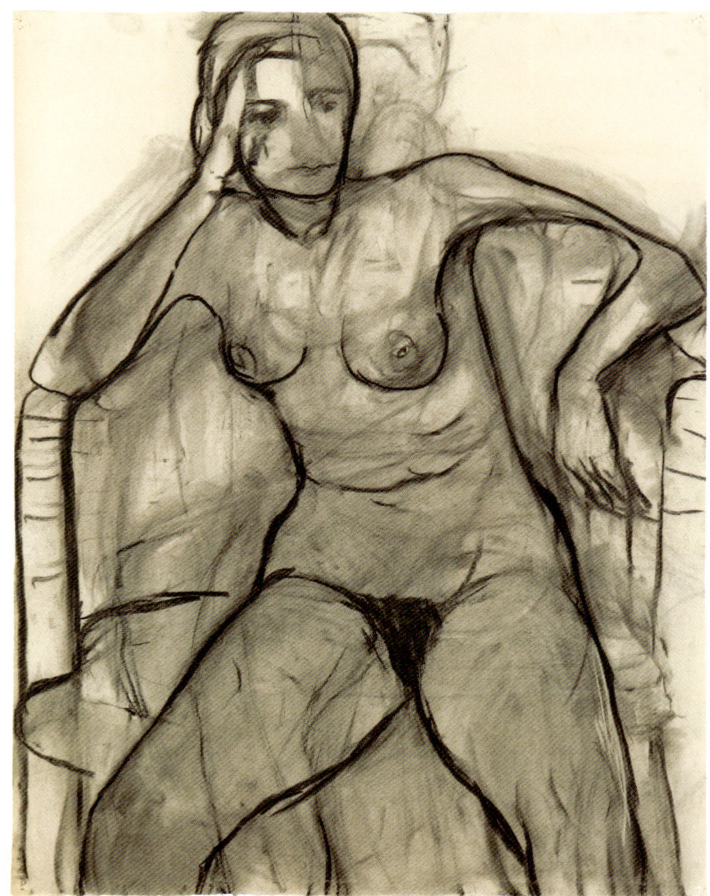

138. *Untitled (Seated Woman)*, 1965
Charcoal on paper, 23 3/4 x 19 in. (60.3 x 48.3 cm)
The Museum of Contemporary Art, Los Angeles, bequest of Marcia Simon Weisman, 96.108 [15]

139. *Untitled (Seated Nude)*, 1966
Charcoal on paper, 25 x 19 in. (63.5 x 48.3 cm)
Private collection [2171]

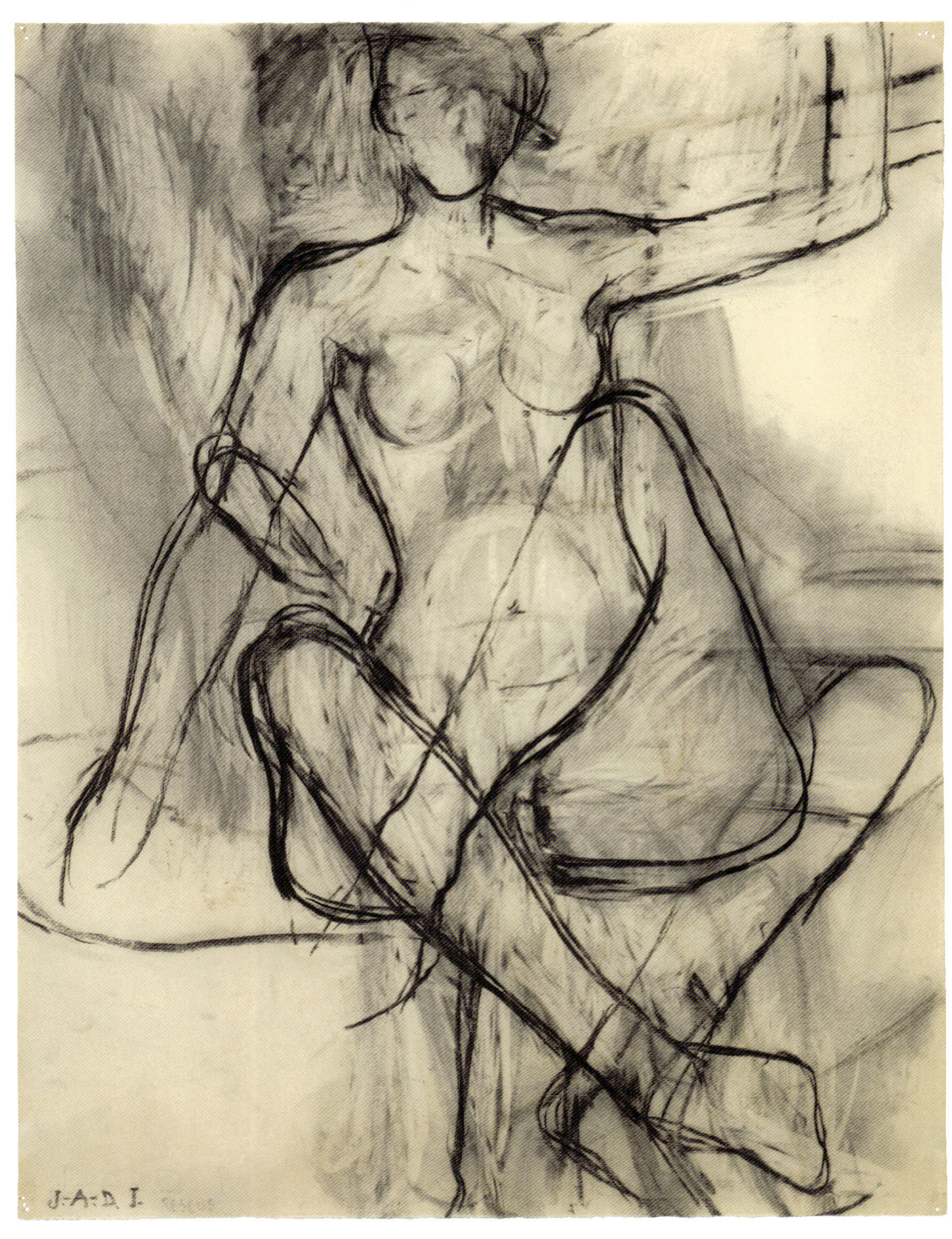

140. *J.A.D.I.*, 1966
Charcoal on paper, 25 x 18 7/8 in. (63.5 x 47.9 cm)
Collection of John Elderfield and Jeanne Collins [598]

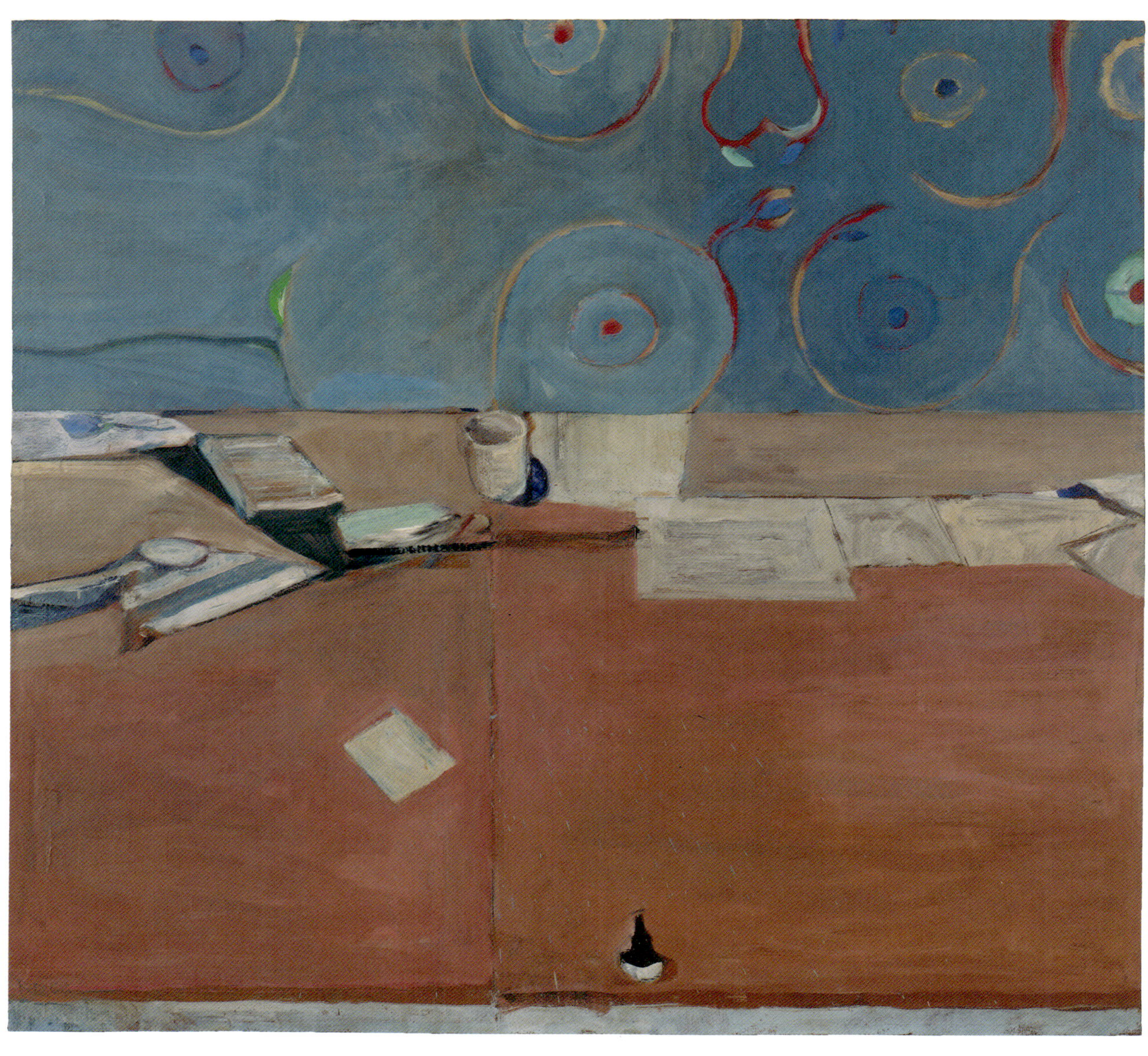

141. *Large Still Life*, 1966
Oil on canvas, 64 1/2 x 70 1/4 in. (163.8 x 178.4 cm)
The Museum of Modern Art, New York, gift of the family of Richard Diebenkorn, 315.2004 [1406]

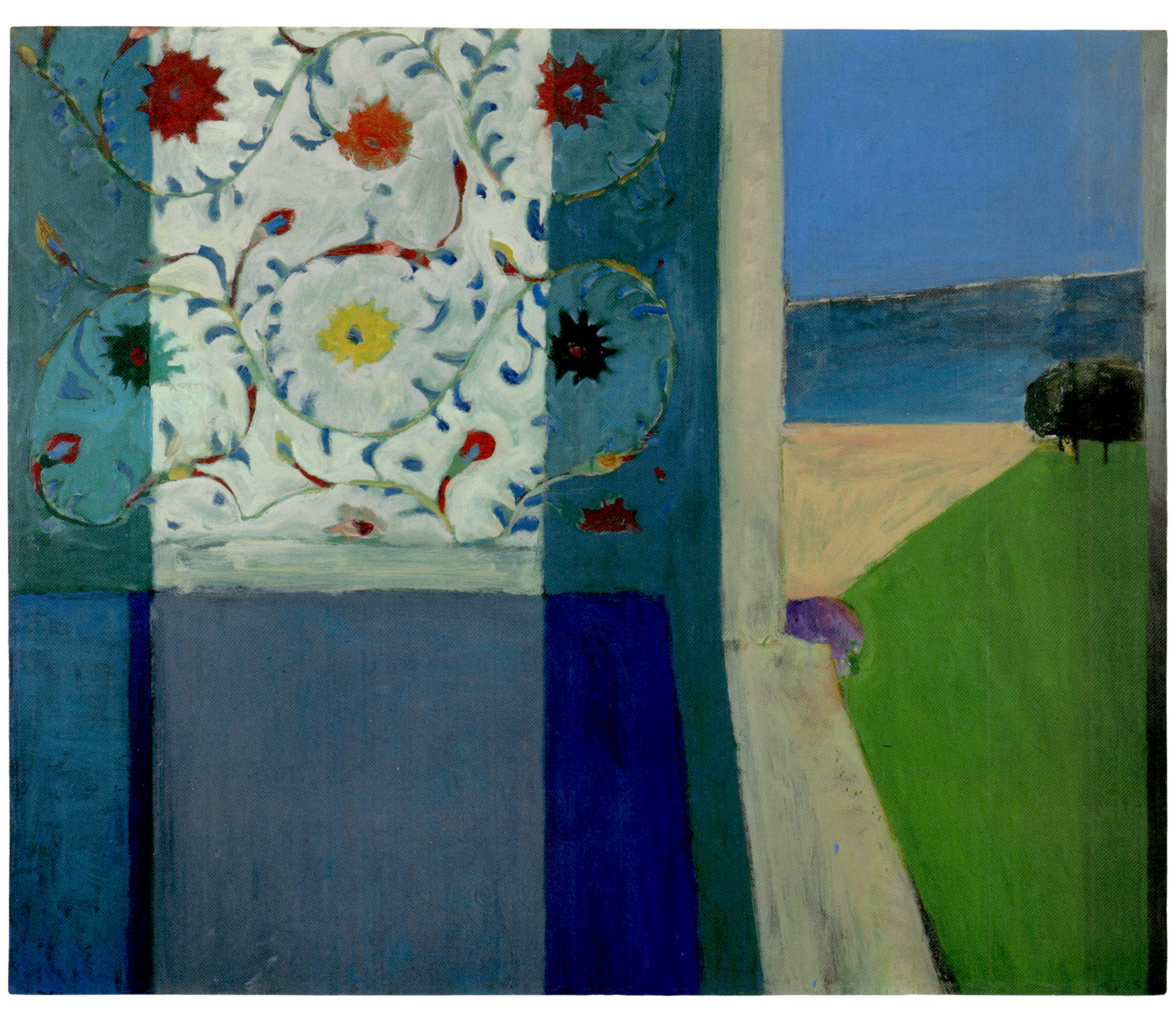

142. *Recollections of a Visit to Leningrad*, 1965
Oil on canvas, 73 x 84 in. (185.4 x 213.4 cm)
Private collection [1404]

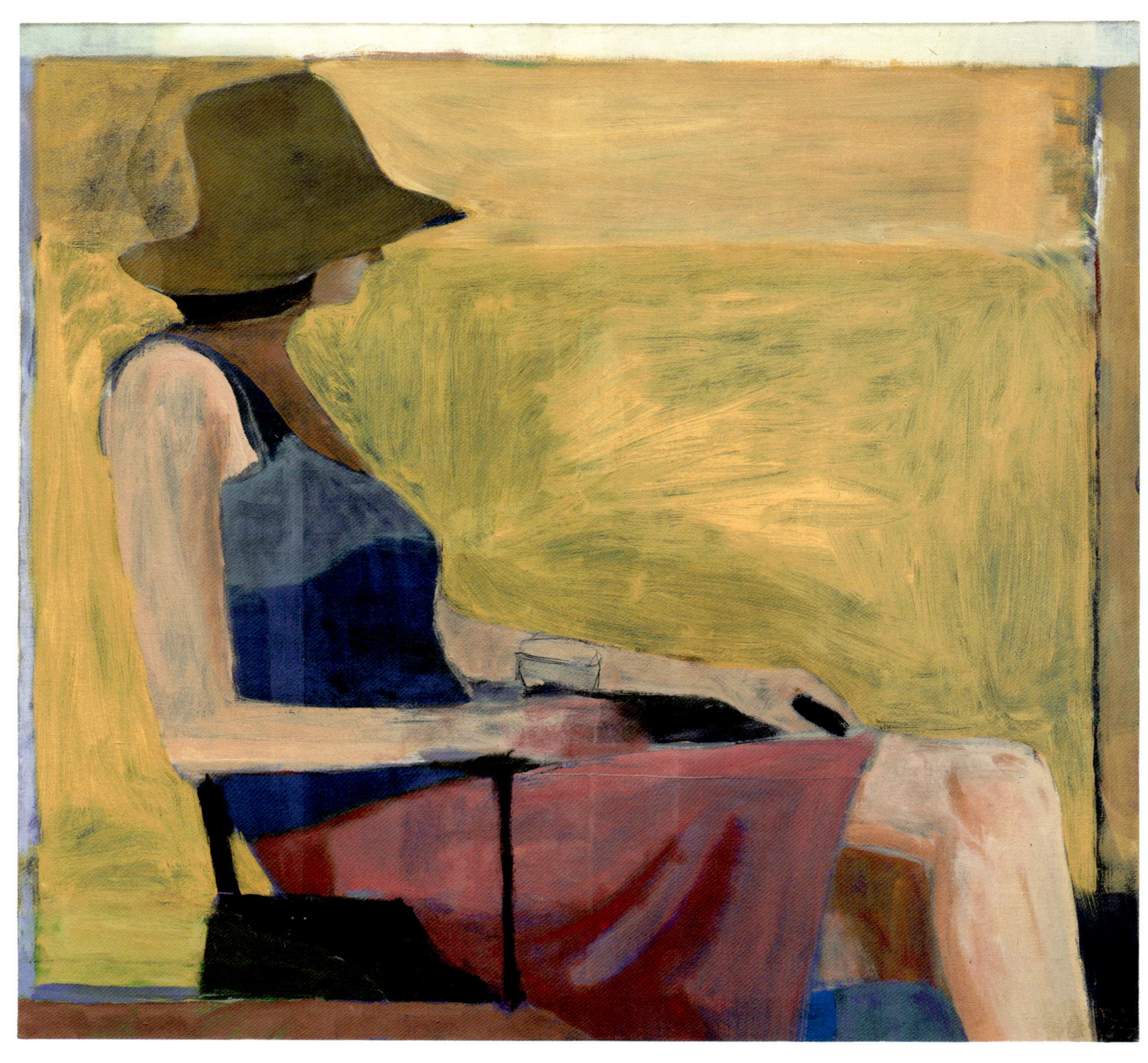

143. *Seated Figure with Hat*, 1967
Oil on canvas, 60 x 60 in. (152.4 x 152.4 cm)
National Gallery of Art, Washington, DC, gift of the Collectors Committee and Mr. and Mrs. Lawrence Rubin, 1991.176.1 [1412]

144. *Large Woman*, 1967
Oil on canvas, 90 x 80 1/8 in. (228.6 x 203.5 cm)
Collection of Gretchen and John Berggruen [1413]

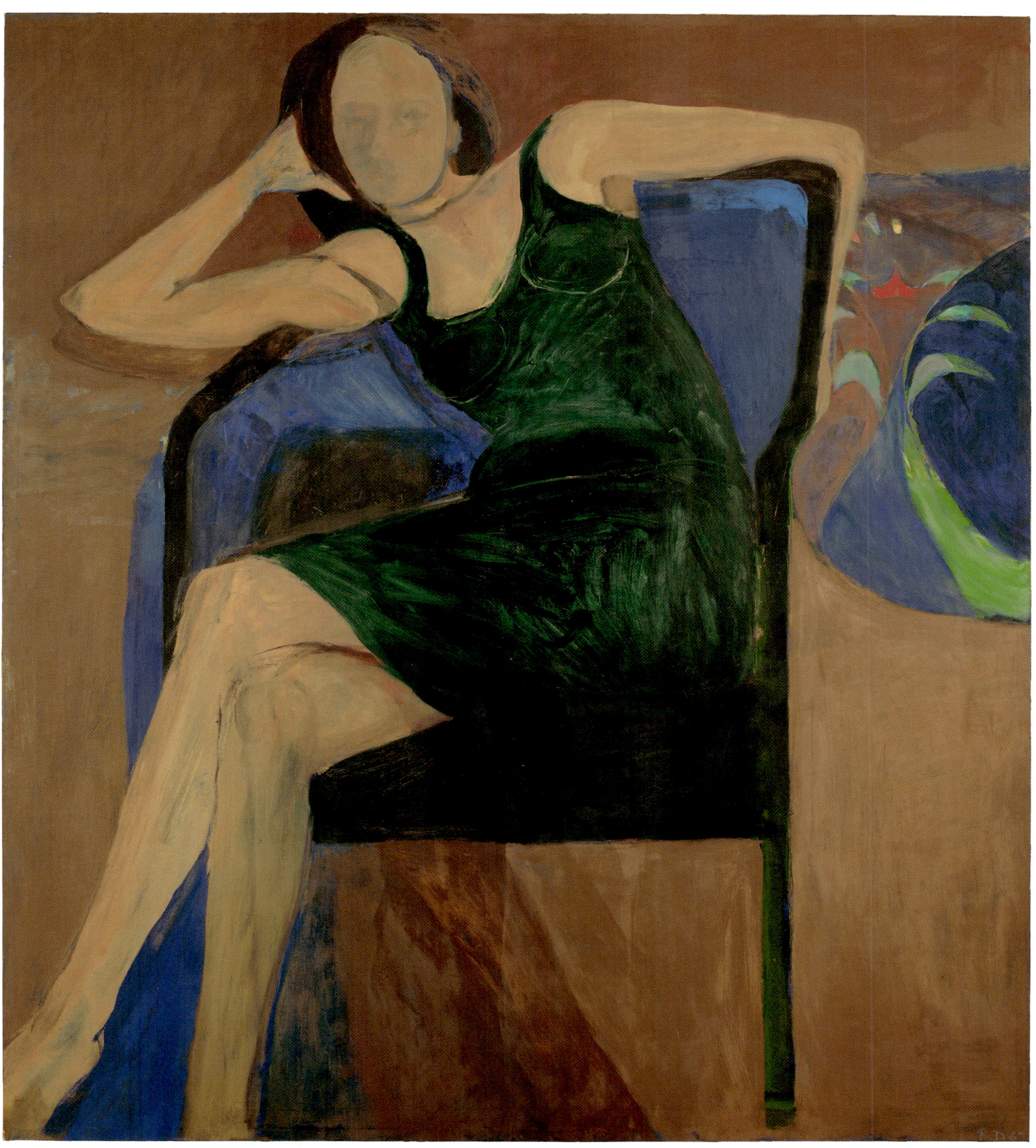

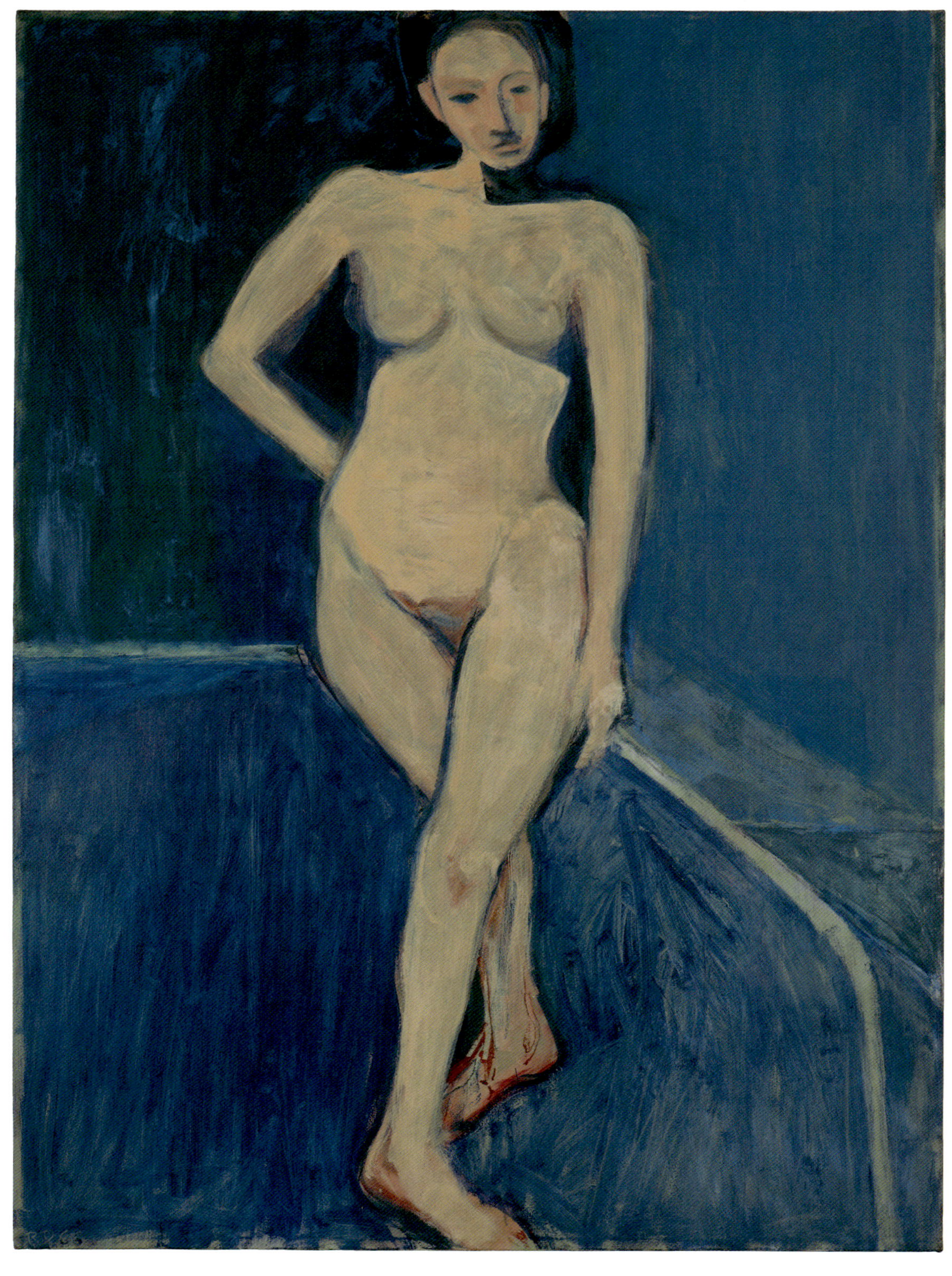

145. *Nude on Blue Ground*, 1966
Oil on canvas, 81 1/4 x 59 1/4 in. (206.4 x 150.5 cm)
Private collection [1408]

146. *Window*, 1967
Oil on canvas, 92 x 80 in. (233.7 x 203.2 cm)
Iris and B. Gerald Cantor Center for Visual Arts at Stanford University, California, gift of Mr. and Mrs. Richard Diebenkorn and anonymous donors, 1969.125 [1414]

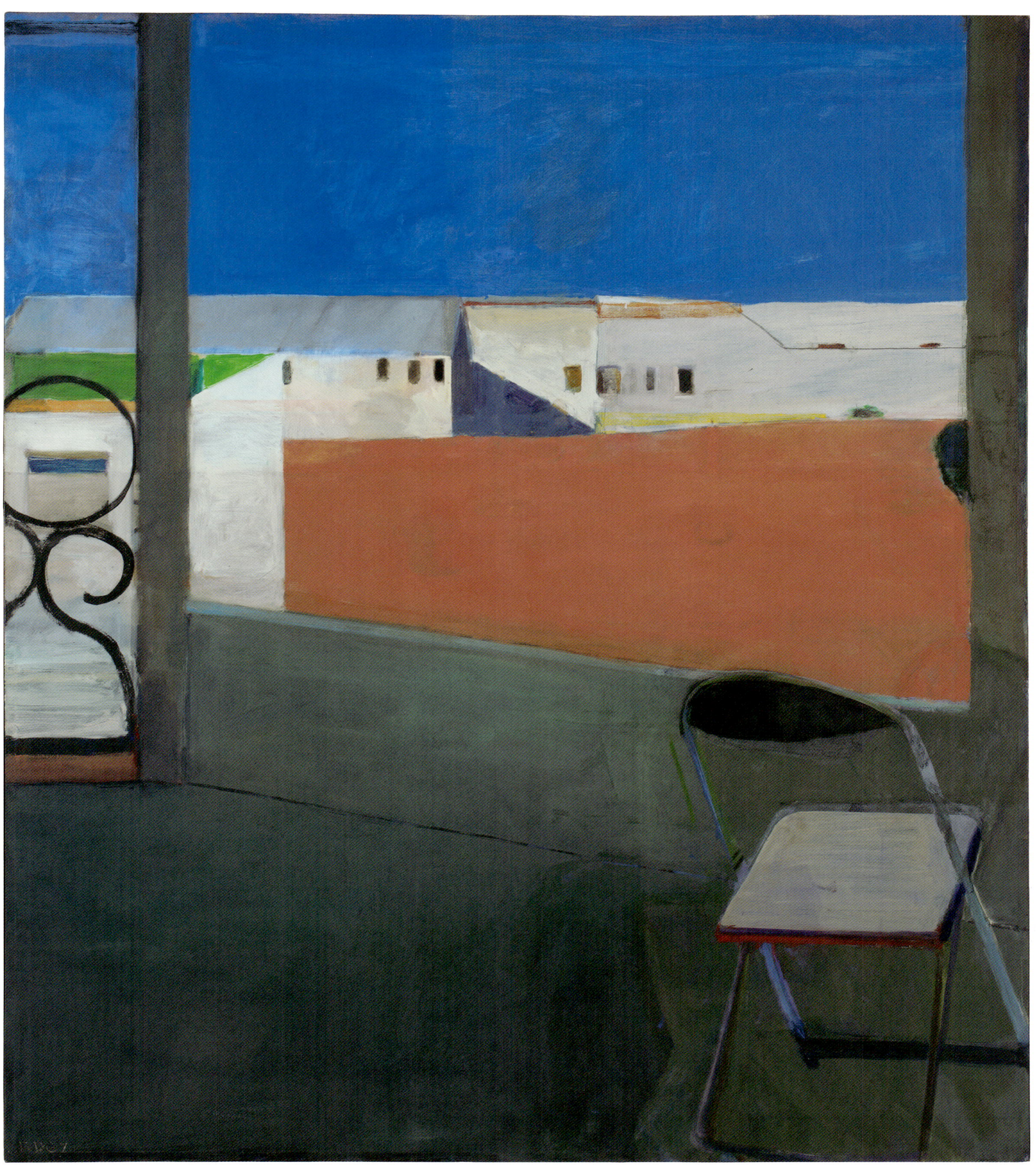

ger's
OFFEE
Oil Color
FULLER
JIM BEAM

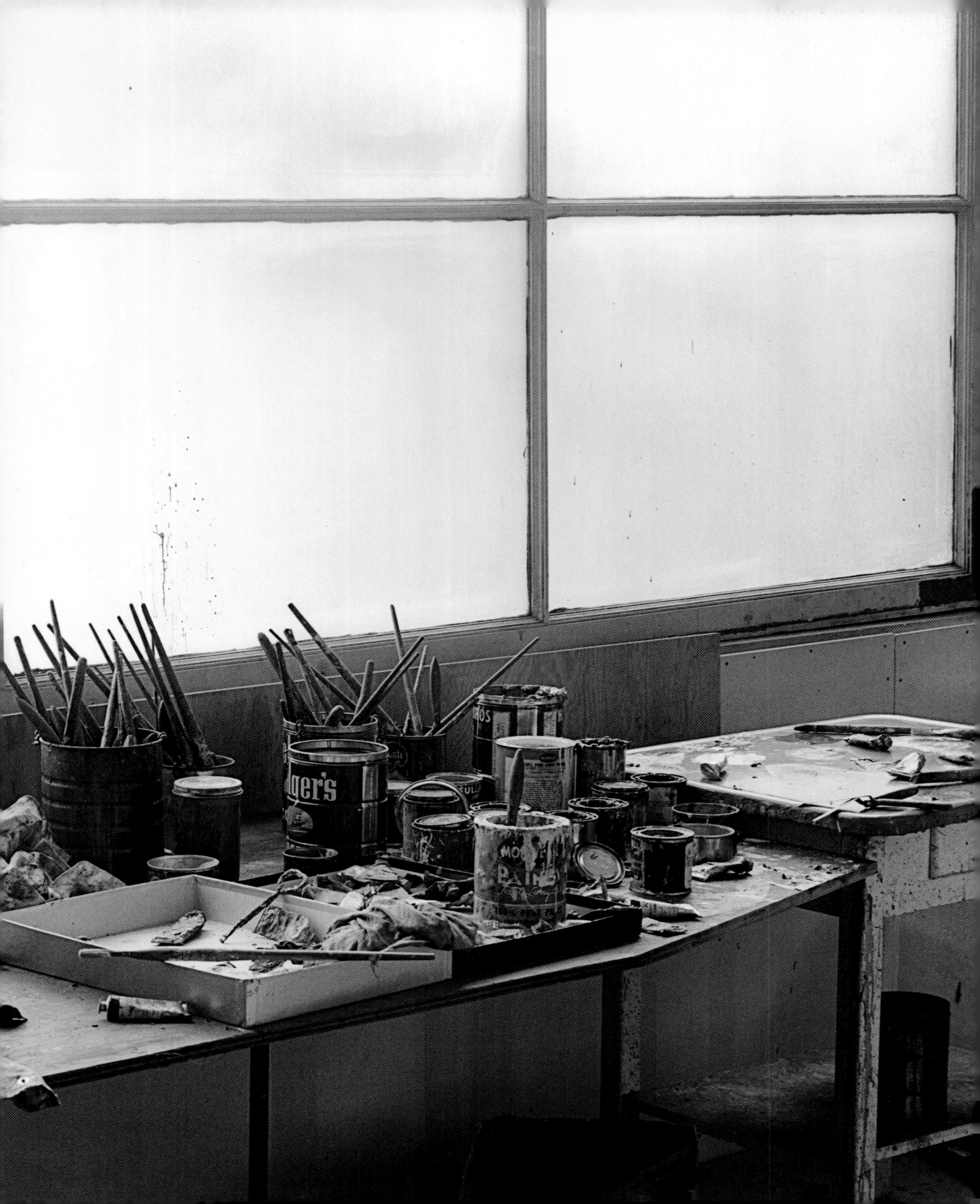

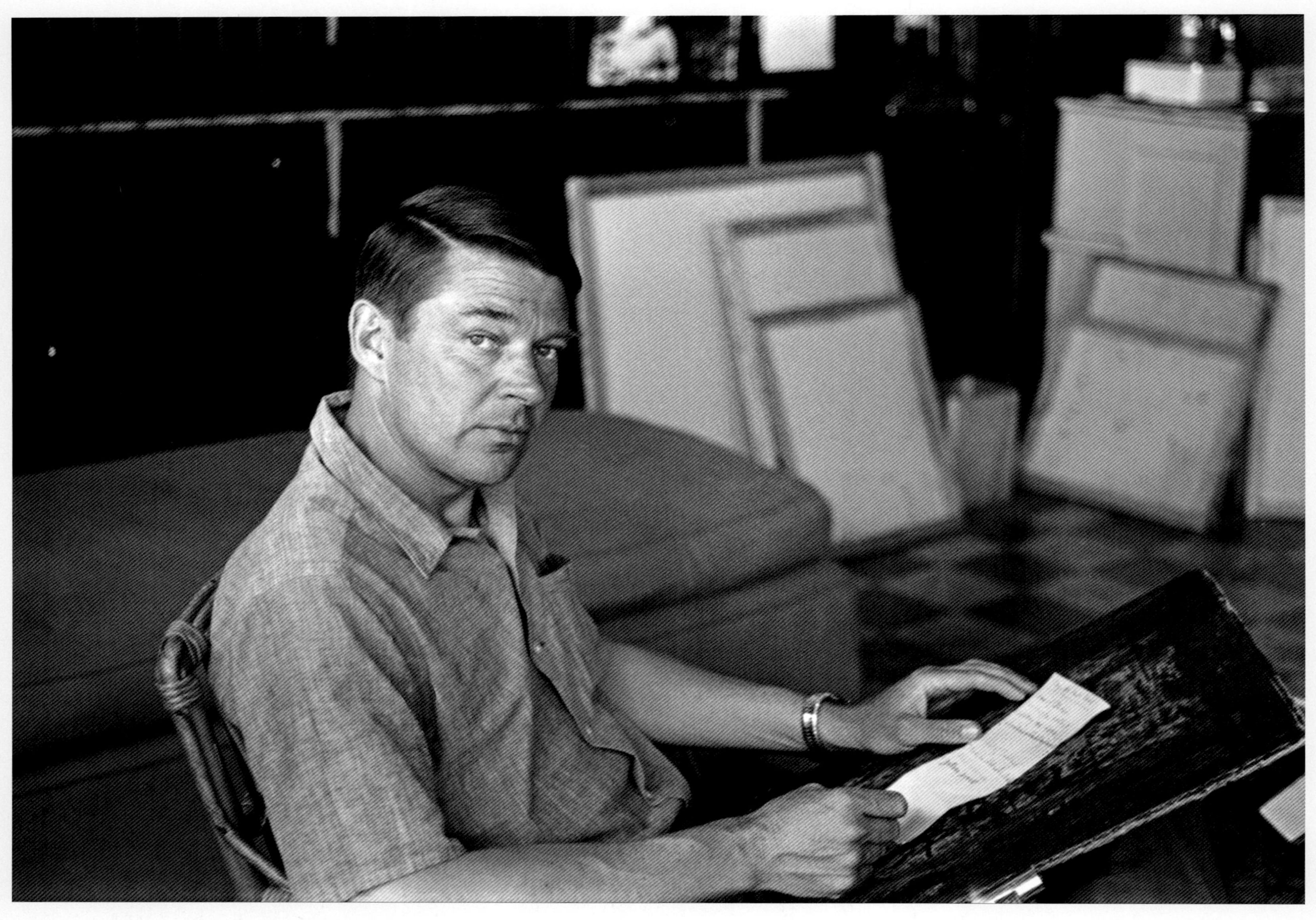

Richard Diebenkorn

A Chronology

Compiled by
EMMA ACKER

With contributions from
Phyllis Diebenkorn, Gretchen Grant,
and Daisy Murray Holman

1922

April 22: Richard Clifford Diebenkorn Jr. (middle name originally Clarence, which he changes at a young age) born in Portland, Oregon, the only child of Richard Clifford Diebenkorn Sr., a hotel supply sales executive, and his wife, née Dorothy Stephens.

1924–early 1930s

Family moves to San Francisco; Diebenkorn grows up at 245 Moncada Way in Ingleside Terraces, a residential neighborhood at the southern end of the city, approximately two miles from the Pacific Ocean.

Frequently spends summers in Woodside, California, with his maternal grandmother, Florence McCarthy Stephens, a civil rights lawyer, writer, radio book reviewer, and amateur artist. She gives him a set of oil paints, encouraging his interest in art, and introduces him to books illustrated by Howard Pyle and N.C. Wyeth and to paintings by Frederic Remington, Charles Russell, and William James. Also gives him reproductions of the Bayeux Tapestry, furthering his interest in heraldic imagery. The card games his mother plays also inspire his interest in the club and spade forms that appear in later work.

Draws from an early age on shirt cardboard and continues to draw throughout grammar school.

1936

May: with his grandmother, sees *Loan Exhibition of Paintings and Drawings by Vincent Van Gogh* at the California Palace of the Legion of Honor, San Francisco (on view May 1–29), which leaves a lasting impression.

1937–1940

Attends Lowell High School in San Francisco, located at the time on Hayes Street between Ashbury Street and Masonic Avenue. Takes some art classes in high school and continues to draw and paint at home. Diebenkorn:

> In the classroom . . . I used strong color, painted loosely, took subjects that other fellows were interested in. . . . At home my work was quite different. It was a sort of elaborate note-taking with reference to my private world. The pictures were tight, rather small, the color was used to identify things . . . the picture being a means of my being transported and brought into real contact with things of importance to me. . . . What I do now combines these approaches.[1]

1940–1943

Enrolls at Stanford University. For the first two years, as part of his general education requirements, studies history, literature, and poetry. Develops a lifelong interest in classical music, particularly the works of Bach, Beethoven, Mozart, and Haydn.

Meets fellow Stanford student Phyllis Antoinette Gilman during his sophomore year.

Signs up to enter the United States Marine Corps shortly after the attack on Pearl Harbor (December 7, 1941).

Despite his father's wishes that he study medicine or law, in his third year at Stanford, takes art courses–studies oil painting with Victor Arnautoff, and drawing and watercolor with Daniel Mendelowitz, with whom he shares a passion for the work of Arthur Dove, Charles Sheeler, and Edward Hopper. Diebenkorn later recalls,

> In my third year there, I had about an hour alone with [Mendelowitz] every week, and that was quite stimulating. He influenced me a lot, and also let me use his studio in the afternoons. Otherwise, I was on my own. I used to drive around, full of enthusiasm, looking for landscapes or cityscapes to paint.[2]

1943

June: marries Phyllis Gilman at Trinity Episcopal Church, Santa Barbara, California.

Called up as an active reserve by the Marine Corps. As part of training for the V-12 program of armed services (to grant bachelor's degrees to future officers from both the Navy and Marine Corps), attends a summer semester at the University of California, Berkeley (UC Berkeley); assigned to study physics and art. Lives on campus and visits Phyllis each weekend at her apartment in San Francisco's Marina district.

At UC Berkeley, studies painting with Erle Loran (who that year published *Cézanne's Composition; Analysis of His Form with Diagrams and Photographs of His Motifs*), drawing with Worth Ryder, and history of art with Eugen Neuhaus. Art department at UC Berkeley embraces a formalist modernism whose exemplars include Paul Cézanne, Pablo Picasso, and Piet Mondrian. Diebenkorn later observes,

> The instruction at Berkeley was really much more rigorous than at Stanford, with everything sort of lumped together—"you don't violate the picture plane," "push-pull," "lateral dynamics," "the opposition of forward and back"—all that sort of thing. Frankly, I thought it verged on being pedantic, though in those days I might have used another expression—"too intellectual"—because Dan Mendelowitz had insisted that art wasn't intellectual. Looking back, though, I feel I got a lot out of it.[3]

With Mendelowitz, visits home of Sarah Stein and the late Michael Stein in Palo Alto, where he encounters the work of Cézanne, Henri Matisse, and Picasso.

Fall: transferred to active duty and attends basic training in Parris Island, South Carolina.

Winter: transferred to Camp Lejeune, North Carolina (where he remains through spring 1944).

FIG 71

Richard Diebenkorn in his Triangle studio on the Berkeley-Oakland border, 1962

1944

Summer: sent to Officer Candidates School in Quantico, Virginia; dismissed from OCS and reassigned to Quantico's photographic section to make maps.

While stationed at Quantico, makes frequent trips to Washington, DC, to visit The Phillips Collection, where he sees works by Pierre Bonnard, Georges Braque, Matisse, and Picasso. Also visits National Gallery of Art and Corcoran Gallery of Art in Washington, DC; Philadelphia Museum of Art; and The Museum of Modern Art in New York. Diebenkorn:

> I wasn't consciously studying; however, at the time I was fortunate in the service to have . . . a bit of free time so I was able to paint quite a bit . . . and then, on liberty, I would go up and look at the paintings in Washington, it was sort of an art school thing for me.[4]

Makes representational drawings, including landscapes and portraits of his fellow Marines, as well as his first abstract watercolors.

1945

January: ordered to report to Camp Pendleton, California, to serve in the photographic section.

While on leave, purchases from San Francisco Museum of Art bookstore the final issue of the magazine *Dyn: The Review of Modern Art* (no. 6, November 1944) and learns of the work of Abstract Expressionists.[5] The issue contains an article by Robert Motherwell titled "The Modern Painter's World" and includes examples of Motherwell's own work, along with that of William Baziotes, Braque, Stanley William Hayter, Roberto Matta, Jackson Pollock, and David Smith. According to Diebenkorn,

> In it were pictures of paintings that were a new breed of cat to me altogether. I remember a couple of very early Robert Motherwells—the only other name that comes to my mind is Pollock. . . . Well, this, at a time when I was looking at French modernism, hit me kind of hard. . . . And so I guess in a very awkward way, I got into this kind of nonobjective or embryo-action painting.[6]

May 23: daughter, Gretchen, is born.

A few weeks later, transferred to Honolulu, Hawaii, in final preparation for combat assignment in Japan, but not deployed. Subsequently returns to live at Camp Pendleton with his family. Diebenkorn:

> I did my first assays at a Cézanne landscape in Hawaii, where I came to know that there was something real in art. I had achieved an excitement, an absorption, an intensity of feeling regarding the means, the artifice of making that was separate from the concern for subject matter.[7]

Winter: honorably discharged from the Marines; returns with his family to parents' house in Atherton, California.

1946

January: enrolls for a semester on the GI Bill at California School of Fine Arts (CSFA, now San Francisco Art Institute [SFAI]), located at Chestnut and Jones Streets on Russian Hill; studies painting with David Park, who quickly becomes a close friend and colleague, as well as with Clay Spohn and Hassel Smith. Begins to paint more abstractly.

The director of CSFA, Douglas MacAgy, has made the school a center for avant-garde art with an emphasis on abstraction (one of MacAgy's first actions is to cover up a Diego Rivera mural on campus), and a strongly creative and experimental spirit pervades the school. Diebenkorn later notes,

> [Surrealism] was very much around that first year I was in art school [1946]. I'm carefully separating this first year, because the Abstract Expressionist thing started to be felt in the second year that I was there. The third year that I was there, it really wiped out the Surrealist influence.[8]

April–May: *North Coast* (1946) and *War Forms* (ca. 1946) included in San Francisco Art Association's *Tenth Annual Watercolor Exhibition*, San Francisco Museum of Art (April 17–May 5).

Fall: $1,200 Albert Bender Grant-in-Aid fellowship in art enables him to live and work on the East Coast. Unable to afford rents in Manhattan, moves with his family to Woodstock, New York, for the winter. Travels to New York City; meets artists such as Bradley Walker Tomlin and Baziotes, and visits Kootz Gallery and The Museum of Modern Art—where he sees work by artists such as Mondrian, Jean Arp, Julio González, Joan Miró, and Kurt Schwitters. In Diebenkorn's words:

> One of the first things I did when I visited New York in 1946 was to go to the Samuel Kootz Gallery and ask to see some of Baziotes' work. . . . Sam Kootz just said, "Well, Baziotes just happens to *be* here in my office." So he took me back, and then they hauled out a bunch of pictures from storage. They were very good to me, and then Bill Baziotes had me to his house for dinner. I took a little package with me and showed him some of the things I was working on.[9]

Paints small canvases influenced by Cubism and by the art of Abstract Expressionists such as Motherwell and Baziotes.

October–November: *Dry Reef and Land Forms* (1946) included in San Francisco Art Association's *Sixty-Sixth Annual Exhibition: Oil, Tempera and Sculpture*, San Francisco Museum of Art (October 10–November 3).

1947

Spring: returns to the Bay Area.

Summer: although Diebenkorn does not take a course with him, Mark Rothko is a visiting professor at CSFA; he also teaches there during the summer of 1949. He shows students slides of work by Pollock, Motherwell, Adolph Gottlieb, and Willem de Kooning, and brings an original painting by Jean Dubuffet to class.

July: sees *Paintings by Clyfford Still* at the California Palace of the Legion of Honor, San Francisco (on view July 2–31), which inspires him to move to larger canvases.

August 25: son, Christopher, is born.

September: lives and works at 40 Bulkley Avenue in the town of Sausalito, on the Bay just north of San Francisco.

Fall: begins teaching at CSFA and is on faculty until January 1950. Teaches life drawing, painting and drawing, and composition.

Reestablishes contact with Park and Smith and meets other fellow teachers Elmer Bischoff, Edward Corbett, and Clyfford Still. Begins weekly studio discussion meetings with Park and Bischoff, soon joined by Smith.

While at the school, becomes associated with two leading students (and veterans, also studying on the GI Bill), John Hultberg and Frank Lobdell, who also live in Sausalito.

Publication of *Drawings*, ed. Frank Lobdell (Mill Valley, CA: Eric T. Ledin, 1947), a portfolio of seventeen lithographs by Diebenkorn, Lobdell, Hultberg, George Stillman, James Budd Dixon, and Walter Kuhlman.

Becomes increasingly aware of contemporary art, in part from reading critic Clement Greenberg's articles in *The Nation* and *Partisan Review*.

1948

February: awarded Emanuel Walter Purchase Prize for *Composition* (1948) at San Francisco Art Association's *Sixty-Seventh Annual Exhibition of the San Francisco Art Association: Oil, Tempera and Sculpture*, San Francisco Museum of Art (February 4–29).

June–July: *Paintings by Richard Diebenkorn*, first solo exhibition, California Palace of the Legion of Honor, San Francisco (June 4–July 1).

Views black-and-white photographs of de Kooning's paintings in the April 1948 issue of *Partisan Review*. Diebenkorn later states, "Seeing de Kooning's work reproduced at that time showed me in a glance what I somehow knew painting could be and what I was flailing around trying to do."[10]

Absorbing the influence of Abstract Expressionist artists such as Rothko, Still, and de Kooning, creates larger, more abstract, and more freely painted canvases.

1949

Fall: awarded a bachelor of arts degree from Stanford, based on his past studies, teaching, and military experience.

December: along with CSFA students and faculty members Smith and Lobdell, participates in a tongue-in-cheek, neo-Dada exhibition organized by Spohn, *The Museum of Unknown and Little-Known Objects*, part of the decor for the school's fund-raiser, Ball of the Unknown.

late 1949 or early 1950

Park takes all his Abstract Expressionist canvases to the Berkeley dump and shifts to painting in a representational mode. Diebenkorn learns of this shift later, after he moves to New Mexico.

1950

January: enrolls on the GI Bill in the Master of Arts program at University of New Mexico in Albuquerque. Diebenkorns spend first eighteen months living in caretaker's cottage on a ranch at 1000 Gabaldon Road, near the Rio Grande, with views of cottonwoods and the mesa on the western side. Diebenkorn's studio is in a Quonset hut that belonged to the university's physical education department.

During his two and a half years in Albuquerque (until June 1952), works through many influences—Bay Area colleagues Park and Smith; Surrealists Miró and Yves Tanguy; Abstract Expressionists Arshile Gorky, Gottlieb, and Motherwell; the light and landscape of his new environment; and the cartoon imagery in George Herriman's Krazy Kat comics—to produce his first mature body of work: 34 extant paintings, at least 250 drawings, several prints, and a few welded metal sculptures.

March: Sausalito paintings and sculptures exhibited in *Paintings and Sculpture by Richard Diebenkorn and Hassel Smith*, Lucien Labaudt Gallery, San Francisco (March 8–30), his first exhibition at a commercial gallery.

1951

February: Park's representational painting *Kids on Bikes* (1950, fig. 32) exhibited at *San Francisco Art Association Annual*, M. H. de Young Memorial Museum, and provokes a controversy between adherents of abstraction and figuration.

April–May: his master's degree exhibition, University Art Museum of New Mexico, Albuquerque (April 29–May 5).

June: receives master's degree from University of New Mexico, Albuquerque.

Late spring or summer: takes his first daytime civilian flight from Albuquerque to San Francisco; it has a lasting impact: "The aerial view showed me a rich variety of ways of treating a flat plane."[11]

During his visit to San Francisco, sees *Arshile Gorky Memorial Exhibition* at San Francisco Museum of Art (May 9–July 9).

June–July: included in *Contemporary Painting in the United States: 1951 Annual Exhibition*, Los Angeles County Museum of Art (June 2–July 22).

Fall: returns to University of New Mexico for a second year, again on the GI Bill.

Painting *Untitled* (1950) chosen for illustration in Motherwell's anthology *Modern Artists in America* (New York: Wittenborn, Schultz, 1951).

1952

Phyllis Diebenkorn completes undergraduate degree at University of New Mexico, with a major in psychology.

Summer: Diebenkorns return to California, staying with Phyllis's family in Spadra, near Pomona, east of Los Angeles. He sees *Henri Matisse: Selections from the Museum of Modern Art Retrospective*, Municipal Department of Art, Los Angeles (July 24–August 15).

Fall: family moves to Urbana, Illinois; Diebenkorn teaches drawing and painting to architecture students at the University of Illinois for 1952–1953 academic year.

While in Urbana, paints the representational oil *Untitled* (ca. 1952–1953), which depicts a group of musicians.

November–December: *Richard Diebenkorn*, first solo exhibition at a commercial gallery, Paul Kantor Gallery, Los Angeles (November 10–December 1), which continues to represent him until 1956.

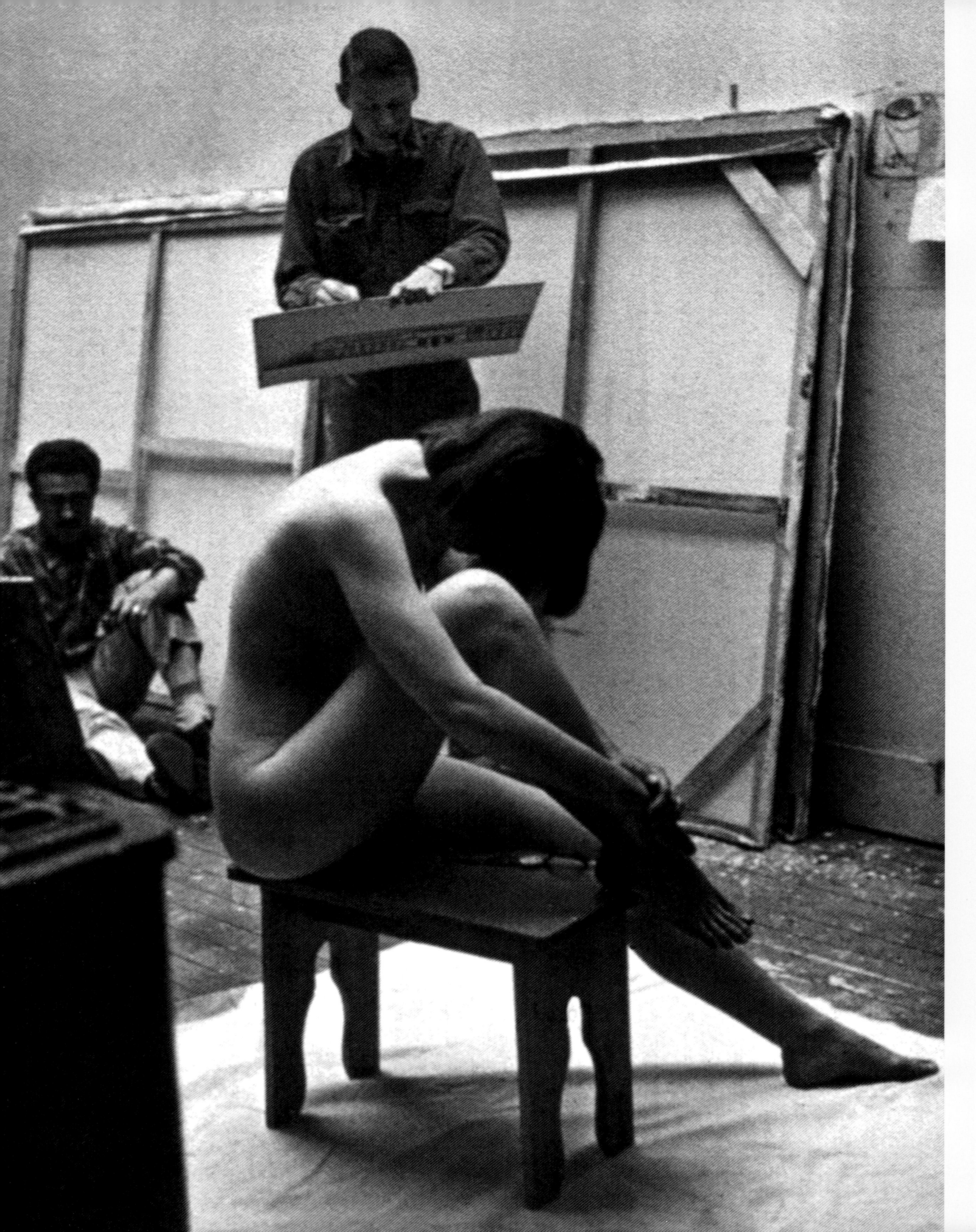

The Berkeley Years

1953

Summer: drives with Phyllis from Urbana to New York; spends summer there living and working at 68 East 12th Street (the artist Jon Schueler's studio). Meets Greenberg and artists de Kooning and Franz Kline. Kline will later encourage Elinor Poindexter of Poindexter Gallery to exhibit Diebenkorn's work.

September: moves back to Bay Area, rents a railroad-style apartment in Berkeley at 2837 Webster Street. Studio is located in the center of the apartment, so family members walk outside to get to the kitchen or living room from the bedroom while Diebenkorn is working.

Phyllis enters the graduate program in psychology at UC Berkeley.

Fall: though continuing to paint and draw abstractly, begins weekly studio visits and drawing sessions from the model with Park and Bischoff. During his absence they have started to work in a figurative mode (in 1950 and 1952, respectively). Draws from the model with Park and Bischoff until Park's death in 1960, when Lobdell joins the group, and thereafter until 1966.

Begins Berkeley series, which will include 58 extant abstract oil paintings produced between the fall of 1953 and early 1956.

Winter: makes the first of two small groups of fetish-like objects.

1954

February: *Richard Diebenkorn*, Allan Frumkin Gallery, Chicago.

February–March: $2,400 Abraham Rosenberg Fellowship for Advanced Studies in Art, administered by San Francisco Art Association, enables him to paint full time. Jury for the fellowship includes painters Park, Karl Kasten, and Ward Lockwood; director of the San Francisco Museum of Art Dr. Grace L. McCann Morley; and critic Alfred Frankenstein.

March–April: *Richard Diebenkorn*, Paul Kantor Gallery, Los Angeles (March 22–April 30).

May–July: included in *Younger American Painters*, Solomon R. Guggenheim Museum, New York (May 12–September 26); travels to Portland Art Museum; Henry Art Gallery, Seattle; San Francisco Museum of Art; Los Angeles Museum of History, Science, and Art; University of Arkansas, Fayetteville; and Isaac Delgado Museum of Art, New Orleans.

August–September: *Three Bay Region Artists (Ruth Armer, Richard Diebenkorn, Ralph Du Casse)*, San Francisco Museum of Art (August 17–September 5).

Moves half a block away to a rented house at 2947 Magnolia Street, Berkeley.

Begins working at a studio located above a Volkswagen dealership at 2751 Shattuck Avenue, Berkeley.

Paints what may be his first representational work of the Berkeley period, the small oil *Untitled (Horse and Rider)* (fig. 16), as well as the small oil *Untitled (Nude)* (fig. 25).

1955

March–May: included in *Twenty Fourth Biennial Exhibition of Contemporary American Oil Paintings*, Corcoran Gallery of Art, Washington, DC (March 13–May 8); travels to Museum of Fine Arts, Boston; then circulated to various locations by American Federation of Arts, New York.

April–May: included in *Giovanni pittori Painters Under 35*, organized by Congress for Cultural Freedom and circulated by The Museum of Modern Art Circulating Exhibitions to Galleria Nazionale d'Arte Moderna, Rome (April 15–May 20); travels to Palais des Beaux-Arts, Brussels, and Musée National d'Art Moderne, Paris.

Continues weekly group drawing sessions from the model with Park and Bischoff, which rotate between the artists' studios. Experiments with producing representational drawings, beginning with still lifes, then moving to interior scenes, landscapes, and figural compositions.

Spring: begins teaching at California College of Arts and Crafts (CCAC, now California College of the Arts [CCA]) in Oakland (intermittently through 1960).

July–October: included in *IIIrd Bienal do Museu de Arte Moderna, São Paulo* (July 2–October 12).

Summer: begins to rethink relationship to Abstract Expressionism after seeing some "pretty poor contemporary work" among second-generation followers. Diebenkorn:

> I came to mistrust my desire to explode the picture and supercharge it in some way. At one time the common device of using the super emotional to get "in gear" with a painting used to serve me for access to painting, but I mistrust that now. I think what is more important is a feeling of strength in reserve—tension beneath calm.[12]

September–October: *Recent Paintings: Richard Diebenkorn*, informal solo exhibition, Art Department, UC Berkeley (September 12–October 12).

October–December: included in *Pittsburgh International Exhibition of Contemporary Painting*, Museum of Art, Carnegie Institute, Pittsburgh (October 13–December 18).

October–December: included in *Vanguard 1955: A Painter's Selection of New American Paintings*, Walker Art Center, Minneapolis (October 23–December 5); travels to Stable Gallery, New York.

November 1955–January 1956: included in *Annual Exhibition of Contemporary American Painting*, Whitney Museum of American Art, New York (November 9, 1955–January 8, 1956).

Late fall: working en plein air, paints *Chabot Valley* (pl. 36), often cited as his first representational work of the Berkeley period (but see *Untitled [Horse and Rider]* and *Untitled [Nude]* mentioned in 1954). Although the subject is recognizable as an urban or suburban landscape, the paint is richly, expressively handled and impastoed, as in his Abstract Expressionist paintings. He recalls,

> Essentially what I did was what I had done at Stanford, is get in the car and go out and look for something that looked like it might make a good painting. . . . I worked right from the canvas . . . and I did it entirely on the spot. . . . It's not intentional, but it certainly does relate to the '55 paintings . . . that I was doing . . . the larger things were done in the studio. So I guess after doing . . . this landscape—and this probably all happened in a week—the landscape and several still lives—then I approached a big canvas with a figure.[13]

FIG 72

Richard Diebenkorn with Nathan Oliveira during a figure drawing session at Theophilus Brown and Paul Wonner's studio, Berkeley, ca. 1956

In a 1983 interview, elaborates on the impetus for this transition:

> In the rush of painting that I did in 1954–55, I had experienced my first kind of opposition. It was a struggle all along, and I was attributing this to my being in a stylistic straightjacket. I felt that perhaps I had too many rules, that there was too much Abstract Expressionism hanging over my head, and so . . . there was a need for change.[14]

December: receives "Guest of Honor" one-man show award and gold medal for painting *Berkeley #27* (1955, pl. 25), which is shown in *Western Painters' Annual Exhibition*, Oakland Art Museum (December 10, 1955–January 8, 1956).

1956

February–March: included in *California School, Yes or No?*, Oakland Art Museum.

February–March: *Richard Diebenkorn: Paintings*, solo exhibition of Berkeley works, Poindexter Gallery, New York (February 28–March 24), which will continue to represent him until 1971. In her review of the exhibition critic Dore Ashton writes,

> The paintings in this show, if studied carefully, present a single landscape under various conditions. Like the Impressionists, Diebenkorn is eager to get down his impression of momentary effects and get it down quickly. . . . In most of the canvases, a raking stroke which moves across and back in steady horizontal rhythms gathers the forms together. Where Diebenkorn wants to suggest contrary natural phenomena, like wind or storm, he executes a flurry of diagonal strokes.[15]

March: wins $75 Seventy-Fifth Commemorative Artist's Council Award for *Berkeley #66* (1956, pl. 39) in *Seventy-Fifth Annual Painting and Sculpture Exhibition of the San Francisco Art Association*, San Francisco Museum of Art (March 29–May 6).

May–July: included in *Pacific Coast Art: United States' Representation at the IIIrd Biennial of São Paulo*, San Francisco Museum of Art (May 15–July 15); travels to Colorado Springs Fine Art Center; Walker Art Center, Minneapolis; Dayton Art Institute; Cincinnati Art Museum; Institute of Contemporary Art, Boston; and Los Angeles County Museum of Art. In the catalogue, Dr. Grace L. McCann Morley discusses what she views as a sensitivity to landscape in work by Bay Area artists:

> The art of San Francisco likewise has its own character. . . . Open country of orchards and wine producing valleys is near, and, within view from every hill on which it stands, are the Bay and the bare mountains encircling it . . . everywhere on the Pacific Coast, the typical landscape, with its contrast of sea and mountains and of fog and brilliant sunshine, appears to have considerable influence.[16]

Summer: buys a house in Berkeley at 217 Hillcrest Road and builds a small studio in the backyard. The studio, about 14 by 21 feet, is at the upper end of a sloping lot, with a single large window overlooking a view of pine trees and hilltops. Stops painting for the two months of building the studio. In a letter to Poindexter dated November 15, writes, "Besides changing my emphasis considerably which has produced only intangible results the stopping this summer to build a studio threw me off much more than I anticipated."[17]

According to the critic Herschel B. Chipp,

> [This period] was a crucial time, for during the previous months he had made a gradual change to a more representational type painting, and he now wondered if this were to be permanent. He admits that during the month when he was not painting, his thinking was still involved with his former abstract landscape style.[18]

Fall–winter: consistently painting in a representational manner. Diebenkorn later states,

> I found a somewhat literal reinforcement of the differences I sought, such as, outside beside interior, sunlight as opposed to gloom, the presence of a person as opposed to emptiness, made the balance a better one and maintained the kind of differences that I sought.[19]

September: *Richard Diebenkorn*, Oakland Art Museum, is first solo exhibition of his representational work (September 8–30). This exhibition results from his 1955 "Guest of Honor" one-man show award at the Oakland Art Museum.

December: wins first prize at *San Francisco Art Association Members' Show*, M. H. de Young Memorial Museum, for *Flowers and Cigar Box*, also known as *Untitled (Still Life with Iris)* (1956, pl. 41).

1957

January–February: *Richard Diebenkorn: Paintings*, solo exhibition of the Berkeley works, Swetzoff Gallery, Boston (January 16–February 9).

January–March: included in *Twenty Fifth Biennial Exhibition of Contemporary American Oil Paintings*, Corcoran Gallery of Art, Washington, DC (January 13–March 10); travels to Toledo Museum of Art.

January–March: included in *LXII Annual American Exhibition*: *Paintings, Sculpture*, Art Institute of Chicago (January 17–March 3).

March: wins $375 prize for *Cups* (1957) in *1957 California Painters' Exhibition*, Oakland Art Museum (March 9–31).

March–April: included in the exhibition *Objects on the New Landscape Demanding of the Eye*, Ferus Gallery, Los Angeles, a survey of western Abstract Expressionism of the late 1940s and early 1950s that includes works by John Altoon, Billy Al Bengston, Roy De Forest, Edward Kienholz, Craig Kauffman, and Still (March 15–April 11).

April: included in *Life* magazine article "Look of the West Inspires New Art."[20]

April–May: included in *Modern Painting, Drawing & Sculpture: Collected by Louise and Joseph Pulitzer, Jr.*, M. Knoedler & Co., New York (April 9–May 4); travels to Fogg Museum, Harvard Art Museums, Cambridge, Massachusetts.

FIGS 73–74

The artist's studio behind his family's home, 217 Hillcrest Road, Berkeley. Photographed by Morley Baer, 1966

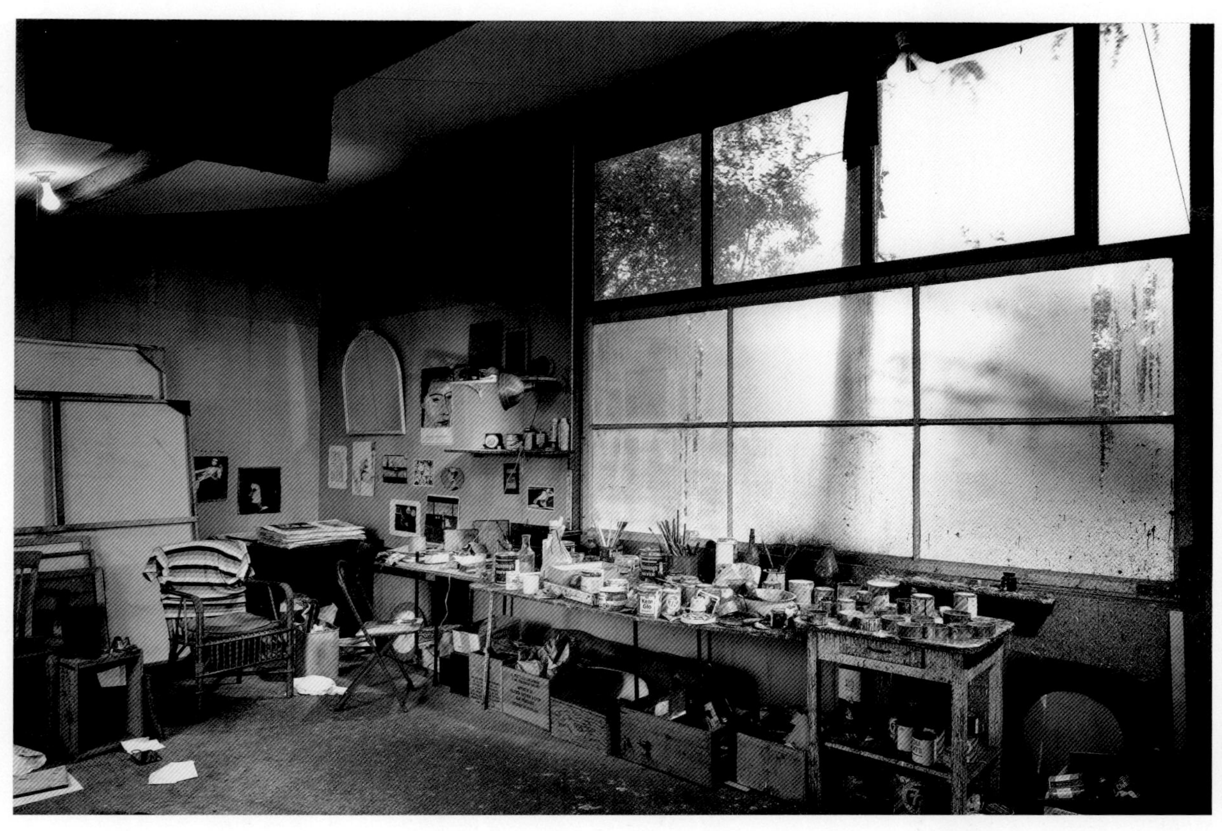

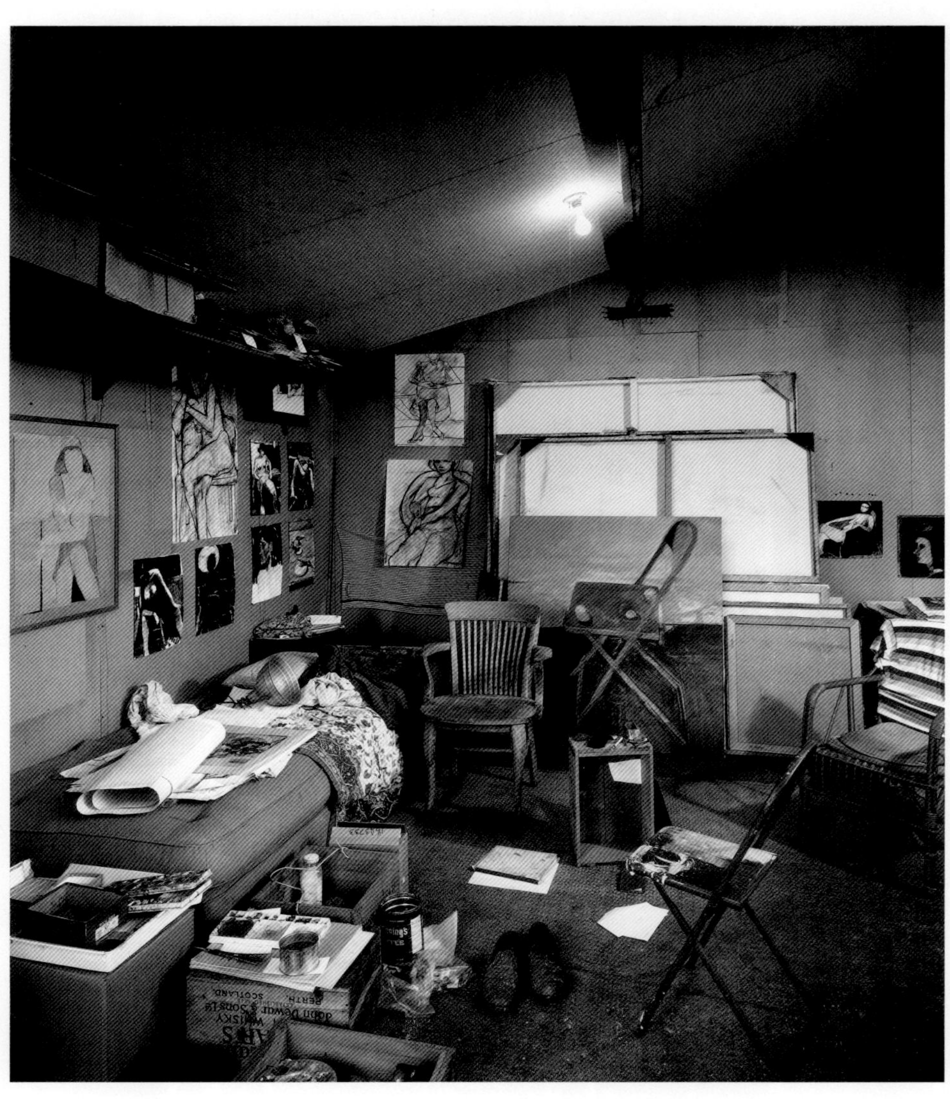

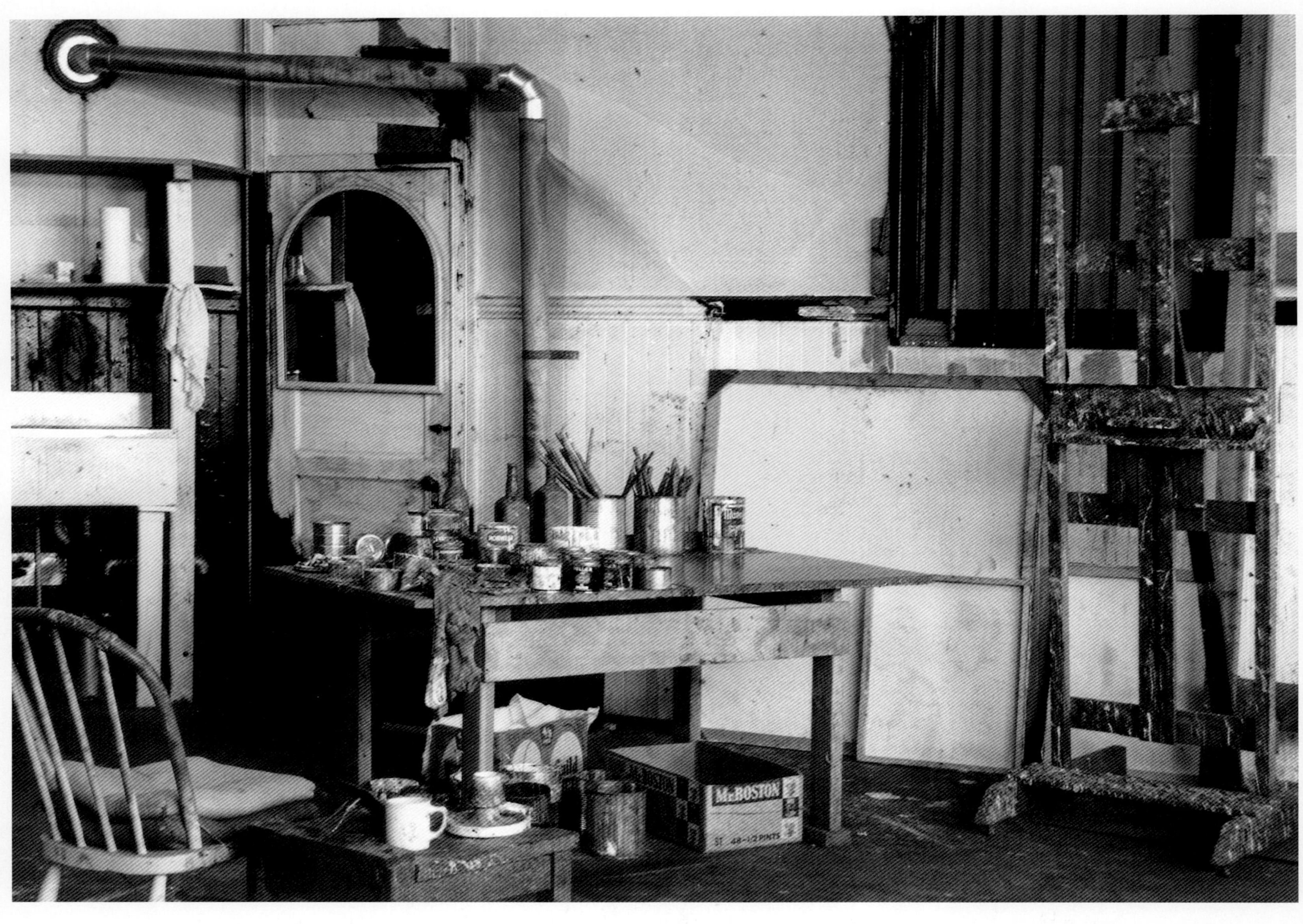

FIG 75

Richard Diebenkorn's Triangle studio on the Berkeley-Oakland border, ca. 1958–1963

May: Herschel B. Chipp's article "Diebenkorn Paints a Picture" is published in *Art News* and introduces his new representational manner to a wider public. The article documents the creation of a figurative painting titled *Woman by the Ocean* (1956, pl. 47) and is illustrated with photographs by Rose Mandel (see pp. 232–237).

Summer: teaches at University of Southern California, Los Angeles.

June–September: included in *American Paintings, 1945–1957*, Minneapolis Institute of Arts (June 18–September 1).

Fall: teaches at Mills College, Oakland.

September: despite reservations about being associated with a movement, is included along with Park, Bischoff, and others in *Contemporary Bay Area Figurative Painting*, organized by Paul Mills, Oakland Art Museum, California (September 8–29); travels to Los Angeles County Museum of Art, The Dayton Art Institute, and Colorado Springs Art Center.

September: wins Women's Board of the Santa Barbara Museum of Art Award of Merit for *Woman and Checkerboard* (1956) in *Second Pacific Coast Biennial Exhibition of Paintings and Watercolors*, Santa Barbara Museum of Art, California (September 10–October 13); travels to California Palace of the Legion of Honor, San Francisco; Seattle Art Museum; and Portland Art Museum.

1958

February–March: *Richard Diebenkorn: Recent Paintings*, solo exhibition of his figurative work, Poindexter Gallery, New York (February 24–March 29). Exhibition is widely reviewed; *Time* magazine reproduces three of the paintings in color in article titled "Edging Away from Abstraction":

> His abstractions recalled the sunlit, freshly green California hills, San Francisco Bay and the Pacific. . . .
>
> The significance of Diebenkorn's recent work is that it points a way for other younger painters to combine the surface richness and excitement discovered through abstraction with a recognizable subject matter. [21]

April–October: included in an exhibition at the American Pavilion of the Brussels World's Fair (April 17–October 19); travels to inaugural exhibition of the United States Information Service Library, London; then, as *Brussels '58—Contemporary American Art*, to World House Galleries, New York.

September 28: makes first trip of many (through 1988) to Santa Cruz Island, off the coast of Santa Barbara, to stay at the home of college friend Carey Stanton. Produces a series of four views looking east from a balcony in the upstairs *sala* of Justinian House at Main Ranch. Exemplifying his movement from representation to abstraction, the third of these views, *Winery, S.C.I.* (1958, pl. 67), includes a view of the nineteenth-century winery buildings on the island. The last in the series, *View of the Ocean, Santa Cruz Island* (1958, pl. 68), is much more abstracted, with the wineries painted out and the ocean painted in.

Winter: begins working at the Triangle studio—a large, parallelogram-shaped space behind a popular bar in an industrial building in Berkeley close to the Oakland border, near the intersection of Ashby Avenue and Adeline Street. Some features of the studio—a large door, transom windows, checkered linoleum floor, and corner sink—are depicted in paintings such as *Corner of Studio—Sink* (1963, pl. 98). Building will be condemned in 1964 and razed to make way for the new Ashby station of the Bay Area Rapid Transit (BART) system. Recalling the studio many years later, Diebenkorn says,

> It was a triangular room at the back of a tavern. I could open a door and look right down the bar at all the regulars. There was a lot of useless furniture built into the wall, and when I pulled it off you could see many different overlapping layers of house paint. The effect was fascinating.[22]

November 1958–January 1959: included in *1958 Annual Exhibition: Sculpture, Paintings, Watercolors, Drawings*, Whitney Museum of American Art, New York (November 19, 1958–January 4, 1959).

December 1958–February 1959: included in *1958 Pittsburgh Bicentennial International Exhibition of Contemporary Painting and Sculpture*, Museum of Art, Carnegie Institute, Pittsburgh (December 5, 1958–February 8, 1959).

1959

January–March: included in *The Twenty Sixth Biennial Exhibition of Contemporary American Painting*, Corcoran Gallery of Art, Washington, DC (January 17–March 8).

June: spends summer teaching at University of Colorado Boulder; lives at 842 Grant Place, Boulder.

Fall: recommences teaching at CSFA.

September–November: included in *New Images of Man*, Museum of Modern Art, New York (September 30–November 29); travels to Baltimore Museum of Art.

December 1959–January 1960: included in *63rd American Exhibition: Paintings, Sculpture*, Art Institute of Chicago (December 2, 1959–January 31, 1960).

1960

Spring: travels to New York with Phyllis; visits The Metropolitan Museum of Art and Frick Collection for the first time. Also travels to Lower Merion, Pennsylvania, to visit Barnes Foundation.

September–October: *Richard Diebenkorn*, first retrospective exhibition of works from 1952 to 1960, Pasadena Art Museum, California (September 6–October 6); travels as *Recent Paintings by Richard Diebenkorn* to California Palace of the Legion of Honor, San Francisco.

David Park dies.

1961

January–February: included in *The Twenty Seventh Biennial Exhibition of Contemporary American Painting*, Corcoran Gallery of Art, Washington, DC (January 14–February 26); circulated to various locations by American Federation of Arts, New York.

March–April: *Richard Diebenkorn*, Poindexter Gallery, New York (March 13–April 8).

May–June: *Richard Diebenkorn*, The Phillips Collection, Washington, DC (May 19–June 26).

June–July: included in *Vanguard American Painting*, organized by Solomon R. Guggenheim Museum, New York; circulated by the United States Information Agency, Washington, DC,

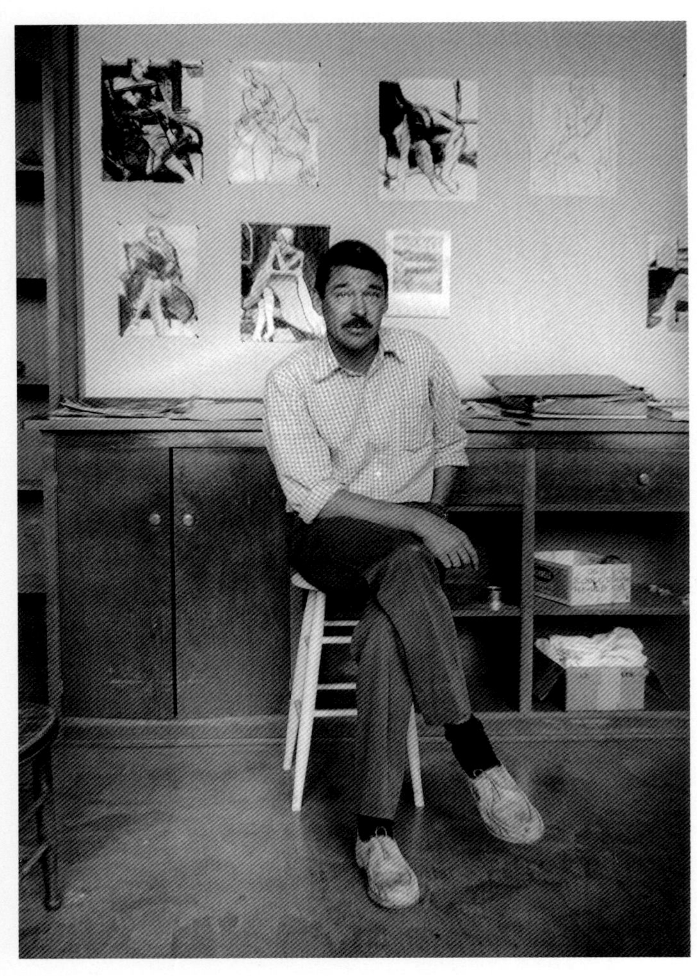

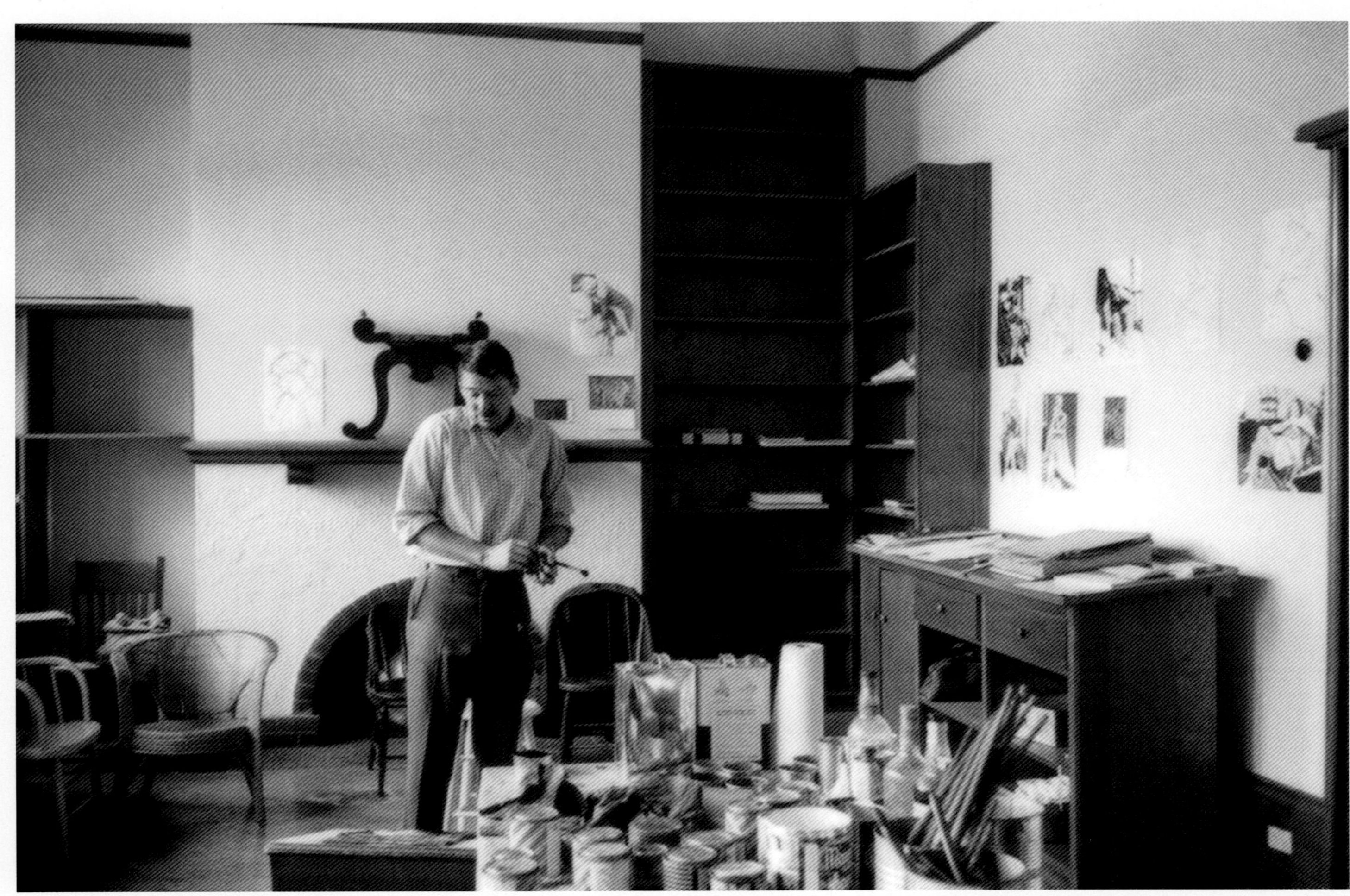

to Galerie Würthle, Vienna (June 19–July 8); travels to Zwerglgarten Pavilion, Salzburg; Kalemegda Pavilion, Belgrade, Yugoslavia; Umetnicki Pavilion, Skopje, Macedonia; Zagreb Museum, Yugoslavia; Modern Gallery, Ljubljana, Yugoslavia; Museum of Modern and Contemporary Art, Rijeka, Yugoslavia; American Embassy, London; and Hessisches Landesmuseum, Darmstadt, Germany.

Summer: visiting painting instructor at University of California, Los Angeles (UCLA); guest artist at Tamarind Lithography Workshop, Los Angeles.

Fall: joins faculty at San Francisco Art Institute (SFAI, formerly CSFA; teaches there intermittently until 1966). Also teaches at the prison in Vacaville, California, and privately in San Francisco.

October 1961–January 1962: included in *The 1961 Pittsburgh International Exhibition of Contemporary Painting and Sculpture*, Museum of Art, Carnegie Institute, Pittsburgh (October 27, 1961–January 7, 1962).

November 23: trip to Santa Cruz Island with Phyllis, Gretchen, and Christopher. The island now includes a newly constructed airstrip and is accessible by plane and by helicopter.

December 1961–February 1962: included in *Annual Exhibition 1961: Contemporary American Painting*, Whitney Museum of American Art, New York (December 13, 1961–February 4, 1962).

1962

April–October: included in *Art Since 1950*, Fine Arts Pavilion, Seattle World's Fair (April 21–October 21); travels to Rose Art Museum, Brandeis University, Waltham, Massachusetts, and Institute of Contemporary Art, Boston.

Late April–early May: on a fellowship, completes a series of lithographs at Tamarind Lithography Workshop, Los Angeles.

May–June: wins the Arts and Letters Grant from the National Institute of Arts and Letters, New York, and is included in *Exhibition of Work by Newly Elected Members and Recipients of Honors and Awards*, National Institute of Arts and Letters, New York (May 25–June 17).

September–October: included in *Art: USA: Now, The Johnson Collection of Contemporary American Paintings*, organized by S.C. Johnson and Son and circulated by United States Information Agency, Washington, DC, to Milwaukee Art Center (September 21–October 21); travels for five years throughout the United States, Europe, and Japan.

October: Greenberg discusses Diebenkorn in "After Abstract Expressionism" in *Art International*:

> [Diebenkorn's] development so far is what one might say the development of Abstract Expressionism as a whole should have been. Earlier on he was the only *abstract* painter, as far as I know, to do something substantially independent with de Kooning's touch (and it makes no difference that he did it with the help of Rothko's design). More recently, he has let the logic of that touch carry him back (with Matisse's help) to representational art, and one might say that this consistency of logic is partly responsible for his becoming at least as good a representational as he was an abstract painter. That de Kooning's touch remains as unmistakable as before in his art does not diminish the success of his change .... Diebenkorn ... has, in effect, found a home for de Kooning's touch where it can fulfill itself more truthfully, though modestly, than it has been able to so far in de Kooning's own art.[23]

October–December: included in *Fifty California Artists*, San Francisco Museum of Art (October 23–December 2); travels to Walker Art Center, Minneapolis; Albright-Knox Art Gallery, Buffalo, New York; and Des Moines Art Center, Iowa.

November–December: included in *The Artist's Environment: West Coast*, Amon Carter Museum of Western Art, Fort Worth, Texas (November 6–December 23); travels to UCLA Art Galleries and Oakland Art Museum, California.

Makes first prints with Kathan Brown at recently founded Crown Point Press in Brown's basement in Richmond, California.

Panelist at a symposium called "Abstract Art–Action or Reaction" at UCLA, moderated by Frederick Wight, director of the university's art galleries.

1963

April–June: *Drawings by Elmer Bischoff, Richard Diebenkorn, and Frank Lobdell*, California Palace of the Legion of Honor, San Francisco (April 27–June 2).

September–October: *Richard Diebenkorn: Paintings 1961–1963*, M. H. de Young Memorial Museum, San Francisco (September 7–October 13).

September 25: becomes first Artist-in-Residence at Stanford University (through June 1964). He and his family live at 1241 Harker Avenue, Palo Alto, and he has a studio on campus on the first floor of the old Union building. His only requirement is to make art during the residency, although students may visit his studio at scheduled times during the week. Of the residency, Diebenkorn says,

> I think it's a good idea. Having a working artist around should be stimulating for the students. Also, I know from experience that teaching and painting don't mix.[24]

In the same article, he states,

> The action in the subject matter can detract from what the artist is trying to do. In my own work, I want the action to be in the painting. My investment is in the moods, colors, and shapes rather than in the situations depicted.[25]

During residency there is a lull in his painting, but he produces a number of works on paper.

October–November: *Richard Diebenkorn*, Poindexter Gallery, New York (October 29–November 16).

1964

April: *Drawings by Richard Diebenkorn*, first solo exhibition of drawings, Stanford University Art Gallery, Stanford, California (April 3–26).

April–June: included in *Painting and Sculpture of a Decade, '54–'64*, Tate Gallery, London (April 22–June 28).

June: father dies in La Jolla, California.

September–October: *Richard Diebenkorn*, Waddington Galleries, London (September 29–October 24).

FIGS 76–77

Richard Diebenkorn in his Stanford University studio, Stanford, California. Photographed by Leo Holub, 1963

Fall: travels abroad with Phyllis under aegis of US State Department's Cultural Exchange Program, as a guest of Soviet Artists' Union. He and Phyllis spend a month in Paris waiting for their visas, then travel for one month in Russia. There Diebenkorn sees Matisse paintings in Pushkin and Hermitage museums and is greatly impressed by the tilted floor planes, patterning, and saturated colors and tonal contrasts in Matisse's work. He and Phyllis also travel to Romania, Yugoslavia, Germany, and England (through winter 1964). As Diebenkorn later states,

> When I was in Leningrad in 1964 I saw at the Hermitage Museum a Matisse picture that must have been—oh, seven feet wide [*Moroccan Café*, ca. 1912–1913]. It's in Alfred H. Barr's Matisse book. He says it's an oil—he's wrong there, it's a gouache—but the important thing is the way the paint's piled up. . . . It was one of Matisse's Moroccan pictures from around 1913, very "decorative," painted in flat, soft, matte colors. It was beautiful, but you felt that if you clapped your hands all the paint would fall off.[26]

An article titled "Russian Bear Hugs Test U.S. Visitor's Mettle," from the December 20, 1964, issue of the *Washington Post, Times Herald*, states,

> [Diebenkorn] took 100 slides of his work to show in Russia. One of the polite criticisms was that his paintings lacked a social message.
>
> "One of the Russians—who generally accepted my work—felt that I had done only half the job," Diebenkorn reported.

In a postcard from the Diebenkorns to Carey Stanton, sent during their October trip to Leningrad, they write,

> Enroute: Leningrad to Tblisi 10–18
>
> Dear Carey, This country is magnificent, wild + superb. We know you would like it.
>
> However it is the artist and the scientist who is of the elite and who lives, eats and DRINKS well. . . . Because of how things are here it is difficult to understand how 3 men went into space + returned. We are continually wined + dined and there are sad farewells wherein we kiss one another. We are headed for Georgia where they REALLY have parties. Love, P. + W. ["W" refers to Diebenkorn's nickname, "Witz."][27]

November–December: *Richard Diebenkorn*, retrospective of work 1948–1963, organized by Gerald Nordland, Washington Gallery of Modern Art, Washington, DC (November 6–December 31); travels to Jewish Museum, New York, and Pavilion Gallery, Newport Beach, California.

December 1964–January 1965: included in *100 Artists for Free Speech*, Berkeley Gallery, a benefit for the Faculty-Student Legal Defense Fund and the Academic Publicity Fund of the University of California (December 22, 1964–January 3, 1965).

Begins making series *41 Etchings Drypoints* with Kathan Brown, Crown Point Press, Berkeley (published in 1965).

1965

Begins late figurative works characterized by flat, planar color areas and geometric compositions.

May–June: *Sam Francis, Richard Diebenkorn: Two American Painters, Abstract and Figurative*, Scottish National Gallery of Modern Art, Edinburgh (May 8–June 7).

October: *Recent Drawings by Richard Diebenkorn*, Paul Kantor Gallery, Los Angeles (October 1–31).

December 1965–January 1966: included in *1965 Annual Exhibition: Contemporary American Painting*, Whitney Museum of American Art, New York (December 8, 1965–January 30, 1966).

Appointed to National Council on the Arts and serves from 1966 through 1969.

1966

January–February: sees *Henri Matisse: Retrospective 1966* at UCLA Art Galleries (January 5–February 27), which includes *View of Notre Dame* (1914) and *Open Window, Collioure* (1914).

May–June: *Richard Diebenkorn: Drawings*, Poindexter Gallery, New York (May 17–June 4).

May: reviewed by Hilton Kramer in the *New York Times*:

> In seeking something richer than his former loyalties [to Abstract Expressionism] permitted him, he has moved—not, I think, programmatically, but in order to fulfill his real gifts—more and more against the historical current. His work thus constitutes both a caution and a challenge to those of his peers who find themselves similarly placed on the historical precipice.[28]

Summer: travels with Phyllis to Southern France and Germany.

September 18: Gretchen Diebenkorn marries Richard Grant.

End of September: moves with Phyllis to Santa Monica Canyon, a neighborhood in Los Angeles, and takes up professorship in art department at UCLA (through 1973). Rents a small windowless studio near the beach on Main Street (at Ashland Avenue) in the Ocean Park neighborhood of Santa Monica, where he works for six months while waiting to move into a larger studio.

September–November: included in *Art of the United States: 1670–1966*, Whitney Museum of American Art, New York (September 28–November 27).

FIG 78

Richard and Phyllis Diebenkorn on the deck of their Hillcrest Road home, Berkeley, with their dog Valentine and view of the neighborhood and the Berkeley-Oakland hills. Photographed by Morley Baer, 1966

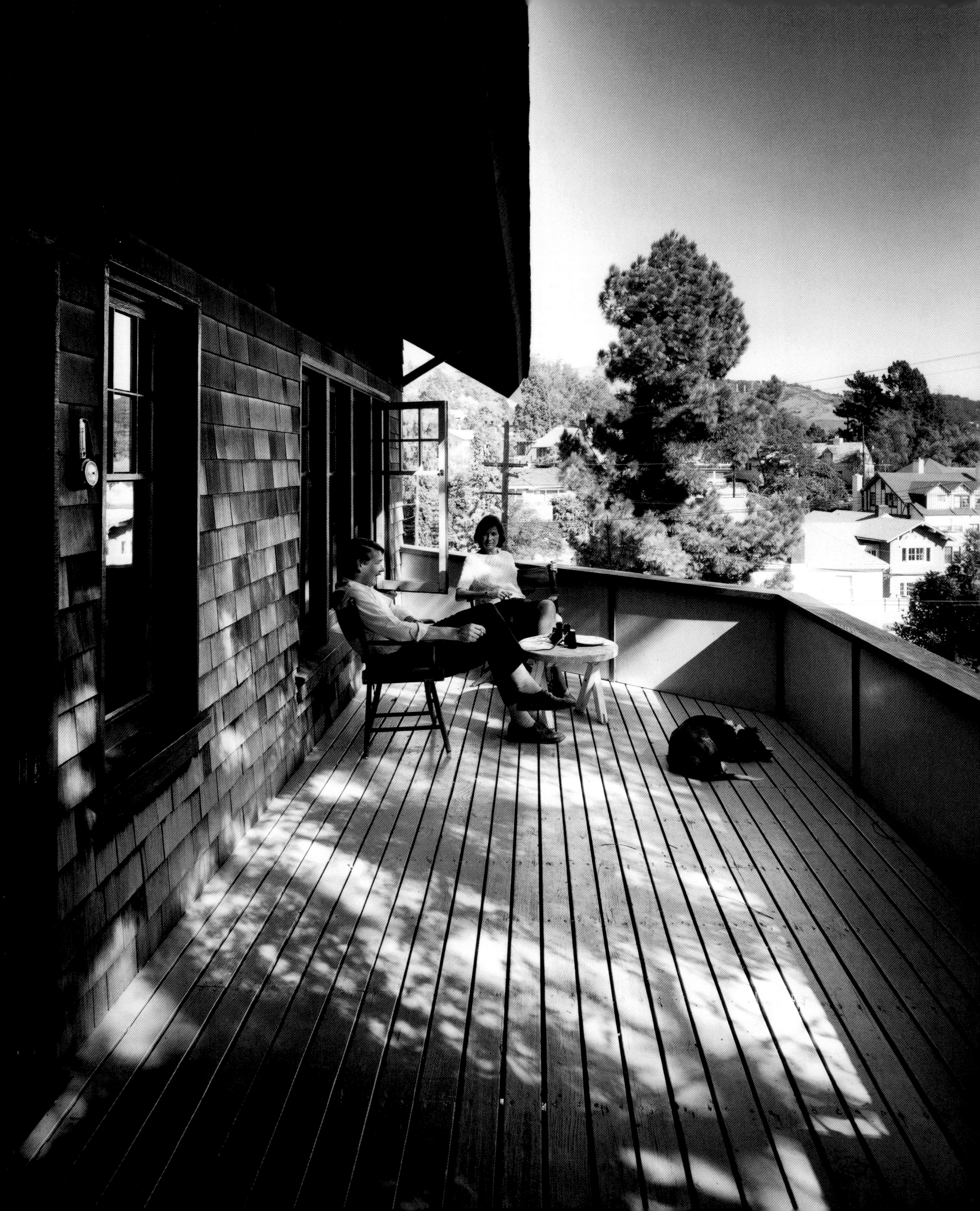

1967

January–February: *Richard Diebenkorn: Works on Paper*, Waddington Galleries, London (January 12–February 4).

Spring: moves into a larger studio space, formerly occupied by Sam Francis, in the same building; there makes his last few representational works. Moves to 334 Amalfi Drive, Santa Monica.

May–June: elected to National Institute of Arts and Letters and included in *Exhibition of Work by Newly Elected Members and Recipients of Honors and Awards*, National Institute of Arts and Letters, New York (May 25–June 25).

December 1967–January 1968: *Drawings by Richard Diebenkorn*, Pennsylvania Academy of the Fine Arts, Philadelphia (December 14, 1967–January 28, 1968).

Returns to abstraction when he begins the Ocean Park series (until 1988), which ultimately numbers some hundred paintings and incorporates the influences of painters such as Matisse, Bonnard, Cézanne, and Mondrian, as well as the marine light and topography of the Southern California landscape.

1968

February: undergoes a back operation that leaves him incapacitated for two months, during which time he makes a second group of fetish-like objects.

May: Ocean Park works shown for the first time in New York, to critical acclaim, in *Richard Diebenkorn*, Poindexter Gallery (May 11–30).

June–October: included in *Venice 34: The Figurative Tradition in Recent American Art*, American Pavilion, *XXXIV International Biennial Exhibition of Art*, Venice (June 22–October 20); travels to National Collection of Fine Arts, Smithsonian Institution, Washington, DC, and Sheldon Memorial Art Gallery, University of Nebraska, Lincoln.

December 1968–February 1969: exhibitions of his representational drawings held at Richmond Art Center (*Richard Diebenkorn Drawings*, December 12, 1968–February 2, 1969), Richmond, California, and at Poindexter Gallery (*Recent Drawings*, December 21, 1968–January 30, 1969), New York.

Awarded the Carol H. Beck Gold Medal, Pennsylvania Academy of the Fine Arts, Philadelphia.

1969

June–July: *New Paintings by Richard Diebenkorn* is the first exhibition of the Ocean Park paintings in Los Angeles, Los Angeles County Museum of Art (June 3–July 27).

Fall: travels with Phyllis to Europe and they visit museums in the Netherlands, Germany, and Italy.

Commissioned by Bureau of Reclamation of the US Department of the Interior to document water reclamation projects along the Colorado and Salt Rivers in Arizona; travels by helicopter to these areas and takes photographs and makes drawings of his aerial views of the landscape. Produces Lower Colorado series—a group of eight works on paper (currently on loan from the Bureau of Reclamation to the Hirshhorn Museum and Sculpture Garden, Smithsonian Institution, Washington, DC), which are later exhibited in the Smithsonian Institution's traveling exhibition *The American Artist and Water Reclamation: A Selection of Paintings from the Bureau of Reclamation*, National Gallery of Art, Washington, DC, 1972.

1970

April 11: Richard and Gretchen Diebenkorn Grant's daughter, Phyllis, is born.

Summer: Christopher Diebenkorn marries Margaret Radin.

1971

Withdraws from Poindexter Gallery, New York, and moves to Marlborough Gallery, New York, which represents him until 1977.

1972

Begins yearlong leave of absence from UCLA.

September 29: Richard and Gretchen Diebenkorn Grant's son, Benjamin, is born.

October 1972–January 1973: *Richard Diebenkorn: Paintings from the Ocean Park Series*, San Francisco Museum of Art (October 14, 1972–January 14, 1973).

1973

Summer: travels to Europe with Phyllis.

Fall: resigns from position at UCLA.

1974

February–March: *Richard Diebenkorn: Drawings, 1944–1973*, first drawings retrospective, Mary Porter Sesnon Gallery, University of California, Santa Cruz (February 17–March 17).

Spring: makes a series of monotypes in Nathan Oliveira's Stanford studio. Among the images explored are the playing-card shapes of clubs and spades, perhaps inspired by his lifelong interest in heraldic imagery.

1975

March–April: *Richard Diebenkorn: Early Abstract Works, 1948–1955*, John Berggruen Gallery, San Francisco (March 12–April 19) and James Corcoran Gallery, Los Angeles (September 1–December 1).

June: awarded an honorary doctorate in fine arts from SFAI.

Summer: moves to a new studio built to his specifications in Santa Monica, on Main Street near Ocean Park Boulevard.

1976

November: achieves true national and international recognition when his major retrospective *Richard Diebenkorn: Paintings and Drawings, 1943–1976*, organized by Albright-Knox Art Gallery, Buffalo, New York, receives widespread critical acclaim (November 12, 1976–January 9, 1977); travels to Cincinnati Art Museum; Corcoran Gallery of Art, Washington, DC; Whitney Museum of American Art, New York; Los Angeles County Museum of Art; and Oakland Museum, California.

Exhibition reviews include the following:

> [Diebenkorn] is not, as the condescending tag once read, a California artist, but a world figure. . . . In short,

> he is a thoroughly traditional artist, for whose work the words "high seriousness" might have been invented.[29]

> Greatness in art is measured not necessarily by how much ground is covered, but by how deeply, how fully and movingly it is explored. . . . As Monet, or Still, or Rothko—indeed as most other great contemporary artists—Diebenkorn demonstrates that it is possible to construct a universe by exploring a single idea to its frontiers.[30]

During Oakland Museum's opening reception for the retrospective, *Scissors and Lemon, II* (1959, pl. 88) is stolen from the gallery. After the *Oakland Tribune* runs a front-page article about the theft, the painting is found in a mailbox, packaged and addressed to a local television station, from a six-member group called the "Art Liberation Front," who had taken the work to protest "the disproportionate attention given to art's high prices compared to aesthetic values."[31]

1976–1979

Creates a series of Ocean Park paintings on cigar box lids.

1977

Returns to Crown Point Press (now in Oakland, California) to make a series of drypoints; continues to make prints with Brown almost every year until his death.

January–March: aerial photographs from the Bureau of Reclamation commission included in the exhibition *Private Images: Photographs by Painters*, Contemporary Art Galleries, Los Angeles County Museum of Art (January 18–March 27).

May–June: *Richard Diebenkorn*, first exhibition of paintings with his new dealer, M. Knoedler & Co., New York (May 7–June 2).

1978

February–June: housesits for friends in Aups, in the South of France, with Phyllis.

July–October: is the US Representative at *38th Venice Biennale* (July 2–October 15).

Awarded the Edward MacDowell Medal, MacDowell Colony, Peterborough, New Hampshire.

1979

Awarded the Skowhegan Medal for Painting, Skowhegan School of Art, Skowhegan, Maine.

Made a Fellow of American Academy of Arts and Sciences, Boston.

1980

Elected a member of American Academy of Design.

Makes a small group of complex club and spade drawings, which he develops extensively the following year and continues to explore throughout the rest of his career.

1981

January–March: *Richard Diebenkorn: Matrix / Berkeley 40*, an exhibition of works from the Berkeley period, University Art Museum, UC Berkeley (January 15–March 8). From the exhibition brochure:

> The Berkeley series shows Diebenkorn's absorption of New York Abstract Expressionism which he adapted to his own Western environment and personal idiom. It is important to recognize, however, that Diebenkorn belongs to the first generation of Abstract Expressionists along with such Bay Area artists as Hassel Smith and Frank Lobdell. His work in Berkeley represents a fully formed achievement contemporary with that in New York which announced the arrival of the American avant-garde on the world scene.

> . . . Diebenkorn's approach to the Abstract Expressionist style differs markedly from that of his New York contemporaries. His line is restrained compared, for example, to the compulsive, energetic line of Franz Kline; Diebenkorn's canvases are composed of flat, brushed, horizontal color patches, whereas in the works of Jackson Pollock colors were dripped and poured. Diebenkorn's color sense is distinctly Californian: warm earth colors dominate as opposed to the blacks, grays and whites that generally characterize the New York school.[32]

April–June: *Richard Diebenkorn: Etchings and Drypoints 1949–1980*, Minneapolis Institute of Arts (April 25–June 21); the show is an expanded version of the 1979 exhibition of intaglio prints organized by Phyllis Plous of the University of California, Santa Barbara Art Museum (June 27–September 2). Travels to William Rockhill Nelson Gallery of Art, Atkins Museum of Fine Arts, Kansas City, Missouri; Saint Louis Art Museum; The Baltimore Museum of Art; Museum of Art, Carnegie Institute, Pittsburgh; Brooklyn Museum; Flint Institute of Arts, Michigan; Springfield Art Museum, Missouri; University of Iowa Museum of Art, Iowa City; Sarah Campbell Blaffer Gallery, University of Houston, Texas; Newport Harbor Museum, Newport Beach, California; and San Francisco Museum of Modern Art.

1982

Made a Fellow of Rhode Island School of Design, Providence.

Awarded an honorary doctorate in fine arts, Occidental College, Los Angeles.

1983

Travels to Kyoto, Japan, to make woodblock prints at a studio established by Crown Point Press.

May–July: "Pentimenti: Seeing and Then Seeing Again" in *Resource/Response/Reservoir—Richard Diebenkorn: Paintings, 1948–1983*, retrospective exhibition, San Francisco Museum of Modern Art (May 13–July 17).

1984

August: mother dies in Santa Monica.

Made an associate of National Academy of Design, New York.

1985

Awarded an honorary doctorate in fine arts, University of New Mexico at Albuquerque.

December: elected to American Academy of Arts and Letters.

1986

May–June: included in *Exhibition of Work by Newly Elected Members and Recipients of Awards and Honors*, National Institute of Arts and Letters, New York (May 21–June 15).

1987

Returns to Kyoto to make more woodblock prints with Crown Point Press.

Awarded the UCLA Medal.

1988

Spring: moves from Santa Monica to Healdsburg, California, to a rural home near the Russian River, overlooking vineyards and scrub-oak hillsides.

November 1988–January 1989: *The Drawings of Richard Diebenkorn*, organized by John Elderfield, The Museum of Modern Art, New York (November 17, 1988–January 10, 1989); travels to Los Angeles County Museum of Art; San Francisco Museum of Modern Art; and The Phillips Collection, Washington, DC.

1989

Undergoes two heart surgeries for a damaged aortic valve.

December 1989–February 1990: included in *Bay Area Figurative Art, 1950–1965*, San Francisco Museum of Modern Art (December 14, 1989–February 4, 1990); travels to Hirshhorn Museum and Sculpture Garden, Smithsonian Institution, Washington, DC, and Pennsylvania Academy of the Fine Arts, Philadelphia.

1990

Produces a series of six etchings representing variations on the theme of a coat on a hanger, as well as a map of Ireland, for the Arion Press edition of *Poems of W. B. Yeats*, which contains poems selected and introduced by Helen Vendler.

1991

July: awarded the National Medal of Arts.

October–December: *Richard Diebenkorn*, Whitechapel Art Gallery, London (October 4–December 1); travels to Fundación Juan March, Madrid; Frankfurter Kunstverein, Frankfurt; Museum of Contemporary Art, Los Angeles; and San Francisco Museum of Modern Art.

1993

March 30: dies in Berkeley.

In the *New York Times*, Michael Kimmelman describes Diebenkorn as "one of the premier American painters of the postwar era, whose deeply lyrical abstractions evoked the shimmering light and wide-open spaces of California, where he spent virtually his entire life."[33]

In *The New Yorker*, Adam Gopnik writes that "Diebenkorn had been, in an unpretentious way, one of the key figures in a great transformation that took place in American art over the past quarter century: the rise of California from a provincial backwater to an artmaking capital equal to New York."[34]

Posthumously awarded the gold medal for painting by American Academy of Arts and Letters.

1997

October 1997–January 1998: *The Art of Richard Diebenkorn*, Whitney Museum of American Art, New York (October 9, 1997–January 19, 1998); travels to Modern Art Museum, Fort Worth, Texas; Phillips Collection, Washington, DC; and San Francisco Museum of Modern Art.

2000

May–June: *Richard Diebenkorn: Representational Drawings*, Galleria Lawrence Rubin, Milan, Italy (May 4–June 1).

November–December: *Richard Diebenkorn Early Abstractions 1949–55*, Lawrence Rubin Greenberg Van Doren Fine Art, New York (November 8–December 9).

2002

April–June: *Figurative Drawings, Gouaches, and Oil Paintings*, Artemis Greenberg Van Doren Gallery, New York (April 25–June 7).

2003

March–April: *Richard Diebenkorn: Figurative Works on Paper*, John Berggruen Gallery, San Francisco (March 19–April 26).

2006

May–August: *Richard Diebenkorn: The Carey Stanton Collection*, Pasadena Museum of California Art (May 6–August 27).

2007

June–September: *Richard Diebenkorn in New Mexico*, Harwood Museum of Art, University of New Mexico, Taos (June 2–September 9); travels to San Jose Museum of Art, California; Grey Art Gallery, New York University; and The Phillips Collection, Washington, DC.

2008

July–November: *Richard Diebenkorn, Artist, and Carey Stanton, Collector: Their Stanford Connection* and *Richard Diebenkorn: Abstractions on Paper*, Cantor Arts Center, Stanford University, Stanford, California (July 23–November 9).

2010

May–June: *Richard Diebenkorn: Paintings and Drawings, 1949–1955*, Greenberg Van Doren Gallery, New York (May 5–June 25).

2011

September 2011–January 2012: *Richard Diebenkorn: The Ocean Park Series*, Modern Art Museum of Fort Worth, Texas (September 24, 2011–January 15, 2012); travels to Orange County Museum of Art, Newport Beach, California, and Corcoran Gallery of Art, Washington, DC.

2013

June–September: *Richard Diebenkorn: The Berkeley Years, 1953–1966*, de Young Museum, San Francisco (June 22–September 29); travels to Palm Springs Art Museum, California.

1 Richard Diebenkorn, in letter dated January 8, 1957, to Joseph Pulitzer, Jr., cited in Charles Scott Chetham and Joseph Pulitzer, Jr., *Modern Painting, Drawing & Sculpture: Collected by Louise and Joseph Pulitzer, Jr.*, exh. cat. (Cambridge, MA: Fogg Art Museum, Harvard Art Museums, 1957), 31.

2 Dan Hofstadter, "Profiles: Almost Free of the Mirror," *The New Yorker*, September 7, 1987, 61.

3 Ibid.

4 Frederick Wight, "The Phillips Collection—Diebenkorn, Woelffer, Mullican: A Discussion," *Artforum* 1, no. 10 (April 1963): 26.

5 Edited by the Austrian-Mexican Surrealist Wolfgang Paalen, *Dyn* was an art magazine published in Mexico City and distributed in New York, Paris, and London from 1942 through 1944.

6 Wight, "The Phillips Collection," 26.

7 Gerald Nordland, "Richard Diebenkorn: Routes to New Mexico," in Gerald Nordland, Mark Lavatelli, and Charles Strong, *Richard Diebenkorn in New Mexico*, exh. cat. (Santa Fe: Museum of New Mexico Press, 2007), 10.

8 Sandra Leonard Starr, "Assemblage Art in California: A Collective Memoir 1940–1969," in *Lost and Found in California: Four Decades of Assemblage Art* (Santa Monica: The James Corcoran Gallery in cooperation with Shoshana Wayne Gallery and Pence Gallery, 1988), 61.

9 Jan Butterfield, "Pentimenti: Seeing and Then Seeing Again," *Resource/Response/Reservoir–Richard Diebenkorn: Paintings 1948–1983* exh. brochure (San Francisco: San Francisco Museum of Modern Art, May 1983).

10 Herman Cherry, in Herman Cherry et al., "Willem de Kooning on His Eighty-Fifth Birthday," *Art Journal* 48, no. 3 (Autumn 1989): 231.

11 Gerald Nordland, *Richard Diebenkorn* (New York: Rizzoli, 1987), 43.

12 Paul Mills, *Contemporary Bay Area Figurative Painting*, exh. cat. (Oakland, CA: Oakland Art Museum, 1957), 12n56.

13 Susan Larsen, interview with Richard Diebenkorn, May 1, 1985, Archives of American Art, Smithsonian Institution, Washington, DC.

14 Butterfield, "Pentimenti."

15 Dore Ashton, "First One-Man Show in New York at Poindexter Gallery," *Arts & Architecture* 73 (April 1956): 11.

16 Grace L. McCann Morley, "Art of the Pacific Coast at the IIIrd Biennial of São Paulo," in *Pacific Coast Art: United States' Representation at the IIIrd Biennial of São Paulo* (San Francisco: San Francisco Museum of Art, 1956), 9.

17 Letter from Richard Diebenkorn to Elinor Poindexter, November 15, 1956, Poindexter Gallery records, 1956–1999. Archives of American Art, Smithsonian Institution, Washington, DC.

18 Herschel B. Chipp, "Diebenkorn Paints a Picture," *Art News* 56, no. 3 (May 1957): 46.

19 Diebenkorn, quoted in Jane Livingston, John Elderfield, and Ruth E. Fine, *The Art of Richard Diebenkorn*, exh. cat. (New York: Whitney Museum of American Art in association with University of California Press, 1997), 53.

20 "Look of the West Inspires New Art," *Life*, November 4, 1957, 65–69.

21 "Edging Away from Abstraction," *Time*, March 17, 1958, 64.

22 Diebenkorn, quoted in Hofstadter, "Profiles," 61.

23 Clement Greenberg, "After Abstract Expressionism," *Art International* 6, no. 8 (October 25, 1962): 25.

24 Diebenkorn, quoted in Bob MacKenzie, "Stanford Artist Pleased with Post," *Oakland Tribune*, March 24, 1963, 4.

25 Ibid.

26 Diebenkorn, quoted in Hofstadter, "Profiles," 69.

27 Quoted in Marla Daily and Paul Chadbourne Mills, *Richard Diebenkorn and Carey Stanton: A Private Collection* (Santa Barbara, CA: Santa Cruz Island Foundation, 2005), 118.

28 Hilton Kramer, "The Diebenkorn Case," *New York Times*, May 22, 1966, D29.

29 Robert Hughes, "California in Eupeptic Color," *Time*, June 27, 1977, 58.

30 Thomas Albright, "Diebenkorn's 'Ocean Park'—A New World," *San Francisco Sunday Examiner and Chronicle*, November 20, 1977, 48.

31 Quoted in Daily and Mills, *Richard Diebenkorn and Carey Stanton*, 58.

32 Connie Lewallen, *Richard Diebenkorn: Matrix / Berkeley 40*, exh. brochure (Berkeley: University Art Museum, 1981).

33 Michael Kimmelman, "Richard Diebenkorn, Lyrical Painter, Dies at 70," *New York Times*, March 31, 1993, A1, B9.

34 Adam Gopnik, "Diebenkorn Redux," *The New Yorker*, May 24, 1993, 97.

Diebenkorn Paints a Picture:

A Selection of Photographs by Rose Mandel

SUSAN EHRENS

When the editors of *Art News* magazine asked art historian Herschel B. Chipp to contribute an article on Richard Diebenkorn for their series highlighting the methodology of significant painters of the twentieth century, Rose Mandel was asked to make the photographs that would illustrate the feature. Born in Poland and educated in Paris and Geneva, Mandel had fled Europe during the Holocaust and settled in Northern California, where she studied photography with Ansel Adams and Minor White in 1946 and 1947, and, in 1948, became the photographer for the department of art at the University of California, Berkeley.

Over a period of two weeks during the fall of 1956, Mandel used her tripod-mounted four-by-five-inch view camera to photograph the serious and habitually private Diebenkorn as he sketched, painted, deliberated on, and repainted a canvas in the studio he had just built in the backyard of his home in the Berkeley hills. This canvas, which ultimately became the painting *Woman by the Ocean* (1956; pl. 47), was made during the critical period when the artist was shifting from an abstract to a more figurative style.

Six of Mandel's photographs tracing the artist's work on *Woman by the Ocean* were published in Chipp's article, "Diebenkorn Paints a Picture,"[1] with no credit line acknowledging her contribution. In fact, Mandel made forty-nine exposures of Diebenkorn at work in his studio.[2] From one image to another, these pictures record the artist's distinctive methodology—his contemplation, reorganization, reshaping, flattening, and redirection—which often resulted in total transformations of his canvases. This extraordinary series provides an unprecedented documentation of Richard Diebenkorn at work.

1 Herschel B. Chipp, "Diebenkorn Paints a Picture," *Art News* 56, no. 3 (May 1957): 44–47, 54–55.

2 Vintage gelatin silver prints of six of these images are held by the Richard Diebenkorn Foundation, Berkeley, and some of these have been published in monographs and catalogues. All forty-nine negatives of Diebenkorn, the interior of his Hillcrest home studio, and his paintings are in the collection of the Rose Mandel Archive, Oakland, California.

For more on the life and art of Rose Mandel, see Susan Ehrens, *The Errand of the Eye: Photographs by Rose Mandel* (San Francisco: Fine Arts Museums of San Francisco; Munich/New York/London: DelMonico Books/Prestel, 2013).

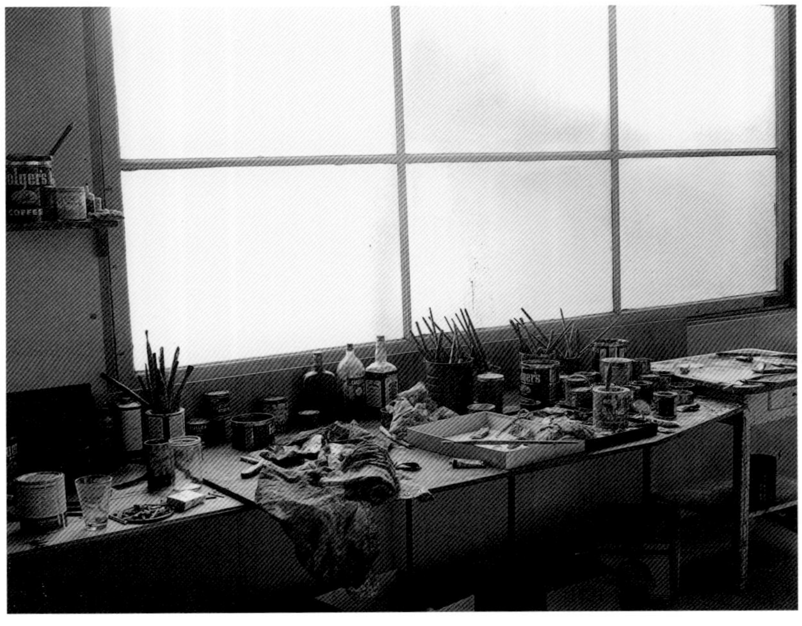

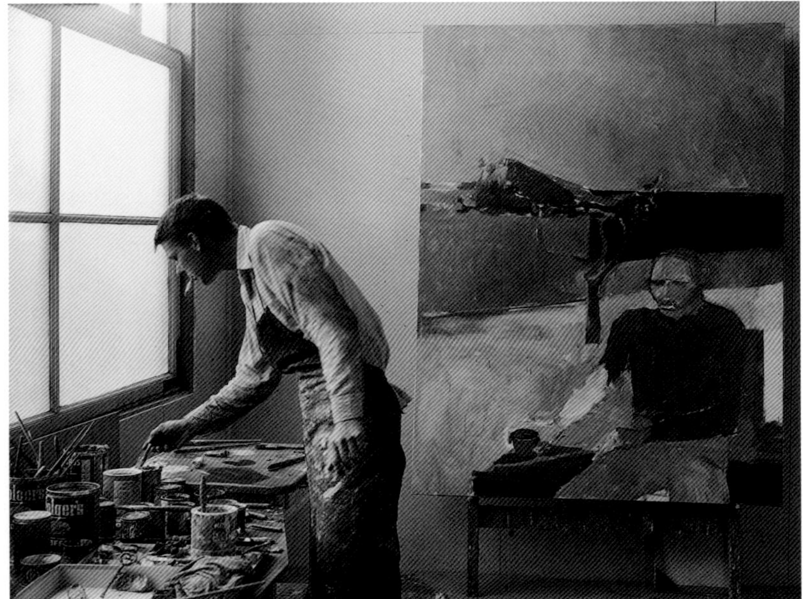

FIGS 79–86

Eight photographs by Rose Mandel, each titled
***Richard Diebenkorn, 1956*, 1956**

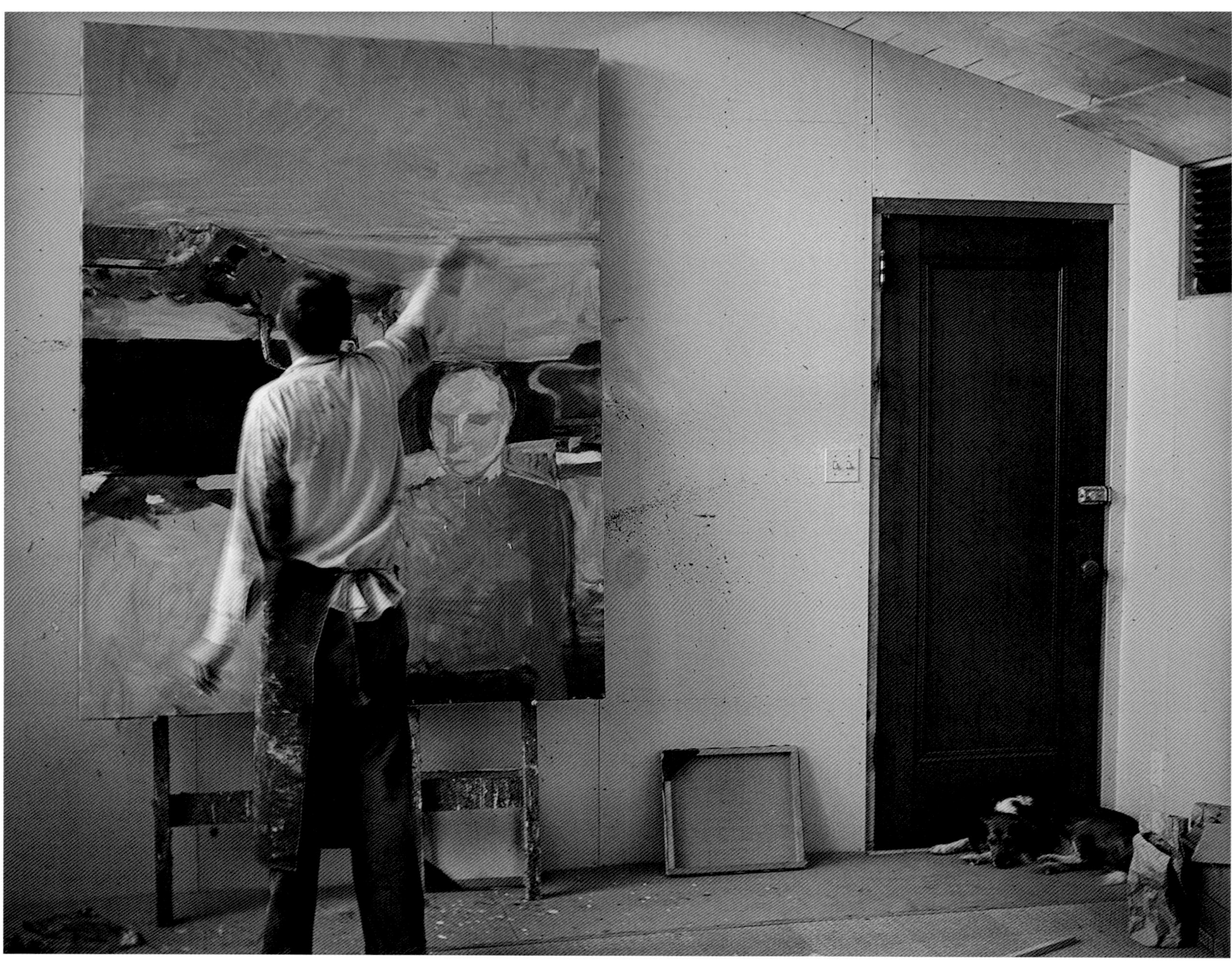

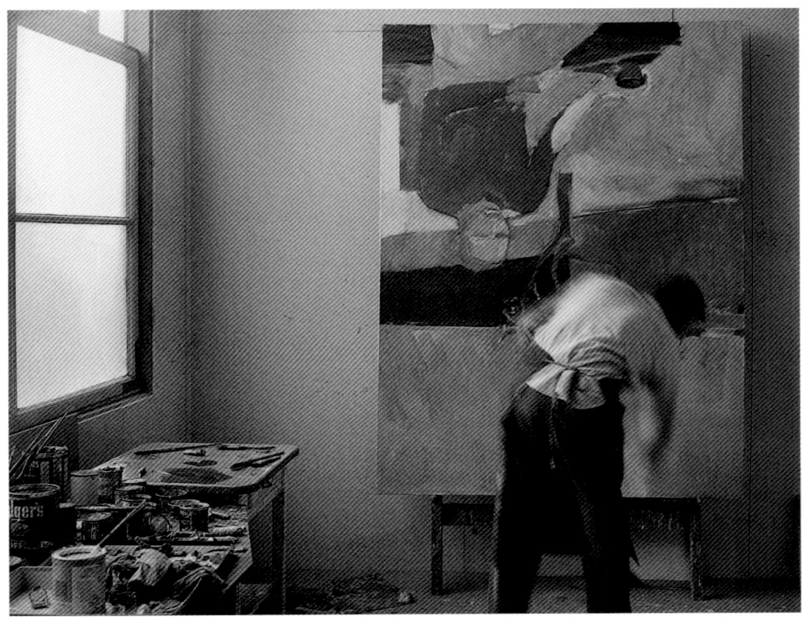

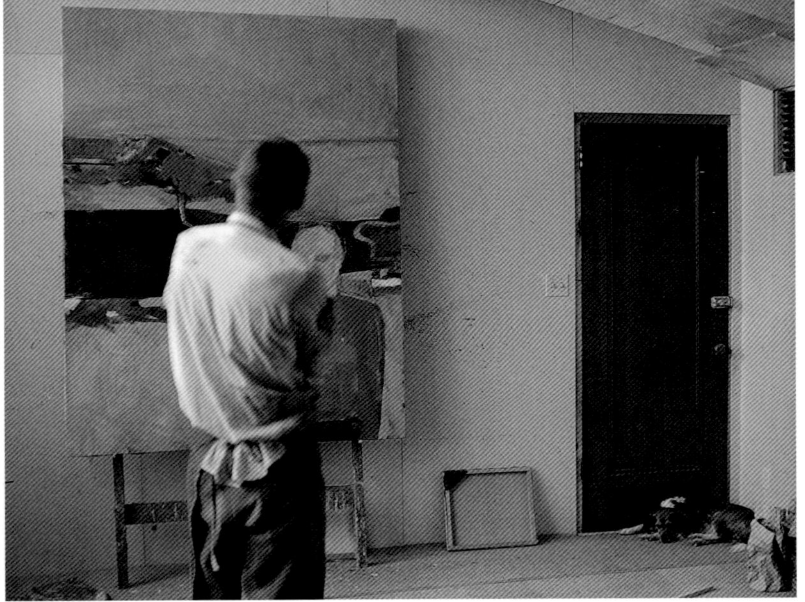

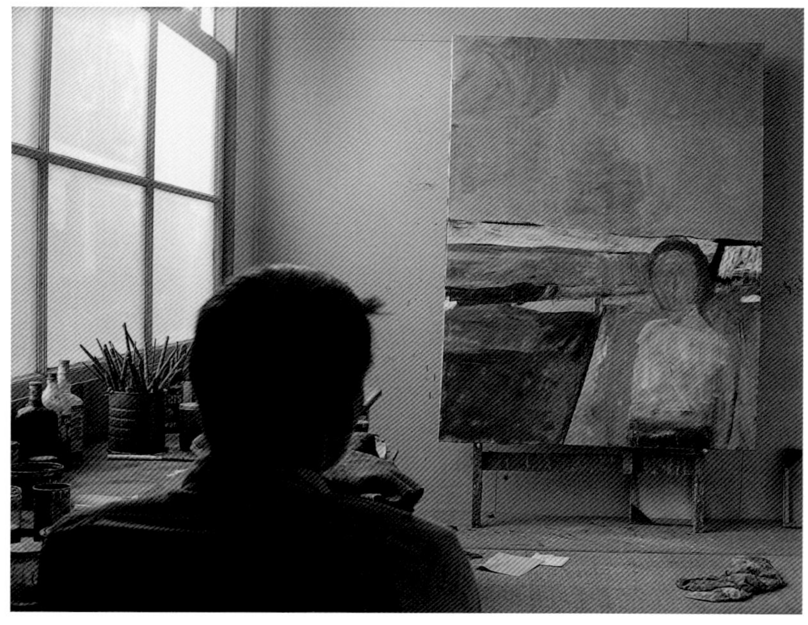

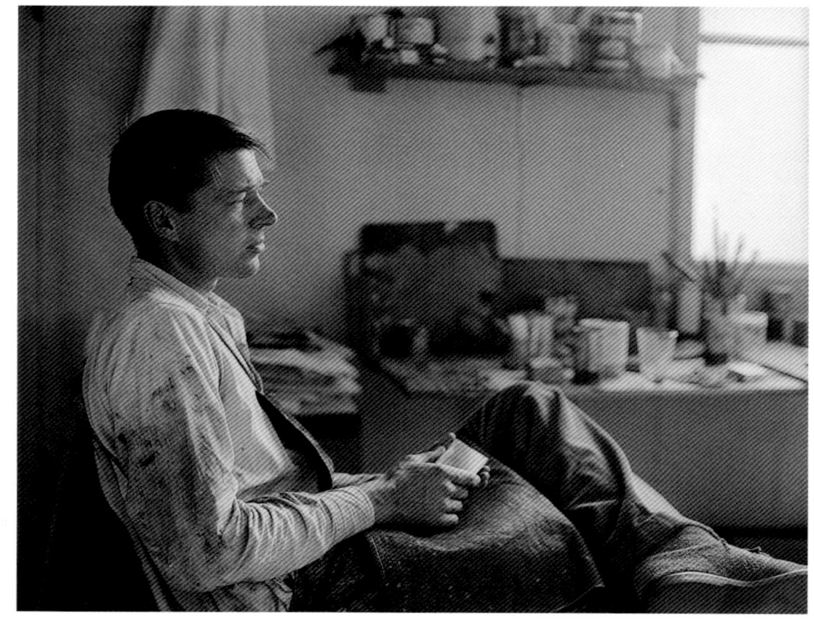

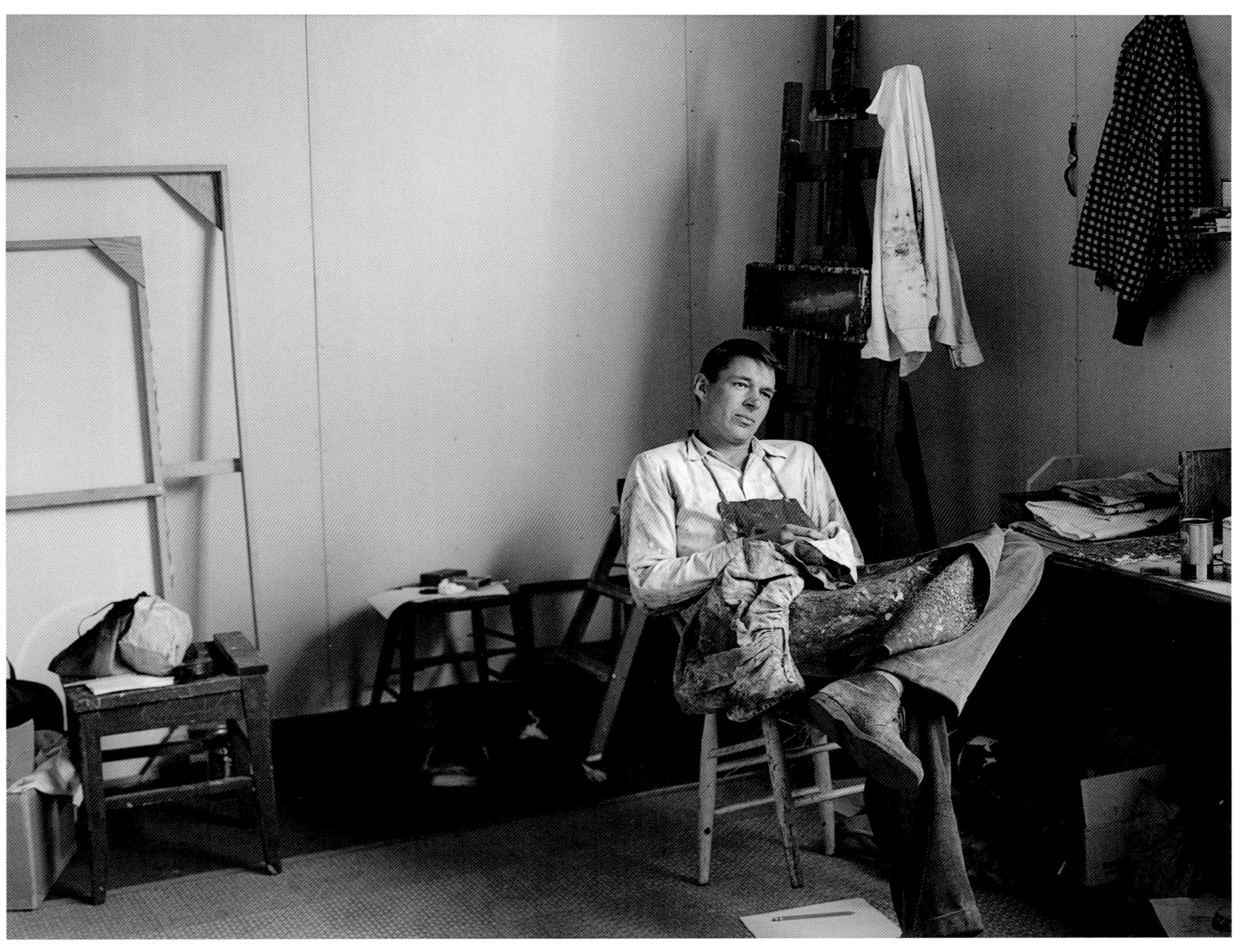

BIBLIOGRAPHY

Compiled by

CARL R. SCHMITZ

The Berkeley Years

Solo and Group Exhibition Publications

1953

Gottlieb, Adolph, Richard Lippold, and Ad Reinhardt. *Exhibition Momentum Midcontinental.* Chicago: Exhibition Momentum, 1953.

1954

Byrnes, James B. *New Accessions USA.* Colorado Springs: Colorado Springs Fine Arts Center, 1954.

Morley, Grace L. McCann. *Eighteenth Annual Watercolor Exhibition of the San Francisco Art Association.* San Francisco: San Francisco Museum of Art, 1954.

——. *Seventy-Third Annual Painting and Sculpture Exhibition of the San Francisco Art Association.* San Francisco: San Francisco Museum of Art, 1954.

Sweeney, James Johnson. *Younger American Painters.* New York: Solomon R. Guggenheim Museum, 1954.

1955

Annual Exhibition of Contemporary American Painting. New York: Whitney Museum of American Art, 1955.

Fifth Annual Oil and Sculpture Exhibition. Richmond, CA: Richmond Art Center, 1955.

Giovani pittori (Painters Under 35). Rome: Congress for Cultural Freedom, 1955.

Graphic Gala: Seeing Art through the Eye. New York: The Artists' Gallery, 1955.

Mills, Paul. *Western Painters' Annual Exhibition.* Oakland, CA: Oakland Art Museum, 1955.

Morley, Grace L. McCann, and E. Morris Cox. *Art in the 20th Century: Commemorating the Tenth Anniversary of the Signing of the United Nations Charter.* San Francisco: San Francisco Museum of Art, 1955.

Morley, Grace L. McCann, Sérgio Milliet, and Marvin C. Ross. *IIIa bienal do Museu de Arte Moderna, São Paulo: Estados Unidos.* São Paulo: Museu de Arte Moderna, 1955.

Morris, Kyle. *Vanguard 1955: A Painter's Selection of New American Paintings.* Minneapolis: Walker Art Center, 1955.

Washburn, Gordon Bailey. *Pittsburgh International Exhibition of Contemporary Painting.* Pittsburgh: Department of Fine Arts, Carnegie Institute, 1955.

Weller, Allen S. *Contemporary American Painting and Sculpture.* Urbana: University of Illinois, 1955.

Whiteside, Forbes. *Three Young Americans.* Oberlin, OH: Allen Memorial Art Museum, Oberlin College, 1955. Included in *Allen Memorial Art Museum Bulletin,* Spring 1955.

Williams, Hermann Warner, Jr. *Twenty Fourth Biennial Exhibition of Contemporary American Oil Paintings.* Washington, DC: Corcoran Gallery of Art, 1955.

1956

Contemporary American Painters 1950–55. Stanford, CA: Thomas Welton Stanford Art Gallery, 1956.

Crehan, Hubert, and Grace L. McCann Morley. *Seventy-Fifth Annual Painting and Sculpture Exhibition of the San Francisco Art Association.* San Francisco: San Francisco Museum of Art, 1956.

Heavenrich, Samuel, and Grace L. McCann Morley. *California Painting: 40 Painters.* Long Beach, CA: Municipal Art Center in collaboration with the San Francisco Museum of Art, 1956.

Morley, Grace L. McCann. *Pacific Coast Art: United States' Representation at the IIIrd Biennial of São Paulo.* San Francisco: San Francisco Museum of Art, 1956.

O'Hara, Frank. *41 Aquarellistes américains d'aujourd'hui* [*41 Contemporary American watercolorists*]. New York: International Program of Circulating Exhibitions, The Museum of Modern Art; Paris: Association française d'action artistique, 1956.

Salmi, Hazel. *Sixth Annual Oil and Sculpture Exhibition.* Richmond, CA: Richmond Art Center, 1956.

1957

Catlin, Stanton L. *American Paintings 1945–1957.* Minneapolis: Minneapolis Institute of Arts, 1957.

Chetham, Charles Scott, and Joseph Pulitzer, Jr. *Modern Painting, Drawing & Sculpture: Collected by Louise and Joseph Pulitzer, Jr.* Cambridge, MA: Fogg Museum, Harvard Art Museums, 1957.

Directions—Bay Area Painting—1957. Richmond, CA: Richmond Art Center, 1957.

Mills, Paul. *California Painters' Exhibition.* Oakland, CA: Oakland Art Museum, 1957.

——. *Contemporary Bay Area Figurative Painting.* Oakland, CA: Oakland Art Museum, 1957.

Morley, Grace L. McCann. *Seventy-Sixth Annual Painting and Sculpture Exhibition of the San Francisco Art Association.* San Francisco: San Francisco Museum of Art, 1957.

——. *The World of Abstract Art.* New York: American Abstract Artists, 1957.

Price, Vincent. *Paintings & Drawings by Living Americans: A Selection by Vincent Price.* New York: Alan Gallery, 1957.

Selz, Peter. *California Drawings.* Long Beach, CA: Long Beach Museum of Art, 1957.

Seventh Annual Oil and Sculpture Exhibition. Richmond, CA: Richmond Art Center, 1957.

Story, Ala. *Second Pacific Coast Biennial Exhibition of Paintings and Watercolors.* Santa Barbara, CA: Santa Barbara Museum of Art, 1957.

Sweet, Frederick A. *LXII American Exhibition: Paintings, Sculpture.* Chicago: Art Institute of Chicago, 1957.

Williams, Hermann Warner, Jr. *Twenty Fifth Biennial Exhibition of Contemporary American Oil Paintings.* Washington, DC: Corcoran Gallery of Art, 1957.

1958

Annual Exhibition: Sculpture, Paintings, Watercolors, Drawings. New York: Whitney Museum of American Art, 1958.

Chetham, Charles Scott, and Joseph Pulitzer, Jr. *Modern Painting, Drawing & Sculpture: Collected by Louise and Joseph Pulitzer, Jr.: Volume II.* Cambridge, MA: Fogg Museum, Harvard Art Museums, 1958.

Contemporary American Art: Brussels Exposition Artists. Flint, MI: Enos A. & Sarah DeWaters Art Center, Flint Institute of Arts, 1958.

Eighth Annual Oil and Sculpture Exhibition. Richmond, CA: Richmond Art Center, 1958.

Fresh Paint—1958. Stanford, CA: Stanford Art Gallery, Stanford University, 1958.

Morley, Grace L. McCann. *American Art: Four Exhibitions.* New York: American Federation of Arts, 1958.

——. *American Painting, 1958.* Richmond, VA: Virginia Museum of Fine Arts, 1958.

——. *Seventy-Seventh Annual Painting and Sculpture Exhibition of the San Francisco Art Association.* San Francisco: San Francisco Museum of Art, 1958.

Painting and Sculpture in the San Francisco Art Association: A Catalog of the Art Bank of the SFAA. San Francisco: San Francisco Art Association, 1958.

Price, Vincent, and Kenneth Ross. *The Collection of Mary and Vincent Price.* Los Angeles: Los Angeles Municipal Art Gallery, 1958.

Smith, Gordon M. *Contemporary Art—Acquisitions 1957–1958.* Buffalo, NY: Albright Art Gallery, 1958.

Some Younger Names in American Painting. Worcester, MA: Worcester Art Museum, 1958.

Sweeney, James Johnson. *American Artists of Younger Reputation: Giovani pittori americani.* Rome: Rome-New York Art Foundation, 1958.

Washburn, Gordon Bailey. *The 1958 Pittsburgh Bicentennial International Exhibition of Contemporary Painting and Sculpture.* Pittsburgh: Department of Fine Arts, Carnegie Institute, 1958.

1959

Baker, Richard Brown. *Paintings Since 1945: A Collection in the Making, Lent by Richard Brown Baker.* Providence: Museum of Art, Rhode Island School of Design, 1959.

Byrnes, James B., and W. R. Valentiner. *Masterpieces of Art: W. R. Valentiner Memorial Exhibition.* Raleigh: North Carolina Museum of Art, 1959.

Culler, George D. *Seventy-Eighth Annual Painting and Sculpture Exhibition of the San Francisco Art Association.* San Francisco: San Francisco Museum of Art, 1959.

McDonough, James V. *New Directions in Painting.* Tallahassee: Florida State University Gallery, 1959.

Megrew, Alden F. *Exhibition of Paintings: 12th Annual Creative Arts Program.* Boulder: Department of Fine Arts, University of Colorado, 1959.

Selz, Peter. *New Images of Man.* New York: The Museum of Modern Art, 1959.

63rd American Exhibition: Paintings, Sculpture. Chicago: Art Institute of Chicago, 1959.

25 Anni di pittura americana, 1933–1958 [25 years of American painting]. Rome: De Luca Editore, 1959.

Williams, Hermann Warner, Jr. *Twenty Sixth Biennial Exhibition of Contemporary American Painting.* Washington, DC: Corcoran Gallery of Art, 1959.

1960

Adlow, Dorothy, *Modernt amerikanskt måleri: 1932–1958* [American modern art]. Göteborg, Sweden: Konstmuseum, 1960.

Culler, George D. *Modern Masters in West Coast Collections: An Exhibition Selected in Celebration of the Twenty-Fifth Anniversary of the San Francisco Museum of Art, 1935–1960.* San Francisco: San Francisco Museum of Art, 1960.

——. *79th Annual Painting and Sculpture Exhibition of the San Francisco Art Association.* San Francisco: San Francisco Museum of Art, 1960.

Jones, Howard Mumford, and Richard B. K. McLanathan. *Art Across America: A Selection of American Art from Collections Open to the Public in Communities of One Hundred Thousand or Less.* Utica, NY: Munson-Williams-Proctor Institute, 1960.

Leavitt, Thomas W. *Richard Diebenkorn.* Pasadena, CA: Pasadena Art Museum, 1960.

Messer, Thomas M. *The Image Lost and Found.* Boston: Institute of Contemporary Art, 1960.

Neuberger, Marie, and Roy Neuberger. *American Art, 1910–1960: Selections from the Collection of Mr. and Mrs. Roy R. Neuberger.* New York: American Federation of Arts, 1960.

Price, Vincent. *Twentieth Century Drawing.* La Jolla, CA: Art Center in La Jolla, 1960.

Sculpture and Painting: Andrews, Diebenkorn, Wilson. Stanford, CA: Stanford Art Gallery, Stanford University, 1960.

Seiberling, Frank. *Main Currents of Contemporary American Painting.* Iowa City: Department of Art, School of Fine Arts, State University of Iowa, 1960.

Seventieth Annual Exhibition. Lincoln: Nebraska Art Association, 1960.

Smith, Howard Ross. *Recent Paintings by Richard Diebenkorn.* San Francisco: California Palace of the Legion of Honor, 1960.

——. *Winter Invitational.* San Francisco: California Palace of the Legion of Honor, 1960.

25th Annual Midyear Show. Youngstown, OH: Butler Institute of American Art, 1960.

1961

Annual Exhibition 1961: Contemporary American Painting. New York: Whitney Museum of American Art, 1961.

Barthelme, Donald. *The Emerging Figure.* Houston: Contemporary Arts Museum, 1961.

Bloch, E. Maurice. *Two Hundred Years of American Painting.* Santa Barbara, CA: Santa Barbara Museum of Art, 1961.

Coe, Ralph T. *The Logic of Modern Art: An Exhibition Tracing the Evolution of Modern Painting from Cézanne to 1960.* Kansas City, MO: William Rockhill Nelson Gallery of Art and Mary Atkins Museum of Fine Arts, 1961.

Culler, George D. *Painting from the Pacific: Japan, America, Australia, New Zealand.* Auckland: Auckland City Art Gallery, 1961.

d'Harnoncourt, René, and William C. Seitz. *VI bienal do Museu de Arte Moderna, São Paulo: Estados Unidos.* São Paulo: Museu de Arte Moderna, 1961.

Friedman, Martin L., and Richard Brown Baker. *Eighty Works from the Richard Brown Baker Collection.* Minneapolis: Walker Art Center, 1961.

Phillips, Gifford. *Richard Diebenkorn.* Washington, DC: The Phillips Collection, 1961.

Schramm, Dorothy, Jim Schramm, and Harris K. Prior. *Art of the Twentieth Century Collected by James S. and Dorothy Schramm.* New York: American Federation of Arts, 1961.

Smith, Howard Ross. *Second Winter Invitational.* San Francisco: California Palace of the Legion of Honor, 1961.

Third Winter Invitational. San Francisco: California Palace of the Legion of Honor, 1961.

Washburn, Gordon Bailey. *The 1961 Pittsburgh International Exhibition of Contemporary Painting and Sculpture.* Pittsburgh: Department of Fine Arts, Carnegie Institute, 1961.

Weller, Allen S. *Contemporary American Painting and Sculpture.* Urbana: University of Illinois, 1961.

Williams, Hermann Warner, Jr. *Twenty Seventh Biennial Exhibition of Contemporary American Painting.* Washington, DC: Corcoran Gallery of Art, 1961.

Works of Art from the Collections of the Harvard Class of 1936. Cambridge, MA: Fogg Museum, Harvard Art Museums, 1961.

1962

Arnason, H. H. *Vanguard American Painting.* London: United States Embassy, 1962.

The Artist's Environment: West Coast. Fort Worth, TX: Amon Carter Museum of Western Art, 1962.

Byrnes, James B. *Painting and Sculpture in Florida Collections.* Gainesville: Department of Art, University of Florida, 1962.

Culler, George D. *Some Points of View–'62.* Stanford, CA: Stanford University Art Gallery, 1962.

Fifty California Artists. San Francisco: San Francisco Museum of Art, 1962.

Fraser, Joseph T., Jr. *One Hundred and Fifty-Seventh Annual Exhibition of American Painting and Sculpture.* Philadelphia: Pennsylvania Academy of the Fine Arts, 1962.

The Gifford and Joann Phillips Collection. Los Angeles: UCLA Art Galleries, 1962.

Hunter, Sam. *Art Since 1950, American and International.* Seattle: Seattle World's Fair, 1962.

Johnson, H.F., and Lee Nordness. *Art: USA: Now, The Johnson Collection of Contemporary American Paintings.* Washington, DC: United States Information Agency, 1962.

Lithographs from the Tamarind Workshop. Los Angeles: UCLA Art Galleries, 1962.

Mills, Paul. *Treasures from East Bay Collections.* Oakland, CA: Oakland Art Museum, 1962.

Recent American Paintings: A Loan Exhibition Sponsored by Art Today. Memphis: Brooks Memorial Art Gallery, 1962.

A Selection of East Coast and West Coast American Painters. London: Gimpel Fils, 1962.

Selections 1934–1961: American Artists from the Collection of Martha Jackson. New York: Martha Jackson Gallery, 1962.

Smith, Howard Ross. *Fourth Winter Invitational.* San Francisco: California Palace of the Legion of Honor, 1962.

Strater, Henry. *Tenth Annual Exhibition.* Ogunquit, ME: Museum of Art of Ogunquit, 1962.

Wagstaff, Samuel, Jr. *Continuity and Change: 45 American Abstract Painters and Sculptors.* Hartford, CT: Wadsworth Atheneum, 1962.

1963

Annual Exhibition 1963: Contemporary American Painting. New York: Whitney Museum of American Art, 1963.

Art Today. Memphis: Brooks Memorial Art Gallery, 1963.

82nd Annual Exhibition of the San Francisco Art Institute. San Francisco: San Francisco Museum of Art, 1963.

Hilles, Susan Morse, and Richard Brown Baker. *Two Modern Collectors: Susan Morse Hilles, Richard Brown Baker.* New Haven, CT: Yale University Art Gallery, 1963.

International Exhibition and Sale of Works of Art in Aid of the Bertrand Russell Peace Foundation. London: Woburn Abbey, 1963.

Leavitt, Thomas W. *Mr. and Mrs. Max Zurier Collection.* Pasadena, CA: Pasadena Art Museum, 1963.

Maxon, John, and A. James Speyer. *De A à Z: 31 Peintres américains choisis par The Art Institute of Chicago.* Paris: Centre Culturel Américain, 1963.

19th Artists West of the Mississippi: The Realistic Image. Colorado Springs: Colorado Springs Fine Arts Center, 1963.

The VII Tokyo Biennale, 1963. Tokyo: Tokyo Metropolitan Art Gallery, 1963.

66th Annual Exhibition: Directions in Contemporary Painting and Sculpture. Chicago: Art Institute of Chicago, 1963.

Williams, Hermann Warner, Jr. *Twenty Eighth Biennial Exhibition of Contemporary American Painting.* Washington, DC: Corcoran Gallery of Art, 1963.

Works on Paper: Avery, Bigelow, Diebenkorn, Feininger, Graves. London: Waddington Galleries, 1963.

1964

Adams, Clinton. *Art Since 1889.* Albuquerque: Art Gallery, University of New Mexico, 1964.

Baur, John I. H. *Between the Fairs: 25 Years of American Art, 1939–1964.* New York: Whitney Museum of American Art, 1964.

Bowness, Alan, Lawrence Gowing, and Philip James. *Painting and Sculpture of a Decade, 54–64.* London: Calouste Gulbenkian Foundation, 1964.

Culler, George D. *Eighty-Third Annual Exhibition of the San Francisco Art Institute.* San Francisco: San Francisco Museum of Art, 1964.

Dorra, Henri. *From the Sterling Holloway Collection.* Los Angeles: UCLA Art Galleries, 1964.

Eitner, Lorenz. *Drawings by Richard Diebenkorn.* Stanford, CA: Department of Art and Architecture, Stanford University, 1964.

Faison, S. Lane, Jr. *Man: Glory, Jest, and Riddle: A Survey of the Human Form Through the Ages.* San Francisco: M. H. de Young Memorial Museum, California Palace of the Legion of Honor, and San Francisco Museum of Art, 1964.

Fraser, Joseph T., Jr. *One Hundred and Fifty-Ninth Annual Exhibition of American Painting and Sculpture.* Philadelphia: Pennsylvania Academy of the Fine Arts, 1964.

The Friends Collect. New York: Whitney Museum of American Art, 1964.

Hope, Henry R., and Reinhold A. Heller. *American Painting 1910 to 1960: A Special Exhibition Celebrating the 50th Anniversary of the Association of College Unions.* Bloomington: Museum of Art, Indiana University, 1964.

Messer, Thomas M. *American Drawings.* New York: Solomon R. Guggenheim Museum, 1964.

Mills, Paul. *2a bienal americana de arte.* Córdoba, Argentina: Ciudad Universitaria, 1964.

Nordland, Gerald. *Richard Diebenkorn.* Washington, DC: Washington Gallery of Modern Art, 1964.

Painting & Sculpture Today. Indianapolis: Herron Museum of Art, 1964.

Paintings from the Fifties: From the Contemporary Collection of the Museum of Art, Carnegie Institute. Pittsburgh: Museum of Art, Carnegie Institute, 1964.

Richard Diebenkorn. London: Waddington Galleries, 1964.

Seven California Painters. New York: Staempfli Gallery, 1964.

Six Americans. Little Rock: Arkansas Art Center, 1964.

Von Groschwitz, Gustave. *The 1964 Pittsburgh International: Exhibition of Contemporary Painting and Sculpture.* Pittsburgh: Museum of Art, Carnegie Institute, 1964.

Wayne, June. *New Dimensions in Lithography: An Exhibition Recently Selected from the Tamarind Lithography Workshop.* Los Angeles: University Galleries, University of Southern California, 1964.

1965

Ashton, Dore. *One Hundred Contemporary American Drawings.* Ann Arbor: University of Michigan Museum of Art, 1965.

Baker, Richard Brown. *Art of the 50's and 60's: Selections from the Richard Brown Baker Collection.* Ridgefield, CT: Larry Aldrich Museum, 1965.

California Printmakers. San Francisco: Printmaking Center of the San Francisco Art Institute, 1965.

The Drawing Society—Regional Exhibition. San Francisco: California Palace of the Legion of Honor, 1965.

Hess, Thomas B., Hilton Kramer, and Harold Rosenberg. *Critic's Choice: Art Since World War II.* Providence, RI: Providence Art Club, 1965.

McCoubrey, John W. *American Paintings from the Bloedel Collection.* Leeds, UK: Leeds City Art Gallery, 1965.

Mocsanyi, Paul. *Portraits from the American Art World.* New York: New School Art Center, 1965.

The Newspaper in American Art: An Exhibition in Honor of the Inter American Press Association. San Diego: Fine Arts Gallery of San Diego, 1965.

1965 Annual Exhibition: Contemporary American Painting. New York: Whitney Museum of American Art, 1965.

Nordness, Lee. *Art: USA—The Johnson Collection of Contemporary American Painting.* San Diego: Fine Arts Gallery of San Diego, 1965.

Sam Francis, Richard Diebenkorn: Two American Painters, Abstract and Figurative. Edinburgh: Scottish National Gallery of Modern Art, 1965.

The San Francisco Collector. San Francisco: M. H. de Young Memorial Museum, 1965.

Sanguinetti, E. F. *Representative Paintings from the American Collection of the Phoenix Museum of Art.* Tucson: Tucson Art Center, 1965.

Selections from the Work of California Artists. San Antonio: San Antonio Art League and Witte Memorial Museum, 1965.

Von Groschwitz, Gustave. *The Seashore: Paintings of the 19th and 20th Centuries.* Pittsburgh: Museum of Art, Carnegie Institute, 1965.

The White House Festival of the Arts. Washington, DC: The White House, 1965.

1966

Alley, Ronald. *American Art of the Fifties and Sixties.* Belfast, UK: Arts Council of Northern Ireland Gallery, 1966.

American Painting and Sculpture. Nottingham, UK: Midland Group Gallery, 1966.

Art, USA: The Johnson Collection of Contemporary American Painting. Omaha: Joslyn Art Museum, 1966.

Baker, Richard Brown. *A Point of View: Selected Paintings and Drawings from the Richard Brown Baker Collection.* Rochester, MI: University Art Gallery, Oakland University, 1966.

Day, Robert E. *Summer Exhibition: 19th Annual Creative Arts Program.* Boulder: Department of Fine Arts, University of Colorado, 1966.

Gerdts, William H. *Contemporary American Still Life.* New York: The Museum of Modern Art, 1966.

Goodall, Donald B., and Mercedes Matter. *Drawings &.* Austin: University Art Museum, University of Texas, 1966.

Goodrich, Lloyd. *Art of the United States: 1670–1966.* New York: Whitney Museum of American Art, 1966.

Henning, Edward B. *Fifty Years of Modern Art, 1916–1966.* Cleveland: Cleveland Museum of Art, 1966.

Hodge, G. Stuart. *Flint Invitational.* Flint, MI: Flint Institute of Arts, 1966.

———. *Realism Revisited: Fifty Years of American Realistic Painting Since the Armory Show.* Flint, MI: Flint Institute of Arts, 1966.

Mills, Paul. *Contemporary Prints from Northern California, For the Art in Embassies Program.* Oakland, CA: Oakland Museum, 1966.

Mocsanyi, Paul. *Contemporary Urban Visions.* New York: New School Art Center, 1966.

Robbins, Daniel. *Recent Still Life.* Providence: Museum of Art, Rhode Island School of Design, 1966.

Scott, David W. *American Landscape: A Changing Frontier.* Washington, DC: National Collection of Fine Arts, Smithsonian Institution, 1966.

Selz, Peter. *Seven Decades, 1895–1965: Crosscurrents in Modern Art.* New York: Public Education Association, 1966.

26th Annual Exhibition by the Society for Contemporary American Art. Chicago: Art Institute of Chicago, 1966.

Selected Articles

Ahlander, Leslie Judd. "From Abstraction to the Image." *Washington Post*, June 4, 1961, G6.

"Artist-in-Residence Won't 'Putter' for Public." *San Jose Mercury*, October 10, 1963, 5NC.

"Art Spectacle in Pittsburgh." *Life*, December 1, 1961, 125–128, 130, 132.

Ashton, Dore. "About Art and Artists: Show at the Poindexter Gallery Offers an Index to Contemporary Trends." *New York Times*, December 21, 1955, 59.

———. "Art." *Arts & Architecture* 73, no. 4 (April 1956): 3, 10–11.

———. "Art." *Arts & Architecture* 75, no. 5 (May 1958): 5, 28–29.

———. "Art: Rebel in the West." *New York Times*, February 25, 1958, 55.

———. "An Eastern View of the San Francisco School." *Evergreen Review* 1, no. 2 (1957): 148–159.

———. "West Coast Artists Score in Painting." *Studio* 165, no. 838 (February 1963): 64–67.

———. "Young Painters in Rome." *Arts Digest* 29, no. 17 (June 1, 1955): 6–7.

Baker, Richard Brown. "Notes on the Formation of My Collection." *Art International* 7 (September 20, 1961): 40–47.

"Berkeleyan Is Top Winner." *Berkeley Daily Gazette*, December 9, 1955, 8.

"Berkeleyan Is Winner of Art Fellowship." *Berkeley Daily Gazette*, March 18, 1954, 16.

Bloomfield, A.J. "Little Blotches Look Like Pieces of Lint." *San Francisco News-Call Bulletin*, November 5, 1960, 19TV.

Campbell, Lawrence. "Reviews and Previews: Richard Diebenkorn." *Art News* 57, no. 1 (March 1958): 13.

———. "Reviews and Previews: Richard Diebenkorn." *Art News* 64, no. 1 (March 1965): 12.

Canaday, John. "Visitors from the West: Fifty Californians in an Exhibition at the Whitney." *New York Times*, October 28, 1962, X15.

Chipp, Herschel B. "Art News from San Francisco: Bay Area Figurative Painting." *Art News* 56, no. 8 (December 1957): 50.

———. "Art News from San Francisco: Diebenkorn and Other One-Man Shows." *Art News* 59, no. 10 (February 1961): 54.

———. "Art News from San Francisco: Group-Show Winners." *Art News* 55, no. 10 (February 1957): 20, 60.

———. "Art News from San Francisco: Pacific Coast Leaders." *Art News* 55, no. 5 (September 1956): 18, 57.

———. "Diebenkorn Paints a Picture." *Art News* 56, no. 3 (May 1957): 44–47, 54–55.

Coates, Robert M. "The Art Galleries." *The New Yorker*, May 29, 1954, 74–77.

Crehan, Hubert. "Is There a California School?" *Art News* 54, no. 9 (January 1956): 32–35, 64–65.

Cross, Miriam Dungan. "Diebenkorn, Oakland Teacher, Making Art History in N.Y." *Oakland Tribune*, March 23, 1958, 8-C.

Dann, Frode N. "Show Spans Artist's Transition." *Independent Star-News* (Pasadena), September 18, 1960, 10.

"Edging Away from Abstraction." *Time*, March 17, 1958, 64–65, 67.

Eichelbaum, Stanley. "An Abstract Artist's Return to Landscapes and Figures." *San Francisco Examiner*, October 23, 1960, 9.

Eitner, Lorenz. "A Living Artist's Example. . . ." *Stanford Today*, Summer 1964.

"Figurative Painters in California." *Arts* 32, no. 3 (December 1957): 26–27.

"Fine Arts in the Market Place." *Life*, September 19, 1960, 12–16.

Frankenstein, Alfred. "'Bay Region Painting' on View at S.F. Museum." *San Francisco Chronicle*, May 22, 1955, 4.

———. "Ethical Feeling in Diebenkorn Art." *San Francisco Chronicle*, September 12, 1963, 39.

———. "Museum Shows Work of Young U.S. Painters." *San Francisco Chronicle*, July 29, 1957, 19.

———. "Oakland Shows There Was No 'California School.'" *San Francisco Chronicle*, February 26, 1956, 28.

———. "Works of Reputable Moderns in the Current Exhibitions." *San Francisco Sunday Chronicle*, October 30, 1960, 24–25.

Fremantle, Christopher E. "New York Commentary." *The Studio* 148, no. 739 (October 1954): 124–126.

Fried, Alexander. "Diebenkorn's Art as Eyed by Some Women Painters." *San Francisco Examiner*, November 13, 1960, 13.

Getlein, Frank. "Painting Has Meaning Again in New Shows." *Sunday Star*, June 4, 1961, D20.

———. "Two Privacies." *New Republic*, December 5, 1964, 25–26.

Gosling, Nigel. "A New Realist." *The Observer* (London), October 4, 1964, 25.

Greenberg, Clement. "After Abstract Expressionism." *Art International* 6, no. 8 (October 25, 1962): 24–32.

Grissom, Sarah. "San Francisco." *Arts* 32, no. 5 (February 1958): 22–23.

———. "San Francisco." *Arts* 32, no. 8 (May 1958): 20–21, 69.

Halbfinger, Andrea S. "Diebenkorn Presents Excellent One-Man Show." *Washington Post*, November 15, 1964, G10.

Hudson, Andrew. "The Painting as Object." *Canadian Art* 22, no. 2 (March–April 1965): 30–39.

"The Human Figure Returns in Separate Ways and Places." *Life*, June 8, 1962, 54–61.

"In the Galleries. . . ." *San Francisco Chronicle*, August 17, 1958, TW25.

Johnson, Ellen. "Diebenkorn's 'Woman by a Large Window.'" *Allen Memorial Art Museum Bulletin* 16, no. 1 (Fall 1958): 18–23.

Jouffroy, Alain, and K. A. Jelenski. "Une grande enquête: Tendances de la jeune peinture" [A grand inquiry: Trends in contemporary painting]. *Preuves* 68 (October 1956): 33–69.

Key, Donald. "Miniature Art Makes Imposing Exhibition at Downer College." *Milwaukee Journal*, October 2, 1960, 5.

Kozloff, Max. "New York Letter." *Art International* 7, no. 10 (January 16, 1964): 33–34.

Kramer, Hilton. "Art Chronicle." *Hudson Review* 16, no. 1 (Spring 1963): 96–101.

———. "The Diebenkorn Case." *New York Times*, May 22, 1966, D29.

———. "The Latest Thing in Pittsburgh." *Arts Magazine* 36, no. 4 (January 1962): 24–27.

———. "Month in Review." *Arts* 33, no. 3 (December 1958): 46, 48–49.

———. "Month in Review." *Arts* 34, no. 4 (January 1960): 42–45.

———. "Pure and Impure Diebenkorn." *Arts Magazine* 38, no. 3 (December 1963): 46–53.

Lanes, Jerrold. "Brief Treatise on Surplus Value; or, The Man Who Wasn't There." *Arts* 34, no. 2 (November 1959): 28–35.

Langsner, Jules. "Los Angeles Letter." *Art International* 6, no. 10 (December 20, 1962): 38–40.

Leider, Philip. "California—after the Figure." *Art in America* 51, no. 5 (October 1963): 73–83.

———. "Diebenkorn Drawings at Stanford." *Artforum* 2, no. 11 (May 1964): 41–43.

Lippard, Lucy R. "New York Letter." *Art International* 9, no. 3 (April 1965): 48–64.

"Look of the West Inspires New Art." *Life*, November 4, 1957, 65–69.

MacKenzie, Bob. "Stanford Artist Pleased with Post." *Oakland Tribune*, March 24, 1963, 4.

McCue, George. "Visit with Richard Diebenkorn: Californian Combines Figurative and Abstract Painting." *St. Louis Post-Dispatch*, May 15, 1960, 5B.

Meyer, Luther. "Abstractionist Back on Track." *San Francisco Call-Bulletin*, March 28, 1958, 16.

Millier, Arthur. "Californians' Oils Impress." *Los Angeles Times*, September 11, 1960, G8.

——. "S.F. Bay Show on View Here." *Los Angeles Times*, November 24, 1957, E8.

——. "West's Artists Display Talent." *Los Angeles Times*, September 22, 1957, E5.

Mills, Paul. "Bay Area Figurative." *Art in America* 52, no. 3 (June 1964): 42–45.

Monte, James. "Reviews: Winter Invitational." *Artforum* 1, no. 8 (February 1963): 46, 48.

Munro, Eleanor C. "Figures to the Fore." *Horizon: A Magazine of the Arts* 2, no. 6 (July 1960): 16–24, 114–116.

——. "Reviews and Previews: Four Landscape Painters." *Art News* 59, no. 3 (May 1960): 15.

Neumeyer, Alfred. "Neue Gegenständlichkeit–Neuer Stil: Richard Diebenkorn weisst einen Weg." *Die Kunst und das schöne Heim* 63, no. 7 (April 1965): 284–285.

Nordland, Gerald. "Art: Innovation." *Frontier: The Voice of the New West* 8, no. 7 (May 1957): 25–26.

——. "Art: New Figures in Perspective." *Frontier: The Voice of the New West* 13, no. 10 (August 1962): 23–24.

_____. "Art: 6 x 5." *Frontier: The Voice of the New West* 7, no. 12 (October 1956): 23–24.

——. "Art: Some Noteworthy Exhibitions." *Frontier: The Voice of the New West* 11, no. 12 (October 1960): 18–20.

——. "Collecting in Los Angeles." *Artforum* 2, no. 12 (Summer 1964): 12–18.

——. "Diebenkorn Retrospective in Washington." *Artforum* 3, no. 4 (January 1965): 21–25.

"Nordland Browsed His Way from Political Science into the Art World." *Washington Post*, August 28, 1966, G7. Andrew Hudson interview with Gerald Nordland.

"'Nudes Now'—Ten Painters: Contemporary Approaches to the Figure." *Art Voices* 5, no. 3 (Summer 1966): 41.

O'Doherty, Brian. "Art: Ethics of Adversity." *Newsweek*, November 30, 1964, 97.

Ostermann, Robert. "Fame and Fortune for Today's Painters: Men Who Lead an American Art Revolution." *National Observer*, February 17, 1964, 18.

"Painter at Stanford for Year in Residence." *Palo Alto Times*, September 28, 1963.

Panza di Biumo, Giuseppe. "The Words of the Collector." *Cimaise* 6, no. 2 (December 1958): 30–31, 35–36.

Peer, Ralph. "Painter Residing Here Gets Critical Acclaim." *Stanford Daily*, October 21, 1963.

Petersen, Valerie. "Reviews and Previews: Richard Diebenkorn." *Art News* 60, no. 1 (March 1961): 13.

——. "Reviews and Previews: Richard Diebenkorn." *Art News* 62, no. 8 (December 1963): 54.

Polley, E.M. "Diebenkorn Art Is Shown at Palace of Legion of Honor." *Vallejo Times-Herald*, October 30, 1960, 46.

Preston, Stuart. "Art History's Many Turning Points." *New York Times*, January 17, 1965, X19.

——. "Painting on View." *New York Times*, March 4, 1956, X14.

——. "Veterans and Newcomers Exhibit Here as Gallery Season Picks Up Speed." *New York Times*, October 1, 1955, 17.

R.R. "In the Galleries: Richard Diebenkorn." *Arts* 30, no. 6 (March 1956): 56–57.

Raynor, Vivien. "In the Galleries: Richard Diebenkorn." *Arts Magazine* 39, no. 6 (March 1965): 54.

Rexroth, Kenneth. "Figurative Art Revival." *San Francisco Examiner*, September 15, 1963, 3C.

"Richard Diebenkorn: Four Drawings." *Artforum* 1, no. 5 (October 1962): 35.

"Richard Diebenkorn: Three Drawings." *Stanford Today*, Summer 1964.

"Richard Diebenkorn Wins Rosenberg Fellowship." *San Francisco Art Association Bulletin* 20, nos. 2–3 (February–March 1954).

Richardson, John. "The Neuberger Collection." *Art in America* 48, no. 2 (Summer 1960): 86–88.

Sandler, Irving Hershel. "New York Letter." *Art International* 5, no. 4 (May 1, 1961): 52–54, 59, 62.

——. "Reviews and Previews: Elmer Bischoff, Richard Diebenkorn and David Park." *Art News* 59, no. 8 (December 1960): 15.

Sarwin, Martica. "In the Galleries: Park, Bischoff, Diebenkorn." *Arts* 35, no. 3 (December 1960): 50.

Schevill, James. "Art: Richard Diebenkorn." *Frontier: The Voice of the New West* 8, no. 3 (January 1957): 21–22.

Seckler, Dorothy Gees. "Problems of Portraiture: Painting." *Art in America* 46, no. 4 (Winter 1958–1959): 22–37.

Seldis, Henry J. "The Development of Richard Diebenkorn." *Los Angeles Times*, April 11, 1965, M32.

——. "A Great Art Gift to the Nation." *Los Angeles Times*, May 29, 1966, K1, K30.

"The Singing Colors and Evocative Scenes of Richard Diebenkorn." *Ameryka* (in Polish; United States Information Agency publication, distributed in Poland), no. 82 (1965): 44–48.

Steif, William. *San Francisco News*, September 2, 1958, 9.

Sylvester, David. "London Views Advanced American Painting of Today." *New York Times*, November 30, 1958, X9.

Temko, Allan. "The Flowering of San Francisco." *Horizon: A Magazine of the Arts* 1, no. 3 (January 1959): 4–23.

Tillim, Sidney. "In the Galleries: Brussels '58." *Arts* 33, no. 5 (February 1959): 55.

——. "In the Galleries: Realism in American Art." *Arts Magazine* 36, no. 9 (May–June 1962): 95–96.

——. "Month in Review." *Arts* 35, no. 7 (April 1961): 46–49.

——. "Month in Review." *Arts Magazine* 37, no. 3 (December 1962): 38–41.

——. "Realism and 'The Problem.'" *Arts Magazine* 37, no. 10 (September 1963): 48–52.

Tyler, Parker. "Reviews and Previews: Richard Diebenkorn." *Art News* 55, no. 1 (March 1956): 51.

Van der Marck, Jan. "The Californians." *Art International* 7, no. 5 (May 25, 1963): 28–31.

Ventura, Anita. "In the Galleries: Richard Diebenkorn." *Art* 32, no. 6 (March 1958): 56.

——. "The Prospect Over the Bay." *Arts Magazine* 37, no. 9 (May–June 1963): 19–21.

——. "San Francisco: The Aloof Community." *Arts Magazine* 39, no. 7 (April 1965): 70–73.

Wallis, Nevile. "Round the London Galleries: Autumn Flowering." *Apollo* 80, no. 32 (October 1964): 324–326.

"What's New: In Art Influences." *Glamour* 31, no. 4 (June 1954): 70–71.

Whittet, G.S. "Figurative Abstraction—Or Abstracted Figuration?" *Studio International* 168, no. 860 (December 1964): 272–275.

Wight, Frederick. "The Phillips Collection—Diebenkorn, Woelffer, Mullican: A Discussion." *Artforum* 1, no. 10 (April 1963): 23–28.

"Work of Abstract-Expressionist Currently Displayed on Campus." *Daily Californian*, September 23, 1955, 7.

Before and After the Berkeley Years

Selected Monographs and Solo Exhibition Publications

Bancroft, Sarah C., Susan Landauer, Peter Levitt, and Anna Brouwer. *Richard Diebenkorn: The Ocean Park Series.* Exh. cat. Newport Beach, CA: Orange County Museum of Art in association with Prestel, 2011.

Brown, Kathan, ed. *Richard Diebenkorn: Etchings and Drypoints 1949–1980.* Exh. cat. Houston: Houston Fine Art Press, 1981.

Buck, Robert T., Jr., Linda L. Cathcart, Gerald Nordland, and Maurice Tuchman. *Richard Diebenkorn: Paintings and Drawings, 1943–1976.* Exh. cat. Buffalo, NY: Albright-Knox Art Gallery, 1976; revised edition 1980.

Butterfield, Jan. "Pentimenti: Seeing and Then Seeing Again." *Resource/Response/Reservoir–Richard Diebenkorn: Paintings 1948–1983.* Exh. brochure. San Francisco: San Francisco Museum of Modern Art, 1983.

Cathcart, Linda L. *Richard Diebenkorn: 38th Venice Biennale, 1978.* Exh. cat. New York: International Exhibitions Committee of the American Federation of Arts, 1978.

Daily, Marla, and Paul Chadbourne Mills. *Richard Diebenkorn and Carey Stanton: A Private Collection.* Santa Barbara, CA: Santa Cruz Island Foundation, 2005.

Elderfield, John. *The Drawings of Richard Diebenkorn.* Exh. cat. New York: The Museum of Modern Art, 1988.

——. *Richard Diebenkorn.* Exh. cat. London: Whitechapel Art Gallery, 1991.

Livingston, Jane, John Elderfield, and Ruth E. Fine. *The Art of Richard Diebenkorn.* Exh. cat. New York: Whitney Museum of American Art in association with University of California Press, 1997.

MacAgy, Douglas. *The American Artist and Water Reclamation.* Washington, DC: Bureau of Reclamation, United States Department of the Interior, 1973.

Neubert, George W. *Richard Diebenkorn: The "41 Etchings Drypoints" Portfolio.* Exh. brochure. Lincoln: Sheldon Memorial Art Gallery, University of Nebraska–Lincoln; New York: American Federation of Arts, 1988.

Newlin, Richard. *Richard Diebenkorn: Works on Paper.* Houston: Houston Fine Art Press, 1987.

Nordland, Gerald. *Richard Diebenkorn.* New York: Rizzoli, 1987; revised edition 2001.

Nordland, Gerald, Mark Lavatelli, and Charles Strong. *Richard Diebenkorn in New Mexico.* Exh. cat. Santa Fe: Museum of New Mexico Press, 2007.

Orr-Cahall, Christina. *Diebenkorn: Works by Richard Diebenkorn in the Collection of the Oakland Museum with the Howard E. Johnson Bequest.* Exh. brochure. Oakland, CA: Oakland Museum, 1984.

Richard Diebenkorn: Early Abstract Works 1948–1955. Exh. brochure. Los Angeles: James Corcoran Gallery; San Francisco: John Berggruen Gallery, 1975.

Scott, Gail R. *New Paintings by Richard Diebenkorn.* Exh. brochure. Los Angeles: Los Angeles County Museum of Art, 1969.

Selected Group Exhibition Publications

Albright, Thomas, Jan Butterfield, Ted Hedgpeth, Peter Plagens, and Moira Roth. *Reflections: Alumni Exhibitions, January 1981.* San Francisco: San Francisco Art Institute, 1981.

Bishop, Janet, Corey Keller, and Sarah Roberts, eds. *75 Years of Looking Forward.* San Francisco: San Francisco Museum of Modern Art, 2009.

Byrnes, James B. *California Centennials Exhibition of Art.* Los Angeles: Los Angeles County Museum, 1949.

——. *Contemporary Painting in the United States: 1951 Annual Exhibition.* Los Angeles: Los Angeles County Museum, 1951.

Freeman, Richard B. *Sixty-Seventh Annual Exhibition of the San Francisco Art Association: Oil, Tempera and Sculpture.* San Francisco: San Francisco Museum of Art, 1948.

——. *Twelfth Annual Watercolor Exhibition: San Francisco Art Association.* San Francisco: San Francisco Museum of Art, 1948.

Geske, Norman A. *Venice 34: The Figurative Tradition in Recent American Art.* Washington, DC: National Collection of Fine Arts, Smithsonian Institution, 1968.

Leering, Jean, Eugen Thiemann, and Zdenek Felix. *Kompas 4: West Coast USA.* Eindhoven, Netherlands: Van Abbemuseum, 1969.

Lewallen, Connie. *Richard Diebenkorn: Matrix / Berkeley 40.* Berkeley: University Art Museum, 1981.

Nash, Steven. *Abstract and Figurative: Highlights of Bay Area Painting.* San Francisco: John Berggruen Gallery, 2008.

Nash, Steven A. *Facing Eden: 100 Years of Landscape Art in the Bay Area.* San Francisco: Fine Arts Museums of San Francisco in association with University of California Press, 1995.

Perkins, Constance M. *Nouvelle figuration américaine: peinture, sculpture, film, 1963–1968.* Geneva: Musée d'Art et d'Histoire, 1969.

Perl, Jed. *A Culture in the Making: New York and San Francisco in the 1950s and '60s.* San Francisco: Hackett-Freedman Gallery, 2006.

Tuchman, Maurice, and Stephanie Barron. *Private Images: Photographs by Painters.* Los Angeles: Los Angeles County Museum of Art, 1977.

Books and Articles

Andreae, Christopher. "Remembering Diebenkorn." *Christian Science Monitor,* April 5, 1993, 14.

Ashton, Dore. *American Art Since 1945.* New York: Oxford University Press, 1982.

——. "Richard Diebenkorn." *Flash Art,* no. 102 (March–April 1981): 8–13.

Brown, Kathan. "Richard Diebenkorn (1922–1993)." *Overview: Crown Point Press Newsletter* (Spring 1993), 1, 6–7.

Coffelt, Beth. "Doomsday in the Bright Sun." *San Francisco Sunday Examiner and Chronicle: California Living Magazine,* October 16, 1977, 22–28.

"Diebenkorn's Art Is Shown." *Albuquerque Journal,* May 2, 1951.

Frankenstein, Alfred. "The Art Galleries." *San Francisco Chronicle,* March 12, 1950, TW27.

Frick, Thomas. "Richard Diebenkorn." *The MOCA Contemporary* (August–September 1992): 4–5.

Gopnik, Adam. "Diebenkorn Redux." The *New Yorker,* May 24, 1993, 97–100.

Green, Eleanor, Robert Cafritz, and Lawrence Gowing. *Master Paintings from The Phillips Collection.* Washington, DC: The Phillips Collection, 1988.

Gruen, John. "Richard Diebenkorn: The Idea Is to Get Everything Right." *Art News* 85, no. 9 (November 1986): 80–87.

Gussow, Alan. *A Sense of Place: The Artist and the American Land.* Washington, DC: Island Press, 1972.

Hazlitt, Gordon J. "Problem Solving in Solitude." *Art News* 76, no. 1 (January 1977): 76–79.

Hinson, Tom E. "Recent Paintings by Richard Diebenkorn and Jack Tworkov." *Bulletin of the Cleveland Museum of Art* 67, no. 2 (February 1980): 31–40.

Hofstadter, Dan. "Profiles: Almost Free of the Mirror." *The New Yorker,* September 7, 1987, 54–55, 58–70, 72–73.

Hopkins, Budd. "Diebenkorn Reconsidered." *Artforum* 15, no. 7 (March 1977): 37–41.

Hughes, Robert. "God is in the Vectors." *Time*, December 8, 1997, 98, 100–101.

Kimmelman, Michael. "A Life Outside." *New York Times Magazine*, September 13, 1992, 58–60, 62, 64.

——. "Richard Diebenkorn, Lyrical Painter, Dies at 70." *New York Times*, March 31, 1993, A1, B9.

Larsen, Susan C. "A Conversation with Richard Diebenkorn." *LAICA Journal*, no. 15 (July–August 1977): 24–30.

——. "Cultivated Canvases." *Artforum* 24, no. 5 (January 1986): 66–71.

——. "Richard Diebenkorn's Retrospective." *Artweek* 8, no. 28 (August 27, 1977): 1, 20.

Lavatelli, Mark. "Richard Diebenkorn: The Albuquerque Years." *Artspace* 4, no. 3 (June/Spring 1980): 20–25.

Machin, Julian. "Richard Diebenkorn: A Rare Interview." *San Francisco Chronicle*, November 17, 1992, D3, D5.

Marmer, Nancy. "Richard Diebenkorn: Pacific Extensions." *Art in America* 66, no. 1 (January–February 1978): 95–99.

"May a Big Month for Art in Albuquerque Circles." *Albuquerque Journal*, May 4, 1950, 8.

Millier, Arthur. "Art Trends Traced at Centennials Show." *Los Angeles Times*, October 2, 1949, D4.

——. "Contemporary Show Offers Rare Chance." *Los Angeles Times*, June 3, 1951, D4.

——. "Northern Californians Show Paintings Here." *Los Angeles Times*, July 10, 1949, D6.

Mills, Paul. *The New Figurative Art of David Park*. Santa Barbara, CA: Capra Press, 1988.

Mills, Paul C. "Richard Diebenkorn: Painting Against the Tide." *Saturday Review*, November 4, 1972, 55–59.

Morris, Gay. "Report from San Francisco: Figures by the Bay." *Art in America* 78, no. 11 (November 1990): 90–93, 95, 97.

Mumma, Phil. "A Quiet Californian is U.S.' Hottest Artist." *The Museum of California* 1, no. 4 (October 1977): 13–15.

Murphy, Richard. "A Painting Should Have Flex." *Horizon: A Magazine of the Arts* 21, no. 7 (July 1978): 66–71.

Richard, Paul. "Diebenkorn's Pacific Heights." *Washington Post*, May 10, 1998, G1.

_____. "The Unbearable Lightness of Painting." *Washington Post*, April 4, 1993, G4.

Roditi, Edouard. "Border Art: California Meets the 'Real Thing.'" *Arts Magazine* 41, no. 5 (March 1967): 50–51.

Rose, Barbara. *American Art Since 1900: A Critical History*. New York: Frederick A. Praeger, 1967.

San Francisco Museum of Modern Art: The Painting and Sculpture Collection. San Francisco: San Francisco Museum of Modern Art, 1985.

Selz, Peter. *Art in Our Times: A Pictorial History, 1890–1980*. New York: Harry N. Abrams, 1981.

Tallmer, Jerry. "Diebenkorn: Painter Against the Grain." *New York Post*, June 11, 1977, 20.

Tarshis, Jerome. "Far West's 20th-Century Art in East Coast Review." *Smithsonian Magazine*, May 1977, 57–61.

Thomas, Elizabeth, ed. *Matrix / Berkeley: A Changing Exhibition of Contemporary Art*. Berkeley: University of California, Berkeley Art Museum and Pacific Film Archive, 2009.

Tuchman, Maurice. "Richard Diebenkorn: The Early Years." *Art Journal* 36, no. 3 (Spring 1977): 206–220.

White, Nan. "Free Form Abstractions Stir Up Controversy in This Area." *San Francisco News*, March 18, 1950, 10.

Wollheim, Richard. "On Thiebaud and Diebenkorn: Richard Wollheim Talks to Wayne Thiebaud." *Modern Painters: A Quarterly Journal of the Arts* 4, no. 2 (Autumn 1991): 64–68.

Unpublished, Archival, Theses, and Dissertations

Bossart, Joan Chambliss. "Bay Area Figurative Painting Reconsidered." MA thesis, University of California, Berkeley, 1984.

Larsen, Susan. Interviews with Richard Diebenkorn, May 24 and 31, June 2, 1977. Archives of American Art, Smithsonian Institution, Washington, DC.

——. Interviews with Richard Diebenkorn, May 1, 2, 7, 1985, and December 15, 1987. Archives of American Art, Smithsonian Institution, Washington, DC.

Lavatelli, Mark. "The Albuquerque Paintings of Richard Diebenkorn." MFA thesis, University of New Mexico, 1979.

——. "The Berkeley Paintings of Richard Diebenkorn." Unpublished manuscript, 1985.

Poindexter Gallery records, 1956–1999. Archives of American Art, Smithsonian Institution, Washington, DC.

Richeda, Noreen Mary. "The San Francisco Bay Area 'New-Figurative' Painters, 1950–1965." PhD diss., University of California, Los Angeles, 1969.

Shaak, Yvette Friedli. "The Bay Area School of Figurative Painting: An Analysis." MA thesis, California State College at Long Beach, 1967.

Tuchman, Maurice. Interviews, 1976. Archives of American Art, Smithsonian Institution, Washington, DC. Interviews with Elmer Bischoff, James Byrnes, Phyllis Diebenkorn, Gretchen Grant, Paul Harris, Walter Hopps, Paul Kantor, Frank Lobdell, Gerald Nordland, Ray Parker, Joann and Gifford Phillips, and Don Weygandt.

Suggested Further Reading

Albright, Thomas. *Art in the San Francisco Bay Area, 1945–1980: An Illustrated History*. Berkeley: University of California Press, 1985.

Boas, Nancy. *David Park: A Painter's Life*. Berkeley: University of California Press, 2012.

Brown, Kathan. *Know That You Are Lucky*. San Francisco: Crown Point Press, 2012.

Burgard, Timothy Anglin, Bruce Guenther, Walter Hopps, Robert Flynn Johnson, Bruce Nixon, and Anthony Torres. *Frank Lobdell: The Art of Making and Meaning*. Exh. cat. San Francisco: Fine Arts Museums of San Francisco, 1998.

Frank, Patrick L. "Abstract Expressionism in San Francisco, 1945–50." PhD diss., George Washington University, 1992.

Hopkins, Henry T., ed. *Painting and Sculpture in California: The Modern Era*. Exh. cat. San Francisco: San Francisco Museum of Modern Art, 1977.

Jones, Caroline A. *Bay Area Figurative Art, 1950–1965*. Exh. cat. San Francisco: San Francisco Museum of Modern Art in association with University of California Press, 1990.

Landauer, Susan. *Elmer Bischoff: The Ethics of Paint*. Exh. cat. Berkeley: University of California Press; Oakland, CA: in association with the Oakland Museum of California, 2001.

——. *The San Francisco School of Abstract Expressionism*. Exh. cat. Berkeley: University of California Press; Laguna Beach: Laguna Beach Art Museum in association with University of California Press, 1996.

Marioni, Tom. *Beer, Art, and Philosophy: A Memoir*. San Francisco: Crown Point Press, 2003.

McChesney, Mary Fuller. *A Period of Exploration: San Francisco 1945–1950*. Exh. cat. Oakland, CA: Oakland Museum Art Department, 1973.

Peabody, Rebecca, Andrew Perchuk, Glenn Phillips, and Rani Singh, eds., with Lucy Bradnock. *Pacific Standard Time: Los Angeles Art, 1945–1980*. Exh. cat. Los Angeles: Getty Research Institute and the J. Paul Getty Museum, 2011.

Plagens, Peter. *Sunshine Muse: Art on the West Coast, 1945–1970*. Berkeley: University of California Press, 1999. Originally published as *Sunshine Muse: Contemporary Art on the West Coast*. New York: Praeger, 1974.

Smith, Richard Cándida. *Utopia and Dissent: Art, Poetry, and Politics in California*. Berkeley: University of California Press, 1995.

Starr, Sandra Leonard. *Lost and Found in California: Four Decades of Assemblage Art*. Exh. cat. Santa Monica: James Corcoran Gallery in cooperation with Shoshana Wayne Gallery and Pence Gallery, 1988.

Note: This checklist documents the exhibition as presented at the Fine Arts Museums of San Francisco and the Palm Springs Art Museum, unless parenthetically noted otherwise. Key to the abbreviations of the museums is as follows: Fine Arts Museums of San Francisco (SF) and Palm Springs Art Museum (PS). This list is arranged chronologically under paintings and works on paper and reflects the most complete information available at the time of publication.

CATALOGUE OF THE EXHIBITION

Paintings

Berkeley #3, 1953 (pl. 2/fig. 23)
Oil on canvas, 54 1/8 x 68 in. (137.5 x 172.7 cm)
Fine Arts Museums of San Francisco, bequest of Josephine Morris, 2003.25.3 [1102]

Berkeley #5, 1953 (pl. 3)
Oil on canvas, 53 x 53 in. (134.6 x 134.6 cm)
Private collection [1104]

Berkeley #7, 1953 (pl. 4)
Oil on canvas, 47 3/4 x 43 in. (121.3 x 109.2 cm)
Mildred Lane Kemper Art Museum, Saint Louis, Missouri, gift of Joseph Pulitzer, Jr., WU 4019 [1106]

Berkeley #8, 1954 (pl. 6/fig. 12)
Oil on canvas, 69 1/8 x 59 1/8 in. (175.6 x 150.2 cm)
North Carolina Museum of Art, Raleigh, gift of W. R. Valentiner, G.57.34.3 [1109]

Berkeley #12, 1954 (pl. 5)
Oil on canvas, 53 1/4 x 43 1/4 in. (135.3 x 109.9 cm)
The Phillips Collection, Washington, DC, gift of Judith H. Miller, 1990.006.0005 [1111]

Berkeley #15, 1954 (pl. 10)
Oil on canvas, 64 1/4 x 53 in. (163.2 x 134.6 cm)
New Mexico Museum of Art, Santa Fe, gift of Mr. and Mrs. Gifford Phillips, 4565.23P [1113]

Berkeley #19, 1954 (pl. 30)
Oil on canvas, 59 1/2 x 57 in. (151.1 x 144.8 cm)
University of Arizona Museum of Art, Tucson, gift of Gloria Vanderbilt, American Federation of Arts, 1962.16.1 [1116]

Berkeley #22, 1954 (pl. 24)
Oil on canvas, 59 x 57 in. (149.9 x 144.8 cm)
Hirshhorn Museum and Sculpture Garden, Smithsonian Institution, Washington, DC, Regents Collections Acquisition Program, 1986, 86.5886 [1119]
(SF only)

Berkeley #26, 1954 (pl. 23)
Oil on canvas, 56 1/4 x 49 1/4 in. (142.9 x 125.1 cm)
Collection of Harry W. and Mary Margaret Anderson, 1969.013 [1121]

Berkeley #33, 1954 (fig. 65)
Oil on canvas, 24 x 20 3/8 in. (61 x 51.8 cm)
Private collection [1132]

Berkeley #23, 1955 (pl. 8/fig. 28)
Oil on canvas, 62 x 54 3/4 in. (157.5 x 139.1 cm)
San Francisco Museum of Modern Art, gift of the Women's Board, 58.1729 [1125]

Berkeley #27, 1955 (pl. 25)
Oil on canvas, 41 3/4 x 44 1/8 in. (106 x 112.1 cm)
Private collection [1127]

Berkeley #31, 1955 (pl. 26)
Oil on canvas, 58 7/8 x 53 1/4 in. (149.5 x 135.3 cm)
Collection of Marguerite and Robert Hoffman [1130]

Berkeley #38, 1955 (pl. 31)
Oil on canvas, 63 3/4 x 58 3/4 in. (161.9 x 149.2 cm)
Carnegie Museum of Art, Pittsburgh, gift of Mr. and Mrs. Sidney M. Feldman, 64.9 [1136]

Berkeley #44, 1955 (pl. 27)
Oil on canvas, 59 x 64 in. (149.9 x 162.6 cm)
Private collection [1124]
(SF only)

Berkeley #46, 1955 (pl. 29)
Oil on canvas, 58 7/8 x 61 7/8 in. (149.5 x 157.2 cm)
The Museum of Modern Art, New York, gift of Mr. and Mrs. Gifford Phillips, 188.1973 [1142]
(SF only)

Berkeley #57, 1955 (pl. 32)
Oil on canvas, 58 3/4 x 58 3/4 in. (149.2 x 149.2 cm)
San Francisco Museum of Modern Art, bequest of Joseph M. Bransten in memory of Ellen Hart Bransten, 80.423 [1149]

Chabot Valley, 1955 (pl. 36/fig. 37)
Oil on canvas, 19 1/2 x 18 3/4 in. (49.5 x 47.6 cm)
Collection of Christopher Diebenkorn [1154]

Still Life with Matches, 1955 (pl. 38)
Oil on canvas, 20 1/2 x 14 1/4 in. (52.1 x 36.2 cm)
Private collection [2394]

Untitled, 1955 (pl. 37)
Oil on canvas, 12 5/8 x 16 in. (32.1 x 40.6 cm)
The Thiebaud Family Collection [3795]

Berkeley #66, 1956 (pl. 39)
Oil on canvas, 41 3/4 x 36 1/2 in. (106 x 92.7 cm)
Collection of Jack and Frances Levy [1153]
(SF only)

Face, 1956 (fig. 40)
Oil on canvas, 6 5/8 x 5 1/8 in. (16.8 x 13 cm)
Private collection [1183]

Flowers and Cigar Box, 1956 (pl. 41)
Oil on canvas, 17 3/4 x 15 5/8 in. (45.1 x 39.7 cm)
Private collection [1184]

Girl on a Terrace, 1956 (pl. 46)
Oil on canvas, 70 1/2 x 65 3/8 in. (179.1 x 166.1 cm)
Neuberger Museum of Art, Purchase College, State University of New York, gift of Roy R. Neuberger, 1975.16.09 [1185]

Man with Glasses, 1956 (fig. 41)
Oil on canvas, 16 1/2 x 13 in. (41.9 x 33 cm)
Private collection [1189]

Seated Man, 1956 (pl. 48)
Oil on canvas, 22 1/8 x 20 in. (56.2 x 50.8 cm)
Collection of Gretchen and John Berggruen [1644]

Woman by the Ocean, 1956 (pl. 47)
Oil on canvas, 79 x 59 in. (200.7 x 149.9 cm)
Collection of the Lisa and Douglas E. Goldman Family [1196]

Beach, 1957 (pl. 65)
Oil on canvas, 17 5/8 x 22 in. (44.8 x 55.9 cm)
Collection of Gretchen and John Berggruen [125]

Girl Looking at Landscape, 1957 (pl. 50)
Oil on canvas, 59 x 60 3/8 in. (149.9 x 153.4 cm)
Whitney Museum of American Art, New York, gift of Mr. and Mrs. Alan H. Temple, 61.49 [1203]

Girl on the Beach, 1957 (pl. 56)
Oil on canvas, 52 1/8 x 57 1/4 in. (132.4 x 145.4 cm)
Collection of Harry W. and Mary Margaret Anderson, 1969.023 [1206]

Girl with Cups, 1957 (pl. 63)
Oil on canvas, 59 x 54 in. (149.9 x 137.2 cm)
Yale University Art Gallery, New Haven, Connecticut, gift of Richard Brown Baker, B.A. 1935, 1975.110.1 [1202]

Man and Woman in a Large Room, 1957 (pl. 52)
Oil on canvas, 71 1/8 x 62 1/2 in. (180.7 x 158.8 cm)
Hirshhorn Museum and Sculpture Garden, Smithsonian Institution, Washington, DC, gift of the Joseph H. Hirshhorn Foundation, 1966, 66.1371 [1214]
(SF only)

Painter, 1957 (pl. 58)
Oil on canvas, 27 3/4 x 17 1/8 in. (70.5 x 43.5 cm)
Private collection [1217]

Seawall, 1957 (pl. 66)
Oil on canvas, 20 x 26 in. (50.8 x 66 cm)
Fine Arts Museums of San Francisco, gift of Phyllis G. Diebenkorn, 1995.96 [1220]

The Table, 1957 (pl. 59)
Oil on canvas, 30 x 26 7/8 in. (76.2 x 68.3 cm)
Des Moines Art Center Permanent Collections, Iowa, gift of James S. and Dorothy Schramm, 1961.49 [1223]

Untitled Landscape, 1957 (pl. 69)
Oil on canvas, 18 1/2 x 13 1/8 in. (47 x 33.3 cm)
Private collection [1212]
(SF only)

Woman in a Window, 1957 (fig. 44)
Oil on canvas, 59 x 56 in. (149.9 x 142.2 cm)
Albright-Knox Art Gallery, Buffalo, New York, gift of Seymour H. Knox, Jr., 1958, K1958:32 [1225]

Man and Woman Seated, 1958 (pl. 49)
Oil on canvas, 70 3/4 x 83 1/2 in. (179.7 x 212.1 cm)
Palmer Museum of Art of The Pennsylvania State University, University Park, 76.6 [1237]

View of the Ocean, Santa Cruz Island, 1958 (pl. 68)
Oil on canvas, 19 1/8 x 14 3/8 in. (48.6 x 36.5 cm)
Santa Cruz Island Foundation, Carpinteria, California, 1988.6 [2538]

Woman in Profile, 1958 (pl. 61)
Oil on canvas, 68 1/8 x 59 in. (173 x 149.9 cm)
San Francisco Museum of Modern Art, bequest of Howard E. Johnson, 84.196 [1246]

Woman on a Porch, 1958 (pl. 74)
Oil on canvas, 72 x 72 in. (182.9 x 182.9 cm)
New Orleans Museum of Art, Louisiana, museum purchase through the National Endowment for the Arts Matching Grant, 77.64 [1248]

Coffee, 1959 (pl. 60)
Oil on canvas, 57 1/2 x 52 1/4 in. (146.1 x 132.7 cm)
San Francisco Museum of Modern Art, fractional gift of Barbara and Gerson Bakar, 94.428 [1253]
(SF only)

Figure on a Porch, 1959 (pl. 73)
Oil on canvas, 57 x 62 in. (144.8 x 157.5 cm)
Oakland Museum of California, gift of the Anonymous Donor Program of the American Federation of the Arts, A60.35.5 [1254]

Man Smoking, 1959 (fig. 39)
Oil on wood panel, 9 3/4 x 8 1/8 in. (24.8 x 20.6 cm)
Private collection [1266]

Scissors and Lemon, II, 1959 (pl. 88)
Oil on hardboard, 13 1/4 x 10 in. (33.7 x 25.4 cm)
Santa Cruz Island Foundation, Carpinteria, California, 1988.17 [1276]

View from the Porch, 1959 (pl. 70)
Oil on canvas, 70 x 66 in. (177.8 x 167.6 cm)
Collection of Harry W. and Mary Margaret Anderson, 1970.018 [1277]

Bottles, 1960 (pl. 42)
Oil on canvas, 34 x 26 in. (86.4 x 66 cm)
Norton Simon Museum, Pasadena, California, gift of the artist, P.1961.27 [1285]
(SF only)

Girl with Plant, 1960 (pl. 62)
Oil on canvas, 80 x 69 1/2 in. (203.2 x 176.5 cm)
The Phillips Collection, Washington, DC, acquired 1961, 0519 [1293]

Landscape with Smoke, 1960 (pl. 71)
Oil on canvas, 54 3/4 x 49 3/4 in. (139.1 x 126.4 cm)
Private collection [1295]

Interior with Flowers, 1961 (pl. 96)
Oil on canvas, 57 x 38 3/4 in. (144.8 x 98.4 cm)
Collection of Gretchen and John Berggruen [1316]

Prisoners' Harbor, Santa Cruz Island, 1961 (fig. 54)
Oil on canvas, 21 1/2 x 25 in. (54.6 x 63.5 cm)
Santa Cruz Island Foundation, Carpinteria, California, 1988.23 [1322]

Sleeping Woman, 1961 (pl. 86)
Oil on canvas, 70 x 58 in. (177.8 x 147.3 cm)
Kalamazoo Institute of Arts, Michigan [1328]

Still Life with Letter, 1961 (pl. 91)
Oil on canvas, 20 5/8 x 25 5/8 in. (52.4 x 65.1 cm)
Collection of the City and County of San Francisco, purchased by the San Francisco Arts Commission for the Hall of Justice, 1967.31 [1329]

Untitled, 1961 (pl. 84)
Oil on canvas, 24 x 22 in. (61 x 55.9 cm)
Private collection [1333]

Ashtray and Doors, 1962 (pl. 92)
Oil on canvas, 29 x 20 3/8 in. (73.7 x 51.8 cm)
Private collection [1335]

Girl with Flowered Background, 1962 (pl. 85)
Oil on canvas, 40 x 34 in. (101.6 x 86.4 cm)
Modern Art Museum of Fort Worth, Texas, Museum Purchase, Sid W. Richardson Foundation Endowment Fund, 1991.11.P.P [1342]

Interior with Doorway, 1962 (pl. 78)
Oil on canvas, 70 3/8 x 59 1/2 in. (178.8 x 151.1 cm)
Pennsylvania Academy of the Fine Arts, Philadelphia, Henry D. Gilpin Fund, 1964.3 [1347]

Interior with View of Buildings, 1962 (pl. 80)
Oil on canvas, 84 x 67 in. (213.4 x 170.2 cm)
Cincinnati Art Museum, Ohio, The Edwin and Virginia Irwin Memorial, 1964.68 [1346]

Reclining Nude, Pink Stripe, 1962 (pl. 82)
Oil on canvas, 30 3/4 x 24 3/4 in. (78.1 x 62.9 cm)
The Metropolitan Museum of Art, New York, purchase, Lila Acheson Wallace Gift, 2001, 2001.664 [1352]
(SF only)

Santa Cruz I, 1962 (pl. 75)
Oil on canvas, 36 x 52 in. (91.4 x 132.1 cm)
Private collection [1355]

Cityscape #1, 1963 (pl. 99/fig. 13)
Oil on canvas, 60 1/4 x 50 1/2 in. (153 x 128.3 cm)
San Francisco Museum of Modern Art, purchase with funds from Trustees and friends in memory of Hector Escobosa, Brayton Wilbur, and J. D. Zellerbach, 64.46 [1374]

Cityscape #4, 1963–1966 (pl. 101)
Oil on canvas, 47 x 53 3/4 in. (119.4 x 136.5 cm)
Collection of Christopher Diebenkorn [1377]

Knife in a Glass, 1963 (pl. 94)
Oil on hardboard, 14 5/8 x 10 3/4 in. (37.1 x 27.3 cm)
Collection of Nancy and Roger Boas [1386]

Studio Wall, 1963 (pl. 97)
Oil on canvas, 45 3/8 x 42 1/2 in. (115.3 x 108 cm)
Private collection [1395]

Untitled (Tomato and Knife), 1963 (pl. 93)
Oil on canvas mounted on board, 5 5/8 x 7 7/8 in. (14.3 x 20 cm)
Santa Cruz Island Foundation, Carpinteria, California, 1988.27 [1396]

Recollections of a Visit to Leningrad, 1965 (pl. 142)
Oil on canvas, 73 x 84 in. (185.4 x 213.4 cm)
Private collection [1404]

Large Still Life, 1966 (pl. 141)
Oil on canvas, 64 1/2 x 70 1/4 in. (163.8 x 178.4 cm)
The Museum of Modern Art, New York, gift of the family of Richard Diebenkorn, 315.2004 [1406]
(SF only)

Nude on Blue Ground, 1966 (pl. 145)
Oil on canvas, 81 1/4 x 59 1/4 in. (206.4 x 150.5 cm)
Private collection [1408]
(SF only)

Seated Figure with Hat, 1967 (pl. 143)
Oil on canvas, 60 x 60 in. (152.4 x 152.4 cm)
National Gallery of Art, Washington, DC, gift of the Collectors Committee and Mr. and Mrs. Lawrence Rubin, 1991.176.1 [1412]

Window, 1967 (pl. 146)
Oil on canvas, 92 x 80 in. (233.7 x 203.2 cm)
Iris and B. Gerald Cantor Center for Visual Arts at Stanford University, California, gift of Mr. and Mrs. Richard Diebenkorn and anonymous donors, 1969.125 [1414]

Works on Paper

Untitled, 1953 (pl. 14)
Ink on paper, 12 x 9 1/8 in. (30.5 x 23.2 cm)
Private collection [5319]

Untitled (Berkeley), 1953 (pl. 15)
Ink, gouache, and graphite on paper,
10 1/2 x 11 1/4 in. (26.7 x 28.6 cm)
Collection of Ann and Robert L. Freedman,
New York [58]

Untitled, 1953–1955 (pl. 12)
Gouache, pencil, and colored pencil on paper,
16 x 13 in. (40.6 x 33 cm)
Collection of Leslie A. Feely [3289]

Untitled (Berkeley), ca. 1953–1954 (pl. 13)
Oil, ink, gouache, and crayon on paper,
13 7/8 x 10 7/8 in. (35.2 x 27.6 cm)
Collection of John and Sally Van Doren, courtesy of
Van Doren Waxter [2154]

Untitled, 1954 (pl. 19)
Watercolor and graphite on paper, 10 7/8 x 8 3/8 in.
(27.6 x 21.3 cm)
Private collection [595]

Untitled, 1954 (fig. 66)
Oil on paper, 17 3/4 x 35 1/2 in. (45.1 x 90.2 cm)
Private collection [3226]

Untitled, 1954 (pl. 11)
Watercolor, crayon, and colored pencil on paper,
14 1/2 x 11 1/2 in. (36.8 x 29.2 cm)
Allen Memorial Art Museum, Oberlin College,
Ohio, transferred from the rental collection to the
permanent collection via Art Museum Gift Fund,
AMAM 1994.27 [4166]
(SF only)

Untitled (Berkeley), 1954 (pl. 16)
Ink on paper, 16 7/8 x 13 7/8 in. (42.9 x 35.2 cm)
Private collection, San Antonio, Texas [333]

Untitled (Berkeley), 1954 (pl. 17)
Ink on paper, 16 3/4 x 13 3/4 in. (42.5 x 34.9 cm)
Collection of Hackett | Mill, San Francisco [335]

Untitled (Berkeley), 1954 (pl. 20)
Watercolor, ink, and charcoal on paper,
14 1/2 x 11 1/2 in. (36.8 x 29.2 cm)
Private collection [2159]

Untitled (Berkeley), 1955 (pl. 22)
Gouache, ink, and oil stick on joined paper,
18 3/4 x 19 in. (47.6 x 48.3 cm)
Art Institute of Chicago, gift of the Diebenkorn
Family, restricted gift of Adele and William Gidwitz,
1996.615 [2152]
(SF only)

Untitled, ca. 1955–1966 (pl. 54)
Gouache, oil, and crayon on joined paper,
19 x 31 1/2 in. (48.3 x 80 cm)
Private collection [2192]

Untitled, ca. 1955–1967 (pl. 127)
Charcoal, chalk, and ink on paper, 17 x 14 in.
(43.2 x 35.6 cm)
Richard and Mary L. Gray and the Gray Collection
Trust [2050]

Untitled, 1956 (pl. 45)
Gouache and ink on paper, 16 x 10 7/8 in.
(40.6 x 27.6 cm)
Private collection, courtesy of Acquavella
Galleries [5907]

Untitled, ca. 1956–1957 (pl. 44)
Gouache and ink on paper, 12 1/2 x 9 3/4 in.
(31.8 x 24.8 cm)
Private collection [738]

Untitled, ca. 1956–1966 (pl. 113)
Watercolor, ink, and torn-and-pasted paper on
joined paper, 15 3/4 x 18 in. (40 x 45.7 cm)
Private collection [65]

The Drinker, 1957 (pl. 43)
Gouache and graphite on paper, 16 3/4 x 14 in.
(42.5 x 35.6 cm)
Yale University Art Gallery, New Haven,
Connecticut, Katharine Ordway Collection,
1980.12.44 [336]

Untitled, ca. 1957–1958 (pl. 55)
Watercolor on paper, 16 x 10 7/8 in.
(40.6 x 27.6 cm)
Collection of Richard Nagler and Sheila Sosnow,
courtesy of John Berggruen Gallery [751]

Winery, S.C.I., 1958 (pl. 67)
Watercolor and graphite on paper, 16 3/4 x 13 7/8 in.
(42.5 x 35.2 cm)
Santa Cruz Island Foundation, Carpinteria,
California, 1988.5 [2534]

Untitled (Seated Woman, Reaching Down),
1960 (pl. 119)
Charcoal on paper, 15 3/4 x 11 in. (40 x 27.9 cm)
Private collection [2176]

Untitled, ca. 1960–1966 (pl. 122)
Graphite and ink on paper, 17 x 13 7/8 in.
(43.2 x 35.2 cm)
Private collection [533]
(PS only)

Untitled, ca. 1960–1966 (pl. 53)
Gouache, crayon, and graphite on paper,
14 x 17 in. (35.6 x 43.2 cm)
Collection of Marguerite Steed Hoffman [2094]

Untitled, ca. 1960–1966 (pl. 117)
Charcoal and ink on paper, 13 7/8 x 17 in.
(35.2 x 43.2 cm)
Richard Diebenkorn Foundation [4305]

Pliers and Match, 1961 (pl. 87)
Oil on paper, 8 1/2 x 10 7/8 in. (21.6 x 27.6 cm)
The Grant Family Collection [2110]

Untitled, ca. 1961 (pl. 90)
Gouache on paper, 17 x 14 in. (43.2 x 35.6 cm)
Collection of Christopher Diebenkorn [2513]

Untitled, 1962 (pl. 64)
Gouache, graphite, and charcoal on paper,
11 x 17 in. (27.9 x 43.2 cm)
Richard Diebenkorn Foundation [922]

Untitled, ca. 1962 (pl. 124)
Ink and graphite on paper, 17 x 14 in.
(43.2 x 35.6 cm)
Private collection, courtesy of Gerald Peters Gallery,
New York [2032]

Untitled, ca. 1963–1964 (pl. 128)
Charcoal on paper, 17 5/8 x 14 3/8 in.
(44.8 x 36.5 cm)
Collection of Gretchen and John Berggruen [928]

Studio Interior, 1964 (pl. 103)
Watercolor on paper, 14 1/2 x 11 1/2 in.
(36.8 x 29.2 cm)
Private collection [468]

Untitled, 1964 (fig. 55)
Ink and conté crayon on paper, 11 1/8 x 17 1/2 in.
(28.3 x 44.5 cm)
Collection of Gretchen and John Berggruen [312]

Untitled, 1964 (pl. 105)
Graphite and ink on paper, 13 7/8 x 16 7/8 in.
(35.2 x 42.9 cm)
Collection of Leslie A. Feely [410]

Untitled, 1964 (pl. 107)
Gouache and graphite on paper, 13 3/8 x 13 7/8 in.
(34 x 35.2 cm)
Collection of John and Sally Van Doren, courtesy of
Van Doren Waxter [665]

Untitled, 1964 (pl. 106)
Ink, charcoal, and graphite on paper, 12 1/2 x 17 in.
(31.8 x 43.2 cm)
Collection of Christopher Diebenkorn [688]

Untitled (Reclining Nude, Side View), 1964 (fig. 56)
Ink and conté crayon on paper, 13 3/4 x 16 3/4 in.
(34.9 x 42.5 cm)
Fleming Museum of Art, University of Vermont,
Burlington, Museum Purchase, 1966.12 [340]

Untitled (Scissors on Cup), 1964 (pl. 111)
Ink, gouache, graphite, and charcoal on paper,
11 7/8 x 17 in. (30.2 x 43.2 cm)
Collection of Christopher Diebenkorn [581]

Untitled, ca. 1964 (pl. 120)
Charcoal on paper, 17 x 14 in. (43.2 x 35.6 cm)
Private collection [582]

Untitled, ca. 1964 (pl. 89)
Gouache on paper, 12 3/4 x 10 7/8 in.
(32.4 x 27.6 cm)
Private collection [655]

Untitled, 1965 (pl. 108)
Gouache, crayon, and ink on paper,
17 1/8 x 14 1/4 in. (43.5 x 36.2 cm)
Private collection, courtesy of the Greenberg
Gallery, Saint Louis [672]

Untitled, 1965 (pl. 109)
Gouache and ink on paper, 13 3/4 x 10 3/4 in.
(34.9 x 27.3 cm)
Collection of Thelma and Melvin Lenkin [4536]

Untitled (Seated Woman), 1965 (pl. 138)
Charcoal on paper, 23 3/4 x 19 in. (60.3 x 48.3 cm)
The Museum of Contemporary Art, Los Angeles,
bequest of Marcia Simon Weisman, 96.108 [15]

Untitled (Still Life with Textured Cloth),
1965 (pl. 110)
Ink and charcoal on paper, 13 7/8 x 16 7/8 in.
(35.2 x 42.9 cm)
Collection of John and Sally Van Doren, courtesy of
Van Doren Waxter [27]

Untitled, ca. 1965 (pl. 131)
Charcoal on paper, 17 x 11 3/4 in. (43.2 x 29.8 cm)
Private collection [579]

Standing Nude, ca. 1965–1966 (pl. 130)
Ink, watercolor, and charcoal on paper,
17 x 12 in. (43.2 x 30.5 cm)
The Grant Family Collection [344]

Invented Landscape, 1966 (pl. 114)
Acrylic on paper, 18 x 23 in. (45.7 x 58.4 cm)
Oakland Museum of California, gift of the Estate of Howard E. Johnson, A84.45.6 [2549]

J.A.D.I., 1966 (pl. 140)
Charcoal on paper, 25 x 18 7/8 in. (63.5 x 47.9 cm)
Collection of John Elderfield and Jeanne Collins [598]
(SF only)

Seated Nude, Profile, 1966 (pl. 135)
Charcoal on paper, 24 x 19 in. (60.9 x 48.2 cm)
Art Institute of Chicago, gift of the Diebenkorn Family, restricted gift of Adele and William Gidwitz, 1998.80 [2179]
(SF only)

Seated Woman, 1966 (pl. 121)
Gouache, crayon, and ink on paper,
30 1/4 x 23 1/4 in. (76.8 x 59.1 cm)
University Art Museum, The State University of New York Albany, 1970:0049 [18]

Seated Woman, 1966 (pl. 137)
Acrylic and charcoal on board, 31 x 20 in.
(78.7 x 50.8 cm)
The Museum of Modern Art, New York, gift of the artist, 253.1990 [599]

Seated Woman, Head in Hand, 1966 (pl. 129)
Charcoal on paper, 25 x 19 in. (63.5 x 48.3 cm)
Collection of Christopher Diebenkorn [2561]

Untitled, 1966 (pl. 115)
Watercolor and graphite on paper, 8 x 10 7/8 in.
(20.3 x 27.6 cm)
Private collection [5892]

Untitled, 1966 (pl. 116)
Watercolor and graphite on paper, 10 7/8 x 8 in.
(27.6 x 20.3 cm)
Private collection [5893]

Untitled (Collage—Woman in a Blue Dress), 1966 (pl. 134)
Cut-and-pasted paper, construction paper, graphite, and ink on joined cardboard, 25 1/2 x 24 7/8 in.
(64.8 x 63.2 cm)
Private collection [2195]

Untitled (Seated Nude), 1966 (pl. 139)
Charcoal on paper, 25 x 19 in. (63.5 x 48.3 cm)
Private collection [2171]

Untitled (Seated Nude), 1966 (pl. 136)
Charcoal on paper, 33 x 23 1/2 in. (83.8 x 59.7 cm)
San Francisco Museum of Modern Art, gift of the Diebenkorn Family and purchase through a gift of Leanne B. Roberts, Thomas W. Weisel, and the Mnuchin Foundation, 96.435 [2181]

Untitled (Striped Blouse), 1966 (pl. 126)
Ink and graphite on paper, 27 1/8 x 22 5/8 in.
(68.9 x 57.5 cm)
The Grant Family Collection [1601]

Untitled (Yellow Collage), 1966 (pl. 133)
Cut-and-pasted paper, gouache, and ink on paper,
28 3/4 x 22 in. (73 x 55.9 cm)
The Grant Family Collection [11]

Reclining Woman, 1967 (pl. 123)
Ink and crayon on paper, 14 x 17 in.
(35.6 x 43.2 cm)
Collection of John and Sally Van Doren, courtesy of Van Doren Waxter [2173]

Seated Woman, Umbrella, 1967 (pl. 125)
Ink and charcoal on paper, 17 x 13 7/8 in.
(43.2 x 35.2 cm)
National Gallery of Art, Washington, DC, gift of Phyllis Diebenkorn, 2000.141.2 [2168]

Sink, 1967 (pl. 104)
Ink, charcoal, and watercolor on paper,
24 3/4 x 18 3/4 in. (62.9 x 47.6 cm)
Baltimore Museum of Art, Thomas E. Benesch Memorial Collection, BMA 1969.2 [342]
(SF only)

Still Life, Cigarette Butts and Glasses, 1967 (pl. 112)
Ink, conté crayon, charcoal, and ballpoint pen on paper, 13 7/8 x 16 3/4 in. (35.2 x 42.5 cm)
National Gallery of Art, Washington, DC, gift of Mr. and Mrs. Richard Diebenkorn, in Honor of the Fiftieth Anniversary of the National Gallery of Art, 1990.101.1 [2347]

INDEX

ACKNOWLEDGMENTS

The Fine Arts Museums of San Francisco wish to thank our President of the Board of Trustees, Diane B. Wilsey, who, alongside John E. Buchanan, Jr., former Director of Museums, and Julian Cox, Chief Administrative Curator and Founding Curator of Photography for the Fine Arts Museums, supported the presentation of this exhibition. Thanks are also given to Richard Benefield, Deputy Director, and Michele Gutierrez-Canepa, Chief Administrative Officer and Chief Financial Officer. Timothy Anglin Burgard, the Ednah Root Curator in Charge of American Art at the Fine Arts Museums, and Steven A. Nash, Director of the Palm Springs Art Museum, organized the exhibition. Along with the Fine Arts Museums' Assistant Curator of American Art, Emma Acker, they also contributed catalogue essays that make significant scholarly contributions to the study of Richard Diebenkorn's work.

A special mention goes to Leslie Dutcher, Director of Publications, who skillfully oversaw the editing and production of this catalogue, with assistance from former Director of Publications, Karen A. Levine; and with support from Danica Hodge, Editor, and Lucy Medrich, Associate Editor. We also thank Ann Heath Karlstrom for her editorial expertise; Todd Foreman and Tessa Lee at Public for their design sensibility; Sue Medlicott and Nerissa Dominguez Vales at the Production Department, and Massimo Tonolli and his colleagues at Trifolio for the beautiful printing of this book; and Patricia Fidler, Michelle Komie, and their colleagues at Yale University Press for their esteemed partnership. This catalogue is published with the generous assistance of the Andrew W. Mellon Foundation Endowment for Publications.

Thanks are also due to the Museums' exhibitions team: Krista Brugnara, Director of Exhibitions; Therese Chen, Collections Manager and Director of Registration; Leni Velasquez, Registrar; Diana Murphy, former Administrative Assistant; Bill White, Exhibition Designer; Bill Huggins, Lighting Designer; Juliana Pennington, Senior Graphic Designer; Elise Effmann Clifford, Head Paintings Conservator; Craig Harris, Manager of Installation and Preparation; and Suzy Peterson, Executive Assistant for the Art Division. Special thanks are also given to Sue Grinols, Director of Photo Services; Randy Dodson, photographer; and Jane Glover, Coordinator, American Art Study Center. Our further thanks go to the members of the Museum's extended staff, including the entire marketing, development, design, installation, education, and public programs teams.

Beyond the Museums, we wish to thank the Koret Foundation, Christie's, and the National Endowment for the Arts for their generous funding of the project. We thank Susan Ehrens and the Rose Mandel Archive for sharing Mandel's photography with us. We also extend our gratitude to the Palm Springs Art Museum for its collegiality and partnership.

Of course, the exhibition would not have been possible without the extreme generosity of our many lenders, both private and public. Not only have they agreed to share their prized artworks with wider audiences but, in many cases, they have also provided information on these works that was helpful for our research and for the exhibition catalogue.

Numerous other individuals deserve our sincerest thanks for their assistance in the development and organization of this complex project. These include John and Gretchen Berggruen of the John Berggruen Gallery; Sven Bruntjen; Peter Fairbanks of the Montgomery Gallery; Leslie Feely of Leslie Feely Fine Art; Michael Findlay of Acquavella Galleries; staff of the Getty Research Institute Library; Michael Hackett of Hackett | Mill; Kathryn Hobart and Douglas Baxter of Hobart Associates; Susan Landauer; Philip Linhares; Laura Paulson of Christie's; Kelly Purcell of Paul Thiebaud Gallery; Barbara Rominski, Head of the Research Library and Archives at San Francisco Museum of Modern Art; staff at the Stanford University Art and Architecture Library; John Van Doren and Dorsey Waxter of Van Doren Waxter; and Warren Weitman of Sotheby's.

Above all, we owe an enormous debt of gratitude to Phyllis Diebenkorn, Richard and Gretchen Diebenkorn Grant, and Christopher Diebenkorn, for lending so generously to the exhibition, and for sharing knowledge and insights about Richard Diebenkorn and his art. We are also indebted to the talented and dedicated staff at the Richard Diebenkorn Foundation, the entity in charge of the artist's comprehensive catalogue raisonné project, for providing invaluable logistical and research support to our catalogue. At the Foundation, we particularly wish to thank Richard Grant, Executive Director; Andrea Liguori, Managing Director; Daisy Murray Holman, Research Associate; and Carl R. Schmitz, Visual Resources and Art Research Librarian, for tirelessly contributing their expertise and resources to this project.

This catalogue is published by the Fine Arts Museums of San Francisco in association with Yale University Press on the occasion of the exhibition *Richard Diebenkorn: The Berkeley Years, 1953–1966*:

de Young Museum, San Francisco
June 22, 2013–September 29, 2013

Palm Springs Art Museum
October 26, 2013–February 16, 2014

Richard Diebenkorn: The Berkeley Years, 1953–1966 was organized by the Fine Arts Museums of San Francisco in collaboration with the Palm Springs Art Museum.

This exhibition is sponsored by:

Koret Foundation

Christie's

National Endowment
for the Arts

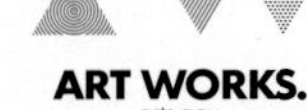

This exhibition is supported by an indemnity from the Federal Council on the Arts and Humanities.

The catalogue is published with the assistance of the Andrew W. Mellon Foundation Endowment for Publications.

Support for the second printing of this catalogue has been provided by the Richard Diebenkorn Foundation.

Second printing, 2014.

Note to the reader:

Bracketed object numbers in captions for Richard Diebenkorn's artworks represent the Richard Diebenkorn Estate numbers.

For works on paper, measurements for prints are of image size and dimensions for drawings are of paper size.

Details:

Front cover: Richard Diebenkorn, *Berkeley #32*, 1955 (detail of pl. 28)

Back cover: Richard Diebenkorn, *Woman on a Porch*, 1958 (detail of pl. 74)

pp. 4–5: Rose Mandel, *Richard Diebenkorn, 1956*, 1956 (detail of fig. 83)

p. 6: Richard Diebenkorn, *Untitled (Yellow Collage)*, 1966 (detail of pl. 133)

pp. 10–11: Rose Mandel, *Richard Diebenkorn, 1956*, 1956 (detail of fig. 85)

p. 12: Richard Diebenkorn, *Berkeley #44*, 1955 (detail of pl. 27)

p. 40: Richard Diebenkorn, *Seated Figure with Hat*, 1967 (detail of pl. 143)

p. 64: Richard Diebenkorn, *Cityscape #1*, 1963 (detail of pl. 99)

pp. 80–81: Rose Mandel, *Richard Diebenkorn, 1956*, 1956 (detail of fig. 84)

pp. 212–213: Rose Mandel, *Richard Diebenkorn, 1956*, 1956 (detail of fig. 79)

Picture credits:

Plates:

59: Rich Sanders, Des Moines. 74: Courtesy of the New Orleans Museum of Art. 90: Ira Schrank, Sixth Street Studio. 102: Courtesy of the Grand Rapids Art Museum. 135: Photography © The Art Institute of Chicago.

Figures:

Foreword, 2: Courtesy of the Richard Diebenkorn Foundation. 1: Fred Lyon / Glamour © Condé Nast 1954. 5: © 2013 Succession H. Matisse / Artists Rights Society (ARS), New York. 7: Copyright 1957. The Picture Collection Inc. Used with permission. All rights reserved. Nat Farbman / Time & Life Pictures / Getty Images. 14: Courtesy of the Grand Rapids Art Museum. 21, 22, 58, 68: Photographed by Joseph McDonald. 31: Photo © Fred Lyon. 32: Courtesy of Hackett | Mill, representative of the Estate of David Park. 33: Courtesy of Hackett | Mill, representative of the Estate of David Park. Photography courtesy John Berggruen Gallery. 34: Photograph by Richard Diebenkorn. 38: Photographed by Steven A. Nash. 42: © 2013 Succession H. Matisse / Artists Rights Society (ARS), New York. Archives H. Matisse. 45: © 2013 Artists Rights Society (ARS), New York / ADAGP, Paris. Solomon R. Guggenheim Museum, New York, USA / The Bridgeman Art Library. 46: bpk, Berlin / Nationalgalerie, Staatliche Museen / Joerg P. Anders / Art Resource, NY. 47: Photo © Hans Namuth, Ltd. 48: © 2013 Succession H. Matisse / Artists Rights Society (ARS), New York. Photo © Christie's Images / The Bridgeman Art Library. 50: The Estate of Elmer Bischoff, courtesy of the George Adams Gallery, New York. Photography courtesy John Berggruen Gallery. 53: Photography © The Art Institute of Chicago. 67: © 2012 by the Morley Baer Photography Trust, Santa Fe. Used by permission—All reproduction rights reserved. 71: Photograph by Phyllis Diebenkorn. 72: William T. Brown Papers. Courtesy Archives of American Art, Smithsonian Institution. 73, 74, 78: © 2013 by the Morley Baer Photography Trust, Santa Fe. Used by permission—All reproduction rights reserved. Photograph commissioned by the Oakland Museum of California. 76, 77: Copyright Leo Holub. 79–86: Copyright Rose Mandel Archive / All Rights Reserved. Original negatives digitally processed by Piet Halberstadt.

Yale University Press
P.O. Box 209040
302 Temple Street
New Haven, CT 06520-9040
yalebooks.com/art

Fine Arts Museums of San Francisco
de Young, Golden Gate Park
50 Hagiwara Tea Garden Drive
San Francisco, CA 94118-4502
www.famsf.org

Leslie Dutcher, Director of Publications
Danica Hodge, Editor
Lucy Medrich, Associate Editor

Edited by Ann Heath Karlstrom
Proofread by Susan Richmond
Index by Susan G. Burke
Designed and typeset by Public, San Francisco
Production management by The Production Department
Color separations, printing, and binding by Trifolio Srl, Italy, using their extended gamut printing system AreaW4

Library of Congress Cataloging-in-Publication Data

Richard Diebenkorn (Fine Arts Museums of San Francisco)
Richard Diebenkorn: the Berkeley years, 1953–1966 / Timothy Anglin Burgard, Steven A. Nash and Emma Acker.
pages cm
Issued in connection with an exhibition organized by the Fine Arts Museums of San Francisco in collaboration with the Palm Springs Art Museum, held at the de Young Museum, San Francisco, June 22, 2013–September 29, 2013, Palm Springs Art Museum, October 26, 2013–February 16, 2014.
Includes bibliographical references and index.
ISBN 978-0-300-19078-6 (hardback) – ISBN 978-0-88401-140-8 (paperback)
1. Diebenkorn, Richard, 1922–1993—Exhibitions. I. Burgard, Timothy Anglin. Nature of abstraction. II. Nash, Steven A., 1944– Tension beneath calm. III. Acker, Emma. Sense of place. IV. Diebenkorn, Richard, 1922–1993. Works. Selections. V. Fine Arts Museums of San Francisco, sponsoring body. VI. Title.
N6537.D447A4 2013
759.13–dc23
2013000126

10 9 8 7 6 5 4 3 2